# The Advancement of Civilisation in the Western World

## Vol. 1

### *Egypt, Greece & Rome*

# The Advancement of Civilisation in the Western World

## Vol. 1
### *Egypt, Greece & Rome*

## BRIAN HODGKINSON

## Originals
Delhi

First Published 2018

© Copyright Reserved with Author

ISBN 13: 978-81-8454-192-2 (Set)
ISBN 10: 81-8454-192-9 (Set)
ISBN 13: 978-81-8454-193-9 (Vol. 1)
ISBN 10: 81-8454-193-7 (Vol. 1)

**Published By**

# Originals

A-6, Second Floor, Nimri Commercial Centre,
Ashok Vihar Phase-4, Delhi - 110 052 (India)
Tel.: +91 11 2730 2453 Fax: 011 4706 1936
Website: www.Lppindia.com,  e-mail: info@Lppindia.com

**Printed At**

D K Fine Art Press P Ltd.
Delhi-110052

**PRINTED IN INDIA**

To Catherine, David, Jean and Ian

# *Acknowledgements*

Many people have helped in the writing of this book over a considerable time. Leon MacLaren provided the initial impulse, Sheila Rosenberg offered invaluable advice in the early stages. Colleagues in the School of Economic Science Teachers' Conferences assisted in the research and discussion of many topics. John Stewart was a permanent source of historical companionship and ideas. I am especially grateful to Felicity Debenham for her interest in hearing the reading of the whole book and suggesting numerous points of development and improvement; and to Yvonne Brook for her care and patience in typing the whole script, despite my repeated amendments. Kenneth Verity offered much advice and encouragement in the elusive art of creative writing. Professor John Dillon of Trinity College, Dublin, also made some valuable comments.

My History pupils at St James' Schools were always a great stimulus, and several visits to Greece and Italy have enabled much to be learnt 'on site' about the ancient world, often with the instruction of my colleagues, Clement Salaman and Margot Camp. Professor John Camp was a most expert and generous guide in Athens.

Barrington Barber drew the maps with his usual sense of space and time. James Armstrong kindly allowed the use of the slides of Egypt. Most of the other photographs were taken by the author.

Thanks are also due to those who enabled the book to be published, especially Nicholas Debenham, William Fox, David Lambert and Simon Lambert.

Finally may I thank my wife, Catherine, for her love and endurance throughout, my son, David, for his continuing interest in all things classical, and my daughter-in-law, Catherine for invaluable technical assistance.

*Brian Hodgkinson*
*Oxford, 2018*

# Introduction

*"...For history is a pattern*

*Of timeless moments."*[1]

SOME YEARS AGO I stood in a courtyard of Hampton Court Palace looking up at Tudor roundals of the Roman emperors, when a bell unexpectedly struck the hour. Was that the very same sound heard by King Henry VIII, Cardinal Wolsey or Sir Thomas More about four and a half centuries before? The worn stone of a Greek temple gave rise to the same thought: that this texture and solidity was what an ancient stonemason felt, the same stone, the same sensation. In such moments there is a connection with the past which has motivated the writing of this book. History is, of course, about time passed, a world of imagination built upon documents, artefacts and books, but the study of history takes place in the present, and therein lies its potentiality for enlightenment. What we hear and see and touch of the past comes to life in the present, and from that living history we may struggle to construct a story that has all the qualities of life.

Although our age has witnessed a century of war and the rise and fall of monstrous tyrannies throughout the world, and now continues in widespread abuses of human nature like drug addiction and economic exploitation, belief in the progressive nature of Man from an ape-like state towards some kind of superabundant material millennium remains. Ancient tradition challenges that belief with the idea of a progressive descent from a Golden Age. From this standpoint, men and women may be seen to rise above the conditions of the lesser ages that follow, but the long-term decline is in the nature of things. Such a tradition offers a modern historian a view of the advancement of civilisation, not through the ideas of social Darwinism, but through the study of great individuals or of ordinary people touched for a moment by a vision of greatness. No one who has studied history seriously can doubt that the finest human qualities, both individual and social - creativity, virtue, law, freedom, for example - were at least as much present in the ancient world as today. Thus the now almost forgotten concept of successive ages of Man from gold through silver and bronze to a final iron age may offer a heuristic principle that enables historians to step a little beyond the prejudices of our time.[2]

The general plan of this book traces the rise of three civilisations. The account of Egyptian civilisation only seeks to outline some of the chief features that enabled it to survive with remarkably little variation for almost three thousand years. Graeco-Roman civilisation, from its obscure beginning in the world of Homer to its collapse in the fifth century AD, revealed much greater diversity, and its final centuries are seen as simultaneous with the rise of the third civilisation, in which we still live, that of Christianity. Whilst Egypt saw the passing of perhaps three cultures, known as the Old, Middle and New Kingdoms, the classical world can be divided into Homeric and Hellenistic cultures, separated by the great war to which Thucydides devoted his exemplary talents. On the other hand, the rise of Christianity did not seem to establish or need a new culture until about the early fifth century AD, a subject with which a second volume, on the medieval world, commences.

What are civilisations and cultures? By what criteria are they identified? Having taken the decisions as to where to draw such lines in time, one may reply, 'Let History speak for itself.' Nevertheless the grounds of the decision itself cannot be ignored. A civilisation is the greatest unity of mankind below that of the human race itself, and a unity which offers to individual men and women within it the possibility of the complete fulfilment of their human potentialities. Every civilisation contains a philosophy, a way of life, that touches the very depths of human experience. Such was the teaching of Hermes Trismegistus in Egypt, of the early philosophers of Greece, and of Jesus Christ in Israel. A culture, as I have used the term, finds its source in the civilisation that contains it. Through culture human life is enhanced by an appeal to the heart and mind, to an innate love of beauty, of harmony, of virtue. Culture raises men and women above the material world and turns them towards the Spirit. How civilisations rise and fall, what causes lie beneath the surface of their glorious achievements and terrible disasters, one cannot claim to know, but it is the fortunate task of historians to continue to search.

---

1. T.S. Eliot, 'Little Gidding V, in *Four Quartets*, Faber & Faber, London, 1959, p. 58.

2. See Chapter 2 for further explanation of the idea of the successive ages of Man.

# Contents

**Part 5: The Rise of Christian Civilisation**

### Index of Maps

*Part I*

# Foundations

*The Sphinx*

# Chapter 1

# A Time to Live

## The Nature of History

IN THE BEGINNING WAS THE WORD and the Word was made flesh, but this beginning was not in time. Whatever is in time has a before and after and is no more a beginning. So, too, the end of all things is not in time, and may therefore be one with the beginning. "Before Abraham was, I am."

History is a process of rebirth. In time, as it appears, all things run forward and hasten to their end. Civilisations rise and fall, an empire dominates the world and falls in ruins, nations have moments of glory and become in their turn dark and contemptible. Great men appear upon the stage, the pride and envy of the world, and are no more when the curtain falls upon their exploits. There is in all this a pattern; for within it, controlling everything from within, is nature, unseen but containing the seeds of growth and change and decay, expressing itself in laws which the wise may discern and from which men of action may profit. Yet nature is not conscious. From it comes no renewal beyond the endless succession of growth and decay. From the acorn comes the oak tree and from the oak tree the acorn. From the idea of empire comes a mighty power over men, and from that mighty power comes hubris and dissolution and, at last, a new idea, different but still of empire, doomed to extinction like all before it.

All this is the material of history, but none of it is the essence. For the essence is rebirth and a true rebirth is a beginning, when something enters the world which is in it but not of it, proceeding from the Spirit, and in its fulness the Word Incarnate. Were time merely the matrix of sequential events in which effect follows cause in a never ending chain, there would be no place for such a beginning. Passing time has no existence outside consciousness; it does not contain consciousness for consciousness contains it. We are aware of the passing of time and, forgetting our awareness, ascribe to time a reality it does not possess, so that we think of ourselves as contained within it, and therefore limit our lives to the brief interval between birth and death. The ancient Egyptians knew better than this; the Sphinx does not believe in the reality of the passing world.

Beyond the sequential character of time there is a connection with another dimension which passes, as it were, at right angles to the line of material events. The connection is the moment now, wherein there is consciousness and an aspect of eternity. Here alone is rebirth possible, for here alone is life. The Orphics believed that to be embodied in the material world was death. To escape from death is to live in the moment now, the ever renewing present which never dies. "Sweet love, renew thy force."[1] In this rebirth lies the point in history, for without it history is indeed a tale told by an idiot, signifying nothing.

Since everything is connected with consciousness, the historian has a choice. He may look outwards at what consciousness reveals, at men in their outer life, working and fighting and multiplying, or he may look inwards towards the source, at their efforts for fulfilment, for realisation, for a life which is conscious and divine. The outward thrust of nature is powerful. It is driven by desire and its works are multifarious and inexhaustibly attractive. Ambition and greed and lust easily compel attention. A conqueror possesses great palaces, fine women and elephants mad with pride. On the other hand, the life of a great contemplative or scholar or artist may appear of little interest. Their fruits are more subtle and need more care to appreciate than the spoils of conquest. Moreover, it is the direction in which they are working which gives value to their endeavours and makes of their work a guide for others who seek, like them, the truth itself. Yet the historian is fortunate, for men of action also may look within towards the source, even in the midst of struggle or movement, finding there true motives and unwearying energy. Nor are the 'evil' men of history to be ignored; they are elemental forces, which may change the outer face of nations and empires. They are forces to be reckoned with, perhaps on the scale of giants, in any rational account of how conscious actions are taken by those who withstand them. How often did the Greeks portray on their temples the struggle of gods with centaurs, of heroes with giants, the victory of civilisation over barbarism? This is not merely a moral struggle of good and bad: it is of conscious forces against the mechanical, of reason against desire.

In history men have understood time in a great variety of ways, and only perhaps in the modern era has it been seen exclusively as stretching before and after like a Euclidean line. In the twelfth century the iconographers who decorated the new churches that spread outwards from the Ile de France to England and Germany placed Christ at the centre of time, and matched the great Christian teachers and saints with their Old Testament forbears. A window in the south transept at Chartres shows the four prophets, Isaiah, Ezekiel, Daniel and Jeremiah, bearing on their shoulders the four evangelists, Matthew, John, Mark and Luke, whilst in the Rose de France of the north transept the Virgin holds the infant Christ, surrounded by the gifts of the Spirit, a circle of angels, the kings of Judah and the twelve minor prophets. The Old Testament takes its meaning and life from Christ, for He redeems time. Like the felly of a wheel upon its hub, time before His coming and time after it are both alike dependent upon Him.

A conception of time as repetitive may have been present in the ancient Egyptian tradition of burying the pharaohs alongside magnificent accoutrements for another life on earth -jewellery, furniture, emblems of office and even games boards - a practice followed also by the Greeks of the second millennium B.C. in the shaft tombs of the grave circles of Mycenae and the Athenian Agora. Their precise beliefs concerning repetition may be unknown, but in some sense time was understood to be cyclical in character rather than merely linear, and the preservation of physical artefacts to be symbolic of this. The megalithic circles of Stonehenge, Avebury and Malta may indicate a similar conception of cycles. No doubt ancient man lived closer to the natural cycles of the seasons - in Egypt the annual flooding of the Nile was the very life force of a civilisation which lasted three thousand years - but this proximity to nature does not explain away such people's cyclical idea of time; it rather shows their readiness to see in the laws of nature the inner truth of time and reality.

The Book of Ecclesiastes contains a profound conception of time, whereby certain times are of special significance and carry a potentiality which reaches beyond the mere future. "A time to every purpose under the heaven, a time to be born and a time to die." The Romans believed deeply in the importance of choosing the right moment for an action: for a battle, a treaty, or the founding of a city. Perhaps from the Etruscans they learnt the arts of divination from the flight of birds or the entrails of a beast. The time taken at the flood led to fortune. To neglect the right moment was to miss for ever an opportunity for action which might affect, not just mundane life, but the life of the Spirit or soul in a world beyond the trammels of sense. Such a view, held by devoted Stoics like the younger Cato, was related to astronomy and to the belief that there are planetary influences the effect of which on human affairs can be studied and turned to good account.

What underlies all these conceptions of time is the recognition that everything begins in the present. Man transcends death, nature and his own past, in that moment. He does not know the future, nor does he know what possibilities are opened to him, but he throws off the chains of passing time when thus awake. For this reason Man is not bound by the mechanical evolution of life on earth. Poppy seeds and acorns, rabbits and apes may be determined in their forms of life and painfully slow movement through generations to a new, more developed adaptation to the physical conditions of the planet earth, but men are not. According to the Vedic tradition of ancient India, Man is of a different order. The Lord God fashioned him in his own image; he is born from the mind of Brahma with the Creator's own form. The order of men, or Manu, is not the order of those bound, the brutes, or Pashu.

In the great creation myths of the world, including Genesis, water, a bonding agent and a symbol of love, precedes the formation of earth. Then follows the growth of vegetation, an animal kingdom, and finally, as a distinct action, the creation of Man. Though consciousness is present in the whole created universe, only humanity can realise this consciousness and turn back towards it, rather than merely be driven onwards by the force of the creative power. All men are born with this possibility, but only some make use of it. Whilst they forget, they are borne forward in life, perhaps through many embodiments as the wheel of time revolves. What they meet on the way is the result of all that has gone before, so that each faces the results of his own past actions. He may redeem the past in the present. Such is the message of Osiris, of Socrates, of Christ, and of Krishna.

Evolution for men is not along the line of passing time, and if there is such evolution for lesser creatures, it does not lead to the creation of men. Man evolves by returning to what he truly is, which is to be one with God. As the Bhagavad Gita tells us[2], we do not see what lies before and after the life of a man; we see but the intervening manifestation, like the flight of a sparrow through the fire-lit hall of Bede's

Northumbrian lord. Reborn into successive bodies, the essence of Man may evolve into higher forms or deteriorate to the level of beasts, or even lower:

> "You shall have the power to degenerate into
>
> the lower forms of life, which are brutish. You
>
> shall have the power, out of your soul's
>
> judgment, to be reborn into the higher forms,
>
> which are divine."[3]

The humble shepherd may become a king, the arrogant despot may be reborn as a common criminal, and the wise man, who has learnt indifference to the passions of the world, may exhaust the inheritance of previous embodiments and become free from rebirth. His freedom is the real evolution for Man. He is at one with Himself. As for the man who degenerates, the imagination of Dante has portrayed him with stark accuracy in the distorted and frozen forms of Hell, where the essence of a man may be locked in the immobility of a tree, for thus he acted in that human life which was his opportunity to evolve. History is the record of this evolution, so far as it can be observed and written down. As men find themselves, they reveal their real nature, as rulers and soldiers, as scholars and artists, as labourers and wise men. The kaleidoscope of their efforts is the pattern of history.

### References:

1. Shakespeare *Sonnet 56.*

2. *Bhagavad Gita*, trans. Shri Purohit Swami, Faber and Faber, London, 1965, ch. 2, v. 28.

3. Pico della Mirandola, 'On the Dignity of Man', trans E. L. Forbes, in *The Renaissance Philosophy of Man*, ed. Cassirer, Kristeller and Randall, University of Chicago, London, 1948, p. 225.

## Chapter 2
# The Ages of Man
## *The Great Cycles*

"Whenever I take up my pen these days, which I do frequently, it comes to mind that I should write something about patience. These iron ages bring us nothing but evil. The Muses impart to us nothing but patience, the virtue required for bearing evils. There is now a need for this transforming alchemy, which turns iron into gold, so that the worst ages, which come as iron because of suffering, may be transformed at least for us into gold through the exercise of patience."[1] *Marsilio Ficino*

*Hill of Cronos, Olympia*

ONLY SINCE THE TIME OF Charles Darwin, little over a century ago, have most men believed that we are descended from more primitive forms of life, that we evolve through successive generations and that, as a consequence, human civilisation tends to improve or progress through time. With such a belief is associated the idea that greater knowledge implies greater complexity, that the simple is naive. For at least five thousand years before the nineteenth century, the general belief was the reverse. Human life was seen as declining; tradition was associated with the memory of better laws and customs; individuals were judged against the standard of the ancient heroes and heroines, the pure and the virtuous of now lamented times. In the early eighteenth century, Jonathan Swift's *The Battle of the Books* debated the question whether the ancients were superior. Are we, who live through an era of nuclear weapons, drug abuse and widespread neurosis, to assume without question that for five millennia the best thinkers of each age were wrong? And even if they were, should we not examine with care the underlying assumption that governed the world for so long, that human life is not a secular progression, but a secular decline from a state of grace? Would history not be more accurate if it studied the societies that held such a view against the backdrop of that view, rather than imposing upon them our idea of progress?

Western literature provides many examples of the belief in a Golden Age. Hesiod and Plato, Genesis and the Book of Daniel, the Renaissance philosopher, Marsilio Ficino and Shakespeare, all draw upon this pervasive and compelling myth. Beyond literature, in the very consciousness of peoples, lies a "memory" of ancestors who lived in such epochs of radical simplicity or heroism, when no man or woman oppressed another, when the land was free and held in common. Such is the racial heritage of the North American Indians, the Bushmen of the Kalahari, the aborigines of Australia and the New Zealand Maoris. Yet nowhere is the belief in the four ages of Man more clearly formulated and developed than in the writings of the Veda. In these the myth is given measure and content. We are told of the precise times of the ages, or *yugas*, the causes of the change from one to another, the essential nature and qualities of each. Scholars may enquire into the deep questions of whether the Greeks, whose language was certainly related to Sanskrit, learnt of the four ages from the Veda, of whether Plato really intended to visit India (as Ficino says),[2] or of Alexander the Great's connection with Indian philosophers. The easier issue is that the Vedic scriptures provide the backdrop that is required to view history as the great majority of people have viewed it; namely as a fall from grace, not as a slow march towards the millennium.

According to the Veda, at the beginning of every great cycle of time, called a *mahayuga* there is a Golden Age, lasting for two-fifths of the whole cycle of four *yugas* which make up one *mahayuga*. A Silver Age follows, then an age of bronze, then of iron, forming with the Golden Age the ratios 4:3:2:1 out of the full time of a *mahayuga*. The human race successively degenerates, until at the end of the Iron Age, or *kaliyuga*, men live like beasts and are destroyed finally by fire and flood. Yet, like the phoenix, Man is reborn, for in all men the Spirit is untouched by the vicissitudes of temporal life. This is the great rebirth, the beginning of history, the dawn of a Golden Age:

"In the beginning, in the Golden Age, men had but one caste, known as Hamsa."[3]

Each *yuga* or age has its special quality: liberality in the Iron Age, sacrifice in the Bronze Age and knowledge in the Silver Age. In the Golden Age, it is meditation. Indeed one myth describes how Brahma was angered by the first men of the Golden Age, who wished to do nothing but meditate. Men do not work in the Golden Age; "all men idle, all". Work is the curse upon Adam and Eve, cast out of the Garden of Eden for partaking of the tree of knowledge of good and evil. As Hesiod relates, the golden race lived like the gods, "with happy hearts untouched by work or sorrow," for the fertile earth gave her fruits unasked and men were rich with the flocks which they tended with loving care. Land was not bound by fences but was common to all, for the elements were acknowledged as freely given to all, for use and not for possession. Air, sunshine, water and earth were sacred, the gifts of the Creator, each a divine force in itself, as the North American Indians believed.

Such a time is described in the Puranas of ancient India. Human life was pure and simple and full of love. There was no sickness, and death came to men, after a long and tranquil life, like sleep, so that they knew no pain nor grief. Beauty was all around them in nature, and what they made was beautiful, for they made it, not as work, but as an act of love, fashioned on the harmony they saw in nature. Where could there be a model for something ugly and mean? They had no need of laws, nor of punishments. Morality did not exist as a code or set of rules, for knowing that they were united in one Self they could bear no ill will, and therefore experienced no greed, anger or lust. The sin of pride had no place in their hearts. Only for certain common activities was any kind of government needed, to organise common worship or large undertakings beyond the bodily power of a few. Their lives were filled with the happiness natural to all creatures; they had no need to seek it, for it was ever-present and only fleetingly did they leave the present and dream of the past or future. Love was rarely hindered by thoughts of claiming anything for oneself.

At certain times in history, groups of men have been inspired to live according to the standards of the Golden Age, holding it as an ideal to which they may aspire, however much they may in fact fall short. The early followers of Christ were such a group, as St Luke relates:

"And the multitude of them that believed were of one heart and of one soul: neither said any of them that ought of the things which he possessed was his own; but they had all things common."[4]

Whenever the teaching of Christ is revived, such an ideal appears again. The simple lives of the original Benedictine monks in the early sixth century bear witness to it, as do those of the twelfth century Benedictines re-inspired by the handful of men who went into the "desert" of the forests of Burgundy to found Citeaux in 1098. St Benedict taught them the cardinal virtue of humility, to deny the personal self with its lusts and temptations, to own nothing, to give everything.

In Florence in the fifteenth century, Marsilio Ficino reminded the members of his Academy that Plato had associated the Golden Age with the rule of a true philosopher. From the Socratic wisdom which Ficino himself revealed through his study of Plato, a new understanding of the life of the Spirit arose in Florence. The darkness and confusion of the late medieval world of Europe gave way there to light and order, to the glorious colour of Botticelli, the profundity of Leonardo, and the harmony of Renaissance architecture that spread from San Lorenzo in Florence to Palladian Venice, to Wren's City of London churches. In a letter to Paul of Middelburg in 1492, Ficino says: "For this century, like a golden age, has restored to light the liberal arts, which were almost extinct: grammar, poetry, rhetoric, painting, sculpture, architecture, music, the ancient singing of songs to the Orphic lyre, and all this in Florence."

That same wisdom had reached England a century before Wren. It found there the greatest of poets in the English language and infused his verse with a unique brilliance of form and content. For a few decades Elizabethan England, like Ficino's Florence, was touched with a unity that transcended its brief span of time. The gentle civility of an Elizabethan manor, the comfortable ease of the town houses of Stratford, the valour of Drake's seadogs, the cultured pomp of the Queen, the immense diligence of her first minister William Cecil, and the glories of Shakespeare's theatre were united in a moment of time which shines through the centuries as a golden age of England.

Just so did the Dutch experience half a century when their culture emerged into the clear focus of great art, when the sixteenth century burghers' families of Amsterdam and Haarlem and Breda seemed to represent a breadth of humanity greater even than that served by the far flung merchant ships which enriched them. In the genre painters of the seventeenth century, the interiors of houses and of reformed churches, the costumes of fine ladies and peasants, the watery land and skyscapes, the ubiquitous sailing ships, cornucopia and pewter, tavern scenes and clay pipes, all indicate the unity of life of a people emboldened by centuries of struggle with the sea. Had they not also, under the heroic leadership of William the Silent, expelled even the dreaded Spanish *tercios*, the finest infantry soldiers in Europe? The climax of Dutch culture was reached in the great masters, Rembrandt and Vermeer. Like their compatriots, the physicist Huygens and the philosopher Spinoza, they were fascinated by the nature of light. In their painting, light becomes all pervasive, softening the forms and colours, defining the texture of skin and cloth, reflecting off gold and bronze, eyes and mirrors, flooding into rooms and drawing deep shadows on walls and furniture.

For the mark of such times when the Golden Age has been remembered is the presence of a greater light. In truth it is the light of consciousness, but even physical light may seem to be more intense, to cast sharper shadows on the marble of the Parthenon, to touch with a warm glow the wheatfields of Beauce below the silhouette of the cathedral of Chartres. For in such midsummer moments there is a connection with the primeval consciousness of Man, when beauty is woven into the fabric of daily life and love is recognised as the cause of all things. Yet for all its apparent perfection the Golden Age cannot last for ever. It, too, is bound by the laws of nature. Though their life is blissful, the men of the Golden Age are not free from dreams, and from these arise the claims of selfishness. Harmony is disturbed and a new order of life becomes inevitable.

Rules of morality are the first product of the Silver Age, since the concept of duty is essential if selfish claims are not to lead to the destruction of society. The Silver Age is an age of knowledge; men retain knowledge of the unity of all things, but the love that flowed freely is now diverted by desire. The impulse to selfish action needs the restraint of duty. Who then is to formulate this duty and who is to ensure that it is not ignored? For this reason, four castes are created in the Silver Age: sages, rulers, merchants and labourers, each with specific duties arising from the natural distribution of ability and energy. The sages are akin to the men of the Golden Age; they meditate, they are pure, simple, contented; they preserve the revealed teaching and make it available to others; they are the counsellors of kings.

The rulers are men of action - kings and warriors, whose duty is to govern. They are full of courage, energy, justice, and skilled in many arts; they are temperate and can govern others from having first learnt to govern their own senses and appetites. They are both loved and feared, for their virtue arouses intense devotion and yet they punish the wrongdoer with tenacity, aware that anarchy is the worst of all states, as the great Indian epic, the *Ramayana*, makes clear:

"In a rulerless land, one may not enjoy the fruits of one's labour in peace; without a king, the army is unable to overcome the enemy in combat. In a rulerless land, men, richly apparelled, no longer drive their mettlesome and handsome steeds or their chariots abroad. In a rulerless land, those versed in the spiritual traditions do not withdraw to the woods and groves to debate together. In a rulerless land, no alms or garlands or confections are offered in homage to the Gods by pious people."[5]

The justice which the rulers administer is what the late Roman Emperor, Justinian, called "the constant will to render to every man his due." His due is what follows from the natural qualities of each member of the community. In the Silver Age everyone carries out the duties proper to him, for the rulers ensure that this is so, knowing that to perform the duty of another is fraught with danger.

The majority of men are merchants or labourers. The former are naturally faithful, trustworthy and charitable. They have the desire to accumulate wealth, but it is tempered by principles of equity. From them the rulers obtain the wealth required to govern the community, for as rulers they own no personal property beyond what is absolutely necessary, whereas the merchants, including those who engage in cattle-rearing and agriculture, control the land on which wealth is created and can bear the burden of the public revenues.

Labourers are free from this burden, on the principle that work is not taxed. Their duty is to labour and to serve. In return they are free from oppression and their bodily needs are easily satisfied from the production of a well-ordered community. Yet, unlike the other three castes, they lack the desire to be pure and hence, like Adam and Eve, are condemned to dig and spin.

These four castes are not determined by heredity, though birth into a high caste may be the result of virtue in former embodiments and birth into a lower one from former vice. Plato asserted that the most important duty of all for the rulers was to ensure that each man and woman occupies his true place in the caste system. The rulers alone have the wisdom required for this perception:

"And God proclaims as a first principle to the rulers and above all else, that there is nothing which they should so anxiously guard, or of which they are to be such good guardians, as of the purity of the race. They should observe what elements mingle in their off-spring; for if the son of a golden or silver parent has an admixture of brass and iron, then nature orders a transposition of ranks and the eye of the ruler must not be pitiful towards the child because he has to descend in the scale and become husbandman or artisan, just as there may be sons of artisans who having an admixture of gold or silver in them are raised to honour, and become guardians or auxiliaries. For an oracle says that when a man of brass or iron guards the State, it will be destroyed."[6]

What gives a Silver Age its great qualities of justice, virtue and prosperity is the character of its great men, the sages and rulers. The precise relationship between the sage and the ruler is also crucial, as Rama - an incarnation - acknowledged when he turned to Vasishtha. The Brihadaranyaka Upanishad defines this by saying that the priest is the root of the power of the king, so that at a coronation the priest anoints and crowns the king, who then sits above him to represent his temporal sovereignty over all his subjects, including priests.[7] The chrism, or holy oil, symbolises the "divinity that doth hedge a king," which lies both in the inner nature of the king and in the divinely appointed position which he holds in the realm; whilst the priest who administers the chrism has the knowledge of this natural order.

Not only does the Silver Age give rise to castes; it also witnesses the descent to earth of the absolute power of consciousness in the form of an earthly creature, an incarnation or *avatara*, meaning 'descent'. Once the pure simplicity of the Golden Age has been destroyed, every succeeding age stands in need of an incarnation, for memory has become too weak, even in the Silver Age, for men to find their way back to the unity within themselves without the presence of that unity in an earthly form. As Krishna, a bronze age *avatara*, says to Arjuna on the battlefield of Kurukshetra, very few men can give their complete devotion to the Supreme Being if it is unembodied.[8] Thus in the Silver Age came Rama, King of Ayodhya, and in the Iron Age came Jesus of Nazareth, the Christ. When suffering overflows, the Supreme Being takes upon Himself an earthly form to ease the lot of the world.

In the great epic of the *Ramayana*, the divine Rama appears as a king in the Silver Age. His father, King Dasaratha, ruled the country of Koshala from his palace in the city of Ayodhya. The city was a model of beauty and good order, its main thoroughfares long and broad, adorned with flowers and sprinkled daily with water, and the houses gracious dwellings with arched porticos. A deep and unpassable moat surrounded the whole city and its fortifications were marvels of military engineering. The nobility lived in mansions and palaces with domes which rose like mountain peaks above the rooftops and with fine gardens replete with every kind of plant. Near the outskirts rose huge trees and mango groves. Sweet scents wafted into every street and courtyard, the sound of trumpets, bugles, lutes and gongs enchanted the ear, and the brilliant colours of the dyed cloth of dress, flag and banner enhanced the splendour of the people. Countless elephants, horses, cattle and mules lived peacefully in the city. Traders from abroad flocked to it and dignified ambassadors met within its walls. The people ate only the best shali rice and drank the juice of sugar cane.

The king was learned in the Vedas, imbued with philosophy, just, strong and beloved by the people. The great horses of his cavalry guard shone with pride and his golden chariot dazzled the eyes of the spectators as it proceeded down the great avenue from palace to council chamber. His counsellors were judicious and respected by all. Nothing unreasonable was commanded to be done and the city was constantly protected from its enemies by strategies appropriate to the time and place of engagement and within the bounds of the lawful action of a warrior. Every man was brave and every woman virtuous. No one failed to perform his proper duties. Merchants were scrupulously honest and craftsmen devoted to skill. Illness and poverty were unknown. The wise performed due sacrifices and knew the science of astronomy. Harmony prevailed in the city of Ayodhya.

Yet, in the nature of life in the Silver Age, some canker grows unbidden within the city. King Dasaratha has promised his wife, Kaikeyi, that he will grant her any wish, since she had saved his life by her care after he had been struck down in battle. When Kaikeyi learns that the king has appointed Rama, his eldest son by his other wife, Kaushalya, to be crowned as heir to the throne, she is filled with jealous love for her own son, Bharata, who does not himself covet the kingdom. Kaikeyi holds the king ruthlessly to his word by demanding that he repudiates Rama and declares Bharata his heir. Dasaratha is shattered, for he knows the worth of his proper heir, Rama, but cannot break his word. Kaushalya, too, is grief-stricken, but Rama accepts the situation with absolute magnanimity, recognising that his father's word is law.

Kaikeyi, in her vindictiveness, asks for Rama to be exiled for fourteen years. The great prince, accompanied by his faithful wife, Sita, and devoted brother, Lakshmana, retires to the forest of Dandaka amidst the universal lamentations of the people of Ayodhya. Not for a moment does Rama question his obedience to *dharma*, the law which reason acknowledges as undeniable, whatever may be the situation, feeling or opinion.

Beyond the impregnable walls of the city Koshala is troubled by a reign of terror. Demons, or *rakshasas*, slaughter or torment the inhabitants, man and beast alike. The *rakshasa* king, Ravana, possesses the gift of immunity from all attack, except by a man. No ordinary man can possibly overcome him. The forces of evil are beyond the competence of mortals; their cause lies deeper. A God/Man is necessary, an incarnation. Rama is born into the Silver Age for this end, in the form of a kshatriya or warrior.

By a piece of deceit Ravana manages to kidnap Sita, so that the assault upon him has become a matter of desperate urgency. Rama seeks him out in the forest and slays him in personal combat. He rescues Sita and they return to Ayodhya, where Rama is received with joy by the people and reclaims the throne.

Rama's dedication to his people is exemplified in his attitude towards Sita. He loves her profoundly and is totally faithful to her. Yet on their return from exile, the question arises amongst the people of whether she preserved her chastity when in the hands of the *rakshasa* king. In fact, she remained pure in body and mind throughout the ordeal, for she is a worthy consort of her divine husband. Rama, however, will not let even suspicion disturb the peace of the city. He orders Sita to undergo a trial by fire to prove her truthfulness. Though he himself never doubts her, he insists that for the sake of the whole people, she must appear to suffer. He knows that perfect innocence is its own protection, that she will enter the fire and remain unharmed. All suspicion is allayed when she survives the terrible ordeal.

The epic of the *Ramayana* explores the roots of life in the Silver Age, for it shows how harmony is disturbed by evil, but re-established by the absolute adherence to *dharma* of a great leader. Rama does not set out as a champion of righteousness to combat all evil-doers. He merely keeps unswervingly to the truth. He knows that his father must keep his word; that those who appeal to him, Rama, for protection from the *rakshasas* must be heard; that Sita must be rescued; that suspicion must be allayed. Each step is the recognition of *dharma*. That alone is sufficient to restore harmony. The grain of evil in Kaikeyi has fulfilled its role; from it the truthfulness of Rama has spread abroad to cleanse the world of the demonic Ravana.

The archetypal silver age hero of ancient Greece was Heracles, son of Zeus and Alcmene, slayer of monsters, protector of men and one received into the company of immortal gods on Olympus when his earthly tasks were completed. His exploits were superhuman and he became for all Greeks the perfect exemplar of courage and nobility of character, champion of the oppressed, defender of women, author of great projects. He has most of the characteristics of an *avatara*, although, unlike Rama, he earned his place amongst the gods by his endeavours on earth.

Throughout his life Heracles is plagued by the jealousy of the goddess Hera, wife of Zeus, who resents the dalliance of the Father of the Gods with Alcmene, mother of Heracles. Hera sends two snakes to kill the infant hero in his cot, but already Heracles masters the evil of the world and strangles the snakes, one in each infant fist. Many years later, the jealous goddess makes him mad, so that he kills his own children. Tormented by remorse on recovering his reason, Heracles visits the Delphic oracle and is told to absolve the crime by offering himself to Eurystheus, King of Mycenae and overlord of Tiryns, to which Heracles himself was rightful heir. Eurystheus lays upon the hero twelve great labours, each seemingly impossible. The obstacle in each labour is some terrible scourge of land and people, some monstrous torment which befalls an age no longer pure. The hero rescues his people; he is their saviour, and becomes the divine victor, the Kallinikos.

Already Heracles has acquired an aspect of a lion, for he wears an invulnerable lion-skin won in previous conflict, and his first labour is to rid the land of the fierce lion of Nemea, which roams abroad terrorising humanity. It, too, has an invulnerable hide, so Heracles strangles it with his bare hands. Henceforth, he wears a garland of wild celery, which grows on graves to symbolise his triumph. He has conquered death. At the Nemean Games the winners remembered his deed with their crowns of the same plant.

Heracles' victories over his other mighty adversaries are similarly won by using no more than his own natural gifts: his hands, his strength, his speed, and the forces of the natural world - water, fire, and even snow. When the Erymanthian boar has to be taken alive by order of Eurystheus, Heracles traps it in a snowdrift. When the filth of the stables of King Augeias has to be removed in one day, Heracles diverts the rivers Alpheus and Peneus, which free the land of Elis from foulness and disease. The brazen-beaked Stymphalian birds are routed by the sound of cymbals, reverberating painfully as the birds fly off in confusion. Fire he uses to destroy the horrible water beast, the Hydra of Lerna. Its fifty heads, one immortal, duplicate themselves when cut off. They are the desires which cannot be destroyed by direct assault. Heracles cuts them off in turn, but cauterises each wound with a flaming brand, like the fire of reason. Only the immortal head remains, writhing under stone by the swamp of Lerna in Argos. Heracles' strength is prodigious. He relieves Atlas of his burden of holding up the heavens, whilst the giant obtains for him the golden apples of the Hesperides, guardian nymphs whom Heracles will not attack. Yet this strength would be insufficient for his tasks were he not helped by the goddess Athena, mistress of wisdom and the arts. The hero surrenders himself to the divine; only thus can he overcome his divine enemy, the goddess Hera.

Heracles is the epitome of ancient chivalry in his attitude to women. Throughout his labours he remains faithful to Megara, his betrothed. He refuses to attack the Hesperides, the daughters of night. Hippolyte, Queen of the Amazons, and her army of female warriors are similarly secure from assault, though Hippolyte's girdle is the prize demanded by Eurystheus. Even the life of the female stag of Cerynea, protected by Artemis, goddess of the hunt, is treated with respect and not taken by the poisoned arrows of the hero. Similarly the violent mares of King Diomedes, son of Ares, god of war, are preserved alive to graze on Mount Olympus, though they were the agents of Diomedes' cruelty to the people of Thrace.

The true victory of Heracles, as of an *avatara*, is over death. In the final labour he is sent to the underworld of Hades, whence no mortal ever returns, to capture the dread three-headed dog, Cerberus, guardian of the entrance. Heracles goes as a mortal, like Christ ascending Calvary, to face death for the sake of humanity. He is ferried across the waters of forgetfulness by Charon, and strangles two of Cerberus' throats, slipping a chain around the third. With the captive hound of hell he emerges triumphant, like Jonah from the whale, like Christ from the tomb. Death is overcome. Greeks of antiquity would write above their doorways:

> "Here dwells the Glorious Victor, Heracles,
>
> The son of Zeus; let nothing evil enter."[9]

Evil means death, for they did not wish to write of death itself, and so the hero became known as Heracles Alexikakos, "Heracles averter of evil", a name first dedicated to him by Telamon, at the sack of Troy. The hero himself has become immortal; his labours over, he is welcomed to Olympus by the company of the gods.

In the Iron Age, corresponding to what is regarded today as historical time, men who rise above the general level, and lead a nation towards a fulfilment marked out by the nature of its people, have something of the Silver Age in them. They inspire others to service; they awake those sunk in apathy; they present a vision of the good and the just for which lesser men may strive. Above all, they recall by word and example the true stature of Man, as the unlimited Spirit discovering itself amidst the limited and the transient.

The English king Alfred the Great was such a leader. He saw clearly the need within his kingdom for those who pray, those who fight and those who labour, and he devoted his life to calling all these orders of men to their proper duties. Almost alone, he kept alive the flickering hopes of the Anglo-Saxon people when they lay prostrate before the fearsome Danish armies in the year 877 AD. What sacrifice did he make of his desire for safety and comfort and reputation, as he hid like an outlaw in the marshes of the Isle of Athelney through the long winter months? Only a strong memory of the truth could have sustained him in such humiliation and brought him to the pitch of valour which rallied the English armies in the spring and beat the Danes at the great battle of Edington. The qualities of a true king shone forth in Alfred and the Anglo-Saxon people responded to them. He was only a shadow of the divine Rama, but the shadow was enough to create a nation.

The Bronze Age is the age of heroes, men no longer pure but of mixed qualities like bronze itself, an alloy of copper and tin. It is an age dominated by the warrior caste, with great virtues like courage, strength, magnanimity, boldness and a spirit of adventure, intermixed with dark aspects of selfishness, with greed, cruelty, lust and arrogance; for knowledge and power have declined and a sea-change comes over human nature. This double quality of the Bronze Age was portrayed by Hesiod as successive ages, first with heroic strength wasting itself in futile conflict and later with greater deeds of exemplary valour.

> "... more just and good,
>
> A godlike race of heroes, who are called
>
> The demi-gods - the race before our own.
>
> Foul wars and dreadful battles ruined some;
>
> Some sought the flocks of Oedipus, and died
>
> In Cadmus' land, at seven-gated Thebes,
>
> And some, who crossed the open sea in ships,
>
> For fair-haired Helen's sake, were killed at Troy."[10]

What especially distinguishes the Bronze Age from the Iron Age that follows it is the heroic mind of the bronze age warrior. He does nothing trivial or vulgar. His mind is set upon actions of great moment. At a word of insult he springs to arms; asks for and gives no quarter; has no regard for petty matters, only for honour and power. Doubt, timidity, meanness, all small-minded vices are unknown to him. The sins of such heroes may be prodigious; good and bad struggle alike for greatness; cruel malevolence a worthy adversary of sublime virtue.

It was inevitable that war would be a constant feature of an age of heroes, but a thread of wisdom still ran through their lives amidst the passions of adventure and the battlefield. They forgot themselves and committed mighty crimes, like Achilles' treatment of the body of the noble Hector before the walls of Troy, but memory returned and the spirit of sacrifice lived again.

Such great leaders arouse love in their followers. The mere presence of their leader amongst them is enough to inspire deeds of heroism, and his words are a touchstone of the truth, to be remembered in the darkest moments of despair or death.

> "... that, when he speaks,
>
> The air, a charter'd libertine, is still,
>
> And the mute wonder lurketh in men's ears,
>
> To steal his sweet and honey'd sentences."[11]

Or as a soldier in the Peninsula War was to put it, more prosaically, he would rather see the long nose of the Duke of Wellington than ten thousand extra infantry.

Of such a character were the ancient heroes, the men of Bronze: Arjuna, whose flag bore the Hanuman"; Karna, "conqueror of hostile cities"; Yudhisthira, "first of charioteers"; Hector, "of the flashing helmet"; Achilles, "peerless son of Peleus"; Diomedes, "of the loud war cry"; Idomeneus, "illustrious spearman"; Castor, "tamer of horses"; Agamemnon, "King of Men".

The end of the Bronze Age with the destruction of the warrior caste is most sharply depicted in the account of the battle of Kurukshetra in the great epic the *Mahabharata*. Towards the end of the fourth millennium BC, it the rich lands of north India, a deadly quarrel arose within the ruling warrior caste. Duryodhana, the eldest son of the blind king, Dhritarashtra, harboured a bitter grudge against his five cousins, the Pandu brothers, despite the efforts of their mutual great-uncle, Bhishma, and others, to make Duryodhana see reason. When the eldest Pandu, Yudhisthira, is crowned with magnificent ceremony in his capital city of Indraprastha, attended by his brothers Bhima, Arjuna, Nakula and Sahadeva, Duryodhana decides to assuage his jealousy by challenging Yudhisthira to a game of dice, for he knows that gambling is the prince's cardinal weakness. The outcome is the ruin of the Pandavas, after a terrible insult to their princess Draupadi, and their exile.

When thirteen years later they return, Duryodhana's jealousy has not abated. He will not give them as much land as would be covered by the point of a pin. They resort to war, and on the field of Kurukshetra two inmense armies, commanded by men of the same family, confront each other. True to the principles of their caste, the leaders agree before fighting to certain rules of noble combat. Car-warriors, elephant riders, horsemen, and footsoldiers must only fight against their own kind. No one should attack a combatant who is already engaged in fighting another, nor one seeking refuge or retreating, nor a warrior whose weapon is broken or who is not clad in armour. Charioteers, animals, men carrying weapons, drummers and conch-blowers are also immune from attack. These rules of civilised warfare are gradually lost sight of as the battle progresses. Their dereliction constitutes and marks out the close of the age of bronze. Even the invincible Arjuna, master of every military art and supreme with the bow, a man of great compassion who weeps at the sight of his kinsmen and peers arrayed against him, stoops eventually to cheating, for he can only kill the mighty Bhishma by hiding behind a warrior whom Bhishma has sworn never to attack. Indeed Bhishma's death is perhaps the heart of the tragedy, for he represents the unity of the whole family, of Kurus and Pandavas, and dies with utter nobility of character, resting on a bed of arrows, bleeding from wounds which have left not a finger's width of unscathed flesh upon his body.

Bhishma is a man of the true stature of a hero. He has done all he can to reconcile the opposing factions within the family. He holds no hatred nor resentment of any kind for the Pandavas, though he commands the Kuru army; indeed he converses with Arjuna and his brothers with kindness and respect during lulls in the fighting. Realising that Duroydhana is implacably jealous, yet unable to break his warrior's code by surrendering or by cowardice, Bhishma finally advises Arjuna how to kill him, Bhishma, by making use of the certainty that he would never break his word. As the great man lies on his bed of arrows he chooses the time of his own death, in accordance with a divine boon, and asks Arjuna for a cushion for his head, and for water. Knowing his great-uncle's nobility, Arjuna fires three arrows into the earth to support the dying man's head, and then a further arrow, with enormous force, strikes a spring from which gushes divine water with the taste of nectar. Just after sunset, as Bhishma dies with the sun, he makes a final appeal to the assembled warriors, entreating them to be reconciled and lay down their arms. Even this, a voice of noble impartiality, redolent with the wisdom of a finer and greater time, cannot move Duryodhana's heart of stone. The war of destruction is ordained in the nature of things.

The degeneration of the heroic standards of behaviour continues apace. Yudhisthira is the very embodiment of truthfulness. No one, friend or enemy, doubts his word; but somehow the great preceptor of the Pandavas, Drona, who taught them to excel all others in the martial arts, but now has risen to command the Kuru army after the deaths of Bhishma and Karna, has to be killed. Neither Yudhisthira's supreme skill in the chariot, Bhima's superhuman strength, nor Arjuna's bowmanship, can fell the redoubtable Drona. A plan is devised to exploit Drona's devotion to his son Ashvatthama, himself a great fighter who later leads the final slaughter of the Pandava host. They will tell Drona falsely that Ashvatthama has been killed.

When Bhima tells Drona this, Drona does not believe him, but then Yudhisthira is persuaded to tell the lie. He, the eldest of the Pandu brothers, is unable to accept the deceit wholeheartedly. He shouts out to Drona that Ashvatthama is dead, but knows that an elephant of that same name has in fact died, so he adds in a whisper 'Ashvatthama, the elephant'. Drona does not hear the qualification. He is devastated with grief and loses his will to fight; but Yudhisthira also, in telling his lie, has departed from the standards of bronze age heroism. He is the king; his defection symbolizes the corruption of the age.

In one respect, especially, the *Mahabharata* makes more explicit than does Homer the real nature of the change from a bronze to an iron age. For in the battle of Kurukshetra the role of Krishna takes on a central significance. He is the incarnation who ensures that the total defeat of the human spirit does not take place, whatever may be the horrors and tribulations of the final days of the age of heroes and however dark the ensuing Iron Age may threaten to become. As Arjuna's charioteer, he exhorts the hero to remember the truth that, though the body falls, the Spirit in man is undying.

> "He who thinks that the Spirit kills, and he who thinks of it as killed, are both ignorant. The Spirit kills not, nor is it killed. It was not born; it will never die; nor having once been, can it ever cease to be; unborn, eternal, ever-enduring, yet most ancient, the Spirit dies not when the body is dead."[12]

As Arjuna swoons with grief and despair on the floor of his chariot, confronted with the internecine battle, Krishna raises him up by the power of pure reason, teaching him that the whole terrible series of events, the passions and violence, are but an illusion, and that no harm will come to one who realises that death is no more than the shuffling off of mortal coils. So, too, is the death of the Bronze Age. Even Krishna cannot prevent it. He sees the inevitable turn of history, the fall of a civilisation. In his compassion he prepares men for what is to follow. If they remember his words, they will know that they are above pain and suffering, and can face the approaching Iron Age with a resolution born of knowledge. The truth has made them free.

The battle of Kurukshetra signified the end of the Bronze Age. According to tradition, it took place in 3102 BC; the Iron Age is said to have begun at midnight on

17th February of that year![13] In the Western world the fall of Troy, dated by modern scholars at c1200 BC, marks the time when the age of heroes, or Bronze Age, ended. In both cases the deaths of so many great warriors reduced the consciousness available to their respective communities and ushered in the new era of darkened lives and relative ignorance. Kurukshetra was the archetypal cataclysm; Troy its distant echo in the West.

For this reason the Trojan War stands as a beacon to which men in the western world, especially the Greeks, have turned for inspiration in the less heroic days of their own time. When Alexander the Great set out upon the great adventure of his conquest of Asia, he took in his personal baggage a copy of Homer's *Iliad* and began his campaign with a detour to the site of Troy to feel for himself the power of the long-dead heroes, Achilles and Hector, Odysseus, Ajax, Diomedes and the rest, who fought before the walls of the ancient city. Such men were the demi-gods of Hesiod: of unswerving courage, magnificent in bearing and action, yet full of pride, unmerciful and prone to greed, especially for the spoils of war. Their weapons testified to the wealth of their society and its emphasis on war: ashen spears were tipped with bronze and bronze swords bore silver-studded hilts, helmets were plumed with horse-hair and breastplates inlaid with scenes of heroism. Bowls and cups in which libations were offered to the gods were of gold, as was the shield of Nestor, king of Pylos. The love for these beautiful appurtenances of heroic society characterised the age, and so it was the choice of beauty by Paris when he awarded the apple to Aphrodite, rather than to the wise Hera or the learned Athena, that led to the terrible Trojan War. Aphrodite promised Paris in return the most beautiful of mortal women as his bride.

The chief quality of the Bronze Age, however, was sacrifice. Before every battle, before every feast, a sacrifice is made to the gods; for, unlike men of the succeeding Iron Age, those of the age of heroes have not entirely forgotten that to devote everything to one's own purposes leads to destruction. By the time of the Trojan War their sacrifices have degenerated. Wine and roasted, freshly-killed meat are poor substitutes for the sacrifice of wisdom which the *Bhagavad Gita* enjoins as the the highest form! Indeed, the Greek dramatists of the classical period made much of the sacrifice by King Agamemnon of his daughter, Iphigenia, who was killed in order to placate the goddess, Artemis, a friend of Troy engaged in detaining the Greek fleet at Aulis by contrary winds. The slaughter of Iphigenia indicates the debasement of the Bronze Age ideal.

For Greeks of the classical period, also, the great expedition to Troy was a memory of that unity of all Greek peoples, lack of which bedevilled their own age. Under the leadership of Agememnon, brother of the wronged Menelaus, the kings of Greece - Tyndareus of Sparta, Odysseus of Ithaca, Idomeneo of Crete, Nestor of Pylos, Achilles of the Myrmidons and many others - loyal to the oaths they had sworn to protect Helen, brought their ships and contingents of warriors. Nine years of war, the sack of Troy and the scattered journeys back to their homeland broke the unity with which they had set out.

Yet the most potent symbol of degeneration is the character of Achilles. This great soldier, whom Greeks and Trojans alike acknowledge as the master of the field, holding the key to victory, refuses to fight, because his pride has been hurt by Agamemnon's demand to hand over the beautiful, captive maiden, Briseis. Nothing induces him to fight in the Greek cause, until the death of his beloved friend, Patroclus, drives him to vengeance. Even when he kills the Trojan champion, Hector, his wrath at the death of his friend has not left him. Vehemently he denies the last request of Hector for an honourable funeral and submits the hero's body to be dragged around the walls of Troy before the eyes of King Priam and the brokenhearted Andromache. At last, he is moved by the intolerable suffering of Priam and hands Hector's mutilated body over to his father. Homer thus portrays Achilles as the hero in the last epoch of the heroic age, one who had not held firmly enough to the ideals of his age, to the real qualities of leadership, to truthfulness, justice and benevolence to all his people. Even the declining hero, however, is a magnificent figure, towering over the common man, contemptuous of material interests and petty concerns, loving honour above life itself:

> "... head tossing his gleaming helmet, four horns strong and the golden plumes shook that the god of fire drove in bristling thick along its ridge. Bright as that star amid the stars in the night sky, star of the evening, brightest star that rides the heavens, so fire flared from the sharp point of the spear Achilles brandished high in his right hand."[14]

Occasionally there appear men, or even individual actions, touched with the glint of bronze, with a special kind of heroism and leadership which reaches out beyond the mundane or anticipated actions of the majority. In our time Winston Churchill was such a man. He had physical courage, of course, in abundance, as he showed when he charged with the cavalry at Omdurman against the fanatical Sudanese tribesmen of the Mahdi, as a war correspondent in South Africa, and when he flew thousands of miles in converted RAF bombers to the great wartime conferences with Roosevelt and Stalin in the Second World War. His moral courage came to the fore, especially, over the question of appeasement in the nineteen-thirties, when he alienated most of his own Conservative Party; but the supreme moment was in 1940. The French army, the victors of 1918, the heirs of the Gallic tradition of *la gloire*, had been driven into a humiliating armistice by a rejuvenated army of young Hitlerite Germans. Suddenly, the 'phoney war' and then a war across the Channel had both given way to an immediate threat of devastating aerial bombardment and the landing on British shores of a triumphant German army, set on reducing Britain to a dependency within a Nazi Empire. In Churchill's voice as he spoke to the House of Commons, and on the radio to the British people, there was an unrelenting determination to fight to the last breath to save the nation and, with it, mankind.

The Vedic tradition teaches that between each age, or *yuga*, there is a period of transition, called in Sanskrit *sandhi*, like the grammatical linking of adjacent sounds which is determined by the character of the antecedent and succeeding letter. Thus the beginning and end of each age are a kind of dawn and twilight in which the qualities of the former age merge with those of the later, until the second predominates. The *sandhi* period is said to last for one tenth of the following age. Since the seeds of the future age are being sown, it contains the essential features of that age and appears, therefore, more extreme in some respects than the greatly extended age which follows. Our own time is said by the Veda to be the *sandhi* period prior to an Iron Age.

As Edward Gibbon wrote, history is little more than the record of the crime and follies of mankind. In recorded history since the fall of Troy, successive cultures have exhibited qualities which have been the antithesis of what gave each culture its original glory. In the ancient world the magnificent literature, art and architecture was, to some degree, dependent upon the profound injustice of human slavery. In the Middle Ages, religious devotion with all that it yielded in great saints and religious art, produced also a degenerative aspect of cruel persecution and intolerance. In the modern era the remarkable development of a scientific culture has led to the growth of hideous weapons of mass destruction and an interest in so-called human engineering. Great men struggle against evil forces within themselves; they are great in spite of much of their own nature, rising above ambition, fear, corruption or disease, to which their weaker brethren succumb.

The *Vishnu Purana* describes conditions in the Iron Age in some detail. The darkness is profound. Men are surrounded by a thick husk which cuts them off from the light of the Self and leaves them powerless. Lifetimes of selfish desires have created this husk, so that they act without reference to reason and almost become automatons, the blind led by the blind. Ignorance and vice overtake their lives; tradition is lost, and society disintegrates. The natural order of the four castes is disregarded or is crudely misunderstood, so that birth, wealth or mere physical powers are thought to make a sage or a warrior, instead of the inherent qualities that constitute virtue. Those are thought wise who are merely learned, those are thought powerful who are merely rich. Men in authority abuse their positions, teaching any opinion, even heretical views that deny the scriptures, or using their power to enrich themselves. No longer do rulers hold land for the benefit of the community, using its product in the service of the people, but for their personal gain, exploiting those who work or driving them away to a life of penury. Merchants and traders extract all they can from their customers and forget the honest dealing that creates prosperity for all. Standards of craftmanship deteriorate and money becomes the only incentive, introducing a haste and shoddiness into economic life which is the ruin of society. Taxation is heaped upon the people, for the natural fund available for the community in the rent of land is appropriated by greedy individuals for their own ends.

According to the *Purana*, women disobey their fathers and husbands and turn to wealthy lords who can provide them with a life of comfort. They become careless, slatternly, immoral. The family is destroyed with the corruption of women. Unnatural vices grow apace. Children are neglected and grow up in ignorance. As the Iron Age advances, the sanctity of marriage is eroded, until young girls are giving birth and boys beget children when they themselves are far from manhood. Vigour and good sense diminish with virtue, until length of life also is cut back and men and women die at twenty years of age, overtaken by pain and suffering, their natural powers broken by abuse.

Men fear death. They watch the sky for impending doom. The rains stop and famine ravages the earth, leaving a desert where once were golden crops and pleasant pastures. As the torment grows, faith disappears and everything is questioned. Of what authority are the scriptures? Who are the wise? Of what purpose is sacrifice or prayer? Is there a God? Indeed, the advance of the Iron Age is measured by the growth of heresy and by the decline in the number of virtuous men, by the lack of effort to achieve virtue and by the loss of respect for teachers of the scriptures. Every man thinks himself the equal of the wise.

The Greek poet Hesiod knew this. In the age of iron, he said, *aidos* and *nemesis* will leave the earth. *Aidos* is the feeling of reverence or shame which restrains men from wrong; *nemesis* is the feeling of righteous indignation aroused especially by the sight of the wicked in undeserved prosperity.

> "Last, to Olympus from the broad-pathed Earth,
>
> Hiding their loveliness in robes of white,
>
> To join the gods, abandoning mankind,
>
> Will go the spirits of Righteousness and Shame."[15]

History has recorded innumerable examples of the ignorance, violence, cruelty and immorality of men in such an age. The prime example from the ancient world of the blindness which denies every vestige of truth and urges on the forces of evil and destruction is given by the Gospels:

> "And the voices of them and of the chief priests prevailed. And Pilate gave sentence that it should be as they required. And he released unto them him that for sedition and murder was cast into prison, whom they had desired, but he delivered Jesus to their will."[16]

The chief priests and scribes of the Jews could not bear the challenge to their authority represented by Jesus. Though he teaches the true law, they claim that his words are heresy. When Pilate wishes to release him, the Jewish mob demand that he is condemned and Barabbas, a convicted criminal, released.

The Bronze Age witnesses passion and cruelty, but in the decline of humanity, this is a giant step further, the triumph of unreason, the stark mistaking of good for evil. It is as though the prisoners in Plato's analogy of the cave have closed a stone over the entrance, consigning themselves to perpetual darkness. Thus entombed, they can only await the Saviour who will roll it back and show them the light of the immortal sun.

The Jewish leaders were merely the first people to make this great denial of Christ's teaching. Many were to follow. The Middle Ages abounds in examples of the denial of the very principles which were everywhere on the lips of churchmen. A celebrated example was the absurd horror of the Fourth Crusade in the early thirteenth century. Supported, with some misgiving, by the omnicompetent Pope Innocent III, the sun to the Emperor's moon, as he called himself, the crusaders set off from Venice, destined for Muslim-held Egypt, but arriving eventually at Constantinople on the pretext of re-instating a Greek prince as Emperor. The real motives of most of the crusaders were revealed when negotiations with the leaders inside the great walled city broke down. Two and a half centuries before it fell to the Turks, Constantinople was stormed and ravished by the soldiers of Venice, France and Flanders.

There was not much fighting in the streets. The invaders had soon taken the Imperial Palace and installed the Venetian Doge and the Frankish leaders in the council chambers of the Byzantine Empire. From there the word went out to the rank and file of the armies that they could sack the city. For nine hundred years it had been the capital of Christendom. It housed the greatest art treasures of civilised Europe, the finest churches, the most splendid houses, and a cultured Christian population. Fury, greed and lust worthy of savages assaulted it without mercy.

Frenchmen and Flemings snatched away whatever glittered and smashed the rest; the Venetians, with a touch of discrimination, carried away the most valuable treasures to adorn their own streets and houses. Thus the exquisite bronze horses, possibly those of the Delphi charioteer of the fifth century BC, became the property of the Venetian Republic and St. Marks. Monasteries, churches and libraries were wrecked. Nuns were ravished in their own convents. In the greatest church of all, Hagia Sophia, soldiers drunk on looted wine, tore down the great silken hangings, broke asunder the silver iconostasis, and trampled on sacred books and icons, whilst a prostitute sat upon the throne of the Patriarch and sang ribald songs to amuse her would-be clients. Outside in the streets, women and children lay dying. "Even the Saracens would have been more merciful," wrote the historian Nicetas. All this was done in the name of the Cross of Christ, as the "Croisade".

In modern history, since the Florentine Renaissance, the horrors of perverted religion have given way to those of perverted science. Not lightly has the twentieth century been called the century of total war. Advancing technology refines the instruments of war. It also creates the capacity for governments to become totalitarian, to enter into every aspect of men's lives, to control their workplace and hearth, their education and feelings. In this century sixty thousand British soldiers were shot down on the Somme in one day, several million Russian peasants were deliberately killed in the name of collectivisation, millions of Jews, gypsies, Slavs and others were murdered in Hitler's concentration camps; the women and children of Oradour-sur-Glane were burnt to death in the parish church on the orders of a Nazi commander; tens of thousands died in the incendiary bomb raid by the R.A.F. on Hamburg; hundreds of thousands when the atomic bombs fell on Hiroshima and Nagasaki. Yet such almost random examples of gross brutality may foreshadow the possibilities that arise from the use of drugs, genetic 'engineering', chemical and biological warfare and other misuses of science.

The terrible events of the *sandhi* period of the Iron Age, such as those which occur today - civil wars, terrorism, the murder and abuse of children, drug addiction, pornography, new diseases of body and mind - all these, are effects. What are the causes? History may only give glimpses into what forces undermine a complete society but in the *Bhagavad Gita*, the Lord Krishna explains how the degeneration which results in such inhuman action may befall the individual:

"When a man dwells on the objects of sense, he creates an attraction for them; attraction develops into desire, and desire breeds anger. Anger induces delusion; delusion, loss of memory; through loss of memory, reason is shattered; and loss of reason leads to destruction."[17]

The worst excesses of modern times mirror those described in the *Vishnu Purana*. The period of transition, or *sandhi*, contains foreshadowings of all that is to come. When the warrior caste was destroyed at Kurukshetra, the time of *sandhi* began. After the turbulence dies down, there may be a plateau of relative peace and prosperity before the cataclysm of the inevitable end of the whole cycle of ages, the twilight of the gods. A great teacher may revive the ancient wisdom, as Marsilio Ficino did in fifteenth century Florence, and for a time the world, or a part of it, may live in the reflected light of former greatness.

To understand the great myth of the four *yugas* only as an explanation of decline, or an inevitable falling-off from goodness and light to an end in evil, misery and darkness, is to ignore its challenge to human intelligence. Each age is a plateau that cannot be raised or lowered to that of the preceeding or succeeding age; but within it the conscious efforts of those who rise above the general standards of the time may draw a society up to achievements of rare and splendid brilliance, just as some may bring it down to unusual depths of degradation. Civilisation advances through recourse to consciousness. As men and women awake to the real potentialities of their own nature, which is divine, so the cycle of a civilisation turns upwards, and for some individuals the life of a higher age may become a living experience, as Ficino described so often in his letters to his friends. Like the human body, mankind may experience secular decline transcended by those times when love or goodness or beauty intercede. Each man or woman may transcend the ills of the body; a society may transcend the age of iron. The record of that transcendence is history.

Every man, even in the Iron Age, faces a choice. At some moment, perhaps frequently, the truth can be discerned, and a step made towards it. How often have the great men of history stood out as those who turned against the current, who did not flinch from this choice? Each meets his Garden of Gethsemane: each is offered the cup. To accept it is to move towards the eternal; to deny it is to be carried away by the headlong force of passing events. History, even of the Iron Age, is concerned with life and not death.

## References:

1. Marsilio Ficino, 'letter to Bernardo Bembo', in *The Letters of Marsilio Ficino*, trans. School of Economic Science, Shepheard-Walwyn, London, 1988, vol. 4, no. 41.

2. Ficino, *Letters*, trans. School of Economic Science, Shepheard-Walwyn, London, 1981, vol. 3, p. 34.

3. *Srimad Bhagavatam*, trans. Swami Prabhavananda, Shri Ramakrishna Math, Mylapore, 1972, Book II, ch. 11, p. 251.

4. *Acts of Apostles*, ch. 4, v. 32, King James Version.

5. *Ramayana*, trans. Hari Prasad Shastri, Shantisadan, London, 1962, vol. 2, p. 328.

6. Plato, *Republic*, trans. B. Jowett, Random House, New York, 1937, Book III, 415.

7. *Ten Principle Upanishads*, trans. Shree Purohit Swami and W. B. Yeats, Faber and Faber, London, 1938, p. 122.

8. *Bhaghavad Gita*, Faber and Faber, London, 1965, ch. 12, v. 5.

9. Diogenes 'Cynicus' in *Epistolographis Graecis*, 36, trans. H. J. Rose, in C. Kerenyi, *The Heroes of the Greeks*, Thames and Hudson, London, 1959, p. 183.

10. Hesiod, *Works and Days*, trans. D. Wender, Penguin, London, 1973, 11. 158-165.

11. Shakespeare, *Henry V*, Collins, London, 1951, act I, scene 1.

12. *Bhaghavad Gita*, ch. 2, vv. 19-20.

13. *Sanskrit-English Dictionary*, M. Monier-Williams, O.U.P., Oxford, 1976, p. 854, col. 1.

14. Homer *Iliad*, trans. R. Fagles, Folio Society, London, 1996, Book XXII, p. 473.

15. Hesiod, *Works and Days*, 11. 197-200.

16. *Luke*, ch. 23, vv. 13-25, King James Version.

17. *Bhagavad Gita*, ch. 2, vv. 61-62.

*Part 2*

# Egyptian Civilisation

## Chapter 3

# God Beyond All Name

### *Egyptian Philosophy and Religion*

"It was there that men, long before others, discovered various religions in what may be called their cradle, and now carefully preserve the origins of worship in their esoteric scriptures. Training in this sphere taught Pythagoras to worship the gods in secret, gave unquestioned authority to whatever he said or ordained, and caused him often to exhibit his golden thigh at Olympia and to be frequently seen in colloquy with an eagle. Egypt taught Anaxagoras to foretell a rain of meteorites and to predict earthquakes by the feel of mud in a well. Solon too was helped by the dicta of the priests of Egypt in framing his legal code, which has given Roman law its strongest support. Plato drew on this source, and it was after a visit to Egypt that he achieved his highest flights in language which rivalled in sublimity Jove himself, and served with glory on the field of wisdom."[1]

*Sailing boat on the Nile*

THE ANCIENT HISTORY of the Middle East offers some evidence that the change from a Bronze Age to an Iron Age took place there about five thousand years ago. Almost simultaneously, in the valleys of the Euphrates and Tigris rivers and in the Nile valley in Egypt, urban life and the art of writing made their appearance. The Sumerians began to use wedge-shaped marks imprinted on wet clay tablets, known as cuneiform, and the Egyptians developed hieroglyphics incised in stone, both ideograms or pictures, and phonograms, or marks indicating sounds. Viewing from the tradition of the four great ages (or *yugas*), writing was not necessarily an improvement, but rather a prerequisite for a new age which could no longer rely on oral communication.

The Sumerians built massive ziggurats at Babylon, Ur and Choga Zambil, like successors to the Tower of Babel, which symbolised the divisions and confusions of tongue of men whose single great Bronze Age civilisation was disintegrating. Near Ur, also, was produced the first work of western literature, *The Epic of Gilgamesh*, whose hero was the archetypal man of the Iron Age, in that he undertook an arduous journey in search of eternal life, forgetful that such a prize was already in his possession.

The country, however, destined to become the bridge over which would pass the wisdom of the primeval ages, was Egypt. Pythagoras, Anaxagoras, Solon and Plato would indeed go there, but so too Joseph, Moses and perhaps Jesus drew from Egypt whatever they required to play their roles in the transmission of the original Word. There in the Nile valley, the brilliant light of the desert, the stark rock of the bordering mountains, the ferocity of the overhead sun and, above all, the purifying, sustaining waters of the Nile, running like the stalk of a lotus plant to the bright flower of the Delta, reminded men of the half-forgotten questions, "What am I?", "What is this universe?" and "What is my relationship to it?"

Out of the east the great Sun God Ra rose in his chariot to climb to his zenith over the green serpent of the Nile, before falling blood-red into the western desert. Through the night he traversed the underworld, where dwelt the souls of the dead, awaiting the call to life, until once more his golden disc appeared above the lip of the sandstone mountains. Not only in the diurnal sun, but also in the regular annual flooding of the great river, which alone made life possible, the Egyptians saw material images of the origin, sustenance and dissolution of the universe itself. The cycle of life and death, birth and rebirth, the pattern of creation, were self-evident; and there, too, was the image of Man, born to experience eternal recurrence, yet like the Nile, unchanging.

In ancient Egypt the seasons drove life before them as dust before the *sirocco*. The lush verdure of the cool season gave way to the parched fields of summer, when, after sweltering nights, the first rays of the morning sun struck like the flames of a furnace and the river turned yellowish-green, depleted below its banks. Later in the year the great head of water from the southern mountains flooded the valley with its miraculous silt and the river changed to rust between the inundated fields. Suddenly the land once more was green with grass and unripe cereals.

The life-giving Nile drains a basin of one million square miles, discharging one hundred thousand cubic feet of water, on average, every second. Nowhere is the flood-plain more than twelve miles wide, until the Delta is reached below ancient Memphis and Heliopolis. So dominant was the great river to the ancient Egyptians that it was worshipped as a god and entered into the meaning of hieroglyphics, so that an ideogram of a ship with full sail meant "south" and of a ship without sail meant "north".

Though the Nile was the basis of existence for the people of ancient Egypt, the spirit of life came from the philosophy whose spokesman was Hermes Trismegistus, "the thrice great", so called because he was the greatest philosopher, the greatest priest and the greatest king. The earliest extant writings of Hermes date only from the first to third centuries AD, but the teaching attributed to him arose a great deal earlier, for it contains the essence of Egyptian wisdom. Hermes' teaching dispelled the idea of any separation between God and Man:

"If you do not make yourself equal to God you cannot understand him. Like is understood by like. Grow to immeasurable size, be free from every body, transcend all time. Become eternity and thus you will understand God. Suppose nothing to be impossible for yourself. Consider yourself immortal and able to understand everything: all arts, sciences and the nature of every living creature. Become higher than all heights and lower than all depths; sense as one within yourself the entire creation: fire, water, the dry and the moist. Conceive yourself to be in all places at the same time: in earth, in the sea, in heaven; that you are not yet born, that you are within the womb, that you are young, old, dead; that you are beyond death. Conceive all things at once: times, places, actions, qualities and quantities; then you can understand God."[2]*

Thus Man is both human and divine: as human he is mortal; as divine, he is immortal and partakes of the nature of the Supreme Being Himself. For this reason Egyptian civilisation presented a deep paradox. On the one hand, it was permeated with religion; its art and architecture, law and customs, daily life, and especially its treatment of death, were thoroughly religious in character, controlled by ritual, bound by formulae, dedicated to the gods. On the other hand, it was intensely earthy and practical, wealthy in gold, its science and mathematics founded on measuring the earth and the stars, its knowledge acute in agriculture and medicine, its gods portrayed as hawks and rams, snakes and bulls. Above all the paradox is compelling on the question of death. The dead are immortal, but they need chairs and tables, ears of wheat and fine clothes, toys and jewellery. It is the soul, or ba, which survives them and yet it is the body which must be preserved in canopic jars and mummy cases. Did the Egyptians believe that God is not other-worldly, that there are not two places, an earth for Man and a heaven for God, that God and Man are in reality One, and the One is here and now, not as flesh and blood, but immanent in flesh and blood? Many tombs of Pharaohs and great officials contained "false doors", marking precisely where the dead man would return into the tomb; some show statues of him returning. Life and death are present together; life is Spirit, death is matter. God is transcendent

---

\* *Marsilio Ficino believed Hermes to be the source of a tradition embracing Orpheus, Moses, Pythagoras and Plato. In Siena Cathedral a large pavement mosaic dating from c 1480AD shows Hermes as a contemporary of Moses.*

and immanent, beyond flesh, but present in it. For this reason the greatest Egyptian sculpture portrays men as simultaneously in life and in death before the great deities, or as the dead, confronting Osiris with the life they have led. Judgement is now, for it is in life that the truth is met, and to ignore it is death.

This cryptic unity was present also in the Pharaoh as the head of Egyptian society. He was both man and god, the touchstone of the immanence of Spirit in the world. He was identified with the great state god, Horus, but he was also the war leader, the high priest who in theory conducted all rituals in the temples throughout Egypt, the architect who laid the cornerstones of the sacred precincts, the owner of all land, the head of the administration. During many years of his reign the work of preparing his tomb would be undertaken, so that on death his body would enter a mausoleum worthy of gods, a mastaba, a pyramid or a rock temple in the Valley of the Kings. Such is the honour due to Man when he is recognised as God.

Except, perhaps, in its beginning Egyptian religion was complex, with a bewildering variety of gods and goddesses, whose roles were never exactly defined or constant. The complexity grew as religion, together with other institutions, degenerated over the enormous length of three millennia from the origin of the civilisation to its collapse in Roman times, but complexity was a result also of three aspects of religion always present in Egypt. For a small, educated group of Egyptians the gods were symbolic; they were the outward symbols of an inner teaching and the forms they were given by artists were no more than evocative portrayals of intangible forces. For the Egyptian state, however, the pantheon was an official system of religious belief, closely bound up with the status and authority of the Pharaoh. The third aspect of religion was the popular, social function of providing festivals and other occasions when the mass of the people could celebrate and express their feelings with little regard to religious meaning. Beyond all this lay a simple and all-embracing monotheism:

*Temple of Luxor: Rameses II*

"God is One and alone, and none other existeth with Him"

and

"God is a spirit, a hidden spirit, the spirit of spirits, the great spirit of the Egyptians, the divine spirit."[3]

The name usually given to God as formless Spirit containing all existence was Atum, meaning "complete". From Atum, but not by his activity, came creation, instigated by the great creator god, called Ptah at Memphis under the earliest dynasties, and later, at Heliopolis, called Ra. Ptah created by means of speech and was always represented in human form, unlike most other Egyptian gods. His creative power was said to be manifest in every heartbeat and every sound. To the common people he was the sculptor of the earth, or the creator of all beings on a potter's wheel. In such a guise the ancient Greeks assimilated him to their god of the forge, Hephaestus. As late as 1000 BC, the Pharaoh Amenemope remembered the creative power of Ptah's speech when he said:

"The tongue of a man is the steering oar of a boat,

And the lord of All is its pilot."[4]

Ra was understood as a universal and benevolent force, creating the sky and the two horizons, like a curtain; when he opens his eyes the day shines forth, when he closes them night descends. The disc of the sun, called the Aten, is his physical manifestation; the hours, days and festivals of the year are at his command; so too are fire and food and the great life-sustaining flooding of the Nile. When the sun descends below the horizon its passage through the night represents the creative force in men and all creatures passing through the underworld of darkness and trial, before death is overcome in the rejuvenation of the dawn; a symbolism recreated later in the legend of Osiris. The Pharaoh, too, was seen as the embodiment of Ra, though usually under the name of the god Horus, depicted as a falcon with an all-seeing eye and swifter in movement than any other creature.

Fundamental to the Egyptian view of life was the concept of order, represented by the goddess Maat, who was the symbol of Law in all its aspects, the natural law of the created universe, the law of human society, both natural to Man and formulated by law-makers, and the correctness or straightness of things. The Sanskrit *dhatu**  Ma, meaning 'measure', perhaps coincidentally carries the meaning embodied in Maat. Devotion to Maat brought with it respect for all forms of law and the ordering of life, both communal and personal, according to natural law. Only through acknowledgement of Maat could the unsurpassed precision of the masonry work of the pyramids be achieved, the exquisite repose of the stone sculptures, the ebony furniture and gold jewellery of the royal tombs, or the massive irrigation system that measured out the floodwaters of the Nile. The Pharaoh was the interpreter of Maat to the people. His divine nature gave him access to the inner causes of things, to the realm of law governed by Maat. Thus, he dispensed justice from this fount of knowledge, spreading order into society whenever he spoke and acted. Provided he himself remained pure, he could not err, for the knowledge of law had no ambiguity, no shadow of turning. For this reason, to harm the Pharaoh, to contaminate him in any way, was the most heinous of crimes, for thus was the divine ordering of the

---

*  *A dhatu is the root or seed-form of a word.*

state endangered. The unity of the kingdom arose from this divine pharaonic power, based not upon supreme force or even upon compelling tradition, but upon the knowledge of natural law available to the pure sovereign. He was not a mere symbol: with his purity the kingdom flourished in unity, with his impurity it declined and disintegrated, for he was the embodiment of Maat. As Amenemope said, "The boat of the covetous is abandoned in the mud, while the skiff of the truly temperate man sails on."

The creative force of Ptah, or Ra, was understood to give rise to the elements: Shu (air), Tefnut (water), Geb (earth) and Nut (sky). With other gods, such as Osiris, Seth, Isis and Nephthys, these elements formed a pantheon of nine gods - including the creator god. Within this ninefold scheme - or ennead - the triad played an essential part, though the composition of triads of gods varied greatly between religious centres and times. What remained constant was the underlying structure of one-three-nine (though at Hermopolis the ogdoad of eight gods prevailed,) indicating the law that three is the number governing creation and events in the created world.

Parallel to this cosmological system was an analysis of Man. Hermes Trismegistus taught that, in truth, Man has his being in God; hence the Atum was both the Spirit of spirits and the innermost Self of Man. Each man also possessed a soul, or ba, which, at least by day, moved freely, uninhibited by the body, like the bird which represented the soul in Egyptian religious art. The soul's immortality rose above transmigration from one lifetime to another, for it was the ka, a sort of individual mind, which transmigrated and was looked after in the tomb, the house of the ka, by offerings of food, until it returned to earth in a new body. Finally, the kaibit was the shadow of the soul, the illusory "me", which each man believes to be himself, until he awakes from the dream of life on earth.

Man's search for eternal life, a central idea in Egyptian culture, was helped by another great god, Thoth, often identified with Hermes Trismegistus and later assimilated into the classical Graeco-Roman pantheon as Hermes/Mercury. Thoth was the inventor of all arts and sciences, the interpreter of god to Man and the divine scribe.

" I am Thoth the skilled scribe whose hands are pure.......who drives away evil, who writes what is true, who detests falsehood, whose pen defends the Lord of All; master of laws who interprets writings, whose words establish the Two Lands."[5]

As though in response to the loss of the oral tradition of the Bronze Age, Thoth's introduction of writing was a basic contribution to human well-being and indicated the place of Egypt as a bridge from one age to the next – it was said that "Ra has spoken, Thoth has written." He was also the chronologer of heaven and earth and, therefore, a mathematician. The baboon was sacred to him, but his real worth was shown in his depiction as a crested ibis with iridescent plumage, which appeared in the hieroglyph for the word "to be radiant". Moreover in his identification with Hermes Trismegistus, Thoth stood for the power of reason, which points to the ultimate truth of Man's unity with God.

The enduring concern of ancient Egypt with the question of life and death was demonstrated in its great monumental buildings - the pyramids, mastabas and rock tombs - and in its sculpture, painting and symbolism. In the widespread use of the scarab, an image of a dung beetle, this concern was expressed at all levels of society and throughout Egyptian history. For the dung beetle was thought to consume its own egg, after laying it in a ball of dung, and hence to be continually reborn, like a microcosm of all natural cycles, especially that of the diurnal sun. As seals and amulets, often exquisitely made, the scarab reminded peasant and Pharaoh alike of the cycle of birth and death and of the immortal soul which looks with indifference upon the repeated drama of nature. Even as late as the fifth century BC, the Greek historian, Herodotus, could describe a rather debased form of the search for immortality:

> "When the rich give a party and the meal is finished, a man carries round amongst the guests a wooden image of a corpse in a coffin, carved and painted to look as much like the real thing as possible, and anything from eighteen inches to three feet long; he shows it to each guest in turn, and says: 'Look upon this body as you drink and enjoy yourself; for you will be just like it when you are dead.'"[6]

## References:

1. Ammianus Marcellinus, *The Later Roman Empire*, trans. W. Hamilton, Penguin, London, 1986, Book XXII, p. 254.

2. *The Way of Hermes*, trans. C. Salaman, D. van Oyen and W. Wharton, Duckworth, London, 1999, pp. 57-58.

3. *The Egyptian Book of the Dead*, ed. E. A. Wallis Budge, Dover, New York, 1967, p. xcii.

4. W. MacQuitty, *The Wisdom of the Ancient Egyptians*, Sheldon, London, 1978.

5. *Book of the Dead*, trans. R. O. Faulkner, British Museum, London, 1985, Spell 128.

6. Herodotus, *The Histories*, trans. A. de Selincourt, Penguin, London, 1972, Book II, pp. 158-9.

*Chapter 4*

# Giants in the Earth

## *The Old Kingdom*

ABOUT THE YEAR 2900 BC an Egyptian king, called Menes, was installed with a double crown, the red crown of lower Egypt on the Nile Delta and the high white crown of upper Egypt, which extended along the Nile valley to the cataracts in the south. He took as his capital the city of Memphis, situated at the junction of the two Egypts. Upper Egypt had conquered its northern neighbour, but the unification was not merely a conquest, for a deeper unity was established. Of the little that is known about the first few centuries of this so-called early dynastic period, we can say that writing made its appearance and with it the use of papyrus. Tombs contained magnificent goods of metal, ivory, ebony and lapis-lazuli. Fine stone vases were produced in large quantities. The new capital was ringed with a great white wall.

*Imhotep's Pyramid*

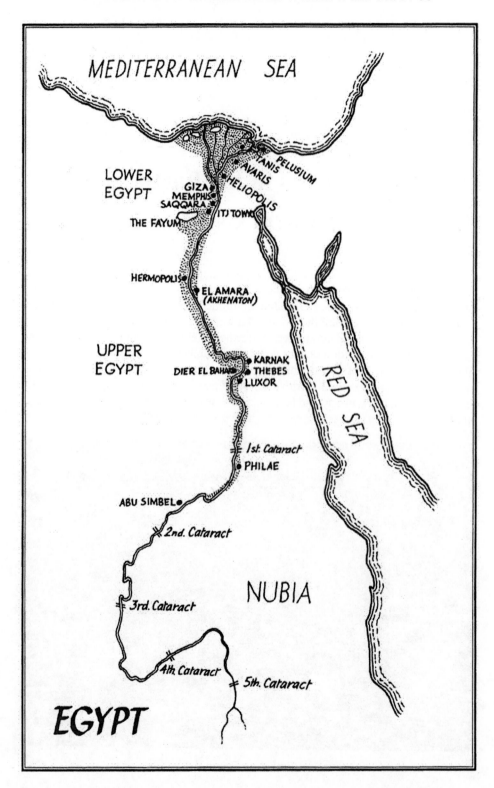

With the third dynasty, a brilliant creative phase began. It was associated above all with a man who may be called the father of Egypian civilisation, known as the son of Ptah and later identified with Hermes Trismegistus. His human name was Imhotep, "he who comes in peace". Grand Vizier to King Djoser, who ruled united Egypt from c2630 BC to c2611 BC, he was at the same time a philosopher, priest and scribe, musician, healer, architect, astronomer and chief minister. This latter role is well attested by the public recognition given to him by King Djoser: Imhotep's name appears prominently in an inscription at Saqqara, a city at the heart of the new development.

There, just west of the Nile, near Memphis, Imhotep built the first pyramid. It began as a simple mastaba, a flat-topped rectangular royal tomb, similar to others built since the time of King Menes; but, using this as a base, Imhotep raised five more layers, each diminishing in size to form a step pyramid. Later pyramids followed this construction, though the steps were filled in to form true pyramids. The buttress walls of the step pyramid, sloping inward, prevented the explosion of the whole mass of stone, a vital structural feature. Imhotep's pyramid was the centrepiece of a group of religious buildings faced with fine white stone and surrounded by a continuous wall. They served as a magnificent funerary complex for Djoser, in particular a place which would provide for every need during his eternal life beyond the grave. The Saqqara constructions clearly served other ends also. For example, Imhotep was the first builder to use solid stone blocks cut as masonry; previous builders had used stone only for foundation walls. This stonemasonry very soon became as fine as at any time in recorded history, for only by exact measurement and fitting could the colossal weight of the pyramids be contained. In addition, Imhotep invented the stone column, creating at Saqqara grooved columns, not entirely free-standing, with shaft, capital and base, remarkably similar in style to the Doric of the classical Greeks two thousand years later. Decoration was not neglected, for the interior of the step pyramid contained halls and corridors lined with green and blue glazed tiles with inlaid faience, showing the name of Djoser, whilst the column shafts were shaped as groups of palm branches and the capitals as formalised palm leaves.

The plant motif was repeated throughout the great courtyard of the funerary complex - where also stood statues of the king and his family, including a colossus. One statue has survived intact, a limestone life-size seated figure identified as the Pharaoh Djoser, the underside of which bears the name Imhotep. This is the earliest known royal portrait and is thought to have been carved by the technique of drawing on three faces of a stone block and carving inward until all three merge, a method to be recommended 4000 years later by Michelangelo. The perfect composure of the figure owes much to the highly refined discipline required by the sculptor. Here was the prototype of all seated statues for the rest of Egyptian history. Originally the statue was placed in the serdab, or sealed chamber, built alongside the step pyramid, its rock crystal eyes peeping out through two holes in the wall. The stillness of the meditative pose, common to all such Egyptian seated figures, reveals the inner strength of Egyptian civilisation.

The step pyramid measures 140 x 118 metres at the base, with a height of 60 metres. Its construction demonstrates a profound knowledge of mathematics, which the later pyramids at Giza indicate was closely related to the study of astronomy.

Imhotep was in fact associated with Thoth as a recorder of the movements of the heavens. Egyptian society, throughout its history, retained a firm belief in the influence of heavenly bodies on human life. Yet Imhotep's later reputation and deification rested more upon his skill in healing by the use of music to restore the inner harmonies of body and mind. His practice and teaching of this ancient healing technique was the inspiration behind the wealth of medical papyri recording incantations, which made Egypt the medical centre of the ancient world and led the Greeks to identify Asclepius, their god of healing, with Imhotep himself. At Epidaurus, Cos, Pergamus and elsewhere the sanctuaries of Asclepius held the restorative spirit of the Egyptian sage. New meaning can perhaps be found in Socrates' famous last jest, as recorded by Plato. Turning to Crito, he said "I owe a cock to Asclepius; will you remember to pay the debt?", a final confirmation perhaps that an ancient teaching received through tradition from Imhotep was to be passed on by his disciples. If so, it was Plato primarily who fulfilled Crito's promise, "The debt shall be paid."[1]

The history written by the Egyptian priest, Manetho, in the third century BC credits Imhotep with a far-reaching reform of Egyptian hieroglyphics. In the southern tomb at Saqqara the inscriptions on the walls were executed with a new and enlivening purity of line, which gave to each glyph the power of a sacred symbol. The new system of ideograms and phonograms was both simpler and more consistent than that which had arisen at the beginning of the third millennium. Under the fifth dynasty the interior walls of the pyramids of Unas were inscribed with the Pyramid Texts, dealing with the passage of the king after death, in similarly perfect glyphs, whose precision carried the sacred character of their meaning. About a thousand years after Imhotep's reforms these Old Kingdom hieroglyphics probably became the model from which the alphabet, the most pervasive of all writing systems, evolved. Imhotep had solved the problem of incapacity to listen to and retain accurately the words of aural language. As the creator of alphabetic writing, he was the great god Thoth, for "Ra has spoken, Thoth has written."

These practical arts - architecture, sculpture, astronomy, music, healing and writing - together with the administrative work of the office of Grand Vizier, were not in reality so diverse. Their hallmark was the measure of the goddess Maat, the harmony of natural law arising from the original sound, the speech of Ptah, creator of all things. Imhotep discovered it in constructions of hewn stone, in music and language and in the carving of glyphs.

In the eyes of the people, his greatest office was as Chief Lector Priest in the temple of Ptah at Memphis, which made him the intermediary between the Pharaoh and the unseen powers of the universe. Only priests and the Pharaoh were allowed to enter the temples. There, the Lector Priest, if the Pharaoh were absent, would make the offering of food sacred by means of incantations, so that it might sustain both living and dead. A communion was established with the spirits of the dead and the sacred food united them with the spirits of the living. The ritual enhanced the awareness of their unity in Atum; it may have been the origin of the later Etruscan and Roman emphasis upon the need to hold sacred the ancestors of the family, the manes.

When a later Egyptian poet seemed to be sceptical about the belief in an after-life, he was perhaps looking for a deeper understanding of immortality than a mere

*Chephren's Pyramid and Sphinx*

*Great Pyramid of Cheops*

revival of the physical body and worldly joys, for the poem was always associated with the name of Imhotep.

> "And no man cometh again from the tomb
>
> To tell of what passeth below.
>
> So feast in tranquillity now,
>
> For none taketh his goods to the tomb,
>
> And none cometh back again."[2]

Such lines suggest that the inner meaning of the pyramid burials was to symbolise the connection with eternity through the present - "so feast in tranquillity now" - rather than to provide for the material welfare of a king resurrected in the future. The poem ascribes these words to Imhotep in keeping with the spirit of his work.

Imhotep, and other master teachers who laid the foundations of Egyptian civilization, created with the pyramids the most substantial buildings in recorded history. The largest, the so-called Great Pyramid of Khufu at Giza, contains about 2,300,000 blocks of masonry with an average weight of two and a half tons each. That of Khafre, adjacent to the Great Pyramid, is only slightly smaller. There is little evidence that the Egyptians lifted these stones into place. What is more likely is that sliding was used. The top surfaces of each row of stones were extremely level, suggesting that they were finally dressed in situ, which would enable the row above to be slid into place. Wet gypsum would have made a good lubricant and about eight men could have pushed one stone. The vast size of the fourth dynasty pyramids makes them landmarks for the age to come; so too does the precision of craftmanship. On the north side of the Great Pyramid for example, the gap between stones nowhere

---

*The shape of the Great Pyramid is deceptively simple, each of the four sides being an isosceles triangle, with the walls sloping at an angle of 51° 51', to meet at a point. The tiniest error in this angle, and in the angles of the corner ridges, would make a considerable error at the top. Its square base is aligned exactly to the four points of the compass. When the white limestone outer cover was in place - only the top of the pyramid of Khafre is still covered - each side measured 230 metres, the height was 146 m and the slanting side from the top to mid-point of base (the apothem) 185 m. The Greek mathematician, Agatharcharides, said that the length of a base side was one eighth of a minute of a degree of longitude (Eratosthenes having discovered for the Greeks the circumference of the earth). This is confirmed by calculation: (230 x 8 x 60 x 360)m = 39,744 kms (actual circumference 40,076 kms). Furthermore, if the perimeter of the base of 920 m is divided by 2pi the result is 146.4 m. Thus the height is equivalent to the radius of a circle of which the perimeter would be the circumference. This means that the pyramid can be seen as a model of the earth's hemisphere on the scale of 1 : 43,200 (i.e. 2 x 60 x 360). Multiplying the height of 146 m by this figure gives the radius of the earth, 6,307 km (actual polar radius 6,357 km). Finally, the Greek geographer Strabo found that the apothem of the Great Pyramid is one stadium long (= 185.5m). Using Eratosthenes calculation, the Greeks defined a stadium as one six-hundredth of a degree of longitude. Hence the architect of the Great Pyramid made the apothem one part in 216,000 (= 43,200 x 5) of the circumference of the earth (600 x 360 = 216,000). Obviously, the square of the apothem is also equal to the sum of the squares of the height and the square of half the base, by Pythagoras's theorem. $(185^2 = 146^2 + 115^2)$. Measurements in metres are approximate; the Egyptians used royal cubits related to the length of the forearm.*

exceeds one fiftieth of an inch. On the east and west sides, the margin of error in squareness is 0.03 per cent. The huge pavement on which it rests has a deviation from the true plane of 0.004 per cent. No mortar was used in the construction.*

The positioning of the Great Pyramid at a point where the diagonals of the base, if extended, would just enclose the Nile Delta, and where a due north line would cut the Delta in half also indicates great accuracy in land surveying, a science which was the origin of the whole system of Egyptian geometry. The relationship between pyramids and the earth was probably subsumed within the study of astronomy, to which the Egyptians were dedicated. Not only did they believe in the unseen influence of the heavens on human life, they also, as an agricultural people, depended upon an accurate calendar and therefore upon a precise science of astronomy. The Greek philosopher, Proclus, claimed that the Great Pyramid had been used as an observatory before it was completed. Its Egyptian name was "the place of the rising and setting sun". There are four interior passages, two facing northwards, two southwards, which could have been used for astronomical observations. At the time of construction the northern passages pointed at Alpha Draconis, the star then nearest to true north, and at Ursa Minor. The southern passages pointed to Orion and Sirius. A reflector, perhaps a pool of water, may have been used to facilitate observations within the pyramid. Such a system enables stars to be observed even by day, since the sky looks dark when seen through a long tube. Proclus' view implies that observations were made for some years, perhaps to construct a calendar and astrological charts, until the final stages of construction blocked the passages and also prevented observation through the "roof. Other evidence supports the connection between Egyptian architecture and astronomy. For example, at the huge temple of Amon-Ra at Karnak, built over a millennium later, the sunlight on the Summer solstice penetrates directly into the inner sanctuary.

About fifty royal pyramids were built in the millennia after Imhotep. They served as royal tombs and typically were accompanied by a mortuary chapel and a valley temple at the end of a causeway. To the valley temple came the Pharaoh's body, brought by barge on the Nile or a canal from the main river. There it would be purified, and sometimes mummified, before being taken along the causeway to its resting place inside the pyramid. Being divine, the Pharaoh was immortal, and since the spiritual realm was seen as immanent in the physical, his tomb was to be as indestructible as possible. Thus the pyramids were constant reminders of eternity and of a life devoted to the Spirit, rather than to the fleeting images of passing time.

Following the exemplary statue of King Djoser at Saqqara, later Old Kingdom sculptors demonstrated that same awareness of eternity. A statue in hard, smooth-surfaced diorite of the Pharaoh Khafre encapsulates the unchanging majesty and unquestionable authority of a rightful ruler imbued with the power of Maat, whilst a bust of Prince Ankhaf in limestone shows a further dimension of royalty, the responsibility and compassion of a sensitive father of his people. The statue of a seated scribe from Saqqara has been described as representing a bureaucrat; if so, Egyptian administration must have reaped untold benefits of efficiency and integrity from the awesome wakefulness of the bright eyes and balanced cross-legged posture. In general, Old Kingdom sculpture established canons of excellence to which not only Egyptian, but Greek and all others, could aspire.

The greatest enigma of all presented by the Old Kingdom was the Sphinx. This great rock-carved lion with a human head, whose name means 'living image', may be merely a symbol of royal majesty from the time of the Pharaoh Khafre, for sculptures of him were found in the adjoining temple. However, there is an alternative view which casts into doubt the whole chronology of ancient Egypt. The Greeks and Romans certainly believed that the Sphinx, and much else in Egypt, was a great deal older than the Old Kingdom: they give dates of between 24,000 and 36,000 years before their own times, claiming that the people of Egypt then were the original followers of Horus and that the land was a green savannah. One major piece of evidence supports this view, namely that the Sphinx, which is heavily eroded, could hardly have been eroded by wind and sand, since it was probably buried in sand for millennia. Water erosion would produce the required effect. Since the last major flooding of Egypt took place about 10,000 - 15,000 years ago at the end of the last ice age, the Sphinx, if it was water eroded, was carved at least that long ago. Plato hints at such an antiquity for Egypt when he describes a tale told by an old man to the Greek sage, Solon.[3] The last ice age contained four periods of relative warmth, so the Greek belief in the green savannah of the followers of Horus is not unreasonable. Plato wrote also of a continent of Atlantis, which disappeared totally beneath the ocean to the west of the pillars of Hercules. Was there a Bronze Age civilisation in Egypt, of which the Old Kingdom and its successors were merely the remnants? Only the Sphinx knows.

The later dynasties of the Old Kingdom could not match the pyramid building of the giants of the fourth dynasty, but the fifth dynasty (c2465-c2325 BC) produced the fine pyramids of Unas with its Pyramid Texts, which became the source for the numerous later so-called "Books of the Dead". These writings seemed to offer a future life for the soul and gave the dead the power to leave the tomb. The true meaning of the "Books of the Dead" may be indicated by the title used by the ancient Egyptians for them, which was "Chapters of Coming-forth by Day". As the philosophy of Orphism later taught, the body is the tomb and the power to leave it resides in the soul, which need not wait upon death to come forth into life. During the fifth dynasty, the Pharaohs began to call themselves regularly the Son of Ra, a title rarely taken under the fourth dynasty, and accordingly to build elaborate sun temples at Abu Gurab, south of Giza. Fine painted relief decorations confirmed the continued quality of artistic work.

However, signs of deterioration from the justice of the early dynasties began to appear. Fifth dynasty nobles constructed larger tombs for themselves and no longer built them closely around the royal pyramid. Under the following dynasty (c2325-c2150 BC) regional governors, or nomarchs, were buried in their own homes, suggesting a degree of independence from royal power contrary to the spirit of pharaonic rule. At the same time, expeditions to Nubia, Libya, Western Asia and Sinai became more aggressive and the Egyptian army became dependent upon foreign mercenaries. The nomarchs began to claim for themselves the produce of land and service previously due only to the king. The priestly caste acquired land from the Pharaohs beyond the needs of the temples, so that priests in Upper Egypt owned land hundreds of miles away in Lower Egypt. Peasants were impoverished and economic decline hastened political disintegration. Fields became dessicated as the irrigation system, so vital to Egyptian life, broke down under the lack of coordinated government. Violence and famine went hand in hand. During the long reign of Pepi

II, the Old Kingdom collapsed. For about two hundred years (c2130-1938 BC) there was anarchy, heightened by marauding groups of Bedouin who entered the Delta.

The first cultural cycle of Egyptian civilisation had lasted about nine hundred years. In the epic scale of the pyramids, in the purity and force of its sculpture, in the precision of its hieroglyphics, in the concentration of justice and authority, in the divinity of the Pharaoh, it had set standards of life for which the later culture of Egypt would strive. New masterpieces would be produced, but these never attained the supreme heights of the earlier giants.

### References:

1. Plato, *Phaedo*, trans. Jowett, Random House, New York, 1937, p. 118.

2. Extract from *The Song of the Harper, From Imhotep to Akhenaten: An Introduction to Egyptian Philosophers*, M. K. Asante, Menaibuc, 2004, p. 82.

3. See Plato, *Timaeus*, trans. Jowett, 22ff.

## Chapter 5
# Renewing Births
### *The Middle and New Kingdoms and the Decline of Egypt*

THE ANARCHY OF THE so-called First Intermediate Period was brought to an end by a Pharaoh of the eleventh dynasty, called Mentuhotep I, whose mortuary complex at Deir-al-Bahri contained fine sculptured reliefs modelled on those of the

*Gold Mask of Tutankhamun*

Old Kingdom. The revival of pharaonic authority brought with it a new faith in the immanence of an Absolute God, now called Amon "the hidden one" and associated with the Sun as Amon-Re. Egypt, however, had changed. People sought a more personal form of religion, perhaps to strengthen their resolve after the breakdown of the previous culture.

An ancient myth described the birth of five children to the sky goddess Nut. Of these, the boy, Osiris, grew up to become the perfect Pharaoh of Egypt ensuring justice and peace and teaching the art of agriculture to his people. He married his sister Isis, who ruled in his stead whilst he went abroad to teach the people beyond his kingdom. Isis, too, was a model of virtue and knowledge, the merciful mother, goddess of fertility and of the earth, like the matriarch goddess of the later Cretans and other Mediterranean peoples.

In Osiris' absence, his brother Seth, the embodiment of evil, plotted to kill him and seize the throne of the Pharaoh for himself. He gathered around him seventy-two conspirators. When Osiris returned, Seth invited him to a great feast, during which a magnificent chest, made of cedar from Lebanon, ebony from Ethiopia and inlaid with gold and silver, ivory, lapis lazuli and precious stones, was brought to the royal table. Seth challenged everyone to see whether they could lie in the chest with a perfect fit. None could do so, until Osiris lay there, for Seth had earlier measured his brother's body by a trick. The conspirators leapt forward and slammed the lid, securing it with nails and molten lead. The chest was taken to the Delta and cast into the sea. Seth proclaimed himself Pharaoh and the grief-stricken Isis could only wander about the whole land of Egypt, seeking her lost consort. The chest came ashore at the ancient city of Byblos on the Phoenician coast, where it lodged in a tamerisk tree, of sweet scent and bark, which slowly entwined it in its branches, until the chest became a part of the trunk itself. So beautiful was the tree that Astarte, the queen of the country, removed the trunk to her palace.

Children on the Delta sea-shore told Isis of the chest set afloat in the sea. She found her way to Byblos and to Astarte's palace. In return for Isis' care for her daughter, Astarte let Isis examine the tamerisk trunk, and the body of Osiris was found by his lamenting queen, who took it back to Egypt. The evil of Seth had not abated. He stole the body and cut it into fourteen pieces to ensure that Osiris could not be reborn. They were scattered far and wide; but Isis was indefatigable. She travelled the length of the Nile and breadth of the Delta to recover them.

Isis either buried the pieces of Osiris' body at fourteen different places, which each became a sacred site, or she buried the complete body at Philae, the holy island beyond the First Cataract. A son was born to her, named Horus, the falcon, the all-seeing eye, the form of the Pharaoh, and the avenger of his father, Osiris. When he grew to manhood he killed Seth and rid Egypt of evil. Hence the living Pharaoh was Horus and the dead Pharaoh was Osiris in each generation, son and father.

Osiris was an *avatara*, an incarnation of God. When he died he went to the under world and became the judge of the dead. His judgement was the truth about every man, for each soul, or ba, came to him in the underworld and answered for the man's actions in life, before his heart was weighed in a pair of scales against the feather of truth, emblem of the goddess Maat. A divine dog, called Anubis, held the scales, whilst a fiendish creature with crocodile jaws waited to devour those found unfit. Osiris did not judge the morality of a person, but his or her purity. To do so he asked the soul to make forty-two confessions, most of which were negative in form. Though they reflected the conditions of life in Egypt, such as the special need to protect the waters of the Nile, they were universal in scope; they included:

| | |
|---|---|
| "Hail Fenti, | I have not done violence to any man. |
| Hail Am-khai-bitu, | I have not committed theft. |
| Hail Neha-hra, | I have slain neither man nor woman. |
| Hail Maata-f-em-seshet, | I have not acted deceitfully. |
| Hail Neba, | I have not purloined the things that belong unto God. |
| Hail set-qesu, | I have not uttered falsehood. |
| Hail Uatch-nesert, | I have not uttered vile words. |
| Hail Hetch-abchu, | I have invaded no man's land. |
| Hail Am-besek, | I have not laid waste the lands which have been ploughed. |
| Hail Thenemi, | I have not set my mouth in motion against any man. |
| Hail Tututef, | I have not committed fornication and I have not committed sodomy. |
| Hail Maa-aut-f, | I have not lain with the wife of a man. |
| Hail Seshet-kheru, | I have not made myself deaf unto the words of right and truth. |
| Hail Serekhi, | I have not multiplied my speech beyond what should be said. |
| Hail Nefer-Tem, | I have never uttered curses against the king. |
| Hail Tem-sep, | I have not fouled running water. |
| Hail Nehab-kau, | I have not increased my wealth, except by means of such things as are mine own possessions."[1] |

The meaning of these confessions was related to transmigration of souls, for the Egyptians did not believe that the life of a man was completed in one embodiment. After death the ba would pass into a higher or lower state according to the purity of the previous life, and might be reborn in another human body or as an animal; hence the attention given to creatures of all kinds: to cats, crocodiles, birds, many of which were mummified. Over a million mummified ibises have been found in a huge underground necropolis at Memphis. The way out of the cycle of death and rebirth, which otherwise was never ending, was through unity with Osiris. Once the Osiris myth had become powerful, it offered this unity to all men, not just to the Pharaoh, who was ensured of it on his death. Every man who could truthfully state the forty-two confessions was proved pure, "sound of voice", and became one with the immortal God.

Osiris was, therefore, the saviour of men. He was the god of life, of rebirth, of vegetation, and of the seed of corn, which later became the supreme symbol in the Greek mystery religions. From the innocent victim of evil, the sacrificed perfect man, he became the judge of all men and the way of salvation. His story is the cycle of life, death and rebirth in nature and in Man.

Of him, Plutarch said:

> "But he himself is at the remotest distance from the earth imaginable, being unstained and unpolluted, and clean from every substance that is liable to corruption and death . . . when men are loosed from the body, and removed into the unseen, invisible, impassible and pure region, this God is then their leader and king."[2]

It is possible that the whole epic story of Osiris and the religious faith associated with him was a living influence on ancient Egypt much earlier than the beginning of the second millennium. The alignment of the southern passages of the Great Pyramid with Orion and Sirius confirm that the Old Kingdom revered Osiris, for he was associated with the Orion constellation, as was Isis with Sirius. The Pyramid Texts refer many times to the star Orion as the Soul of Osiris and to the departed Pharaoh as joining Osiris in Orion:

> "Live and be young beside your father (Osiris), beside Orion in the sky."[3]

Moreover, the configuration of the three main pyramids at Giza follows remarkably that of the three stars of Orion's belt, notably in the slight offsetting from alignment of the smallest pyramid. If this architectural "mapping" of the constellation was intentional, it shows both that the stellar rather than solar element in Egyptian religion was predominant, and that the Osiris myth was a powerful influence long before the reign of Mentuhotep, probably as an oral tradition. That the human soul may become, and indeed has been, a star was a belief familiar enough to Plato:

> "he (the Creator) divided the whole mixture into souls equal in number to the stars, and assigned each soul to a star... He who lived well during his appointed time was to return and dwell in his native star, and there he would have a blessed and congenial existence."[4]

Whatever its origin, the story of Osiris revived Egyptian religion at the beginning of the second millennium. The kingdom awoke once more to its heritage of high civilisation. A single administration was established once more for the whole country, mines and quarries were re-opened, trade routes revived. In c1938 BC the Chief Vizier of the Pharaoh assumed the throne when his master died. Ruling as Amenemhat I, he took the title of "renewing births" in the spirit of the Osiris myth and completed the restoration of pharaonic authority. A new capital, called Itj-towy, was established just south of Memphis, though Thebes remained a great religious centre. The frontiers were secured by vigorous campaigns, especially in the south in Lower Nubia. A tomb inscription in Upper Egypt recorded the achievement of the founder of the great twelfth dynasty:

> "His majesty had come that he might crush iniquity, arisen as Atum himself, and that he might repair what he had found ruined, what one town had seized from another, and that he might enable the towns to know their boundaries with each other, their boundary stones being secured like heaven, and their water rights, according to what was in the documents and verified according to antiquity, through the greatness of his love of Maat."

Needless to say, Amenemhat met opposition to his reforms. He was assassinated, but he had taken care to have his son crowned as Sesostris I.

This Pharaoh began the great temple at Karnak, which remained for the rest of Egyptian civilisation as probably the most impressive of all its temples. For several generations the twelfth dynasty continued the work of Amenemhat. Under Sesostris III, the illegitimate power of the nomarchs was completely broken. All land was restored to the Pharaoh, except much temple land, and a just system of taxation was re-introduced, based upon the surplus product of land. Herodotus wrote of it:

> "It was this king, moreover, who divided the land into lots and gave everyone a square piece of equal size, from the produce of which he exacted an annual tax. Any man whose holding was damaged by the encroachment of the river would go and declare his loss before the king, who would send inspectors to measure the extent of the loss, in order that he might pay in future a fair proportion of the tax at which his property had been assessed. Perhaps this was the way in which geometry was invented, and passed afterwards into Greece."[5]

The system was very precisely measured out. The annual tax was related to the extent and depth of the flooding by the Nile in the period mid-August to September each year, for on the water and silt of the great river all fertility depended. Hence those nearest the banks of the river paid the highest taxes. Since the government needed revenue - paid in kind in wheat, barley and other produce - in advance of its expenditure, the assessment was made by means of nilometers, which were gauges at intervals along the river, indicating by their reading of depths the level of later flooding downstream. In addition, annual taxes had to be adjusted every year, when land boundaries changed as a result of flooding. The effect of this naturally just system was that the marginal farmer on poorly irrigated land was free from the burden of tax, and an even level of agricultural prosperity was maintained. By the end of the reign of Sesostris III, no more elaborate tombs of nomarchs were to be seen. The office of nomarch reverted to its original status, as that of a royal appointee with no inheritable rights.

Under the early dynasties of the Middle Kingdom, Amon became, at Thebes, the supreme deity of Egypt. The Pharaohs were believed to be his sons. Their majesty, however, never attained the sublimity of the third and fourth dynasties of the Old Kingdom. They needed military force to consolidate their power. Sesostris III built eight large forts each side of the Nile near the Second Cataract, primarily in order to control Nubia, and he also campaigned in Syria. Sculpture of the twelfth dynasty shows the Pharaohs as careworn, yet noble, figures; for the only time in Egyptian history they are portrayed as humans in need of support from their people, whom they did indeed serve well. Artistic heights could still be reached. The polished granite figure of Princess Sennuwy, for example, sits in serenity and balance, with the exquisite profile of a Helen or Cleopatra, a meditative ideal of beauty, portraying the inner being rather than the outer form.

Egypt of the twelfth dynasty was rich; it developed the mineral resources of Nubia and the desert near the Red Sea: iron, copper, tin, gold and precious stones. It built palaces, forts and temples, using plentiful supplies of granite, sandstone and limestone.

It developed the marshy area of the Fayum, west of the middle Nile, by a vast drainage scheme, building there a huge labyrinth, which may have been a model for that at Cretan Knossos and astonished Herodotus fourteen hundred years after its construction. Egypt of the Middle Kingdom was granted a long period of stability and a strong remembrance of the glories of the early Pharaohs.

After the zenith of imperial power reached by the twelfth dynasty, however, Egypt became weaker and subject to attack from abroad, especially from Asia, where the Hittite and Mittani peoples were exerting pressure in Syria and Palestine. Into the Nile Delta from the east came settlers called Hyksos or "foreign peoples" who by about 1630 BC were powerful enough to become Pharaohs. Nevertheless, they tended to adopt Egyptian customs and during their rule the native culture was not greatly affected. For example, the Rhind mathematical papyrus, which amongst much else gave a calculation of pi, was written under a Hyksos Pharaoh. The movement of the Hykos into Egypt was a foretaste of the general disturbance in the whole eastern Mediterranean, associated with the fall of Cretan and Mycenean culture and perhaps even the war between Greeks and Trojans. So, too, was the migration of the Jewish people into Egypt, culminating in the Exodus under Moses, probably in the reign of Merneptah of the nineteenth dynasty. It was as though the end of the great Bronze Age was approaching.

Eventually an Egyptian leader was strong enough to expel the Hyksos and had himself crowned Pharaoh as Ahmose in c1539 BC. His New Kingdom dynasty, the eighteenth, contained some of the most glorious and also most bizarre events of Egyptian history. Sixty years after Ahmose, his descendant, Tuthmosis III, became Pharaoh when a boy, so that his step-mother Hatshepsut ruled as regent with great panache for fifteen years, supported by a Vizier, Senenmut, whose versatile talent recalled the great Imhotep. Under his guidance, Hatshepsut sent an extensive trading mission to Punt on the Horn of Africa, which returned with exotic riches : perfumes, oil, myrrh, ivory, panther-skins and ostrich plumes. She also built a magnificent temple for her tomb in the Valley of the Kings at Deir-al-Bahri, its huge colonnaded terraces cut out of the solid rock.

Tuthmosis was not content with the reflection of his stepmother's fame. Within a year of becoming king in his own right, he led a huge military expedition to Palestine to face an Asian coalition, and at Megiddo in c1478 BC inflicted an overwhelming defeat on the Asians, so that for three generations Egyptian power in Western Asia was dominant. His forbears had learnt from the Hyksos the use of the horse and the wheel; the elaborate chariots bear witness to the wealth of the eighteenth dynasty. Tuthmosis III was perhaps Egypt's greatest general. In the south the empire was extended beyond the Fourth Cataract, and in the west the Libyans, also, were defeated. Military success was put to good use through the control of conquered territories by local princes, supported by Egyptian envoys, whilst trade developed; for example, in the Sudan, where the important trading and garrison town of Napata was founded. Artistic activity was stimulated by foreign contact; new temples were built and existing national shrines extended. Sculpture and painting looked back to the Middle Kingdom for models and precious minerals available in the new territories were welcomed by craftsmen. In short, the reign of Tuthmosis III was a time of great prosperity.

By the fourteenth century BC, however, faith in the all pervading power of Amon had diminished. Amenophis III, though a powerful and skilful ruler, who gained much by diplomacy and built the Colossi of Memnon in his temple near Luxor, allowed the cult of Aten, god of the sun's disc, to grow at the expense of Amon and the traditional pantheon. Already the rays of Aten with their slender bands granting beatitude to Pharaohs and men, were appearing on temple and monument reliefs. When his son, Amenophis IV, succeeded him, a revolutionary change was imminent.

The new king was a strange, intellectual man, with a gaunt frame, neck and elongated skull, long chin and high, protruding cheek bones, a physique which became the model for the original, and sometimes grotesque, art of his era. He soon took the cult of Aten to an extreme conclusion. At first other gods - except Ra - were ignored; then they were officially proscribed and their insignia destroyed. Amenophis IV changed his name to Akhenaten, "servant of Aten", and founded a new capital city, called Akhetaten, "horizon of the Aten", on the east bank of the middle Nile, where a line of hills make a level horizon for the rising disc of the sun. New priests and officials were appointed; those associated with the other gods were now a disaffected force within the state. The presence of soldiers at Akhetaten showed that the Pharaoh correctly feared a counter-revolution.

Akhenaten and his influential and beautiful queen, Nefertiti, gave a strong impulse to new forms of art, all centred on the worship of the Aten. The Pharaoh was Aten's son and was depicted under the winged sun-disc whose rays were arms or mercy and sustenance. Yet he was also shown in homely scenes with his family, in unkingly poses, reclining or nursing children. He was at once dignified and awkward, divine and domestically commonplace. Tradition was eschewed; innovation was inventive yet sometimes trivial. Free standing sculptured figures of Akhenaten are strangely powerful, for the Pharaoh is like a man possessed, intent on a single idea, yet slightly mocking, with his hollow cheeks and huge bony frame.

Akhenaten had a vision of the one supreme God. He recalled the religion of his predecessors, the distant Djoser, Khufu and Khafre: the Atum, from which all gods and men were generated; Ptah of Memphis speaking creation into existence; Ra as the solar form of Atum; but he did not understand the strength of age-long habits and ideas. His people were attached to multiplicity, to a pantheon of gods, and so the vision of unity was condemned.

When Akhenaten died in c1335 BC, his successor, Smenkhare, reigned very briefly and was succeeded by the ten-year old Tutankhaten, probably Akhenaten's son by another wife, Kiya. The priests and officials of Amon, those who looked back eighteen years to the old forms of life, took control. The boy Pharaoh was renamed Tutankhamun, after the breath (ankh) of Amon. Akhetaten was razed to the ground. The gods were restored, though Aten remained, a god amongst gods, to grace the gilded chair of Tutankhamun, which was buried with other treasures in his tomb in the Valley of the Kings. The "Hymn to the Aten", perhaps composed by Akhenaten himself, also remained:

"When thou risest in the morning and shinest as Aten by day thou dost put to flight the darkness and givest forth thy rays. The two lands rejoice, they awake and stand on their feet, for thou hast aroused them. They wash their limbs and take up their clothes, their arms do adoration to thy rising. All the land performs its labours. All cattle rejoice in their pastures. The trees and herbs grow green. Birds and winged things come forth from their nests, their wings doing adoration to thy spirit How manifold are thy works! They are concealed from us. O sole god to whom no other is like! Thou didst create the earth according to thy desire when thou wast alone, men and cattle, all goats, and all that is upon the earth and goeth upon its feet, and all that is in the sky and flieth with its wings....... Lord of every land, who risest for them, disk of the day, great of might. Thou art in my heart."[6]

For all its magnificence, the vision of Akhenaten could not overturn the nature of the Egyptian people, which Plato recognised and which he knew was proof against innovations, even of a religious genius like Akhenaten:

"....their young citizens must be habituated to forms and strains of virtue. These they fixed and exhibited the patterns of them in their temples; and no painter or artist is allowed to innovate upon them, or to leave the traditional forms and invent new ones...their works of art are painted or moulded in the same forms which they had ten thousand years ago ...if a person can only find the natural melodies, he may confidently embody them in a fixed and legal form."[7]

The reign of the young Pharaoh, Tutankhamun was unexceptional, dominated as it was by a general who seized the throne for himself after Tutankhamun's death, but a quirk of history has granted the boy king a new kind of immortality. In 1922 Lord Carnaervon and Howard Carter, British archaeologists, discovered his tomb in the Valley of the Kings. In it was not only the Pharaoh's mummified body, but - since the tomb had been missed by looters - the greatest hoard of Egyptian treasures ever found. Though the quality of the craftmanship could not attain that of the Old Kingdom, the profusion of superb artefacts demonstrated the magnificent wealth and culture, even of the New Kingdom. The furniture included a chest with ivory and ebony marquetry, a folding camp bedstead, an ivory headrest, a gaming box with animal legs and feet and the great throne with its gold embossed Aten symbol. Of ornaments, there were bracelets, fan-shaped earrings with amber, blue and turquoise inlays and a "Birth of the Sun" pectoral chain with ibises and blue scarabs. Gold sandals, shabtis (figures of men said to perform the king's duties after his death), fire making apparatus, fly whisks of hair, an ornamental alabaster boat, garlands of flowers, a golden fan showing Tutankhamun hunting, a walking stick with a handle carved as prisoners of war, a linen dalmatic adorned with tapestry and needlework - these and much more indicate the range and beauty of the Pharaoh's possessions and the gamut of materials available in his society. Outstanding, perhaps, were the chariots found in the tomb. Their elegant, light frames were encased entirely in gold, embossed with traditional patterns and scenes and edged with semi-precious stones and polychrome glass. They were sprung with leather thongs and pulled by horses decked with sumptuous trappings, surmounted by a crest of ostrich feathers. A tablet of Akhenaten says: "His Majesty ascended a great chariot of electrum, like Aten when he rises from his horizon and filling the land with love.. ."

Howard Carter himself has described his immediate impression of the mask of Tutankhamun when he opened the king's golden coffin:

"The beaten gold mask, a beautiful and unique specimen of ancient portraiture bears a sad but calm expression suggestive of youth overtaken prematurely by death. Upon its forehead, wrought in massive gold, were the royal insignia - the Nekhebet vulture and Buto Serpent - emblems of the Two Kingdoms over which he had reigned. To the chin was attached the conventional Osiride beard wrought in gold and lapis-lazuli-coloured glass; around the throat was a triple necklace of yellow and red gold and blue faience disk-shaped beads; pendent from the neck by flexible gold straps was a large black resin scarab that rested between the hands and bore the Bennu ritual. The burnished gold hands, crossed over the breast, separate from the mask, were sewn to the material of the linen wrappings, and grasped the Flagellum and Crozier - the emblems of Osiris. Immediately below these was the simple outermost linen covering, adorned with richly inlaid gold trappings pendent from a large pectoral-like figure of the ba bird or soul, of gold cloisonne work, its full-spread wings stretched over the body."[8]

After Tutankhamun a final blaze of pharaonic glory was to come with Ramesses II of the nineteenth dynasty. Early in his reign he won victories against the Hittites, notably at Kadesh in c1274 BC, though the Hittites themselves claimed a victory; and also against sea-raiders, called the Sherden, whose attacks heralded much greater unrest in the eastern Mediterranean. Ramesses was a master of propaganda, presenting his achievements in fulsome inscriptions; yet the magnificent scale of his numerous buildings marked him as a ruler with a residual sense of majesty. At Abu Simbel in Nubia, four enormous seated figures of Ramesses dominated his new Great Temple. At Karnak he completed the Hypostyle Hall - so large that St Paul's Cathedral in London could fit into it - which had a forest of 134 giant columns. Yet often Ramesses effaced the names of earlier Pharaohs and carved his own cartouche (i.e. his name within an oval ring) in place of them on monuments and other works. Moreover, his grandiose building projects were usually shoddy; often surface ashlar covered hastily packed rubble.

The specious glory of Ramesses II's reign was symptomatic of the collapse of the long-standing values of Egyptian civilisation. When, probably in the reign of Merneptah (c1226-1223 BC), the Jews, who had settled in Egypt four hundred years before, abandoned Egypt under the leadership of Moses, they took with them gleanings of the knowledge preserved for millennia by the Pharaohs and the priests of the temples. It was as though, after the extravagant efforts of Akhenaten to return to some form of monotheism, the Egyptians were deprived, or deprived themselves, of their perennial wisdom. The sea-raiders, probably from Phoenicia, hurled themselves once more upon the Delta; perhaps in the course of wrecking the beautiful culture of ancient Crete. Ramesses III saved his country from their worst excesses by a great victory. Egypt was not to suffer the apparent fate of Troy, whose destruction by the Greeks was soon to mark the symbolic end of the Bronze Age in the west; but never again would it rise to the heights of even the eighteenth dynasty, far removed as that was from the majesty of the Old Kingdom. All over the ancient world the Bronze Age warriors were entering an Odyssey of the unknown. Peoples were on the move. Culture was buried beneath cinders and volcanic ash. The strength of Egypt enabled it to withstand for some while the forces of disintegration. Ramesses III

*Karnak: Entrance Way*

*Karnak: Rameses II*

survived a strike of workers in the royal necropolis and a harem conspiracy. Wholesale plundering of tombs began, indicative of a breakdown in the age-long spiritual awareness of the people. From the loss of the Asiatic Empire, there were serious economic effects. By the time of the twentieth dynasty, a tenth of all land was in the hands of temples, so that gradually priestly usurpation of power and wealth strangled economic life. Finally, the country was divided between a priestly dynasty, ruling from Thebes, and a Pharaoh ruling the Delta from the city of Tanis.

Foreign influence grew stronger, as native institutions declined. Libyans entered the country from the west and military tribes, called the Meshuresh, even formed a Libyan dynasty in the Delta. Later, the Nubians advanced from the south and engaged in a struggle with northern dynasties. Religion resembled government in its fragmentation and decay, as the worship and mummification of creatures like ibises, cats and crocodiles assumed huge proportions at ancient religious centres, like Memphis. In the seventh century, the warlike Assyrians burst into the country through the buffer states of Syria and Judah. Assurbanipal, whose dynasty boasted in brilliant stone reliefs of the royal slaying of lions and of the flaying alive of enemy captives, overran it in c665 BC, before the Babylonians abruptly destroyed Assyrian power.

For a brief period in the sixth century, under the Pharaoh Amasis, the light shone again in Egypt; once more the traditional forms of temples and sarcophagi were revived. From his capital of Sais in the western Delta, justice was again dispensed by an Egyptian Pharaoh; Herodotus for instance, said of him:

> "Amasis established an admirable custom which Solon borrowed and introduced at Athens where it is still preserved; this was that every man once a year should declare before the Nomarch, or provincial governor, the source of his livelihood; failure to do this, or inability to prove that the source was an honest one, was punishable by death."[9]

With Amasis the line of Pharaohs who retained a connection with ancient wisdom probably came to an end. In 525 BC, a year after Amasis' death, Cambyses of Persia defeated the Egyptians at Pelusium and incorporated the country into the Persian Empire. For nearly two hundred years, Egypt was subject to the Great King, though there were occasional revolts, stiffened with Greek mercenary soldiers. When Alexander the Great shattered the armies of Darius III, he broke the Persian hold on Egypt, then briefly worshipped at the shrine of Amon in the western desert to demonstrate his fidelity to the religion of the Pharaohs. Greek rule endured under the Ptolemies until the subjection to Rome.

Ancient Egypt was like a bridge that passed from the Bronze Age into the Iron Age, over which crossed a system of knowledge offering salvation to those living in darkness. The Old Kingdom, dedicated to the unity of Atum and foreshadowing the words of Hermes Trismegistus, preserved that knowledge, and through the teaching of Imhotep and other masters allowed it to inform great works of language and music, mathematics and astronomy, medicine, architecture, sculpture and other arts of Man. It was an age of giants. After its culture expired at the end of the third millennium BC, the second culture of the Middle and New Kingdoms could not rise to the heights of its predecessor, but it created the glorious fruits of the twelfth and eighteenth dynasties, not least the prosperity of the people and the magnificence of the Pharaohs, reflected in the tomb of Tutankhamun. In its nurture of the myth of Osiris, this culture offered a way of human redemption. When the time of dissolution came upon Egypt, as it came to Crete and Mycenae and Troy, the Jewish people probably took with them knowledge of the ultimate unity of Man and God, the secret of ancient Egypt, the mystery in the tomb, the seed of resurrection:

"The One forever is: the other passes away. The One, indeed, is Truth: the other is the shadow of reality."[10]

Yet not only to Moses was it given to transmit what Egypt bequeathed. For Greece, also, was to take much of the groundwork of civilisation and culture on which to build her own unique contribution to the welfare of Man.

## References:

1.  E. A. Wallis Budge, *Egyptian Religion*, Kegan Paul, London 1900, p. 156.

2.  Plutarch, *Moralia IV.*

3.  *Pyramid Text* 2180, trans. R. O. Faulkner, Clarendon, Oxford, 1969.

4.  Plato, *Timaeus*, trans. Jowett, Random House, New York, 1937, pp. 41-42.

5.  Herodotus, *The Histories*, trans. A. de Selincourt, Penguin, London, 1972, Book II, p. 169.

6.  W. MacQuitty, *The Wisdom of the Ancient Egyptians*, Sheldon, London, 1978, pp. 55-7.

7.  Plato, *Laws*, trans. Jowett, Book II, pp. 656-657.

8.  H. Carter, *The Tomb of Tutankhamun*, Book Club Associates, London, 1972, ch. 16, pp. 129-130.

9.  Herodotus, *The Histories*, Book II, p. 199.

10. *The Divine Pymander of Hermes Trismegistus*, Shrine of Wisdom, Godalming, 1955, p. 18.

*Part 3*

# Graeco-Roman Civilisation:

## *Homeric Culture*

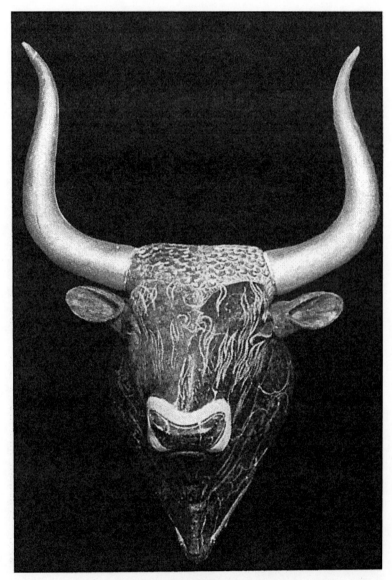

*Cretan Bull*

## Chapter 6

# Minotaur

### Theseus and Ancient Crete

IN THE LAND OF CANAAN in Palestine there lived, according to legend, a son of the great sea god, Poseidon, named Agenor, who originally had come from Egypt. He had five sons and one beautiful daughter called Europa. Indeed, she was so fair that the father of the gods, Zeus himself, fell in love with her. Turning himself into a snow-white bull, he joined the herd of cattle belonging to Agenor and became so docile that Europa played with him and climbed on his back. He ambled gently down to the seashore and, to the amusement of his rider, into the shallow waves. Gradually, he edged outwards from the shore until he could swim, and then, as Europa suddenly realised her peril, the bull swam vigorously away to sea. Zeus took the captive Europa to the island of Crete, where she bore him three sons, of whom one was Minos, later King of Crete, whose name may be derived from the Egyptian Menes.

The consequences of this escapade by the father of the gods were to be redeemed by a hero, Theseus, companion of Heracles and founder of Athens. He was born from an illicit union of Aegeus, King of Athens, and Aethra, a princess of Troezen, who brought him up discreetly in her own city, until he was old enough to be told about his father, the King. Aegeus had left a pair of his sandals and a sword under a huge rock at Troezen with instructions to Aethra that, if Theseus could lift the rock, he should bring the sandals and sword to Athens as means of identification. Theseus had little difficulty in lifting the rock, but, keen to emulate Heracles, he announced that he would travel to Athens along the coast road, which was beset with brutish men who murdered travellers, rather than travel by sea as his mother enjoined him.

The road proved a worthy challenge to the aspiring hero. Amongst those whom he encountered was Sinis, the pine-bender, whose practice was to bend two huge pines until he could affix a victim's arms and legs to them. When he released the pines, the victim was torn in half. Sinis was overcome by Theseus, the inventor of the art of wrestling, and tied to two bent pines and projected, like his victims, into a grisly death. Similarly, the more technically inclined Procrustes was punished by Theseus with his own cruel invention. His victims had been bound to a bed and made to fit it exactly by being racked or sawn into shape. The whole road from Troezen to Athens was cleared of such vile torturers, and the region of Attica thus prepared for its later emergence under Theseus as a prosperous city, grown rich on trade.

Crete, however, provided the greatest adventure, worthy of Heracles himself. Minos, son of Zeus, now King of Crete, married Pasiphae, daughter of Helios, god of the sun, and a nymph of the island. The sea-god Poseidon offered to Minos a beautiful white bull for sacrifice, but Minos made the mistake of keeping it for himself, whereupon Poseidon caused Pasiphae to become unnaturally infatuated with the bull, conceiving by it a monster with the body of a man and the head of a bull. King Minos, in his shame, sought the advice of the engineer Daedalus, who constructed an ingenious labyrinth in the city of Knossos as an underground prison for the queen's appalling offspring, the Minotaur.

This was not the king's sole cause of grief, for one of his sons was killed in Athens. In revenge, Minos invaded Attica, besieged Athens and, when it surrendered demanded as tribute that seven youths and seven maidens should be sent every nine years to be thrown to the Minotaur. When Theseus heard of this cruel demand, he volunteered to take the place of one of the youths, despite the entreaties of his father, Aegeus. Each nine years the ship with its mournful cargo had carried a black sail. Now Theseus stowed on board a spare sail, a white one, promising to hoist it on the return voyage, if he succeeded in killing the Minotaur. As he set foot in Crete, Minos' daughter, Ariadne, caught sight of this noblest of the seven youths and fell deeply in love with him. Contriving to meet him in secret, she gave him a ball of thread and a sword, the thread on the advice of Daedalus, and the sword because she knew the terrible power of her monster half-brother, the Minotaur.

Theseus entered the labyrinth, tied the end of the thread to the door and. unwinding the thread as he went, made his way to the centre where the Minotaur had his lair, amidst the bones of the dead Athenian youths. After a short struggle, the Minotaur was slain. Theseus followed the thread back to the entrance. He gathered his companions and the faithful Ariadne and set sail for home. At the island of Naxos they stopped to provision the boat and here Theseus first showed signs of human weakness, for he deserted the woman who had defied her father and risked her life to save him. Ariadne was left behind on Naxos, her love unrequited, even scorned. Perhaps Poseidon, who knew everything about Crete, punished Theseus for his pride, for the hero forgot to raise the white sail on his ship.

King Aegeus stood each day on the Acropolis at Athens looking out towards the sea from the high point on the south west corner - where much later would stand the little temple of Athena Nike - scanning the horizon for a sail. At last he saw one; it was black. Distraught with sorrow, his reason gone, he plunged over the cliff edge. The sea on which he had gazed so ardently became known as the Aegean.

Chastened no doubt by his singular adventures, Theseus duly became king of Athens. Once in office, he laid the basis for future greatness: the settlements of Attica, which were little more than villages, were united under the leadership of Athens, an act of foundation later celebrated in the annual festival of the Synoikia, dedicated to Athena. Each village gave up its law court and self-government in return for access to the law courts and administration in the city of Athens itself, but the promise of self-government in the greater unity of Athens was held out for all the people of Attica, when peace and order prevailed there. Strangers were invited to settle in the enlarged city, for Theseus anticipated the future reliance of Athens on a broad commerce and a generous outwardlooking foreign policy. With a similar intention he introduced money coinage, stamped with an ox, and began the Isthmian Games in honour of Poseidon, the god upon whose favour Athens would ever depend. Most important of all, he divided the people of Athens into three groups, similar to the castes of the Silver Age; a class of nobles charged with the highest duties of government, law and religion, providing education and protecting what was sacred; husbandmen, caring for the land and responsible for the material wealth of the state; and thirdly, the majority of the people, who were artificers of all kinds, living by the work of their hands. Though this hierarchy was based upon ancient law, it did not preclude a democratic tendency in the state, as indicated by Homer's reference to the uniquely "sovereign people" of Athens. On the eighth day of each month the Athenians paid homage to Theseus, along with Poseidon, because eight is the number of stability, the cube of the first even number, for he built for them a foundation as immovable as the vast oceans of the god.

Theseus is a legendary figure, presented as living some time before the Trojan war which brought the Bronze Age to an end. In fact, Crete had been a relatively obscure backwater to the mainstream of eastern Mediterranean civilisation during the third millennium BC, though its villages were well developed and its artefacts skilfully made. Copper came into common use and the olive was cultivated. Egyptian influence was present in the manufacture of fine jewellery and seals in gold and ivory. Immigration from Asia Minor brought a new strain into the native population and probably gave rise to a creative fusion of blood and of cultures. To the north, the islands of the Cyclades experienced similar immigration and a related culture, specialising in marble and stone vases, so that this whole maritime area acquired a potential for new development based upon Egyptian and Asian influences, but enlivened by the spirit of independence of sea-going peoples. Indeed, just after the beginning of the second millennium a completely new culture arose in Crete, centred upon the building of palaces, most significantly at Knossos and Phaistos, and characterised by the smelting of bronze, the use of the rapier sword, and a pictographic form of writing, soon to become a linear script.

The earliest palaces were destroyed by earthquakes, but finally, at Knossos in particular, the height of the palace culture was reached soon after 1600 BC. For two hundred years Knossos became the lodestone of the Mediterranean, drawing to itself traders and diplomats from Egypt and Syria, exporting fine ware, food and timber, creating dependencies in the Cyclades, at Miletus on the Ionian coast and on the island of Cythera, close to the Peloponnese. The sea-lanes from the Aegean to Egypt passed through the ring of Cretan dependencies and, since Crete was a maritime power capable of defending itself entirely by its naval forces, its prosperity was assured. Envoys carrying gold and silver vessels are portrayed in an Egyptian tomb in Thebes, and an inscription there reads "the coming in peace of the Great Ones of Keftiu and of the Isles in the midst of the sea", probably referring to Crete as Keftiu. Egyptian subject matter - cats and papyrus, for example - were used as motifs by Cretan artists in frescoes and on pottery.

The strong connection with Egypt and Syria explains the origin of some elements in Cretan society, in particular the central place of the king and the palace. The great palaces at Knossos, Phaistos, Mallia and Zakro, similar in form to those in Syria and on the Euphrates, were each the hub of a local economy. At Knossos, for example, huge jars, or pithoi, were used to store wine, olive oil and cereals - possibly twenty-five thousand litres of olive oil - with an elaborate accounting system in operation. The splendid throne room at Knossos with its wavy backed throne of alabaster and frescoes of proud griffins was the seat of royal administration and justice. Above all, the palaces were the centre of the prolific artistic output of this late type of a bronze age culture.

Cretan art was not imitative of the Egyptian, though it borrowed a few of its themes. Indeed, it displayed a buoyant originality in every form it utilised. The architecture of Knossos makes creative use of light wells, which penetrate the two or three storeys of the palace and send a mellow sunlight through the rooms and staircases. Even the columns are curiously inverted in shape, the thickness at the top producing a rather squat effect, unlike the upward-tapering columns of mainland Greece. In layout, the palace is a strange cross between careful design and a gradual accretion of rooms as occasion demanded, with the final result of labyrinthine complexity. To a stranger, from mainland Greece, for example, it would indeed have appeared as a labyrinth. A real labyrinth, if there were one, may have been modelled on the huge Egyptian labyrinth in the Fayum west of the middle Nile to which Herodotus refers,[1] but the word itself could also have come from the Carian word 'labrys', meaning a double-axe. The palace at Knossos contained many carvings of this ritual emblem.

A palace orientated culture was common to both Crete and the areas of southern Greece, especially in the Argolid, which were in the forefront of civilised life in the second millennium BC, notably at Mycenae. Yet the palace system certainly originated in Crete with the first palaces at Knossos and Phaistos in the period 1900 to 1700 BC, with the implication that Mycenae and the other mainland centres received the idea from the island. By 1600 they were rivals of the great Cretan palaces for trade and cultural influence throughout the Aegean and eastern Mediterranean, but even then Cretan preponderance in fine art, craftmanship and building methods was retained; Cretan pottery styles, for example, were superior and were adopted at Mycenae. Cretan script known as Linear B, constructed at Knossos about 1450 BC, almost certainly by Greek invaders with the aid of native Cretans who had earlier developed their own hieroglyphics (Linear A), was transmitted to the mainland, and at Mycenae and Pylos utilised for the elaborate accounting procedures of the palace economies on the lines laid down at the Cretan palaces. In all these features of the palace, Crete was the exemplar, if not the origin, of what became characteristically European.

The palace frescoes portray animated people and creatures: young boys gently boxing, Parisian style young women with pretty black ringlets of hair, an arrogant prince with a monstrous head-dress, fat comfortable porpoises and mammoth bulls over which lean young athletes of both sexes leap with unbelievable agility. Pottery, too, is rich with idiosyncratic design; patterns that curve round jars with natural spirals, octopuses that cling in all-embracing rotundity, harvesters with scythes, singing in noisy unison. Even the huge storage pithoi are decorated with indented wavy rings. Jewellery and small seals are intricate and made from fine materials: gold, ivory, faience and steatite. Probably most expressive of all is the rhyton, or drinking vessel, found in the palace at Knossos, made of black steatite with horns and eyes inlaid with shell and rock crystal, an image of the strange blend of religion and entertainment embodied in the ritual bull leaping. Here in Cretan art is portrayed a new emotional attitude to life, almost romantic in its expressionism, distinctly not Egyptian, nor Asiatic, indeed recognisably European.

One dominant and distinctive feature of the art of the palaces was a love of natural forms, indicating an awareness of unity with nature and a joy in its movement and exuberance, which has been persistent in European culture into modern times. Unlike the serious and hieratic art of Egypt, Cretan art turned to the ever-present world of plants and animals, birds and fishes. In the early second millennium, Kamares ware pottery was decorated with marvellous patterns in emphatic colours - black, white, orange and red - which was not copied from nature, but reflected it in partially abstract shapes. Later, especially at Knossos, nature was represented directly, but still with an element of witty yet disingenuous abstraction; for example, in frescoes, which made no attempt to present a dimension of depth, but settled for an overtly naive flatness, akin in this respect to Byzantine art. The effect is to highlight the natural naivety of non-human forms of nature, the immediacy of trees and plants, the innocence of animals, the vacant weightlessness of fish, the airiness of birds. Humour was never far distant, as in the exquisite gold pendant of two wasps sipping a drop of honey.

When translated into the human form, this art showed a childlike simplicity; boys box without animosity, women preen themselves without guile, a prince struts without hiding his regality. It is a world devoid of the dualism of pretence - each is what he is - a natural world, touched with a memory of a Golden Age.

According to Homer, there were ninety cities in Crete at the time of the Trojan war. At Knossos and elsewhere cities attended upon the palaces, and substantial roads connected them with other centres. Viaducts and aqueducts bore further witness to the engineering skill symbolised by the legendary figure of Daedalus. Maritime trade was very extensive and ship-building, using the great timber resources of the island, was clearly an important industry. The economy relied upon an elaborate system of barter, involving the storage of large quantities of staple goods, like olive oil, wine and cereals, which itself gave rise to accounting recorded by means of the linear scripts (which utilised decimals). Material comfort was of importance to the Cretans; they had bath-rooms, and even lavatories, of a modern type, though no hot water systems. Secular life was attractive, and in no way inhibited by religion. Perhaps they even believed in romantic love, as the story of Ariadne suggests! In all this they were forerunners of Europe.

There is a marked absence of tokens of war in the remains of ancient Crete: few weapons, paintings of soldiers or their accoutrements, no fortifications. King Minos certainly fought abroad in Greece, and a navy, probably recruited from merchant ships in time of war, guarded the coasts and kept open the sea-lanes, but on the island peace prevailed and an artistic culture could flourish undisturbed. Though Zeus himself was reputed to have been born on Mount Lasithi, near the greater peak of Ida - for his mother Rhea could only thus hide him from his dreaded father Cronos, who swallowed his children to prevent their usurping his power - Cretans worshipped especially a female goddess of nature, in accordance with many Mediterranean peoples. The benign influence of this mother goddess appears in both the peaceful nature of Cretan society and in the natural and gentle character of its art.

Nevertheless, war came to the Cretans and brought their fine culture to an abrupt end. It followed upon natural disasters. About 1450 BC, the great palaces, with the exception of Knossos, were destroyed. On the island of Thera to the north of Crete a huge volcanic explosion sent a great tidal wave southwards to flood the lower parts of Crete. Volcanic ash accumulated in thick layers on agricultural land. Only Knossos survived, though it was damaged. Some time after these calamities, Knossos was invaded, probably by Greeks from the mainland, perhaps from Mycenae. They built at Knossos their typical chamber tombs - the Cretans had little use for elaborate burials - and placed weapons with their dead, but most significantly they developed the new script. It remains a possibility that the final destruction of Knossos was carried out by a great raid of the "sea people" from the eastern end of the Mediterranean, those same raiders who would have invaded Egypt had not the pharaoh Rameses III stopped them in the delta. Either way, the collapse of Cretan society, from earthquake, flood or invasion was another symptom of the drawing to an end of the age of heroes.

The zenith of Cretan culture in the mid second millennium was an experiment. It was as though Zeus, in gratitude for his mother's courage in saving him from the wrath of Cronos, felt a nostalgic love for the island of his birth, for the rocky heights of Ida and Lasithi and the thick forests of cypress and cedar, pine and oak, and, thus compelled, brought there his beautiful paramour, Europa, to give birth to a new society of men, close to nature but artistic, with a zest for living and a contempt for war; as though in his intoxication he forgot the age of bronze and the fierce warriors, who soon would destroy themselves and their ethos in the fratricidal siege of Troy. And so he experimented with an idyll, an island of "sounds, and sweet airs, that give delight, and hurt not"; but this island, too, had its Caliban, for out of the mixing of the cultures of Egypt and Syria, that by now were becoming degenerate, came the strange monster of the Minotaur. The Egyptian God, Ptah, creator of all things by the Word, was now worshipped as a bull, the god Apis; and King Minos' queen, Pasiphae, daughter of the Sun-god, was corrupted by lust. The unnatural union of a woman and the white bull, offered by Poseidon, not for such uses, but for sacrifice, could yield only evil. The Minotaur was the degeneracy of the ancient civilisation of the Middle East. It had to be slain. The Cretan experiment had failed and must end.

Theseus was the hero who would pluck salvation from this nettle of corruption. He killed the Minotaur with the help of the love of an uncorrupted woman, Ariadne. The good that was still there, the seeds of language, the appreciation of beauty, the knowledge of kingship, were taken to the mainland to enter the palace culture of Mycenean Greece, but the evil, the depravity of mind which was leading the Egyptians to worship the bull and the ibis, had to be destroyed by reason, the sacred and golden chord which showed the way out of the labyrinth.

### References:

1. Herodotus, *Histories*, trans. A. de Selincourt, Penguin, London, 1972, Book II, p. 188.

## Chapter 7
# Agamemnon's Return
### *Mycenaean Society*

AT MYCENAE IN THE ARGOLID on the mainland of Greece stands the great fortress and palace of King Agamemnon, legendary leader of the Greek expedition which fought for nine years at Troy in the thirteenth century BC. A narrow passage, flanked by enormous walls of undressed, but carefully interlocking, stone blocks, leads uphill to the magnificent Lion Gate, a huge entrance made of a rectangular frame of four blocks, with the lintel supporting a triangular structure in order to

*Lion Gate, Mycenae*

carry the weight away from its centre. Within the triangle two lionesses face each other, their front paws resting on a column which tapers downwards - evidence that Cretan influence was significant. More lies in the fine quality of the art work of the palace, especially the decoration of walls, pottery and jewellery, all of which became lighter, more inventive and closer to nature, as Cretan artisans brought their skills from "the great island".

From an undistinguished mainland society a new culture arose rapidly after 1600 BC, reaching its apogee, with the aid of Cretan influence, by about 1400 BC. Two rings of shaft graves - unknown in Crete - in which one or more bodies of kings or nobles were buried in deep vertical shafts, together with the rich trappings of aristocracy, prove that an indigenous culture was present on the mainland, though itself influenced by Egyptian and Middle Eastern practices. In the shaft graves were magnificent weapons and jewellery in gold, silver, electrum and ivory, and most notable of all, death masks of repoussee gold, one of which led the German archaeologist, Heinrich Schliemann, to send a telegram to the Kaiser claiming that he had looked upon the face of Agamemnon. In fact, the death masks are probably from the sixteenth century, three hundred years before the Trojan war. The weapons testify that this was a military aristocracy; bronze thrusting swords with elaborate hilts and pommels and bronze daggers, one with a complete scene in gold, electrum and niello of a spirited lion hunt on its blade, were undeniably the possessions of a proud and artistically cultured warrior caste. Very large shields, like sections of a cylinder, long spears for thrusting rather than throwing, and splendid conical helmets made from boars' tusks were also part of the warriors' equipment; and the grave stones above the shafts at Mycenae have engravings of chariots, recalling the chariot-borne warriors of Egypt and the Hittite Empire, who met at Kadesh in c1274 BC.

Clearly war was a dominant feature in the lives of the palaces of the mainland; hence also their massive fortifications - Cyclopean, as later Greeks called them, in wonder at the feat of moving these colossal stones. A brilliant irrigation project near Gla in Boeotia bore witness to another kind of engineering skill. The low lying area is naturally marshy, but ditches and dykes recovered it for agriculture, and the fortress of Gla, with a containing wall two miles long, protected the area from marauders. The need for such a fortress reinforces the picture of a fairly unstable society, centred on strong-points and guarded by intelligent, alert and well-equipped military forces under aristocratic leadership, a picture confirmed by Homer, whose kings - Agamemnon of Mycenae, Menelaus of Sparta, Odysseus of Ithaca, Nestor of Pylos, Ajax of Salamis, Diomedes of Argos and the rest - only really co-operated when a major war against non-Hellenes was in progress.

A hint of a broader society is given by an inscription in Linear B, a script used at several palaces after its origination at Knossos, referring to land held "from the demos", meaning the local community, and possibly akin to the free land systems of medieval Europe, like the Saxon open field. Such economic freedom could co-exist with an hierarchical type of society in which the warrior caste had political and military authority. Though this caste held great wealth - "rich in gold" is Homer's epithet for Mycenae - they did not themselves acquire it as merchants or employers of labour, but from some form of rent from land held as dynastic estates, perhaps alongside that of the demos. Spoils of war, no doubt, supplemented their wealth.

The military aspect distinguishes the mainland culture clearly from that of Crete. In the Argolid such fortified palaces were built at Tiryns, Asine and Dendra, and

*Beehive Tomb, Nestor's Palace, Pylos*

*Grave Circle, Mycenae*

further afield Pylos, on the west coast of the Peloponnese, Thebes and Gla in Boeotia, Athens and the region of Messenia all had similar constructions and a military aristocracy. Mycenae, however, was the most powerful, as the role of Agamemnon indicates. Tiryns was its outpost, guarding the southern entrance to the plain of Argos, as Dendra guarded the eastern route to Mycenae. Asine was a port from which part of Agamemnon's host probably set sail for Troy.

Accompanying many of these fortress palaces, also, throughout Greece were the strange beehive tombs, built into the side of a hill with only the top of the dome emerging above. The so called "Treasury of Atreus" at Mycenae is the finest of these; indeed, it is the largest enclosed space known to have been built until Hadrian's Pantheon of the second century AD. The interior walls are corbelled inwards towards the top, and the faces shaped to take account of both the vertical and horizontal curvature. The entrance is a long passage, or dromos, walled on either side and culminating in a tall, rectangular doorway with a lintel weighing approximately 120 tons. Elaborate half-columns and sculptured ornamentation decorated the entrance, despite its being totally buried in earth after the entombment of the kings or nobles.

There was trade on a substantial scale, for copper from Cyprus, Egyptian gold, lapis-lazuli and ivory from the Middle East, exotic stones and papyrus, perhaps even tin from Cornwall, were all imported; whilst timber, wine, and especially pottery were exported as far afield as southern Italy, Rhodes, Syria and Palestine. During the reign of Akhenaten in Egypt much Mycenean pottery was brought to El Amarna. Traders were a social group, together with bards, doctors and special craftsmen, who were not tied to a locality, as were warriors and small farmers, but travelled and formed a leaven in the international community. Mycenaean culture made this practical; the Argolid, for example, had a good road system, supported by bridges and culverts and linking the principal palace fortresses. The fall of Knossos to Greek invaders after 1450 BC undoubtedly widened the markets for mainland traders and brought a greater prosperity.

*Ancient Mycenae*

The heart of the palace was the megaron, or great hall, built round a hearth and entered by a columned gateway, a scheme influencing later Greek architecture with its propylaea. Here in the megaron the king held court, a king who was at once political leader, chief judge, commander-in-chief and chief priest. The king's person was probably considered sacred, as was his tomb, and his authority was undisputed, even in assemblies, where, though advice could be given, the king had the power to decide. In this, Egyptian influence may have been preponderant, though the general aristocratic tradition of the age ensured that it would be so at Mycenae and elsewhere. No temples have been found at Mycenae; yet this may show only that the priestly caste were content to eschew office and offer their wisdom at the feet of the ostentatious warriors.

Certainly the megaron would have witnessed acts of regal generosity, for gift offering and hospitality were cardinal rules of the warrior caste. The offer of rich gifts to friends, peers, suitors, and dowries was a custom accounting no doubt for much of the magnificent weaponry and jewellery. When Agamemnon sought to win over the recalcitrant Achilles, he offered him seven tripods, untarnished by flames, ten talents of gold, twenty cauldrons of gleaming copper, twelve prize-winning horses and seven women skilled in fine crafts, and much more after the promised sack of Troy. Not that such gifts were only used as bribes or rewards; gifts were an integral feature of the heroic life, for meanness was second only to cowardice as an execrable vice. Hospitality was similarly valued, for no stranger was to be turned away, and a warrior like Odysseus, who for so long enjoyed the call of adventure and the sea, could at least rely on a noble and generous welcome from his own caste and from social inferiors in Ithaca, like the swineherd Eumaeus, who took great care over the stranger he did not recognise as his lord and master.

Yet despite all this magnificence the story of the Trojan war describes the dusk of a bronze age civilisation, the drawing down of blinds; just as in the East the battle of Kurukshetra marks the same end, the death of warriors, brought down by their wilful pride and insolence. The passions unleashed by war get out of control. At Kurukshetra, the rules of warfare successively crumble as the fighting intensifies, so that even the noble Yudhisthira tells a lie on the battlefield. At Troy, Achilles forgets the honour due to a worthy adversary and vilely desecrates the body of Hector before the eyes of Andromache and King Priam. When Achilles relents, it is not through reason but through the awakened memory of his own old father Peleus, when Priam begs him on bended knee to hand over his son's body for proper funeral rites. And the final sack of Troy is a merciless act of debauchery, unworthy of heroes who claim to venerate a code of honour.

Greece, and the Argolid in particular, fell into a state of anarchy and economic disintegration after the Trojan war. The culture of Mycenae, of Tiryns and Pylos, and the other palace fortresses, declined; trade faltered, treason and civil war appeared, to turn the fine weapons upon themselves and stain the glorious megarons with blood. The story of Agamemnon's return from Troy exemplifies this in its starkest form. His fleet returns to the bay of Nauplia, within sight of the cyclopean battlements of Tiryns, the stronghold of Mycenae at the head of the plain. As he is conveyed towards his palace, a plot is prepared against his life. In Mycenae his queen, Clytemnaestra, has taken a lover, Aegisthus, during Agamemnon's long absence at Troy. With his help she plans to murder the king when he returns. From the palace gate - the Lion

Gate - a carpet of the finest material leads up the broad ramp to the palace, and the aging king, weary but light of heart, walks to the colonnaded doorway of the megaron, no doubt to be welcomed with loving arms by his queen. He is offered a bath to refresh himself before the homecoming feast. Outwardly the scene has every mark of a hero's return - the joyous servants, the respectful warriors, the brightly coloured deckings of the inner palace, the bustle of preparations for a feast, the smell of roasting flesh and warm wine, the glitter of the fire in the great hearth on gold and silver, on goblets and sheathed daggers.

As Agamemnon steps out of his bath, Clytenmaestra offers him a purple bath towel, but ignoring his outstretched arms she hurls it over his head. Aegisthus emerges from behind a screen with an axe. It crashes down on the king, splitting his skull. This foul crime, born of lust and ambition, the calculated murder of a king, a husband, a returning warrior, marks the death of Mycenaean society. It symbolises the collapse of the palace system which had begun so peacefully in the island of Crete. The Trojans are avenged. Two innocent victims of the Trojan War, Hector's wife Andromache, and Iphigenia daughter of Agamemnon and Clytemnestra,* have been requited. Trojan and Greek will fall together into a dark age, the end of an era.

*Bath, Nestor's Palace, Pylos*

Yet memory has not been destroyed. It rests in the minds of the bards, who will sing of the Trojan war and its heroes, of Odysseus and his voyages, until the great Homer will formulate it for generations of Greeks to read and recite. From it they will draw their understanding of the gods, whose intervention turned the course of

* *See p. 19.*

war, raised and destroyed heroes, brought Odysseus and his men to death or salvation. They will learn, too, of *arete*, the excellence of a man, his fine tuning as a soldier, a statesman, a speaker or a craftsmen; of reason and courage, those twin virtues of Odysseus, which surmount every obstacle of man and nature; and of hubris, the overweening pride which leads men to challenge the gods themselves and break their powers against the divine wrath that will not be so offended. Above all, they learn of the journey that men make in search of themselves, the journey that Krishna explains so carefully to Arjuna, and that Odysseus finds for himself through long experience with the help of Athena, goddess of wisdom.

Social and economic collapse brought invaders into the territory of Mycenaean culture. They came from the north and north-west of Greece, settling for a while north of the Gulf of Corinth at Doris, which gave rise to their name of Dorians. Doris was near Delphi, "the rocky threshold of Apollo", which became the greatest religious centre of the whole Greek world, and the Dorians retained their reverence for the god - though Zeus and Athena also were close to their hearts. Legend claimed that the invaders were led by the sons of Heracles, returning to claim their birthright in the Argolid, for Heracles had been lord of Tiryns before he was committed ta serve his task master - Eurystheus, King of Mycenae. In any case, the Dorians spread themselves well beyond the Argolid, into Laconia, Messenia, Corinth and Megara in the Peloponnese - the island of Pelops, king of Mycenae - and yet further into the islands of Cythera, Melos, Thera, Rhodes, Cos and Crete. Arcadia, in the uplands of the northern Peloponnese, was not invaded, remaining an ancient and reputedly idyllic enclave with a dialect akin to that of Cyprus. Laconia received the harshest treatment. Its population was enslaved to work the land for their Dorian masters, and here began the history of a mainstream of Greek civilisation, the Dorian Spartans.

Athens was relatively untouched in its eastern promontory. There the Ionic dialect was retained and from there later waves of emigrants moved across the Aegean to people the Cyclades - except Melos and Thera - and the coast and islands of Asia Minor. This division between Doric and Ionic Hellenes was to run like veins of rock through Greek history, in its art and language, politics and warfare. When the two strains met and fused, which rarely happened, the genius of Greece reached a pinnacle of brilliance, as in the Acropolis of Athens, where Doric and Ionic orders of architecture stand alongside one another in a unique union.

Thucydides said that the Dorians occupied the Peloponnese eighty years after the Trojan war. Certainly a wave of destruction swept over the palace fortresses about 1200 BC. It was to be many centuries before anything approaching the cultured life of Mycenaean Greece was to be re-established. The age of heroes had run its course. The Dorians lacked the civilised life of those they replaced or enslaved, but they, too, were to find a teacher who would transform them into a resemblance of former glory.

## Chapter 8

# One is the Race of Gods and Men

## *Culture and Religion*

FROM THE FALL OF MYCENAEAN Greece until the eighth century BC is usually referred to as a Dark Age. Yet in the eighth century appeared the institutions and forms of art which became the great strands in the rich tapestry of later Greece, such as the polis, the Olympic Games, a new written language, and colonisation. From what did these basic institutions grow? Whatever their origin, it lay in a period of history about which little is known.

The collapse of civilisation and culture in the eastern Mediterranean was far reaching. After about 1100 BC, according to modern archaeology, economic life in Greece was primitive and few signs of culture can be discerned, until protogeometric* pottery

*Apollo from pediment of the temple of Zeus, Olympia*

---

\*   *A style using only geometric shapes, like circles and triangles, for decoration, mainly on the shoulder and belly of the vase.*

emerged about two centuries later. Nevertheless, somewhere in the simplicity of the Dorian and Attic villages arose the knowledge required for a renewal of civilised life. Some bold spirits turned away from the world of the senses and looked for something more trustworthy. One such man may have become, in the minds of his benefactors, the demi-god Heracles or even the shining god Apollo, for these two, hero and god, presided over much that was dearest to the Greeks for a thousand years.

By the eighth century, a new way of life had emerged, no longer a palace culture centred upon a king, nor a nobleman's estate of the type admired by Homer, but a city-state, or polis, a political atom, for it was the smallest self-contained unit in which every member could find full expression of his humanity. The new men of this culture loved above all to strive for excellence, or arete, and the polis was the means for achieving this, whether it were perfection in speaking, in fighting, in throwing a pot, or ploughing a straight furrow. This ideal found its most obvious expression in the Olympic Games, which probably began several hundred years before the first record of victors in 776 BC. For the ideal was not that of a specialist, whom the Greeks viewed as a crabbed slave to a particular craft, rather like their limping god of the forge, Hephaestus, but that of a master of all he touched, like Achilles or Odysseus, who brought to each task a shaft of the golden light of Phoebus Apollo himself. Thus could a race, a boxing match, a discus- or javelin-throw, become actions of great beauty, full of speed and strength, power and elegance. Man was not divided into separate powers of emotion, mind and body; he was a unity, spirit embodied in action:

> "For the Gods give all the means of mortal greatness,
> They grant men skill,
> Might of hand and eloquence,
> My praise is ripe for one."[1]

This sense of unity held the Greeks back from undue analysis of themselves and the world. Acuteness of mind and precision of language were turned instead to explore questions about unity, rather than disunity. The Ionian scientists came to ask not what are the parts of something or of the universe itself, but of what one substance is a thing, or the universe, made. What is it in itself, not what does it divide into? Greek political thinkers asked not what are the alternatives to the polis, but how may the polis itself grow or decline, for the polis was the unity of social man. A great mathematician, like Pythagoras, did not seek to translate number into something else, like sets, but to find what secrets number already contained. Nor in their art did they dissect natural form. They believed that beauty lies within nature, especially within human nature. Therefore they would enlarge, magnify, this beauty. They would not follow the Cretan love of the miniature; they would make monumental statues, temples that would be seen from afar by homeward bound mariners, theatres which would carry the human voice to every stone seat of a hillside, warships of triple banked oars which would churn the sea into a white froth, and a philosophy which would see in man an immortal and indivisible soul.

It was a culture which put forth strong roots in the Italian peninsula, also, amongst the south Italian and Sicilian colonies of Magna Graecia, around the Black Sea, and, with the Romans, spreading to every shore of the Mediterranean. The Ionian coast of Asia Minor became a particularly rich field for Greek culture, yielding fine cities like Ephesus, Miletus and Mytilene and the earliest Greek writers of philosophy.

Within this supremely artistic culture of the Mediterranean, which drew upon the natural beauty of colour and form in sea and limestone, there arose also a sense of Greek nationality, tenuous, fiercely proud when threatened from without.

The idea of the polis was given specific form by the great lawgivers, Lycurgus and Solon; the Greek language received an alphabet from the Phoenicians - according to Herodotus from the obscure Cadmus, who took it to Thebes - and religion was partly, though never wholly, systematised, through the Homeric epics and the *Theogony* of the Boeotian poet, Hesiod.

All Greeks distinguished themselves from those who were ignorant of the Greek tongue, *barbaroi*, though Greeks acknowledged that the profounder aspects of religion, at Delphi for example, were appreciated by Syrians and Africans and other non-Greeks. What had brought Greeks together in nationhood was the unity found in their common struggle before the walls of Troy. Much of Homer's power over the Greek mind was from recalling this unity of struggle and sacrifice. Mycenaeans, Spartans, Ithacans, Cretans, men from Tiryns, Argos, Pylos, Aegina, Troezen, mainlanders and islanders alike, had all sent contingents in a common cause. Their palace culture and ample estates were no more, but the memory of this great display of unity was not lost. Reminded by the metrical charm of Homer, they could recapture this unity, and though each polis became a microcosm of the new culture, it carried within it also a sense of nationality. Every Greek polis would worship with similar rites at the statues and altars of the gods in the city temples, every Greek could converse freely with his compatriots, and so much was a common law respected that a polis would be represented in another polis by a member of the latter one. However strong a polis became - and Athens became overwhelmingly strong by the mid-fifth century BC - a common danger would draw taut the threads that united Greeks. If the sanctity of Olympia was threatened, common cause was soon made against the miscreant. When the Games were held, in every fourth year, violent animosities would bow before a national truce. When the Phoenicians or Persians attacked Greek territory, they might face a sudden alliance. Nothing demeaned Sparta more than its eventual desperate call upon the Great King for help against Athens in the Peloponnesian War of 431-404 BC. By then Greek nationality was doomed and would make way, ere long, for the stronger breed of Rome.

At a critical point in Homer's Iliad, Zeus, the father of the gods, allows the rest of the gods to enter the battle, according to their sympathies for either the Greeks or the Trojans.

"And with that command Zeus roused incessant battle. Down the immortals launched to the field of action - their warring spirits split the gods two ways. Hera went to the massed ships with Pallas Athena, Poseidon who grips the earth, and Hermes god of luck who excels them all at subtle twists and tactics - and the god of fire flanked them, seething power, hobbling along but his shrunken legs moved nimbly. But Ares swept down to the Trojans, helmet flashing, and pacing him went Phoebus with long hair streaming and Artemis showering arrows, Leto and River Xanthus and goddess Aphrodite strong with eternal laughter."[2]

As unrestrained partisans, the gods enter the battle, protecting their favourites, interfering with the other side, even attacking each other in their zest for action. How then are mortal men responsible for their own individual actions? Did the Greeks deny that man had free will? Could a people who believed so much in valour and initiative and intelligence displayed in action really repudiate the autonomy that such virtues require? Where then is arete? Homer answers such questions, not theoretically, but in the substance of his epic narrative. One example may suffice: that of the Trojan warrior, Agenor, as the Greeks pour towards the gates of Troy, led by the dreaded Achilles. Agenor is a noble youth, but he is full of misgivings, as he sees Achilles bearing down upon him. Yet, because he is noble, the god Apollo breathes daring into his heart. Agenor braces himself and waits for Achilles without a tremor; then challenges him in combat. His spear strikes Achilles on the greave, without injuring him. As the great Achilles prepares in his turn to strike, Apollo hides Agenor in a thick mist and sweeps him away from the battlefield to safety. It is divine intervention; but it has not negated the will of men. Agenor is infused with courage, because he is already noble; he has earned the breath of daring and is worthy of Apollo's inspiration.

This is not all that Homer implies, for the gods are forces within men, given names and forms by the poet. Agenor draws upon a divine force within himself. Where else could it be? Neither Homer, nor any educated Greek, believed in visible, tangible gods moving about the earth like massy ghosts. When Agenor makes a supreme effort of courage, he finds within himself divine power, for that is what makes the effort supreme. The god and the force are one and the same. Greek life and art are rich with pictorial and plastic creativity. Thus for the Greeks the gods could easily be portrayed in human form; fighting, loving, quarrelling, being partial; beautiful like Apollo and Aphrodite, ugly like Pan, limping like Hephaestus. In later literature and art, perhaps, the names and forms became too dominant. Audiences became gullible, as Plato warns often enough, but Homer and Hesiod, who first formulated the Greek Pantheon, were not.

Plato, or rather Socrates, said that the one God used other gods to create men. He gave Man the immortal spark of Himself, the soul of each, and left the gods to furnish them with everything else human.[3] So each god gave a force of his or her own to each human, the spiritual or emotional powers within by which human faculties are motivated. Agenor is noble, therefore daring and fearlessness work within him.

The Greeks were not systematic in their religion, but they had an unyielding faith in the existence of unseen things. Socrates, in the fifth century BC, did not have to convince them of a totally new idea, that the world of sense objects is not real; he only needed to remind them of an idea that went back into the depths of their culture. The Greeks of Homer's time would have agreed more easily. According to Socrates, everything has an inner nature or essence, called a soul in animate creatures. These essences are divine agencies and, as he said at his trial, how can one believe in divine agencies without believing in the divinities which instruct them? Thus Socrates answered the charge that he did not believe in the gods, but he did not say that he could see them.

On the heights of Olympus in north-eastern Greece dwelt the chief gods, or Pantheon: Zeus, the thunderer; Poseidon, the Earthshaker, ruler of the sea; Phoebus Apollo; Athena of the Flashing Eyes; Demeter, goddess of earth and grain; Hera, jealous queen of Zeus; Hephaestus, god of fire and the forge; Hermes, messenger of the gods and ruler of the winds; Artemis of the Golden Distaff, goddess of the moon and hunting: Hestia, goddess of hearth and home: Ares, Sacker of Cities, god of war; and Aphrodite, goddess of love and beauty. An older tradition still preserved the memory of the goddess of the earth, the ancient Gaea, worshipped in the Aegean for centuries before the pantheon of the epic poets, and connected with this sense of a divine Earth were the nymphs or spirits of springs, trees and mountains, and the gods of rivers. Within the earth lived the great race of Titans, sons of Uranus or Heaven, who deposed their father and were themselves defeated by the youthful Zeus.

The Greek myth of creation begins with the unmoving and unlimited Chaos - not chaos in the sense of confusion and lawlessness, but in the proper sense of without form - from which arises Earth, and from Earth, Heaven. One of Heaven's sons is the Titan Cronos or Time, for time can only be created by the movement of heavenly bodies, but Cronos rebels, castrates his father and becomes ruler of all. Knowing that his offspring may displace him, Cronos swallows them as soon as they are born to his consort, Rhea, but Rhea desperately escapes to Crete, where Zeus is born near Mount Ida. Rhea wraps a huge stone in swaddling clothes, which Cronos swallows, inducing him to spew out the previous victims of his jealousy. Zeus overcomes Cronos and rules the world in his stead, for even Time succumbs to divine Justice. His own son, Apollo, becomes the means for the redemption of men, for justice may be more than men can bear, and when sin drives them to despair they may turn to a redeemer for salvation from eternal retribution.

Other aspects of the genealogy of the gods, as described by Hesiod, strikingly represent the generation of forces:

> "Hateful strife bore painful Toil,
> Neglect, Starvation and tearful Pain,
> Battles, Combats, Bloodshed and Slaughter,
> Quarrels, Lies, Pretences and Arguments,
> Disorder, Disaster - neighbours to each other -
> and Oath, who most harms men on earth,
> when someone knowingly swears false."[4]

In contrast, the union of Zeus and Memory brings forth the Nine Muses, guardians of all forms of poetry and music.

Yet above both the conflict and the harmony of the wilful gods, the divine forces of Creation, the Greeks recognised a higher unity, containing even Zeus and the whole immortal pantheon, as well, of course, as humanity. This unity was not often stated, though there are a few hints in the Ionian philosophers, like Heraclitus:

> "Listening not to me, but to the divine account it is wise to agree that all things are one."[5]

and in the poets, like Pindar:

> "Single is the race, single
> Of men and gods;
> From a single mother we draw both breath."[6]

And in Plato the unity known to Socrates as the Good is the only true reality.

This unity was inherent in the Greeks' way of life, actions and art, as though they half remembered it and allowed the memory to shape their lives, if not to govern them.For their fundamental concepts went deeper than the gods. Beyond natural forces, either in men or the world, were justice, nemesis, necessity, arete. These were inexorably lawful - that everything had in principle a perfection of its own, for example - because they all arose from the final principle of law itself. That there was one law, which was the very form of law, is an evident belief of all Greeks. How else could their art convey such an ubiquitous measure or order? Before the temple at Delphi, the seven wise men had inscribed "Nothing in excess" and "Know thyself. The former maxim was founded upon the complete lawfulness of everything, for excess is the breaking of the laws. The latter showed the origin of that lawfulness, for the source of law lies within oneself.

At Olympia, on the west pediment of the great Temple of Zeus within the sacred enclosure known as the Altis, stood a huge figure of Apollo, his right arm extended in a gesture of irrefutable authority, his magnificent head turned to look along the arm at the creatures he commands. They are centaurs, dominated by their lower nature as beasts, for they are seizing the Lapith women at the wedding feast of the Lapith king, Peirithoos. Though it is upon the temple of Justice, or Zeus, it is the light of reason which commands the passions. Apollo is not the sun-god Helios, but the inner light which shines within the mind, revealing good and evil alike, subduing those creatures which seek darkness, amongst them lust. For Apollo is the purifier, the washer-away of sin as shown in the terrible sequence of events beginning with Agamemnon's return from Troy. After the murder by Clytemnaestra and her lover Aegisthus, Orestes, the dead king's son, avenges his father by killing his mother and Aegisthus. He thus incurs the guilt of matricide, even though the ancient law has enjoined upon him the act of vengeance. In his cycle of tragedies the fifth century dramatist, Aeschylus, makes Apollo both the instigator of Orestes' revenge and the god to whom Orestes appeals as a suppliant. The goddess Athena finally decides on Orestes' acquittal before the court of the Areopagus in Athens, but Apollo is the purifier, who alone absolves the killer from blood guilt and the awful curse which possesses his family.

Apollo fulfills the role of saviour. As Egyptians sought refuge in Osiris, so Greeks turned to the serene son of Zeus, of whom Plato said:

> "He is the god who sits in the centre, on
> the navel of the earth, and he is the
> interpreter of religion to all mankind."[7]

Delphi was the home of his shrine, where a great navel-shaped stone, or Omphalos, marked the centre of the world. Nearby, at a fissure in the earth, sat the priestess of Apollo on a tripod. She would descend into the fissure to receive from the Pythian oracle the answers to the questions of suppliants. She drank pure water from the Cassotis spring and chewed laurel leaves, until she came forth and spoke the oracle's answer in a language which only the priests of Delphi could interpret. Throughout the Greek world the oracle was revered, though its answers were obscure and often ambiguous, as King Croesus found to his cost.[8] Apollo had killed the Python, a snake which guarded the Earth's oracle, and made himself master of it, in place of Gaea. He seized some Cretan sailors to serve as priests by disguising himself as a dolphin (Greek, *delphis*), thus giving to the place the name of Delphi. That knowledge really stemmed from the oracle was indicated by the fact that even Socrates respected its

*Temple of Apollo, Delphi*

*Theatre at Delphi*

pronouncements. Indeed, it was the Delphic oracle who said that Socrates was the wisest of the Greeks. Too shrewd to take the oracle literally, he proved subsequently that his wisdom consisted in realising that he knew nothing, whilst other Greeks were unaware of their own ignorance.

Apollo was the god of prophecy, an art which Socrates explained as hearing an inner voice "which always forbids, but never bids"[9] and which was close to that knowledge of law so familiar to the Greek mind. Music, medicine and archery were Apollo's special province also. His lyre was the symbol of both musical and healing skills, for its harmonious sound would soothe away all ills. (His son, Asclepius, the father of Greek medicine later identified with the Egyptian sage, Imhotep, used more mundane cures, since Hippocrates of Cos is said to have copied down the inscriptions of cures written on the temple walls in Cos by Asclepius' patients. These however owed much to Apollo, for some took the form of experiencing therapeutic dreams in the god's temple. Archery was associated with Apollo's power to bring sudden death, as though from an arrow shot. He was said to destroy at a distance, though Plato said that his reputation as a destroyer arose from a misunderstanding about his name, which should really be "the mover together,"[10] befitting the god of harmony.

This last quality lay at the root of Apollo's power. Harmony destroys disharmony, the excess measure of sound inherent in everything corrupt or evil. Thus Apollo is the purifier, the absolver from all impurities, and this is why he can take the load of sin from the shoulders of his suppliants. Sacred to Apollo were swans, who sing when death approaches, but not in sorrow, for they divine a blessed future. He was the great reconciler of conflict. Between man and man, polis and polis, Greece and her enemies, he pacified antagonists, bringing reason to the causes which separated them. Under Apollo's influence, the doctrine of a life for a life was replaced by a more humane idea of punishment, as the story of Orestes demonstrates (see p. 80). No shrine was more sacred than that of Delphi, and none could disturb its tranquillity. When the Persians approached it, they were driven back by a landslide.[11]

Whenever Apollo entered the assembly of the gods, they all rose to honour him. As son of Zeus, the mind of God, Apollo was the soul of the world, and therefore around him, the unmoving mover of the universe, revolved the eight spheres, whose own souls were the eight Muses. Each Muse created a form of music or poetry; the ninth and greatest, Calliope, Muse of epic poetry, was the harmony of all eight. No wonder that aspiring poets washed their hands in the sacred waters of the Castalian spring that runs from the hillside at Delphi. In the same spirit did Plato say that the greatest officer of state, in charge of education, should be elected in the Temple of Apollo, for the lord of the Muses is the master of education.[12]

The worship of Apollo replaced that of Gaea, the earth goddess, at Delphi some time in the eleventh to ninth centuries BC. The change marks the rise of a new culture. At its centre, Apollo of the Golden Locks sat on the navel of the earth, below the great twin crags of Mount Parnassus, looking down beneficently upon the sacred olive groves of the Krissaean Plain far below.

Greek religion was in no way a department of life. Greeks lived under the authority of the gods, who made their lives intelligible, justified their actions and explained the consequences. For the unseen forces were known to be causes of events, and Man had to take full account of these forces. To pretend to be free from them, or to have the power to overcome them, was hubris and led to inevitable disaster. Freedom lay in understanding them and acting in harmony with them, like in intelligent sailor with wind and tide. Thus the Greeks were rarely in danger of being caught up in materialism or thorough-going hedonism, since they did not believe inj the final reality of the visible and tangible world. Not for them the ideas that the production of ever more physical goods, or material power over others, make for the good life. Proud though Athens became of her fifth century empire, it was never of such a low order as that, as Pericles, according to Thucydides, made clear in his great funeral oration.[13]

*Temple Colums at Bassae*

Decisive events in Greek history were influenced by this belief in the divine and causal world. When the Spartans delayed their departure for Marathon in 490 BC because the moon was not yet full, no one in the ancient world condemned them for it (though it is fair to ask whether a few voices may have been raised if the Persians had won!). The Athenians credited the victory to the goddess Athena, and the two semi-divine heroes, Theseus and Heracles, whom they believed were present on the battlefield. Even if the causes of victory were the moral vigour of the Athenian hoplites, pride in their polis, and martial strength, yet the inner forces of these were believed to be the goddess and the heroes, invisible, but present and efficacious, at Marathon. So too, the work of the farmer and sailor were managed with a knowledge of underlying causes, which acted at precise times - a time to plant and a time to set sail, as Hesiod explained in his "Works and Days". Action had to be in the particular moment, when the divine forces were conducive to its success, and of course, the participant had to be present in that moment also, so that the causal chain would be complete, from god to mind, from mind to hand. Socrates could not be executed in his Athenian prison until the ship returned from the sacred island of Delos. Apollo would not tolerate sacrilege; and so the grace of Apollo made possible the last great philosophical dialogue between the master to his disciples, concerning death and the immortality of the soul. Who dare say that this was not the grace of a god, of Apollo, the purifier and redeemer of Man?

> "In everything the Mean is right, and to know
> The Moment is best."[14]

The history of ancient Greece is only explicable in the light of Greek understanding of divine forces. Most tangible as evidence of this were the Greek cities themselves. Their finest buildings were dedicated to the gods and would not have existed without divine inspiration. The Parthenon frieze, over which the genius of Phidias presided, was scarcely visible from the ground, for it was serenely mounted high up under the shadow of the colonnade. Only the gods could see it in its full artistry. As for the lonely eminence of the temple at Bassae in the north-western Peloponnese, even the modern traveller must venture to it in the spirit of a pilgrimage. Though the great chryselephantine statues of Athena on the Acropolis and of Zeus in his temple at Olympia have been lost, the majestic figure of Poseidon (or perhaps of Zeus), found beneath the sea off Cape Artemesium, is ample proof of the devotion the Greeks felt towards the unseen forces that governed, but under wisdom, did not dominate, their lives.

### References:

1. Pindar, 'Pythian I, III, in *The Odes*, trans. C. M. Bowra, Penguin, London, 1969, p. 133.
2. Homer, *The Iliad*, trans. R. Fagles, Folio Society, London, 1996, Book XX, 11. 37-48, p. 427.
3. See Plato, *Timaeus*, trans. B. Jowett, Random House, New York, 1937, 41.
4. Hesiod, *Theogony*, trans M. L. West, O.U.P., Oxford, 1988, 226-232, p. 10.
5. J. Barnes, *Early Greek Philosophy*, Penguin, London, 1987, p. 102.
6. Pindar, 'Nemean VII', in *The Odes of Pindar* (Classics) trans. C. Bowra, Penguin, London, 1969, p. 206.
7. Plato, *Republic*, trans. Jowett, Book IV, 427.
8. See Herodotus, *Histories*, trans. Aubrey de Selincourt, Penguin, London, 1972, Book I.
9. See Plato, *Phaedrus*, trans. B. Jowett, 242.
10. Plato, *Cratylus*, trans. B. Jowett, 405.
11. See Herodotus, *Histories*, Book VIII, p. 536.
12. See Plato, *Laws*, trans. B. Jowett, Book VI, 766.
13. Thucydides, *The Peloponnesian War*, trans. R. Warner, Penguin, London, 1972, Book II.
14. Pindar, 'Olympian XIII, III', trans. Bowra.

## Chapter 9
# Since Peace is in the Land
### The Greek Polis

"What I would prefer is that you should fix your eyes every day on the greatness of Athens as she really is, and should fall in love with her. When you realise her greatness, then reflect that what made her great was men with a spirit of adventure, men who knew their duty, men who were ashamed to fall below a certain standard."[1]

THUS DID THUCYDIDES EXPRESS Pericles' pride in Athens, when the Athenian leader gave the funeral oration for the dead at the end of the first year of the Peloponnesian war. Yet such words might have been spoken in many of the Greek poleis. By the mid-fifth century BC, Athens was the largest polis in the Greek world, with perhaps over 300,000 inhabitants, but greatness was not to be measured by size,

*Wash Basins at Nemea*

as Pericles would have been first to admit. The greatness of the Greek polis lay in its heightening of life, in the exhilaration of men breathing the fine air of real human achievement. The Athenian citizen in that year, 431 BC, could look up from the Agora, or market place, beyond the towering walls of the Acropolis with their fragments of columns from the unfinished temple begun after the battle of Marathon, to the glorious elegance of the just completed Parthenon and the great gateway of the Propylaea leading to it.

For Athens' frequent antagonist, Sparta, greatness lay in the martial splendour and supreme resolution of her warriors. For the Corinthians, it was the artistic and commercial genius which had made her black figure pottery supreme in the markets of the eastern Mediterranean, and the power and fecundity of her wide-ranging fleet. Even little Sicyon could boast a fine treasury at the sacred site of Delphi, and the handful of Elians took pride in their guardianship of Olympia, which housed a sanctuary of Zeus and the most famous of all stadiums. The variety of the Greek genius found its expression in the rich diversity of the poleis themselves.

Nor was there uniformity within the polis. By the standards of most later societies, and of the great contemporary empire of Persia, all Greek poleis were small communities; yet they were large enough to enable each citizen to find in the life of the community a place for his or her arete, or excellence. Skill of every kind was fostered by the face-to-face nature of the animated, competitive and essentially social life of both citizens and resident foreigners. The orator would be regularly tested in the Assembly, the craftsman would display his wares in the Agora, the artist or stonemason would offer his work to gods and men alike in the temple, the actor, musician and dramatist would he heard by all at the great religious festivals. Even the philosopher was open to public praise or derision. When Aristophanes entered "The Clouds" for the Athenian drama festival - and was placed third and last - he offered up Socrates to public ridicule as a naive agnostic, who taught that the clouds were gods and that the worse case could be the better one.

Everyone knew what everyone else was doing and saying; but personal concerns were tempered by a universal interest in what concerned everybody. For in view of the small size of the polis, a war, a drought, a crop failure, a new temple, a new play or the death of a leader, directly affected each individual for good or ill.

"We do not say that a man who takes no interest in politics is a man who minds his own business; we say that he has no business here at all."[2]

A Spartan who survived the annihilation of his comrades at Thermopylae, because he was sick with inflammation of the eyes, was treated with such disdain by everyone in Sparta that he made certain of his own death at the later battle of Plataea. He had nowhere to hide. A victor in the Olympic Games, on the other hand, might eat at the public expense in his native city for the rest of his life, for his achievement was the pride of everyone.

How could the polis be so small and yet so complete, a self-sufficient association securing the good life, as Aristotle described it?[3] The answer lies in the small demands that the Greeks made on material things. Socrates was not alone in needing only the simplest of garments and plain food. Greeks only ate meat at festivals and were satisfied with cheese, figs, olives, bread and a little wine. Their homes were devoid of elaborate furniture and unnecessary ornament. Hence specialisation within the polis enabled these needs to be met with only limited recourse to trade. (Though fifth century Athens, being exceptionally large, depended on heavy corn imports.) No polis was a mere town. It included some country areas around it, so that agriculture, and perhaps fishing, sheep farming, timber and mineral production were integral parts of its economy, and the population of the rural areas had full citizenship alongside the town dwellers.

Poleis were formed by the process of *synoikismos*, which Theseus had used to create the polis of Athens. Villages were grouped together and given common institutions. Athens and Sparta were early examples: Elis and Mantinea were late examples in mid-fifth century BC. Yet the polis was never a mere collection of people. Aristotle was only endorsing a common assumption when he wrote that it was natural for man to live in a polis.[4] For the Greeks believed that every polis was founded upon justice, and justice was a natural law, not a man-made contrivance. Thus the polis was divinely appointed, and without it a man was unnaturally isolated, separated from his own nature. Moreover, the natural distribution of qualities marked out labourers, traders, warriors or even the wise, as in the myth of the Silver Age.* When this division was acknowledged there was justice, for all lived and worked in the way best suited to their natural capacities.

> And is justice dimmer in the individual, and is her form different, or is she the same which we found her to be in the State? For the just man does not permit the several elements within him to interfere with one another, or any of them to do the work of others.[5]

The Greek poleis differed greatly in their constitutions. Athens evolved into a democracy; Sparta was a timocracy, founded on military virtues, though becoming in its decline an oligarchy; the Ionian poleis in the sixth century were tyrannies. Many poleis veered from oligarchy to democracy, or vice versa. The constitutional forms, however, concealed the fundamental common pattern of the four classes, which matched Plato's concept of justice and confirmed the intuitive Greek belief that justice lay at the root of every polis.

The Greeks loved excellence. They naturally sought out the best men as rulers, whatever the constitutional form. Peisistratus, Cleisthenes, Miltiades, Themistocles, Aristides, Pericles, differed greatly in their political persuasion, as did the constitution during the century for which they led Athens; but all were men of political genius, intelligent, courageous and charismatic. Similarly, in Sparta the apparent sovereignty of the two kings was tempered by the power of the Assembly, which decided all issues submitted to it by the Council, and which elected the members of the Gerousia, or Senate, and, later, the ephors. Hence the influence of the best natural leaders from amongst the several thousand Spartans could always be felt. The wise, too, had their role to play, whatever the constitution. They could educate each generation, be it in private homes or collectively in the Sparta agoge** They could speak through drama and literature, and were welcome in every cultivated circle, like the Boeotian Pindar in Aegina and the Athenian Xenophon in Sparta.

---

\*    *See pp. 10ff.*

\*\*   *See p. 102.*

*Treasury of Siphnos frieze; Quadriga in front of altar*

*Temple at Nemea*

So, too, the traders and labourers of Greek poleis were usually free to find their own mode of expression in their work. Most poleis welcomed foreigners and benefitted from their skills, often as traders or craftsmen. Athens certainly gained much from Solon's explicit encouragement to them to settle there. Some of the stonemasons who worked in Athens on the great Periclean rebuilding programme also worked at Persepolis on the palace of the Great King, for the masons' marks show this. Metics, as the resident foreigners were called, worked side by side with citizens and even slaves, on the metopes of the Parthenon, for example. It was not status that mattered, but the quality of work. They were free men, in the fullest sense of freedom to express their inherent genius.

Indeed, the real greatness of the Greek polis lay in its unique fusion of justice and freedom. This was not the mere negative freedom to escape the dangers of violence or other harm. It was the positive freedom found in a union of endeavour, a rising to the challenge of human perfection. Culture was intrinsic to the Greek polis. The beauty of its public buildings and its religious festivals and processions, replete with literature, music and drama, were an integral part of the way of life; not to be jealously guarded, but open to all Greeks, even sometimes to barbarians. Participation in this public culture, dedicated to the gods, was a higher freedom, a freedom of the mind, which at its finest could even point the way to spiritual liberation, as in the Eleusian Mysteries, or in the catharsis of the greatest tragic drama.

The religious festivals and dramas at Athens were paid for by the richest citizens, who also financed the navy, under the general idea of liturgies or public duties. This economic justice underpinned the harmony of the polis. No polis could possibly pretend to be a nation, for Greek nationality was a much broader concept bound up with language, religion and law; but the polis was an economy, enlivened by the local variety of these three principles. A polis had its local dialect; its religion acknowledged the national pantheon, though it had its own special gods also, like Apollo Karneios at Sparta and Athena Promachos at Athens. As for law, all Greeks acknowledged a natural law whose working in human affairs was inexorable, but they chose to meet its exigencies in a variety of ways, according to their constitutions and legislation. Whilst rich Athenians, for example, bore liturgies, that is, undertakings to pay for a public event, like a drama festival, in Sparta the whole ruling class had to observe the law concerning common messes. In both cases the growth of a parasitical leisure class was avoided, but by different legislation. Thus the economy of the polis was subject to the overall guidance of national principles, and these in turn reflected the abiding culture of the Greek people.

Hesiod has described the fruition of life under justice in the polis:

> "But when the judges of a town are fair
> To foreigner and citizen alike,
> Their city prospers and her people bloom;
> Since peace is in the land, her children thrive;
> Zeus never marks them out for cruel war.
> Famine and blight do not beset the just,
> Who till their well-worked fields and feast."[6]

The geography of Greece was not the cause of the institution of the polis, but was conducive to it. The numerous islands, long headlands, and river valleys isolated between high ranges of limestone mountains made self-dependent communities almost a necessity, and encouraged the development of virile local strains of national life. In a society whose ideals were those of the Homeric warrior, the great table-like rocks at Corinth, Argos, or Athens were sure to sprout military fortifications, especially where springs were found alongside. Similarly, the strategic position of Mycenae amongst its ring of hills, or Sparta below the towering and almost impenetrable barrier of Mount Taygetus, were sure to be exploited. Even Thebes, on a low rise about the central, fertile plain of Boeotia, dominated the area and controlled the routes northwards to the highlands of Aetolia and Phthiotis and south to Attica, the isthmus of Corinth and the Peloponnese. Such places were centres of concentration of military, economic and cultural forces. The ancient roads wound through the mountains to them, or the sea stretched its almost tideless waters into their gulfs and harbours, linking them permanently with the islands and colonies, to make the political network of the Greek nation. Not least, the beauty of land and sea, the one white with limestone and mottled with the variant greens of dark conifer and paler oak, vine and olive, the other changing with the sky from brilliant blue to the wine-darkness of Homer, made of Greece the natural home of a profoundly rich culture nurtured in the poleis.

Though allegiance to the polis dominated the lives of most Greeks, except in the remote areas of Arcadia and the north-west, there were institutions which acknowledged the idea of nationality. An amphictyony, or league of neighbours, arose in the "dark ages", based on Anthela, near Thermopylae, and dedicated to the nature goddess, Demeter. It was associated with the sanctuary of Apollo at Delphi. On the island of Euboea, close by Anthela, a very ancient apsidal building at Lefkandi may have been used by the amphictyonyic council. Its size - over forty-five metres long - and colonnaded style, and the rich tombs next to it, suggest that the amphictyony was a powerful force for unity, even before the poleis first arose in the late ninth century. Thessalians, Boeotians, Euboeans and probably other peoples from central Greece were members of the league. Its prestige continued for centuries, until even Philip of Macedon elected to join it in the fourth century BC. Members were bound not to cut off running water from any polis which belonged to it.

In 582 BC the league instituted the quadriennial Pythian Games in the stadium at Delphi, in the shadow of Mount Parnassus, high above the sacred way and the place where the oracle gave its cryptic advice. Panhellenism, a term used by Homer in his Catalogue of Ships, in book II of the *Iliad*, found its strongest emotional force in devotion to Apollo, the god who sat at the navel of the earth. Also in the sixth century began the Nemean and Isthmian Games, both held every two years. Other sites, religious in character, fostered this sense of national identity, but outstanding in such essentially Greek inspiration was Olympia in the far west of the Peloponnese.

### References:

1. Thucydides, *The Peloponnesian War*, trans. R. Warner, Penguin, London, 1972, Book II, p. 149.
2. Thucydides, *The Peloponnesian War*, Book II, p. 147.
3. Aristotle, *The Politics*, trans. T. A. Sinclair, Penguin, London, 1962, Book I, ch. 2.
4. Aristotle, *The Politics*, Book I, ch. 2.
5. Plato, *Republic*, Random House, New York, 1937, Book IV, pp. 442-443.
6. Hesiod, *Works and Days*, trans. D. S. Wender, Penguin, London, 1973, 11. 225-231, p. 66.

## Chapter 10
# The Crown of Wild Olive
### The Olympic Games

IN THE YEAR 48O BC, whilst the huge land and sea forces of Xerxes were bearing down upon Greece, the great athlete Phayllos of Croton sailed from his home in Magna Graecia to take part in the Olympic Games, which were not to be stopped, even by the Great King of Persia. This was perhaps the only chance Phayllos would ever have of winning the precious crown of wild olive, which distinguished an Olympic victor. Nevertheless, when his ship approached the Greek mainland, he heard news of the Persian invasion and set sail for Salamis. There he commanded the only western Greek ship in the famous battle that destroyed the Persian fleet and saved Greece from conquest. It was a greater honour.

*View of Temple of Hera, Olympia*

What had Phayllos of Croton sacrificed? The crown of wild olive was the finest tribute of all to a Greek competitor in any of the numerous games held throughout Greece - finer than the pine crown of Isthmia, the wild celery of Nemea, even than the laurel of Delphi - for Olympia was the first great venue of the games, where the ideal of athletic excellence was first established. The ideal was not that of a specialist, even though all competitors had to swear on oath that they had trained for ten months in their own cities, and for one month preceding the games at Olympia itself, in the Gymnasium and Palaestra (for boxing and wrestling). The ideal remained the arete of the whole man, the unity of spirit, mind and body. The events themselves did not allow for much specialisation. Only in the Pentathlon, for example, were there field events, where the discus and javelin were combined with running, long jump and wrestling. Above all, the games were a religious festival in honour of the gods and heroes: of Zeus at Olympia, Apollo at Delphi, Poseidon at Corinth, and Heracles at Nemea. Thus athletic perfection was sought as the dedication of mind and body to the divine forces. This has been well expressed by a modern translator of the Boeotian poet Pindar, whose Odes praised the victors of the Games:

> "His central theme is the part of experience in which human beings are exalted or illumined by a divine force, and this he commonly compares with light. At such times the consciousness is marvellously enhanced, and a man's whole being has a new spaciousness and confidence..... What Pindar conveys in song is precisely the enhancement of consciousness which his athletes enjoy in the moment of triumph."[1]

*Stadium at Nemea*

Olympia is a place of great peacefulness, especially at the Hill of Cronos, overlooking the ancient stadium. At such places, perhaps, came that heightening of consciousness from which arose the new culture of Greece after the destruction of the Mycenaean palaces. Long before the games at Olympia there had been a sanctuary to Gaea, the ancient earth goddess, mother to the Titans, the gods and the human race. She was Nature itself, source of the created universe. At the green and symmetrical Hill of Cronos a cleft in the rock gave rise to her oracles. To the men who revered her she gave peace. Later, a shrine to Cronos, her son, was built there by people who were called the people of the Golden Age, according to Pausanias.[2] The displacement of Cronos by his son, Zeus, was marked by Olympia's dedication to the father of the gods, so that in the fifth century BC Phidias made at Olympia his greatest work of sculpture, the colossal chryselephantine statue in the Temple of Zeus.

This masterpiece became the first of the seven wonders of the ancient world. It was seven times lifesize, 12.40 metres high, including the base. Zeus was seated on a throne, and if he had stood up would have burst through the roof of the temple. The face and bare parts of the body - arms and feet - were made of sheets of ivory, fixed on the armature, or wooden frame, whilst the robe, sandals, beard and hair were of gold. A silver olive wreath crowned the head. Precious stones adorned the throne. The eagle, which carried the souls of heroes to the home of the gods on Mount Olympus, surmounted the sceptre which he held in his left hand. The Zeus of Olympia was not only the hurler of thunderbolts, but also the "Kindly One", full of love for Man. His face expressed serenity and gentleness. In this work Phidias captured the spirit of the place, and one who saw it wrote:

> "If a man with a heavily burdened heart, who has drunk the cup of grief and sorrow in life and whom sweet sleep visits no more, happens to stand before the statue, he will forget wretched things which afflict a man's life."[3]

Various legends surround the origin of the games at Olympia. Heracles is said to have begun them after invading Elis, in which Olympia is situated, in order to recover from King Augeias what was owed for the cleaning of his stables. Then King Pelops is said to have revived them in honour of Zeus, after winning the kingdom of Pisa, next to Elis, from King Oinomaos, the father of his bride, Hippodameia. Pelops had to defeat Oinomaos in a chariot race, for only thus would he win his bride, but the king's horses were offspring of the winds, and had already defeated many suitors. These had been put to death, since Oinomaos feared a rival, after an oracle hid warned him about his future son-in-law. Pelops won by suborning the king's charioteer to fill the hubs of the king's chariot wheels with wax, so that when they became hot and melted the wheels fell off. On the east pediment of the Temple of Zeus at Olympia this story is portrayed, with the anxious faces of the charioteers bearing witness to its fatal outcome, but also perhaps to the dangers of chariot racing in the games. In one race, for example, only one of forty-one chariots finished the course, which consisted of many laps of two 180° turns.

Homer tells in the *Iliad* and the *Odyssey* of games being held amongst the Greeks at Troy after the funerals of Hector and Patroclus, and in the idyllic land of the Phaeacians, when Odysseus was shipwrecked there. A chariot race began the events before the walls of Troy, followed by boxing, wrestling, running, armed combat, discus, archery and javelin. At Phaeacia, Odysseus was taunted by the arrogant Euryalus, whereupon he picked up a huge discus, much heavier than others and, without bothering to remove his cloak, hurled it far beyond the marks of the Phaeacian competitors. These Homeric contests indicate an antiquity for the idea of the Olympic Games, which goes back beyond the traditional founding date of 776 BC and places them near the beginning of the new culture. The *agon*, or contest, between military heroes, between Hector and Achilles, Ajax and Odysseus, was transmuted into the athletic contest, a struggle for supremacy that involved the same total concentration of will and strength, but was not so deadly.

A most significant story tells of Apollo directing Iphitos of Elis to refound the games in order to save Greece from plague and civil war. This may refer to a refounding in the ninth or eighth centuries, for since 776 BC, when records began, the idea of a Sacred Truce was ever after associated with Olympia. Iphitos, Lycurgus of Sparta and Cleosthenes of Pisa made such a truce; the Eleians recorded; it on the bronze Disc of Iphitos kept in the Temple of Hera inside the Altis, and seen by Pausanias almost a thousand years later.[4] This was the divine work of Apollo, the peacemaker, for Elis itself became sacred territory immune from war, and for the month of the games, every four years, all wars ceased throughout Greece. When Sparta invaded the city of Lepreon in Elis in 420 BC, it was heavily fined and barred from the games, despite the immense power and prestige of the Spartans.

Each Olympiad - the period of four years from one Olympic festival to the next, which was used by the Greeks as a dating system - was named after the current winner of the short running race, called the stade. This consisted of one length of the stadium, about 192m, and was the only race until 728 BC. Koroibcs of Elis was the first recorded winner in 776 BC. Gradually other events were introduced, a two stade race, a twenty-four stade race, wrestling, pentathlon, boxing, and the pankration, which was a combination of wrestling and boxing, in which only eye-gouging and biting were ruled out. In one wrestling contest, the winner died from the victorious hold with which he pinned down his opponent! Significantly, in 520 BC a hoplite race was introduced, for fully armed heavy infantry. Thirty years later at Marathon,

*Krypte (stadium entrance), Olympia*

the Athenian hoplites ran about one mile downhill before crashing into the ranks of the Persians, in order to confuse the Persian archers and to surprise their infantry with the speed and momentum of their approach.

Equestrian events were introduced about the year 700 BC in a hippodrome adjoining the stadium. Rich men, often from the wealthy cities of Magna Graecia, owned the horses and chariots and hired the trainers and charioteers, and also received the accolade of victory. Alcibiades of Athens was a frequent winner, near the turn of the fifth century. Boys' events were also introduced. Unmarried women attended the games as spectators, and the Priestess of Demeter welcomed the athletes when they processed into the stadium through the arched entrance, or Krypte, at the initial ceremony. From a one day festival the games grew to occupy five days, from 472 BC onwards. Athletic excellence for women was recognised in the running races of the Heraia, a festival at Olympia held in honour of the goddess, Hera, wife of Zeus, whose temple jay inside the Altis, just below the Hill of Cronos. Hippodameia, daughter of Oinomaos and wife of Pelops, is said to have founded them.

As for victory, Pindar wrote many times of what it meant for a Greek youth to win the crown of wild olive:

*Starting line, Olympia*

"But if, my heart, you would speak

Of prizes won in the Games,

Look no more for another bright star

By day in the empty sky

More warming than the sun,

Nor shall we name any gathering

Greater than the Olympian."[5]

The wild olive was cut from an ancient olive tree growing by the Temple of Zeus, by a boy with a golden knife. Such was the honour of the Olympian wild olive that the king of Sparta fought in battle alongside a crowned Spartan victor. Sparta had no walls, but when elsewhere a victor returned to his own city, a gap would be torn in the city walls to allow for his entrance in a four-horse chariot. The story of Diagoras best illustrates the victor's renown. He was the greatest wrestler in the Greek world, with numerous victories at the Olympic and other games to his credit. When he returned to Olympia as a spectator, his two sons were competing, one a wrestler, one a boxer. Both won their events. After they were crowned, they rushed across to their father and carried him shoulder high around the stadium to the applause of everyone present. Above the noise, the stentorian voice of a Spartan rang out, "Die now Diagoras, for you will never reach Olympus." Not being a god, no greater moment of achievement could be reached by a mortal. When the two brothers arrived at the Krypte to leave the stadium, Diagoras was found to be dead!

Herodotus tells another story of the moral effect of Olympia. It was the year 480 BC, just before Phayllos of Croton set sail from Italy and after Xerxes had defeated the Spartans at the heroic battle of Thermopylae, where Leonidas and three hundred Spartiates died in the narrow pass. Some Arcadian deserters told the Persian general, Mardonius, that the Greeks were celebrating the Olympic festival of athletic contests and chariot races. The Persian interrogator asked what was the prize for which they contended, to which the Arcadians replied that it was a wreath of olive-leaves. Whereupon the Persian, Tritantaechmes, cried out in front of everybody, "Good heavens, Mardonius, what kind of men are these that you have brought us to fight against - men who compete with one another for no material reward, but only for honour!"[6]

Great men from every walk of life attended the games as spectators: statesmen, soldiers, artists, playwrights, philosophers. When in 476 BC Themistocles, the Athenian who had defeated the Persians at Salamis, entered the stadium; the crowd rose as one man to acknowledge his saving of the Greek nation from the Persian invasion of Xerxes. Later, Georgias of Leontini and Isocrates of Athens used the games as an opportunity to remind all Greeks of the need for unity. Victories over barbarians were glorious, but victories over fellow Greeks were to be counted as a disaster, except - they might have added - in the Games.

What then had Phayllos of Croton sacrificed? Coming from the city of Pythagoras, he realised that even an Olympic victory counted for nothing when compared with the love of freedom. And so he fought at Salamis, instead of competing for the wild olive at Olympia. Plato would have approved his decision:

"The Olympic victor is deemed happy in receiving a part only of the blessedness which is secured to our citizens, who have won a more glorious victory and have a more complete maintenance at the public cost. For the victory which they have won is salvation of the whole State; and the crown with which they and their children are crowned is the fulness of all that life needs."[7]

## References:

1. Introduction to Pindar, *The Odes*, trans. C. M. Bowra, Penguin, London, 1969, p. xvi.

2. Pausanias, *Guide to Greece*, trans. P. Levi, Penguin, London, 1971, vol. 2, p. 215.

3. Dion Crysostome; quoted in *Olympia Complete Guide*, Spyros Photinos, Olympic Publications, Athens, 1982.

4. Pausanias, *Guide to Greece*, vol. 2, p. 256.

5. Pindar, 'Olympian, I, I', in *The Odes of Pindar* (Classics) trans. C. Bowra, p. 64. For Hieron of Syracuse, winner in the horse race.

6. See Herodotus, *Histories*, trans. A. de Selincourt, Penguin, London, 1972, Book VIII, p. 533.

7. Plato, *The Republic*, trans. B. Jowett, Random House, New York, 1937, Book V, p. 465.

## Chapter 11
# Obedient to their Laws
### *Lycurgus & Sparta*

THE DORIAN PEOPLES who had invaded and settled in the Peloponnese after the collapse of Mycenaean culture were divided into three tribes, but soon they developed the common form of the polis, a change which may have taken place first of all amongst the Dorians who had settled as far afield as Crete. The Dorian polis was characterised by a very strong allegiance to the state and a military temper, which together overrode the tribal system, reducing it to the regulation of family and cult matters, such as the inheritance of family houses and family religious rites. This tendency was hastened, if not caused, by the need to maintain control of the large indigenous population overrun by the Dorians. Probably owing to the break down of government amongst them, these peoples were reduced by the Dorians to the level of serfs, working the land on condition that up to half the produce was given to their

*Base of Doric column*

masters. Some also became personal slaves. In one place, in particular, conditions saw the rise of a society which has profoundly influenced European history to the present day. Below the rugged and towering line of the Taygetus mountains lies, to the east, the broad enclosed valley of the Eurotas. Commanding this fertile region lay the polis of Sparta.

"Art, 'poiesis', is creation, and Sparta created not things in Words or stone, but men."[1]

For at least five hundred years, from the ninth to the fourth century BC, Sparta was renowned throughout Greece as the polis which bred the finest soldiers and the most virtuous citizens. So much were the Spartans esteemed that, in a crisis, many other states begged Sparta for just one of her citizens to lead them to victory. Thus in the Peloponnesian War, when an Athenian expedition to Sicily threatened to take Syracuse, the Syracusans turned for help to Sparta and were saved by the generalship of the Spartan Gylippus.

Many stories are told of the qualities of the Spartans. An old man once wandered about the stadium at the Olympic games looking for a seat, whilst the crowd jeered at him. When he reached the area where the Spartans sat, every young man, and even some older ones, rose to offer him a place. The crowd applauded them, and the old man said with a sigh, "All Greeks know what is right, but only the Spartans do it."[2]

The austerity of the Spartans was also proverbial. They ate very simply in communal dining halls; their black broth, made from pork cooked in blood, was notorious. A foreigner from one of the more comfortable parts of the Greek world was entertained in Sparta and remarked afterwards. "Now I understand why Spartans do not fear death!"[3] Another story indicates the simplicity of their dress. The philosopher, Diogenes, was also at Olympia and saw some young men from Rhodes very elaborately dressed, and called out, "Affectation!". Then he saw some Spartans dressed most austerely - they were only allowed one tunic a year - whereupon he cried, "More affectation!"[4] In fact, it was not really affectation. Spartans were taught as children to possess only what was strictly necessary to perform their function in the community, so that they grew up with no desire whatsoever for finery.

In speech, also, they were taught a perfect economy of language, giving rise to the word "laconic" from Laconia, the region around Sparta. The Spartan king, Charilaus, once said that men of few words need few laws.[5] A Spartan, who was recommended to go to hear a man who could imitate the voice of a nightingale perfectly, replied simply, "I've heard the nightingale herself."[6] If a boy failed to give a laconic reply to a question from his troop-leader, he was bitten on the thumb.

Above all, however, the Spartans were renowned for their courage and skill as soldiers. It was taken for granted that no other people, Greek or barbarian, could defeat them in an equal encounter, and time and again they won battles in which they were heavily outnumbered. When finally at the battle of Leuctra in the year 371 BC, they were beaten in an evenly matched fight by the Thebans, the whole of Greece stood amazed. It had required the tactical genius of the Theban leader, Epaminondas, and the long training of his "Sacred Band", to overturn Spartan supremacy, even in its decline in the fourth century. Indeed, the Spartans themselves believed that they had given the Thebans too much practice over the centuries in their own manner of fighting. If a Spartan returned from a battle where his king or most of his comrades had died, he was treated with disdain by the whole city, perhaps until the end of his days. A Spartan mother was said to have told her son to return from battle either with his shield or on it.

What then was this art of creating men that the polis of Sparta uniquely possessed? Earlier, the Dorian peoples who settled in Sparta had built a city where art and fine craftsmanship flourished, so that it was known for its pottery, jewellery, musicians and poets, like the lyric poet Alcman, who instituted a festival to Apollo in Sparta. The chief characteristic of Dorian art in this aristocratic period was its simplicity and its connection with the artefacts of daily life. However, Alcman himself said that fine lyre-playing matched iron weaponry. Music, in particular, was used in education and became associated with military training and battle songs.

By the ninth century a reform of the laws became necessary, probably because the kings, who ruled in pairs by ancient tradition, were no longer to be entirely trusted to safeguard the interests of the people. At this point, about 825 BC, there appeared one of the great lawgivers, Lycurgus, himself the son of a Spartan king and brother and uncle of kings. Lycurgus was regent for his infant nephew and ensured that the child should become king in his own right, despite attempts by the dowager queen to seize power through Lycurgus' position as regent. Once his nephew was firmly established, Lycurgus travelled for some time in Crete and Egypt, to study the wisdom and law of those ancient centres of civilisation. Thales of Crete was said by Plutarch to have paved the way for Lycurgus with his soothing music, which reduced the internal strife in Sparta. Realising that a thorough reform of the laws was required, Lycurgus drew up a new constitution from which the great qualities of the later Spartans arose. It gave to the polis the gift of *eunomia*, or law and order. As though stringing a lyre, Lycurgus laid down the conditions for the creation of finely tuned men.

Before introducing it, Lycurgus took the new constitution to Delphi to seek the approval of Apollo. The god of harmony confirmed his desire for eunomia and promised that his constitution would excel all others. The statement which Lycurgus brought back to Sparta was known as the Great Rhetra. Henceforth, the citizens of Sparta would assemble in the open air to *apellaze*, or celebrate a festival of Apollo, and there conduct their political affairs. They would elect from the noblest families a Senate, called the Gerousia, of twenty-eight men over sixty years of age. The two kings, hereditary rulers by tradition, acting ex officio, made up the Gerousia to thirty. It decided upon what matters should be put to the *Apella*, or Assembly, for approval and acted as the court in criminal cases, though it could not give the death penalty. Between the kings and the people now stood a body of elder statesmen, who would prevent either from veering to extremes of monarchy or democracy. Thus was the Greek principle of a harmonious mean conducive to unity.

Lycurgus divided the land of Sparta into nine thousand equal lots and the rest of Laconia into thirty thousand. In principle, each full Spartan citizen, or Spartiate, received one lot, so that land-holding and citizenship went hand-in-hand, but little is known about how this system operated, for example, whether a land bank was held by the state. The absence of a dominating and valuable city centre in Sparta - unlike Athens - would have prevented the accumulation of great economic rent in private hands, especially if lots were not hereditary. Nevertheless, over centuries, inequalities did appear, implying that land-holdings at some point became hereditary and/or marketable to some degree. Spartiates did not themselves work the land: serfs, or helots, farmed the land in Sparta, and in Laconia the population, known as *perioeci*, paid tribute from produce of the thirty-thousand lots. So long as the Spartiates fulfilled the role of ruling and protecting the whole state, they were a true warrior caste, appropriating the rent of land for the uses of government and defence.

No Spartiate practised a craft. Indeed, Lycurgus banned all crafts deemed unnecessary and discouraged the importing of useless goods by introducing iron as a means of exchange. Foreign traders would be loth to acquire iron bars in payment. Moreover, the Spartans themselves had no incentive to accumulate such a cumbersome store of wealth. Only much later did Spartans become notorious for their susceptibility to foreign luxuries, available when they were abroad.

The most potent of Lycurgus' reforms was neither political nor economic, but educational. A course of education, called the *agoge*, was instituted for boys, and separately for girls, from the age of seven until the age of eighteen. Weak babies were selected by the Gerousia to be exposed to die on the slopes of Mount Taygetus, whilst healthy children left home at the age of seven to live in groups of fifteen under a master and older boys. Their education was of a military character, though most became literate; gymnastics, weapon training, tests for hardship and initiative, were central to it. Their rations were sometimes deliberately insufficient, and they were expected to supplement them by stealing. If caught, they were beaten severely. A religious aspect was introduced when boys had to steal cheeses from before the altar of Artemis Orthia in the face of their elders equipped with whips.

Acceptance of such a regime for boys depended upon the attitude amongst parents that their children were the responsibility, not of themselves, but of the whole community. Spartan adults, in principle, treated all children as subject to parental discipline from any citizen. Boys were trained under the watchful eyes of Spartiates, who attended the gymnasia expressly to give advice, praise or rebuke to those who would become their successors as the defenders of Spartan renown and honour. Girls' training included a wide range of athletics, even javelin throwing, for Spartan women were as much integrated into the life of the community as were men. King Leonidas' wife, Gorgo, was asked how it was that Spartan women could rule men, to which she replied, "Because we are also the only ones who give birth to men."[7] Nor was marriage merely a domestic matter. Spartiates considered it shameful to indulge overmuch in sexual relations, so that men were encouraged to sleep at the common mess and only visit their wives surreptitiously. Plutarch thought that the Spartans of Lycurgus' time allowed community of wives to some degree, whilst he insisted that this in no way led to immorality. He believed that the older Spartiates, without any sign of jealousy, would sometimes allow their wives to mate with a young, fit man in order that fine children should be produced. However, very little is known for certain about Spartan marriage customs, and the stability of Spartan society and the high moral and physical standing of Spartiates suggests that the family was a stronger unit than appears from the emphasis put upon male common messes and the martial aspects of women.

Nevertheless, common messes were a fundamental element in the reforms of Lycurgus. It was a condition of becoming a full Spartiate that a man, after the two years of military training that followed his schooling, should be accepted into a common mess, where he ate and spent much of his time. Each member brought a monthly contribution of barley, wine, cheese and figs, the produce of his lots of land. Even the kings of Sparta were expected to meet this condition. The famous black broth supplemented this austere diet.

Such severe laws created men who put a very high value upon courage and honour. The state became a timocracy, its citizens devoted to its defence, proud of their education, unwilling to admire other states where gentler arts were practised or where wealth was taken as a sign of merit. Such an example of timocratic men living in the heart of Greece affected the tone of Greek life for centuries. All Greeks grudgingly admired the Spartans and they, in turn, held themselves high in their own esteem, not as individuals but as a polis where eunomia was ever present. Examples abound of the Spartiates' love of valour. No athletic contest was allowed which involved 'hand-raising' - the sign of submission in wrestling and other sports - for every Spartiate entered a real combat ready to defeat his enemy or to die. The fourth century Spartan king, Archidamus III, on seeing an arrow shot from a catapult, when it was first brought from Sicily, shrewdly exclaimed: "By Heracles, man's valour is done for!"[8] A much earlier king, Sous, was once besieged in a rugged, waterless area. He agreed with the enemy, who were guarding a spring, that he would surrender the territory if all the Spartans could drink from the spring. Oaths were taken, and the Spartiates drank; all except King Sous, who merely splashed himself with water, and then called upon his men to withstand the enemy again, because not all had drunk from the spring.

Such shrewd intelligence pervaded their military practices, arising perhaps from their sparing use of language. During a war the rigorous discipline was relaxed as unnecessary, since circumstances were a discipline in themselves. If the enemy fled, they were not pursued very far, for this encouraged them to flee rather than stand and be killed. Spartan dead were buried in plain graves, the bodies wrapped in the soldier's red cloak and olive leaves; and mourning ceased completely after eleven days.

One condition became the Achilles' heel of Spartan society. Originally, the helots and perioeci, as conquered people, were probably treated no harsher than elsewhere in Greece. Lycurgus' reforms, indeed, may have weakened any sense of injustice, by making the lives of the masters little better in some respects than that of the helots! However, about one hundred years after Lycurgus, Messenia to the west was conquered, which imposed a much greater strain on the relatively few Spartiates, who now controlled a much larger territory than a typical polis. Sparta became almost a society under siege. Harsher treatment of helots and perioeci was inevitable. Even so, Plutarch claims that it was only after a great earthquake in 460 BC had led to a rebellion in both Laconia and Messenia that real oppression of the inferior peoples began.[9] War was then declared on the helots every year, so that they could be killed without pollution from blood guilt. Young men, as part of their early military training, were said to have been armed with daggers and sent out individually to live off the country and murder troublemakers amongst the helots. Collectively, they were called the *krypteia*, or secret force; a new and sinister feature was thus introduced into Spartan society, which probably had much to do with its later degeneracy and eventual collapse. Whatever the effects of the krypteia, there was no further revolt of helots until after the battle of Leuctra in 371 BC. By then, helots had for some while been able to earn their freedom, though not citizenship, by fighting bravely for Sparta. The Spartan general, Brasidas, had about seven hundred ex-helots fighting under him in Thrace in the Peloponnesian War.

When Lycurgus had completed his work, he made the Spartans take an oath to abide by his constitution until he returned. He went again to Delphi, where the oracle enjoined obedience on the Spartans; then he disappeared, never to return. Even his ashes were never to be sent back to Sparta, on his instruction - in case this became an excuse for defection from the laws. After Lycurgus, other reforms did, in fact, take place. A law was made allowing the kings and Senate to ignore a decision of the Assembly of the citizens, if it were regarded by the Senate as "crooked." This prevented any movement towards democracy, though Lycurgus had not envisaged the Assembly's power to decide issues placed before it as in any sense democratic, since the citizens were by their education timocrats rather than common men.

Another later reform in the early seventh century was the creation of five ephors or judges, chosen annually by the Assembly and responsible for watching over the actions of the kings. As Spartan society degenerated in later centuries' the ephors became the virtual rulers of the state, moderating any tendency towards tyranny in the kings or oligarchy in the Gerousia.

Plato, a great admirer of Sparta and Dorian Crete, whose institutions were akin to it, made one broad criticism. Spartans were marvellously inured to pain and hardship, but they could be susceptible to pleasure, for they were unaccustomed to it.[10] Somewhere in Sparta's history the idea that pleasure should be driven out of society and out of the lives of Spartiates came to influence the otherwise healthy austerity of Lycurgus. Thus deprived, Sparta became too avidly militaristic. In the fifth century no art flourished there; the lyre was unstrung. By the fourth century, the Athenian wit, Stratonicus, could propose for the best government of Greece that the Athenians should manage the mysteries and religious processions; that the Eleans manage the Games; and that the Spartans should be whipped for the others' mistakes![11]

Lycurgus brought to Sparta an ideal of justice that is close to that of Plato. Spartiates were to be selected and trained as the best of men, an aristocracy who looked for unity in the denial of themselves. As warriors, guided by the wisest amongst the older men, they eschewed all work as traders and labourers, leaving this to those whom birth and circumstance offered no more. Perhaps few Spartiates ever really saw beyond the principles of timocracy, but even so the Spartan polis never entirely lost the vision of eunomia which Lycurgus had created.

Plutarch made a final judgment upon it:

"All the same it was not Lycurgus' main aim at the time to leave his city as the leader of so many other cities. Instead his view was that happiness in the life of a whole city, as in that of one individual, derives from its own merits and from its internal concord: it was to this end that all his arrangements and his structures were combined, so that Spartans should be free and self-sufficient, and should have the good sense to be thus for a very long time. Lycurgus brought into the light of the day, not paper theories, but a functioning constitution which is quite unmatched. To those who suspect that it is impracticable for a theoretical structure to be centred upon a Sage, he has exhibited his whole city practising philosophy, and has deservedly won greater renown than all those who have ever governed so far among the Greeks."[12]

## References:

1.  H. D. F. Kitto, *The Greeks*, Penguin, London, 1957, p. 95.
2.  Kitto, *The Greeks*, p. 93.
3.  Kitto, *The Greeks*, p. 93.
4.  Kitto, *The Greeks*, p. 93.
5.  'Plutarch', in *Plutarch on Sparta*, trans. R. J. A. Talbert, Penguin, London, 1988, p. 3.
6.  'Plutarch', trans. Talbert, p. 32.
7.  'Plutarch', trans. Talbert, p. 158.
8.  'Plutarch', trans. Talbert, p. 132.
9.  'Plutarch', trans. Talbert, p. 41.
10. Plato, *Laws*, trans. B. Jowett, Random House, New York, 1937, Book I, 634.
11. 'Plutarch', trans. Talbert, p. 44.
12. 'Plutarch', trans. Talbert, p. 45.

## Chapter 12

# Model Cities

### *Colonisation & Solon*

FOUNDED UPON THE PRINCIPLE of justice and suited to the development of *arete*, the Greek polis was bound to multiply in most places where Greeks lived. By the eighth century BC, the growth took a new form with the planting of colonies abroad by poleis, which became mother cities to their colonial children. Groups, probably of up to a few hundred members of a polis, under the leadership of an aristocratic founder, chosen by the mother city, set sail to sites recommended by traders or adventurers. Most sites were coastal or on river estuaries, ideally on spits of land, as at Syracuse in Sicily, easily defensible and with natural harbours. Ionian experience in settling the west coast of Asia Minor was useful, and cities like Miletus and Clazomenae were enthusiastic colonisers. North Africa, particularly Cyrenaica, (named after the very early colony of Cyrene), the northern Aegean, the coasts of

*Temple of "Ceres", (dedicated to Athena), Paestum*

the Black Sea, Southern Italy and Sicily were the main areas settled. An early reluctance to take to the sea was overcome, and maritime enterprise, in trade also, became a permanent feature of Greek life.

Amongst the most notable foundations were the Corinthian Syracuse in 834 BC, Tarentum, the only Spartan colony, founded in 707 BC, Croton, an Achaean colony founded in 703 BC (both at the foot of Italy) and Byzantium, of later fame, founded by the little polis of Megara in 660 BC. When the Megarans began by founding a colony on the east bank of the Bosphorous, the Delphic oracle called them blind men for not appreciating the superior site of the west bank, where the Golden Horn was to become the glory of the late Roman Empire. Of great significance for the future, also, was the foundation by the Euboeans of Cyme, near modern Naples (the colony of Neapolis), for Cyme influenced the new nation of Rome, offering a written alphabet and new gods, Heracles and Apollo, Castor and Polydeuces. The Cymean Sibyl, prophetess of Apollo, became the source of oracles containing the destiny of Rome.

Apollo was the guardian of Greek colonisation. As though intent upon preserving the unity that all Greeks acknowledged, every mother city consulted the Delphic oracle about the proposed foundation and every colony acknowledged, above its human founder, Apollo Archegetes, Apollo the Leader, creator of harmony, curer of ills. Thus at Croton, where Pythagoras would soon dwell, the coins bore the emblem of a Delphic tripod.

Greeks, educated on the adventures of the sea-borne Odysseus, could hardly fail to venture abroad. Yet there were further reasons why colonisation became so powerful a movement. In the eighth century population expanded. Often poleis were hemmed in by mountains or infertile land or, as in Asia Minor, by hostile peoples. Moreover, the system of land tenure was imperceptibly changing. Traditionally, land was held in families under the guiding authority of the *phratry* (brotherhood) and *genos* (group of families). Each family of citizens had a lot, which was shared equally by the sons and could not be alienated. Growing population made some family lots inadequate. The ability of families to work as a unit and to co-operate within the *genos* declined. As the idea of individual ownership of land reared its hydra head, eldest sons began to claim the family land. Amongst the Boetoian farmers, Hesiod berated his brother, Pelens, for his greed for land. Younger sons began to look elsewhere for a livelihood. Colonisation was to hand. Their grievances chimed in with the urge to spread the idea of the polis and with the spirit of adventure.

How the land was to be held was the central question for a new foundation. The political institutions could be modelled on those of the mother city, be it Ionian, Dorian, or Achaean; but the distribution of land was an open question, looking backwards to a commonality and family units, or forwards to the heedless growth of individual ownership. The usual method seems to have become the distribution of new colonial land in equal lots amongst the first group of settlers. At Syracuse, these were the *Gamaroi*, an aristocracy of "those who share the land." The new polis, as a result, was often laid out on a regular grid pattern, perhaps with further lots outside the city walls in similarly regular agricultural strips. Such a system produced a superficial fairness and equality, but it contained a tendency towards injustice, which only a few men, like Solon and Plato, could discern clearly. As the new polis developed, the productivity and value of lots of land changed relatively; those nearest to the centre usually acquired the greatest value. Though the sale of lots was often prohibited, as it had been in early Greek poleis, the extra value yielded higher income for the owner. In short, economic rent was the inevitable outcome, and the rent remained in the hands of owners, unless some measure was taken to counter this source of inequality. As new settlers arrived, the situation became more acute. Their lots would be peripheral, perhaps on very poor land. Eventually new settlers and impoverished older ones would find themselves without land, being forced to hand over or sell what they had in payment of debts. In later centuries a universal tendency towards a division in the poleis between landed and landless, rich and poor, produced the characteristic internal strife of both mother cities and colonies. Oligarchs and democrats tore their cities apart during the Peloponnesian war.

Plato's solution was simple. In a new colony, every citizen should have at least two lots, one near the centre of the city, one on the outskirts, the two together being as equal as possible in productivity or value to every other dual holding The number of lots must not be changed and alienation of lots should be a criminal offence, carrying the severest punishment. His choice of 5,040 for the number of lots had a practical meaning, for it is divisible by every number up to 10, so that as new settlers arrived, or circumstances changed, adjustments could be made within the system of a fixed number of lots. For example, the number of families could be such as to require any number of lots each, between one and ten. Also, public duties, like military service, could be allocated easily, for each group of, say, five or nine lots might be responsible for one hoplite or horseman. 5,040 is not a magic number; it represents the principle that landholdings should be flexible without being freely alienable. Such a system implies that land is ultimately the property of the colony as a whole, and that citizens hold lots from the colony and not absolutely as their own property. It was Plato's attempt to recommend a land law which would retain some measure of justice.[1]

At the beginning of Greek colonisation perhaps some token of justice in land-holding was present. The citizens on the best land may have borne the public expenses, especially of defence, but as corruption spread, and men like Solon were needed in the mother cities to restore a sense of justice, the colonies inevitably bred inequality and strife. Greek culture was strong enough to retard the economic decay, but the current of decline which Plato himself recorded, of aristocracy, through timocracy, oligarchy and democracy to despotism, ran deeply in mother cities and colonies alike.

Solon, whose wisdom the Lydian king, Croesus, and the Persian, Cyrus the Great, had both learnt to admire, himself founded a colony in Cyprus, known as Soli. It soon became the finest city on the island. At that time Solon was in self-imposed exile from Athens for ten years, for, like Lycurgus at Sparta, he wanted the new constitution which he had given his native city to be tested by experience, without any possible recourse to its author. Meanwhile, he not only founded Soli and met Croesus, but also travelled in Egypt, studying philosophy at Heliopolis and Sais.

The Dorian laws of Crete had influenced Lycurgus and led him to bring the musician, Thales, to prepare the ground for reform in Sparta. Likewise, the Athenians sent to Crete for the philosopher and musician, Epimenides of Phaestus, when their city was in a state of grievous unrest from economic disparities and political faction. Epimenides became a friend of Solon, and made the people ready for reform by sanctifying the city and bringing the harmony of music to its citizens. Already Solon had won their respect by his public recitation of verse; in particular, when he had restored their spirits during a wearisome war with Megara for the island of Salamis.

Solon was a lawgiver, like Lycurgus, creating a community based upon natural law. Nevertheless, he also took full account of time and conditions. When Solon was asked whether he had provided the best laws for the Athenians, his reply was that they were the best that they would accept. He was appointed archon, or magistrate, with power to legislate, in the year 594 BC, although it is possible that his reforms were in fact introduced twenty years later. Athens was suffering from terrible internal disorder and from the harsh legislation of Draco, who about thirty years before had introduced the death penalty for almost every crime, in a crude attempt to restore order.

The underlying problem was economic. Wealthy families within each of the four tribes into which Attica was divided were owed debts by poorer families, who owned less land, or by "guildsmen" who owned no land, but lived by the exercise of a craft. These debtors had been forced either to give one-sixth of the produce of their land every year to their creditors, or to sell themselves into slavery to pay off their debts. Some had even become slaves in foreign lands in order to obtain the money that their creditors in Attica demanded. The sixth-partners, or *hectemorioi*, like feudal serfs, were bound to the land, and left with the minimum produce to meet their families' needs. Solon swept all this aside. In his own words, he:

"uprooted the mortgage stones that everywhere were planted and freed the fields that were enslaved before."[2]

Solon brought back the debtors from abroad, cancelled existing debts and prohibited the selling of a debtor into slavery. This discharge of burdens marked by a public sacrifice, or *seisachtheia*, obviously upset the creditors; yet Solon was careful not to alienate them entirely by redistributing land on a large scale, as the poorest class wished him to do. As he said, "In great affairs you cannot please all parties."[3] His aim was simply to go as far as possible in the direction of justice, without arousing irreconcilable conflict. There was indeed conflict in the period after his legislation, as factions grew up to oppose or support his reforms, but nevertheless the practical test of the seisachtheia was that the community remained sufficiently purged of economic injustice to become the seed-bed for the flowering of Athenian culture in the fifth century. The courage he needed for such reform is indicated by the fact that even some of his "friends" operated as swindlers, and bought land by borrowing heavily in advance of the general cancellation of debts!

Other economic provisions were made by Solon. Any man who had not been taught a trade by his father was not obliged to support him when he was old, a reform probably learnt from King Amasis of Egypt, who ruled at Sais. The silver coinage used in the eastern Mediterranean by important trading states, like Samos, was adopted by Athens, thus releasing her from subservience to her trading neighbour, Aegina, and stimulating her economic expansion overseas. Exports of olive oil and pottery were encouraged, but other exports banned. Imports of corn were ensured by the development of the port of Sigeum near Troy, an Athenian colony which Solon himself helped to found.

New weights and measures guaranteed the accuracy and honesty of trade, but the boldest and most imaginative of the new policies was the welcome extended to foreign craftsmen to settle in Athens, and even to qualify for citizenship. Solon saw clearly that, unlike Laconia, Attica was a land of infertile, rocky soil, unsuitable for the wide-spread cultivation of cereals. Only olive trees could grow freely on the sparse limestone hills and narrow plains. Therefore, the economic prosperity of Athens lay in manufacture and export, in the development of skilful crafts, such as pottery, woodwork, metal working and jewellery. Foreigners could teach such crafts and become grateful citizens of an open trading community. Athens would turn its back on the Boeotian Hesiod's fear of the sea. Trade would grow alongside the general growth of Greek colonisation. In the long-run the Corinthian domination of the Mediterranean market for pottery would yield to the black-figure ware of Athens. The wise law that a father should teach his son a craft played a part in this transition to an economy of skill and initiative.

*The Temple of Apollo, Corinth*

Nor was the land of Attica to be neglected. Its water supply was largely artesian. Solon laid down rules for the proper distribution and sharing of wells. Planting of trees was carefully regulated, so that, for example, olive and fig trees, which have especially far-reaching roots, had to be planted at least three hundred feet from those of another owner.

Once the basic economic conditions had been set to rights, Solon turned his attention to political reforms. Recognising that the period of timocracy had expired, as men turned to wealth rather than to honour, Solon introduced a political system in keeping with oligarchy. Wealth replaced birth as the criterion of political power. In the Council of the Areopagus, for example, the highest body in the state, members had been chosen exclusively from a few ancient families, the *enpatridae*, who also unduly influenced the election of the nine archons. Solon created a wider class of citizens, defined by wealth, any of whom could be elected to the Council of the Areopagus. This class was composed of citizens whose land was capable of producing at least 500 bushels of corn, or its equivalent. At the same time, an annual census of income was introduced.

Three other classes defined by wealth were created by Solon. The criteria were 300 bushels, 200 bushels and less than 200 bushels in potential annual income from land. The four classes were called respectively: *pentacosiomedimni* (five hundred bushel men), *hippeis* (knights), *zeugitae* (ploughmen) and *thetes* (hired labourers). Lesser offices in the state were open to the second and third classes; though the *thetes* could not hold office, they were given the right to vote in the Assembly, or Ecclesia. Since the Assembly passed laws, elected officers and also acquired judicial powers, the *thetes* felt that they had some responsibility in affairs of state. Solon established also a new Council of Four Hundred, one hundred representing each tribe, and known as the Boule, which presented business to the Assembly and selected cases for the Assembly when the latter acted as a judicial body. This Council helped to preserve a balance between the Council of the Areopagus and the Assembly itself, for the Areopagus consisted of the *pentacosiomedimni* and the Assembly contained *thetes*. Had not the oracle at Delphi advised Solon to "Seat yourself now amidships, for you are the pilot of Athens"?[4]

In addition to his economic and political reforms, Solon carried through law reforms concerning the civil duties of citizens. The abolition of enslavement for debt was one of a series of changes making Athens a more humane and enlightened society; so too was the abolition of excessive dowries, for these were a cause of greed and disrespect for women. Public slander was forbidden, and double restitution by the offender for theft was enforced. These legal reforms, together with the others, were posted on revolving wooden tablets in the Agora, for all to see and know. Such measures were introduced with the aim of making justice attractive to the citizen, so that Athens would become a city where those not the victims of a crime were as keen to punish the offender as those who were the direct victims.

The sixth century saw the rise in many Greek poleis of the rule of tyrants, autocratic governments, not necessarily maleficent, but a threat to the creation of a harmonious and free society based on justice. These tyrannies were especially vigorous in the Ionian areas of coastal Asia Minor; on Samos, for example, the tyrant, Polycrates, was noted for his powerful navy and splendid engineering projects. Athens did not avoid this trend towards tyranny, for it was a stage in the movement away from aristocracy towards democracy, probably at the point when the growth of individual land ownership gave rise to the marked accumulation of wealth in fewer hands. Extremes of wealth and poverty arose, factions developed as a result, and one particular faction leader seized power for a while. As Theognis said, "From corrupt judges arise factions and civil bloodshed and single rulers."[5] Commercial wealth compounded the underlying maldistribution. Thucydides wrote that tyrannies were established in the poleis as revenues were increasing. This was not the tyranny which, according to Plato, follows upon democracy and takes deep root from the demagogue, whom the people demand should restore order in the aftermath of the collapse of democracy - as happened in the fourth century. These sixth century tyrannies were short-lived; they were an aberration of the earlier phase, oligarchy.

Solon saw what was happening. He could not totally avert the rise of tyranny in Athens, but he defused it. Having warned the people against Peisistratus, the powerful leader of the faction known as "the Hill", to the north-east of the city, where many poorer farmers lived, Solon found on his return from his travels that Peisistratus was about to seize power. Solon was disgusted; the people of Athens were "of foxy ways and foolish wits." Nevertheless, when Peisistratus became tyrant and the Assembly accorded him an armed bodyguard, Solon continued to speak out for liberty. The reforms of ten years previous had ameliorated economic division, and political responsibility had been distributed more widely. Peisistratus' position was unstable. Twice he was forced to leave Athens; twice he returned. For a short while, until Solon died (about 560 BC), the tyrant even listened to his advice. Athens flourished; great building projects, like the Temple of Olympian Zeus below the Acropolis, black-figure pottery, and a renewed Great Panathenaic Festival, all bore witness to the vigour of a polis touched with the spirit of justice.

When the rule of tyrants - of Peisistratus and his sons - passed away, Athens emerged into a new light, ready for an age of glorious achievement, when the genius of artists, writers and craftsmen under intelligent political leadership would set standards of creative work for centuries to come. How had Solon made this possible? The laws which he had introduced rested upon the natural justice of the polis. His classes of citizens - *pentacosiomedimni, hippeis, zeugitae* and *thetes* - were reflections of the wise men, warriors, merchants and labourers of ancient law. The overt criterion in a period of oligarchy had to be wealth, but it was a flexible system. Moreover, shares in the public expense, notably defence, were proportional to wealth, as the name *hippeis* (knights) indicates. Freeing the land from the dreaded mortgage stones, restoring the self-respect of men on their own lots of land and welcoming foreign traders and craftsmen enlivened the whole of society, and encouraged the proper allocation of talents and duties. The gifted man, who worked well, could acquire wealth; the lazy or stupid, who inherited wealth, might soon lose it. Solon had not established justice, but he had shown Athens the direction towards it. She would never become the ideal city which Plato later described in his "Laws", but Solon made no idle boast when he wrote:

"I stood guard with a broad shield before both parties, and prevented either from triumphing unjustly."[6]

Herodotus tells the simple story of how Solon's fame became known to the most powerful man of his time, the Persian king, Cyrus the Great. Croesus, king of Lydia, had entertained Solon, when the latter was travelling during the ten years for which he had promised to leave Athens, whilst his constitutional reforms bore fruit. The immensely wealthy Lydian king had asked Solon who was the happiest man he had ever met, to which the sage replied, Tellus, the Athenian, who had died bravely for his city and left a fine and prosperous family. Croesus was greatly offended, expecting Solon to say that he, Croesus, was the happiest. When challenged on his opinion, Solon replied that no man should be called happy before his death, for fate may overturn any man's fortune before he dies. When Cyrus captured Croesus he decided to put him to death by fire. He placed the Lydian on the top of a huge pyre of wood, together with other captives, and the wood was lit. As the smoke gathered around the unfortunate Croesus, he called out in despair the name of Solon, in memory of his wise advice concerning happiness. Struck by the name, Cyrus ordered his interpreters to find out what Croesus meant. On hearing the story of Solon's understanding of happiness, Cyrus was moved to save his enemy's life, but the fire was too far advanced to be stayed. Whereupon the god, Apollo, who presided over the Delphic shrine, brought a sudden storm to burst over the pyre, quenching the flames. Croesus himself became a companion and adviser to the Persian king after his narrow escape from immolation.

## References:

1. Plato, *Laws*, trans. B. Jowett, Random House, New York, 1937, Book V, 737-8.

2. Plutarch, 'Life of Solon', in *The Rise and Fall of Athens*, trans. I. Scott-Kilvert, Penguin, London, 1976, 15, p. 57.

3. Plutarch, 'Life of Solon', 15, p. 867.

4. Plutarch, 'Life of Solon', 15, p. 55.

5. *Theognis*, quoted in N. G. L. Hammond, *A History of Greece to 322 B.C.*, O.U.P., Oxford, 1977, 51, p. 146.

6. Plutarch, 'Life of Solon', 15, p. 60.

## Chapter 13
# The Tomb of the Body
### *Pythagoras; Egyptian & Eastern Influences*

THE IONIAN COAST OF Asia Minor, a strip of Greek territory with river valleys, mountains and islands squeezed between the Aegean Sea and the barbaroi of the hinterland, witnessed in the early sixth century the beginning of an intellectual movement vital to European civilisation. Thales of Miletus, the first of these early thinkers, was followed by the great mathematician Pythagoras, a native of the island of Samos. It was Thales who advised Pythagoras to study in Egypt. According to one ancient writer, Pythagoras spent twenty-two years there, besides perhaps visiting Crete and Babylon, where he may have met the Zoroastrian Magi. Certainly much that Pythagoras later taught was based upon the learning of Egypt, particularly the divine nature of the natural elements, the importance of symbols, and the use of geometry as a training for the mind.

*Sphinx of the Naxians*

Pythagoras was born about the year 570 BC. When the tyrant, Polycrates, took control of Samos in 535 BC, Pythagoras emigrated to Croton on the heel of Italy and established a school of philosophy there. It was a highly practical school: the students were taught to find measure in their own lives; unnecessary talking, excessive sleep, gross appetites of any kind were forbidden. Wealth and worldly success were viewed with contempt, and everything in the school was held in common. Rigorous intellectual discipline included the mathematical studies for which Pythagoras is best known to posterity. The theorem that the square of the hypoteneuse of a right-angled triangle equals the sum of the squares of the other two sides was said by Pythagoras to demonstrate, *inter alia*, the nature of justice, which has an invariable distribution of power, despite the dissimilarity of all instances where it is present (since there are innumerable forms of right-angled triangles.) Other mathematical theorems original to Pythagoras were the proof that the internal angles of every triangle add up to two right angles, and the idea of the incommensurability of the sides and the diagonals of a square. The latter follows from the proof that for any square of side one unit, the diagonal, $\sqrt{2}$, cannot be expressed as a fraction of the form n/m, where n and m are both integers. This enabled number to be distinguished from extension in space, a step which helped to form the quadrivium of studies developed in the Middle Ages.

The training of students in such mathematical disciplines was no mere intellectual pastime. Its real purpose was defined by Plutarch:

> "All the so-called mathematical sciences are like smooth flat mirrors in which traces and images of intelligible truth are reflected. But it is above all geometry which, according to Philolaus, being the origin and native city of the others, turns and elevates the mind which is purified and gently released from perception."[1]

What the Ionian philosophers, Thales, Anaximander, Anaximenes, Heraclitus and others had in common was to seek the one essential principle of all things, whether they called it fire, air or simply eternal, unchanging Nature. Pythagoras and his successors in southern Italy, like Parmenides and Empedocles, followed the same line of enquiry. They looked for an underlying unity that pervades the universe, and Pythagoras, especially, saw liberation as the identification of oneself with that unity.

Pythagoras laid the foundations of European music when he discovered the natural octave by using a string, possibly made of brass, to demonstrate the basic intervals. A half cut produces a note one octave higher, a two-thirds cut produces the fifth chord, and a three-quarters cut the fourth chord, giving the arithmetical ratios 2:1, 3:2 and 4:3. This was not a mere empirical demonstration, for Pythagoras taught that number was the root of all created things, so that the numerical ratios expressed the natural law inherent both in musical harmony and in humanity.

The Pythagoreans as a school particularly revered the special form of the elementary numbers known as the tetractys, a triangle made up of a base of four points and an apex of one point, viz:

This symbol contains all numbers up to and including ten, the number which has been the principal base of European number systems to the present day. The Pythagorean concept of number, like the Vedic, held that the numbers from one to nine actually are the elements or gods. Elements, gods and numbers are the same. According to Plutarch, the Pythagoreans called the number one Apollo, because it rejected plurality, the number two Strife and the number three Justice, because it intervenes between the deficiency and excess of injustice. The nine heavenly bodies of the solar system were seen by Pythagoras as the nine numbers, or gods, in extension, rotating with the "harmony of the spheres," a music accessible only to those whose hearing was refined by study of the infinite and the perfect. Much later, philosophers like Boethius and Marsilio Ficino were to teach similar principles of a divine harmony.

Number and symbolism were not all that Pythagoras studied in Egypt, for he met there, also, the idea of reincarnation, according to which the soul moves in a recurring cycle from one embodiment to another, taking each time a new body, in keeping with its actions in former lifetimes. Whatever the mind dwells on at death may determine the character of the next embodiment. This principle of reincarnation is probably what the Egyptians themselves believed, with their "false doors" through which the soul returned when re-united with a body.

Pythagoras is said to have remembered his own previous embodiments, or some of them at least. One story told that he recognised a warrior's shield when travelling through Argos, and burst into tears. On the back of it, he claimed, was the name Euphorbus, for he had been Euphorbus, a Trojan warrior killed by Menelaus in the Trojan War. The name was indeed there on the shield. Pythagoras' concept of reincarnation was closely related to his teaching on how to live a good life, for he said that an evil life would lead to embodiment as an animal (hence the vegetarianism of his disciples). The cultivation of virtue had the practical aim of liberation through evolution to a higher form.

This doctrine of the reincarnation of the soul profoundly affected Greek and later European thought. It permeated the mystery religions of Dionysus, Demeter and the Orphics, and influenced the writings on death and immortality of Plato. Moreover, it passed into the early Christian religion. Until Clement of Alexandria in the late second century AD, Christians accepted the idea of reincarnation, but it was later rejected. The idea of immortality of the soul only became Catholic doctrine at the Lateran Council in the sixteenth century. Christians came to believe merely in the ideas of the resurrection of the body and the passage of the soul through hell, heaven and, perhaps, limbo. Such thinkers as Dante, Pico della Mirandola and Ficino saw further into the nature of the soul's immortality, and their writings show the influence of Pythagoras' doctrine.

The teaching that Pythagoras established at Croton spread from there to many places in Magna Graecia and Greece itself. His disciples were devoted to him, and their practices were continued for many generations, becoming the seedbed for later movements in Greek philosophy, notably Platonism and Stoicism. In southern Italy the Pythagoreans became influential in politics, though this produced a reaction, especially in Croton itself, where in the mid fifth century BC their meeting houses were burnt down, and about fifty of them were slain. Their master had anticipated this when he said that the keystone of political knowledge is that nothing is pure among things that exist! A hundred years after this disaster the school at Croton finally closed.

When Pythagoras brought this philosophy to Greece, the culture of Apollo and of Homer was already old. Internal strife in the poleis, of the kind which Solon so wisely remedied at Athens, was widespread. Tyranny, though sometimes benevolent, bore with it the corruption of power. Hesiod had complained of the incipient greed of land-hungry farmers. From Croton a revitalising wisdom flowed out to Greek-speaking lands, reminding Greeks of the ancient knowledge enshrined at Delphi as "Know thyself". Who was that self? Was it separate or was it a soul united with Apollo himself, the soul of the world?

In Plato's *Timaeus*, Pythagorean ideas on the nature of the soul, number and astronomy are brought together in a way which suggests that the surviving fragments of Pythagoras' own ideas indicate a universal teaching about Man and reality. For Plato writes of the soul of the universe permeating all corporeal things and bringing to them an unseen harmony, based upon number. The heavens exhibit a divine proportion, at one with the harmonies of music, and are themselves contained within the universal soul. For good reason Pythagoras was called the son of Apollo - the soul of the world and the god who presided over harmony.

The Ionian philosophers were distinguished by a cool reason, which at times was contemptuous of any mystical tendency, but Pythagoras and his followers successfully united reason with intuitive understanding. In him the influence of Egypt is clearly discerned. From about 620 BC this influence had flowed into Greece with increasing momentum. A change of attitude amongst Egyptian rulers, induced by the brief political unification before the arrival of the Persians, opened doors to enquiring and acquisitive Greeks. Psammetichus II, for example, employed Ionian mercenaries, one of whom left a witty inscription on the leg of the colossal statue of Rameses II at Abu Simbel: "Cut by Archon son of Amoebichus and by Axe son of Nobody."

More importantly, in c610 BC the Milesians founded the Greek trading community at Naucratis on the western outlet of the Nile. This became a major port, particularly for the importing of Greek pottery, and the Pharaohs gave it a monopoly of Greek trade with Egypt. Amasis, in particular, in the mid sixth century, patronised it with generous privileges, like shrines for Greek gods. The Hellenion, built by Ionian Greeks - Chians, Rhodians, Milesians and others - was the greatest of these, coinciding with the acme of Ionian commercial prosperity.

Amidst this economic intercourse more subtle forces were at work. Amasis respected Greek culture; he gave one thousand talents of alum to help rebuild the temple of Apollo at Delphi. During his reign Pythagoras was probably in Egypt, meeting there, according to Herodotus, the priest of Heliopolis, Oenuphis. Perhaps at this time also the archetypal sage, Imhotep, became the deified Asclepius, the Greek god of healing. Certainly Egyptian medical practices, in ophthalmology and gynaecology for example, passed into Greek medicine. In architecture the Ionic order of Greece was stimulated by the example of Egyptian temple building, with its use of the faceted column and simple capitals.

Sculpture, particularly, showed the powerful influence of Egyptian art on Greece. In the late seventh century BC, the Greeks suddenly began to make massive and

*Statue of Kore*

*Statue of Kouros*

*Grain sculpture at Eleusis*

*Sanctuary at Eleusis*

*Lekythos at Eleusis, probably showing Demeter and Kore*

startlingly new statues of young men (kouroi) and maidens (korai). Both kouroi and korai are magnificent idealisations of the human form, dignified, upright, poised for action, and with an enigmatic smile on their lips. They are not portraits, but were dedicated to gods or used as monuments on graves, like the heroic Anavyssos Kouros made about 525 BC for the grave of a fallen warrior. The Kouros of Sounion is an awe-inspiring figure, nearly ten feet tall. Egyptian monumental sculpture is clearly the model from which this art form developed, but the Greeks were loathe to copy, and so modified the austere rigour of the Egyptian style with a masterly native touch. The Egyptian use of a stone block to strengthen the work, thus preventing completely free standing figures, was ignored, partly because Greek craftsmen had the benefit of iron tools (rather than bronze tools which require heavier pressure). Kouroi and korai stand with weight equally distributed on both feet, giving a sense of potential movement, unlike Egyptian statues where the weight is statically on the back foot.

Most significant, perhaps, of the Greek innovations was the tension and animation of the face in the statue. The calm, self-controlled Egyptian expression gave way to the intense interest and emotive force of the youthful Greeks, tempered with the harmony of Apollo.

These great sculptures are the exuberant expression of a new ideal. Man has moved to the centre of the stage, even perhaps at the cost of upstaging the gods. A century later the Athenians would dare to decorate the Parthenon with human figures, and to portray the gods as little larger than their human companions in the frieze of the Panathenaic procession. Such an attitude may end in hubris, but in its origin in the seventh century it had the sense of a truth freshly realised - Man is divine, in himself absolute. Why then should he not be portrayed as a colossus, a king of creation, or divinely beautiful, like the Kouroi.

Pythagoras taught that number was the essence of all things. This sculpture that accompanied him out of Egypt was built upon number. For the Egyptians had used, since the beginning of their civilisation, a system of measuring sculptured figures by means of a grid drawn on the stone block. The sculptor then cut into the block from three faces. Moreover, the system of measurement, like other ancient systems, used the human body as its module. The principal unit was the cubit, the distance from the elbow to the tip of the thumb. Six handbreaths, measured across the four finger knuckles, made up one cubit, whilst four cubits made a fathom. A complete canon of such measurements enabled Egyptian artists for three millennia to insist upon constant measures for every form of art and to achieve perfectly proportioned representations of the human form. The Greeks adopted this canon in the seventh century BC. In Samos, the home of Pythagoras, two sculptors, Telekles and Theodorus, were the first to make a statue - of Pythian Apollo - using the Egyptian grid, probably with the canonical proportions. By the fifth century, Protagoras of Abdera could proudly say that man is the measure of all things. The kouroi were the physical symbols of this philosophical truth.

Just as in the maturing period of Egyptian civilisation, in the second millennium BC, there arose a new form of religion with the profound mythology of Isis and Osiris, so in sixth century BC Greece, the mystery religions arose to meet a need which orthodox religion could not satisfy. A mystery was a secret rite practiced by devotees, committed not to reveal it to the world at large. As with the cult of Osiris, this exclusive character was later modified, so that at Athens, in particular, the Eleusinian Mysteries were open to all who chose them, including slaves. Even then, the inner nature of the Mysteries was not disclosed.

The teaching of Pythgoras was closely related to Orphism. The Pythagorean, Philolaus, said:

> "The old theologians and prophets testify that the soul has been yoked to the body as a punishment and that it is buried in it as though in a tombr."[2]

which was a characteristic belief of Orphism. Orpheus himself was an obscure figure from Thracian legend, but it was Egypt that provided the core of the Orphic teaching. How was the soul to be raised from its entombment in the body? Osiris had risen from death, and his devotee could become one with him by leading an exemplary life, which would enable him to pass the test before his Master in the underworld. Hence Orphism held to an austere way of life, with the control of desire and the eventual elimination of material concerns. The devotee died to the world.

Orphism represented this spiritual aim in mythologies enacted in its rites. At Eleusis, it used the cult of Demeter, goddess of grain. Demeter's daughter Kore, or Persephone, was raped by Hades and imprisoned in the underworld, until she rose each year to a new life in the world above, like germinating grain, symbol of the rebirth of life out of death. Similarly, Dionysus was a god whose myth told of his death at the hands of the Titans, and whose resurrection enacted the return to life of the divine element in Man. Since the Titans had devoured his limbs, he rose from their ashes, which represented the mortal body of Man. Dionysus, like Orpheus, had Thracian origins, and essentially this was the same teaching of Man's quest for immortality.

There was a darker side to the mystery religions of Greece. Dionysus became also a god of unrestrained passion, associated with frenzied rites which were restricted to women, and the eating of raw flesh. This intrusion into the pure meaning of Orphism probably came from Phrygia in Asia Minor. Its corrupt doctrine and practice were partially tempered by Greek restraint, so that it could be incorporated into the Eleusinian Mysteries and the theatre, of which Dionysus became the patron god. At Delphi, Apollo and Dionysus were reconciled and, at Athens, the Dionysian festivals of drama grew out of the choruses sung during Dionysiac ceremonies. The association of Dionysus with the Cretan Zeus also helped to tame the ecstasy of the Phrygian god.

The rhetorician, Themistius, wrote this of the Eleusinian Mysteries:

> "The soul at the moment of death experiences the same impressions as those who are initiated into the Great Mysteries.... made perfect, free, and walking unrestrained, a man can celebrate the Mysteries, a crown on his head; he lives amongst pure and holy men; he sees the crowd of non-initiates on earth, wilfully plunging into filth and darkness, and dallying with evil through their very fear of death, instead of believing in the bliss of the life to come."

During the zenith of Athenian culture and power in the fifth century BC the Eleusinian Mysteries were adopted by the city as a major cult. The fearlessness of her hoplites and sailors, the energy and boldness of her statesmen, the profound imagination of her artists and dramatists, and the sheer enthusiasm of her life and people owed not a little to the contempt for death and the faith in the divine spirit of Man engendered at Eleusis.

## References:

1. Plutarch, *Table Talk* 718E.
2. Clement, *Miscellanies* III iii 17.1.

# Chapter 14
# The Gates of Heaven
## *Reforms of Cleisthenes & the Battle of Marathon*

UNDER THE TYRANT, PEISISTRATUS, who controlled Athens during the middle decades of the sixth century, the Eleusinian Mysteries were encouraged and became a potent force in the lives of many Athenians of all classes. A third figure, beside the two goddesses, Demeter and Persephone, in the cult of Eleusis was the youth, Triptolemus, honoured by Demeter for his hospitality to her, when she had wandered the earth deprived of her daughter by the king of the underworld. Demeter rewarded Triptolemus with the gift of seeds of grain and the instruction to spread this gift throughout the world, as a bas relief at Eleusis shows in its portrayal of Triptolemus holding a stalk of corn, between his benefactress and her daughter.

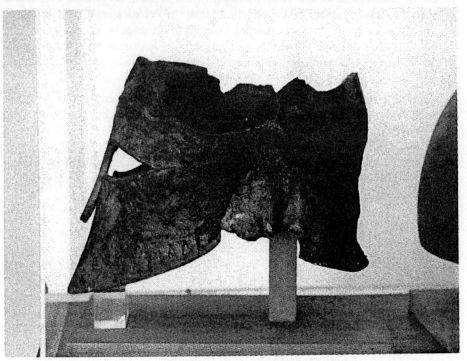

*Helmet of Miltiades, National Museum, Athens*

The seeds of Triptolemus were like the fundamental ideas forming in the minds of Athenians at the time. For in the fifth century in Athens lived and worked the most consummate artists in paint, stone, bronze and clay, the finest writers of poetry, prose and drama, the most courageous and persuasive leaders on the battlefield and in government, and, in Socrates, the wisest teacher of the art of living and dying. This height of human excellence lasted but a moment, as the culture of Apollo and Homer burnt itself out in a flame of unique brilliance.

Solon had established the conditions for the development of a free community in Attica, not bound by land monopoly or debt, and taking upon itself responsibility in government and warfare commensurate with wealth and ability. During the sixth century, a backbone of free farmers upheld the economy of Attica, and the benevolent tyranny of Peisistratus and his sons preserved a degree of order. New problems, however, emerged. A desire for more self-government grew in reaction to the rule of one family, however public spirited it might have been. Moreover, the diverse geographical conditions of Attica led to inevitable conflicts of interest between regions. Along the coast, the fishermen and small farmers often opposed the interests of the townsmen of the plain in Athens itself. Above the city, in the hills encircling it, the more remote farmers, with their herds of sheep and goats, and olive trees rooted in the rocky soil, formed a third group, whose economic interests were peculiar to them.

In this situation there arose a man whose insight into the political needs of the time was acute. Cleisthenes came from one of the oldest and most aristocratic families, the Alcmaeonids, whose political life was haunted by an ancient curse, incurred when an act of sacrilege had been committed against a political opponent. Cleisthenes came to the fore as a leader in the struggle against the Peisistratids. The tyranny had degenerated; the tyrant, Hippias, reacted violently to opposition. With the aid of the Spartan king, Cleomenes, Hippias was expelled, but Cleomenes expected a grateful oligarchy to pursue a pro-Spartan policy in Athens, whereas a popular movement was, in fact, growing apace.

Cleisthenes placed himself at the head of this movement, aware that the future lay with it. A further intervention by Cleomenes was defeated by the power of the majority of citizens, who surrounded the small Spartan force on the Acropolis. All that remained from the participation of Sparta in Athenian affairs was that Athens emerged as a member of the Spartan-led Peloponnesian League, for she had been obliged to join this when Cleomenes' aid had been sought to expel the tyrant, Hippias.

For Cleisthenes, the moment for political action had arrived. In 507, he carried through the Assembly (or *Ecclesia*) of the citizens a sweeping measure of political reform. Its basis was a fundamental change in the system of tribes, or *phratries*. The existing four Ionic tribes were groupings of clans, each dominated by a few old aristocratic families. Many people were excluded from citizenship. The tribes were scattered throughout the three geographical regions of coast, plain and hill. Hence the Council of Four Hundred and the Assembly were swayed by the dominant families or by economic interests from the regions. Either way, there was little chance of the interest of the whole polis gaining its rightful place in public issues. In a brilliantly conceived revision of the tribe system, Cleisthenes swept away the disparate interests which had been so dominant.

He took as the unit for his new tribes the existing local grouping of people in a deme. These demes were small, but varied in size naturally, according to such local conditions as terrain, work and remoteness. Demes were now collected together into a new unit called a *trittys*, with exactly ten *trittys* in each of the three regions of coast, plain and hill. The *trittys* was a nominal unit only, with no corporate existence or officials of its own, unlike the deme, which as a local body was enlivened by personal loyalties. The key step was then to take one *trittys* from each of the regions to form a new tribe, making ten tribes in all from the thirty *trittys*. Thus each tribe drew a third of its membership from each geographical region of Attica. Economic interests were divided; no longer would each region voice its claims and complaints without reference to the interests of the whole polis, for the new tribes became the focus for political debate and representation. Within a tribe, economic interests would need to be reconciled, but the tribe itself would naturally present the views of all three regions of Attica.

This new system of tribes was linked with the creation of a new Council (or *Boule*) of Five Hundred, to replace the old Council of Four Hundred. The demes put forward a number of representatives, according to the size of the deme, and from these fifty were elected by lot to sit in the new Council as representatives of each tribe. The Council became the administrative organ for the polis. It prepared the agenda for the Assembly, which could only debate and vote on proposals from the Council. It managed the finances of the polis and all other questions of executive government, such as law and order and the control of markets and festivals. These tasks required a smaller body than 500. For this, the year was divided into ten and each tribe administered the whole polis for one tenth of the year. The fifty members currently in control were called the *prytany*, and from them one was selected by lot each day to be chairman, or *epistates*. Thus every member of the Council had about a 70% chance of being epistates during the year, for re-election was ruled out. In 406 BC, at a crucial point in the trial of Athenian admirals, Socrates became *epistates*. The Council also had some judicial powers; in particular, it could hear impeachments. However, the central questions of making treaties and declaring war were reserved to the Assembly.

Associated with the new tribes, also, were military reforms. Each tribe now contributed a regiment of hoplites and a squadron of cavalry to the army of Athens. In command of each tribal contingent was a general, or *strategos*, making ten generals, who led the army under the nominal command of the ancient officer, the *polemarch*. *Strategoi* were later to become the most important officials in Athens; it was in this capacity that Pericles led the democracy for thirty years. Since the *strategos* was elected by his tribe, there was every chance that he would be a man whose reputation for leadership and valour qualified him for the office. Indeed, for a long time the *strategoi* were aristocrats, educated for authority.

These reforms brought in the course of a generation a political ripeness to Athenian society. The citizenship was extended fairly, beyond those who had been favoured by the old tribal leaders. Through the system of election by lot to the Council and to the *epistates*, many citizens acquired a sense of responsibility and administrative skill of great significance when Athens faced the trials associated with its supreme achievements in the fifth century. The Councils' role as a steering committee for the Assembly prevented the direct democracy of the latter body becoming the source of rash decisions, at least until the emergence of the demagogues thrown up by the stresses of the Peloponnesian War at the end of the fifth century. Above all, Athenian people were given a sense of true political authority, of considering issues from the standpoint of the polis itself, for Cleisthenes had hit upon the solution to factional economic disputes, namely the creation of political units, the new tribes, which were each a microcosm of the whole polis. It was a stroke of genius, underpinned by the substantial economic justice of Solon's earlier reforms. Within twenty years the Athenian polis was to pass the supreme test of standing alone against a foreign invader of unsurpassed might.

The Achaemenid dynasty who ruled the Persians had been subject to the more numerous Medes for centuries, when the Achaemenid Cyrus II resolved to free himself from their subjection. In 550 BC his revolt was successful, and the Median empire was suddenly transformed into a Persian one. Next, Cyrus moved westwards to confront the rich kingdom of Lydia in Asia Minor, ruled by King Croesus, himself related by marriage to the Medes. Croesus, according to Herodotus, consulted the Greek oracles for their advice about the approaching war, for he was influenced by the Ionian Greeks on the western coast of Asia Minor. When the Delphic oracle passed the test of divining what Croesus was doing at a certain point in time - he was stewing a tortoise and a lamb together in a bronze pot - the king decided to listen to the Delphic advice, namely that if he set forth with his army he would destroy an empire. With unrestrained confidence he left his capital of Sardis to meet Cyrus, his expected victim. After an inconclusive battle at the river Halys, Croesus withdrew casually to Sardis to reprovision his army. Cyrus was too quick for him. The Persian king bore down upon the city, discovered a way over the walls by hearing of a Lydian soldier who had climbed down after dropping his helmet outside, and took the city by storm. Croesus had fulfilled the Delphic prophecy. He had destroyed an empire - his own!

The triumph of Cyrus the Great over Croesus meant the end of any real political independence for the Ionian Greek states of the littoral and islands of Asia Minor. Their prosperity, based upon trading freely in the eastern Mediterranean with their compatriots and with Egypt and Cyprus, waned in the second half of the sixth century BC, especially when Cyrus' son, Cambyses, added Egypt to the Persian Empire in 525 BC and restricted Greek interests there. The thriving Ionian poleis, such as Miletus, Mitylene, Ephesus and Clazomenae, which had nursed the emerging genius of Greek philosophy, were frustrated in their desire for political autonomy. Though the tyrants who now ruled them were Greek, the Persian satraps on the mainland kept a jealous eye upon them and directed their economies towards the great empire centred upon distant Susa.

In 522 BC Darius succeeded Cambyses, obtaining the throne with dubious legality, but bringing to it a masterly and ambitious talent for government over his immense dominions. The empire stretched from Cyrenaica in North Africa to the banks of the Indus, and from the Caucasus to the Persian Gulf. Twenty-two satrapies brought to the Great King their absolute obedience and massive tribute. Even to the Greeks, whose political ideal of the independent polis was so utterly contrary to this extensive imperialism, the Persian monarch was known simply as "the King". His military power, which would soon be felt across the Aegean, was based upon an aristocratic and much feared cavalry, heavy infantry, and a myriad of provincial troops of all kinds: Assyrians armed with spears and wooden clubs, Scythians with the sagaris, or battle-axe, Indians with cane bows, long-robed Arabians, Ethiopians in leopard skins, and more of many races. Partly for military purposes, Darius built a splendid road system throughout the empire, notably the Royal Road from the Greek city of Ephesus on the Ionian coast to his capital city of Susa, a distance of over 1500 miles, or three months journey on foot. In the hills of central Persia, Darius also built a new summer capital at Persepolis, endowed with a fine palace, which Alexander the Great was to burn to the ground.

Darius was a cultivated man, devoted to Zoroastrianism, yet sufficiently respectful of the religion of Greece to spare the sacred island of Delos when it was at his mercy. The absolute nature of his rule could brook no interference, however, and, like most empires, his was sensitive to disturbances on, or near, its far-flung borders. The Persians were interested in the mineral deposits of Thrace, across the northern Aegean. When the Greek ruler of Miletus, Histiaeus, proposed to found a Greek colony there, they carried him off to Susa for safe custody. His son, Aristagoras, ruled Miletus in his stead and connived with the Persians to take the Greek island of Naxos in the Cyclades. He quarrelled with the Persian admiral; the enterprise was ruined, and Aristagoras resolved on a much bolder course to save his fortunes, namely to lead a revolt of the Ionian Greeks. He may have been encouraged in this by his father Histiaeus, who is said by Herodotus to have sent a slave to him from Susa with a message enjoining revolt branded on his forehead. In 499 BC the revolt began.

Alone the Ionian Greeks had little chance, even had they been fully united. On land they were hopelessly outnumbered; at sea they were quite strong, but the Phoenician navy was stronger, and fought for the empire. The Ionians' only hope lay with an alliance with their fellow Greeks. Aristagoras himself went to Sparta and entreated King Cleomenes; but the Ionian tyrant overplayed his hand by envisaging a Spartan conquest of the Persian Empire. When Cleomenes was told that it was three months journey from Sparta to Susa, he dismissed Aristagoras from his court.

At Athens and Eretria, on the island of Euboea, the answer was more favourable, for they were of Ionian blood. Athens promised twenty ships, Eretria five. These ships were the beginning of troubles between Greeks and barbarians, according to Herodotus.[1] The Greek allies marched inland from the Ionian coast to the important Persian city of Sardis on the Royal Road. A fire broke out, by intention or accident, and the city was burned to the ground. The wrath of Darius was terrible when he heard the news. He bade a servant remind him of the Athenians three times every evening as he dined.

No more help was given by Athens and Eretria. Aristagoras proved a poor leader, fleeing to Thrace, where he was soon killed, and Histiaeus, though he persuaded Darius to send him to suppress the revolt and then briefly led it, was later captured and crucified by the Persians. In 494 BC, near the island of Lade, off Miletus, a major naval battle saw the utter defeat of the Ionians, despite brave efforts by the sailors of Chios. The revolt had failed, but its consequences were momentous.

Persia had a strong impulse to extend her power westwards. She coveted Thrace, and she knew that the Ionians might never be reconciled to her rule whilst Greek brothers lived freely across the narrow Aegean. Now, in addition, Darius had a burning desire to avenge himself upon the troublesome peoples who had dared to fire a city on the Royal Road. The king's son-in-law, Mardonius, was sent to conquer Thrace and Macedonia, and to punish the two offending cities. In 492 BC, Mardonius overran northern Greece, but a great storm wrecked his fleet off Mount Athos in the Chersonese. Athens and Eretria had been granted a respite, but not for long.

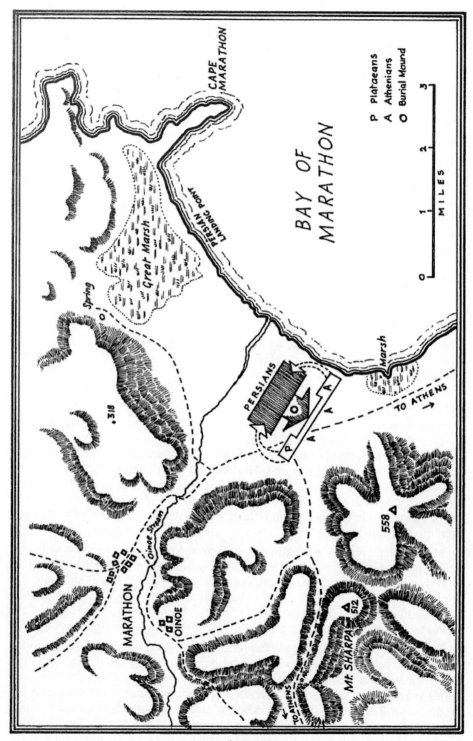

*Battle of Marathon*

Two years later the Persians returned under the command of Datis and Artaphernes, and this time their force consisted of an army of about 25,000 troops, carried across the Aegean by the Persian fleet. Many Greek states had already submitted to the Great King's demand for "earth and water", tokens of submission given to his envoys and symbolic of the hegemony that Persia was now demanding on the Greek mainland. Athens and Eretria stood alone to face the wrath of Asia. Even then, Athens had only just disengaged herself from a local war with her naval rival Aegina, an old enemy which contemplated "*medizing*", or joining Persia, in her own self-interest. The pressure of Sparta, which had a more generous view of Greek loyalties, and a sharp defeat at the hands of the Athenian navy, taught Aegina a lesson.

Meanwhile, the Persian force besieged Eretria. Athens sent 4,000 soldiers from her colony on Euboea to help her ally, but they were advised by an Eretrian friend to depart, for there was a *medizing* group within the city. After a short resistance, Eretria was betrayed. The Persians burnt it to the ground. Sardis was half avenged.

The Athenian aristocrat, Miltiades, ruler of a city in the Chersonese for many years, had returned and been elected one of the ten *strategoi*. The nominal military leader was the *polemarch*, Callimachus. When news arrived that the Persians had landed in the bay of Marathon to the north-east of Athens, a debate began in the Assembly on what measures to take. The Persians had brought with them the ex-tyrant of Athens, Hippias, son of Peisistratus, hoping to reinstate him as a ruler sympathetic to Persian interests. It was probably on his advice that they landed at Marathon, where his father had returned many years before, and where the plain was suitable for the deployment of cavalry. The presence of Hippias, whether or not the Assembly knew of it, made the question of the internal unity of Athens a crucial issue. Miltiades' firm advice to the Assembly was for the army not to stay in the city and withstand a siege, but to march boldly to Marathon to confront the enemy. He was opposed by those who considered him rash, and saw safety on the Acropolis, the ancient citadel, and by those, unknown as yet, who secretly hoped to betray the city to the Persians and to reinstate Hippias. Others warned of the danger, if they marched to Marathon, of missing the advancing enemy, for there were two roads, one over the heights of Mount Pentelicus, one along the coast; but the convincing rhetoric of Miltiades touched a chord in the imaginative and daring mind of the citizens assembled on the hill of Pnyx, to the west of the Agora. It was September; the river beds were dry and the countryside was brown from weeks of hot sun.

The army that left Athens lacked cavalry and archers. Its whole strength lay in the citizen hoplites, about 10,000 of them, heavily armoured in bronze helmets, breast plates and greaves, carrying swords and long spears. The *strategoi* wisely chose the mountain road to Marathon, for the large Persian force could not easily take the longer and lower coastal road without being spotted by scouts. They camped on the lower, eastern slopes of Mount Pentelicus. Here they were joined by a thousand hoplites from their sole active ally, Plataea, a small city, indebted to Athens for help against the powerful city of Thebes, which sought to dominate Boeotia. A runner, Pheidippides, had been sent from Athens to Sparta with a call for assistance, but the Spartans had replied that they would come at the full moon in a few days time, for they were engaged in religious observances.

From the hills the Greek hoplites could see the Persian army camped near the Great Marsh to the north-east along the coast. The Persian fleet lay off to sea, ready to carry their victorious soldiers to Athens in triumph. The *strategoi* ordered their

*Burial mound at Marathon*

*Modern copy of "The Warrior of Marathon"*

men to cut down trees and build stockades on the lower slopes to inhibit an attack by the deadly enemy cavalry. Caution still ruled many of the Greek leaders. At a council of war five of the ten *strategoi* advised defensive measures awaiting a move by the enemy, whose force outnumbered theirs by well over two to one. Miltiades spoke out strongly for a direct and prompt attack, relying on surprise and the favourable ground of the Greeks. The deciding vote belonged to Callimachus as *polemarch*. To his credit, he voted with Miltiades. Operational command was given to the man who had counselled boldness from the beginning.

At dawn the Greek hoplites moved forward, at first slowly and silently, then gathering pace. To cover the long Persian line, they were forced to stretch out their own line, but, making a virtue of necessity, they strengthened the wings at the expense of the centre. On the left wing were the Plateans. Once within a mile of the leading Persian ranks, the Greeks broke into a run, coasting easily downhill, in the style of the Olympic race in full armour. The Persian archers, caught by surprise, could not judge the range of their arrows as the Greeks closed fast upon them. The Persian cavalry was nowhere to be seen. Some Ionian deserters from Darius' forces had told the *strategoi* that it was not at the Persian camp. Where it was is unknown; perhaps the horses were being watered away to the north, for the stream of Oenoe near the camp had run dry. They may have been embarked, ready for the voyage to Athens. The Persian commanders had been either careless, or arrogant.

Herodotus' description of the engagement is brief:

"The struggle at Marathon was long drawn out. In the centre, held by the Persians themselves and the Sacae, the advantage was with the foreigners, who were so far successful as to break the Greek line and pursue the fugitives inland from the sea; but the Athenians on one wing and the Plataeans on the other were both victorious. Having got the upper hand, they left the defeated army to make their escape, and then, drawing the two wings together into a single unit, they turned their attention to the Persians who had broken through in the centre. Here again they were triumphant, chasing the routed enemy, and cutting them down until they came to the sea, and men were calling for fire and taking hold of the ships. It was in this phase of the struggle that the War Archon Callimachus was killed, fighting bravely, and also Stesilaus, the son of Thrasylaus, one of the generals; Cynegirus, too, the son of Euphorion, had his hand cut off with an axe as he was getting hold of a ship's stern, and so lost his life, together with many other well known Athenians.........

"In the battle of Marathon some 6400 Persians were killed; the losses of the Athenians were 192. During the action a very strange thing happened: Epizelus, the son of Cuphagoras, an Athenian soldier, was fighting bravely when he suddenly lost the sight of both eyes, though nothing had touched him anywhere - neither sword, spear, nor missile. From that moment he continued blind as long as he lived. I am told that in speaking about what happened to him he used to say that he fancied he was opposed by a man of great stature in heavy armour, whose beard overshadowed his shield; but the phantom passed him by, and killed the man at his side."[2]

By their unswerving devotion to their poleis the men of Marathon set a standard for the whole of Greece. Never again would Greeks stand in fear of overwhelming might. They had proved that courage, self-discipline and intelligence could triumph over numbers; that the human spirit, nurtured on free institutions, cannot be overborne. Marathon was to stand as the beacon to which all would turn for inspiration in the struggles ahead, against a second and mightier Persian invasion and against the more subtle assaults of political disunity. In the *Poikile Stoa*, or painted colonnade, at the Athenian Agora, the great painter, Polygnotus, portrayed three stages of the battle: the charge downhill and hand-to-hand fighting, the enemy fleeing in disorder, and the slaughter at the ships. Callimachus, who died in the place of honour on the right wing, Cynegirus, Epizelus, and Aeschylus, the dramatist, were all portrayed, as was Darius himself. Yet the greatest honour was given by Polygnotus to the gods and heroes, who were thought to be present on the field of battle: Theseus, founder of Athens, Athena, protecting goddess, and Heracles, the archetypal hero from another and greater age. The Greek line of battle had been drawn up to attack with its right wing adjoining a small precinct devoted to Heracles. He had not failed them.

As the Persian fleet sailed away, the *strategoi* realised that the danger had not passed. The enemy was still strong enough to take the unguarded city. Moreover, some Greeks saw a signal flashed from the heights of Mount Pentelicus to the fleet by a polished shield reflecting the rays of the sun. It indicated treachery at Athens. The conspirators within the city had completed their preparations. Miltiades gave the order and the army marched back along the mountain road, leaving a section to guard the battlefield. By a forced march, they reached Athens well before the Persian fleet. When the first boats approached the beaches at Phalerum, the crews and soldiers could see the victorious army drawn up to meet them on the plain behind the beaches. Even fear of the Great King would not compel the Persian troops to face once more the long hoplite spears and steel-edged bronze swords. The fleet turned for home. The expedition had failed.

On the following day, the vanguard, two thousand strong, of the Spartan army arrived at Marathon. They inspected the battlefield and the Persian bodies, and paid their respects to the dead of Athens and Plataea. They, too, learnt that the Athenians, for all their easy-going ways to Lacedaemonian eyes, could fight in defence of freedom with unsurpassed nobility. They also learnt how a Persian host might be defeated by a skilful choice of ground and time. It was a valuable lesson for men who made soldiering their chief pride, and who would bear their own share of the burden when Persia attacked once more.

The battle of Marathon was a supreme moment in history, when a few thousand men became briefly aware of the need of the time:

"Nothing can be more welcome to a soldier than a righteous war... Blessed are the soldiers who find their opportunity. This opportunity has opened for thee the gates of heaven."[3]

For those who died at Marathon, there was immortal fame. For those who lived, the gates of heaven were to open on earth.

### References:

1. Herodotus, *The Histories*, trans. A. de Selincourt, Penguin, London, 1912, Book V, p. 379.

2. Herodotus, *The Histories*, Book VI, pp. 429-430.

3. *Bhagavad Gita*, trans. Shri Purohit Swami, Faber, London, 1978, ch. 2, vv. 31-2.

## Chapter 15
# Triumph of the Greeks
### *The Persian War*

DARIUS' RESOLVE TO DESTROY the resistance of the Greeks did not abate. He set about building up greater forces by land arid sea, knowing that an invasion across the Aegean was no longer sound and that only a massive force, crossing the Hellespont and supplied by an off-shore fleet, might ensure success. His plans were spoilt by a rebellion in Egypt, to which he had to divert whatever forces he had already prepared. A year later, in 486 BC, he died. His son, Xerxes, a less cultured man than Darius, but of equal ambition, continued with the invasion plans, after snuffing out the Egyptian revolt.

The man responsible for Darius' defeat at Marathon, Miltiades, hardly outlived the king. Few instances illustrate better the ingratitude of the Athenian people towards their leaders on occasion. Miltiades, as an aristocrat and ex-tyrant in the Chersonese,

*Treasury of Siphnos Frieze; Lions of Cybele, Apollo and Artemis*

was later under attack from the more democratic elements in the city. When he led an expedition to the island of Poros, to punish it for medizing, his failure there - where he was severely wounded - gave his opponents the chance to bring him to trial. The court fined him the huge sum of 50 talents, having commuted the death sentence, probably out of respect for his earlier services. Shortly afterwards Miltiades died of his wounds. His son, Cimon, managed to pay the fine. Such treatment was a hint that Athenian society hid a self-destructive tendency, which would emerge as a cause of its collapse.

A man of different stamp was already on the political stage in anticipation of the renewal of war. Themistocles came from humbler origins than both his great rival, Aristides, and Miltiades. Even before Marathon, Themistocles had introduced his constant theme of the vital importance for Athens of sea power, for he had advocated the construction of a great port at the natural harbour of the Piraeus to replace the open beaches of Phalerum. Now, as news of Persian preparations filtered back from travellers and Greek spies, he redoubled his efforts to convince the citizens that he was right.

*Silver mines at Laurium*

Aristides, a man of exemplary and rational character, in contrast to the ebullient and susceptible Themistocles, steadily opposed him, seeing in the hoplite army and the Spartan example a surer defence. In 482 BC a crucial new factor appeared in the struggle: an especially rich vein of silver was discovered in the mines at Laurium, near Cape Sunium. How was this influx of wealth to be used? The mines were state property, rented to tenants; in the year 483/2 the rents yielded 100 talents. Many in the Assembly wanted this huge windfall to be distributed amongst the citizens. Themistocles saw that this was an opportunity to enlarge the fleet. With the skill of a born politician he convinced the Assembly that more warships were needed for the continuing sea war with Aegina. His real aim was to build a fleet to match that of the Persians. In fact, the two aspects were linked, for if the Persians reached Attica, a hostile Aegina might *medize*, making Athenian sea-power in the Saronic Gulf quite inadequate. Keels for 100 triremes were laid down in the following year. The success of Themistocles marked the temporary eclipse of his rival, Aristides. Every citizen had the right to name on an ostrakon, or piece of pottery, the politician whom he most wished to see banished. Provided a total of six thousand votes were recorded, he who was named most was the victim. By this procedure of ostracism, dating from the time of Cleisthenes or soon after, Aristides was banished for ten years from Athens, though without loss of property.

Another constitutional change was introduced in this period. In 487 BC the archons, previously elected, were chosen by lot. From its traditional position as the highest magistracy, the archonship sank in importance, for the best men would seek power by other means than chance. Henceforth, the *strategoi* would be the leaders of the Athenian state, their authority now reaching into the political sphere.

Whilst the Athenians were rapidly completing a fleet of 200 triremes and training the crews, who were from artisan backgrounds, unlike the wealthier citizens who fought as hoplites, Xerxes sent a vast army to cross the Hellespont, accompanied by a large navy. A violent storm destroyed the bridge which ran from Asia to Europe. With barbaric fury, Xerxes ordered that the sea should be given 300 lashes with whips and a pair of fetters be cast into it, and that the engineers who had built the bridge should be beheaded. A further mark of Xerxes' despotism was his treatment of a Lydian noble, who asked that his eldest son should be spared from fighting, as another four sons were already serving in the army. Xerxes treated the request with contempt and ordered that the eldest son should be cut in half. The two halves of the body were then placed each side of the road and the army marched between them. An Ionian Greek was brave enough, nevertheless, to give Xerxes a truthful answer, when he was asked about the readiness of the Spartans to fight against enormous odds:

> "...fighting together they are the best soldiers in the world. They are free - yes - but not entirely free, for they have a master, and that master is Law, which they fear much more than your subjects fear you. Whatever this master commands, they do; and his command never varies: it is never to retreat in battle, however great the odds, but always to stand firm, and to conquer or die."[1]

Sparta was the natural leader of Greece at this critical moment. Her military prestige was unique and unaffected by her religious scruples before Marathon, since all Greeks acknowledged their validity. She was the leader of the Peloponnesian League, which meant ability to organise and control an allied army. Yet when the Greek states met in congress at the Isthmus to consider joint action, she did not insist on using the existing League as the means of fighting Persia. A new league was formed, to be known simply as "the Greeks". It was a display of unity not witnessed since the days when Agamemnon had summoned the host that went to Troy. Thirty-one poleis were represented there. Some in the north were preparing to *medize*. The Congress sent envoys to others of the Greek race, to Crete and Corcyra, to Syracuse and to Argos, Sparta's old enemy. These yielded nothing, beyond a Corcyran naval contingent which dallied en route to the scene of action and played no part. Gelon, the powerful tyrant of Syracuse, was sympathetic, but had his own problems in Sicily,

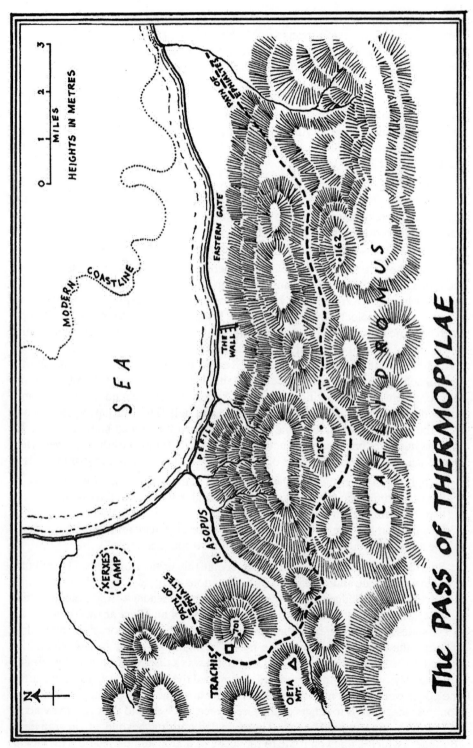

*The Pass of Thermopylae*

soon to be resolved. The Spartans allowed every polis one vote each in the Congress, including themselves, Athens and Corinth, by far the most powerful three states present at the Isthmus. Spartan generosity and moral leadership were rewarded: the Congress accepted a Spartan commander on land and on sea - Athenian naval power was resented - and gave the supreme commanders full powers of decision. This concession by the individual poleis proved vital in the great campaigns that were to follow. It meant that co-ordination between army and navy was possible; that rapid and firm commands could be given; that the choice of where to fight was relatively free from political influence. The latter point was of vital importance in a war where the huge Persian forces could easily turn a position, and where the great superiority of Persian cavalry made any engagement on a lowland plain lethal for the Greeks.

In such circumstances every Greek asked himself what the Delphic oracle might pronounce upon their fate. For Sparta the answer was in the form of a cruel dilemma: either the city would be lost, or a Spartan king would die. It was not to be forgotten when the test came. For Athens, the oracle was yet fiercer: "But all is ruined, for fire and the headlong God of War speeding in a Syrian chariot will bring you low." So terrible was this prophecy that the envoys returned as suppliants and were given a second response: ".....the wooden wall only shall not fall." Solving this riddle cost a few Athenians their lives and led others to salvation through its interpreter, Themistocles. Some said that the wooden wall was the thorn hedge surrounding the Acropolis, and those who persisted in this belief stayed on the Acropolis when the Persians reached Athens. Themistocles came forward and persuaded most people that the wooden wall was the navy. Since the oracle also said, "Divine Salamis, you will bring death to women's sons, when the corn is scattered, or the harvest gathered in,"[2] Themistocles' interpretation made more sense, as the island of Salamis was likely to witness a sea battle for the defence of Attica.

Xerxes' vast army was advancing ponderously through Thrace, having successfully crossed the now repentant Hellespont. To avoid the danger of yet another disaster to the fleet, the Great King ordered a canal to be dug for his ships, across the peninsula of Mount Athos. As his combined forces moved along the coast of mainland Greece, the Greek Congress made a false start in their defensive manoeuvres. They marched north to Thessaly and occupied the Pass of Tempe, only to find that it could be easily outflanked. Their withdrawal was the right military decision, but it ensured that the Thessalians, with their superior cavalry, would *medize*, for Thessaly was left virtually defenceless. Worse still, most of the states north of Attica *medized* also.

King Leonidas of Sparta, leader of the confederate army, decided that the best defensible position north of the Isthmus of Corinth was the pass of Thermopylae, on the coast of Locris opposite the northern end of Euboea. Here ran the only route through the mountain mass of eastern Greece. If it were defended, Attica would be safe; if not, the next defensible site was the Isthmus of Corinth. Naturally the Athenians were keen that the confederate army should advance to Thermopylae. The Spartans did not appear to be so enthusiastic; they sent only 300 Spartiates, together with a few thousand other Peloponnesians, including helots, though once again they pleaded delay for the observance of religious festivals.

The pass at Thermopylae - so named because of the hot sulphur springs in the neighbourhood - was a narrow passage a few miles long between the mountains and the Gulf of Malia. Half way along it lay a low stone wall, built in earlier campaigns. To the west, the direction from which the Persian army would advance, a mile from the wall was a defile, no more than an ox-cart in width, through which the enemy would have to filter if they were to attack. As a defensive position, it would have been completely impregnable, but for one defect: a mountain path led up the hillside from the Persian side, along the slopes and back down to the pass near the village of Alpeni, behind the Greek position. Leonidas knew about the path and sent a force of 1000 Phocian infantry to defend it near its highest point. As yet, Xerxes did not know of it. Not far from where the battle was to be fought was the sacred site of Anthela, associated with the Amphictyonic League, and also a precinct of Heracles (as at Marathon), from whom Leonidas claimed descent.

Sea power was likely to be decisive in the outcome. If the Persians held the coastal waters and, in particular, the channel of the Euripus between Euboea and the mainland, their fleet could always turn any holding action by the Greek army, or even attack far south of the main action on land. If the Greek fleet dominated the coast, then the vast Persian host would sooner or later be trapped without supplies. Consequently, the Spartan naval commander, Eurybiadas, no doubt with the strong support of his Athenian subordinate, Themistocles, stationed his fleet in the Malian Gulf, near Artemisium on Euboea. The land and naval actions were to be fought out more or less simultaneously over a period of a few days.

Meanwhile, Xerxes sent a man on horseback to spy on the Greeks in the pass at Thermopylae. All he could see were a few of the Spartans on guard near the low wall. They were combing their hair. He reported this to Xerxes on his return, and the king asked his Greek adviser what this could mean. His reply echoed what he had said earlier:

> "It is the common practice of the Spartans to pay careful attention to their hair when they are about to risk their lives. But I assure you that if you can defeat these men and the rest of the Spartans who are still at home, there is no other people in the world who will dare to stand firm or lift a hand against you. You have now to deal with the finest kingdom in Greece, and with the bravest men."[3]

Xerxes did not really believe that the Greek army of 9,000 men would try to oppose his immeasurably larger force, estimated by Herodotus at over two million fighting men, but even by modern authors at over two hundred thousand. So he waited west of the pass for four days, expecting them to retreat. On the fifth day, realising perhaps that time was not really on his side in a land devoid of rich crops and pasture, he ordered the attack. Leonidas moved his men forward from the defensive wall into the mile long stretch between the wall and the defile. As the Persian foot-soldiers debouched into the pass, they met the dreaded long spears of the Greeks. Wave after wave of Asian troops flung themselves against the Greek position, with no possible escape from the carnage. The first day saw no progress at all for Xerxes' forces; nor did the second day, even when the cream of his army, the ten thousand "Immortals" - so called because a dead man was instantly replaced - were launched through the defile. For the Greeks, it was akin to fighting in a stadium; indeed the Spartiate, Dienekes, treated it as lightly, even at the time when the Spartiates were doomed. When told by a native of Trachis that the Persian archers were so numerous that their arrows would blot out the sun, he replied, "This is pleasant news that the stranger from Trachis brings us: if the Persians hide the sun, we shall have our battle in the shade."[4]

Whilst the courage of the 9,000 Greeks withstood all that Xerxes' huge army could throw against them, the treachery of one Greek, a Malian called Aphialtes, betrayed them. He told Xerxes of the mountain path and offered to guide the Persians along it. The Immortals, led by their commander, Hydarnes, set out at the time of lamp lighting and during the night filed slowly and silently along the path. As dawn approached, the Phocians near the summit heard the faint crackle of dry oak leaves and saw the Persians approaching, dimly lit as they marched towards the rising sun. The Phocian force, greatly outnumbered, retired to the heights behind them and prepared to withstand an attack; but the Persians were not to be diverted. They ignored the Phocians and began to descend the path towards Alpeni.

Leonidas' rearguard, east of the low wall, saw the Immortals first, and carried the news forward. A council of war was held by the Greek leaders. Just what they decided is not known. Leonidas ordered all but the 300 Spartiates and a small force of Thebans to retreat eastwards beyond Alpeni, before the Immortals egressed into the pass. A contingent from the small polis of Thespiae refused to abandon the Spartiates and stayed with them. This decision of Leonidas may have been based upon a plan to trap the Immortals themselves in the pass, by closing the narrowest part and bringing back the main Greek army in their rear. If so, it placed an enormous burden upon the tiny force of Spartiates, Thebans and Thespians, for they were sure to be assaulted from both directions. Nevertheless, if the main Greek army of about 8,000 returned, there was some chance of destroying the elite Persian force and thereby breaking the morale of the rest. Whether this was the plan or whether the main force were straightforwardly retreating, the outcome was the same. They did not return. The Spartiate force was itself bottled up, facing an attack from each end of the pass.

An old seer, Megistias of Acarnania, had foretold that the Greeks would be betrayed and surrounded. Leonidas ordered him to join the forces retreating eastwards. He refused, but sent his son back with them. An hour before noon, Leonidas led his men out beyond the wall and across the mile-long pass, still littered with Persian bodies. Xerxes was about to attack with his main force. In the belief that they would die wherever they fought, the Spartiate force was led by Leonidas through the narrow defile and deployed on the wider plain beyond, where they would have room to fight in uninhibited fashion. When the assault came, with the Persian infantry driven forward with whips, the Spartan spears pierced for some while the wicker shields and padded breasts of the enemy, but gradually the wooden shafts of the spears were shivered and the Spartiates drew their steel edged swords.

At this point, the Immortals in the eastward end of the pass advanced. It was about this time that Leonidas fell, in the thick of the battle beyond the defile. A furious skirmish developed around his body, worthy of the field of Troy around an Achaean or Trojan hero:

"....four times the Greeks drove the enemy off, and at last by their valour rescued it. So it went on, until the troops with Ephialtes were close at hand; and then, when the Greeks knew that they had come, the character of the fighting changed. They withdrew again into the narrow neck of the pass, behind the wall, and took up a position in a single compact body - all except the Thebans - on the little hill at the entrance to the pass, where the stone lion in memory of Leonidas stands today. Here they resisted to the last, with their swords, if they had them, and, if not, with their hands and teeth, until the Persians, coming on from the front over the ruins of the wall and closing in from behind, finally overwhelmed them with missile weapons."[5]

Xerxes had little of the generous humanity of his father Darius. He ordered the body of Leonidas to be decapitated and then crucified. The Spartan king had known of the Delphic prophecy that:

>"Either your famed, great town must be sacked by Perseus' sons,
>
>Or, if that be not, the whole land of Lacedaemon
>
>Shall mourn the death of a king of the house of Heracles."[6]

Did Leonidas fight to the end with the slender hope of a Greek counter attack from his main force, or was his death an act of self-sacrifice to save his people? Either way it was the response of a trained Spartiate, who valued honour above all else, and death in battle as a noble and worthy end. Whatever its motive, it inspired all Greeks who remained free from the yoke of Persia to renew their efforts, and it taught the Great King that here, at last, he confronted men who were proud to claim from his Immortals the title of the bravest soldiers in the world. Though Thermopylae was a military defeat, it was a moral triumph to rank forever in the stories of nations fighting for self preservation against overwhelming odds.

Much later, when the Persian threat was over, the Amphictyonic League erected columns and epitaphs at Thermopylae. The most famous of these read:

>"O Stranger, tell the Spartans only this,
>
>That we lie here obedient to their laws."[7]

The Greek confederate navy had not been idle. The much larger Persian fleet had split its forces, with one large contingent sailing around the east of Euboea to trap the Greeks in the Epirus. Off the southern tip of Euboea a great storm, fortuitously for the Greeks, had wrecked this contingent. On the days of the action of Thermopylae several engagements had been closely contested at sea. By holding their own, the confederate navy had ensured that the main Greek land forces should not be at the mercy of turning movements by sea. Valuable lessons were also learnt, especially by Themistocles, about the capacity of Greek ships to ram their adversaries. He may also have learnt the use of bribery, for it was said that the Euboeans paid him a very large sum to persuade Eurybiadas and the Peloponnesians to fight so far north of the Isthmus of Corinth. In any case, the navy had performed well, if not as gloriously as the army, which left 20,000 Persians dead.

After the battle of Marathon it had been Themistocles, the Athenian, who, almost alone, had been convinced that the Persians would return to seek nothing less than the conquest of Greece. His advocacy of sea power had been opposed by Aristides. Wisely, the Athenians now recalled Aristides from his exile, for he was a selfless and courageous leader, who would prove his worth soon enough. The struggle at Artemisium was proof that Themistocles' view of sea power had to be taken seriously.

Though Eurybiadas remained as commander of the confederate navy, increasingly Themistocles exerted control over the course of events.

The crucial question was where the Persian fleet should be challenged to a major engagement. In this, political interests threatened the unity which alone made victory possible. The Peloponnesians thought of fighting at, or even south of, the Isthmus of Corinth; already they were building defensive works across the Isthmus, for Attica was now abandoned to the enemy. On the other hand, the Athenians and their brave little allies, the Plataeans and Thespians, though forced to sacrifice their land and homes, were resolved to fight at sea near their own territory. Their families were evacuated to Aegina, Salamis and Troezen; only the last was south of the Isthmus. The evacuation was ably administered by the Council of the Areopagus, the body of elder statesmen, who invoked both the Delphic reference to "divine Salamis" and the favour of the goddess, Athena, to encourage the people to abandon their homes. A dog, belonging to Xanthippus, father of Pericles, was so distraught at being left behind that he swam right across the straits, following his family's boat, until he reached the beach of Salamis, where he collapsed and died. A few men stayed behind: the treasurers of the temples and some stout hearts who believed that "the wooden wall" was the stockade around the Acropolis.

At first Themistocles could not move the confederate council of war to fight so far north. The decision was made to sail to the Isthmus. At this point Mnesiphilus, an old friend and teacher of Themistocles, approached him and insisted on the need to fight at Salamis, for Greek unity depended upon it. Mnesiphilus belonged to a tradition of teachers of wisdom, especially wisdom applied to political life, which stretched back to Solon. He had long been an adviser of Themistocles, and at this juncture his influence may have been decisive. Before the council of war met again, Themistocles saw Eurybiadas and won him over. Even so, the council would not budge. If reason could not convince them, then Themistocles was prepared to use other means. He sent a faithful slave to Xerxes himself, with a message that he, Themistocles, sympathised with the Persian cause and therefore was informing the king that the Greek fleet was about to sail out of the Bay of Salamis for the Isthmus. If the king could send a squadron to the western end of the island of Salamis, the escape would be prevented, with the Greeks trapped in the straits behind the island. Xerxes believed him. After all, the possibility of Athens *medizing* in the present circumstances, where retreat to the Isthmus was what the Peloponnesians were themselves advocating, was great; at least to one who had not known the men of Marathon.

During the night an Egyptian squadron was detached from the Persian fleet and sent to patrol the western end of the straits. In the morning observers told the Greek admirals of the predicament. Aristides, now in his rightful position in command of Athenian troops, came to Themistocles with the same news. Both men set aside their long standing enmity. The shrewd democrat explained his plan to the proud aristocrat.

As the sun rose over the eastern heights of Attica, the Greek fleet deployed in the channel between Salamis town and the sanctuary of Heracles on the mainland. Above the sanctuary Xerxes had chosen a spot to sit, surveying the engagement that must ensue. Of 380 Greek ships, 310 were triremes, low in the water and with reinforced prows for ramming the enemy hulls. Marines with spear and sword stood ready above the bands of oars to board every Persian vessel which came alongside or was shattered by ramming. Outside the narrowest part of the strait, 1200 Persian vessels awaited the order to advance, led by the huge Phoenician triremes, larger, higher and faster than the Greek. Xerxes had sent out soldiers to garrison the island of Psyttalea in mid-channel, to save Persian ships and slaughter Greek survivors who swam there.

The rising sun caught the Greek ships with its rays as they backed water towards Salamis. In the shadow of the heights, the Phoenician triremes advanced into the straits. For a while only missiles were exchanged between the fleets. It was Themistocles who controlled the timing of the engagement, for he had convinced Eurybiadas that he knew exactly how to defeat the huge armada confronting them. As the wind strengthened to its accustomed force, the higher Persian boats swung out of line in the choppy water. Swiftly the Greek triremes rowed forward, low in the water, accelerating under the unison of 150 oars to reach their maximum speed at the point of impact on the enemy hull, or whilst racing alongside to break like sticks the triple banks of Persian oars. Dire congestion made the Persian fleet incapable of manoeuvre. Turning, or backing water, only brought terrible collisions; going on meant running the gauntlet of the coordinated Greek attack. As the splintered fleet lost its momentum and floundered, hundreds of Persian rowers and marines were cut down, or were flung or jumped into the water, where most drowned.

Those Persians who swam to Psyttalea did not find the expected help, for Aristides and his Athenians had landed there and slaughtered the whole Persian garrison. The enemy sailors who reached the island and collapsed exhausted on the beaches were killed like stranded seals.

On his throne above the battle, Xerxes raged and despaired. Some Phoenician commanders, who reported to him with explanations of their difficulties in the melee below, were summarily decapitated. When Xerxes saw Queen Artemisia of Halicarnassus gallantly ram and sink a trireme, he exclaimed that his women had become men and the men women. In fact, she had rammed a Persian ship, either by mistake or because it was in the way of her flight from the battle!

At last, the Persian armada, or what remained of it, extricated itself from the narrow waters. The Greeks regrouped, for a Persian counter attack would still leave them heavily outnumbered; but there was no heart in the Persian sailors. The sea-tossed mariners had emulated the hoplites at Marathon, though this time with the aid of the Peloponnesians and even former enemies, like the Aeginetans, who in fact had held the most exposed position on the right of the Greek line. Withdrawal of the remnant of the Persian fleet was inevitably followed by withdrawal of the army, under Xerxes and his brother-in-law, Mardonius. They had sacked Athens, before the battle at Salamis had circumscribed their future movements. On the Acropolis the valiant Greek defenders had died, after withstanding a siege, until some Persian infantry had clambered up the precipitous sides. There too the temples had been burnt with a fire profanely unworthy of Zoroaster. Sardis had been avenged in full.

News of Xerxes' retreat incited Themistocles to sail to the Hellespont and destroy the bridge there, but more cautious counsel prevailed. Whereupon the wily Athenian sent a message to the Great King, telling him that this tactical failure to prevent the Persian retreat arose from his, Themistocles', persuading the Greeks from further action. Much later, this message was used to attack Themistocles when he finally went into exile under the protection of the Persian king, though it is more likely that if was not double-dealing, but a subtle means of speeding Xerxes on his way in the belief that the bridge was about to be destroyed. For Xerxes was fully aware of Themistocles' earlier deception at Salamis and was likely to disbelieve the message. Themistocles, like all Greeks of any education, was brought up on Homer. As a man drawn to the sea, he must have thoroughly imbibed the adventures of Odysseus. In warfare his cunning lies were almost worthy of the hero who had deceived Polyphemus the Cyclops with the name of Nobody. In any case, Xerxes left Mardonius in command of the bulk of the army to winter in Thessaly, and himself returned to Sardis with the rest. A splendid procession entered the avenged city, but missing from it was the sacred-chariot of Ahura-Mazda, the supreme god of Persia. It had been lost in Greece.

Yet the Persian army had not been defeated. Only command of the sea had passed to the Greeks. Xerxes could not believe that his vast empire could yield ground to such a pygmy nation, some of which had come over to him without fighting. He prepared for a campaign the following year. Meanwhile, the temper of the Persians was shown when they massacred the whole population of Olynthus in Chalcidia in a marsh near the town, after suspecting it of disloyalty. Mardonius' position was perhaps stronger for having shed many of the low quality troops, who had returned with their king to Persia. His army numbered about 300,000 and had the use of the splendid Thessalian cavalry and contingents from the other *medizing* states, notably Boeotia. When the campaign began in the summer of 479 BC, the position of the Athenians looked little better than when the Persian army had marched south from Thermopylae a year earlier. Everything turned upon Greek unity. Was that sense of a common culture, of the religion of Apollo of Delphi, of the *arete* of the contestants at Olympia, still strong enough to unite the Peloponnesians and those Greeks north of the Isthmus who were too proud to offer earth and water to the barbarian? The matter was by no means certain.

Alexander of Macedon brought to Athens a Persian offer of terms, not ungenerous in the circumstances. The noble reply of Aristides, made when Sparta had not yet shown any inclination to march north beyond the fortified Isthmus, was that Athens would never submit to Persia "so long as the sun keeps his present course in the sky."[8]

To the Spartan envoys the Athenians said this: "There is not so much gold in the world nor land so fair that we would take it for pay to join the common enemy and bring Greece into subjection. There are many compelling reasons against our doing so, even if we wished: the first and greatest is the burning of the temples and images of our gods - now ashes and rubble. It is our bounden duty to avenge this desecration with all our might - not to clasp the hand that wrought it. Again there is the Greek nation - the community of blood and language, temples and ritual; our common way of life; if Athens were to betray all this, it would not be well done. We would have you know, therefore, that if you did not know it already that so long as a single Athenian remains alive we will make no peace with Xerxes."[9]

Envoys were then sent from Athens, Plataea and Megara to demand that the Spartans march. Refusal might lead to an Athenian change of heart and an alliance with Persia; so said the envoys, though they did not mean it. Sparta realised that the Persian fleet, reinforced by the Athenian, would render the fortifications at the Isthmus utterly useless. Still she hesitated to send her infantry forward, probably because the

Isthmus defence had to be completed before fighting began. When, at last, the message was handed by the ephors to the envoys, 5000 Spartan infantry were already a day's march on the road to Attica. With them were 5000 *perioeci*, each with an attendant helot. Never before or since had such a Spartan force left the Peloponnese. The die was cast, and the unity of "the Greeks" was not shattered.

In charge of 8,000 Athenian hoplites and 600 ever loyal Plataeans was Aristides. At the Isthmus, all the Greek forces converged, making about 110,000 with the contingents from Corinth, Euboea and western Greece. Without contention they accepted the leadership of Pausanias, who commanded the Spartans as regent for his infant cousin, the son of Leonidas. Mardonius congratulated himself on drawing the Peloponnesians forward from the fortifications of the Isthmus. His skilful diplomacy, playing on the potential division between the states north and south of the Isthmus, had worked effectively enough, for he had little doubt that his huge army with its core of pure Persian infantry and its Thessalian cavalry could easily deal with a force well under half its size and lacking cavalry. But, unlike the Spartans, he had learnt nothing from Marathon. He had not seen at first hand the effect of superior armour, long spears and the Greek love of freedom.

Pausanias' aim was to free Thebes from Persian control and push back the Persian held territory well beyond the border with Attica. South of Thebes, the heights of Mount Cithaeron flanked the city of Plataea. The foothills would be good ground for Greek infantry and unsuitable for cavalry. At the head were the Athenians on the left wing, to the east the Spartans and Tegeans. The Persian forces began to use their mounted archers to harass the Greeks, as they reached lower ground to the north. What was worse, they captured and fouled the spring of Garaphia, which supplied the Greeks with water. After days of enduring the ordeal of missiles and shortage of water and food - for their supplies were being intercepted by the enemy also - the Greek army began an orderly retreat to some higher land, called "the Island", between two streams, just east of Plataea. Mishaps soon occurred. The Greek centre mistook the way and ended up close to the walls of Plataea, where they played very little part in the battle. The Spartans were seriously delayed by an obstinate commander, Amompharetus, who considered it unworthy of Spartans to withdraw in the face of the enemy. As the whole Spartan force hesitated, the Athenians under Aristides on the left wing also remained in position, unsure of Spartan intentions. At last, Pausanias abandoned Amompharetus and his men, and ordered a general move southwards. Yet he could not cut off all aid from so brave a man. He dallied a mile or two from the Spartan remnant, until Amompharetus, realising the futility of his position, turned to rejoin the main Spartan force. His insubordination might have wrecked the whole endeavour of "the Greeks".

The Persians under Mardonius saw the Greek forces, along the whole front, withdrawing in apparent confusion. Arrogantly, Mardonius boasted to his commanders of his own prescience of Greek inconstancy. He allowed, or perhaps could not prevent, a wild advance by the Persian host on both Spartan and Athenian wings. Hordes of barbarians rushed upon the re-united Spartans, as they adopted a defensive posture on slightly rising ground. Pausanias sent an urgent message to the Athenians a mile to his left, calling upon their love of freedom and proclaiming that this was the moment of its greatest trial. Aristides could not respond. His men were already engaged in a desperate struggle with a larger and well trained force of Boeotian *medizers*. The Spartans were to fight with only the small force of Tegeans by their side.

Mardonius had not lost his head. He sent in the cavalry first and held the infantry behind a rampart of wicker shields. Continuous harassment by missiles must eventually break the Spartan ability to remain on the defensive. Pausanias was well aware of this. Time after time he asked for omens of success to enable him to attack, but always the entrails of the victims were unfavourable. A shrine to the goddess, Hera, stood nearby. Desperately he appealed to her. Now the omens were favourable. The Spartans rose and moved forward in close order. Regardless of the immense force of the enemy, they advanced down the slope, not as swiftly as the men of Marathon, for they were trained to attack at half speed to the steady sound of flutes. Though the best troops of Mardonius took the weight of the attack, they could not withstand the pent-up martial spirit of their enemies:

"First there was a struggle at the barricade of shields; then, the barricade down, there was a bitter and protracted fight, hand to hand, close by the temple of Demeter, for the Persians would lay hold of the Spartan spears and break them; in courage and strength they were as good as their adversaries, but they were deficient in armour, untrained, and greatly inferior in skill. Sometimes singly, sometimes in groups of ten men - perhaps fewer, perhaps more - they fell upon the Spartan line and were cut down. They pressed hardest at the point where Mardonius fought in person - riding his white charger, and surrounded by his thousand Persian troops, the flower of the army. While Mardonius was alive, they continued to resist and to defend themselves, and struck down many of the Lacedaemonians; but after his death, and the destruction of his personal guard - the finest of the Persian troops - the remainder yielded to the Lacedaemonians and took to flight. The chief cause of their discomfiture was their lack of armour, fighting without it against heavily armed infantry."[10]

Aristides' men had won their battle on the left wing. Their approach to join the Spartans was welcomed, for the Athenians were much more skilful at the siege operations that were now required. A huge multitude of terrified Persian troops were crammed into the stockaded camp. Rapidly the Athenians broke in; then followed unremitting slaughter. Pausanias spared none. He knew of the Persian treatment of Olynthus and other Greek peoples, and he had reason to fear a renewed Persian onslaught, which would be enhanced by survivors of this battle.

News of the great victory reached the confederate fleet in the Aegean. At Samos the Persian fleet lay uneasily at anchor, for the islanders were close to revolt under their pro-Persian tyrant. Leotychidas, the Spartan admiral, sought to give battle, but the Persians crossed to the mainland, sent the Phoenician ships away and beached the rest. Then they joined forces with the Persian host, which was camped near Cape Mycale. Leotychidas landed his men and swiftly attacked the camp. Ionian Greeks, realising that the time was ripe to strike for their freedom, deserted the Persian army *en masse*. The confederate forces destroyed the camp with sword and fire. Thus Greek mastery by sea and land brought to the whole Ionian coast and islands a freedom from Asiatic dominion, for which the Ionians had first fought in vain over twenty years earlier.

Before the decisive battle had been fought at Plataea every confederate Greek had taken an oath under the shadow of Mount Cithaeron: "I shall fight to the death; I shall put freedom before life; I shall not desert the officers - alive or dead; I shall carry out commands; and I shall bury my comrades-in-arms where they fall and leave none unburied."[11] The dead were in fact buried within the territory of Plataea, a small polis which had won the gratitude of all Greece for its part at Marathon alongside Athens. The anniversary of the battle was for centuries to be honoured with a religious ceremony at Plataea, with representatives from all "the Greeks". Games would be held in honour of liberation. The Plataeans were dedicated to Zeus as an inviolable and sacred people; their chief magistrates ended the annual sacrifice on behalf of the Greek dead with the words "I drink to the men who died for the freedom of the Greeks."[12]

The Delphic oracle had foretold a victory on the soil of Attica. When it became clear that the battle would be fought near the northern slopes of Cithaeron, the Plataeans had offered to move the boundary stones northwards to leave the battlefield within the border of Attica. They had willingly given land from their small polis in the greater interest of all Greece. It was a sacrifice which few peoples in history have been ready to make. To offer both men and land in the cause of freedom were acts of rare nobility.

## References:

1. Herodotus, *The Histories*, trans. A. de Selincourt, Penguin, London, 1972, Book VII, p. 477.

2. Herodotus, *The Histories*, Book VII, pp. 488-9.

3. Herodotus, *The Histories*, Book VII, p. 514.

4. Herodotus, *The Histories*, Book VII, p. 519.

5. Herodotus, *The Histories*, Book VII, p. 519.

6. Herodotus, *The Histories*, Book VII, p. 517.

7. Herodotus, *The Histories*, Book VII, p. 228. trans. D. L. S. Hodgkinson, pers. comm.

8. Herodotus, *The Histories*, Book VIII, p. 574.

9. Herodotus, *The Histories*, Book VIII, pp. 574-5.

10. Herodotus, *The Histories*, Book IX, p. 602.

11. N. G. L. Hammond, *A History of Greece to 322 BC*, O.U.P., Oxford, 1977, p. 250.

12. Hammond, *A History of Greece*, p. 250.

## Chapter 16

# Alliance into Empire

### *The Delian League*

THE PERSIANS DID NOT LIGHTLY give up their possession of the northern Aegean and Ionian coast after their defeats at Plataea and Mycale. Persistence was needed to drive them out. One local Persian commander even immolated himself rather than retreat from or surrender the city he guarded. The Spartan, Pausanias, remained in command of the Greek forces for a while, but his character became increasingly unstable. To non-Spartiates he behaved with intolerable arrogance. Soldiers were flogged and even forced to stand all day with iron anchors on their shoulders. Even Sparta was horrified when he began to act and even to dress like an eastern autocrat. He was recalled by the ephors, whilst the Greek soldiers and sailors looked more and more to the two Athenian aristocrats, Aristides and Cimon, for leadership. On the evidence of a slave, Pausanias was proved to have connived with

*Treasury of Athenians, Delphi*

the Great King. He fled for sanctuary to the temple of Athena of the Brazen House in Sparta, where he was walled in - his own mother helped in the work, it was said - and starved to death.

Sparta was unable to force a replacement general upon the confederate forces. The debt to Athens was re-inforced by the unquestioned justice of Aristides and the charm and generosity of Cimon, making Athenian leadership of the alliance irresistible. Sparta did not show a readiness to commune with other Greeks, but in Attica the concept of Greek unity, centred upon the city of Athena, was appealing to those who had seen their polis emerge triumphant from the trials of the Persian wars. They accepted readily the offer of leadership; a new organisation replaced "the Greeks", a league of all those Greek states outside the Peloponnese who were still united by fear and anger towards Persia. Sparta remained at the head of its Peloponnesian League of the main states south of the Isthmus of Corinth, except Argos, which still smarted from an overwhelming defeat by Cleomenes of Sparta in 494 BC. As the poleis along the Aegean shore were released from Persian control by the continued efforts of the Athenian-led alliance, they one by one joined the new league.

Aristides was the architect. His reputation for justice made him widely acceptable as arbitrator of the conditions on which states joined the league. Tribute in ships or money was an essential feature, if military power were to be effective. How was it to be fairly assessed? On the basis of economic resources and, in the case of the Ionian coast, of the existing tribute list drawn up with surprising equity by Darius after the Ionian revolt, Aristides calculated what each state should pay. The total came to 460 talents a year, rather less than the cost of the Parthenon, built a generation later, and enough to equip a large navy. Military service was expected, also, from all member states. Some states paid tribute in money, others in ships but, as time passed, this balance moved heavily towards tribute in money. On the little island of Delos, sacred to Apollo, was housed the treasury of the league, under the control of officials called Hellenotimiae, significantly all Athenian. To mark the formation of this Delian League, lumps of iron were flung into the sea as each new member ceremoniously joined, symbolising either the permanence of the union, which would only be dissolved when the iron rose to the surface, or, as later cynics put it, the fate of those who dared to challenge its authority.

Meanwhile, Athens had taken a further step to mark her new role as leader. On the ardent advice of Themistocles (see ch.15), she set about the construction of fortified walls around both the ancient city and the port of Piraeus. Even Aristides had come to acknowledge the significance of a strong outlet to the sea for war and commerce. Now Piraeus was to be developed with wharves and equipment worthy of a great maritime power and to be protected by its own walls. The Spartans objected on the specious grounds that a fortified city north of the Isthmus would be a base for future Persian incursions once it had fallen. Themistocles offered to negotiate. Whilst he delayed in Sparta, the citizens of Athens set to work. Suspicion grew in Sparta, so Themistocles suggested that observers were sent to Athens, at the same time warning the Athenians to hold the Spartan observers as hostages. When the wall was substantially finished, he admitted the fact in Sparta.

In 472 BC Athens committed an act of outright imperialism. The city of Carystus on Euboea had not joined the Delian League. Remembering the place of Euboea, with its long flank guarding the channel in front of Attica in the struggle with the Persian fleet at Artemisium, the Athenian leaders could not tolerate such an omission. Carystus was reduced by force and compelled to join the League. No longer could it claim to be a league of voluntary co-operation to meet a common danger. Though the member states all had one vote in the council, which met at Delos, Athens, from the beginning, controlled the votes of the numerous small states, leaving the larger ones, like Chios, Lesbos or Samos, to choose between compliance or resistance by force. The same year saw the ostracism of Themistocles, who was accused of taking bribes.

The case of Carystus was followed by that of Naxos, which was forced to remain in the League after declaring its secession. No peace treaty had been made with Persia. Athens had good reason to claim that the integrity of the League should not be jeopardised. Her treatment of the Naxians, however, cast her motives in doubt, for they were deprived of autonomy and made subjects of Athens. The confederation was undergoing a metamorphosis into empire. Nevertheless, a major victory against the Persians soon justified its existence as a military organisation under Athenian leadership. At the mouth of the Eurymedon river in Pamphylia, Cimon won a great double victory on sea and land. His fleet destroyed 2000 Phoenician ships and, when the enemy troops landed, his hoplites routed them. Persian humiliation was complete. With the spoil of battle, Cimon financed the construction of a huge wall on the south side of the Acropolis in Athens.

The need for a defensive league was no longer so acute. The northern island of Thasos decided in 465 BC to test Athens' will to maintain her hegemony. Once again the answer was the same. Thasos was besieged; Athens was interested in the rich timber-bearing land of the nearby Thracian shore - although her attempt to found a colony there was frustrated by the Thracians - and her commercial ambitions brooked no rival near the entrance to the Euxine. Thasos took the significant step of appealing for help from Sparta. Fortuitously for Athens, the Spartans just at that time became deeply involved in a major domestic problem. An earthquake wrecked their city; in the ensuing chaos the Messenian helots and some *perioeci* revolted, fleeing to Mount Ithome, whose slopes afforded them hope of a long defence. Sparta could send no help to Thasos. Instead, they asked help in their turn from Athens, aware that in siege operations - as at Plataea - the Athenians were their superiors. A furious debate took place in the Athenian Assembly. For the first time, the growing rift between pro-Spartan and democratic elements broke out into acrimonious argument. The democratic leaders, Ephialtes and Pericles, demanded that no help be given. Cimon supported the old dual leadership of the Hellenes. He was voted 4000 hoplites to join the Spartans. Meanwhile, the Athenian navy jealously patrolled the waters around Thasos.

The Spartans were disappointed by the Athenian assistance. Helot resistance was stiffened by desperation. Lack of immediate success led the Spartans to question the motives even of Cimon. They told the Athenian army that they were no longer needed. It was a rank insult, never to be forgotten by men whose general was the son of Miltiades. The humiliating return from Mount Ithome marked a change in Athenian perception of Greek nationality. The case of the democrats against Sparta had been won by default. Athens would carry the standard of Greece alone, at the head of her loyal subject allies, not in tandem with the Peloponnesian League, whatever the past glory of their co-operation.

The following year, 461 BC, Cimon was ostracised. His opponents, Ephialtes and Pericles, had already carried through democratic reforms during his absence at Mount Ithome. The venerable Council of Aeropagus, made up of past archons and therefore above the hazards of election and lot, was deprived of all powers, save those of trying cases of homicide, caring for the sacred olive trees of Athena and helping in supervising the property of the Eleusinian deities. Previously the Areopagus had the vital duty of reviewing the legality of acts of the Assembly and of the Council of Five Hundred, and could also inquire into the morality of individuals. In future, Athens would rely on the self-regulating power of the Assembly and the moral force of public opinion, both of which were dangerously dependent upon the high-mindedness of individual citizens.

Then Thasos surrendered and, possibly much later, so did the helots and *perioeci* on Mount Ithome. Through resentment, and perhaps generosity, the Athenians offered a new home outside the Peloponnese to the survivors of the latter revolt. The Spartans allowed them to settle at Naupactus on the north coast of the Gulf of Corinth, where they would defend Athenian maritime interests near its western entrance. Thasos was more harshly dealt with. Her walls were razed, her fleet confiscated, her mines ceded to Athens, and her status reduced to that of a subject state. Not long before, Aristides the Just had died.

With the virtual elimination of the Areopagus from political and legal authority, democracy had taken a giant step forward. Aristides, Cimon and the rest of the older generation of leaders who accepted Cleisthenes' reforms, but saw them as *isonomia*, or equality under the law, rather than as a springboard for direct democracy, were losing their preponderance in Athens. When Aeschylus' play "The Seven against Thebes" was first performed, at the lines:

> "His aim is not to seem just, but to be so.
>
> His mind is a deep-ploughed field, from which he reaps
>
> A harvest of wise counsel. . ."[1]

the whole audience turned to look at Aristides. He was a great admirer of Lycurgus and followed his teaching in remaining poor throughout his public life, despite greater opportunities for receiving bribes than perhaps anyone else, as assessor of the tribute for the Delian League. When he was elected to supervise the public accounts of Athens, his enemies, who found they could no longer embezzle money, had him prosecuted for presenting the accounts falsely. His friends supported him enough to avoid any fine; indeed they had him re-elected. For some while he appeared to turn a blind eye to the misappropriation of funds by men taking bribes and suchlike, but when the time came for his re-election, this time with enthusiastic canvassing by those who had benefited illegally, he rose to speak in the Assembly:

> "When I carried out my duties well and faithfully, I was disgraced. But now that I am throwing away most of your money to thieves, everybody thinks I am an admirable citizen. So far as I am concerned, I am more ashamed of the honour you are paying me now than I was of my conviction, and I am sorry for you, because you evidently find it more praiseworthy to pander to a set of rogues than to stand guard over the wealth of the state."[2]

After his ostracism, when he had written his own name on the ostrakon on behalf of an illiterate citizen, he uttered a prayer as he left the city, asking that no crisis might befall the Athenians which would force them to remember his name. Such magnanimity had been repeated when he had returned to fight against the Persians - pardoned by the citizens - for he gave all his support to Themistocles, his political enemy, recognising in him the man who knew how to save the polis. Perhaps, also, he was influenced by having fought alongside Themistocles, in the centre of the Athenian line at Marathon, where the brunt of the Persian attack was borne. At Plataea, it was Aristides who helped to select the place where the Athenian and Plataean hoplites were stationed on the slopes of Mount Cithaeron, near an ancient temple dedicated to the Eleusianian goddesses, Demeter and Kore, indicating perhaps that Aristides had some connection with the Eleusianian mysteries which he valued in a moment of great trial. Alone amongst Athenian statesmen, Aristides received the unqualified praise of Plato, that most austere judge of character:

"Such good and true men, there have been, and will be again, at Athens and in otherstates, who have fulfilled their trust righteously; and there is one who is quite famous over all Hellas, Aristides, the son of Lysimachus."[3]

When Aristides' grand-daughter, Myrto, was destitute, she was cared for by Socrates himself, which suggests that the tradition of philosophy had not passed Aristides by.

Cimon had been a protege of Aristides, but lacked his foresight. As time passed and the Persian threat receded, the allies became lax about the need to maintain a system of defence. Rather than send ships and troops to the joint forces of the League, they were prepared to commute these for money tribute, thus relieving themselves of the hardships and discipline of military life. Athenian *strategoi* or generals, were usually severe on allies who lapsed in this way, but, according to Plutarch, Cimon adopted a different attitude. He treated the allies very leniently in this respect, not demanding ships or services, but being content with regular payments, or sometimes unmanned ships. As a result, the allies gave up military training and any sense of public duty to the Greeks as a whole, whilst the Athenians were trained even more than before at sea and on land and in the spirit of service to their own polis as mistress of the allied states. The natural result was the evolution of an imperial system, in which the ruling and ruled replaced the original relationship of a confederation of allies.

Plutarch, however, greatly praised Cimon as a general, and saw the mid-century as a turning-point in Athenian history in another respect:

"After his death no Greek general was to win another brilliant success against the barbarians. Instead, a succession of demagogues and warmongers arose, who proceeded to turn the Greek states against one another and nobody could be found to separate or reconcile them before they met in the headlong collision of war."[4]

In fact, some steps on the road to civil war were taken before Cimon's death, but after his ostracism. In 461 BC, Athens made an alliance with Argos, the sworn enemy of Sparta, and in 460 BC Megara joined this alliance, which immediately threw Corinth into a state of hostility towards Athens. Megara lay on the Isthmus between her larger neighbours of Athens and Corinth, both of whom disliked her interference with their trade. Alliance with Athens extended the growing competitive force of

Athens, from her brilliant new red-figure pottery, for example, right up to Corinth's own borders. Long walls were built connecting Megara with its eastern port of Misaea. Corinth, a great commercial city at a superb site for trade, now found itself facing an Athenian sea empire, *thassalocracy*, to the east in the Aegean, to the Athenian controlled port of Naupactus at the head of the Gulf of Corinth and to a fortified border to the north insulating both Megara and Athens from attack. Henceforth, Corinth would look southwards for support.

The year 459 BC was perhaps the zenith of Athenian military prowess. A stone has survived recording the names of members of one Athenian tribe, who died fighting in that year.

"Of the Erechtheid tribe. These are they who died in the war, in Cyprus, in Egypt, in Phoenicia, at Halieis, in Aegina, at Megara, in the same year:"[5]

177 names follow.

Sparta could not stand by indefinitely, watching the steady growth of Athenian power. In 457 BC, just as Athens' own long walls were completed, making her effectively an island supplied by an overseas empire, the Spartans marched north, crossed the Gulf of Corinth by ship and intervened in a local war on behalf of their ancient homeland of Doria, against the Phocians. But, despite a victory at Tanagra, the red-cloaked Spartan hoplites had to wend their way uneasily though the passes of the Isthmus to return home. They had not stopped Athenian expansion. For ten years Athens was to control a land empire in central Greece, in addition to her thassalocracy.

*Attic black figure amphora*

*(Achilles & Penthesilea)*

*Attic red figure amphora*

*(Thetis & Achilles)*

In 454 BC an Athenian force in Egypt was almost wiped out, despite naval re-inforcements, by a Persian army. The Athenian Assembly responded by a signal mark of empire: they voted to move the treasury of the League from Delos to Athens, on the grounds that the Persian fleet now threatened the sacred island. The *Hellenotimiae* had always been Athenian, and the tribute money in Delos, which had accumulated considerably, was indisputably under Athenian control, but now the face of imperialism could not be concealed.

Democracy, also, was growing apace. After the attack on the powers of the Areopagus, Ephialtes had been secretly murdered, almost certainly by conservative extremists. Pericles emerged clearly as the leader of the democrats. Faced by the need for a wider distribution of offices to replace the work of the Areopagus, he had already persuaded the Assembly to vote for the payment of judges in the *heliaea*, or law courts. In 457 BC he went further and made the archonship open to the *zeugitae* class, which had provided many of the hoplites who fought bravely at Tanagra. By 451 BC Pericles even introduced pay for the *dikastae*, or jurymen; a sweeping move, since the jury list numbered 6,000 in order to provide for the very large juries, often several hundred, and for the extra cases brought to Athens by the imperial system. Together with this measure, pay was introduced for the Boule of 500, the archons and other magistrates. Most Athenian citizens could by then expect to occupy several paid offices at various times in their adult life, a feature which Aristotle later regarded as the principal criterion for judging a state to be democratic.

Both Athens and the Peloponnesian League were becoming war-weary by the end of the decade of the 450s. In 451 BC they negotiated a five year truce. Two years later, peace was at last declared between Greece and Persia, after a struggle lasting over forty years. Greeks and Persians mutually agreed to refrain from attacking each other's coasts. The Ionian coast was acknowledged to be Greek, for at the River Eurymedon Persian claims to western Asia Minor had been shattered. With peace on all fronts, what choice would Athens make about the future of her own citizens and empire?

One choice had already been made. In 451 BC the definition of Athenian citizenship was narrowed to make only children of two citizens hold such a title themselves. Foreign residents, or *metics*, continued however to be treated generously; though without political rights, they were protected by the law and had full economic freedom. Solon's initiative in encouraging foreign traders and craftsmen was still bearing fruit for the Athenian economy, especially now that the Piraeus was a prosperous port, serving the whole region of Greek penetration, from the northern shores of the Euxine to the western colonies in Gaul and North Africa. A choice had already been made on the question of empire also, for in 450 BC groups of settlers went out from Athens to Euboea, Naxos and Andros to create cleruchies where the settlers remained citizens of Athens with full political rights and duties. In the fourth century, when fears arose of a renewal of Athenian imperialism, this system of cleruchies was especially disliked. Cleruchs were literally "holders of plots of land". States, like Naxos, that had revolted saw their land parcelled out amongst citizens from the conquering mother city.

The real decision on empire probably came in 449 BC, when Athens, under Pericles' guidance, issued an invitation to all the Greek States, except only those of

Magna Graecia, to meet for a Panhellenic Congress to discuss the rebuilding of the temples destroyed by the barbarians - which Athens earlier had sworn would be left as ruins to mark the sacrilege - the votive offerings to the gods, and the clearing of the seas from the scourge of piracy. It was an offering of Athenian moral hegemony, which Sparta in its pride, could not accept. The Congress did not meet. Pericles was too skilful a politician not to realise that the offer alone gave Athens its opportunity to assert its leadership. Yet it was not an easy policy. Peace with the Peloponnesians made it harder for Athenian leaders to demand high expenditure on ships, fortifications and soldiers. Peace with Persia made the Delian League look like, at best, an anachronism, at worst, an engine for imperialist ambition. Pericles, in fact, had other and greater ideas. Athenian leadership was to be moral and cultural. Upon the foundation of the Delian League would be built an empire of the human mind and spirit such as no Greek, even the noble forefathers of Athens herself, had ever witnessed.

In 447 BC work began on the Parthenon. Pericles, with the aid of a circle of intellectuals who were his close associates - Phidias, Ictinus and others - drew up a great building programme, especially for the Acropolis. A huge new entrance would adorn the western end, the paintings of Polygnotus would be housed in a new gallery, an Odeon built with columns resembling ships' masts would rise below the south wall of Cimon, new gymnasia would serve the people; above all, the temple to Athena - the Parthenon - and a chryselephantine statue of the goddess would show the world that the Athenians revered the divine forces which had saved them from destruction at the hands of the barbarians. How would the cost of this magnificent conception be met? The funds of the Delian League, said Pericles, had been paid in return for the security which Athens had so ably provided. Whilst her navy and soldiers ensured that security was unbreakable, then the mother city had every right to use the surplus funds to beautify herself in honour of her gods. It was a powerful argument, but it did not convince everyone, even within the city. The conservative opposition complained bitterly:

"The Greeks must be outraged. They must consider this an act of bare-faced tyranny, when they see that with their own contributions, extorted from them by force for the war against the Persians we are gilding and beautifying our city, as if it were some vain woman decking herself out with costly stones and statues and temples worth millions of money."[6]

For the year 449 BC no tribute list had been inscribed on the great pillar. Tribute may not have been paid. For the following year, several states paid reduced amounts or defaulted, but Athens would not tolerate insubordination; the system of collection was tightened up, with identifiable seals being used for every contribution and independent statements sent on the consignment of money. By 447 BC all arrears had been collected.

The die was cast. The finest marble was dragged in from Mount Pentelicus. The architects sent back any blocks with the trace of a fault. The empire on the sea grew apace: cleruchs were sent to the Chersonese, to Lemnos, to Imbros; but clouds were gathering. To save some captured hoplites, the Athenian Assembly voted to withdraw altogether from Boeotia. The land empire had lasted merely a decade.

*Temple of Aphaia, Aegina*

*Temple of Aphaia, Aegina*

Then Euboea revolted. Strategic necessity could not allow a withdrawal here, so Pericles himself led a force to subdue the islanders. Megara was in revolt also. Pericles returned to face the Megarans, now supported by an expedition from none other than King Pleistoanax of Sparta. The moment of peril was acute for Pericles and for the whole structure that Athens had erected over thirty years. An Athenian army under Andocides only escaped annihilation in the Megarid by marching through narrow passes above the shores of the Corinthian Gulf, whilst the Spartans blocked the main road to the east. Suddenly the crisis dissolved. King Pleistoanax, with the habitual lack of Spartan resolve beyond the Peloponnese, abruptly withdrew. Rumour had it that Pericles had bribed him. Euboea was quickly reduced when Pericles returned there.

Lessons had been learnt on all sides by the sharpness of the crisis. A thirty years peace was concluded in 446 BC to replace the five year truce. Athenian imperialism drew in its claws, for Megara regained its independence, together with its ports of Nisaea and Pagae; Achae and Troezen were evacuated and both sides agreed to make no alliances with each others' existing allies. Only neutral states might be enlisted in the league of their choice. Even the autonomy of Aegina, "the eyesore of the Piraeus," was guaranteed, though it remained a payer of tribute. Probably the loss of the Megarid, with its long walls guarding against invasion from the Peloponnese, was the most serious loss for Athens; a fact which goes some way to explain Pericles' apparently unreasonable insistence upon the harsh Megaran decree fourteen years later, which brought the great civil war one step nearer.

For Athens, in particular, the period of peace that followed the thirty years treaty was immensely fruitful. The great building programme proceeded apace and the arts flourished, including the theatre, which developed a new competition for comic drama to accompany the existing one for tragedy. One event, however, marred these halcyon days of Athenian culture. In 440 BC the powerful island state of Samos, one of the three, with Lesbos and Chios, which still possessed its own fleet, revolted over the question of whether it, or Miletus on the mainland, should control the city of Priene. Pericles himself took command of the fleet of 44 ships, but having overthrown the aristocrats in Samos, he heard on his return that the exiles had obtained the aid of the Persian Satrap in Sardis and had expelled the new democratic government. Pericles returned to defeat the Samian navy and to besiege the recalcitrant islanders. It took nine months before the overwhelming power of the Athenian navy could break the Samian will to resist. The proud island of Polycrates and Pythagoras was reduced to starvation before it acknowledged Athenian hegemony. The Samians were not utterly humiliated, for they were not compelled to pay tribute, but they surrendered their ships, pulled down their walls and paid a huge war indemnity of 1500 talents. Henceforth they were subjects of Athens.

Soon after, Pericles underlined Athenian interest in the northern Aegean by leading a naval expedition into the Euxine. Corn supply was becoming a matter of prime concern as the city of Athens and the Piraeus grew with the increase in craftsmen, both citizen and metic, commercial interests and administration. The route for corn from the Euxine shores was becoming a life-line, and there were men, certainly in Corinth and probably in Sparta, who would be only too ready to cut it.

Athenian imperialism and Athenian democracy were together leading inexorably to war with Sparta and her allies. As the oligarchic character of the state gave way slowly to the democratic, so a conflict with the decadent timocracy of Sparta became imminent. Once the Delian League, formed initially for the defence of Greek freedom against the threat of Persian imperialism, began to change into an Athenian empire such a conflict became inevitable, for Sparta saw that, unchecked, Athenian power would sooner or later stifle the independence of all who refused her domination. Democracy and empire were linked: the taxation of allies for mutual defence financed the offices held by the democratic citizens, and appeals to the Assembly played upon the acquisitive instincts of the people.

The fifth century BC in Greece was a period of turbulence; old ways of life were giving way to new. The magnificent martial zeal of Lycurgan Sparta, though its dwindling power would concentrate to win the final cataclysmic civil war of the Greek peoples, was to be eclipsed by the generative forces in Athenian culture. These could not prevent Athenian military disaster, but they could create a new culture of the Hellenes to woo the later Roman masters of Greece. Great men, including the heroes of the wars against the barbarians, and statesmen, artists and thinkers, were to be cast aside, disgraced, killed, in the severe evolution of events, but they found their chance of fulfilment amid such worldly storms.

### References:

1. See Plutarch, 'Life of Aristides', trans. I. Scott-Kilvert, (Seven Against Thebes, 592f.) in *The Rise and Fall of Athens*, Penguin, London, 1976, p. 112.

2. Plutarch, 'Life of Aristides', trans. Scott-Kilvert, p. 113.

3. Plato, *Georgias*, trans. Jowett, Random House, New York, 1937, 52b.

4. Plutarch, 'Life of Cimon', trans. Scott-Kilvert, p. 163.

5. J. B. Bury and Russell Meiggs, *A History of Greece*, MacMillan, London, 1979, p. 220.

6. Plutarch, 'Life of Pericles', trans. Scott-Kilvert, p. 177.

## Chapter 17

# The Classical Moment

## *Athenian Culture*

IN THE CONSTRUCTION OF their fifth century empire the Athenians were accused of *polypragmosyne* - an excessive curiosity and meddlesome busyness. Certainly they showed remarkable energy and ambition, which led them into all kinds of enterprises in government, colonisation and war, but nevertheless they retained a measure of the wisdom they inherited from the great men of the past. In the midst of action there remained a glimmer of peace. Though Greece learnt much from Egypt, Athens' unique contribution lay in this unity of energetic expression and detachment of Spirit - in art, politics, literature and warfare. With this philosophy they offered themselves totally in battle; they devoted mind and limb to the finest art; they strove unremittingly in the debates of the Assembly or the law courts. Measured by the yard stick of the Spirit, the world was not real, and the part to be played could be entered as fully and dispassionately as in a theatre.

*Parthenon, Athens*

"Man's life is a day. What is he?

What is he not? A shadow in a dream

Is man: but when God sheds a brightness,

Shining life is on earth

And life is sweet as honey."[1]

The art of the first few decades after the battle of Marathon has been described as the serene style. Even before 490 BC, the sculptors who worked on the Temple of Aphaia at Aegina produced figures with a truly majestic self-control and nobility. An archer kneels on one knee to draw his bow with perfect balance, with a back and braced arm that Ares himself could not have surpassed in firmness. A dying warrior falls, the round shield still attached to his wrist by a thong, with a look of sublime disregard for pain and death. Outwardly human, inwardly divine, these figures represent a true appreciation of the nature of Man.

In Athens, two sculptors in particular, Myron and Polycleitus, continued in the severe style with such works as the *Discus-thrower* and the *Spear-bearer*, both in bronze, which was considered the finest material for large-scale sculptures. Myron captures the moment when the discus-thrower is poised to throw, when the arc of the extended arms crosses the arc of the bending torso, making a perfectly balanced form in one plane. Despite the force about to be uncoiled, the thrower's face has the calm attention of an athlete whose rhythmic power arises from stillness. Polycleitus called his spear-bearer a "canon", and wrote a book to explain the proportions of this archetypal man, which was in fact taken as a model by many later sculptors. Though walking forward, with the long spear over his left shoulder, the figure is completely at rest, the weight on the right foot and the left shoulder slightly raised to balance the higher right hip. By contrast the bronze figure, probably of Zeus throwing a thunderbolt, found in the sea off Cape Artemisium, exhibits dynamic action in the moment of potential before the arm is swung forward. Man is the measure of all things, even though it is the king of the gods who is portrayed. The sculptor surely does not intend to represent a god as a man, so much as Man divine.

Another bronze figure, not Athenian, the "charioteer of Delphi", though engaged in less vigorous action, presents a moment of heightened tension, for he is standing controlling the four horses of his chariot in a race in the stadium at Delphi. The eyes, painted realistically, focus intently on the track ahead of the horses, and the long chiton falls in deep folds. The charioteer suggests an image used later by Plato in *Phaedrus*, where he likens the human soul to a chariot drawn by two horses, one obedient, one unruly. Only when the charioteer, or reason, eventually gains control of the unruly steed does the soul find its true way.

By the middle of the century the severe style was evolving into a form, especially in relief work, made famous by Phidias, the friend of Pericles. When the decision was taken to build a new temple of Athena on the Acropolis after peace was made with Persia in 449 BC, Pericles commissioned, not Myron nor Polycleitus, but Phidias to take charge of the whole sculpture programme on the temple. Phidias himself created the colossal statue of Athena within the cella, on the lines of his huge statue of Zeus at Olympia already completed. On the frieze around the cella, and therefore within the peristyle, the Panathenaic procession, which presented a sacred peplos, or woollen garment, to Athena, is portrayed in relief. The white marble figures would have stood out originally against a bright red background, and details like hair, swords and reins of horses, were picked out in bronze, or even gold. Yet what distinguishes the work most is the contrast between the magnificent moving panorama along the ends and sides of the cella and the dispassionate expressions of the human participants. The riders, especially, whose mounts raise their forelegs with the fierce spirit of horses forced to advance flank to flank, maintain a cool detachment.

Nowhere in the Greek world had artists so boldly portrayed men on temples, though the gods are portrayed also at the end of the frieze, sitting in amiable expectation of the honour to be paid to Athena, and the pediments and metopes show, not only gods, but also heroes, Amazons, Lapiths and centaurs. Greeks from outside Attica were often critical. No doubt the Peloponnesians, and disgruntled allies of Athens, called it hubris and decried the implication that Athenians were deified. Yet the deeper meaning was that men are, in truth, divine.

*Workshop of Phidias, Olympia*

Almost nothing has survived of ancient Greek painting, except small-scale work on pottery. After Marathon the works of Polygnotus were very highly regarded. He was said to have mastered the art of expressing the emotions of his subjects, like Socrates' description of the greatest sculpture as representing the "workings of the soul". Certainly painting on pottery, from as early as the archaic period, showed a fluidity of line and simplicity of form through which the figures in action are full of emotional power. Usually they are heroes and gods. Telling incidents from the great stories from Homer, or often of Hercules and the Olympian Pantheon, capture a heightened moment: the judgement of Paris, Achilles slaying the Amazon queen, Penthesilea at Troy, the young Hercules dawdling reluctantly to school, or, in his maturity, wrestling with the Nemean lion, Aphrodite riding a goose, Dionysus in a ship surrounded by dolphins. The immediacy and emotional directness brings the viewer into the present moment. The place of such pottery in houses and temples, at weddings and funerals, at parties and symposia awoke individuals and community alike from the dream of daily life. For Greek pottery was never purely monumental. Wine cups, libation bowls, storage jars, wedding gifts and funerary vessels had a highly practical use in a social context, even if the very best of them were kept as unique objects of beauty.

About 520 BC Athenian red figure pottery appeared, gradually replacing the black figure of the archaic period. For a while, both kinds of figuring were used together on some pots. Black figures were painted onto the red clay surface and details of faces and costume, for example, could be shown by incising on the black to make red lines show through. When red figures were used by painting the surrounds in black, details could be more accurately added by painting them on in black with a fine brush. This was perhaps less important than the development of perspective in the same period. Classical pottery of the fifth century began to foreshorten figures, giving much greater depth to the picture, and also to place them in non-linear relationships, both developments for which Polygnotus may well have been responsible in his large-scale paintings on wooden boards or as frescoes. Perspective did not merely add to a sense of physical reality, but helped the viewer to experience the work as a unity, in which he participated. In the case of pottery, perspective had the additional advantage of harmonising with the actual contours of the pot, so that a horse's flanks, or a satyr's belly, had a natural rotundity. For a brief period in the fifth century, Athenian white pottery appeared, usually in the form of *lekythoi*, or oil-flasks. These were used at marriages and also at funerals, when they would be buried; the white ground paint could not survive much exposure. Skilful outlines and details were drawn in matt paint and washes in colour laid over the figures. A typically fine example by the so-called Achilles painter shows a Muse with a lyre seated on Mount Helicon with a carefully drawn nightingale at her feet.

In pottery, painting and sculpture Man was at the centre of the artist's vision, whether the subjects were historical figures, heroes or gods, for all were shown in human form. Often the governing idea was of other ages, when the divine qualities of men, attributes of a higher nature, were more evident. Historical men were not portrayed, though the recent heroes of Marathon could be generally indicated, as on the Parthenon frieze and in the Painted Stoa, but the Bronze Age heroes of Troy were identified, reminding fifth century Athenians of a nobler realm. The labours of Hercules might bring them into a world of men who measured themselves against the full forces of evil with the help of the gods; as on a metope of the Temple of Zeus at Olympia, where Athena stands gently behind Hercules, who bears the weight of the world for Atlas. Even, occasionally, there is a hint of the Golden Age, as in the perfect compassion of the face of Apollo on the pediment of the same temple, or in the rapt attention of a maenad watching a butterfly on an amphora by the Kleophrades painter.

In the *Statesman* Plato explained how the idea of the mean, or "Nothing in excess", applies to art:

"All these arts are on the watch against excess and defect,…. and the excellence of beauty of every work of art is due to this observance of measure."[2]

The Florentine architect, Alberti, was to say the same much later when he defined beauty as a state which is made worse by any addition or subtraction. The Parthenon, built on the Athenian Acropolis between 447 BC and 438 BC by Ictinus and Callicrates, with the sculptures completed under Phidias' direction in the following six years, is the perfect exemplar of this principle. From the eighth century, temples of wood and clay had been constructed on the lines of the ancient megaron, or rectangular room of the early palaces, with a growing use of wooden columns. In the sixth century, stone temples appeared and the idea of proportion gained strength, probably under the influence of Pythagorean schools, so that two distinct orders of architecture arose, the Doric in mainland Greece and Magna Graecia, and the Ionic in Ionia and the Aegean islands. Large Doric temples were built at Paestum, for example, in Southern Italy, making use of such skilful techniques as entasis, the tapering of columns towards the top to prevent the appearance of an upward spread of the column given by the eye. By 500 BC the temple of Aphaia on Aegina used columns and capitals of a refined simplicity and adorned with magnificent sculptures on the pediments and metopes.

With the Parthenon this technical and aesthetic mastery made possible a final act of creative audacity. To the essentially Doric style were added Ionic features: slimmer, taller exterior columns; a continuous frieze around the cella; and interior Ionic columns, four in the small Treasury room, and a double-tiered screen of columns around the chryselephantine statue of Athena in the cella itself. This merging of Doric and Ionic in one building was matched by the juxtaposition of styles on the whole Acropolis, and indicated both the brilliant judgement of Athenian architects and the unique position which Athens briefly occupied as the focal point of the Dorian and Ionian strains of Greek culture in the fifth century BC.

As an architectural unity the Parthenon exemplifies the idea that "those arts into which arithmetic and mensuration enter, far surpass all others".[3] The influence of Pythagorean mathematics is present in the proportions of the whole building. Many refinements help the eye, encumbered by the sensible world, to appreciate the inner harmony founded upon number. The stylobate, or base, is very slightly arched to prevent any sense of hollowness; the columns have a gentle entasis and lean slightly inwards; the space between columns becomes less towards the four corners, and the corner columns are slightly thicker. Thus the architect has removed the need for any correction by the mind of what the eye sees. Every measurement is based upon a module, which for the Parthenon is the radius of a column measured at its base. Thus all parts of the temple and most spaces between parts are commensurable.

No expense was spared on the construction of the Parthenon. It was built of Pentelic marble throughout, including the roof tiles, even though it was the largest temple in mainland Greece, a few metres longer than the great temple of Zeus at Olympia. Phidias' chryselephantine statue of Athena inside the cella cost more than the rest of the temple, mainly owing to the huge quantity of gold and ivory involved. The main structure required a tremendous amount of highly skilled work by sculptors and masons - on fluting the Doric columns of the peristyle, for example. The eight by seventeen columns, making 46 in total, each have 20 flutes carved in situ, with the characteristic sharp edge of the Doric style. The famous relief frieze on the outside of the cella is 550 feet long, and the superb, almost free-standing, metopes of Lapiths and centaurs, Amazons, heroes, gods and giants, number no less than 92.

*Erechtheion, Acropolis, Athens*

*Pediment on Parthenon*

This apotheosis of Greek art, taken in its entirety, was more than the glorification of a city state, however great and proud it had become. The great men responsible for it - Pericles, Phidias, Ictinus, Callicrates, and others unknown - set a beacon upon the rock of the Athenian Acropolis which would shed its light upon the western world for ages to come and inspire all future architects with a standard of absolute beauty.

Yet the whole programme of work on the Acropolis included much more. The Propylaea, or monumental gateway, built at the more accessible western end between 437 and 432 BC by Mnesicles, is a brilliant combination of Doric porticoes and a central Ionic passageway. The asymetrical Erechtheum, near the north wall, is thoroughly Ionic, with tall, slender columns with scroll capitals and south porch of elegant caryatids. So too is the small temple of Athena Nike, built above the south side of the Propylaea during the later stages of the Peloponnesian War. The whole plan of the Acropolis, even had the programme been completed, had no obvious symmetry. Yet its beauty awoke the memory of a greater life beyond the concerns of the city, so that Athenians could live in the world without being entirely of it.

Below the Acropolis, on the south side, was the theatre of Dionysus, firstly a mere circular floor 60 feet in diameter forming the orchestra where the chorus danced and sang, and by the mid-fifth century containing wooden tiers of seats and a low building, or skene, as a backdrop and changing room. Here were performed the works of the greatest Greek dramatists - Aeschylus, Sophocles, Euripides and Aristophanes - during the century after the victory of Marathon. Adjacent to the theatre were temples of Nature and of Dionysus. The theatre originated with the Dionysian rites brought into Greece from Asia Minor in the sixth century; hence its origin was religious and sacred festivals remained the occasion for performances, especially the Spring festivals connected with fertility and rebirth.

For the great tragedians natural law and moral law were one and the same, for the moral law was binding on all men. From human action followed consequences as inevitable as the chain of cause and effect in the physical world of vegetation and inanimate things. Man has choice and will, but the choice once made, the will once exerted in action, the law ensures that the consequences flow inexorably. Only enlightened choice may avoid the worst consequences, and all too often enlightenment arises only from experience, when suffering has awoken the participants to their real condition.

> "Truths more than mortal, which began
>
> In the beginning, and belong
>
> To very nature - these indeed
>
> Reign in our world, are fixed and strong."[4]

The rule of Peisistratus saw the emergence of the theatre. In 534 BC, Thespis, said to be the very first actor, performed in Athens; only to be berated by the aged Solon for inducing people to believe in lies. It was Aeschylus, however, who took the crucial step of introducing a second actor, thus enabling dialogue to develop beyond the point of mere interplay between actor and chorus. In his *Oresteia*, Aeschylus portrayed the movement of natural law through the dreadful cycle of the accursed house of Atreus, ruling dynasty of Mycenae. Already tainted by the hideous crime of his father Atreus, Agamemnon allows his own daughter, Iphigenia, to be cruelly sacrificed, supposedly to placate the winds which are preventing the Greek fleet's voyage to Troy. His wife, Clytemnaestra, embittered by the loss of her daughter, takes a lover, Aegisthus, during the king's ten year absence at Troy. On Agamemnon's return he is cynically murdered by the lovers, now as much possessed by lust as by the spirit of vengeance. Crime has bred crime, but more remains. Agamemnon's son, Orestes, in his turn seeks vengeance for the murder of his father. By killing his mother and her lover, he himself incurs the wrath of the gods. Only Athena, patroness of the city of Aeschlyus, ends the terrible sequence by casting her vote to acquit Orestes, when he is tried before the Athenian Court of the Areopagus. "Evil's nature is to multiply," sing the Chorus in Agamemnon. The natural law works from generation to generation, for:

> "While Zeus holds his throne,
>
> This maxim holds on earth: the sinner dies.
>
> That is God's law."[5]

Athena's intervention arises, not from abrogation of the law, but from the honourable intention of Orestes, whose choice to avenge his father accords with the will of Apollo, even though the necessary slaying of his mother incurs the curse of matricide.

Much later in the fifth century, Euripides, though he seemed to question the final benevolence of Providence, still held to the underlying Greek recognition that the moral law was natural law, enforced by the will of the gods. In The *Bacchae*, Dionysus himself appears before the sceptical King Pentheus to teach him that denial of a god leads only to destruction. Pentheus only has to acknowledge the power of the god and to allow his devotees to worship him freely and to practise his rites. With this acknowledgement, the god would remain pacific and enjoin his devotees to do no harm to man or beast. Without it, Dionysus becomes a force of destruction. The women who follow him become possessed. They tear to pieces the living flesh of animals and, finally, set upon Pentheus himself and leave his body as bloody fragments in the once peaceful forest.

> "When mind runs mad, dishonours God,
>
> And worships self and senseless pride,
>
> Then Law eternal wields the rod."[6]

Yet it was Sophocles, standing between Aeschylus and Euripides in point of time, who plumbed the depths of the moral law, for he recognised that man's usual awareness of morality is incomplete. What of men who suffer when no culpable action has been committed? What of King Oedipus, great ruler of Thebes, saviour of the city from the scourge of a sphinx? He conquered the sphinx by answering its riddle, but a greater riddle confronted him. Someone had murdered his predecessor; the murderer was unknown. Gradually the truth revealed itself that the hand that struck down the old king was that of the unwitting Oedipus. Worse still, he had married the widowed Queen Jocasta, his own mother, thus fulfilling the fearsome prophecy of Apollo from which Oedipus had once fled. Nowhere in his earlier life was there an overt intention to act thus. Why did these bestial acts occur? That is the real riddle which Sophocles poses. The awareness of the moral law is driven deeper, beyond the surface of the mind to an area where things are known that are not dreamt of in ordinary experience.

Reason draws from the story of Oedipus the idea that men live, not one life on earth, but many; that in an earlier life Oedipus had contemplated such terrible acts of patricide and incest, and that in this life he has committed them in apparent innocence. The tragic drama of Sophocles hints at the teaching of Pythagoras on reincarnation.

Sophocles extended his treatment of moral law in another direction in *Antigone*, where he contrasted it sharply with convention or man-made law. Antigone, daughter of Oedipus, insists that her brother, who died attacking Thebes to win the throne from the other son of Oedipus, should be properly buried with religious rites, whilst the new king, her uncle, refuses such honours on the grounds that his nephew was a rebel. The king's standpoint has its own rationale, but it resolutely ignores the god-given law that demands proper obsequies and family duties. Bravely Antigone stands by her intuitive understanding of the prior claims of the gods, and is driven by the king to hang herself in the desert prison where she has been entombed. No political pretext nor wilful resolution can curb the inexorable claims of the moral law. The king himself only learns this by the horror of seeing his own wife, son and niece all die as a result of his intransigence. The unwritten laws of justice are:

"... not of yesterday or today, but everlasting,
Though where they came from, none of us can tell."[7]

*Theatre, Epidaurus*

The effect of Greek tragedy was to draw from the audience their own recognition of the working of natural, or moral, law. This purification, or catharsis, stripped bare the limitations which each placed upon himself, perhaps deep in his consciousness. Thus freed, even momentarily, he might move closer to the reality within. In *Oedipus at Colonus* Sophocles shows the death of the old king, after a life of intense suffering, as a peaceful and holy disappearance from earth. Within the torment of appalling sin and guilt and self-inflicted pain had arisen a new peace, not as the world gives.

"Born thus, I ask to be no other man

Than that I am, and will know who I am."[8]

As for the comedy - which became an integral part of dramatic festivals when competitors for the prizes had to present three tragedies and one comedy - it balanced the emotional impact of such plays as the Oresteian Trilogy or the Theban Plays of Sophocles. A work such as Aristophanes' *The Clouds* might not produce catharsis, but it enabled Athenian audiences to laugh at leading figures in society, even in this case Socrates - quite unfairly associated with the Sophists - and to take leave for a while of the demanding life of a citizen in the new democracy. Under the harrowing of war, after 431 BC, such relief was probably vital. The unique blend of wit, ribaldry and topical allusion at such a time said much for the genius of the city and for the philosophic spirit that it had inherited.

The cathartic function of the theatre was most obvious at Epidaurus in the Argolid, since performances there were enacted next to the greatest sanctuary devoted to healing in the whole of Greece. Asclepius, the god of healing, son of Apollo and identified with the Egyptian sage, Imhotep, presided over the sanctuary, which contained temples, baths, a gynasium and a circular building, or tholos, which probably housed the sacred serpents peculiar to Asclepius. Healing was the special power of serpents, arising from their connection with the earth and the chthonic, or earthly, deities. When patients came to the sanctuary, they spent a night in the sleeping ward, during which they might be shown in dreams the suitable treatment for their illness. The shock of contact with the supernatural world through dream hastened the cure. Attending performances in the theatre might have aided by catharsis the process of recovery.

Greek drama was essentially religious. Nevertheless, outside the theatre, Athens created a form of literature - narrative history - which was secular in tone and offered explanations which did not rely directly upon divine forces. In the case of Herodotus there remained a strong sense of destiny leading men into situations where great causes could be put to the test, notably the cause of Greek freedom in the face of Persian aggression. Herodotus, however, was prepared to see religious features of all societies, including the Greek, as no more than deeply held conventions, as when he compared the reactions of people who ate their dead relatives to those of people who burned them. Each found the others' practices abominable, yet both were convinced of their own sacred duty towards the dead. Stronger than his belief in religious norms was an awareness of a divine justice which formed the nexus of events and ensured that ultimately good prospered and evil perished.

Writing nearer to the final collapse of Athens in the great civil war of the Greeks and taking that as his subject, Thucydides went much further than Herodotus in eschewing divine causes. For him the causes of action are human choice and the reasons that determine it. These he examined with discrimination, so that debates in the Athenian or Spartan Assemblies are reconstructed and accounts given in full of the circumstances in which decisions were taken. The justification for such meticulous recording and explanation lies in his subject matter, for he believed that "if one looks at the facts themselves, one will see that this was the greatest war of all". What makes his history a great work of literature, however, is not only the thoroughness of his analysis of reasons and circumstances, but also the brilliantly evocative narration of crucial events - Pericles' funeral oration, the siege of Pylos, the death of the Spartan general, Brasidas, at Amphipolis, the massive naval battle in the great harbour at Syracuse. Such clarity of observation produce, as he himself claimed, "a piece of writing not designed to meet the taste of an immediate public, but done to last for ever."

Such, in brief, was the culture centred upon fifth century Athens. It formed a classical canon which was never fundamentally developed beyond that point of harmony then achieved. Architecture, sculpture, pottery, vase painting, drama and the writing of history were given standards of excellence to which generations of Europeans would aspire. Pericles, in Thucydides' account of his funeral oration at the end of the first year of the Peloponnesian War, understated the case when he said that "our city is an education to Greece," for it has since educated humanity. Looking back from the fourth century BC, Isocrates said,

> "Athens has so far outrun the rest of mankind in thought and speech that her disciples are the masters of the rest, and it is due to her that the word "Greek" is not so much a term of birth as of mentality, and is applied to a common culture rather than a common descent."[8]

The achievements of classical Athens were prodigious, but what was their true measure? Socrates, who was not bound by the limitations of time and place, knew that fine buildings could not retain virtue, nor walls hold fast against corruption. He indited all the statesmen of his polis, even Themistocles, Cimon and Pericles, for their failure to teach the people true values, and cites the ingratitude of the populace to their leaders as injustice rebounding upon its perpetrators.[10] What was Athens but a city briefly touched with the divine light of a cultural revival, before the forces of degeneration held sway once more? The leaders of Athens could do no more than show courage and goodwill, as the contagion of war and internal strife spread throughout Greece.

### References:

1. Pindar, 'Pythian VIII', *The Odes*, trans. C. M. Bowra, Penguin, London, 1988, p. 237.

2. Plato, *Statesman*, trans. B. Jowett, Random House, New York, 1937, 284.

3. Plato, *Philebus*, trans. Jowett, 57.

4. Euripides, *The Bacchae*, trans. P. Vellacott, Penguin, London, 1973, 11. 893-6.

5. Aeschylus, *Agamemnon*, trans. P. Vellacott, Penguin, London, 1961, 11. 1562-4.

6. Euripides, *The Bacchae*, trans. Vellacott, 11. 883-5.

7. Sophocles, *Antigone*, trans. E. F. Watling, Penguin, London, 1974, 11. 455-6.

8. Sophocles, *Oedipus Rex*, trans. Watling, 11. 1084-5.

9. Isocrates, *Panegyricus*.

10. Plato, *Georgias*, trans. Jowett, Random House, New York, 1937, 519.

## Chapter 18

# The Saving Bulwark

### *Pericles*

WHAT CAUSED THE REMARKABLE flowering of Greek culture in fifth century Athens? Several conditions were necessary, though none of them was the root cause. The first was security. Marathon, and the great battles from Thermopylae down to the Eurymedon, had ensured that the Persian threat became insignificant. The armed force of the Delian League, especially at sea, guarded against a resurgence of Persian power in the Aegean Sea, Ionia and northern Greece. There remained the threat of civil war amongst the Greek states. After the repulse of the Athenians by Sparta at Mount Ithome, relations between the two major states never really recovered, and Greek military unity was seen to have been a fleeting response to the challenge of the Persian wars. Disputes within the Delian League were a frequent irritation, especially to Athenian empire-builders. Nevertheless, internecine warfare did not

*Triklinos (banquet hall) in Kerylos Villa, Beaulieu-sur-mer*

reach serious proportions, perhaps because the Spartans were reluctant to be committed outside the Peloponnese and the Athenian land empire in Boeotia only survived for a decade. Athens, in particular, found increasing security in her naval power, for as the contributions by the allies in ships declined, her own navy grew correspondingly, financed from the allied money tribute. With the rebuilding of Piraeus, the construction of the long walls and a great navy, Athens was secure in her *thassalocracy*.

A deeper security than this had arisen, however, from the exhilarating experience of Marathon and the other victories. The Greek states who had fought so courageously against the might of Persia grew immensely in self-confidence, but none more so than Athens. At Marathon, the Athenians, with the Plataeans, had fought first and alone against an enemy whom all Greeks till then feared as an immeasurably powerful and alien tyranny. Victory was a triumph of spontaneous valour and intelligence, which nothing could surpass, nor erase from memory. No feat of the Spartans, not even the stand of the 300 of Leonidas at Thermopylae, nor the great counter-attack of Pausanias at Plataea, could quite equal this victory of Miltiades' citizen hoplites, the vanguard of all the Greeks. Those who had fought there were the elite for all time to come in the eyes of Athenians. The survivors formed an association of old comrades, an aristocracy of the brave, numbering amongst them Aristides, Themistocles, Xanthippus, Aeschylus and the father of Pericles, which met to honour those who had died on the field of battle. At the Painted Stoa, and, later, on the Parthenon frieze, every Athenian was reminded of this first of victories. The nine thousand or so survivors of Marathon were an appreciable proportion of male citizens; with their families they formed a leaven in the body politic, raising it to a pinnacle of self-confidence. For a generation, at least, Athenians were immune from self-doubt, secure in the pride of selfless courage.

The second condition, dependent upon the first, was Athenian prosperity. Solon had laid the foundation for this and Peisistratus had assisted by some shrewd measures to help the hill farmers, such as relieving them of taxation. As the empire developed in the fifth century, trade became centred more and more upon Piraeus and the city, particularly when common coins, weights and measures were imposed throughout the empire. Wheat, especially, was imported in great quantities from the Euxine shores, as well as from southern Italy and Sicily and, when conditions permitted, from Egypt. Red-figure pottery was a major export, but with a large flow of tribute Athens could afford to run a large import surplus, indicated perhaps by an extract from a comedy staged in Athens in the 420s:

"From Cyrene silphium and ox hides, from the Hellespont mackerel and all kinds of salted fish, from Italy salt and ribs of beef... from Egypt sails and rope, from Syria frankincense, from Crete cypress for the gods; Libya provides abundant ivory to buy, Rhodes raisins and sweet figs, but from Euboea pears and fat apples. Slaves from Phrygia... Pagarsae provides tatooed slaves, Paphlagonia dates and oily almonds, Phoenicia dates and fine wheat-flour, Carthage rugs and many-coloured cushions."[1]

The tribute money also made possible the payment of jurors, magistrates and many other state officials, including even actors. After 447 BC, of course, the

Parthenon and the rest of the Periclean building programme were financed explicitly from the treasury of the League, after its move from Delos to Athens. State revenue came also from court fines and fees, harbour dues, market taxes and the leasing of mines, especially the silver mines at Laurium, and other public property. Even the stalls in the Agora bore a charge paid into the public revenue, so that some of the rent of urban land accrued for community purposes, like the rent of mines and harbours. Liturgies, in the form of sponsoring a chorus, fitting out and maintaining a trireme and financing religious festivals were paid by the rich, whose income came primarily from land.

Prosperity arose, too, from the generous treatment of metics, or resident aliens, for these were often skilled and industrious men, many from the allied territories, who contributed much, especially to work on the new buildings. Though not citizens, they had economic freedom and were protected by the law. Attica was, in effect, the centre of a more or less free trading area of great extent, and its maritime power and efficient port at the Piraeus enabled it to gain from specialisation within the area and from the rent accruing at the economic and political hub. Such prosperity, with its reasonably just distribution, was a major condition of cultural development.

The third condition was a high degree of personal freedom. Solon had established the basic equality of rights, or *isonomia*, with regard to personal liberty and judicial procedure. "I enacted laws in the spirit of equality for base-born and for high-born, according straight justice to each."[2] A habeas corpus act protected every citizen from illegal arrest. The Assembly was given the power to sit as a law court, called the Heliaea. For the first time the people, or a group of them selected by lot, could be jurors and judges. Cleisthenes followed this by extending the principle of *isonomia* to the electoral system. Local and state officials in deme, tribe or Council were now to be elected by citizens, regardless of birth and wealth. Perhaps more important still was the principle of equality in speaking. From the time of Cleisthenes onwards, the Athenian state, according to Herodotus, was an equality in rights, in speech and in power (*isonomia, isegoria, isokratia*). This equality did not, of course, extend to slaves, who made up probably about one quarter of the population in the fifth century. Slaves had no legal rights, but were treated well in some cases, particularly in domestic service or if they were skilled craftsmen. The great majority of slaves were barbarians captured in war; their work enhanced the quality of life of Athenians, though a few citizens, like the dramatist Euripides, were troubled by doubts about the morality of slavery.

Cleisthenes had established a degree of representative democracy through the Council of Four Hundred. Divisive regional interests had given way to a more generous view of the unity of the polis with his reform of the tribe system. When Ephialtes and Pericles brought Athens closer towards direct democracy with the transference of powers from the Court of the Areopagus to the Assembly and the Heliaea, the individual citizen acquired a remarkable degree of responsibility for and control over political and legal issues. His voice in debates and court actions might affect the decision. So long as the citizens were tolerably educated and not swayed by powerful emotion, such democratic power was a form of freedom for all. For to take part in deciding questions which affected the welfare of all acted as a check upon arbitrary government, and thereby reduced lawless interference with the freedom of individuals.

Athenian democracy also created politically educated citizens, who would speak and vote in the Assembly with a measure of good sense and informed opinion. For by the time of Pericles' ascendancy in the mid-century the magistracies were largely in the hands of citizens chosen by lot. The ordinary citizen could hold such offices, because he received payment for doing so. As a magistrate, and as a judge or juror also, the citizen learnt to act responsibly, to enquire into the facts, to try to be impartial, to make rational decisions with a view to the general interest. What better education could there be for membership of a democratic Assembly? Every Athenian male had a fair chance of becoming president of the Assembly - a post held for a single day and filled by lot - a market commissioner for a full year, a member of the Council, a deme magistrate, or a juryman repeatedly. Between the years 442 and 440 BC, Sophocles was chairman of the board of Treasurers of the Delian League, a general under the command of Pericles on the expedition to reduce Samos, and the first prize-winner, with his *Antigone*, at the Dionysia.

The system was open to abuse. Juries of several hundred citizens might be swayed by emotion and some jurors might enrol on the list of 6,000 as a means to eke out a living on the pay. The Assembly became subject to the influence of demagogues when after 431 BC the Peloponnesian war threatened the stability, and even the existence, of the polis. As early as the mid-century, the Heliaea voted to execute the whole board of Delian Treasurers, presumably for some form of corruption, and only when one member remained alive was it found that the charge was false. Nevertheless, for several decades the new democracy brought many citizens to a pitch of public responsibility and to a sense of lively participation in the whole polis. Such men could not be narrow-minded experts, nor disorientated intellectuals. They were free, not to be isolated individuals, but to be active members of the community. Amongst their achievements was the free choice of a great man as their leader.

All these aspects of personal freedom enabled the Athenians to express themselves creatively in the decades of cultural achievement: Phidias to direct the revolutionary portrayal of men on the Parthenon sculptures; Polycleitus to establish a new canon of the human figure; Ictinus and Callicrates freely to blend the Doric and Ionic orders; metic craftsmen to work alongside citizens, and even slaves, on carving the capitals and flutes; Sophocles to portray the tragedy of patricide and incest in the theatre; Euripides to question the ancient myths and the status of women; the sophists to teach how to win the worse case; and - the greatest blessing of freedom - Socrates, at least for a time, to offer to all who would listen his unique teaching on the immortality of the soul.

Security, prosperity, freedom; but a fourth condition was necessary, namely, leader ship, particularly for a people of great energy and ambition never far from the dangerous state of polypragmosyne. From the moment when Miltiades took charge of the hoplites at Marathon, until Pericles died of the plague in 429 BC, the Athenians were blessed with great leaders. Aristides was the noblest of them in his courage and love of justice; Themistocles the shrewdest in his judgement of what served the interests of the city; Cimon the best soldier in his single-minded devotion on the field of battle; but Pericles was that rare phenomenon, a philosophic statesman.

His rise to power is questionable in its motives, for he co-operated with Ephialtes in 462 BC, when the measures were passed to weaken greatly the Court of the

Areopagus during the absence of Cimon. When Ephialtes was murdered, presumably by embittered conservatives, Pericles took over the leadership of the democratic elements in the state. He may not have then believed unquestionably in the merits of the extended democracy. He himself was debarred from the Areopagus, because he had never been an archon, an office by then selected by lot. Only ex-archons sat in the Areopagus. For an ambitious politician in his early thirties, conscious of his own powers, it was perhaps natural to support a change which made his position so much more promising. In any case, he became a democrat for whatever motive and later was probably one by conviction. His treatment of Cimon was honourable enough, for when the latter's ostracism occurred, Pericles spoke with great restraint against a man who stood for political ideas quite opposed to his own, and he even proposed his recall a few years later.

Pericles dominated Athens politically for thirty years, or at least for the fifteen years after the ostracism of his later opponent, Thucydides. How was this possible in the democracy of the fifth century? The position he held was that of *strategos*, of which there were ten, one for each tribe. Every year he had to be elected to the position. The Assembly were free to reject him, as they did after an unsuccessful year of war in 430 BC. Thus his ascendancy arose from his own ability, from his commanding presence and transcendent rhetoric, combined with an unimpeachable honesty and great skill as a statesman, general and diplomat. In the Assembly, which met in the open air on the hill of Pnyx above the Agora, his rhetoric often won the majority over in causes which were finely balanced, like the decision to tighten the conditions of citizenship or to ostracise Thucydides. His teacher in this art had been Anaxagoras, a philosopher whom he later had to save from persecution, who taught that mind was the ultimate force in the universe and that speech arises from it. Pericles had obviously learnt to speak from a meditative point within himself, yet he was capable of adapting what he said to his audience with great precision. He knew how to play upon the emotions, to pick up the "atmosphere" on the crowded hillside, to encourage the response he wanted and to deflect the unwelcome one. The ponderous hulk of the democracy was deftly steered.

This was not mere demagogy. Behind the rhetoric lay carefully thought out proposals, plans made from a consistent political standpoint: protection and growth of the empire, which Athens had acquired in the previous generation, steady opposition to Sparta and her allies, the maintenance of a strong navy and external trade, especially in wheat imports, and the glorification of Athens as the centrepiece of Greek culture. At any time new circumstances or new potential leaders might present a challenge. The Assembly might swing violently in its views or remain inert when action was needed; direct democracy was an unpredictable beast. Pericles' genius was that he usually knew how to tame it. The terrible judicial error when all the Treasurers of the League, bar one, were executed, was a rare failure.

Examples abound of his skill as a statesman and diplomat. When he called for a conference to be held at Athens of all Greek states after the Five Years Truce of 451, to deal with the rebuilding of the temples, the payment of sacrifices to the gods and the freedom of the seas, he had calculated that Sparta would have to choose between acknowledging Athenian leadership by attending at Athens or leaving the field open to leadership by Athens if she did not attend. It was a masterly stroke which gave Athens great prestige when these three tasks were successfully dealt with. Brilliant also was his control of the acute crisis of 447/6. It might not even have arisen if the Athenian general Tolmides had heeded Pericles' advice not to march with only 1000 hoplites into Boeotia. They were wiped out at Coronea by an army of Boeotian oligarchs, who promptly declared Boeotia independent of Athens, reversing the decision at Oenophyta ten years before. Euboea then revolted, and when Pericles himself took an army there he was confronted with yet another revolt in Megara and a Spartan army north of the Isthmus of Corinth. His swift return and negotiations, probably assisted by bribing the young Spartan king, turned the Spartans round; he could not recover Megara, nor the land empire in Boeotia, but he did recover Euboea quickly by force. His action was a masterpiece of decisiveness, swift movement and shrewd compromise. He knew the danger of losing the strategically vital dependent ally of Megara, but there was no alternative. Tolmides should have listened to him. Clearly Pericles was not a tyrant; if he had been, the whole thing might not have happened!

A broad view of the needs of both Athens and its empire was apparent in Pericles' interest in the supply of wheat. The city alone had a population of perhaps 350,000; Attica could not feed it adequately. Building a third long wall was Pericles' response to the growing threat from Sparta, for it ensured the ability to maintain contact with the Piraeus, even in the event of a break-in by an enemy army through the southernmost wall. In 436 BC, no doubt with growing awareness that war might be inevitable, Pericles himself took an expedition into the Euxine, the first ever appearance of a strong Athenian force beyond the Bosphorous. It was a demonstration of strength to the Greek colonies on the Euxine shores and to those near the sea route to Athens, such as Byzantium, which had unsuccessfully joined Samos in revolting four years previously. Grain from this area was by then even more important for Athens than that from Sicily or Egypt. That her supplies were reasonably safe, until the final disastrous battle of Aegospotami in 404 BC, was largely due to Pericles' foresight.

Two examples in particular show that holding the office of *strategos* was not a mere cover for political leadership. Pericles' active military service included operations in the Corinthian Gulf in 454 BC and, of course, in Euboea and the Isthmus, but he excelled as a general in the Chersonese, when he took a thousand colonists to support those already there. Thracian tribesmen were perpetually harassing the colonists, so Pericles build a fortified line across the whole neck of the Isthmus and managed to expel all the Thracians. This operation in defence of an Athenian colony became a model for later military operations of the same type.

Secondly, in 440 BC occurred the serious revolt at Samos. Not only did Pericles again take personal charge of a naval force; he defeated a larger Samian fleet and conducted siege operations for nine months after the Samians had bravely recommenced their resistance. Samos was finally reduced. The threat to Athenian hegemony had been acute, for Sparta and her allies came close to deciding to intervene. Perhaps for this reason the cruel decision had been made - by Pericles or the Assembly is not known - to brand the Samian captives with the mark of the Samian state; to which Samos responded in kind by branding the Athenian owl on the foreheads of their captives. Afterwards, Pericles hastened to put Athens in a stronger position to fight a major war. The Assembly gave him its wholehearted support, entrusting to him "tribute of cities, and cities themselves to bind and to free, walls to build and walls to overthrow, treaties and rule and peace and prosperity too".[3] When chosen to deliver the funeral speech for those who had fallen in the revolt, he said that the youth of Athens had passed away as the Spring passes away from the year. Such a phrase carried a prophetic hint of the passing away of many seasons of Athenian manhood in the terrible war that was to come.

There is much evidence that Pericles' tone of speaking and style of life were philosophic. Anaxagoras had taught him to give small regard to popular forms of religion and superstition. Once when he was at sea with the fleet, an eclipse of the sun threw the sailors into a panic, including the helmsman of Pericles' trireme. With great presence of mind, Pericles held his cloak open in front of the man and asked, "What is the difference between this and the eclipse, except that the eclipse has been caused by something bigger than my cloak?"[4] In his great funeral oration at the end of the first year of the Peloponnesian War, as recorded by Thucydides, his words abound in a philosophy which makes nothing of the hopes and fears of earthly life and everything of that which transcends them:

"Taking everything together then, I declare that our city is an education to Greece, and that in my opinion each single one of our citizens, in all the manifold aspects of life, is able to show himself the rightful lord and owner of his own person, and do this, moreover, with exceptional grace and exceptional versatility...

As for success or failure, they left that in the doubtful hands of Hope, and when the reality of battle was before their faces, they put their trust in their own selves. In the fighting they thought it more honourable to stand their ground and suffer death than to give in to save their lives. So they fled from the reproaches of men, abiding with life and limb the brunt of battle; and, in a small moment of time, the climax of their lives, a culmination of glory, not of fear, were swept away from us...

They gave to the city their lives, to her and to all of us, and for their own selves they won praises that never grow old, the most splendid of sepulchres - not the sepulchre in which their bodies are laid, but where their glory remains eternal in men's minds, always there on the right occasion to stir others to speech or to action. For famous men have the whole earth as their memorials."[5]

During his career Pericles met much criticism and abuse. After Ephialtes' murder he was clearly in danger of his life. He consistently faced all this with a philosophic, or as it was said, an Olympian, calm. Like the sculptors of the serene style, he knew the secret of peace amidst action. Perhaps the most testing trial for such a man was the mockery of the comic poets, who called him "squill-head" because of his bulbous cranium. Telecleides described him sitting on the Acropolis at his wits' end, "at one moment top-heavy with the load of the cares of state, and at another creating all the din of war by himself, from that brain-pan of his, which is big enough to hold eleven couches."[6] He faced these barbs as he faced the fear of the assassin's knife much earlier, and dealt with a hostile Assembly as coolly as he dealt with the Spartan army at the Isthmus or the Samian fleet on the high seas.

For all this repose of mind, Pericles was not a cold nor unfeeling man. When he left his home in the morning, he kissed the woman he loved, Aspasia, making no attempt to conceal their relationship - for his earlier marriage had been set aside on the grounds of incompatibility. During the terrible plague at the beginning of the Peloponnesian

War, he lost most of his close relatives and friends and was never seen to weep, even at the funeral rites or by the grave; but the depth of his feeling was finally exhibited, when his only surviving son from his marriage, Paralus, also died. Even then no emotion escaped him, until finally he laid a wreath on the young body; then he broke into a passion of sobbing, a thing he was never seen to do before or after.

By nature Pericles was an aloof aristocrat, devoted to his work, not convivial, and perhaps with few intimate friends. Serious, industrious, with a strong sense of morality, he probably found it hard to relax and to distinguish between his public persona and himself. In this, he was the type of a national leader. Yet his study of philosophy brought enough detachment for him to rise above the needs of Athens alone and to glimpse in the culture of the polis a greater destiny. For what made Pericles a truly great man was his decision to introduce the building programme centred on the Acropolis. The threat from Persia was more or less over, the allies in the League were pressing for an end to the tribute system, a large section of opinion within the city, led by Thucydides, was strongly opposed to his policy, which was seen by them as both unjust and extravagant. Pericles was far too intelligent not to appreciate the point of view of his critics both at home and abroad. It would have been easy to unwind the threads of the League, to close the accounts of the Treasurers and settle for a sensible policy of withdrawal from empire and retrenchment in Attica. But a greater vision came to him, a vision of an Athens that would be remembered for centuries, even millennia to come; of a city that would educate mankind in the beauty of works done for the glory of God. He himself lived in touch with an intellectual world where the forms of things were not material nor approximate; a world of more use to humanity, and to the Athenians themselves, than was the world of political advantage and tidy agreements. If the sheep farms of Samos, or the Euboean orchards, had to bear a little more tax, what was that besides the golden glow of Athena within the exquisite colonnades of the Parthenon or the elevating majesty of the Propylaea, which raised the visitor to the Acropolis to a higher awareness of himself. There was, in addition, the argument that Pericles used publicly: that as Athens continued to guarantee the absolute freedom of the allies from Persian interference on land and sea, the continuation of the tribute was perfectly fair. If good management enabled the mother state to maintain a powerful navy and save much of the tribute for other purposes, that was her affair. Should she provide a navy inefficiently and thus avoid the charge of extravagant expenditure on beautiful buildings?

The Periclean building programme gave all Athenians, citizens and others alike, a glimpse into a world of pure beauty. It also enabled many hundreds of men to find fulfilment through their service in the production of such great works. From the immense scope of Phidias' creative imagination to the stonemason's cutting of a knife edge to the Dorian fluting, every man working on the temples and other constructions found the opportunity to devote brain and eye and hand to a work of self-fulfilment. In one sense, the building programme provided employment and stimulated the economy, but the real opportunities that it created for craftsmen were much greater. Here was the Greek ideal of *arete*, for the buildings and for the men who created them:

> "Each work possessed a beauty which seemed venerable the moment it was born, and at the same time a youthful vigour which makes them appear to this day as if they were newly built. A bloom of eternal freshness hovers over these works of his and preserves them from the touch of time, as if some unfading spirit of youth, some ageless vitality had been breathed into them."[7]

Pericles undoubtedly played a key role in the events that led up to the outbreak of the great war in 431 BC. He was still dominating the Assembly at the time when the Athenians decided to support Corcyra against her mother city, Corinth, and when Potidaea was ordered to raze her walls to the ground, both of which antagonised Sparta. As for the Megaran decrees, which made war inevitable by presenting Athens as a state prepared to go to any lengths to exert her will, he was definitely the author of them. He probably knew that the war with the Peloponnesians would have to come, for Spartan resentment had grown steadily, even from the time over thirty years before when Athens had shown its displeasure at being expelled from Mount Ithome. Spartan meddling in the affairs of Boeotia, and encouragement of the rebellions in Euboea and Megara in the mid-century had made Athens more suspicious in her turn. Thasos and Samos had each appealed to Sparta for help, and only the caution of Corinth had prevented a major war over the Samian affair in 440 BC. Moreover, Athenian democracy stood irreconcilably opposed to the oligarchy in Sparta, now that both systems had declined from the more timocratic kind of state of earlier times, which had enabled them to co-operate over the Persian wars. And, more immediately, Pericles had seen at first-hand what a near run thing was the suppression of Samos, when the Samian fleet had threatened to control the Aegean. Perhaps the time was ripe for war.

Certainly Pericles cannot be completely absolved of the charge of aggression. His first known political act was to demand, unsuccessfully, a forceful policy in Thrace. He was responsible for sending out cleruchies to the Cheronese, Euboea, Naxos, Andros, Lemnos and Imbros, a policy which the allies resented, since it meant Athenian garrisons and the taking of land by Athenians, contrary to the general Greek practice of denying land holding to foreigners. He himself led several military expeditions to enforce the will of Athens upon recalcitrant allies. Yet his defence was simple: his generation had inherited an empire; the best policy was to maintain and enrich it.

Pericles died in 429 BC, having caught the plague for a second time. For a while he had suffered the disappointment of rejection by the Assembly, because of the apparent failure of his war policy. Following his directions, the people of Attica had brought everything - families, goods and herds - within the long walls, while the Spartan army ravaged the land. Then the plague had broken out in the cramped and unhealthy conditions. Opinion turned against Pericles and he was suspended from office, only to be re-instated when the unstable Assembly found itself leaderless in the crisis. As he lay on his death-bed, apparently unconscious, his friends were talking of his political and military exploits. Suddenly he spoke in a clear voice, rebuking their praise of his successes and adding that his real claim to fame was "that no Athenian ever put on mourning because of me."[8] These were his last words. In his own eyes he had always striven to act justly, so that no one had died as a result of his own personal ambition or wilfulness. It was the boast of a true leader of men.

"Henceforth the public life of Athens was to be polluted by a rank growth of corruption and wrongdoing, which Pericles had always checked and kept out of sight, thereby preventing it from taking an irresistible hold. Then it was that that power of his, which had aroused such envy and had been denounced as monarchy and a tyranny, stood revealed in its true character as the saving bulwark of the state."[9]

### References:

1. Quoted by R. Meiggs, *The Athenian Empire*, O.U.P., Oxford, 1999, p. 264.

2. N. G. L. Hammond, *History of Greece to 324 BC*, O.U.P., Oxford, 1977, p. 159.

3. Hammond, *History of Greece*, p. 316.

4. Plutarch, *The Rise and Fall of Athens*, trans. I. Scott-Kilvert, Penguin, London, 1976, p. 202.

5. Thucydides, *The Peloponnesian War*, trans. R. Warner, Penguin, London, 1976, Book II, pp. 147-9.

6. Plutarch, *The Rise and Fall of Athens*, p. 167.

7. Plutarch, *The Rise and Fall of Athens*, p. 179.

8. Plutarch, *The Rise and Fall of Athens*, p. 205.

9. Plutarch, *The Rise and Fall of Athens*, p. 206.

# Chapter 19

# A Vision of Hidden Things

## *The Philosophy of Unity*

SECURITY FROM EXTERNAL AGGRESSION, a prosperous society, the freedom of individual citizens and the intelligent leadership were the conditions which enabled the great cultural movement of the fifth century to take place. One essential cause was present also: a practical philosophy which had entered Greece by the time of Pythagoras at the latest. In Plato's dialogue, *Protagoras*, it is said that the art of the sophists was of great antiquity; that these teachers disguised themselves and included among them were Homer, Hesiod, Orpheus, Agathocles, who pretended to be a musician, and Pythocleides the Cean. In this instance, the real meaning of sophist is a wise man, and not the meaning acquired in the late fifth century, when sophists were professional teachers of rhetoric, much criticised by Socrates and by Plato himself.

*Telesterion at Eleusis*

One of Agathocles' pupils was Damon, an expert on rhythm, who taught, according to Plato, the doctrine that "when modes of music change, the fundamental laws of the state always change with them."[1] Damon was a friend, and perhaps a teacher, of Pericles; moreover, he taught music to no less a person than Socrates. Pythocleides the Cean was an associate of Pericles also. The link between the circle of Pericles and that of Socrates can be drawn closer. Pericles' mistress, Aspasia, taught Socrates rhetoric, a fact confirmed by his remark in Plato's *Menexenus* that she had composed the great funeral oration of Pericles. Since she came originally from Miletus, she may have met the Milesian teaching, exemplified by Anaxagoras, the philosopher who most influenced Pericles.

Although Socrates later rejected Anaxagoras' view of the central role of mind in the universe, he was an admirer of Pericles' political ability, calling him magnificent in his wisdom and the only educated man in political life. A pupil of Anaxagoras, called Archelaus, taught Socrates and was the first Athenian-born philosopher in the tradition of the Ionian school. Probably as influential as the Ionians, however, were two philosophers from Elea in Southern Italy, Parmenides and his follower, Zeno; the latter went to Athens and taught possibly Socrates and certainly Callias, a friend of Pericles and the man who negotiated the peace with Persia in 449 BC.

But what had these various philosophers from Ionia, Magna Graecia and Athens in common? Were they as diverse in their ideas as might appear from the arguments recorded later by Plato and others? If so, they could not have caused such a profound expression of thought and emotion as occurred in Athens in the ninety-odd years after the battle of Marathon. Only fragments of their teaching survive; amongst the fragments there is great diversity. Yet it is the diversity of a mosaic, of which each fragment is a part.

Anaxagoras, for example, writes that sensible appearances are "a vision of hidden things" and that the original cause of the change from infinite, unchanging Being is "separation by Mind, or Nous." This places Anaxagoras firmly in the school of Parmenides, a key figure in the line that stretches from Pythagoras to Socrates. Parmenides taught that the single, eternal reality of Being appears as multiplicity of changing forms, so that "all is one" and the belief that there is any real change is illogical. His pupil, Zeno, supported this fundamental monism by attacking the opposite view, that multiplicity and change, or motion, are real. Basically, Zeno argued that, if multiplicity were real, then the units that comprise it must be either divisible or indivisible. If divisible, then each one must be infinitely divisible, because a homogenous unit cannot be divisible only at certain points. If indivisible, then how could each unit have magnitude, which in principle must be divisible? Therefore, in the first case, there must be infinitely small parts of units and, in the second, there must be units of no magnitude. In neither case could there be a universe made up of a real multiplicity of finite sense objects. His paradoxes about change, or motion, of which "Achilles and the tortoise" is justly famous, are similar, for they try to prove that, because an apparently moving object must pass through an infinite series of points, it can never get to any distant point in a finite time. Zeno relies upon an intuitive recognition that the idea of infinity shows that all seemingly finite experience is unreal; hence the conclusion, following Parmenides, that what is real must be non-sensible and infinite i.e. Being.

Parmenides himself used an argument about time to prove that Being is eternal:

"How might what is then perish?

How might it come into being?

For if it came into being it is not,

nor is it if it is ever going to be."[2]

Parmenides' explanation of the apparent existence of multiplicity is that men impose names upon the one indivisible Being:

"Hence all things are a name which mortals lay down and trust to be true - coming into being, perishing, being and not being, and changing place and altering bright colour."[3]

Hence Anaxagoras could conclude that "separation by Mind", or naming, is the cause of the apparent change from Being to multiplicity.

Common to all these philosophers, to Parmendies, Zeno, Anaxagoras, Archelaus and, no doubt, to Agathocles, Damon, Pythocleides and Aspasia, was the realisation that the world of the senses is unreal and transient - whilst reality is one and unchanging. Pythagoras had taught the same and Socrates was to teach it again with an unsurpassed conviction. Meanwhile, it remained to enlighten a few generations of Athenians, and probably many more Greeks whose achievements are less vaunted. For the philosophers explained the source of that peace within action which was the hallmark of fifth century Athens. There is no peace in multiplicity and change, only in unity and stillness. But where are these to be found, if not within oneself? The world contains only things in movement. Hence the ancient words inscribed at Delphi, "Know Thyself" were understood afresh in the light of the teaching that the only reality is hidden behind the world of sense objects in one Being. For some, at that time, the connection was made: the one Being is Oneself; the shackels that bind men to the idea of a separate individual self were broken. "I enquired into myself, said Heraclitus.[4]

The influence of Pythagoras ensured that the doctrines of Parmenides and his followers did not become merely theoretical, for the Pythagorean schools taught self-discipline, through moderation in the use of the senses and other practices. Orphism, too, was a potent force in the fifth century, connected not only with the Pythagoreans, but also with the Eleusinian mysteries. For many Athenians, including women, metics and even slaves, the rites of Demeter and Persephone at Eleusis were the means for evoking the ancient truths of the culture, reaching back to Apollo, the soul of the world. Every year, in September, the initiates went down to the sea-shore and cleansed themselves in the warm sea. Carrying the image of Iacchus, or Dionysus, they walked in solemn procession along the Sacred Way, over Mount Aegaleos to Eleusis, where they entered the temple of the two goddesses, late at night, by the light of hundreds of torches. A great new telesterion, or Hall of Initiation, was built in the time of Pericles and here the rites would be enacted, recalling the rebirth of the soul within the tomb of the body, the awakening of consciousness from the dream of the world.

Such a teaching is implicit in the work of the greatest Athenians. It underlay the work of the sculptors of the serene style and of the marvellous poised figures of the Parthenon frieze. It gave to the architects on the Acropolis a pure harmony of form and absence of all excess. From it the tragic playwrights could draw their understanding of the inexorable working of Man's nature, of the need for justice, even of reincarnation into a life predetermined by previous embodiments. Above all, it inspired all those who lived by it with a self-confidence which could disregard the perils of the age - the harsh experience of war, the agony of the plague, the torment of failure and ridicule in politics or art - and rise to the contemplation of life as no more than a dramatic illusion.

### References:

1. Plato, *Republic*, trans. B. Jowett, Random House, New York, 1937, Book IV, 424.

2. J. Barnes, *Early Greek Philosophy*, Penguin, London, 1987, p. 134. (cf. *Bhagavad Gita*, ch. 2, v. 16.)

3. Barnes, *Early Greek Philosophy*, p. 135.

4. Barnes, *Early Greek Philosophy*, p. 113.

## Chapter 20

# Death of a Culture

### *The Peloponnesian War*

FOR TWENTY-SEVEN YEARS, from 431 to 404 BC, the Greeks fought amongst themselves, until they destroyed the glorious culture which had begun nine centuries before in the peace of Olympia and on the lofty slopes of Mount Parnassus. The war brought to a head the accumulating evils present in every polis, but perhaps most glaring in Athens itself, where the light of that culture shone most brightly. Within the polis men became bitterly divided between party factions - oligarchs and democrats - who sought their own interests in the name of justice. Each party gave a loose allegiance to the Spartan-led Peloponnesians or to the Athenian empire, so that whilst the two sides fought each other on land and sea, the populations inside the poleis contained traitors who really favoured the other side. Thus, worse even than the

*Reconstruction of a Greek warship on the River Thames*

terrible casualties in the battles, were the suffering and crime which occurred within the walls of cities, torn apart by fanatical mobs or ruthless tyrants.

The war brought out the virtues of good men, where these still survived. From their example Greece would be rebuilt when the war was over, but such exceptions to the general growth of greed and narrow self-interest could not stem the tide. War, and especially civil war, degenerated as it proceeded, like the great Trojan War and the war that brought even Arjuna to despair on the field of Kurukshetra. Prisoners were slaughtered; the dead were not properly buried; whole armies and fleets were betrayed; women and children were wiped out in vengeance or blood-lust.

Amidst the horror, a few men watched with philosophic calm, aware of the inevitability of it all, sustained by the recognition that ultimately it was only a terrible illusion. Sophocles continued to write his profound dramas with no apparent mention of the war. The lovely Ionic temple of the Erechtheum was built on the Acropolis, whilst the threat of famine hung over the population of Athens; and Socrates genially discussed questions of philosophy with all who chose to engage him in conversation in the Agora.

The cause of the war lay deeply embedded in the events which led up to it. Thucydides' view was this:

"What made war inevitable was the growth of Athenian power and the fear which this caused in Sparta."[1]

Since Sparta, at the head of the Peloponnesian League, was certainly the most formidable opponent of Athens, his judgement was no doubt correct, but Corinth, too, was gravely disturbed by the same fear and, in fact, played a most significant part in the events preceding the outbreak of war. Moreover, her commercial rivalry with Athens, and her proximity to Attica, gave her more obvious grievances than Sparta, whose fear arose from a more subtle rivalry for political dominance and moral hegemony.

Athens' treatment of her allies was the overt reason for fear amongst the Peloponnesians. She had not tolerated the defection of any member of the Delian League. She had forced states to join the League, when she deemed it essential in her own interest. She had sent out citizens to establish cleruchies in allied states by taking land, often the most valuable land, a practice contrary to the whole tradition of Greek landholding, which had always been confined to the citizens of a polis. In her own case, Athens was zealous to limit land-holding to her own citizens. Such blatant imperialism culminated in the harsh treatment of Samos in 440 BC, when the proud islanders were made to tear down their walls, hand over the remains of their fleet and pay the outrageously large indemnity of 1500 talents. When a serious problem arose over the Corinthian colony of Corcyra in western Greece, those who remembered Samos remembered also that Pericles had recently led an expedition into the Euxine. If the corn supply was of such importance to these meddling Athenians, they would be unlikely to stand by whilst there was trouble near the sea route to Sicily, an island rich in corn. They had already shown an interest in the balance of power in Magna Graecia.

Corcyra was involved in a dispute with its own colony, Epidamnus, which appealed to the mother city, Corinth, for help. When Corinth turned upon Corcyra and threatened war, the Corcyrans realised that their traditional neutrality left them without support, and appealed in their turn to Athens, offering the tempting prospect of a defensive alliance with the major naval power in the Ionian Sea. Though, under the terms of the Thirty Years Peace of 446 BC, neutral states could join either the Athenian or Spartan alliances, such a preponderance of naval power would be, in the circumstances, a serious aggravation of the already tense state of affairs. In 433 BC Corinth sent a fleet to enforce her will on Corcyra. Athens sent a contingent of ships with instructions to intervene only if the Corcyrans were in danger of defeat. Sure enough they were, and Athenian and Corinthian ships met in direct combat.

At Potidaea, in Chalicidice, Athens again came into conflict with Corinth. Potidaea was a colony of Corinth, but an ally of Athens. Fearing action there by Corinth, the Athenians ordered Potidaea to dismiss her Corinthian magistrates and to pull down her fortifications. When the Potidaeans refused, Athens sent troops to besiege the city. Chalcidice was a sensitive area; it abutted on to Thrace by the Euxine, and its ports were a threat to the corn trade.

By this time Pericles had probably decided that war was inevitable. In 432 BC he persuaded the Assembly to issue a set of decrees prohibiting the adjoining state of Megara - a pariah since she had made common cause with Corinth about fifteen years before - from trading in any port within the Athenian empire. It spelt the ruin of the little polis on the Isthmus, for as Aristophanes pithily wrote:

"No Megarian on land

Nor in market shall stand,

Nor sail on the sea

Nor set foot on the strand."[2]

Cruel though it was, the Megaran decree was a powerful blow in the conflict itself, rather than a cause of the war, for Megara guarded the road from the Peloponnese to Thebes, and the Boetian alliance was a key to Spartan hopes of victory, since it placed Athens inside a military pincer. Perhaps, also, Pericles' pretext for the decrees, that Megara had invaded lands sacred to the goddesses of Eleusis, was not entirely spurious.

Corcyra, Potidaea and Megara; these were more than enough to make a *casus helium* for Corinth, whose interest in all three was intimate. They were collectively enough to stir the lethargic Spartans to action. Reluctantly - for even her king, Archidamus, spoke against declaring war - Sparta made the fatal decision, after an exchange of empty ultimatums on both sides. Nemesis had overtaken Greece, though few men knew it when the war started.

Pericles outlined a clear war policy to the democracy of Athens. Essentially, it was the policy of Themistocles adapted to a Greek civil war: to avoid pitched battles against greatly superior land armies; to create a siege economy within the city, the Piraeus and the long walls, sustained by the Athenian navy; to harass the enemy from the sea by cutting his sea routes and landing raiding parties around the coast to burn and run. It might have brought victory, if Pericles had not died so soon, or if his successors had proved as canny as he. Sparta could hardly have been roundly defeated by such methods, but to force her into a conditional peace would have saved Athens and her empire, for the question at issue was whether Athenian power and pride could be humbled. To preserve these was to win.

The first year of the war saw a pattern that was to be repeated with harrowing effect. The Peloponnesian army invaded Attica in the Spring and ravaged the land. Vines, olive trees, orchards, the small-holdings of the sturdily independent Attic farmers, now cooped up within the fortified city, were torn down. From the city walls the populace of Attica watched the smoke rising over the land they had tended for generations, and perhaps glimpsed a distant patch of scarlet, or flash of sunlight, from the Spartan hoplites.

Worse was to come. Conditions within the city deteriorated rapidly as more and more people and livestock crowded in. The population of Attica was about 320,000, of which about 170,000 were citizens; the area within the city walls was little more than one square mile. Before long there was plague. Its symptoms were a terrible burning feeling in the head, followed by nausea, ulcers, diarrhoea, fever and terrible agitation. Most people who caught it died within about ten days, but if they lived longer it was only to prolong the suffering, for then they might experience paralysis or outright madness. Bodies were heaped up indiscriminately or burnt without ceremony. Indeed, religious rites were ignored, as despair overtook reverence for the gods. Morality and general respect for law and order broke down, so that many who doubted for their survival thought only of using the time that was left to them for pleasure, regardless of others and of their own souls. Yet a few men and women had the strength to hold on to the ancient values. They were the ones who continued to visit the sick, even when it was virtually a death warrant to do so. But for them Athens would surely have been utterly destroyed by the very gods who had made her great. In the death throes of a culture, the greater power of civilisation could not be quite extinguished.

The most notable victim of the plague was, of course, Pericles. After his death, when the plague abated, power gradually passed into the hands of popular leaders, men like Cleon, a leather dealer and self-made politician, who knew how to sway the Assembly and was a shrewd judge of the drift of events. For a year or so the war went well for Athens, despite the annual ravaging of the land. A capable admiral, Phormio, won victories in the Corinthian Gulf, and Potidaea fell to the Athenian besieging forces. Then an event occurred which showed the Athenians what dangers lay within the apparent unity of their system of alliances. For Mytilene on the Ionian coast rebelled, at the same time claiming leadership of the important island of Lesbos, one of the only two remaining naval powers within the alliance, apart from Athens herself. Mitylene connived at Spartan support. Fortunately for Athens the Spartan navy was too cautious to seize the opportunity. The revolt was suppressed by the Athenian general, Paches; and then the full import of how degenerate Athenian leadership had become under the demagogues was shown. The Assembly passed a resolution to put all the adult male citizens of Mitylene to death and to send all the women and children into slavery. A trireme was despatched with the dreadful orders.

The next day, partly from the protestations of some Mitylenians in Athens, and partly from the conscience of some Athenian citizens, the matter was brought before the Assembly again. Once more Cleon spoke out for the same punishment, bringing into the open the attitude which had grown up after so many years of hegemony over fellow Greeks:

"If, however, whatever the rights or wrongs of it may be, you propose to hold power all the same, then your interest demands that these (the Mitylenians) rightly or wrongly, must be punished. The only alternative is to surrender your empire, so that you can afford to go in for philanthropy."[3]

Realising that a mere appeal to sympathy, or even to a sense of justice, might fail in the existing mood of the Assembly, especially when the war situation made rebellion seem doubly dangerous and culpable, a cool-headed, humane man, Diodotus, rose to speak for amendment of the sentence. Cleverly he argued that the long-term political interest of Athens demanded a less drastic punishment. If other rebels within the empire knew that their fate would be death if they were to fail, then their resistance would be prolonged to the last man and their cities would be reduced to rubble.

Better, he argued, that only the leaders, who would be oligarchs, should be executed and the rest of the people encouraged to become loyal and secure members of the alliance, welcoming Athenian protection. Thus he secured the votes of those for whom the interests of Athens were paramount, in addition to the votes of those who were already appalled by the impending act of vengeance. A new resolution was passed; a trireme was fitted out at great speed with instructions to overtake the first one and countermand its orders.

A deadly race began across the Aegean Sea. The first trireme had a lead of twenty-four hours, but it had no cause for great speed. The second was provisioned with wine and barley, which the crew consumed whilst rowing. They rowed without stopping, taking it in turns to sleep; luckily, there was no head wind. As they arrived in the harbour at Mitylene, Paches was preparing to carry out the executions, having read his orders shortly before. The Mitylenians were saved from slaughter and slavery; Athenian democracy from itself.

Sparta had no more regard for humanity than her enemy when she was roused to anger. The valiant little polis of Plataea, the ancient ally of Athens, eventually fell after a prolonged siege. Half the garrison had escaped one night with great daring, by crossing the double wall built by the besiegers, but the other 200, with 25 Athenians, were brought before the Spartan officers and asked "Have you done anything to help the Spartans and their allies in the war?" The inevitable answer of "no" was followed by immediate execution. Thus died the descendants of the brave men of Marathon. Their city was razed to the ground. Athens did nothing to help Plataea, pleading the excuse of other war commitments.

Within Corcyra, where the war could be said to have begun, a civil war broke out in 427 BC, which was the first of a series of civil wars within many poleis. Everywhere opinion polarised between democrats and oligarchs, the former looking for Athenian support, the latter to Sparta. In Corcyra the violence used against political, and also personal, enemies was boundless; men were slaughtered in every conceivable way; suppliants were dragged from temples or even butchered on the altars; some were walled up inside buildings; many hung themselves in order to avoid worse forms of death. Fear became endemic. Fathers and sons betrayed each other. First one party, then the other, anticipated its opponents in the violence of its attack in order to pre-empt them. Outside help was called for without compunction, if the other side seemed too threatening, so that love of the polis itself was prostituted to party advantage.

Partnership in crime became the strongest link between men and, from the corruption of morals, an insidious new corruption emerged, the corruption of language:

"To fit in with the change of events, words, too, had to change their usual meanings. What used to be described as a thoughtless act of aggression was now regarded as the courage one would expect to find in a party member; to think of the future and wait was merely another way of saying one was a coward; any idea of moderation was just an attempt to disguises one's unmanly character; ability to understand a question from all sides meant that one was totally unfitted for action. Fanatical enthusiasm was the mark of a real man, and to plot against an enemy behind his back was perfectly legitimate self-defence. Anyone who held violent opinions could always be trusted, and anyone who objected to them became a suspect. To plot successfully was a sign of intelligence, but it was still cleverer to see that a plot was hatching."[4]

Thucydides drew a conclusion from these internal civil wars and revolutions, which is a most significant reminder that this was indeed the end of a culture:

"As a result of these revolutions, there was a general deterioration of character throughout the Greek world. The simple way of looking at things, which is so much the mark of a noble nature, was regarded as a ridiculous quality and soon ceased to exist."[5]

Almost every year until 425 BC the Spartan army invaded Attica to destroy the crops. In reply the Athenians drifted away from the policy laid down by Pericles and commenced land operations, particularly under an enterprising general, Demosthenes. After failing to make progress in Aetolia, he won a decisive victory in the west over the Ambraciots, whose army was almost annihilated. Such boldness led the Athenian leaders to look yet further west, beyond the Ionian sea, to Sicily, where nemesis would strike them hard before the war was over. A proposed expedition thence landed at Pylos on the west coast of the Peloponnese; delay encouraged the Athenian hoplites to fortify the place. It lay just north of the long narrow island of Sphacteria. The Spartans, hearing of this encroachment on their territory, sent a force which landed on Sphacteria. Athenian naval power now exerted itself by taking control of the open sea and the landward bay, thus surrounding the island. Spartan hoplites were besieged within the Peloponnese, an extraordinary situation, of which the Athenians were quick to appreciate the possibilities. A truce was made under onerous conditions for Sparta, which surrendered most of her fleet as a pledge. Representatives of each state met to resolve the situation, but Athens was not to be bought off with offers of peace.

Nevertheless, the Athenians could find no way of ejecting the Spartans from Sphacteria, until Cleon challenged Nicias, one of the *strategoi*, in the Assembly. Irritated by Cleon's persistent taunts, Nicias eventually responded by offering the command of a force to Cleon himself, who had no experience whatsoever of military leadership. The Assembly warmed to the irony of such an offer and cried out that Cleon must accept. To turn it down would have cost Cleon his political future. So he accepted, though ensuring that he would be amply provided with over 10,000 troops, and promised to complete the task in twenty days.

*Island of Sphacteria, Pylos*

They landed on the southern end of Sphacteria and for a while made little progress against the 440 Spartiates encamped further north. Only when an accidental fire stripped the cover of brushwood, and smoke blew into the eyes of the Spartans, could the Athenians take advantage of their numbers and move forward up the three mile long island towards the final redoubt of the northern tip, opposite Pylos. Harassed by light-armed troops, by arrows from 400 archers and by the blinding smoke, the Spartans withdrew in good order to the rocky heights behind them. There they were beyond the danger of direct assault, but a Messenian soldier showed the Athenians a narrow cleft, ending in a hollow just below the highest peak of the sheer north wall. As the Spartans settled with relief into their seemingly impregnable posts, looking down upon the mass of Athenian troops below to the south, a handful of soldiers appeared on the heights above and behind them. Like the 300 men under Leonidas at Thermopylae, the 300 or so Spartans left on Pylos knew what it meant to be surrounded; but much had changed since the great days of the Persian wars. Sparta had become an oligarchy in which some Spartiates were wealthier than others. The krypteia, probably created after the helot revolt at Ithome in the 460s, had corrupted the Spartan youths, who were taught to murder helots without compunction. In the course of the current war 2000 helots were murdered, instead of being granted the freedom promised as a reward for fighting bravely. And so, when the men on Sphacteria felt the approach of death, they did not turn their minds towards the immortality that their grandfathers had won at Thermopylae, but instead laid down their arms and surrendered to their Athenian enemies.

> "This event caused much more surprise among the Hellenes than anything else that happened in the war. The general impression had been that Spartans would never surrender their arms whether because of hunger or any other form of compulsion; instead they would keep them to the last and die fighting as best they could."[6]

This Athenian success had several effects. It enhanced the reputation of Cleon, and with him that of the other demagogues, vis-a-vis the *strategoi*; it gave Athens 292 priceless hostages; and it left a doubt in everyone's mind about the invincibility of Sparta. Holding the hostages enabled Athens to prevent the annual ravaging of Attica by the Spartan army and to negotiate for peace more or less when she chose.

In the year 422 BC the Spartans suffered perhaps as great a loss in the death of their general, Brasidas. He was not a typical Spartan, except in his steady courage and sense of duty. In other respects he was more Athenian in character, full of initiative, energetic, diplomatic, capable of arousing devotion and friendship, particularly amongst neutral peoples who would be useful to the Peloponnesians. He had taken the strategically placed city of Amphipolis, an Athenian colony in Thrace, by offering the inhabitants generous terms. Cleon came with an army to besiege it and was himself killed outside its walls. With the death of Brasidas there, too, the chances of peace improved, for these two men had become the driving force on each side for the continuation of the fight to the bitter end. So in 421 BC Nicias negotiated peace with Sparta, though it did not save the people of Scione in Chalcidice from an act of Athenian brutality. They also had revolted two years before, looking to Brasidas for support. Now all the male population were put to the sword by an imperial power, outraged by the defection of a key city near the precious sea route to the Euxine.

Really the peace was no more than a truce, because it dealt with none of the underlying problems. Both sides agreed to hand back most of the places they had captured in the war, though Athens refused to relinquish Nisaea (to the outrage of Megara) and two Corinthian cities. Athens agreed to ask only for tribute money at the level set by Aristides, not at the recently inflated level, from the recovered cities. All captives were to be handed back, including those from Pylos. Sparta's main allies were disgusted at the terms; Corinth especially felt that the war left her in a worse position than when it began. When Amphipolis refused to return to the Athenian fold, even though Sparta had agreed to this, Athens, too, no longer regarded the peace as anything more than a truce.

For five years the situation in this great civil war of Greece was confused, whilst the participants manoeuvred for position before the final decade of conflict between the two fundamentally opposed camps of Ionian and Dorian forces. For a short while, Athens and Sparta even became allies, owing to the intervention of Argos, previously neutral, which in conjunction with Corinth and other Peloponnesian states, posed a serious threat. Soon, however the original antagonists reappeared as champions of the democratic and oligarchic interests. Opposition to Athens amongst those who had resented her imperialism was once more heightened, when an expedition was launched against the island of Melos, which had for long stood almost alone in refusing to pay tribute assessed upon it by Athens. A brilliant but destructive man, Alcibiades, strangely an associate of Socrates, had come forward to demand the prosecution of Melos. Previously he had sided with one of the demagogues, Hyperbolus, but when a vote of ostracism was proposed, aimed at Nicias, Alcibiades, fearing that Nicias' supporters might write "Alcibiades" on the sherds, turned round and opposed Hyperbolus, who was himself ostracised. Such a manoeuvre was a portent of Alcibiades' future conduct. Meanwhile his counsel was followed to attack Melos.

According to Thucydides, negotiations took place between an oligarchic government in Melos and the Athenians, in which the Athenian delegates bluntly expressed the view that justice is dependent upon the relative power of the participants, and that

> "our opinion of the gods and our knowledge of men lead us to conclude that it is a general and necessary law of nature to rule wherever one can."[7]

Whilst such a denial of justice, the very principle upon which the idea of the polis was founded, was being spoken on the island of Melos, in Athens itself Socrates was carefully rebutting such a view and leading those who would listen back to the recognition that justice is the rule of reason over the passions. Thus had the work of rebuilding begun, even whilst the collapse of values was gathering pace; but Socrates could not save Melos. After a brief siege, she was inexorably overwhelmed. Once more, as at Scione, came the sickening process of putting to death all the adult males and selling the women and children into slavery. This time no second trireme raced across the sea to stay the hands of the executioners.

Melos had been settled originally by men of Dorian stock. Sparta could not be indifferent to this brutal action by her short-lived ally. The self-destructive war was reborn. The lull in the fighting had revived the Athenians' confidence. They now decided, in 415 BC, upon a scheme of surpassing boldness; to attack the Dorian communities in Sicily, thereby ensuring their own control of the western sea routes, denying the Peloponnesians any help from Magna Graecia and greatly enriching themselves at the expense of the people of Sicily. Some Athenians, notably Nicias, thought the scheme foolhardy, especially when Sparta and Corinth lay undefeated beside them on the mainland of Greece. Alcibiades, however, convinced the Assembly of the immense prospective gains and, ironically, Nicias was appointed, with Alcibiades and another general, Lamachus, to command the expedition.

Just before it sailed an act of gross sacrilege occurred in Athens. Statues of Hermes in front of temples and private houses were mutilated during the night. A rumour spread that Alcibiades and his friends were responsible. It is more than likely that the whole outrage, including the rumours, was the work of Corinthian infiltrators, since Corinth was the mother city and protector of Syracuse, the prime target of the Sicilian expedition. Nevertheless, Alcibiades was charged and was refused the right to be tried immediately, because his Athenian enemies knew that his present popularity would ensure his acquittal. So the fleet set sail with this taint overhanging one of its commanders.

134 triremes, carrying 5100 hoplites and numerous additional troops, except cavalry, left the Piraeus to the accompaniment of wild rejoicing and ceremonious farewells:

> "When the ships were manned and everything had been taken aboard which they meant to take with them on the voyage, silence was commanded by the sound of the trumpet, and the customary prayers made before putting to sea were offered up, not by each ship separately, but by them all together following the words of a herald. The whole army had wine poured out into bowls, and officers and men made their libations from cups of gold and of silver. The crowds on the shore also, the citizens and others who wished well to the expedition, joined together in the prayers. Then, when the hymn had been sung and the libations finished, they put out to sea, first sailing out in column,

and then racing each other as far as Aegina. So they made good speed on their way to Corcyra, where the other force of their allies was assembling."[8]

It was the zenith of Athenian pride and overweening confidence. They knew little of Sicily, not even how large it was, or which cities would support them. A shrewd Syracusan leader, Hermocrates, as long ago as 424 BC, had persuaded the pro-Athenian cities of Sicily to end their war with Syracuse and her Dorian allies in the interests of Sicilian security against overseas attack. Thus the Athenians who arrived in Sicily obtained very little help, even from Ionian cities.

The three commanders, Nicias, Alcibiades and Lamachus, had different ideas about how to proceed, but finally they adopted Alcibiades' plan to negotiate for help from other cities before attacking Syracuse, which in fact allowed Syracuse, under Hermocrates' forceful leadership, to prepare their own forces more effectively. Meanwhile, the state trireme, "Salaminia", arrived from Athens with instructions to arrest Alcibiades and bring him to Athens for trial. Now that the initial enthusiasm for the expedition in Athens had abated, his prospects for clearing his name were less than before. Alcibiades was no Socrates, prepared to face an unfair trial on a charge which he knew to be false for the sake of the law itself. At Thurii, where the "Salaminia" called on the return voyage, he escaped and made his way to Sparta. When Lamachus as killed later on, Nicias was to remain as the senior commander, the man who, more than anyone, had spoken out against the whole scheme.

When, at last, the Athenians invested the city, whose Great Harbour made it the finest and wealthiest port in Magna Graecia, the Syracusans were hard pressed, for their citizen army faced the experienced troops of Athens and her allies, so that they lost the preliminary skirmishes. The Athenians built a long wall, intended to cut the whole city off from communications on the landward side, but they failed to complete the northern section down to the rocky north coast. In response the Syracusans built counter walls at right angles, to prevent the Athenian wall from reaching the Great Harbour in the south. Inside Syracuse the situation was becoming desperate, as hope of outside assistance dwindled. At this critical stage, the foolishness of the democratic Assembly in Athens in intervening to recall Alcibiades on a matter which had nothing to do with the direct control of war operations, told decisively against the Athenians. For Alcibiades spoke to the Spartan Assembly, describing the very plans which his own ambition had nurtured for the conquest of Sicily. Perhaps he was hoping to return to Athens with Spartan support as a tyrant, who would dispel the "acknowledged folly" of the democracy, as he now called it. Perhaps he was merely vindictive. Either way, he gave the Spartans brilliant military advice: to send a general to help the Syracusans and to fortify Decelea in northern Attica. The former advice was to bring disaster upon the Sicilian expedition; the latter was to prove a thorn in the side of Athens for the rest of the war by threatening Athenian communications with the Euripus and Euboea and by inhibiting the cultivation of the land.

The Spartan general, Gylippus, was despatched forthwith. He collected a force in some Dorian cities on Sicily and made his way to Syracuse. Now in a mood of confidence, Nicias had neglected to complete the northern part of the Athenian encircling wall, even though he had news of help coming to the Syracusans. Gylippus seized his opportunity, marched into Syracuse and realised immediately that a new Syracusan counter-wall would prevent the Athenians from ever completing their own fortifications. A race to complete the rival walls got under way and, not surprisingly, the Syracusans, under the direction of Gylippus and knowing their lives were at stake, won it. Their wall was then continued up along the heights of Epipolae to the north of the city, threatening the Athenian's own position, and, ominously, their escape routes.

Nicias was ill, suffering from a disease of the kidneys. He wrote to Athens, asking for reinforcements and to be relieved of the command. The Assembly would not release him, but sent out an amazingly large force, almost as powerful as the original one, under the command of the competent general, Demosthenes. They arrived just after a sea battle in the Great Harbour, in which the Syracusans adapted their tactics more successfully than the Athenians to the constricted space. By strengthening and shortening the beaks of their vessels, they were able to manoeuvre and ram the long-beaked enemy. Even on the element they had made their own, the Athenians were losing their grip.

Demosthenes saw that the only chance of success now lay in breaking through the Syracusan counter-wall. A brave attack was launched over the heights on a moonlit night, but a spirited defence led by Hermocrates drove the Athenians back. Then, to the horror of the besieging army, the besieged forces in Syracuse were themselves reinforced by fresh troops from the Peloponnese, Boeotia and the Dorian cities of Sicily. For the Athenians the time to make a tactical withdrawal had undoubtedly arrived. Only Nicias held out against it, with his usual reluctance to change an established position, however bad, in favour of one of uncertain value. Then suddenly the full moon suffered an eclipse. Nicias' irrational caution was confirmed by superstition. The army interpreted the sign as a warning that the plan to move was dangerous.

Syracuse knew that the initiative was now in their hands. They forced the Athenian fleet to meet them once more in the harbour and destroyed many of their ships. Desperation now seized upon the Athenian army. Only the sea offered the hope of a final escape from the nightmare in which they seemed to be embroiled, as they sat in the late summer heat looking down upon the great arc of the harbour below them and over their shoulders at the fortified Syracusan wall, stretching westwards across the heights of Epipolae. Many crowded into the Athenian ships in the harbour, determined to fight their way out to the open sea. A touch of nobility came now to the bemused Nicias, and wanting nothing more than to hand over the responsibility to another general, he found the strength to speak to every shipload of men and encourage them with words that appealed to their native valour and love for their city and families at home. To the sound of a paean, sung with a common and heartfelt emotion, the fleet drew across the harbour to engage the enemy. Across the harbour entrance lay a barrier of ships bound together by chains. What followed in described graphically by Thucydides:

"All the time that one ship was bearing down upon another, javelins, arrows, and stones were shot or hurled on it without cessation by the men on the decks; and once the ships met, the soldiers fought hand to hand, each trying to board the enemy. Because of the narrowness of the space, it often happened that a ship was ramming and being rammed at the same time, and that two, or sometimes more, ships found themselves jammed against one, so that the steersman had to think of defence on one side and attack on the other and, instead of being able to give their attention at one point at a time, had to deal with many different things in all directions; and the great din of all these ships crashing together was not only frightening in itself, but also made it impossible to hear the orders given by the boatswains."[9]

After a terrible struggle, the power of the Syracusans, fighting in their own harbour and with the simpler task of merely preventing the Athenians from breaking out, prevailed. Abandoning their ships, the Athenians fled to their camp, knowing now that they had to escape by land immediately or die where they were, with no prospect of fresh supplies. Hermocrates showed his cool-headedness at this juncture, for the Syracusans wanted nothing more than to rejoice at their great victory in the harbour. He demanded that the routes out of the city be heavily guarded, but the other leaders turned down his request. Still he persisted and hit upon a clever scheme. He sent a few of his men to the Athenian camp with instructions to show sympathy and advise them not to set off immediately that night because the roads were guarded, but to prepare a more systematic retreat the following day. Nicias was taken in by this, despite the fact that he had informants inside the city, and the Athenians actually delayed their departure by two whole days. Meanwhile, of course, Hermocrates and Gylippus had managed to organise their forces; road blocks were set up and the whole army deployed to trap the escaping mass of the enemy.

Athenian sick and wounded were left behind, notwithstanding their desperate entreaties. Men turned to go, knowing that the Syracusans would show little mercy towards their friends and relatives still lying in the camp. Altogether 40,000 men set off along the dusty road into the hills:

"No Hellenic army had ever suffered such a reverse. They had come to enslave others, and now they were going away frightened of being enslaved themselves; and instead of the prayers and paeans with which they had sailed out, the words to be heard now were directly contrary and boded evil as they started on their way back, sailors travelling on land, trusting in hoplites rather than in ships."[10]

Once more, Nicias showed great courage and leadership in the deplorable situation which was largely of his own making. His exhortation "that to be brave now is a matter of necessity" drew more scraps of determination from the wreck of an army, but all knew that only the gods could save them from the heat, the lack of provisions and the pursuing enemy. It was not long before the end came. The rearguard under Demosthenes was caught first; then later the rest were trapped, as they incontinently rushed down to a river to slake their raging thirst. Many were cut down as the drank. Those who were captured were mainly sent to the stone quarries of Syracuse, though the leaders, including Demosthenes and Nicias were executed. How far from the glories of Athens were these miserable men, who had set out with such fanfares and panoplies not long before!

"There were many of them, and they were crowded together in a narrow pit, where, since there was no roof over their heads, they suffered first from the heat of the sun and the closeness of the air; and then, in contrast, came on the cold autumnal nights, and the change in temperature brought disease amongst them. Lack of space made it necessary for them to do everything on the same spot; and besides there were the bodies all heaped together on top of one another of those who had died from their wounds or from the change of temperature or other such causes, so that the smell was insupportable."[11]

A few men escaped this ordeal by pleasing some Syracusans who liked to hear them reciting lines of verse from Euripides' plays. They had been listening carefully, in those far off days when they had basked in the evening sunlight on the grassy bank of the theatre of Dionysus!

The Sicilian expedition failed because of the errors of Nicias, and the stupidity of the Assembly in first appointing him and then in interfering with the situation for political reasons. It failed also because the Sicilian Greeks discovered a brave and resourceful leader in Hermocrates and were given a single Spartan general, Gylippus; yet the real causes of failure lay deeper. Pericles had said, when the war began, "I have other grounds of confidence, if you will refrain from trying to win more territory." He knew that to administer well the empire which his generation had inherited was one thing; that to insist on taking more was another. Could the men who went to Sicily have sworn that their sole purpose was to hasten the defeat of Sparta and her allies in the war? Pride and greed had found a lodgement.

Such a massive defeat was bound to affect the relationship between Athens and her allies. In 412 BC, Chios, Teos, Lebedus, Mytilene, Cyme and others broke out in revolt against their weakened mistress. More ominous still for Athens was the entry of Persia into the war, when Sparta made the humiliating Treaty of Miletus under which she acknowledged the Great King's claim to the Ionian coast of Asia Minor in return for financial help. Such disasters caused an upheaval in Athens. In the Summer of the year 411 BC, the oligarch party in Athens seized power and held it until the Athenian sailors took matters in their own hands and obtained enough support to re-introduce democracy. The democratic navy built on success by winning a series of battles against the Peloponnesian fleet. Even the opportunity for a negotiated peace presented itself, but the new democracy could not see beyond the brief tide of success to a longer term settlement, and so ignored perhaps the last opportunity to save Athens from a final disaster.

Those who saw the impending doom inherent in the persistent clash of arms between Greek poleis were not confined to a handful of Athenian intellectuals, like Euripides in his *Women of Troy*, or the mocking Aristophanes, whose heroine, Lysistrata, bade the women of Athens to strike to compel the men to make peace. In far-off Leontine in Sicily, the sophist, Georgias, looked askance at the Spartan connivance with Persia and seized the opportunity at the Olympic games of 408 BC to speak out to the assembled Greeks against a misalliance that brought the victors of Plataea to fight against the victors of Salamis, alongside the common enemy of both. What would Leonidas say now to his fellow countrymen who took Persian gold to pay men to kill Athenians? "Rather," said Georgias, "go to war against Persia."

Two years later an event occurred which also underlined the decline in ancient standards under the stress of war. A great naval battle was fought south of Lesbos, near the islets of the Arginusae. It left the Athenians victorious, but at the heavy cost of 25 ships with their crews. Many of the sailors had clung to the wreckage, hoping for rescue. When a storm blew up, the Athenian commanders were unable, or unwilling, to go to their assistance. Reports of the victory were overshadowed by the tragedy of the drowned sailors. Eventually the admirals, eight of them, were summoned for trial before the Assembly. Feelings ran high; many present were friends and relatives of those hundreds of men who had drowned. Set upon vengeance, the Assembly ignored the well established custom not to bring a case against a group of accused men collectively. One man only objected to this want of proper procedure, the *epistates* for the day, Socrates, the philosopher.

Though threatened himself with death by his inclusion in the charge, he continued to object to the motion before the Assembly. Nevertheless, it was passed. The sentence was death and loss of property. Two admirals had failed to appear. Six, including Pericles, son of the great statesman, were executed. Even the supporters of the generals had lacked the courage to act legally to oppose the motion, for they could have passed a motion of *graphe paranomen*, making the proposers of the collective charge liable to an action for illegal procedure. Socrates alone looked to the law, and spoke out in its defence, come what may.

In Sparta a man arose who was to be the instrument of bringing the benighted democracy to its knees. Lysander was one of the few remaining Spartan leaders not corrupted by gold, whether Spartan or foreign; but he was inordinately ambitious and also exceedingly competent. After operations near Rhodes and Attica, he sailed to the Hellespont with about 200 ships, knowing that the Athenians could not leave him there to threaten their whole logistical situation. 180 Athenian triremes followed him. They stopped opposite his position at Lampsacus, where the Spartan fleet had an excellent harbour. The Athenian fleet lay on open beaches, at Aegospotami, or "Goat's rivers". For four days the Athenians sailed across the straits, tempting Lysander to engage. Alcibiades, from the castle in the neighbourhood to which he had retired after various flirtations with Persia, now advised the Athenian commander to move his ships from their exposed position on the beaches. He ignored the advice. On the fifth day Lysander struck. Whilst the Athenians heedlessly ate their dinner, following their usual abortive challenge to the Spartan fleet, Lysander sent his full force across to destroy the empty boats. Twenty Athenian triremes escaped to sea. The rest were wiped out. Several thousand Athenian captives were put to death. The disaster for the fleet was total. The city of Themistocles could not have met a more stupendous humiliation. Where it took place was fitly named; the goat of tragedy was in full cry.

The state trireme, "Paralus", arrived at Athens during the night with the news. Everyone knew the significance of the destruction of the navy:

> "As the news of the disaster was told, one man passed it on to another, and a sound of wailing arose and extended first from Pireus, then along the long walls until it reached the city. That night no one slept. They mourned for the lost, but more still for their own fate. They thought that they themselves would now be dealt with as they had dealt with others - with the Melians, colonists of Sparta, after they had besieged and conquered Melos, with the people of Histiaea, of Scione, of Torone, of Aegina and many other states."[12]

In fact, Sparta had not quite forgotten the unity that had once save the Greeks from Persia. Despite the protestations of her allies, especially of Corinth, she was merciful. The Athenians had to hand over all the remaining fleet, except 12 triremes;

to pull down the Long Walls; to give up all foreign possessions; to allow all exiles to return; and to become a dependent ally of Sparta; but her people were spared. As the walls were dismantled to the music of flutes, the successful allies thought that freedom had dawned.

"Whence come wars…? Whence but from the body and the lusts of the body?" asks Socrates in Plato's *Phaedo*.[13] The end of the fifth century saw the degeneration of the Greek poleis into a state of widespread materialism. Selfishness, and in particular, greed, was rife in all classes of society, as much in Sparta and her allies as in those states in the Athenian camp. The war was essentially an extension of the divisions within each polis, arising from this materialism, into the relations between the poleis. For the dominant features of the degeneracy of Athens and of Sparta, as the two leading states, were essentially the same. The people of Athens, having acquired power through the democratic reforms that took place in the course of the century, used it increasingly to oppress those who were deprived of power, not so much within Athens, as outside amongst their allies. Whilst in Sparta, the Spartiates, from acting as a genuinely superior ruling caste, turned into an oppressive minority, terrorising their subjects, the helots and *perioeci*, with the dreaded *krypteia*. When the Athenians slaughtered the men of Scione for daring to rebel, they unwittingly emulated the Spartiates, who murdered 2000 helots to whom they had promised freedom. At root, the democracy at Athens, the spider in the web of empire, was no different from the oligarchy in Sparta, the gaoler of a Laconian prison.

Men had degenerated; that was the real cause of the internecine war and the troubles, like the plague in Athens, that went with it. There were no more like the immovably honest Aristides; no more like Leonidas, prepared to die for the high ideals of freedom and courage. Some fought bravely enough, but they fought for a lesser cause, for a faction, or the seizure of territory. Greek civilisation still gave some the decency to be merciful, or to respect the suffering of others, but the number of such men dwindled, so that, as the war went on, justified killing was often replaced by atrocities. The paradox remains that even at the height of the war Athenian culture produced some of its finest works. Phidias and Sophocles and Euripides stood, as it were, within earshot of the teaching of Socrates in the Agora, the source of another culture, in which the spirit of Man would revive yet again, freed from the morass of greed and lust and war.

### References:

1. Thucydides, *The Peloponnesian War*, trans. R. Warner, Penguin, London, 1976, Book I, p. 49.
2. J. D. Bury & R. Meiggs, *A History of Greece*, MacMillan, London, 1979, p. 247.
3. Thucydides, *The Peloponnesian War*, Book III, p. 217.
4. Thucydides, *The Peloponnesian War*, Book III, pp. 242-3.
5. Thucydides, *The Peloponnesian War*, Book III, p. 244.
6. Thucydides, *The Peloponnesian War*, Book IV, p. 289.
7. Thucydides, *The Peloponnesian War*, Book V, p. 404.
8. Thucydides, *The Peloponnesian War*, Book VI, p. 429.

9.  Thucydides, *The Peloponnesian War*, Book VII, pp. 523-4

10. Thucydides, *The Peloponnesian War*, Book VII, p. 528.

11. Thucydides, *The Peloponnesian War*, Book VII, p. 536.

12. Xenophon, *Hellenica* (A History of My Times), trans. R. Warner, Penguin, London, 1981, ch. 2, p. 104.

13. Plato, *Phaedo*, trans. B. Jowett, Random House, New York, 1937, 66.

*Part 4*

# Graeco-Roman Civilisation:

*Hellenistic Culture*

## Chapter 21

# A Draught of Hemlock

### *The Teaching of Socrates*

DURING THE PELOPONNESIAN WAR any Athenian, or stranger, who happened to walk down to the Agora on a day when normal business was going on there, stood a good chance of seeing Socrates. Anyone could speak to him. That was why he came to the Agora, or thereabouts, for he wanted to find out what men thought and, if they welcomed his help, to enquire with them into all sorts of questions, above all questions about the good life. Often he was to be found in the Stoa of Zeus, or in the fountain house, or near the Bouleuterion, or in Simon's shoe shop, or perhaps strolling along the Panathenaic Way, which led up to the Propylaea.

Of course, he knew many of the more important men in Athens. His father, Sophroniscus, was a friend of Aristides, and he himself knew Pericles well and some

*The Athenian Agora near Socrates' Prison*

of the Periclean circle: Aspasia, Alcibiades and his uncle, Axiochus, and Callias. Archelaus, the pupil of Anaxagoras - Pericles' philosophy teacher - was with Socrates in Samos, probably in the year 440 BC, when Socrates may have been a soldier in the expeditionary force there. In those early years, when he was thirty or so, Socrates met several young men from Megara and Thebes, who were interested in philosophy. They remained devoted friends, even through the war which divided them, for when Socrates died in 399 BC some of them were with him; Eucleides and Terpsion of Megara, and Simmias and Cebes of Thebes, for example. The Megarans followed the teaching of Parmenides, whilst the Thebans were Pythagoreans, and Socrates clearly welcomed their earlier training as a sound basis for the study of philosophy, just as he was very willing to make good use of the ideas of the Orphics and even of the symbolism of the Eleusinian Mysteries.

His own earlier interest had been in natural philosophy, but he soon realised that this would never satisfy him, for the questions which he felt to be most fundamental were those concerning Man's life and how it was to be ordered. As he said, "the unexamined life is not worth living." He had thought that Anaxagoras' doctrine of Mind as the root cause of everything offered the hope of real knowledge, until he read Anaxagoras' book and discovered that the explanation reverted to the elements of fire, water and so on, with no reference to the teleological account that Socrates expected. Later, whilst he sat in prison awaiting execution, Socrates explained exactly what was so inadequate about such kinds of first causes:

"I am able to bend my limbs, and this is why I am sitting here in a curved posture - that is what he (the natural philosopher) would say; and he would have a similar explanation of my talking to you, which he would attribute to sound, and air, and hearing, and he would assign ten thousand other causes of the same sort, forgetting to mention the true cause, which is, that the Athenians have thought fit to condemn me, and, accordingly, I have thought it better and more right to remain here and undergo whatever sentence they impose."[1]

Socrates points out that conditions are not causes. Without bones and muscles the body cannot move, but one does not act because of them. One acts because one chooses to act.

Such cool reasoning in these dire circumstances was in keeping with how Socrates had lived his life. As an ordinary Athenian soldier, serving in the citizen army, often against the dedicated soldiers of Sparta, Socrates had distinguished himself by his unobtrusive, but resolute, courage. In the fighting at Potidaea he saved the life of Alcibiades; after the battle of Delium, a serious Athenian defeat, he had shown exemplary self-control in walking away from the battlefield with no sign of fear and with such clear intent to defend himself that enemy soldiers preferred to attack those who looked scared.

His courage was by no means just physical, as he proved when the admirals were convicted by an unjust procedure after the battle of Arginusae. A similar incident occurred when the thirty tyrants were in control of Athens. They seized power from the democracy soon after the Athenian surrender to Sparta in 404 BC. One of their many victims was a rich man, Leon of Salamis. They ordered Socrates and four other men to arrest him, but Socrates simply went home and did nothing. The other four did arrest Leon, and Socrates was only saved from the wrath of the tyrants by their rapid fall from power. It was another example of Socrates' regard for law, which finally cost him his life.

Socrates' teaching had two aspects: one, a critical examination of any philosophical view; the other, a directing of the mind towards the truth. These were not really distinct, because he held that the approach to truth was a process of stripping away falsehood, but nevertheless those who submitted to his questioning must often have felt that the critical aspect had a special sting. How thorough going he was in this stripping away is shown by his interpretation of the Delphic oracle's pronouncement that he, Socrates, was the wisest of men. For in believing that this was so - only because he realised that he knew nothing and that others thought that they did - Socrates was committed to exposing all claims to knowledge as spurious. This necessarily led him to do battle with such famous intellectuals of the day as Georgias of Leontini, Protagoras of Abdera, and Prodicus of Ceos. Since these, and others like them, were sophists - professional teachers to whom the wealthiest and most successful Athenians sent their sons for the kind of training in rhetoric that would lead to a brilliant career - Socrates was really taking on the intellectual establishment of the time.

His method was to ask for clear definitions or explanations of what his opponents meant, which usually they were incapable of giving when it came to a serious concept, like justice or goodness. He was not asking for mere definitions in words by means of synonyms or circumlocution, but rather for the essence of the concept; what it really was in itself. In this, he was going beyond a merely critical method of arguing. That everything had such an essence was the other aspect of his teaching, the direction towards the truth. For his own standpoint was not that of a sceptic, questioning everything to destruction. He had trained himself to see the world in the light of reason, so that what appeared to the senses was seen as illusory, when compared with the essential world which only the mind itself perceived. Thus to him, justice, goodness, equality, beauty and other pure concepts, or Ideas, could be discerned by the intellect through the recognition of them in, but not of, the world of sense experience. Hence Socrates' questioning was designed to lead the mind from the falsity of sense objects, to a recognition of, for example, the beauty in them; then to an acknowledgement of the existence of pure beauty.

A multiplicity of pure ideas, however, would not satisfy the reason of Socrates. What gave rise to these? What was their cause?

"... then thought begins to be aroused within us, and the soul perplexed and wanting to arrive at a decision asks 'What is absolute unity?' This is the way in which the study of the one has a power of drawing and converting the mind to the contemplation of true being."[2]

The final source of pure ideas must therefore be that absolute unity, which Socrates calls the Good. Hence the philosopher seeks to find himself in the Good, for only thus would that unity be absolute. The whole aim of Socrates' teaching was, therefore, to lead a man to know himself:

"Now I have no leisure for such enquiries; shall I tell you why? I must first know myself, as the Delphian inscription says; to be curious about that which is not my concern, while I am still in ignorance of my own self, would be ridiculous."[3]

For Socrates was the great exponent of the Delphic inscription, "Know Thyself". All else - science, politics, rhetoric - was nothing if it were not founded upon the one certainty of self-knowledge. This was why Socrates had abandoned science and scorned the efforts of Anaxagoras. This was why he would play no more part in public life than he believed was necessary for a responsible citizen, and why he irritated those whose status depended upon their claims to know and yet who had not found themselves.

Xenophon, a pupil and admirer of Socrates, has described one level of this knowledge of oneself:

> "And isn't this obvious", said Socrates, "that people derive most of their benefits from knowing themselves and most of their misfortunes from being self-deceived? Those who know themselves know what is appropriate for them and can distinguish what they can and cannot do;... Self knowledge also enables them to judge the quality of others; and it is through their relations with others that they provide themselves with what is good and guard against what is bad for them."[4]

A deeper level of self-knowledge than this was found in Socrates' teaching on the immortality of the soul. It was there that he drew close to the Orphic doctrines and the Eleusinian Mysteries, often referring to their imagery of sleeping and waking, of purification and regeneration. Socrates brought reason to bear upon these, without denying the power of the ancient imagery. "What is purification, but the separation of the soul from the body?[5] For the soul is the principle of life in men; it cannot therefore die, for it contains life, not as a definition in words, but as an essential element, which resists death, just as the oddness of the number three resists the idea of being even. That the soul has been present before birth, which the Orphics affirmed, is shown by the recognition of things which cannot have been learnt by sense experience, such as the truths of pure geometry, or the recognition of pure beauty.

Socrates referred to the previous existence of the soul in other bodies, as in the Orphic teaching on reincarnation. The souls of the evil, said Socrates, become imprisoned in other bodies. Men who have been gluttonous, immoral or drunken pass into asses and animals of that sort. Those who have chosen injustice, tyranny and violence pass into wolves, hawks and kites. Those who practise the civil and social virtues, such as temperance and justice, acquiring them by habit but without philosophy and reason, become a social kind of creature, like bees or ants, or even again enter into the form of men. Only philosophy teaches the escape from this everlasting cycle of reincarnation.

The acid test of Socrates' trust in his own teaching on the immortality of the soul came when he was tried before an Athenian court on charges of corrupting the young and of impiety towards the gods of the city. The man responsible for the charge was Anytus, a leader of the democratic party, which feared a return of the thirty tyrants and suspected Socrates of secret sympathy for them, since he had not fled with the democrats during the tyranny. Moreover, he had often been critical of Athenian democracy, on the grounds that it let judgements be made, not by the best, but by the majority. Worse still, three of Socrates' associates, Alcibiades, Critias and Charmides, had been noted opponents of the democracy. Alcibiades had conspired with Sparta and Persia, and Critias was "the most deceitful, violent and bloody" of the tyrants, according to Xenophon. In fact, all three had gone to Socrates because they were seeking their own advancement and thought he had the key to it. None were amongst the inner circle of real pupils and friends, like those who were with him when he died. Thus the underlying reason for the prosecution of Socrates was probably political: that the democratic party saw him as a troublemaker and source of disaffection.

Why then did Anytus not openly charge Socrates with political wrongs? The reason was that when the democrats were restored to power they granted an amnesty to their opponents, hence they could not openly proceed against them. Probably few people really believed that Socrates had corrupted the youth of Athens, or that he had shown impiety. The sophists had done much more to corrupt people, for they really did what Aristophanes quite wantonly accused Socrates of in *The Clouds*: they made the weaker argument appear the stronger. As for impiety, everyone knew that Socrates was quite particular about paying reverence to the gods of the city and was quite the most religious man of his time in his devotion to spiritual matters.

Nevertheless, he was brought to trial before a jury of about 500 citizens. Socrates' defence was an eloquent statement of all that he had been doing: to lead men to value virtue and to care for their own souls. As for his religious beliefs, he was quick to point out that his confidence in divine forces implied a sure belief in divine beings. The jury, however, could not rise above their prejudices; their blindness confirmed that Athens had degenerated out of all recognition from the days of Aristides and Themistocles. By a majority of 280 to 220 they found him guilty. Under Athenian law the prisoner had the right to propose a punishment as an alternative to the prosecution's demand, in this case for death. Socrates, with supreme indifference, proclaimed that he should be rewarded with maintenance in the *prytaneum* at the expense of the city, like an Olympic victor or other hero, but that he would defer to the court and ask for a fine of one mina - a derisory amount. His friends, amongst them Plato, cried out to him to say at least thirty minae, which he did; but the jury were further alienated by all this. They voted by a larger majority for the death sentence.

Socrates' execution was delayed for over a month, because the sacred ship, which went annually to Delos to commemorate the voyage of Theseus to Crete, had just set sail. No executions could be carried out till it returned. Here was the perfect opportunity to escape, as Socrates' friends, especially Crito, urged him to do. His reason for staying to await execution was simple. The laws of a state enjoin obedience on all who willingly live under them:

> "But he who has experience of the manner in which we (the laws) order justice and administer the state, and still remains, has entered into an implied contract that he will do as we command him."[6]

Socrates knew that every state rests upon the acceptance by its members of an obligation to obey the law, even when the law appears to conflict with their interests. He would countenance no special pleading in his own case. Even though he was unjustly condemned, the procedure had been correct and the decision of the jury clearly expressed. What also convinced him of the need to stay was the fact that no inner voice told him to flee or avoid punishment. This inner voice, or sign, always warned Socrates against actions which were wrong or harmful, though it never enjoined him to do anything. It was the call to a measured life, to that avoidance of excess which was the counterpart of "Know Thyself" at Apollo's shrine in Delphi. And now the sign was silent. To die in obedience to the law was a measured end for such a man as Socrates.

When the ship returned from Delos, the time had come for the execution. On the day affixed, Socrates conversed with those special friends who would carry on his work. He had defined what it was: "God orders me to fulfil the philosopher's mission of searching into myself and other men." They would form schools for that purpose: Plato's Academy in Athens, Eucleides' School at Megara, Echecrates' at Elis, Antisthenes' Cynic School and others. He bade farewell to his wife and allowed a select few to stay when the executioner brought in the hemlock, the Athenian means of execution. So calm and untroubled was Socrates that the executioner, who had seen men rave or despair at approaching death, gave his instructions and then burst into tears before retiring. Plato has recorded the final moments:

"Then raising the cup to his lips, quite readily and cheerfully he drank off the poison. Hitherto most of us had been fairly able to control our sorrow; but now when we saw him drinking, and saw, too, that he had finished the draught, we could no longer forbear, and in spite of myself my own tears were flowing fast; so that I covered my face and wept; not for him, but at the thought of my own calamity in having to part from such a friend. Nor was I the first; for Crito, when he found himself unable to restrain his tears, had got up, and I followed; and at that moment, Apollodorus, who had been weeping all the time, uttered a loud and passionate cry which made all who were present break down except Socrates. 'What are you doing, you strange people?' he said. 'I sent away the women mainly in order that they might not misbehave in this way, for I have been told that a man should die in silence. Be quiet then, and have patience.' ... He was beginning to grow cold about the groin, when he uncovered his face, for he had covered himself up, and said - they were his last words: 'Crito, I owe a cock to Asclepius; will you remember to pay the debt?' 'The debt shall be paid,' said Crito, 'is there anything else?' There was no answer to this question; but in a minute or two he moved, and the attendants uncovered him; his eyes were set, and Crito closed his eyes and mouth.

"Such was the end, Echecrates, of our friend, of whom I may truly say, that of all the men of his time whom I have known, he was the wisest and justest and best."[7]

The cock to Asclepius, god of health, was paid for a final recovery from the fitful fever of life. It acknowledged also Socrates' debt to the great tradition, which stretched from Imhotep, the wisest of Egyptians, through Asclepius, his Greek deification, to Socrates himself, the "gadfly" who woke men from sleep. For Crito and his colleagues the promise to pay the debt meant their dedication to teaching the way of truth that their master had followed.

Socrates was a man who rose above the culture into which he was born. That culture was dying in the fifth century despite its valedictory beauty, but from it was arising the Hellenism that spread throughout the Mediterranean world. Though the elements of Hellenism were drawn from classical Greek art and architecture and literature, the inner meaning of it came from the teaching of Socrates.

The clash of Greek arms and the murderous affrays of citizens in the Peloponnesian War were the death rattle of the polis. It had fulfilled its role over the centuries from the first foundations by legendary figures like Theseus, through the great restatements of law by Lycurgus and Solon, to the practical reforms of Cleisthenes and the Spartan ephors. The growth of selfishness and greed, however, was irreversible within the context of the polis. Civil war was almost endemic during the last thirty years of Socrate's life. Greek fought Greek with a ferocity previously reserved for barbarians. Party fought party within the walls of cities, striving for power and then using it to slaughter fellow citizens, who had become implacable enemies. Despite the glories of the new Acropolis, Athens was no place now for the arete of the citizen, for the building of an excellence of human skill in the service of the state, especially of an excellence of character - the truly virtuous man. Greatness of character, as Socrates himself knew only too well from long experience, could only be wrested now from the forces of destruction by following the inner light of reason.

In his teaching on the immortality of the soul, Socrates gave to the Greek world a new and unique form of the ancient tradition that offered self-realisation. The soul partakes of the Absolute Good; through the soul each man may find that Absolute within himself. Those who gathered round the master knew that he had shown them the way of escape from the apparent horrors of their world as it crashed down around them, demolished by crime as surely as the Long Walls were torn down to the sound of Spartan flutes.

The soul was not merely individual; it was one and the same as the Good. It was unique and, at the same time, universal. This cornerstone of Socrate's teaching became the foundation for the new culture. For once the polis was destroyed men turned to another unity for their fulfilment, and they found it in the comprehensive nature of the soul. In looking within they found at the same time universality. Hence there was in truth only one great human society, and the source of men and womens' fulfilment became a larger unit than the polis, not of one place, nor of one people, not even necessarily Greek. The empires of Alexander the Great and of Rome were heirs of this idea.

Thus the teaching of Socrates engendered a new culture to replace that which had come to a glorious end in the classical art of Athens. Socrates created nothing of his own - no art, no literature, no mathematics; but he enabled new men to be born, who would lay the foundations of Hellenism and ensure that Greece would pour forth its learning upon fresh generations. As he said of himself, he was a midwife:

"It is quite clear that they never learned anything from me; the many fine discoveries to which they cling are of their own making. But to me and the god they owe their delivery."[8]

### References:

1. Plato, *Phaedo*, trans. B. Jowett, Random House, New York, 1937, 98.

2. Plato, *Republic*, trans. Jowett, Book VII, 524.

3. Plato, *Phaedrus*, trans. Jowett, 230.

4. Xenophon, *Memoirs of Socrates*, trans. A. S. Benjamin, Bobbs-Merrill, Indianapolis, 1965, Book IV, ch. 2.

5. Plato, *Phaedo*, trans. Jowett, 67.
6. Plato, *Crito*, trans. Jowett, 51.
7. Plato, *Phaedo*, trans. Jowett, 117-118.
8. Plato, *Theaetetus*, trans. Jowett, 150.

## Chapter 22
# Scourge of Tyranny
### *The Career of Epaminondas*

NOTHING DEMONSTRATED the collapse of the ancient culture more clearly than the behaviour of Sparta in the years that followed her victory in the Peloponnesian War. What would the great Lycurgus, maker of just men, have thought of the Spartiates who now enslaved the cities of Greece? Spartan military governors, or *harmosts*, were appointed, sharing their rule with groups of oligarchs sympathetic to Spartan interests. It was said that in many cities the will of a Spartiate was the law. Lysander himself boasted that his countrymen cheated boys with dice and men with oaths. Within the territory of Sparta, the Lycurgan system of land tenure had broken down. No longer did each citizen hold a small piece of land, just enough for his needs as a member of the warrior class. Alienation of holdings had enabled some to become rich and made others poor. The link between land and citizenship was broken, with the consequent erosion of the body of free and equal citizens.

*A view near Sparta*

It took a great man to free Greece from Spartan degeneracy. Epaminondas was the son of a poor Theban nobleman, who found the means to educate him in philosophy; so he studied under Lysis of Tarentum, a Pythagorean, and may have been influenced by Simmias and Cebes, Theban friends of Socrates. A soldier of great tactical ability, he became a generous and merciful statesman, relatively free of personal ambition. Unfortunately for his own city and for Greece herself, the Thebans were not equal to the task of fulfilling his ideals. When he died it was his example, not any tangible Theban achievement, that lived on to guide future generations.

For some years intermittent warfare had ranged over northern Greece, until a peace conference met in 371 BC. The settlement, which Athens and Sparta agreed upon, included the condition that Thebes should not sign the peace treaty on behalf of the whole Boeotian League, but that each Boeotian city should sign on its own account. Thebes would not accept this attempt to strike at its traditional leadership of the League. Its refusal gave Sparta the excuse she wanted to attack Thebes. A Spartan army lay in wait on the western border of Boeotia. Avoiding the obvious route, it marched through the mountains to Creusis on the Gulf of Corinth and was only stopped short of Thebes by Epaminondas' army on the plain of Leuctra. The young Spartan king, Cleombrotus, was confident of victory. Under his command were 1000 cavalry and 10,000 hoplites, of which 1,200 were Spartiates, whilst the Theban army numbered only 600 cavalry and about 6,000 hoplites.

The Theban cavalry was superior to the Spartan. Moreover, the Theban hoplites contained an elite group of 300, known as the Sacred Band, under the notable commander, Pelopidas. These men were the most courageous and dedicated warriors in Thebes, taught to fight in pairs, each man alongside his best friend, for whom he would die without hesitation. They were placed on the left of the Theban line to form the nucleus of a spearhead of hoplites drawn up fifty deep, instead of the normal twelve deep formation adopted by the Spartans. Epaminondas had created a tactic involving a bold offensive against the more numerous Spartan line. The opposing cavalry engaged first and the Spartan horses were driven back on to their own lines. Immediately Epaminondas ordered the reinforced left wing to advance at the double, led by Pelopidas. The centre and right wing were given the command to advance only later, so that the Theban line converged on the enemy *en echelon*.

The fifty deep head of hoplites smashed into the thin line of Spartiates holding the place of honour on the right of the Spartan line. For a few minutes the line held, but Cleombrotus fell, mortally wounded. The Spartiates around him fought desperately to rescue their king and even managed to carry him to the rear, but as rank after rank of the best Theban hoplites leapt into the fray, the Spartan line could not hold. As it broke, the disciplined Thebans turned to either side to roll up the enemy line. With the Spartiate head cut off, the body could not survive. The allied troops fled to the rear, even before they had been seriously engaged. 400 Spartiates, one third of their force, lay dead on the field. The remainder retreated to their camp, temporarily secure behind a ditch. A truce was agreed for the burial of the dead.

At Leuctra, for the first time in the history of Greece, the Spartan army had lost a major battle in which the enemy did not outnumber them. The Theban hoplites had become the finest troops in Greece. By striking at the enemy's strongest point with overwhelming force, they had broken his will to fight. Leuctra profoundly affected the whole of Greece. At Sparta, the number of Spartiates, already low, now reached a critical level, so that men up to the age of 58 were called to arms and Spartan strategy turned to defence of their position in the Peloponnese, rather than aggression in northern Greece. At Athens the news of Leuctra was received coldly, for the Athenians did not welcome a new major power threatening the revived league which they themselves now led. All could see that a decisive change in the balance of power between the Greek poleis had taken place. Epaminondas saw further; he realised that the days of the autonomous polis had ended, that new forms of social organisation were required. His military campaigns of the years after Leuctra had this need in mind, though superficially they were directed at the conclusive reduction of Spartan imperialism and the prevention of a new imperialism in Athens and even in Thessaly, where successive tyrants threatened aggression.

Three times within five years Epaminondas, as Boeotarch, one of the five magistrates of the Boeotian League, led expeditions into the Peloponnese, campaigning in Winter, contrary to Greek practice. The Spartan women saw a hostile army on the city boundaries - it had no walls - for the first time in two centuries. Epaminondas, however, withdrew from an all out assault on the city; probably because his intention was never destruction, but rather to induce the enemy to adopt a rational and non-aggressive policy. More significant than any clash of arms was the establishment of two new political units in the Peloponnese, both anathema to Sparta and both progressive in their organisation and aims.

Before his first expedition into the Peloponnese, Epaminondas promised the Messenian people, helots of Sparta, that he would wrest their homeland from its overlords. The Messenian exiles in Naupactus, descendants of those settled by Athens after the final Messenian war, flocked to join Epaminondas as he marched into Spartan territory. The success of the campaign enabled him to fulfil his promise. At Mount Ithome, sanctuary and citadel of the Messenian people, where they had fought so desperately for their freedom a century before, he laid the foundations of a new city on the southern slopes, and the walls of an acropolis on the summit. The Messenian helots, awoken by their deliverer, rose in arms, and hailed Epaminondas as the father of their nation. Messene grew in strength and Sparta, though long resentful, could not recover it.

In the northern Peloponnese, Epaminondas revived the ancient, but defunct, Arcadian League. There too he founded a city, a federal capital, Megalopolis - the Great City - siting it in the most central and most fertile plain of Arcadia. Commissioners were summoned from each Arcadian state, though two declined, to plan the construction. Settlers from each tribe were encouraged to live there. A federal army was levied; the five thousand hoplites, known as the *apariti* became a significant force in Peloponnesian affairs. Contributions to a federal revenue were also raised. Government of the League was to be by means of a Federal Assembly, the "Ten Thousand" - unfortunately large - an administrative council, meeting in turn at three cities of the League, and magistrates elected by constituent states. Essentially the League was democratic, but some limitation on this was set by a property qualification. After the death of its founder, the Arcadian League was short-lived, but it stood as a model for federal systems at a time when evolution towards larger societies than the polis was a natural development.

To limit the imperialistic tendencies of Athens, whose naval hegemony was once more stretching far into the Aegean, Epaminondas took the imaginative step of building a large Boeotian fleet. Traditionally an exclusively land power, Thebes now led an expedition to Byzantium and so emboldened the cities threatened by Athens that some withdrew from alliance with her. Later, in 362 BC, both Athens and Sparta were humbled by the Boeotarch, when he led a fourth expedition into the Peloponnese.

Mantinea had left the Arcadian League and joined Sparta. Epaminondas brought his army of 30,000 hoplites and 3,000 cavalry south of Mantinea to split the alliance, and once more threatened Sparta itself, where the aged king, Agesilaus, earlier responsible for much of the Spartan terrorising of 'liberated' cities, organised a desperate defence. Again Epaminondas stopped short of an assault to the death, and chose instead to seize Mantinea. By chance a brigade of Athenian cavalry arrived from the north and drove off the Theban cavalry. An allied army of 20,000 hoplites and 2,000 cavalry, with contingents from Mantinea, Sparta, Athens, Elis and Achaea, then managed to block Epaminondas' forces in a narrow valley south of Mantinea. Now began the final exhibition of his genius as a field commander. The tactics of Leuctra were repeated but refined. Once again the Spartiates, with the Mantineans, held the right wing, with the rival cavalry deployed facing each other between the lines. This time, however, Epaminondas ordered his whole line to march north-westwards towards the hills, as though declining battle that day. Under cover from the dust raised by the cavalry, the Thebans strongly reinforced their left wing with their elite hoplites, including the Sacred Band. Unconcerned, the Spartan forces took their midday meal, some soldiers even finding shelter in the woods to the rear.

At this point Epaminondas sounded the advance. His cavalry charged in a deep wedge, supported by slingers and javelin-throwers. Behind them marched the Theban hoplites, shoulder to shoulder. On the extreme right, the Argives, allies of Boeotia, were some distance from the enemy line, *en echelon* with the Thebans. A mixed force of cavalry and infantry were posted in some foothills on the extreme right, to prevent the Athenians on the enemy left from swinging round to engage in the main battle. On the Theban left, the blow from the cavalry and Theban hoplites in 50 deep formation shattered the Spartan line; cavalry and hoplites fled in confusion and the triumphant Thebans swung to their right to cut off the retreat of the rest of the enemy forces.

One brave Spartan then changed the course of history. Standing firm as the ranks disintegrated around him, he plunged his javelin into the breast of Epaminondas. The Theban leader was carried from the field to the shady hillside. As news of his wound spread through his army, the organised pursuit of the enemy halted. The impending death of their leader drew the fire from the victorious troops. Victory was theirs, but grief overbore their elation. Whilst the javelin remained in his body, Epaminondas called for two noble Thebans, whom he named as his successors in command, but both were dead. That peace must be made was Epaminondas' final reply. He signalled for the javelin to be removed and the gush of blood took away his life.

Thus died one of the noblest of the Greeks. In warfare he was a consummate leader, prepared to fight in the front line whenever needful, yet capable of complete tactical control in the heat of an engagement. His contribution to military tactics affected the history of warfare; the attack *en echelon* ended once and for all the supremacy of an inflexible line of heavy infantry, advancing to engage at every point simultaneously. His combination of cavalry, infantry and slingers, and the timing of their engagement, instructed all later commanders. Philip of Macedon was a hostage at the Theban court for some while in his youth, and absorbed there the lessons of Theban success at Leuctra and elsewhere. Macedonian domination, for good or ill, owed something to the brilliant originality of Epaminondas.

His contribution to political organisation was as great. The imperialism of Athens and Sparta had been primarily self-seeking. It had antagonised both dependent peoples, by a policy of divide and rule, and other powers, by aggressive and acquisitive acts. Under Epaminondas, Theban hegemony tried to combine and lead the weaker states, especially those which feared Sparta in the Peloponnese and Athens in the Aegean. When other Theban leaders showed a tendency towards old-style imperialism, as at Orchomenus where the male population was slaughtered after a rebellion, Epaminondas protested strongly. He respected the independence of cities, yet encouraged the formation of federal organisations as a means of ending the internecine warfare which had plagued Greece for centuries. The Boeotian League itself, the Arcadian and Thessalian Leagues, and also those of Aetolia, Achaea and Western Locria, were all treated by him as self-governing bodies. His aim was to extend the spirit of self-reliance and autonomy beyond the city to a greater unity, ultimately perhaps to the unity of all Greeks in benevolent fellowship. In this he could not succeed - the mind of Greece was not prepared for it - but Epaminondas showed Greeks the way out of their political myopia. If they could not rise to his high ideals, then others - Macedonians and Romans - would learn of them. He had met the need of his time and place to rid Greece of the tyranny of a decadent timocracy. In doing so he had created a vision of free and equal peoples uniting for mutual prosperity. Part of his epitaph has survived, which exaggerates his immediate achievements:

> "by our counsels Sparta was shorn of her glory,
>
> sacred Messene received her children at last,
>
> Megapolis was crowned with walls by Theban prowess,
>
> and all Greece was free and independent."[1]

Ultimately what hindered Epaminondas was the inadequacy of the people of Thebes, the instrument of his policies. They had not imbued the spirit of Pythagoras and Socrates. Not only at Orchomenus did Epaminondas protest at their barbarity, for they remained relatively uncultured and lacking in vision. He called upon them "to bring the Propylaea of Athens to the forecourt of the Cadmea," but it was not in their power to do so.

After his death, as though in deference to his wishes, all mainland Greek states, with the sole exception of Sparta - unyielding on the issue of Messenia - bound themselves by oath to observe a "general peace and alliance". They undertook to settle disputes by negotiation and to defend one another against aggression. A new federal court was created, and probably federal revenues were collected. Yet, when the Greeks of Ionia called for help against the tyranny of the Great King, the united Greeks of the mainland opted for a cautious neutrality. Within a year, Athens was making separate alliances, contrary to the spirit of the new call for general agreement. Boeotia responded by sending troops into Arcadia to protect her interests there. As practical politics the ideal of Epaminondas was a failure in the context of fourth century Greece, but, as a principle to guide all who sought amity between states and an end to war, it remained a living force.

## Reference:

1. Hammond, *History of Greece to 324 BC*, O.U.P., Oxford, 1977, p. 510.

*Chapter 23*

# Philosopher Kings

## *Plato's Political Philosophy*

"Until philosophers are kings, or the kings and princes of this world have the spirit and power of philosophy, and political greatness and wisdom meet in one, and those commoner natures who pursue either to the exclusion of the other are compelled to stand aside, cities will never have rest from their evils."[1]

A PUPIL OF SOCRATES, Plato became the most influential teacher and writer of the new Hellenistic culture. He was born about 428 BC, a year after the death of Pericles. On his mother's side he was a descendant of Solon. When the terrible news of Aegospotami broke upon the people of Athens and the war that had divided Greece for a generation came to an end, Plato was twenty-four. The whole of his child hood and youth had passed under the shadow of enemy soldiers ravaging the land of Attica, of fierce debates about the conduct of war, of expeditions by land and sea

*Stoa of Attalus at the Athenian Agora*

setting off and returning, triumphant or broken by defeat, of moods of exhilaration or despair, heightened by the ironic probing of Aristophanes in the theatre. In such circumstances the sensitive mind of the young Plato was bound to turn to questions of the meaning of life and of the proper regulation of men in communities. Despite the war, Athens was a powerhouse of intellectual and artistic life; the final days of her valedictory glory were approaching. Through his social connections he could meet statesmen, sophists, poets, dramatists, artists and friends of Pericles. When the war ended he experienced the brief rule of the Thirty and the democratic reaction. As a youth he seemed destined for politics, for he was wealthy, well-connected, intelligent and handsome, but he rejected such a life on realising that in contemporary Athens, where demagogues or extreme oligarchs vied for power, there was no place for an honest man in public life. Yet his passionate interest in politics remained.

In 387 BC he founded the Academy in Athens, using the land of an olive grove about a mile from the Agora, where he taught the practical philosophy he had learnt from Socrates. Only after 900 years, perhaps the lifetime of a culture, was it to be formally closed by the Emperor Justinian, though the original teaching lost its direction long before. Twenty years later, in 367 BC, Plato made one sustained effort to bring his political ideas directly to bear on public life, when he went to Syracuse as tutor to the nephew of his friend, Dion of Syracuse. The boy was heir to the throne and Plato tried to teach him the principles of philosophy, so that he would approach the ideal of a philosopher king. The attempt was unavailing, for the young king banished Dion and rejected Plato. A second visit to Syracuse by Plato even proved dangerous to him; Dion himself was later murdered.

*Excavations near site of Academy*

Plato had been profoundly affected by the manner of Socrates' death. Afterwards he studied with a fellow pupil of Socrates, Eucleides, who founded a School at Megara, then with some Pythagoreans in Magna Graecia, particularly Archytas of Tarentum, who later supported Plato's efforts in Syracuse. After that he went to Egypt to study, following the example of Pythagoras himself. According to Marsilio Ficino, Plato then "intended to go on to the Magi and the Indians, but because of war in Asia he gave up this plan."[2]

As a teacher Plato made it clear that speech is the most powerful means of awakening men to the truth; yet he was also a supreme literary artist, whose Greek prose has the quality of poetry. Indeed the core of his teaching was expressed in an analogy. Imagine, he writes, a deep cave, in which men sit looking inwards, chained by their necks and legs, so that they cannot turn round to see the entrance. Behind them blazes a large fire and between them and the fire runs a low wall. Along the top of the wall someone places objects, shaped like men or animals or other things, and these are moved about, casting shadows on the far wall of the cave in front of the chained men. They look at these with interest, giving them names and learning how they move, in what sequence and so on.

One man manages to break loose and leaves the cave. The daylight outside hurts his eyes, so for a while he can hardly see anything and stumbles blindly about. Then gradually, he recognises the land outside, the sky, and finally the Sun itself. The utter slavery and unreality of the world inside the cave dawns upon him, but he knows that he cannot neglect his fellows in the cave. Reluctantly, he returns. Now the darkness numbs his senses and, once more, he stumbles, until his eyes are accustomed to the feeble light of the fire. He tries to inform the prisoners of their plight, but they are unwilling to listen. Most regard him as a madman, and they continue in their preoccupation with shadows, even revering those who have become expert in predicting the movements on the walls.

These moving shadows are what most men experience as the world around them. They are entirely subjective experiences of things. The objects moving behind the chained men are the actual things of the material world, which are experienced when perception is cleared of ordinary errors and things are seen objectively through the senses. To perceive these objects, the first move away from the shadows has to be made, by turning round towards the entrance to the cave. Nevertheless, everything within the cave belongs only to the sensible world. What is outside belongs to the intellectual world, which also has two parts. The lower part consists of men's beliefs. They include names and ideas, but these are derived from the higher part of the intellectual world, the region of Forms, the real nature of things in themselves.

Forms are eternal and unmoving. They include justice, beauty, equality, number, and ratio. Though beyond sense perception, yet they can be known, for just as the light of the Sun illumines physical things, so the light of the Good - "the source of reason and truth"[3] - illumines the intellectual world.

In *The Republic* Plato outlines the education of a philosopher king. Once the pupil knows for himself that only the Good is real, he needs no further education; but first he must proceed through a rigorous course of instruction in gymnastics, music, mathematics and dialectic. The latter subject is the crowning gem, which casts light upon all impediments to knowledge. Plato was taught by Socrates that learning is only the re-acquisition of pre-natal knowledge, so that dialogue between teacher and pupil eliminates step by step what has been superimposed upon the truth. Those brought to this state of enlightenment have no time for personal ambition, the usual stuff of politics. Like the man who re-enters the cave, they enter political life as a duty, not by appetite, and serve their fellow men out of compassion for their plight. Nor do they pander to the short-sighted wishes of those whom they serve. The true, not the spurious, interests of the people are promoted, with the laws and the administration of the state directed towards the good of the soul.

Plato knew that only a few could ever become such ideal rulers. He taught that men are by nature of different castes, carrying within them, as he said, an element of gold or silver, bronze or iron. Only those of a superior nature are fit to govern, but these may not necessarily be born into the higher castes, for ignorance has led to admixture of castes. Hence the rulers include within their purview the vital task of selecting the children who contain elements of gold or silver, gifted with wisdom or martial skill.

According the Plato, there is a natural progression of governments, repeated time after time, from the best to the worst. Beginning with aristocracy, the rule of the best, government falls to the level of timocracy, the rule of men of honour, then to oligarchy, the rule of the wealthy few, then to democracy, rule by the *demos*, or majority of the people, and finally to tyranny. Such degeneration follows natural law.

Aristocracy is the rule of a group of wise men, educated as true guardians of the state, indifferent to wealth and holding no land as private property. They exhibit the four cardinal virtues of wisdom, courage, temperance and justice. One amongst them may be the king. Plato knew that such a government does not usually last long. Even such men may be ignorant of the laws which determine the most propitious time for human birth. Their children may be less fit to rule than they, even though the best are selected, and will neglect some aspects of education, like music. Soon the very power to select the best will itself be weakened. The new rulers will claim land for themselves and even begin to enslave their subjects. Under aristocracy all men are as free as their natures allow; under timocracy, freedom becomes limited to the few. The timocrats are proud, ambitious and value honour above all else. Soldiers first and foremost, though they respect culture they do not cultivate it in themselves. Secretly they also covet wealth.

Soon the children of the timocrats, often encouraged by their mothers, grow critical of their fathers' apparent disdain for wealth and openly aspire to it. Values change from a respect for honour and courage to a respect for material wealth. The rulers acquire what they can, depriving their subjects of all but the necessities of life. "The accumulation of gold in the treasury of private individuals is the ruin of timocracy."[4] Private property in land is the root of this accumulation. Even citizenship comes to be defined by wealth, and so government has become an oligarchy.

Oligarchs, in their turn, become weak through idleness. Their children are ill-educated and prone to all kinds of unruly desires. So too, the mass of the people, deprived of their rights by the oligarchs, become resentful and violent and find leaders amongst the younger, discontented men of the ruling class. Then there is violence and revolution. Oligarchy gives way to democracy, a condition of apparent freedom, for desires proliferate and society indulges all kinds of appetites, previously restrained by superior rulers. This freedom, however, is not liberty, but licence, both in the individual and in the state. The rule of reason is totally overthrown. Faction struggles with faction. Leaders offer the people what they want, and are soon overthrown when circumstances or tastes have veered round in a new direction.

Divisions between the rulers of a democracy are endemic. Such an unstable society cannot last long. Eventually civil war breaks out, or a swift seizure of power puts an end to factional disputes. Either way, the leader of the reaction sets himself up as a tyrant. He is the party-leader in the civil war against property, for he gets his most vehement support from those without property, who have little to lose by taking violent action. Once installed in power, he appoints a personal bodyguard. The state is at his command, for so long as he can master the dangerous forces he has let loose.

In his political philosophy Plato was imbued with the ideas of the great thinkers of Greece, not only of Socrates, but of Pythagoras, Hesiod and Homer. Aristocracy, as he envisaged it, looked back for its model to an age even beyond the time of the legendary heroes of the Trojan war; to the age of Theseus and even of Hercules. Such rulers were demi-gods, men who became divine when they died, whose lives were devoted utterly to the welfare of the people and to the destruction of their enemies. The Homeric heroes were closer in time to Plato. Achilles and Hector, Odysseus and Ajax were the supreme timocrats, instant in their defence of honour, unmatched in courage, yet often contemptuous of lesser mortals and therefore prone to arrogance and hubris. Lycurgus, too, gave Plato the model of the timocratic state, and he found much to admire in the ancient Dorian states of Crete and Sparta, if not in their contemporary conditions.

With oligarchy, Plato recognised the historical development of Greece as recorded by tradition and the evidence of writers and inscriptions. The Athenian constitution of Solon was clearly suited to the condition of oligarchy which prevailed in the sixth century BC. Solon's division into classes was based upon wealth. Membership of the Areopagus was limited to the *pentacosiomedimni*. The lowest class, the *thetes*, could not hold office, only having the right to vote in the Assembly. His laws were the best that the people would accept. Oligarchy could not be uprooted, but it could be turned to advantage by moderating its extreme tendency towards inequality, in particular by freeing the fields that were enslaved before.

By the end of the sixth century the move towards democracy was under way. Cleisthenes acknowledged this by his wise refoundation of tribes, which appeased sectional interests and gave democracy a sure footing in the local deme. Democracy hastened forward in the fifth century under the reforms of Ephialtes and Pericles, but the latter knew how to bring a touch of superior statesmanship and culture to the *demos* and raise it a little above the level of mere self-interest and faction. After Pericles' death, as Plato grew up, he saw the transformation to the final stages of democracy taking place in Athens: the rise of demagogues, the appeal to passions, the growth of violence, hatred and corruption, especially under the strain of a long drawn-out war. And, finally, he saw the triumph of the thirty tyrants, two of whom, Critias and Charmides, were his acquaintances. Above all, he saw Socrates killed by a relentless faction, as the dying democracy briefly asserted itself. Even as Plato taught and wrote, Sparta set up its tyrannical *harmosts* in the previously independent cities of Greece, whose will became law for the city and whose Spartan garrisons were personal bodyguards.

This pattern was to be repeated in Roman history. Indeed, it had begun in Italy long before Plato was writing. Numa, traditionally known as the second king of Rome who gave the Romans their religious institutions, was certainly an aristocrat. Romulus, and the other early kings, were timocrats, engaged in fighting to preserve the infant state from its enemies. Servius Tullius, however, introduced reforms remarkably similar to Solon's in Athens, which took account of the decline of society into an oligarchy; for he made landed property the criterion for distributing both military obligations and political power. Under the Roman Republic, the laws of Sextius and Licinius in 367 BC and of Hortensius in 287 BC, opening the senior magistracies to the richer plebeians, were necessary reforms that further marked the growth of oligarchy. By the end of the second century BC oligarchy was under threat from the stirrings of democracy, the *populares* leaders, Marius and then Caesar, riding to power on the discontent of the dispossessed in Rome and Italy. Nor was it long before tyranny seized its opportunity, as the generals, who became arbiters of the state, abused their trust, so that civil war could end only in the rule of one man. Fortunately, that man, Augustus, was himself touched by the very ideal that Plato had delineated, and around him were men who had learnt something of the noble ideas of Greece. Hence government did not degenerate into the darkest tyranny.

The philosopher king was a potent ideal. Unrealisable in fourth century Greece, as Plato himself found in Syracuse, it remained a standard for the best minds and characters, who, catching a glimpse of its austere nobility, strove towards that perfection of virtue in government. To a man who had studied *The Republic*, or had been instructed in one of the numerous schools influenced by Plato - he sent teachers of law from the Academy to the Arcadians, the Ilians and the Pyrrheans, for example - the sordid ambition of demagogues and tyrants was no longer attractive. To govern well in the interests of all, to remain incorruptible, to stand indifferent to the clamour of mobs and sycophants, to hold fast to the truth in the face of taunts and threats, and even of death, these were close to the heart of the ruler educated in the ideal of the philosopher king.

In the fourth century BC, the needs of the time drew forth the ideal. With the collapse of the polis, a new form of political organisation was required. From Socrates' fundamental teaching on the human soul, individual yet universal, could spring the notion of a state fit to house all men, irrespective of local allegiance, tribe or even race. A state ruled by a philosopher king would demand piety, respect for humanity and the rule of law, and eschew petty squabbles with neighbours and narrow provincialism. Thus the seeds were sown for the empire of Alexander and the wide-ranging Hellenism that became a fertile field for the spread of Christianity, and for the rule of Augustus, that would extend the protection of Roman law to citizens from Spain to Syria and from the Cheviot Hills to the Sahara.

Epaminondas was the first to be impelled by such a principle of universality. The federal organisations that he set up and acknowledged in Greece were mainly short-lived, but the idea was planted to fructify in the minds of Philip and Alexander of Macedon. Aristotle, who was Alexander's tutor, did not follow his teacher Plato in many respects, but he retained an immense reverence for him, and through Aristotle and perhaps others, including his father, Philip, Alexander learnt to transcend narrow distinctions and open his new empire to all, so that Europeans and Asians might live and fight, and even rule, alongside one another. The old limitation of Greek and barbarian could be laid to rest. Alexander's posterity could not see so far. The Hellenistic world became, to some degree, a Greek preserve, with islands of urban Greek culture in the midst of unchanging Asian societies. Yet what counted in the long-run was that the ideal should yield peace rather than war, friendship rather than hatred, justice rather than despotism; and wherever the philosopher king was remembered, these were the fruits. In explaining the decline of government, in particular in laying down the principles of aristocracy, Plato had shown the way out of the cave of degeneracy. After tyranny new men might arise, government could be rejuvenated, a new cycle could begin.

### References:

1. Plato, *The Republic*, trans. B. Jowett, Random House, New York, 1937, Book V, 473.

2. *The Letters of Marsilio Ficino*, trans. School of Economic Science, Shepheard-Walwyn, London, 1981, vol. 3, p. 34.

3. Plato, *Republic*, trans. Jowett, Book VII, 517.

4. Plato, *Republic*, trans. Jowett, Book VIII, 550.

## Chapter 24

# Son of Zeus

### *Alexander the Great*

IN THE FOURTH CENTURY BC, one man especially was the medium for the expansion of the new Hellenistic culture beyond the land of Greece. Alexander the Great was a supreme man of action. Despite defects of character, including a passionate anger, on occasions uncontrollable, he possessed many qualities of the Homeric heroes, whom he greatly admired. Wherever he went he carried a copy of the *Iliad*, and he invaded Asia with Achilles in his mind's eye. Hellenistic culture itself looked back to the Mycenaean age of the Trojan war. Macedon, Alexander's kingdom, retained features of that age. The king was an hereditary monarch, ruling

*Alexander the Great*

a tribal society through nobles who had a personal kinship with the king. From these he selected his Companions, a warrior elite, who served him with a fierce and proud loyalty in war and peace. The king was not only war leader and executive ruler, he was also judge, priest and treasurer, and with him the state itself was identified, for example in the making of foreign treaties. He owned all the land, so that his subjects paid rent to him as tenants. From the Companions he chose the Council; but his power was not unlimited, for the Macedonian people elected each successor in the royal line and could even vote to depose him. Moreover, the nobles wore the same dress as the king and spoke to him with frankness, facts which became of great importance when Alexander introduced Persian elements into his court.

The Macedonian kings believed that they were sprung from Zeus; Philip II claimed to be a descendant of Heracles, son of Zeus. His earliest coins were stamped with Heracles' head; his first city-foundation was Heraclea. Isocrates asked Philip to consider all Greece as his fatherland, in keeping with his heroic descent. Deep within Philip, and within his son Alexander, ran the conviction that, like Heracles, they were born to benefit mankind through arduous but noble labours.

Alexander was born into a position and place suited to his ambition. His father, Philip, had established a complete hegemony over the Greek city-states by the time Alexander came to the throne. Philip himself was a man of extraordinary power and determination. In his youth he spent a few years in Thebes as a hostage and there learnt a great deal about the arts of governing and of warfare from the example of Epaminondas. Perhaps there, also, he acquired the taste for Greek philosophy which led him as king to make his capital, Pella, into a cultured city in contact with the Platonic Academy in Athens, and welcoming the orator, Isocrates, the philosopher, Aristotle and companies of Athenian actors.

Philip transformed Macedon from a loosely knit tribal society into an efficient, centralised state of imposing military power. He forced the hill tribesmen of the interior to recognise his authority and provide regular troops. The army itself was radically improved. The infantry was organised into phalanxes, open in array and armed with the *sarissa*, an exceptionally long spear (about 6 metres); of the sixteen ranks of the phalanx the front five could now engage the enemy simultaneously. The phalanx was designed to hold the enemy hoplites, whilst the Macedonian cavalry charged into their flanks. This combination of infantry and cavalry, together with the use of oblique lines when attacking, were clearly influenced by Epaminondas. Elite troops known as Royal soldiers, consisted of heavy cavalry and elite infantry (*hypaspists*). During Philip's reign the torsion catapult was developed, making cities more vulnerable to besieging armies. Later, the mathematical relationship between weight of missile and distance projected was calculated precisely. It was a factor in the change from polis to kingdom.

The death of Epaminondas had shattered the power of Thebes. Rarely had a state depended so much upon one man for authority and influence. Its decline left Greece without a dominant power for the first time for over a century, a condition sure to attract the ambitious king of Macedon, whose predilection for Greek culture made him look southwards for empire, rather than northwards to the barbarians beyond Thrace or in the Balkans. He had already subdued the tribesmen of Illyria after coming to the throne in 359 BC. Then he took Amphipolis, so coveted by Athens, conquered Thessaly and intervened directly in Greek affairs by declaring himself champion of Apollo before defeating the Phocians, who were accused of abusing the lands of Delphi.

At this point there emerged in Athens the great orator, Demosthenes, who saw that Philip threatened the independence of the Greek poleis, and who was prepared to match with sharp words the *sarissas* of the Macedonians. Despite opposition in Athens, notably from another master of oratory, Aeschines, Demosthenes spoke out on every occasion when Philip approached closer to an outright invasion of central and southern Greece, calling especially upon the Athenian tradition of self-defence. Would Athens allow herself to be bought off in exchange for acknowledging the hegemony of Philip?

"But this was not in her blood, nor in her competence, nor in her nature. None could ever persuade her at any time to join herself to the cause of strength without right, or gain safety at the cost of slavery. In the struggle for the highest crown of honour and glory, she has lived with danger all her days. We regard this with such pride, we feel it as so fitting to the character of our country, that we heap the highest praise on the generations who maintained it. And that is right... Athenians of that day (the Persian wars) looked for no speaker, no leader who should secure them slavery with comfort. They did not even ask for life, unless freedom could be coupled with it. Every man of them believed he was born not to his father and mother alone, but to his country."[1]

Philip gave further evidence of his aggressive intentions when he took the important city of Olynthos in Chalcidica and enslaved the whole population. As head of a confederacy, Olynthos was the last bulwark against Macedon in the north. In 346 BC, Aeschines persuaded the Athenians to make the Peace of Philocrates, which sacrificed the Phocians to Philip and gave him control of the pass of Thermopylae. Moreover, Macedon took the place of Phocas on the Amphictionic Council, making Philip a potential arbiter of Greek affairs. On the hillside below Parnassus, the Macedonian king presided in the Delphic stadium over the Pythian Games, as the free Greeks competed for the wreath of bay. Though Demosthenes continued to denounce the intentions of Philip, the influence of his opponent, Aeschines, was strong. Philip himself probably wanted to avoid a war with Athens. He respected Athenian culture and history, and he needed the help of the Athenian fleet if he were to fulfil his greatest ambition, to lead an allied force in an invasion of Persia. Hence for some years Philip bided his time, securing his hold on Thrace in the extreme north-east and elsewhere.

In 339 BC, for the second time, a sacred war concerning Delphi broke out. This was Philip's opportunity. Charge and counter-charge of sacrilege were levelled by Athens and by her enemies in the Amphictionic League, the latter counting on support from Macedon. By clever diplomacy, Demosthenes detached Thebes, a potential enemy of Athens, from an alliance with Macedon. Philip intervened in the sacred war, whilst Athens and Thebes remained neutral. When his army reached Elatea, on the northern border of Boeotia, Philip halted. What were his intentions? The Greek world waited, its whole future depending on the next step of this prince from a hitherto little regarded northern state. In Athens, Demosthenes furiously argued his case that the freedom of Athens was irrevocably in the scales. He succeeded in getting himself appointed as one of the ten envoys sent to Thebes to discuss the crisis. The Theban leaders faced a choice between supporting Philip, and therefore probably sealing the fate of Athens, and supporting Athens, with the certain outcome of a confrontation with the famed army of the Macedonians. Demosthenes convinced them that the first option would lead to their becoming a feeble satellite of Philip and perhaps to the loss of their command over the Boeotian cities. Thebes and Athens would stand or fall together.

The decisive battle took place in the extreme north-west of Boeotia, at Chaeronea. The Macedonians advanced first in *echelon*, the *hypaspists* making first contact on the right wing. Philip then used a feint; the *hypaspists* stepped back, keeping order, but drawing the inexperienced Athenian hoplites on to them, so that the Greek line began to edge to the left, with the danger of being outflanked. On the Greek right, the Theban Sacred Band did not move, facing alone the heavy Macedonian cavalry. Into the gap in the Greek line charged Alexander with his Companions. They turned on the Sacred Band and destroyed them to a man. Following the cavalry, the phalanxes of the Macedonian centre drove into the ever-widening gap, then turned to their right to roll up the Greek infantry. On the far left, the Athenians were trapped on the rising land and were slaughtered or captured at will by Philip's *hypaspists*. Macedon had won a total victory. The Greek polis had found its nemesis at the hands of a king.

Was this the end of the freedom of the Greeks, as the famous royal lion of Chaeronea, set up on the battlefield, seemed to indicate? Athens had substantially lost its freedom when it had killed its greatest citizen in 399 BC; Thebes, when its heroic leader had died on the field of Mantinea; Sparta, when it failed to discipline its *harmosts* after victory in the Peloponnesian war. These greater states of Greece now had to submit to the Macedonian conqueror. Thebes was treated harshly and a Macedonian garrison put into the Cadmea; Athens escaped lightly, for Philip did not wish to make it a permanent enemy; Sparta found that its traditional subject peoples in the Peloponnese were confirmed in their independence. Philip did not enslave the Greeks. The small poleis found themselves freer for a while than previously. The Amphictionic Council became the arbiter of inter-state disputes. At Thebes, Corinth and Chalcis, however, Macedonian garrisons remained, called by some "the fetters of Greece". Pride in the polis, however, had foundered. The new system was to be monarchy; if not under Philip, then under his son, Alexander, and then under the kings who would succeed him in the Greek parts of his empire.

A meeting of the Greek states at Corinth appointed Philip hegemon with power to execute all decisions of a new League of Corinth. Now, at last, he could plan the invasion of the Persian empire, which he had long desired. Another side to his nature intervened to cut off such hopes of glory. Macedonian law did not insist on monogamy for the king. Philip rashly decided to marry a young princess, Cleopatra, despite the intense jealousy of his first wife, Olympias, mother of Alexander and a passionate woman from the royal house of Epirus. At the wedding feast, the bride's uncle, Attalus, arrogantly called for a legitimate heir, thus casting doubt upon Alexander's legitimacy and Olympias' honour. Alexander's response was to throw his drinking cup in the face of Attalus; Philip had to be restrained from drawing his sword on his own son. Alexander and Olympia fled from the court into exile. The incident strengthened the emotional bond between Alexander and his mother, of whom he later said that one tear from her could outweigh the entreaties of all his generals.

A year later Philip was murdered. The assassin bore a grudge against Philip and was probably acting for the aggrieved Olympias. Alexander was not himself implicated. Such was Philip's reputation that no-one believed that the nineteen year old son could take over successfully the position won by his father. Many Greek states planned to rebel against the yoke of Macedon, and the unruly tribes of Thrace and Illyria in the north also sought to take advantage of their conqueror's death. A great shock awaited them all; they were to meet a divine force, embodied in the fair-haired Macedonian prince, who within ten years was to rule half the civilised world.

Having dealt swiftly with a rebellion in Thessaly, Alexander went to Corinth to be elected general of the Greeks for the invasion of Persia planned by Philip before his death. Thus ensured of his authority, he had turned northwards and defeated in turn the Thracian tribesmen and the Illyrians, when news came that Thebes, the key city of central Greece on the plain of Boeotia, had also revolted, besieging the Macedonian garrison in the Cadmea. Without resting after his labours in the north, Alexander marched his army southwards to Thebes. It could not withstand his assault and, once within the walls, the Boeotian allies of Alexander, long anxious to shake off the domination of Thebes, ran amok and slaughtered six thousand Thebans. The Greek Confederacy, which had elected Alexander their general, then voted to raze Thebes to the ground and sell the surviving population into slavery. Only the house of the poet, Pindar, was spared, on the explicit orders of Alexander. This harsh treatment of one of the great cities of Greece was never forgotten by Alexander; it lay upon his conscience and influenced his later measures as a conqueror.

By the year 334 BC Alexander was ready to set out for Asia Minor as the leader of the Greeks against the Persian empire of Darius III. Though he became the master of that empire and opened half a continent to Greek influence, he was doing no more initially than taking up the torch laid down by his father, who had claimed revenge for the humiliation of Greece in the Persian wars of the fifth century. Only Sparta stood aloof, as she had a century and a half before on the formation of the Delian League.

Was there any further justification, beyond that of avenging ancient Persian aggression, for this assault upon a foreign empire? The best reason was that the Ionian coast was essentially Greek in population and had earlier in its history been free from Persian control. Sparta had condemned the Ionian Greeks to Persian domination as part of the bargain for Persian gold in the great war against Athens, and when the notorious "King's Peace" was made in 386 BC, Persia was left as the arbiter of Greece, with an iron hand on Ionia.

Xenophon's "ten thousand" had earlier shown the relative weakness of Persia, by marching through hundreds of miles of the Great King's territory with impunity, after failing to put the pretender, Cyrus, on the Persian throne. The expedition demonstrated the moral decline of Persia. After the defeat of the Greeks at Cunaxa, and Cyrus' death, the satrap, Tissaphernes, offered to meet the surviving Greek leaders to discuss the possible employment of the hoplites as mercenaries in Egypt. At the meeting he treacherously murdered all twenty-five generals, which is how Xenophon came to lead the expedition out of Persia. Moral decline had been continuous since the death of Darius I after Marathon. During the fifth century weak kings led to the palace rule of women, treacherous intrigues, and reliance on savage practices, like the roasting of opponents in slow furnaces. Satraps became hereditary sub-kings rather than royal officials, wielding private armies, and the Great King's own army became heavily dependent on Greek mercenaries. The ancient and equitable system of 'bow" land, whereby self-sufficient farmers held their land on condition of fighting as archers, or infantry, for the King, was breaking down, as absentee landlordism and great hereditary estates replaced it. Indebtedness, arising from the need to pay mercenaries and from borrowings abroad, hastened economic decline. Zoroastrianism was diluted by the introduction of Asiatic polytheism by Artaxerxes II; Nature gods appeared alongside the one God of Zoroaster's teaching. In Egypt temples were violated by King Ochus, so that Persian rule was seen as both oppressive and sacrilegious.

Darius III, the Great King whom Alexander confronted, exemplified this miserable condition of the once mighty empire of Cyrus the Great. He himself had been satrap, with a tenuous claim to the throne of Persia as a great nephew of Artaxerxes II. A courtier, called Bagoas, had poisoned both King Ochus and his son. Bagoas placed Darius on the throne, most other claimants having been killed; whereupon, Darius promptly poisoned Bagoas. This was the monarchy which Alexander sought to replace. In Egypt and Babylon, the people greeted Alexander as a deliverer from oppression. To the Greeks of Ionia he gave freedom to form democratic governments and to become his free allies. Elsewhere in the empire many satraps and soldiers turned to him readily, especially when he showed his respect for their beliefs and customs, and married the beautiful Roxana, princess of Sogdiana. For Alexander, therefore, the invasion of Asia was justified, also, as a mission to liberate the people of the Persian empire from a corrupt monarchy.

30,000 infantry and 5,000 cavalry crossed the Dardanelles with Alexander. His first action in Asia Minor was to visit the ancient site of Troy, where he crowned the tomb of Achilles, from whom he claimed descent. His close friend, Hephaestion, cast a garland upon the grave of Patroclus, whose death before the walls of Troy had induced Achilles to fight.

The first encounter with the armies of the Great King was at the River Granicus. The Persian leaders made brave attempts to kill Alexander himself, by charging desperately into the thick of the *agema*, or royal guard, but the superior tactics of the Greek cavalry and phalanx of spearmen eventually broke the Persians. Alexander sent 300 captured panoplies to the Acropolis in Athens with a dedication from "Alexander and the Greeks, except the Spartans."

Most of Asia Minor now fell into Alexander's hands, though only after hard marching and fighting, and such problems as that at Gordion, where legend foretold that the dominion over Asia would go to whoever could untie the knot which bound the chariot of Gordius to its yoke. Alexander is reputed to have drawn his sword and cut the knot in half. As Alexander freed the Greek cities of the Aegean coast - Ephesus, Priene, Miletus and others - he set up democratic governments to replace the pro-Persian oligarchies. These cities remained free allies of Alexander throughout his career, unlike the subject cities of his empire in Asia, or the Confederacy cities of Greece, of which he was hegemon.

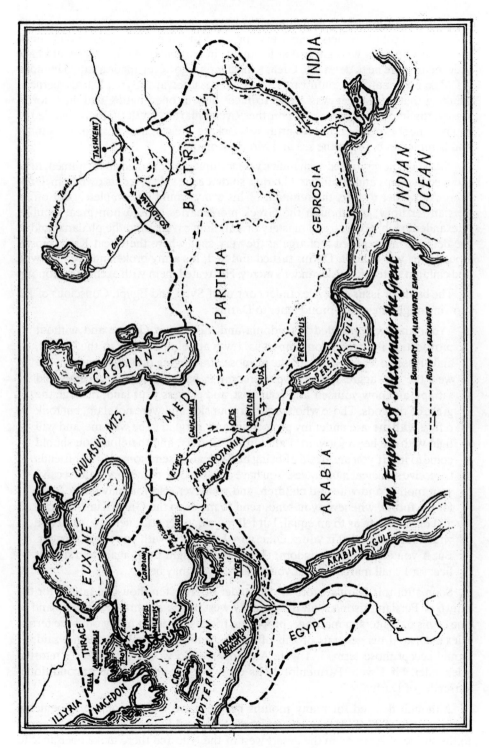

*The Empire of Alexander the Great*

At last the Emperor Darius himself confronted the invader. With him was not only a huge host of soldiers from every corner of his empire, but also 15,000 Greek mercenary hoplites who knew that for them, in particular, Alexander would have little mercy were he to defeat the Great King. Darius, however, made a stupid blunder. As Alexander marched southwards along the coast towards Syria, Darius, perhaps thinking that Alexander was afraid to meet him in open battle, marched north-westwards into the narrow plain on the River Pinarus, south of Issus, where the room to manoevre his enormous army was lacking. He was now north of Alexander and hemmed in between the sea and Mount Amanus.

Alexander never missed such military opportunities. He turned about immediately, retraced his steps and confronted Darius, so that each side faced its own homeland. Were Alexander to lose, the remnant of his army would be completely cut off in Persian territory; but though the Greek mercenaries caused him great trouble, Alexander exhibited his usual mastery of handling cavalry and the phalanx, and at the decisive moment led a charge at the very spot where the Great King himself stood in his war chariot. Darius turned and fled; his army broke and even his wife and children were left to Alexander's mercy. He treated them with exemplary honour.

The battle of Issus gave Alexander control of Syria and Egypt. Conscious of his growing might, he sent a proud letter to Darius:

"Your ancestors invaded Macedonia and the rest of Greece and without provocation inflicted wrongs upon us. I was appointed leader of the Greeks, and crossed over into Asia for the purpose of avenging those wrongs; for you were the first aggressors. I have overcome in battle, first your generals and satraps, and now yourself and your host, and possess your land, through the grace of the gods. Those who fought on your side and were not slain, but took refuge with me, are under my protection, and are glad to be with me, and will fight with me henceforward. I am lord of all Asia, and therefore you should come to me. If you are afraid of being badly treated, send some of your friends to receive sufficient guarantees. You have only to come to me to ask and receive your mother and wife and children, and whatever else you may desire. And for the future, whenever you send, send to me as to the Great King of Asia, and do not write as to an equal, but tell me whatever your need be, as to one who is lord of all that is yours. Otherwise I shall deal with you as an offender. But if you dispute the kingdom, then wait and fight for it again and do not flee: for I shall march against you wherever you may be."[2]

Soon after this Darius wrote to Alexander offering ten thousand talents for the return of Persian prisoners, all the territory west of the Euphrates and the hand of one of his daughters in marriage, proposing friendship and a treaty on these terms. Alexander told his generals of this offer. The leading general, Parmenio, said, "I would accept those terms if I were Alexander." "So would I, by Zeus", retorted Alexander, "if I were Parmenio!"[3] His reply was to demand the unconditional surrender of Darius.

Although delayed for many months by the brave defence of the Phoenician maritime city of Tyre, Alexander conquered Syria and Egypt. He took care to travel to the shrine of Ammon in the desert west of the Nile and there make obeisance to the father god of Egypt. Greek tradition associated Ammon with Apollo and recognised the shrine as ranking with Delphi and Dodona in the homeland of Greece. As conqueror of Egypt, Alexander was now Pharaoh, and accordingly was granted the honours of a god. Some conception of his own divine qualities seemed to become evident to him at the shrine of Ammon; soon he was to present himself as superior to even his fellow Macedonian nobles, the Companions, to whom previously he was no more than first among equals. In Egypt, too, he founded the great city of Alexandria, which became the centre of Hellenistic culture and a rival to Rome itself in centuries to come. Many more, perhaps seventy, Alexandrias were founded throughout Asia, but this, in Egypt, was the greatest of them all.

In pursuit of the Great King, Alexander now led his army north-eastwards into the heart of the Persian dominions. Eventually, at Gaugamela, Darius raised another huge host to confront him. The site of the battle was just east of Nineveh, a seven mile wide, level plain between low hills and rough land by the River Tigris. Darius had chosen the ground well, for he could manoeuvre his great army of 40,000 cavalry, 16,000 heavy infantry, innumerable light infantry and 200 scythed chariots. Alexander's forces were heavily outnumbered. Even with reinforcements, he only mustered 7,000 cavalry and 40,000 infantry. Unlike Darius, he took care to rest his troops before the battle by fortifying his camp against a night attack.

The problem Alexander faced was to avoid encirclement on the plain by the immense cavalry forces of the enemy, before his main forces, which were superior in quality to the Persian, were engaged. Accordingly, he advanced quickly and in *echelon* with his right wing in advance, reinforced by the Companions, with his own *agema* at its head. Cavalry were ranged on both wings of each army, with the infantry, mainly phalanxes, in both centres, supported on the Persian side by chariots. Alexander's deployment allowed for the rapid formation of a defensive rectangle, if encirclement came, for he ranged a second line of infantry behind the first, with orders to face rearwards, if necessary.

The first engagement came on the extreme right. Successive cavalry actions resulted in the failure of the Persian horse to outflank Alexander's right wing. Suddenly, the Persian chariots charged in the centre, cutting down the Greek infantry with their churning scythes, but the javelin men transfixed many of the drivers and horses and the phalanxes opened their ranks to let the chariots pass through. Alexander's right wing was now close enough to charge. The Persian infantry was moving slowly forward: part of its long line veered leftwards towards the action on the wing. This was the time and place to win an empire. As a gap opened in the Persian line, Alexander led the *agema* and Companions in a headlong charge of the great war horses into the ranks of enemy footsoldiers. The wedge-shaped elite of cavalry smashed through and shattered the Persian line. The battle, however, was by no means over, for on the Greek left, Parmenio, in command of the Thessalian cavalry, faced a charge by the heaviest Persian cavalry and was halted. This disrupted Alexander's line, for the phalanxes next to the Thessalians turned to help them. Into this gap charged, in their turn, Indian and Persian cavalry, breaking through and threatening the Greek rear. An element of luck now favoured Alexander, for these horsemen were under orders to rescue the Persian royal family from Alexander's baggage train. They annihilated the guard there, but the second line of Greek infantry now faced about and drove them off. Parmenio, however, had asked for help from Alexander.

Frustrated in his desire to wipe out the Persian centre, Alexander led the Companions back across the field to relieve his general. In the dense dust cloud of battle, he rode straight into the returning Indians and Persians, strengthened by Parthian cavalry also. A fierce encounter left sixty Companions dead, but Parmenio was relieved.

Darius, the Great King, turned and fled, when he saw Alexander's initial break through, which threatened his own position in the rear of the centre line. Bessus, commanding the Persian left wing, also rode off the field when he saw Darius depart. Then a general flight set in. Alexander returned to lead the pursuit. He did not believe in letting a defeated army fight again. The Persian army was hunted down far into the night, despite the collapse of many Greeks and their horses with exhaustion.

This was the decisive victory. Darius' army was utterly broken. Henceforth, only the eastern satraps, like Spitamenes of Sogdiana, would continue the fight with armies drawn from a few provinces at the most. Moreover, Gaugemala opened up the nerve centre of the empire. Babylon lay at the mercy of the conqueror, then the way was open to the Persian Gulf and the great expanses of Parthia and beyond, to the towering mountains of the Hindu Kush.

This time his own generals and satraps lost faith in Darius. As Alexander rode hard, ahead of his main army, to overtake the king, the satrap of Bactria, Bessus, struck Darius down, to leave him dying as Alexander reached him. Bessus escaped to be captured later and executed for treason by the new sovereign of Persia. Perhaps unwillingly, for he did not usually resort to torture, Alexander allowed his new Persian supporters to insist on the mutilation of Bessus before execution.

At Persepolis, the Persian capital where the palace of the Great King had been magnificently constructed and sculptured with the aid of Greek craftsmen, Alexander did show a streak of crude vengeance. He burnt the palace to the ground, seemingly in fulfilment of his aim to avenge the burning of the Acropolis at Athens by the Persians 150 years before. Soon afterwards, when the conquest of much of central Asia was completed, he turned on his own general, Parmenio, though perhaps with some cause. Parmenio's son, Philotas, was found guilty by an army court of implication in a plot to murder Alexander. After Philotas' public execution with the javelins of the army, Alexander swiftly sent orders for Parmenio himself to be killed. Under Macedonian law the male relatives of a man convicted of treason could be executed.

Following the conquests of Bactria and Sogdiana, a worse incident betrayed a change in Alexander's character. Another of the Macedonian generals, Cleitus the Black, argued with Alexander, when both had been drinking heavily. Speaking for his fellow Macedonians, who were resentful of the attention which Alexander gave to his new Persian followers, Cleitus, principal lieutenant of Philotas, claimed that Alexander owed everything to the courage of the Macedonians, who were now being slighted. Alexander turned to two Greeks and said, "Don't you feel like demi-gods among beasts?" Cleitus thrust out his hand towards Alexander: "This saved your life at the River Granicus,"[4] which was, in fact, true, and taunted him further. Alexander's temper gave way. He seized a spear from a guard, but was held back by those near him. Cleitus was forcibly dragged from the room. Unfortunately he burst loose and rushed blindly back. The king ran him through with the spear.

Alexander suffered terrible remorse. For three days he shut himself up without food. The army began to see itself leaderless a thousand miles from home. At last, Alexander was persuaded to eat and the soothsayers declared that the god, Dionysus, had been angry with Cleitus for a neglected sacrifice. A resolution was passed by the army that Cleitus had been justly executed. The historian, Arrian, commented later that many kings had done evil, but only Alexander repented.

Nevertheless, great triumphs were still to come. Not content with the conquest of central Asia, Alexander pressed on to India. He crossed the River Indus and defeated Indian rulers, despite their use of war elephants, which no cavalry could face in battle for the terror of the horses. One ruler, King Porus, greatly impressed the Greeks by his courage and bearing. Brought severely wounded before Alexander and barely able to stand, he replied, when asked how he wished to be treated: "Like a king."[5] So impressed was Alexander that he restored Porus to his kingdom as a vassal and even left him in charge of the Punjab when the Greek army finally left. Alexander also met some philosophers of the Brahmin caste, whom he treated with great respect, though they insisted that in their utmost material poverty they owned no less than him, the master of half the world. At last, at the River Beas, the limit of his men's endurance was reached. They refused to go further, despite Alexander's own enthusiasm to continue till he met the ocean (which he thought was not far beyond the Indus). Under no other commander would a western army have penetrated half as far into Asia. Even the armies of Imperial Rome made little headway beyond the Euphrates.

Yet Alexander faced his disappointment with a renewed initiative. He planned a voyage of discovery for his general, Nearchus, along the coast from the mouth of the Indus to the Persian Gulf, whilst he himself marched his army across the desert of Gedrosia, to meet Nearchus near Babylon. In fact, Gedrosia was almost the charnel house of the whole expedition, for the heat and aridity of the desert had been underestimated.

Once back in the civilised land of southern Persia, Alexander drew together the threads of his new empire and reviewed how it had been administered in his absence. He found corruption amongst both the Macedonian and Persian officials, whom he had chosen to rule the provinces. Many were dismissed, some executed and the most powerful, the Macedonian, Harpalus, chief financial officer, who was guilty of gross embezzlement, fled to Greece to be tried and executed later at Athens. Alexander was no doubt disillusioned by this evidence of the degenerate character of many of his close associates. A greater blow was in store for him. His dearest friend, Hephaestion, Patroclus to Achilles, fell ill and died. Even the most elaborate and expensive funeral that the ancient world could remember did not assuage Alexander's suffering. A year later, in 323 BC, he too was taken ill, worn down with hard living and gruelling campaigns and with the bitter setbacks of the latter years. He died at Babylon, the city he would have made the capital of his vast Asian empire, where the races of East and West might have mingled in amity under a ruler beyond the prejudices of nations and religions, a universal sovereign. It was eleven years since he had crossed the Dardanelles with his army.

Alexander was more than a great commander of men and an efficient ruler of Greeks and barbarians. After his appointment by the League of Corinth as commander-in-chief for the invasion of Asia, he went to see the famed philosopher,

Diogenes of Sinope, who was then living in Corinth, hoping to elicit some words of praise from him. The philosopher was basking full length in the sun. As Alexander approached, Diogenes raised himself on one elbow. The king greeted him and asked whether he might do anything for him. "Yes," replied the philosopher, "you can stand a little to one side out of my sun."[6] Far from being angered by this off-hand treatment of majesty, Alexander was full of admiration for the man's independence of spirit and said that, if he were not Alexander, he would choose to be Diogenes.

Philosophy remained an interest for him, even though he broke with his tutor, Aristotle, and quarrelled with Callimachus, the Aristotelian who accompanied him on his expedition to Asia. Certainly his freedom from racial and national prejudices showed a Platonic strain in his thinking, capable of seeing in all men a common humanity.

He knew that a lasting empire must transcend the ideas and customs of nationalism, including the deeply-rooted Greek distinction between Greeks and barbarians. In Asia, he himself married the beautiful Roxana, daughter of Oxyartes of Sogdiana; at Susa, 80 of his officers married daughters of the Iranian aristocracy and 10,000 of his troops married their native concubines. 30,000 Asian youths were trained as Macedonian infantry for the army, whilst Asiatic cavalry was enrolled in the *hipparchies* and Persian nobles in the *agema*. Alexander himself often wore Persian dress. These generous measures aroused antipathy amongst the Macedonians, proving how much Alexander's own conception of empire rose above the common ideas of the time. Perhaps they showed that he was to some degree an impolitic idealist, but from such an attitude was born the spirit of Hellenism which profoundly influenced Rome and which drew its inspiration from a Socratic transcendence of common opinion.

In Persia, Alexander initiated the ceremony of prostration in his presence, but the justification for this was probably political. In Asia, prostration had no religious significance; it was the correct procedure in the presence of the Great King. In Greece, however, it indicated reverence for a god. Hence the Greeks especially resented it and saw it as evidence of Alexander's self-deification. So he gave up prostration, but retained deification, for which his motives were political. As a god, he could claim rights in Greek states otherwise legally denied to him. For the Greek city states were only subject to him as hegemon - or in Ionia were simply free allies - and he demanded that they allow the return of exiles, especially when these were soldiers who had loyally served him. Deification was merely a means to a political end, though a dangerous one. When Sparta replied to the request for deification with the laconic decree: "Since Alexander wishes to be a god, let him be a god,"[7] Alexander probably respected the independence of mind which lay behind it. Only perhaps at the shrine of Ammon in the Libyan desert did Alexander have some genuine glimpse of divine qualities within himself, although he never revealed to anyone precisely what the priest of Amon-Re had said to him.

His loyalty and trust in friends could be unbreakable. On one occasion he received a letter from Parmenio warning that Alexander's personal physician, Philip, had been bribed by Darius to poison him. Alexander told no-one of the letter and when he next met Philip, who handed him a cup of medicine, he simply gave the letter to the doctor, looked him in the face as he read it, raised the cup to his lips and drained it to the last drop. Alexander looked on, smiling, as the bewildered doctor lifted his hands to heaven and protested his innocence before the gods.

As for physical courage, Alexander knew nothing of fear, or if he did, completely mastered it. On attacking a citadel held by a particularly warlike Asian people, the Malli, Alexander found his troops lacking in initiative; so he led them up a scaling ladder. The enemy managed to smash the ladder and hurl missiles at him. He promptly jumped down from the top of the wall into the compound and fought, with only two of his guards who had followed him, against the mass of Mallian troops. A sheet of flame seemed to surge from his body, so that the Mallians drew back; but recovering themselves they rained blows on his armour with sword and spear. Then an arrow pierced his breastplate and lodged in his ribs. A scimitar was raised above his head; one guard died trying to intervene; the other fought the attackers off for a moment. When all seemed lost, the Macedonians burst into the citadel and killed every Mallian. Alexander was grievously ill, but he recovered.

As a military leader, Alexander excelled in the brilliance of his response to new forms of warfare: at Tyre, a naval siege was required to take the island fortress; scythed chariots and Indian elephants caused him no real problem; nor did the Parthian mounted archers, who could fire facing in reverse. Near Derbent in Sogdiana, the native garrison called down from the Sogdian rock that only flying men could capture it, for the vertical face seemed unclimbable, especially in the winter snows. Alexander called for volunteers. Three hundred men came forward and went up it with ropes and pegs. One in ten fell to his death. When the rest reached a crag above the fortress, they hoisted an agreed signal to the army below. Alexander called on the garrison to go and look at his flying men. The garrison surrendered. What kind of a man could arouse such devotion in his troops?

A modern historian wrote this of Alexander:

"Whatever else he was, he was one of the supreme fertilising forces of history. He lifted the civilised world out of one groove and set it in another; he started a new epoch; nothing could again be as it had been. He greatly enlarged the bounds of knowledge and of human endeavour, and gave to Greek science and Greek civilisation a scope and an opportunity such as they had never yet possessed. Particularism was replaced by the idea of the "inhabited world", the common possession of civilised men."[8]

With Alexander the idea of a universal society progressed further. For all his ferocious energy and consuming ambition, Alexander was a man of the broadest sympathies; not for him the narrow confines of Macedon, nor even the richly endowed peninsula of Greece. Only the world would satisfy his taste for limitless movement and diversity of race and culture; and "the world" lay eastwards, into the vast territory of the Great King. When the victories had been won, the ideas could flow out into a new form of society, Greek in inspiration, but treating Greeks and *barbaroi* for the first time as equals, so that even Alexander's generals grew jealous and grumbled at the oriental vanity of their leader. The empire was indeed short-lived and the Hellenistic kingdoms which Alexander's successors established never, in fact, achieved racial and cultural integration, but the idea which Alexander had glimpsed lived on to inspire the Romans, whose talent for law and government made it a practical possibility. In their *jus gentium*, or law of nations, and in their belief in the rule of law, to which St Paul appealed as a Roman citizen, they carried forward the idea of a universal society. Men were not to be confined to the walls of a polis, nor human excellence to the *arete* of a citizen within a polis. A broader expanse of human endeavour opened before the eyes of the men of the Hellenistic and Roman culture.

Alexander was a vehicle, especially for the transmission of Greek culture to the eastern Mediterranean, Persia and central Asia. Accompanying his army were scientists, naturalists, geographers, engineers and the historian, Callimachus. Cities, roads, trade and commerce developed to link these previously alien areas with the Greek homeland, so that when the new power of Rome produced a stronger political unity, there would be a common world for Roman law and indeed for the teaching of Christ. Not least, the popular form of the Greek language - *koine* - would facilitate the spread of Greek ideas and their fusion with Christianty, in such works as St John's Gospel. Men were looking for the spiritual unity that they seemed to have lost. Alexander laid part of the groundwork for its rediscovery in Christ.

As for the connection with India, when the last general from Alexander's army left in 317 BC, it seemed that no deep roots had been planted and little brought back to Europe, but in memory and imagination the effect was permanent. Four centuries later, the Emperor Trajan sought unavailingly to reach India. More immediately, Chandragupta, within a decade of Alexander's death, began to create a great empire there. He had met, and possibly even assisted, Alexander, perhaps the inspiration for a universal dominion. Chandragupta's grandson, Asoka, became one of the most powerful, yet humane, rulers in the whole history of India.

Alexander lived and died a man of the sword, intent on conquest, if superior to most conquerors in his generosity to the conquered. Warfare and adventure bred in him a callousness which even his contact with Greek philosophy could not prevent. The killing of Parmenio in cold blood, and the hot-blooded murder of Cleitus, seemed to weaken his hold on the blood-lust of his army after the taking of cities in distant Asia and India. Perhaps his men were beyond such restraint, for they were exceedingly tired and yearning to return to the west. Despite all this, the magnanimity of his character cannot be gainsaid. At Opis, near Babylon, shortly before he died, the army almost rebelled at his decision to send home many of the veterans. A compromise was reached and, after a moving scene of reconciliation, he offered a great prayer for peace, for the partnership of men of all races in the commonwealth of his empire, and for the people of the known world to live in unity of heart and mind. All men, he declared, are the sons of one Father.

### References:

1. Demosthenes, 'The Crown', trans. A. N. W. Saunders in *Demosthenes and Aeschines*, Penguin, London, 1974, pp. 302-303.
2. Quoted in J. B. Bury and R. Meiggs, *A History of Greece*, MacMillan, London, 1979. pp. 457-8.
3. Plutarch in *The Age of Alexander*, trans. I. Scott-Kilvert, Penguin, London, 1979, pp. 285-6.
4. W. W. Tarn, *Alexander the Great*, C.U.P., Cambridge, 1999, p. 74.
5. Tarn, *Alexander the Great*, p. 96.
6. Plutarch, in *The Age of Alexander*, p. 266.
7. *Plutarch on Sparta*, trans. R. J. A. Talbert, Penguin, London, 1988, p. 134.
8. Tarn, *Alexander the Great*, p. 145.

## Chapter 25

# Our Fathers' Mingled Blood

### *The Foundation of Rome*

HELLENISTIC CULTURE WAS soon to be borne upon the strong arms of Rome. The Greek civil war that ended in 404 BC had dealt a death blow to the idea of the polis. New forms of government were required. From a tiny settlement on the Tiber hills in the eighth century BC, Rome had grown steadily, through the turbulent period of the early kings, to become a mature Republic with a balanced constitution, capable of ruling Italy, before embracing Greeks and barbarians alike in a single empire. The new culture, supported by Rome, enriched the world with its mathematics, literature and law; later it was to nurture the birth of Christian civilization.

Some time in the early centuries of the first millennium BC, the Etruscan people settled in the area between the Arno and Tiber rivers on the west coast of Italy. They

*Forum, Rome*

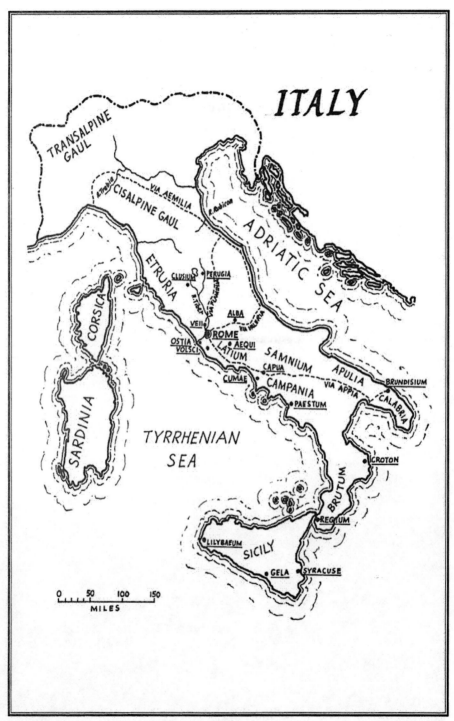

*Italy*

probably came from Asia Minor: Herodotus says from Lydia, and linguistic evidence suggests the island of Lemnos. Virgil, writing in the first century BC, believed them to be Greeks from Arcadia in the Peloponnese, whom Aeneas from Troy hailed as "our fathers' mingled blood." They built poleis on the Greek model and, like the Greeks, failed to unite as a nation, so that they were inevitably eclipsed by the Carthaginians, Syracusans and, of course, by the Romans. In religion they looked back to the Mycenaeans, and even to the Egyptians, for they believed strongly in immortality and made elaborate tombs, enriched with the property of the dead and wall-paintings of the after-life. Some tomb chambers were circular, with corbel vaults, like the great "bee-hive" tombs at Mycenae. Others were rectangular chambers, cut in rock and decorated with wall-paintings of dancing women, lyre players and other signs that the future life was joyous. Only later was a dismal underworld depicted, guarded by the three-headed dog, Cerberus, and containing a demon of death.

According to Virgil they venerated Heracles. Etruscan respect for the great hero who laboured for mankind was reflected in their institution of kingship. The early kings of Rome may have been Etruscans; the curule chair, or throne, and the insignia of the axes and rods, or fasces, representing the authority of the magistrates abroad and at home, symbols of Roman authority through the centuries, were Etruscan in origin. From Etruria, too, came the Roman belief in augury, the interpretation of natural signs to yield prophecies, especially from the entrails of animals and the flight of birds. Even writing was attributed to the Etruscan hero, Evander. He was said, also, to have instituted the annual fertility rites of the Lupercalia.

Etruscan art was the initial inspiration for Roman art. The Roman temple was derived from the Etruscan, which was distinguished by a large open portico, terracotta ornamentation and columns partly based on Greek Ionic and Corinthian orders. In Rome itself a very large Etruscan temple was dedicated in 509 BC on the Capitoline hill, only being replaced after 83 BC, when it burned down. The Etruscans learnt from the Greeks in southern Italy how to construct arches using archivolts - trapezoid stones which make the arch self-sustaining - and they combined such arches with pilasters; for example, in imposing city gateways, like the Porta Marzia at Perugia. This combination of the true arch and Greek orders became the basis of all later Roman architecture. The huge fortified walls of Etruscan cities were a further influence on Rome.

Much Greek pottery found its way to Etruria, confirming the prosperity of its maritime trade - and its piracy. More important artistically was the development of Etruscan sculpture, which resembled the Greek archaic style of the sixth century BC, perhaps indicating some common influence from Egypt. Etruscan works were in terracotta and had the generous scale, smooth bodies, braided hair and happy smiles of their Greek counterparts. On sarcophagi, as at Cerveteri near Rome, the figures recline on a couch with the quiet repose of men and women at a symposium. By contrast, a brilliantly ferocious, bronze she-wolf evokes Rome's legendary origin in the suckling of Romulus and Remus when they were abandoned by their evil guardian.

Though the cities of Etruria - Fiesole, Volterra, Arezzo, Perugia, Orvieto, Clusium, Veii and others - retained their legal independence from Rome until they were absorbed into Roman Italy after the Social War in 89 BC, they declined, like the Greek poleis; nor did the Etruscans recover from an overwhelming naval defeat by the Syracusans in 474 BC. Their unique place at the beginning of Roman history, however, gives them a lasting significance. Etruscan religion, institutions and art introduced the early settlement on the Tiber to a significant culture.

Virgil, writing in the first century BC, knew that Rome owed its culture to others, especially to Greeks and Etruscans; but he recognised the real worth of Rome in its contribution to law and government:

> "Let others better mold the running mass
>
> Of metals, and inform the breathing brass,
>
> And soften into flesh a marble face;
>
> Plead better at the bar; describe the skies,
>
> And when the stars descend, and when they rise.
>
> But, Rome, 't is thine alone, with awful sway,
>
> To rule mankind, and make the world obey,
>
> Disposing peace and war by thy own majestic way,
>
> To tame the proud, the fetter'd slave to free:
>
> These are imperial arts, and worthy thee."[1]

Romans could not match the artistry of the Greeks, but they had a profound regard for law which enabled them to govern with justice. They welcomed into one state all people who acknowledged Roman authority, and knew how to maintain a respect for the gods and yet to tolerate any religious beliefs which did not conflict with political obedience. By nature Romans were industrious, conscientious, devoted to the land and its cultivation, brave in their own defence, self-disciplined, loyal to the family and the state.

Though it became an imperial power ruling half of the civilised world, Rome was in essence a nation, dependent upon the culture which the Greeks created. National law, language and religion were the strands from which were woven its enduring strength. The Twelve Tables, on which the basic laws of Rome were engraved in the forum, originated with Solon, for they were brought to Rome in 451 BC by commissioners sent specially to Athens for the purpose; but they touched a resonant chord in the hearts of Romans. St Paul knew this when he appealed successfully to be judged as a Roman citizen under the rule of law. The genius of the language of Latium, a small area to the south of the Tiber, gave rise to the verse of Virgil, the eloquence of Cicero and, much later, the power of St Jerome's Vulgate. In religion, Rome incorporated its original few gods, which were not anthropomorphic, into the Greek pantheon, making a lawlike system capable of further development, as the gods of conquered peoples were assimilated. A natural piety enabled most Romans to see beyond the claims of the physical world and to dedicate their lives to these gods.

From the beginning Romans had to fight in self-defence against the warlike tribes which pressed upon them. Their sense of law made their armies disciplined and efficient; natural courage made it formidable; and united with devotion to the gods and state, these qualities made their armies invincible. Roman soldiers could be cruel, like Caesar, when he cut off the hands of every captive warrior of Vercengetorix' army in Gaul, but they could be honourable, too, like Camillus, when he refused to accept the betrayal of the city of Falerii into his hands by a treacherous citizen; whilst the Roman centurion, whose faith astonished Jesus, proved that even a battle-hardened soldier could retain a profound humanity.

The birth of Rome took place in the early period of the culture which lasted from about 1300 BC to 400 BC. Little is known about its origin. Two legendary accounts both point to a founder, or *pater patriae*, who embodied the essential qualities of the nation. Virgil describes the Trojan, Aeneas, who sailed to Italy and there founded a settlement near the mouth of the Tiber, but did not himself build Rome. Livy, and later Plutarch, refer to the foundation of Rome by Romulus, a descendant of Aeneas and the first of a line of kings of Rome.

Aeneas is a direct link with the Homeric heroes. As a Trojan warrior, he was courageous, resourceful, magnanimous, hospitable and careless of life and death. His seaborne adventures were second only to those of Odysseus, and equally subject to the whims of the gods. Juno, the wife of Jupiter, father of the gods, as protectress of Carthage did not want Aeneas to fulfil his mission of founding a city which might surpass Carthage in wealth and glory. She almost succeeded in wrecking his fleet in a fierce storm, but Aeneas had his own divine protectress in his mother, Venus. When he landed safely at Carthage, however, Queen Dido fell deeply in love with him. Only the intervention of Mercury prevented him from neglecting his mission altogether; the founder of the greatness of Rome heard the voice of reason amidst the blandishments of the senses. Thus he escaped from Carthage, leaving behind him a city devoted to his destruction, which centuries later fought Rome in three terrible wars.

> "Rise some avenger of our Libyan blood,
>
> With fire and sword persue the perjur'd brood;
>
> Our arms, our seas, our shores, oppos'd to their's;
>
> And the same hate descend on all our heirs!"[2]

In Italy he met adversity also. In order to marry the beautiful Latin princess, Lavinia, he fought to the death with her suitor, Turnus, a prince of Argive blood, whose cause Juno naturally supported. Aeneas' mission, however, could not be gainsaid. Jupiter himself declared that the gods must stand aside and let fate determine the outcome, for the need was that Rome should be founded. Overcoming every difficulty, Aeneas made the initial settlement of his people, which bore fruit three centuries later in the time of Romulus.

The twins, Romulus and Remus, were said to be the sons of the god, Mars, later the Roman god of war, and grandsons of the legitimate king of Alba in Latium, who had been deposed by his brother. As babies, they had been abandoned on the banks of the River Tiber, but were saved by a shepherd after a she-wolf suckled them - which gave rise to the famous emblem of Rome. When they grew up, they overthrew the usurper and reinstated their grandfather in Alba. On the hills above the Tiber, where the shepherd had cared for them, they founded the new city, but Romulus chose a square hill, which later was called the Palatine, and Remus a hill later called the Aventine: they had become rivals to rule the city. The Etruscan custom of divination by means of birds was used to decide the contest. Remus first saw six vultures, Romulus then saw twelve. Should priority or number decide the issue? Only the death of Remus during the construction of a city wall finally settled matters.

Aeneas, like the Etruscans, especially revered Heracles, now renamed Hercules, who had laboured incessantly to purify himself and his people. Romulus, too, introduced into Rome, now named after him, the worship of the deified Hercules, the only god foreign to the people, showing "his respect for that immortality which is the prize of valour."[3] He gave the people laws, appointed twelve personal attendants, called lictors, and adopted the Etruscan use of the curule chair of state and the purple-bordered toga of office. From the year of Romulus' accession, traditionally 753 BC, the Roman people dated their calendar, so that all later years were numbered *ab urbe condita*, (after the founding of the city).

Fugitives from local tribes were allowed to enter Rome. Population expanded, but there were not enough women. Romulus ordered a great festival to be held, inviting to it the neighbouring Sabine people. At a given signal during the festival all the marriageable Sabine maidens were seized and the Sabine men driven off by armed force. The Roman men seeking wives treated their captives honourably, marrying them with full rites and showing them love and respect. When, some while after, the Sabine men returned to Rome to do battle, the Sabine wives rushed out and pleaded with them not to attack their Roman husbands, whom they dearly loved. A reconciliation was made. Romans and Sabines became one people, and later, Numa, the greatest of all Roman kings, was of Sabine blood.

According to Plutarch, the Sabines believed themselves to be a colony of Lacedaemonians. That they were worthy comrades in arms of the Romans was proved by their treatment of Tarpeia, daughter of the Roman captain of the guard. She had opened the gates to the Sabine army, in return for a promise of what the Sabine warriors wore on the left arm - a golden bracelet - but once inside the city, the Sabine leader, Tatius, threw not only his bracelet but also his buckler at her. When all the warriors followed him, Tarpeia was buried alive under the weight of armour. The Romans named a high precipice on their citadel the Tarpeian Rock, and ever afterwards threw traitors from there to their deaths.

The great Julii family, whose brightest star was Gaius Julius Caesar, claimed descent from Aeneas, and thus from the goddess Venus, Aeneas' mother. When Virgil wrote his epic work, he was drawing together the threads of belief that linked all Romans to the heroic wanderers from Troy. The noblest leaders of the ancient Republic were worthy to claim ancestors who wore the crested helmet of Hector and sailed forth from the burning city in search of a new life of triumphant adventure. Did not the Etruscans speak a language of the Eastern Mediterranean, perhaps of Lemnos, so close to Troy, build cities like those of the Greek poleis and venerate kingship? Not just in the mind of the Latin poet was the connection established between Rome and the heroes of Troy; in the mind of the Roman people it had been remembered for generations.

### References:

1. Virgil, *Aeneid*, trans. J. Dryden, Airmont, New York, 1968, Book VI.

2. Virgil, *Aeneid*, trans. Dryden, Book IV.

3. Livy, *The Early History of Rome*, trans. A. de Selincourt, Penguin, London, 1976, Book I, p. 42.

## Chapter 26
# Sacred Fire
### *Numa Pompilius*

THE LEGEND OF AENEAS indicates that the foundation of Rome sprang from the Greek culture of the eastern Mediterranean, transmitted to Italy through the Etruscans and Magna Graecia. Roman religion however, appears to have been largely the creation of Romulus' successor, Numa Pompilius. According to Livy and Plutarch, he was a Sabine, called to the throne on the death of Romulus in 715 BC by the need for a successor acceptable to both Romans and Sabines. An agreement was made that a king should be elected by the Romans from amongst Sabine candidates. The Sabines acknowledged that Numa was their worthiest man, a philosopher, indifferent to wealth and status, pious and self-disciplined, a man of justice and peace, who defined courage as the ability to control one's own passions. His lack of ambition led

*Temple of Vesta, Forum, Rome*

him to refuse office, claiming that no-one should willingly change a life of contentment, until the people's representatives told him that government was the service of God. At his coronation he would not wear the crown until the proper omen was presented. When a flight of birds came into view on the right side of the sky at the ceremony on the Capitoline Hill, he allowed the crown to be placed on his head. His first act as king was to disband Romulus' 300 bodyguards, for he said that with the people's trust he did not need a bodyguard and without that trust he did not want to rule.

To Numa's eyes the Roman people, including now the Sabines, were like a high-spirited war horse. Energetic, proud, brave and capricious, they lacked the finer qualities that arose from spiritual practices. He instituted a priesthood to supervise public and private ceremonies, prayers and augurs trained in the art of divination - the understanding of omens, notably the flight of birds, storms and movements of celestial bodies. Numa's religious ceremonies were simple. Sacrificial offerings were of wine or flour; only later were living creatures slaughtered for sacrifice. The temples were unadorned; no images of any kind were used, because Numa taught that divine forces were unseen, and for 170 years this absence of images was a feature of Roman temples. Omens were natural signs that the time was ripe for action. No important action of a religious, political or military nature would be taken in Roman society without an omen being sought. Numa's initiation of augury, drawing upon Greek and Etruscan practices, implied that the present flight of a bird, or conjunction of planets, in some way contained the future, so that the favourable time to act could be well chosen. As Shakespeare's Cassius says:

> "And when the cross blue lightening seem'd to open
>
> The breast of heaven, I did present myself
>
> Even in the aim and very flash of it!"[1]

To assist with this judgement of time Numa recreated the Roman calendar, which had twelve lunar months, with an intercalary month of 22 days every second year. March, named after the god Mars, he relegated from first to third month; instead, the first month was named after Janus, the two-headed god of beginnings and protector of peaceful arts, who looked before and after, and god, also, of entrances, gates and doorways. February, the second month, became the time of purification. To Janus, Numa built a temple, the gates of which were to be closed in times of peace and open in times of war. For the 43 years of Numa's reign the gates remained closed. Thereafter, only once were they briefly closed again - at the end of the first Punic War in 241 BC - until Augustus introduced a new pax Romana after the battle of Actium in 31 BC. Of Numa's reign, the poet, Sacchylides, said, "Over the iron shield the spiders hang their threads".

Peace was, for Numa, the natural human condition. Every effort was to be made to avert war, especially unjust war. He appointed officers, called Fetiales, to negotiate on behalf of Rome with foreign peoples. Their function was sacred; they followed precise rules and invoked curses on the unjust, including even Rome, if she contemplated an unjust declaration of war. War was to be the last resort in support of a just cause. Even the king could not declare war without the assent of the Fetiales. Thus began the tradition of fair dealing, including the proper treatment of defeated enemies, which enabled Rome to gather to her side many people seeking the protection of justice. From this beginning Roman lawyers were later to develop the great concept of the law of nations, regulating the conduct of nations one to another.

Romans were taught by Numa to have the utmost good faith in their dealings with everyone. The word of a Roman was to be unbreakable; his pledge was a sacred act. A temple of Faith was constructed to ensure that this was never forgotten. An annual ceremony of truth-keeping saw the priests brought in a covered wagon, symbolising that truth is unmanifest, to the temple, where they carried out the rites with hands swathed to the fingers, to indicate that truth is preserved inviolable in the right hand. The practical effect of this insistence on speaking the truth was profound. In the first Punic War the general, Regulus, returned to Carthage to face a cruel death, because he had so promised his captors. Roman standard bearers would die in battle clinging to the standard, for they had given their word to protect it.

Related both to peace and to good faith was the god Terminus, whom Numa introduced as the guardian of boundaries. Romulus had not deterred the Romans from taking territory from neighbours, but Numa recognised that justice in dealing with land was a prerequisite of peace. Boundaries were made sacred. The boundary stones were seen as a protection against violence from either side, a measured limitation to possession, rather than a claim to it. For this and other reasons Numa's influence extended beyond Rome; he was revered for his wisdom and justice by all the adjacent peoples of Italy. If land was justly acquired from defeated enemies, Numa ensured that it was fairly distributed amongst the citizens of Rome; the neglect of such a practice later caused revolution and civil war. All Roman territory was divided by Numa into *pagi* or districts, each inspected to check that land was not wasted or abused. To overcome any lingering sense of division between original Romans and Sabines, he set up groups of craftsmen - potters, blacksmiths, goldsmiths, carpenters, musicians and so on - each group containing both peoples and uniting them in love of their own profession or trade. On the feast of Saturn, also instituted by Numa, labourers and masters shared all in common.

The gods, Janus, Fides and Terminus, and the three great ancient deities of northern Italy, whom the Romans knew as Jupiter, father of the gods, Juno, his consort, and Minerva, an Etruscan goddess of thunder - later identified with the Greek Athena - were not described by Numa as anthropomorphic beings, but as great, unseen forces. Romans came to see events as guided by this unseen world, waiting to be acknowledged. Of course, the Greeks, too, believed in this world and of the need to propitiate its forces, but their strong imagination and artistry led them to form images of the gods with bewildering ease, whilst retaining some memory that the images themselves were unreal. The Roman mind was less imaginative and close to the richer soil of Italy. It only later borrowed the Greek tendency to see gods in human, or animal, form. Most of the early gods of Rome, including Mars, were initially agricultural in their qualities, for the people were farmers; they studied the sky and wind, sun, rain and soil. Gods were elements: space, air, fire, water, earth.

Gradually, as Roman religion degenerated, alongside the decline of society and government, the number of gods became legion, so that an event like the growing of corn, or childbirth, was seen as controlled in minute detail by a whole series of gods and goddesses, and individual objects, like the broom, the axe and the mortar, were each associated with a god or goddess. This was a perversion of the tradition, but its root was the idea that every event is controlled from within by a divine force; that the growth of ears of corn or the birth of a child is the unfolding of hidden forces, and that respect for these is the beginning of wisdom. The multiplication of gods stemmed, also, from Numa's original teaching that the name of the god is its essence. Priests had to be absolutely exact in their language and ritual to avoid mis-naming, for name and divine force were fundamentally the same. The spirit of ancient Egypt had entered Numa Pompilius.

Central to Numa's innovations was the building of a temple to the goddess Vesta. Fire was sacred to her, so the circular temple contained a holy flame at the centre, never to be extinguished. Numa appointed the fire to be worshipped as the origin of all things. Two young maidens, the Vestal Virgins, were appointed to guard it, who later were increased to four, then to six. They were selected at an age of between six and ten, and took vows of absolute chastity. For ten years they were trained; for another ten they practised as priestesses; for ten final years they trained initiates. After these 30 years they were free either to marry or to remain as highly honoured figures in Rome. The Vestal Virgins were the emblem of the purity of the Roman race. They stood for the sanctity of womanhood and the preservation of the morality of the family and people. A terrible punishment was inflicted upon any Vestal Virgin who broke her vow. She was flogged by the High Priest and then buried alive in a tomb, furnished with a couch, a burning candle and a supply of food, to prevent unseemly death from starvation. On average, less than one such case of the corruption of a Vestal Virgin occurred in every century of Roman history. Romans believed that, if the sacred fire went out, then Rome itself would be destroyed. Vesta was the most beautiful of the Roman divinities; she became, also, the goddess of the hearth, to whom thanks were offered before eating.

These were only some of Numa's gifts to the Roman people. He also preserved the family by introducing reverence for the souls of ancestors - the *Manes* - so that the Roman family, under its paterfamilias, became an immensely strong institution, based upon not one or two generations but a succession into the remote past. Thus could the Fabii, the Metelli, the Scipios, the Julii and many other great families contribute to the life of Rome for centuries.

Numa introduced, too, practices - sacrifices, processions and choral dances - which gave an artistic and harmonious character to Roman religion, and did much to soften the rough and warlike nature of the people. On the other hand, he also appointed dancing priests, called Salii, who invoked Mars by shaking sacred shields in time of war; for fighting, like everything, was to be authorised and supported by divine forces, especially when it had been ordained by the Fetiales in a just cause. Indeed the Sabines' belief that they were a Lacedaemonian colony suggests that the Roman people were dedicated to fighting as a form of self-discipline, like the Spartans. Plutarch even thought that a Spartan called Pythagoras, who won a prize at the sixteenth Olympiad, in the third year of Numa's monarchy, may have visited Rome and advised Numa on the laws of Lycurgus.

Numa was a deeply spiritual man, called to rule as king of Rome. He was indeed a philosopher king, reluctant to re-enter the cave, but recognising his duty to serve his fellow men as the service of God. He liked to wander in groves or desert places, to commune there with divine forces. To the Romans he gave what he himself loved, the *pax deorum*, the peace of the gods. When he died, in 672 BC, he was buried in a stone coffin, alongside another which contained all his sacred writings, for he believed that wisdom must be taught by the voice, not by reading. His own pupils, particularly the priests, would pass on his teaching and practices. Four hundred years later this was respected when the second coffin was discovered. The Roman Senate ordered the books to be burnt to prevent the corruption of the teaching if the books were made public. Even long after has death, he protected the Roman people:

> "Men of all classes took Numa as their unique example and modelled themselves upon him, until the effect of this change of heart was felt even beyond the borders of Roman territory... Rome's neighbours came to revere her so profoundly as a community dedicated wholly to worship, that the mere thought of offering violence seemed to them like sacrilege."[2]

Roman piety was an enduring force that sustained Rome under the early kings, the Republic and the Empire, until, a thousand years after Numa, the Emperor Julian could still appeal to the pagan gods in a final attempt to turn back the growth of Christianity. During the early days of the Republic in the fifth century BC, however, it received a powerful transfusion from Greek religion. From the Greek colony of Cumae (or Cyme), near Naples, gods of the Greek pantheon were introduced to Rome, and the oracle there was recognised as of divine authority. The utterances of the Sibyl priestess of Apollo were written in the *libri fatales*, or Sibylline Books, and placed in the care of one of four priestly colleges in Rome, to become a great source of Roman prophecy. Apollo later became one of the twelve-fold Roman pantheon, and the legendary Hercules was reinvigorated by Greek practices of worship.

In the early fourth century, the rites of *lectisternium* and *supplicatio* were introduced, in conjunction with the gradual grafting of the Greek pantheon on to the Roman collection of gods. *Lectisternium* was the worship of gods whose images were placed on couches to receive rich offerings from devotees. *Supplicatio* was a public processional ceremony to propitiate or render thanks to the gods. By this time Roman religion was prone to use images, which for the more intelligent worshippers were merely symbols of divine forces, but for the ignorant had become idols. After a plague epidemic in Rome, the cult of Asclepius was also introduced from Epidaurus in 293 BC, beginning a fresh wave of Greek religious importation and also the systematic study of medicine. By the late third century, a *lectisternium* marked the synthesis of Roman and Greek pantheons, and the poet, Ennius, could list the great gods of Rome as Juno, Vesta, Minerva, Ceres, Diana, Venus, Mars, Mercury, Jove, Neptune, Volcanus and Apollo. Some, like Ceres, Diana and Neptune, were much enhanced by their association with Greek gods and goddesses, like Demeter, Artemis and Poseidon. It was a far cry from the native religion of Numa, who spoke of union with God, unadulterated by images and poets' tales. Yet something remained of the simple Roman faith in a divine world, unseen but potent, and few Romans ever forgot to pay obeisance to those forces which might kill them for their sport or offer what the natural world gave those who acknowledged its origin.

### References:

1. Shakespeare, *Julius Caesar*, act I, scene 3.

2. Livy, *The Early History of Rome*, trans. A. de Selincourt, Penguin, London, 1976, Book I, p. 56.

## Chapter 27

# Brave Days of Old

### The Kings of Rome

HISTORIANS IN THE ANCIENT WORLD had little doubt that under Numa Pompilius Rome had been governed by an aristocrat, a philosopher king. As there was no hereditary succession of kings in Rome, the Senate, which was composed of the heads of the *gentes* or clans, chose the king, but the choice was submitted to a general assembly of all the people, the *Comitia Curiata*. Numa had been chosen king

*A view in the Forum at Rome*

for his reputation for justice and piety. His successor, Tullus Hostilius, was chosen for timocratic qualities more like those of Romulus.

Tullus was young, strong, brave, even reckless, and he viewed the long peace under Numa as merely an occasion for the Romans to lose their ambition and martial spirit. Circumstances favoured his election as king by the Senate and people, for there was a running battle going on with the Albans over accusations by both sides of cattle-stealing. Tullus was set adamantly upon war, rather than negotiations, to settle the problem on the border with Alba, but the Alban king, Mettius, was wiser. When both sides were committed to war and their armies lay entrenched, facing each other, five miles from Rome, he made a proposal to Tullus. Albans and Romans were kindred people, he claimed, both sprung from the Trojan stock which had followed Aeneas to Italy. Their common enemy, the powerful Etruscan state to the north, threatened them by land and sea. Were they to weaken each other in the present conflict they would both become the prey of the Etruscans. Should they not settle their differences more rationally? Three warriors from each side could fight in mortal combat to decide the issue.

The proposal appealed to the good sense of the Romans and yet satisfied the aggressive ardour of Tullus. Moreover, both Albans and Romans could draw upon a trio of brothers noted for their martial skill and patriotism, the Curiatii of the Albans and the Horatii of the Romans. The terms were simple: that the losing state would submit to the victors; subjection or mastery would be the spoils. With appropriate solemnity, priests sanctified the compact. A precise form of words was used by the Fetiales, and the earliest treaty of the Romans was made in these critical circumstances.

Romans and Albans assembled on the level ground on which they would otherwise have fought a full scale battle. From their ranks stepped forward on either side the three brothers, Horatii and Curiatii, armed for hand to hand combat in cuirass, helmet, greaves, buckler and short sword, the thrusting weapon of the disciplined soldier.

A Roman soon fell, mortally wounded, then another. Although the Albans were themselves wounded, all three remained on their feet, confident of victory, as they closed upon the third Roman. Despair rose up in the hearts of his watching countrymen. How could one defeat three? A life of slavery was the dark vision of every Roman.

Livy describes the outcome:

"The young man, though alone, was unhurt. No match for his three opponents together, he was yet confident of his ability to face them singly, and, with this purpose in mind, he took to his heels, sure that they would be after him with such speed as their wounds allowed. Not far from the scene of the first fight he looked back. His three enemies were coming, strung out one behind the other, the foremost almost upon him. He turned and attacked him furiously. A cry rose from the Alban army, 'Your brother! Save him!' But it was too late. Horatius had already killed his man and, flushed with triumph, was looking for his next victim. The Roman's cheer for their young soldier was like the roar of the crowd at the race when luck turns defeat into victory. Horatius pressed on to make an end. He killed his second man before the last, near though he was, could come to his aid."[1]

The third, and most seriously wounded, Alban was soon dispatched. Outside the Capena gate of Rome, the sister of the victorious Horatius watched the arrival of her brother and the bodies of the five dead warriors. She had been betrothed to one of the Curiatii brothers. Across her brother's shoulder was slung a cloak, which she herself had made for her dead lover. Overcome with grief, she loosed her hair and called upon his name. That his sister, a Roman, should grieve amidst the triumph of her brother and her people was too much for Horatius. He drew his sword and thrust it into her heart. "So perish all Roman women who mourn for an enemy," he cried.

King Tullus shrank from the prosecution of a man who had killed his sister in such circumstances. Though formally condemned to be scourged to death, Horatius was reprieved. Nevertheless the Roman sense of justice compelled him to be humiliated. A piece of timber was slung across the roadway and Horatius was made to pass beneath it with covered head, as under a yoke of submission. Much later a whole Roman army was to undergo the same ordeal at the hands of an enemy leader who was too humane to kill his captives. Tullus made a statesmanlike settlement with the Albans. Although forced to give up their possessions and become absorbed into the Roman state, they were allowed to keep their arms for use in future struggles with the enemies of Rome.

After Tullus Hostilus there probably followed a period of Etruscan monarchy, until, a native king, Servius Tullius, was elected, following unrest amongst the people of Rome. Servius' reign, from 578 to 535 BC, coincides with the time of Solon's reforms in Athens. The needs of both cities were similar: the ideals of timocracy were giving way before the love of wealth. Ancient systems of holding land, to which in early Rome all citizens had equal access, were breaking down, as individuals demanded greater property rights. Hence, Servius, perhaps knowing of Solon's measures, introduced reforms which related land-holding closely to the chief public burden in the state, the provision of armed soldiers for its defence.

Servius divided the population of Rome into seven classes. The richest, whose families had held land since the earliest days of Rome, were to be known as knights and to equip themselves as cavalry, though their horses were provided by the state and maintained by a tax on rich widows. The highest class of infantry were recruited from men whose wealth from land amounted to about ten times that of the lowest assessed class. These had to equip themselves with all the armour and weapons of heavy infantry, able to fight in the front ranks. Engineers, whose equipment was expensive, were included in this first class. The second and third infantry classes, with between three-quarters and half the landed property of the first class, omitted some expensive armour; the fourth class, worth half the third, were unarmoured, fighting with spear and javelin only. The fifth and lowest class of infantry made do with slings and stones, and included in their ranks buglers and trumpeters. The remainder of the population, perhaps the majority, were exempt from military service.

These reforms were a wise readjustment of the cost of defending the state, the main public burden of a simple and small agrarian society. In this way they helped to preserve the economic freedom of Romans by proportioning taxation to the rent of land and leaving weaker citizens with some independence, as Solon had done in Athens. Political conditions, also, were affected. Servius arranged that each class, including the knights, was grouped into centuries, one century providing one hundred armed men of the required type. Although the old assembly of the people, the *Comitia Curiata*, based upon *curiae*, or groups of *gens*, remained, a new assembly, the *Comitia Centuriata*, became more influential. Voting in this assembly was by centuries, but the superior centuries voted first, the inferior ones only voting if a decision had not been reached. Since the knights and the first class of infantry composed together 98 centuries, against the 93 of the remaining classes, the political effect was oligarchy, the rule of the wealthy few. Executive power still lay with the king, and the fundamental laws of Rome were either customary or had been laid down by Numa Pompilius.

The Servian reforms indicate that conflict had arisen in Rome between the older, wealthiest families and the rest of the population. The former were the patricians, claiming descent from the founder citizens, the latter the plebeians, people whose ancestors, or they themselves, had entered Rome since its foundation - Albans, Etruscans, refugees from neighbouring lands - or men impoverished by misfortune or weakness. For centuries this conflict was to influence Roman history. The Senate, the senior political organ, which advised the king and from whom kings were chosen, was entirely patrician. In principle, the patricians were a warrior class, ruling as a timocracy and motivated by honour, but by the sixth century BC Rome had ignored the vital condition, emphasised later by Plato, that rulers must select their successors from amongst the children of any class. Hence the patrician class had become a closed order, denying to able plebeians the opportunity to serve the state in a political or judicial capacity. Fortunately for Rome, a few patricians were later to realise the need for more liberal conditions in the constitution and to pass laws through the Senate and assemblies which opened the door to natural talent.

The last king of Rome, Tarquin the Proud, probably an Etruscan who had seized power in the city by murdering Servius Tullius, ruled without consulting the Senate. Patricians were disregarded or abused by Tarquin; plebeians were forced to work at his command on public works, intended to glorify him and perpetuate his name. A great new temple was built on the Capitoline Hill. The land for it was cleared of all other buildings, including sacred ones - except for the temple of Terminus, who proved his immovable nature by resisting demolition. In addition, tiers of seats were constructed in the Circus, and a huge sewer for the whole of Rome, the *Cloaca Maxima* (or Great Sewer), was built by forced labour.

One of Tarquin's sons, however, initiated his father's downfall. According to Livy, it began when a snake suddenly slid out of a wooden pillar in Tarquin's palace. So ominous was this event that Tarquin sent two of his sons to Delphi to consult the oracle of Apollo. With them went their cousin, Lucius Junius Brutus, whose last name was given for his stupidity. Brutus had realised that the best security against Tarquin's violence and greed was to appear incapable of being a threat or a rival; hence his 'brute' nature was assumed. On his visit to Delphi he presented the priest there with a hollow stick of cornel-wood, containing a gold rod - Livy suggests that it was symbolic of Brutus' character. One of Tarquin's sons asked the oracle who would rule next in Rome; the reply was that supreme authority would reside with whoever of the three first kissed his mother. Whilst the two brothers drew lots to decide who this should be, Brutus fell upon the ground and kissed the earth.

Meanwhile, Tarquin was at war with the city of Ardea. His third son, Sextus, a dissolute young man, conceived a passion for the beautiful and virtuous wife of his kinsman, Collatinus. This lady, Lucretia, was a young Roman noblewoman - industrious, chaste, devoted to her husband and to the principles for which he stood. Not suspecting Sextus' motives, she entertained him generously when he called upon her. Collatinus was away in the Roman military camp. During the night Sextus returned to Lucretia's room. He threatened that if she would not share her bed with him he would kill her, together with a male slave, and leave their bodies together, whilst he claimed to all the world that he had surprised them in Lucretia's bedroom. So Lucretia yielded to Sextus.

The following morning, after Sextus had fled, Lucretia called for her father and her husband. With them came Brutus and Valerius, two future leaders of Rome. Lucretia told them of Sextus' crime, then plunged a dagger into her heart. This terrible act of release awoke in Brutus recognition of his duty to the Roman people. Throwing aside his years of pretence, he showed a resolution which astonished his kinsmen and all who knew him. He organised the people to overthrow the whole family of the Tarquins. Sextus was killed when he sought refuge in Gabii. His father, Tarquin the Proud, was driven out of Rome, with the curses of those he had misgoverned.

The rape of Lucretia symbolised the evil forces that needed to be purged from the state, for the destiny of Rome could not be fulfilled without purification. Lucretia sacrificed herself for her husband's honour and for the honour of Rome, whilst Sextus had betrayed himself:

> "Pawning his honour to obtain his lust;
> And for himself himself he must forsake -
> Then where is truth if there be no self-trust?"[2]

Amongst the Etruscans, Tarquin Superbus found refuge. Indeed, in Lars Porsena, king of Clusium, he found ready support for an attempt to regain his lost kingdom. Porsena gathered a huge Etruscan army, marched south against Rome and captured the Janiculum hill, overlooking both the Tiber and the wooden bridge which alone gave entry to the city. The people of Rome were near to panic. The Senate, fearing that Tarquin might be re-admitted by the populace, rapidly passed measures which modified the oligarchic character of the government. The monopoly on salt, a vital product found in great quantities on the banks of the lower Tiber, was brought under public control; the plebeians were exempted from tolls and taxes; taxation instead was borne wholly by the rich. Thus from this emergency the state reverted to a condition of justice which it soon forgot when the crisis passed. However, the plebeians were reconciled to their leaders and, at least, would not betray them.

From the surrounding countryside farmers and their families flocked into the city, together with Roman soldiers. As the Etruscans moved down from the Janiculum, it was evident to one man, the captain of the guard, Horatius Codes, that the wooden bridge must be demolished. He rallied some soldiers to begin the task, but there was no time, unless the bridge could be defended at the further end. Horatius himself marched across and stood at its narrow entrance. Two noble Romans, Spurius Lartius and Titus Herminius, shamed by his solitary courage, ran over and stood by him:

> "As that great host, with measured tread,
> And spears advanced, and ensigns spread,
> Rolled slowly towards the bridge's head,
> Where stood the dauntless three."[3]

The Etruscan army stopped, baffled by the audacity of the three men. Then a few of their finest soldiers stepped forward to engage the Romans, but were quickly cut down. More followed and met the same resistance. Meanwhile, the Roman soldiers on the city bank worked with furious energy, sawing and hacking at the wooden supports of the bridge. It began to creak. Lars Porsena, fearing the prospect of a lengthy siege, shouted orders for his spearmen to advance. Horatius now ordered his companions to withdraw across the bridge. A flight of spears wounded him, but he kept on his feet, barring the way. As the Etruscans charged forward, realising that they had to brush him aside by sheer numbers, the bridge collapsed in a tangle of splintering timber. Horatius leapt into the swiftly flowing Tiber, swam to the bank, and collapsed in the arms of soldiers. As Livy says, "It was a noble piece of work - legendary maybe, but destined to be celebrated in story through the years to come."[4]

Porsena besieged the city for some while. Horatius was held in the highest honour, not least because he had recalled the people of Rome to their tradition of courage in the defence of their city. Later, he was granted as much land as he could drive a two-oxen plough round in one day; and a statue of him was erected in the Roman Forum.

At least one other Roman nobleman showed the same courage as Horatius Codes. Gaius Mucius was appalled at Rome's subjection to a siege by people whom Rome had often defeated in battle. He asked the Senate for permission to leave the city, knowing that otherwise he might be thought a deserter. Under his cloak he carried a dagger, as he went at night through the Etruscan lines. The next morning he stood in the large crowd attending upon Lars Porsena, whilst the Etruscan army was being paid. A senior official, splendidly attired, sat next to the king, dealing with the business of the day. Mistaking him for the king, Mucius suddenly rushed out of the crowd and plunged his dagger into his heart. Mucius was seized and brought before Lars Porsena. Despite his intense disappointment and his hopeless situation, Mucius spoke out firmly: "I am a Roman; my name is Gaius Mucius. I came here to kill you - my enemy. I have as much courage to die as to kill. It is our Roman way to do and to suffer bravely." He told the king that many others would try where he had failed. Porsena, in rage and alarm, ordered that Mucius be burned alive, unless he divulged the whole plot. At this, Mucius cried out: "See how cheap men hold their bodies when they care only for honour!" and he thrust his right hand into a fire kindled on an altar nearby for a sacrifice. He let it burn, as though unaware of the pain. Astonished beyond belief, Porsena ordered his guards to drag Mucius from the altar. "Go free," he said, "you have dared to be a worse enemy to yourself than to me. I should bless your courage, if it lay with my country to dispose of it. But, as that cannot be, I, as an honourable enemy, grant you pardon, life and liberty."[5]

Mucius told Porsena that there were three hundred young men who had sworn to make an attempt upon the king's life. Mucius' courage, however, had awoken Porsena's humanity. He offered generous terms to Rome; the siege was relieved, captured territory was returned by Rome to the Etruscan city of Veii, and hostages were taken but well treated. Gaius Mucius, the cause of this good fortune for Rome, became known as Scaevola, the left-handed man. His nobility of character confirmed what Tarquin's expulsion had indicated: that Rome, under the oligarchy then prevailing, was not ripe for tyranny.

### References:

1. Livy, *The Early History of Rome*, trans. A. de Selincourt, Penguin, London, 1976, Book I, pp. 60-1.
2. Shakespeare, *The Rape of Lucretia*, 11. 156-8.
3. Macaulay, *Horatius* v. xxxv.
4. Livy, *The Early History of Rome*, Book II, p. 116.
5. Livy, *The Early History of Rome*, Book II, p. 118-9.

## Chapter 28

# Destined to Grow Great

### *The Republic Conquers Italy*

ROME HAD LOST HER KINGS, but not her love of virtue. *Virtus, pietas, fides*: these ensured her a glorious future. For two hundred and fifty years after the expulsion of Tarquin, Rome had to fight for her survival against enemies in Italy, until by the mid third century BC, she was mistress of the whole land from the River Arno in the north to the toe and heel of the peninsula. Throughout these wars what sustained her was the recognition that above each citizen stood the state, above that the gods, and above them the one indefinable power which kept the fire in the temple of Vesta forever burning.

Brutus and Valerius became the chief magistrates of the new Republic that was formed. Under the title of consul each fulfilled many of the duties of a king, but could veto each other's acts. Apart from the problem of relations between the patricians

*Temple of Castor, Forum, Rome*

and plebians, Rome had to deal with the threat from the nearby cities of Latium to the south. War followed, until in 493 BC a peace treaty was made between Rome and the newly created Latin League. For some while Rome was little more than an equal partner with such Latin cities as Tusculum, Corioli, Ardea and Lanuvium. Then a new enemy appeared south of Latium: the Volsci. They and the Aequi, to the east, troubled the Romans for half a century, mainly because, as hill-tribes, they coveted the flat pasture-land of Latium and Rome's position on the Tiber at its lowest bridging point. War with the Volsci brought to the forefront of Roman public life a patrician, Gaius Marcius, known as Coriolanus after his capture of Corioli.

Coriolanus was contemptuous of the plebeians and of their claims for more rights in land and government. So much so that plebeian anger led to his expulsion from Rome and his acceptance of Volscian hospitality. He resolved to lead a Volscian attack upon Rome, though persuading his new allies to preserve the property of Roman patricians. His military boldness and leadership were enough to turn the scales of war against the Romans. Rome was besieged by a Volscian army; its situation became desperate. Uncertainty and fear grew within the city, until the women of Rome decided to take matters into their own hands. They marched to the home of Coriolanus' mother, Volumnia, and his wife, Vergilia, and pleaded with them to help. Volumnia was an aged Roman matron, brought up to love the city and acknowledge that her children were its servants, if necessary prepared to die for it. Taking Vergilia and her two grandsons with her, she left Rome and walked through the Volscian lines. Begging an audience with her son, she besought him to show mercy upon Rome, to negotiate peace between the country of his birth and his new allies:

> "Even to pray to the gods, which others may find a comfort in their misfortunes, has become impossible for us, since we cannot ask them in the same breath to make our country victorious and to keep you safe. When we pray for you, we are calling down a curse upon Rome, such as the bitterest of her enemies could desire, and your wife and children are compelled to sacrifice either their native land or yourself. As for me, I shall not wait for the war to decide this issue for me. If I cannot prevail upon you to prefer friendship and harmony to enmity and strife, and thus become the benefactor of both countries rather than the scourge of one of them, then you must know - and let there be no doubt of this - that you shall never attack Rome unless you trample first upon the dead body of the mother who bore you."[1]

Coriolanus listened in silence, then raised up his mother, who had fallen at his feet, and cried out, "You have saved Rome, but you have destroyed your son." The next morning he marched the Volscian army out of Roman territory. Not all the Volscians blamed Coriolanus for what he had done, but those who did organised a conspiracy and killed him.

Thirty years later, in 458 BC, war with the Aequi led to a dramatic incident which showed how the best Romans had the courage and military genius of Coriolanus without his pride and rashness. An elderly patrician, famed for his powers of leadership, Quinctius Cincinnatus, had been reduced to poverty by the folly of his son. Forced to sell all he possessed in order to redeem his son's debts, he moved to a three acre farm beyond the city on the west bank of the Tiber. Whilst Cincinnatus dwelt there, living as a humble citizen farmer, the Roman army, under a timid consul, was surrounded by a force of Aequi, who walled the Romans into their camp with earthworks. Such was the reputation of Cincinnatus for patriotism and military prowess that every voice in Rome called for his return. He was appointed Dictator, a special office giving supreme power in an emergency to one man for a maximum term of six months. A mission sent from Rome found him quietly ploughing his fields. They told him to fetch his toga. On donning it, he was saluted as Dictator.

Once in Rome, Cincinnatus organised a relief army with amazing speed. Every able bodied man was ordered to obtain weapons, twelve stakes and five days' bread ration. They marched out to the place of the besieged camp. Darkness had fallen when they arrived. Cincinnatus rode round the camp, outside the lines of the Aequi; then ordered his men to build a palisade, completely encircling the Aequi and their own circle of earth works. Meanwhile, the consul had heard the arrival of the relieving army, and ordered his men to launch a diversionary attack. By the morning the Aequi realised that they were hopelessly trapped between the two Roman armies. They begged for fair treatment, if they surrendered. Cincinnatus gave them his word. He compelled the Aequi, every one of them, to walk under a yoke of spears. Then they were allowed to return to their hills to the east of Rome. Cincinnatus was loaded with praise and honours. Though he rewarded only the relieving army with the spoils of victory, the army of the consul presented him with a golden circlet in gratitude. As for Cincinnatus himself, he was devoid of ambition and resigned the Dictatorship after fifteen days.

Gradually the Volsci and the Aequi were forced by Roman arms to make treaties with Rome, which reduced their power to threaten her. Though Rome took land from defeated enemies, she remained faithful in principle to the directions of Numa Pompilius when he created the Fetiales and insisted on fighting only in a just cause. Treaties often gave the defeated people many of the rights of Roman citizens, though usually without the right to vote in the assemblies of the people, which constituted the ultimate sovereign power in Rome.

The Etruscan city of Veii, however, only a few miles north of Rome, remained a powerful rival throughout the fifth century BC. As early as 477 BC the great patrician family of the Fabii had tried to solve the problem that Veii presented for Rome by offering to take upon itself, exclusively, the defence of Rome from any attack by Veii. Valiantly all the male members able to bear arms, 306 in all, had marched behind the crimson cloak of their leader, out of the right hand arch of the Carmental Gate - later called the "Unlucky Way." For a while they had gained an ascendancy over the army of Veii, until one day they were ambushed. Despite breaking out, they were again surrounded on a small hill and annihilated, though one youth returned to Rome and became a hero in later wars.

Veii was finally defeated in 396 BC by a Roman patrician, Furius Camillus, who was appointed Dictator several times during days of great peril for Rome. In 406 BC Veii was besieged by the Romans, but the natural strength of its site on a hill in the wild, volcanic country of Etruria enabled the Veians to hold out for ten years. Camillus took Veii eventually by mining operations in the tufa rock, when he synchronised an attack on the citadel, mounted from tunnels, with a general assault. The story was later told that, as the tunnellers were about to break out into the citadel, the king of Veii was conducting a sacrifice. A priest who was present said that whoever cut up the entrails would possess Veii, whereupon a bold Roman officer sprang from the tunnel, seized the entrails and carried them back to Camillus to be cut up.

There is no doubt that Camillus was a pious man. He ordered that one tenth of the rich spoils of Veii should be devoted to Apollo at Delphi, who had contributed to the Roman victory when the Pythian Apollo had answered Roman supplicants with the prophecy that Veii would fall when the Alban Lake, south of Rome, was drained. Camillus had seen to it that the lake, which was excessively high, was drained. Now he proposed a votive offering of a huge golden ornament to Apollo, paid for by each soldier giving one tenth of the value of his personal plunder from Veii. This proposal was not popular. It reinforced the existing belief amongst the common people that Camillus was a die-hard patrician. Later a popular Assembly voted for his exile, a decision which the Veians might have seen as divine retribution for his cruel decision to sell the whole free population of Veii into slavery.

Before his exile, however, Camillus gave one outstanding instance of Roman awareness of justice. A smaller city than Veii, but a similarly resistant one, Falerii, was under siege by Camillus' army. Each day, as the Roman troops sat in their encircling positions outside the walls, a schoolmaster of Falerii took the boys in his charge for a walk beyond the town. These boys were the sons of the most eminent citizens of Falerii. The Roman soldiers took little notice of this harmless enterprise; indeed, they failed to observe that the schoolmaster was leading his party further and further each day towards the Roman lines. Finally he walked through the lines, followed by the boys. He asked to see the Roman commander. Then he proposed that the boys would be ideal hostages to force the leaders in Falerii to surrender their city. Far from rewarding the schoolmaster, Camillus treated him with contempt as a traitor to his city and a man who had utterly abused his trust. He ordered him to be stripped and his hands tied behind his back. The boys were each given a stick and told to beat the master back to the city gates. When the citizens of Falerii heard the boys' story, they were amazed at the spirit of justice of the Roman general. They resolved that to live under such justice was better than under their own regime. Falerii was freely offered to Camillus by its own citizens.

A worse military threat to Rome than Veii or Falerii now appeared in the far north of Italy. Throughout the fifth century Celtic tribes from Gaul had been moving through the Alps to settle in the great plain of the Po valley, displacing earlier Etruscan settlers. The Gauls were fine warriors, using long swords and renowned for the ferocity of their infantry. A huge horde, led by their king, Brennus, were roused to attack Rome, after the Roman envoys had forgotten their own sacred rules of diplomacy and assaulted the Gaullish leaders at a parley. A Roman army, hastily deployed without auguries being taken, was almost wiped out at the River Allia, a few miles from Rome, a day which lived long in Roman memories as one of the greatest humiliations in their history. In desperation the Romans recalled Camillus from exile, but there was little he could do. The Roman citadel was reinforced, but the rest of the city could not be defended after the losses at the River Allia.

At this moment of acute crisis a decision was taken that all the fighting men, together with some of their families, should garrison the citadel, that the remaining plebeians should escape from the city as best they could, but that the older patricians, by their own choice should remain in the lower city to die with honour. When the

Gauls entered the Colline Gate, they found strangely empty streets ; only the citadel was obviously prepared for fighting. They wandered through the pubic places and thoroughfares, looting, and gazing at the Forum and the temples, until they grew wary of a trap, so acute was the silence. At the fine houses of the patricians the Gallic warriors stood unwilling to enter, aware of some human presence which they feared and respected. When they slowly crossed the thresholds, they found in the open courtyards patricians, dressed in ceremonial toga, or the full uniform of a military consul, seated on ivory-inlaid curule chairs. Each had taken a solemn vow, repeating after the Chief Priest that they offered themselves as a sacrifice for their country and the Roman people. Their grave eyes expressed the majesty of the gods. For a while the Gauls stood entranced. Then one of them, on an impulse, touched the beard of Marcus Papirius. The aged Senator struck him promptly with his ivory staff. The spell was broken. The Gallic warriors unsheathed their long swords and a terrible massacre was committed, until the marble pavements of the courtyards ran with noble blood.

One particular act of courage by a young Roman nobleman bears comparison with the collective sacrifice of the older generation. The Gauls besieged the citadel tightly, unwilling to allow anyone to escape through their lines. Despite this, Gaius Fabius Dorsuo, from the same Fabii family who had laid down their lives against Veii, resolved to carry out the family duty of the annual sacrifice, on behalf of Rome, in the temple on the Quirinal Hill. Within the citadel he put on a toga, girt up in ceremonial fashion, took the sacred vessels and made his way down the steep slope towards the enemy. Ignoring the sentries and every other Gallic soldier, he walked through the lines, contemptuous of challenges and threats of violence. At the Quirinal he entered the temple and, with due solemnity, performed the rite to the gods, omitting nothing. Then he walked back, at the same measured pace, with a look of calm resolution, content with having served the gods. The Gauls made no move to stop him.

One night the Gauls decided to climb up and surprise the citadel guards, for they had discovered a steep ascent near a shrine. Many of them reached just below the wall at the summit without disturbing anyone, even the Roman watch dogs. Piety had restrained killing the geese sacred to Juno, even though the soldiers and their families were desperately short of food. Now the sacred geese saved them in return, for a fierce cackle began when the geese heard the Gauls moving below the wall. One officer, Marcus Manlius, was first to awake, and alone, he rushed to the wall and pushed back the first Gaul, whose falling body took others with it. As Manlius bravely fought off other Gauls, the remainder of the Roman guards ran to the scene and the attackers were killed or fell to their deaths. Disheartened, the Gauls offered generous terms to the Romans in the citadel. A truce was made and the Gallic army departed from Rome in return for gold.

Camillus expressed his love for Rome in a speech he made in 386 BC after the retreat of the Gauls. The city had been ruined by fire and pillage. Some of those who returned to it, especially the plebeians, considered leaving it in order to settle in Veii, now that Veian land was available to them. A mass exodus from Rome was a likely outcome. Camillus would not harbour such thoughts, disloyal to the tradition of the place that had been graced by Aeneas, Romulus, Numa Pompilius and the heroic leaders of old.

"We have a city founded with all due rites of auspice and augury; not a stone of her streets but is permeated by our sense of the divine; for our annual sacrifices not the days only are fixed, but the places too, where they may be performed: men of Rome, would you desert your gods - the tutelary spirits which guard your families, and those the nation prays to as its saviours?... Not without reason did gods and men choose this spot for the site of our city - the salubrious hills, the river to bring us produce from the inland regions and sea-borne commerce from abroad, the sea itself, near enough for convenience, yet not so near as to bring danger from foreign fleets, our situation in the very heart of Italy - all these advantages make it of all places in the world the best for a city destined to grow great."[2]

The speech had a profound effect upon the Roman people. Yet their unique blend of religious and prosaic qualities was displayed when what finally decided them to stay in Rome, according to Livy, turned out to be a seemingly trivial event. Whilst the Senate was debating the whole issue, a troop of soldiers on guard-duty marched up outside. Their centurion gave the order to halt and added, casually, "We might as well stop here." The Senators inside heard his words. It was taken as an omen, the proposal to migrate was rejected, and the work began on rebuilding the ancestral city.

Though war with the Volscians, Aequi and Etruscans continued intermittently after the departure of the Gauls, Rome had acquired an ascendancy over her neighbours not seriously challenged. A shrewd policy of "divide and rule" was followed by the Roman leaders. Defeated cities were allowed trading and even political rights with Rome, but were debarred from entering into treaties with each other; hence they became dependent upon Rome and looked upon her as a benevolent and usually just protector. However, a new area of conflict opened up to the east and south of Rome. The Samnites were a hardy, mountain people, given to raiding the less warlike tribes of Campania, south of Latium. When the Campanians appealed for help from Rome in 343 BC, in return for ceding sovereignty over their territory to Rome, the Romans seized the opportunity.

Rome's first war against the Samnites was won after a decisive battle at Mount Versuvius, but war broke out afresh in 327 BC. This time the valiant highlanders won a great victory, which ranked with the Allia as a major disaster for Roman arms. Trapped in a narrow defile, called the Caudine Forks, a Roman army, led by both consuls, surrendered to the Samnite general. The consuls negotiated a treaty, under which Samnium would be recognised as a free and independent state with the restoration of lost territory, and Rome would receive back her army unscathed. Nevertheless the Romans were made to walk "under the yoke," as a sign of complete submission. Six hundred hostages were kept by the Samnites; the remainder of the Roman army slunk back to Rome, only to find that the Senate would not confirm such a humiliating treaty. With honourable restraint the Samnite general allowed the six hundred hostages to return to Rome. He had miscalculated, for the Roman consuls did not have the power to bind Rome by a treaty, but he had excelled the Romans in respect for humanity and natural justice.

Between 304 and 298 BC there was a brief peace between Rome and Samnium. In the third war, Rome was faced by a coalition of Samnites, Etruscans and Gauls, but she won a great victory at Sentinium, north of the Appenines. Rome had learnt much in these long Samnite wars. To defeat the warlike tribesmen in hilly country required a more flexible military organisation and tactics. The heavy infantry was given a screen of slingers and javelin throwers and the long cylindrical shield, or *scutum*, replaced the small, round shield. More important was the change from the solid phalanx to the more open maniple formation, under which a legion comprised 30 maniples of 120 men each. Maniples would fight as semi-independent units, with space for each man to use his short sword and spear, but with each maniple keeping in general line of battle with its neighbours. This enabled rapid movement around the flanks of the enemy and simplified any change of direction, since the whole line did not have to redeploy as one mass. War in Italy had brought the Roman armies to a new pitch of technical achievement, before war abroad would test them on a yet greater scale.

From Greece in 281 BC came a final challenge in Italy, with the arrival of Pyrrhus, king of Epirus. His elephants severely tested the new Roman methods of fighting, but the heroism of the Roman infantry made his successes immensely costly - giving rise to the term "Pyrrhic victory". His attempt to gain a foothold in southern Italy failed; Appius Claudius, the Roman Censor, laid down the proud maxim that Rome would never negotiate with an enemy on Italian soil, a maxim to be strikingly remembered when Hannibal brought his Carthaginian army to harass Italy for nine long years. Pyrrhus himself crossed swords with the Carthaginians in Sicily, but was finally driven back to the Greek mainland after a defeat by the Romans at Beneventum in 275 BC.

Rome had conquered Italy. *Virtus, pietas, fides*: her victories had been built upon these - the steady faith of the citizen in battle, fighting for his homestead, family, and state; the piety of the nobles who led them, like Camillus at Falerii and Dorsuo at the Quirinal temple; the virtue of every Roman who remembered the sacred flame of Vesta, of Lucretia who had sacrificed her life to honour, of Veturia who offered her motherhood to Rome, of Cincinnatus who, in his own misfortune, obeyed the call to serve his country.

When Pyrrhus had marched on Rome he found the gates of the cities on his route closed to him. Loyalty to Rome overrode the opportunity for renewed independence. Whence came such devotion from cities which had once fought so fiercely against their present mistress? The peoples of Italy, conquered by Rome, recognised the nobility of their conquerors, for the Romans treated them mercifully and with political good sense. Though "divide and rule" remained a tenet of Roman policy, each defeated people or city was offered some kind of alliance with Rome. The terms of the alliance were adjusted to meet each individual case. Favoured cities, like Tusculum, were granted the status of *civitas optimo iure*, with their citizens having the full rights of Roman citizens and undertaking military service and tax liabilities. Less favoured were people like the Picentes, who were *cives sine suffragio*, with private rights, but denied the right to vote in Roman elections. A third category were allied peoples with no citizen rights, but some local independence. Many of the colonies founded by the Latin cities had this status; for example, Beneventium. All these types of allies gave military service under Roman leadership, but in the south of Italy were a group of cities, such as Thurii, which supplied ships, rather than soldiers, and were known as *socii navales*, or naval allies. Payment of taxes or tribute was not widely enforced, except in return for Roman citizenship, so that all the allies felt that, though they were under firm Roman leadership, especially in foreign policy, they were not exploited. Some contained Roman garrisons, but of these many accepted them willingly as a defence against local tribesmen. There were, in addition, Roman colonies, such as Ostia and Tarracina, comprised of Roman citizens.

This network of alliances was gradually reinforced by the building of fine roads, centred upon Rome. The Via Appia was the first to be built, in 312 BC, stretching 132 miles from Rome to Capua. Trade between the allied peoples and Rome naturally grew apace. What had become the nation of Rome, founded on the hills above the Tiber, was expanding into the whole of Italy. In 273 BC, Ptolemy II, king of Egypt, offered a treaty of friendship, or grant of *amicitia*, with Rome, acknowledging that the city was now a power on the world stage. How would she fare, when she faced the greater challenges beyond the shores of her fertile and hospitable homeland?

## References:

1. Plutarch, 'Life of Coriolanus', trans. I. Scott-Kilvert in *Makers of Rome*, Penguin, London, 1972, p. 48.

2. Livy, *The Early History of Rome*, trans. A. de Selincourt, Penguin, London, 1976, Book V, pp. 398-401.

## Chapter 29

# Natural Justice

## *Growth of Roman Government and Law*

NUMA POMPILIUS HAD briefly raised Rome to the level of an aristocracy, though the spirit of early Rome was essentially timocratic. After the degenerate rule of Tarquin, the new Republic, formed in 509 BC, soon moved towards an oligarchy in which the great patrician families held sway. At first an understanding of law, innate in the Rome people, asserted itself, with a demand by those not born into the

*Curia (Senate house), Forum, Rome*

charmed circle of patrician families for a share in political power. In 494 BC the plebeians refused to serve in the war against the enemies who surrounded Rome: Aequi, Volscians and Sabines. They marched out to the Sacred Mount beyond the city, threatening to found a city of their own. Pride alone could not defend Rome; the patricians yielded. An assembly of plebeians, the *Concilium Plebis*, was formed, though the older assemblies of all citizens, the *Comitia Curiata* and the *Comitia Centuriata*, remained. The *Concilium Plebis* was empowered to elect two tribunes, officers who represented plebeian interests, whose persons were held sacred, and who had the remarkable constitutional power to veto legislation.

Ten years later the question of land reform arose. The original Roman land system was based upon natural justice. Though households held small parcels of land, most land was held by clans and farmed collectively. Numa had ruled that each *pagus*, or district, was inspected to prevent any abuse of land. By the time of the Servian reforms, most clan land had been distributed amongst individual families, but public duties were borne by the landholder - to serve in the army, to assist the king and to construct public buildings. The very word for the city walls became *moenia*, or "tasks". Thus no direct taxation was necessary. Only in a crisis, such as war, was a *tributum*, or tax, enforced and even this was often repaid later.

As success in war brought foreign land into the possession of the Roman state, the treatment of this became a vital issue. State land was rented out to tenant farmers, in return for payments made in produce. Also, land for common pasturage brought in a similar public rent. However, by the early fifth century some patricians were holding state land free of any rent. In 485 BC a consul, Spurius Cassius, boldly demanded a more just distribution of state land, both new land won from recent enemies and land misappropriated by patricians. Vested interests were too powerful. Spurius was accused of treason, tried and executed. He was the first of many Romans who struggled against the gradual neglect of economic duties.

Nevertheless a more generous outlook towards citizens' political and economic equality under law was fostered by Greek influences, centred on the Aventine Hill in Rome. Greek traders built there a temple to the divinities of grain and wine: Ceres, Liber and Libera (the Greek Demeter, Persephone and Dionysius). Commercial disputes were settled there, and from the cities of Magna Graecia in the south came artists, priestesses and philosophers. Even the effect of Pythagorean schools, that had spread from Croton, may have reached as far as Rome. The Aventine became a rallying point for plebeians in their dispute with the patricians.

Greek influence came to the fore in 452 BC, when the demand arose for written laws to prevent patrician abuse of unwritten law. A commission of three men was sent to Athens to obtain a copy of the laws of Solon. When they returned, a board of ten, known as *decemvirs*, were empowered to govern Rome and to write the laws. What they produced, with the assistance of two more *decemvirs* appointed later, were the famous Twelve Tables, a statement of fundamental law carved on stone tablets and set in the Forum for every Roman to see. Even in the time of Cicero, four hundred years later, Roman schoolboys learnt the Twelve Tables by heart. By them the liberty of the citizen was guaranteed; no one could be executed on the order of a magistrate without a final appeal to the *Comitia Centuriata*, and a strict law of libel punished offenders with loss of civil rights. Such civil duties gave Rome a renewed measure of freedom and nurtured the growth of men who would rule half the civilised world. The spirit of Greece breathed upon the young republic.

The following decade saw further important steps in refining the constitution. The offices of *quaestor*, to handle public finance, and *censor*, to keep a census of the population and to preserve public morality, were created. Military tribunes were also appointed to ensure more competent leadership in Rome's wars. By the *Lex Canuleia* of 445 BC, the marriage of patricians with plebeians was at last permitted, a change long demanded by the plebeians, who resented the rigidly hereditary system by which patrician status was held.

At the founding of Rome in the eighth century, land had been recognised as a sacred gift to the whole people. Free land became an ideal which the Romans long remembered. Under the enlightening influence of Greek philosophy, Rome in the fourth century BC awoke to the fact that this birthright of free land was being overridden by private interests. Even the well-established oligarchy were touched by the note of universality which entered Italy from Greece. If every man has an immortal soul, then each has a right to life and to the necessary means of life; hence access to land is a universal right. This principle was acknowledged in a remarkable law passed in Rome in 367 BC. It followed a long struggle by two tribunes, C. Licinius Stolo and L. Sextius Lateranus, to introduce legislation limiting holdings of public land. The law of 367 BC limited such holdings to 500 *jugera* (300 acres), thus enabling a far wider distribution of the land acquired by the state from successful wars. Moreover public land was to be held in return for rent paid to the Roman state; the economic duty to return to the community the surplus which it created was acknowledged. Since 500 *jugera* was a suitable limit on what one family could actively farm, the duty of each man to maintain himself and his dependants once more became practicable. The days of the self-sufficient, industrious Roman farmer, the mainstay of Rome's strength, exemplified by Cincinnatus, were revived. The vision of Camillus, in his speech after the retreat of the Gauls, might yet be brought to fruition.

The Licinian law also eased the problem of indebtedness by ruling that all debts were to be reduced by the interest already paid; and it gave political equality by the requirement that one consul was to be plebeian. A generation later the *Lex Poetelia* ended the irksome practice of making debtors bondsmen, whose personal liberty was forfeited to the creditor. In 304 BC legal procedure was made public, thus preventing the obscuring of procedure in favour of the patricians, who previously had control over it; and in 300 BC the *Lex Valeria* reiterated the right of all citizens to appeal to an assembly of the people against a capital sentence.

The now artificial distinction between patricians and plebeians was finally broken down by the *Lex Hortensia* of 287 BC, making decrees passed by the *Concilium Plebis* binding on every citizen. By this time all the important magistracies were open to plebeians. Those who aspired to the highest offices had to pursue the *cursus honorum* - the scale of magistracies - beginning with the lowest, such as *aedile*; but birth was no longer a disqualification. A poor plebeian might succeed in the army, where courage and skill were greatly valued, and then climb the whole ladder of civil authority to the consulship.

Rome of the fourth and third centuries BC remained, however, an oligarchy. Even the Licinian law could not prevent an accumulation of wealth in private hands, for only the holding of public land was limited to 500 *jugera*, so that families might still become extensive landholders. Moreover, the rapid acquisition of public land from success in war led to the gradual abuse of the limitation, especially as captives were available as slaves to work new land. Thus as civil and political freedom flourished for Roman citizens, economic freedom slowly diminished and, by the late second century, great internal crises brought the Republic to its knees.

Essentially, the Roman Republic was ruled by the Senate, whose members had all held senior office as magistrates. Before any bill was put before an assembly of the people, the magistrate proposing it would consult the Senate. Over foreign affairs, war and finance the Senate had undisputed customary authority, even though a vote in the *Comitia Centuriata* was formally necessary for war and peace. *Senatus consulta*, or resolutions of the Senate, in the form of advice to magistrates, were the practical means of government on major issues; the assemblies became increasingly ill-suited to make general decisions as more and more citizens lived far beyond the city of Rome, in colonies or in allied states with voting rights. Natural authority abounded in the Senate, where political, military and financial expertise was perpetually renewed as magistracies expired. What enhanced this authority was an understanding of natural law derived from the earliest days of Rome. Numa, in particular, had given to the Romans the idea that natural forces - the gods - govern the universe and that a well-ordered society should revere these forces, the gods of the city and of the hearth. Moreover, in creating the *Fetiales*, who ensured that dealings with foreign nations were just, he had laid the foundations for the Roman concept of *jus gentium*, a law of nations in accord with natural law.

A great new development of Roman principles of natural law came in the third century BC, at the time when the teaching of Socrates and Plato fructified in the Italian peninsula. Already the influence of Magna Graecia - of the Sibyl of Cumae, prophetess of Apollo, of the philosophers of Velia who taught that "all things are many in name, but in nature one,"[1] and of the Greek traders on the Aventine - were turning Rome towards the ideas of Greece, so that the Socratic culture of the fourth century, with its spirit of universality, was welcomed in Rome.

The new teaching took the form of Stoicism. Zeno, a philosopher from Cyprus, born in 333 BC, following in the footsteps of Socrates himself, taught in the Athenian Painted Stoa. Though Epicurus from Samos and Diogenes from Sinope also attracted influential followers at about the same time, Zeno's Stoicism was the development of Socratic teaching which most appealed to the Roman mind. All three schools, Epicurean, Cynic and Stoic, placed ethics at the centre of their system. *Eudaimonia*, or well-being, became the main concept of Hellenistic philosophy. Zeno, particularly, taught that one should expel from the mind everything which disturbs it, such as desire and delight, fear and grief. Since these are founded upon false belief, then their removal is the work of philosophy. In this, Zeno may have been influenced by Pyrrho of Elis, who had accompanied Alexander the Great to India and learnt from Indian ascetics that the senses are unreliable and that tranquillity arises from the absence of false judgements.

Educated Romans were well prepared for such a message. The just treatment of foreigners, instituted by Numa, made for an easy acceptance of the Socratic idea of the soul. If the soul were both universal and individual, then all men possessed it. It was but a small step for Roman lawyers to see that the *jus civile* for the citizens of Rome need not differ essentially from a *jus gentium*. Already the *praetor peregrinus* administered law for foreigners within Roman territory.

Natural law was seen as the foundation of all law, as later Cicero wrote: "There will not be different laws at Rome and at Athens, or different laws now and in the future, but one eternal and unchangeable law will be valid for all nations and all times..."[2] As the individual found peace, or *ataraxia* (untroubledness), within himself by expelling false ideas, so would peace between men be found by expelling falsity. Likewise, the law of nations would be just if false ideas of greed and self-aggrandisement amongst nations were expelled.

For the Stoic the good life was a series of perfectly appropriate actions, performed in the knowledge that they conformed to nature. Reason was the faculty that made such practical judgements. Hence the Stoic studied nature and sought within himself the power of reason. By the use of reason he became immune from all vicissitudes of fortune, for his actions were measured out to every circumstance, whether apparently good or ill. Conformity to nature was self-sufficiency. Such an austere ideal made of the Roman nobility a class of men who could face perils and disasters with a cool indifference. Once resolved upon a course of action, they would see it through to the end.

Stoicism fitted the Roman character like a glove. To study nature in the elemental forms of fire, air, water and earth appealed to men whose ancestors, for centuries, had tilled the rich soil of Italy under the Mediterranean Sun, and whose early gods included these very elements of nature. To seek reason came easily to a people who had learnt from Numa Pompilius to avoid images and to speak the truth. The breath of Greek wisdom brought new life to the ancient practices of Rome. In the dangers that lay ahead - the great wars with Carthage and in the east - her armies and citizens would stand firm, because her best leaders held to the universal reason that each discovered within himself. As Chrysippus, a head of the Stoic school in Athens, said, "the first thing congenial to any creature is its own constitution and its awareness of that."

### References:

1.  Plato, *Sophist*, trans. B. Jowett, Random House, New York, 1937, 242.

2.  Cicero, *De Republica*, trans. C. W. Keyes, Loeb, London, 1988, Book III, 23.

## Chapter 30
# Tempered in the Fire
### *War with Carthage*

ROME HAD INHERITED the mantle of Greece in southern Italy. Sicily now became the next battleground in the expansion of Rome; for the first time a move was made towards overseas empire. Though Sicily contained many Greek states, like Syracuse, ruled by the tyrant Hiero, the island was under the influence of Carthage, the powerful commercial city on the north African coast, founded by Phoenician colonists from Tyre in the ninth century BC. The Phoenicians were an oriental people, whose alphabet, taken into Greece by Cadmus, became the source of the alphabets of Europe. They were fine seamen and avid traders. At Carthage their energy and enterprise had flourished, to the extent that they dominated the trade of the western Mediterranean.

*Roman Warship carved on Rhodes*

By the third century BC, their government was an oligarchy, self-perpetuating and derived from about a hundred wealthy families. The local native peoples of north Africa were ruthlessly held down to serve the interests of their masters. In war, captives would be sacrificed in hundreds to placate the oriental gods of the Carthaginians. Even their own generals were put to death, often by impalement, when they failed in battle.

In Sicily the Carthaginians held several major cities, notably Lilybaeum on the west coast. It was inevitable that they would clash with the Romans. The two nations were both outward-looking, both relatively wealthy, both capable of bringing to areas poorer in resources and initiative a spirit of enterprise. Yet when they first confronted one another their motives differed radically. Carthage sought land, sea-routes, markets and money. Rome sought security for herself and her allies, peace and integrity for Italy, and her own undisputed leadership in attaining these ends. When the conflict was over, more than half a century later, Roman motives had undergone a significant change.

Earlier, Rome and Carthage had made treaties of common interest against Etruscans or Greeks. With the eclipse of these powers in Italy and the western Mediterranean, the two great cities now confronted one another. Trouble arose at Messena on the Sicilian coast, facing the toe of the peninsula. A group of brigands from Campania controlled the city. They played one power off against the other. In 264 BC war broke out and developed into a struggle for the control of Sicily.

The first Punic War ('Punic' was the Roman term for the ancient Semitic language of Carthage) lasted over twenty years. In the words of the Greek historian, Polybius, "it dragged on like a boxing-match, in which swift blows are struck and parried, but no plan or policy is intelligible to the bystanders."[1] Carthage was predominantly a sea-power, for her leaders were merchants, who preferred to hire mercenaries as soldiers rather than trust the suppressed peoples of her empire. Thus victory could only be won by skilful use of the sea and by the chance of a superlative general to lead the hired army. On the other hand, Rome had the finest army since Alexander's, but almost no navy. She had relied on allies in southern Italy to provide what ships she needed.

As in the Peloponnesian War a century and a half before, sea power versus land power brought stalemate. Sicilian cities changed hands and were ruthlessly besieged. Armies camped outside, while populations starved. Fleets brought supplies and reinforcements. The Romans felled forests at break-neck speed to build galleys - quinqueremes and triremes copied from their enemies. Carthaginian generals were cruelly put to death by their compatriots.

Despite some disasters in naval battles and even more in storms, the Romans developed a naval power which eventually beat the Carthaginians at sea. Their tactics were an outcome of their military training. On board their ships they carried 120 legionaries and a strange construction called a *corvus* (or crow), consisting of a gangplank, wide enough for two soldiers, about 40 feet long, and hinged to the deck and held vertically by ropes to a mast near the prow. Underneath protruded a large iron spike, which, when the gangplank was released, embedded itself in the deck of an enemy ship. The legionaries rushed across and made short work of the enemy.

In all the confused events of the long war two men stand out, each typifying the virtues and ambitions of his countrymen. Hamilcar Barca became the Carthaginian general in Sicily, half-way through the war. His surname, Barca, meant 'lightning' and in warfare he lived up to the name. He attacked the Romans and their allies so swiftly from carefully selected points in the island that for a time victory was within sight; but resolution in adversity was a supreme quality of his opponents, as the action of the consul, Atilius Regulus exhibited.

A great naval victory at Ecnomus, off the south coast of Sicily in 256 BC, gave the Romans the opportunity to invade the African coast. Regulus took command of the invasion forces, which at first were strikingly successful, until the Carthaginians acquired a Spartan soldier and adventurer, Xanthippus, to command their defence. Using tactics that recalled Marathon and anticipated Hannibal's victory at Cannae, Xanthippus crushed the advancing Roman army between his cavalry wings. Regulus was captured, and after a period of captivity was ordered to go to Rome to address the Senate concerning the war. He gave his word to return to his captors. Both sides were seriously weakened by the war; many people in each city wanted peace. The Carthaginians expected that an appeal to the Senate from a captive general would win peace on favourable terms. They misjudged the nature of a stoic Roman. Regulus harangued the Roman leaders for their feeble war effort and lack of martial spirit, declaring that peace should never be made until Carthage were utterly defeated. The Senators were completely won over to a policy of relentless war. Regulus was true to his word. He returned to Carthage, where the incensed rulers put him to death by locking him inside a barrel, which had iron spikes fastened to the inner surface.

Eventually, by 241 BC, Carthage was beaten into surrender, when it could no longer supply the cities it still held in Sicily. The peace terms were not oppressive. An indemnity of 1600cwt of silver was demanded and Carthage withdrew from Sicily. The island was now a Roman preserve. Yet again Rome made independent treaties with some city states, but there was a difference from earlier conquests, for Sicily became a province under a Roman *praetor*. Romans came to occupy lands incorporated as *ager publicus*, and the Carthaginian system of tribute payments was partly retained. An overseas empire was in the making. When, three years later, Rome supported a rebellion in Sardinia by Carthaginian mercenaries, she showed that a new acquisitiveness had entered the mind of her rulers, for both Sardinia and Corsica were stripped away from Carthage. The note was sounded for a renewal of war.

Now Rome was to be tested by military genius of the highest order in the greatest foreign war that Republican Rome ever fought. At the age of nine, Hannibal Barca, at the behest of his father, Hamilcar, swore a solemn oath never to rest until Rome was utterly defeated. Supreme as a military strategist, as a tactician of foresight and ingenuity, as a leader able to arouse sustained loyalty through every turn of fortune, Hannibal was the fire that tempered the maturing Republic. The sword was wielded against him by two other great masters of warfare, each possessed of a special martial quality necessary for his eclipse. His audacity in taking the war into Italy brought forth the unswerving perseverance of Fabius Maximus, whilst his final defence in Africa was confronted by the enterprise and resolution of the young Publius Scipio, whose father had died bravely in Spain earlier in the war.

Hannibal had no constructive aims. He was not offering a concept of political liberty or authority, nor a standard of culture. He scarcely offered even the commercial ideals of his native Carthage, ruled by a tight oligarchy of merchants. Indeed, he needed to overcome the oligarchs' caution and fear of losing their hard-earned wealth by appealing to the populace and playing upon motives of revenge and xenophobia. He stood simply for war, for a fight to the death against the old enemy. During the war his policy towards prisoners was to release, or treat leniently, all who were not Romans i.e. Latins and other allies of Rome, but to kill, or throw into chains, every Roman. On the field of Cannae the Roman wounded had their throats cut where they lay the morning after the battle. Against this unremitting pursuit of war and vengeance, Rome was compelled to draw upon her inmost resources of courage, determination and ability. Fabius and Scipio were the finest leaders of their generation, but their virtues were found, also, in numberless Romans, from a consul like Paullus who shunned the chance to escape from the slaughter of Cannae, though seriously wounded, to the women of Rome, who obeyed the order of Fabius not to mourn too long for their dead husbands and sons.

After its defeat in the first Punic War, Carthage had built a hegemony in Spain over the Celtic tribes, exploiting with success the mineral wealth of the country. Rome, occupied with threats from the Gauls in northern Italy and from Illyria, took little interest in Spain, beyond making a treaty with Carthage limiting Punic expansion northwards to the River Ebro. The city of Saguntum, south of the Ebro, however, had an agreement with Rome which Hannibal refused to acknowledge in a local dispute in 218 BC. Using the Saguntum affair as a pretext, he persuaded Carthage to offer Rome an ultimatum. Rome chose war, unaware of the scale of the future conflict. Hannibal knew that Roman resources of manpower in Italy made a repetition of the first Punic War the probable outcome, unless Italy itself were invaded. He decided to take an army through southern Gaul and across the Alps.

With about ninety thousand foot-soldiers and twelve thousand cavalry, he had in addition twenty-nine elephants, whose use was mainly to spread terror amongst enemy infantry and, even more, amongst enemy horses. The Gauls were hostile to both Carthaginians and Romans, but their resistance to both was light whilst they saw them as transient intruders. Hannibal brushed them aside and reached the high Alps to the east of the Rhone. The mountains were his first serious enemy. It took fifteen days to cross them. Though he had left Spain in the Spring, delays meant that the first snow of Winter was falling, as the vast army wound its way up the narrow paths where the great glaciers lay in the valleys above the Rhone. Mountain tribes opposed their progress, and night operations by picked troops were required to hold the points commanding the passes; but the final decision to advance into Italy was made when, near the beginning of the descent, an enormous wall of sheer rock covered in soft snow and ice sloped down precipitously before the vanguard of the army.

Undeterred, Hannibal ordered enormous fires to be built from all the available wood on the mountainside. These were lit, spaced out carefully on the rock face and refuelled, until the rock surface was extremely hot. Then all the supplies of wine and vinegar that could possibly be spared were flung upon it. Great cracks opened up with sharp explosions that echoed round the Alpine cirques. Then parties of men using picks cut enormous steps down the slope for the elephants. Many had survived the rigours of the climb, and now they ponderously lumbered down to the easier pathway below.

Only about 20,000 infantry and 6,000 cavalry reached Italy with Hannibal. Against what the citizen army of Rome was capable of putting in the field, this was a small force, but it was tempered in the unique experience of a long march through Spain and Gaul, engagements with warlike Gallic tribes and fierce contingents of tough mountain people, and the magnificent accomplishment of crossing the Alps.

When the news reached Rome, an army was sent to meet the invader. Hannibal defeated it at the River Trebia, forcing the Romans to abandon their hold on the Po Valley, where the Gauls were easy recruits for Hannibal. At the next major encounter, in the Spring of 217 BC, Hannibal showed his tactical genius. He set up an ambush in the valley at the bottom of which lay the waters of Lake Trasimene in Etruria. The Romans were approaching a narrow defile, which formed the entrance to the valley. Beyond it the road followed the edge of the lake below steep hillsides, which allowed no room to deploy troops for battle. At the end of the valley a slope of fairly open country faced down upon the road and lake.

Hannibal ranged a large part of his army on the far hillside, confronting the Romans at a distance of a mile or two as they emerged from the defile at the valley entrance. He wanted them to see these troops and to advance, believing that they were numerically far superior to the Carthaginians and had them in full view. He knew, too, that the Roman leader was impetuous and that his men were set upon the glory of destroying the invader of Italy. Hannibal's best troops were concealed on the slopes above the lake, alongside the road. They waited silently behind rocks and trees, as the Romans marched out of the defile. Then a small party crept down and occupied the defile, making retreat impossible. The Romans were sealed in the valley.

At the command of Hannibal, all the Carthaginian troops on every slope, those seen and those unseen, descended with warlike cries, magnified by the still waters of the lake. The Roman column, strung out, incapable of forming up defensively and with no expectation at all of a flank attack, was a vulnerable target. Each Roman fought in ignorance of the nature of the battle and of the whereabouts of the enemy. Men were pushed back into the lake. Some in desperation swam out into its calm waters, only to drown under the weight of their clothes and armour. Others clambered back out of the water to be slaughtered by Carthaginian horsemen who rode down to the sands to wait for them, swords in hand. The Roman army was virtually wiped out, whilst Hannibal lost only a few hundred men. He gained a moral ascendancy which took two superlative generals and fifteen years to dispel.

The Romans now chose a man of destiny to continue the struggle. Fabius Maximus, whose ancestors had fought as a single family against Veii, was appointed Dictator with supreme power. His Master of the Horse was a rash young nobleman, called Minucius. Fabius was the only man to appreciate fully that Rome faced a military genius in command of a dedicated army. He decided that he would avoid pitched battles. Every attempt by Hannibal to manoeuvre, or tempt him into an open engagement, was resisted. Instead, Fabius' army hung upon the heels of the Carthaginians. They tracked them as they marched through the dissected uplands of central Italy. They ambushed small groups of foragers in the steep valleys. They made sudden and brief assaults when Hannibal's column was extended or delayed, or occupied in such work as breaking camp, or besieging a city.

Only Hannibal understood the wisdom of Fabius' tactics. Amongst the Carthaginian soldiers the Roman general's policy was called rank cowardice and the Roman army was sneered at as a gadfly, which they longed to crush in a single decisive engagement. What was much worse for Fabius was that in the Roman army itself their general was considered lethargic by most and contemptible by some. Unfortunately, Minucius was foremost amongst those who scorned the tactics and mettle of his general. So much did he voice his criticism of Fabius that eventually he was given equal rank as general by the frustrated people of Rome, who wanted a victory over the invader. Fabius' response to this slight to his courage and military judgement was to claim his right to divide the army, rather than exercise joint command with a man whose courage he respected, but whose judgement he held at nought.

Now with half an army, Fabius continued his former tactics. When even those loyal to him began to question whether some engagement with Hannibal might not be tried, he remained adamant. Opinion and popularity weighed for nothing with him against his own knowledge of what the circumstances required. Rome had to beat Hannibal. Fabius knew that the only way was by wearing him down slowly and inexorably. Rome was all; his own reputation was of no account. Even when Hannibal took to ravaging the country of Rome's Italian allies, Fabius was unmoved. He remained on the hillsides, watching the fires of the burning villages, hearing the screams of the terrified families, as the Carthaginians ran amok in the lovely valleys of the Apennines. No word to advance passed his lips, despite the entreaties of his subordinates, despite appeals to the Roman sense of friendship with allied people, despite invocations to Roman honour.

Hannibal then employed a more subtle tactic. He ravaged the land around Fabius' own estates and left these alone in isolated prosperity, hoping to raise suspicions amongst the Roman people that Fabius may have come to a treacherous bargain with him. At this, Fabius went to Rome and sold the estates. With the proceeds he repaid some debts owed to Romans who had lent funds for the war effort and risked losing them in the general impoverishment of the public treasury.

At last Minucius could hold his hand no longer. With his half of the army, he moved closer to Hannibal. An attractive site for a camp was a flat area on a low hill, naturally defended by the long slopes and the view, which commanded the whole area. Hannibal deliberately sent a small party of cavalry to occupy it, under the gaze of Minucius' forces, as though a camp reconnaissance was in progress. Minucius fell into the trap. He would contend the use of the best site. He committed his main body of troops to advance to take the hill. When they were fully exposed on the slopes, Hannibal sent his own men swiftly upon them from concealed positions dug into the surrounding plain. As though from nowhere, a large army was soon upon the rear of Minucius' men. They fought back in confusion, troubled too by the smaller party of cavalry charging down upon them from the hill. Annihilation faced one half of the Roman army.

No one had counted on the foresight and unselfishness of Fabius, who had not neglected to defend the half of his army now under Minucius' control. He had observed the foolish advance and the swift recompense of Hannibal, and now he, too, engaged his half of the army, catching Hannibal, for once, by surprise. Fabius' troops were only too ready to fight in open battle with the enemy. Hannibal was in danger of being routed, caught as he was in an unexpected pincer movement. He gave the order to withdraw, with a joke to his companions: "Did I not tell you that the cloud we have seen hovering over the mountain tops would burst one day like a tornado?"[2] It was not a defeat, but a significant check. Fabius refrained from reprimanding Minucius, but his men were garlanded by those whom they had rescued. Fabius was hailed as their saviour and Minucius himself, awakening to his own stupidity, generously acknowledged how blind he had been.

Fabius' policy and conduct were Stoic in inspiration: the attentive watching of the enemy's movements, the patient refraining from action, the disregard for public opinion and the faith in a lawful sequence of events which would reveal the time to intervene. He had been appointed Dictator for six months; when this time expired in 216 BC, two consuls were chosen by the people. Paullus was strongly supported by the Senate and Varro was a demagogue claiming to represent the general demand for a more vigorous pursuit of the war. Both took command of the army in accordance with the constitution of Rome, each commanding on alternate days. When Paullus left Rome for the next campaign, Fabius gave him some advice:

"Hannibal is on foreign and hostile soil, far from home and country, surrounded by every menace, every danger; for him there is no peace on land or sea; no towns receive him, no protecting walls, nothing he sees can he call his own; he has nothing to live on beyond the plunder of a day. He now has hardly a third of the army with which he crossed the Ebro; more of his men have died of hunger than fallen in battle. Can you then doubt that inactivity is the way to defeat an enemy who is daily growing more decrepit?

"But you will have two generals against you, for the wishes of Varro will play straight into the hands of Hannibal. Steel yourself to ignore the tongues of men who will defame you. Truth often comes near to extinction, but is never quite put out. Never mind if they call your caution timidity, your wisdom sloth, your generalship weakness. Hannibal will despise a reckless antagonist, but he will fear a cautious one."[3]

Fortified by these words, Paullus took his army southwards towards Apulia, where Hannibal had resorted to constant plundering in the more fertile plains beyond the hard mountain backbone of Italy. The Romans caught up with him near Canusium in the east, not far from the Adriatic coast. Each side pitched camp near the River Aufidus. When Carthaginian parties of horsemen provoked the Romans, Paullus insisted on restraint and refused to engage the enemy, for it was his day of command. The next day Varro drew up the Romans for battle without even consulting his colleague. Paullus was helpless, bound by law to obey, as his men crossed the river from their camp and arrayed themselves on the plain. Hannibal moved immediately to take the opportunity for which he had longed since the day of Lake Trasimene. Over eighty thousand Roman and allied soldiers formed a long line, with the allied cavalry on the left wing, facing the Numidian cavalry of Hannibal, the Roman legionaries and allied infantry in the centre and the Roman cavalry on the right. Hannibal placed his weaker Gallic and Spanish troops in the centre with his African infantry on their flanks and the light cavalry on his left. He had already gained an advantage in facing north-east away from the hills, whence a hot local wind, the Volturnus, blew dust into the eyes of the Roman army.

The auxiliaries and lightly-armed troops of both sides met first, but soon Hannibal's light cavalry pressed down upon the Roman right wing, squeezed between the river and the thick ranks of infantry. The Romans were pushed back in hand to hand struggles, with each man striving to fling his opponent from the saddle; but the legionaries in the centre were in their turn pushing back the bare-chested Gauls and the Spaniards in their white, purpled-edged tunics. Soon the line of Hannibal's army was bent inwards like a crescent, as the Roman infantry forced home its advantage, intent on fulfilling the command of Varro to avenge the earlier defeats of Roman arms. Fabius would not have fallen into such a trap, nor would his pupil, Paullus, both students, like Hannibal, of Greek warfare. The Numidian cavalry had driven their Roman counterparts off the field and returned promptly with great discipline to join the assault on the wings. With the African infantry, they closed in behind the Romans in a ring of steel. They were reinforced, also, by five hundred cavalrymen who had played a clever trick on the enemy. Riding over to the Romans and flinging down their arms, they had pretended to abandon the Carthaginian cause, though concealed beneath their tunics were short swords. In the heat of battle they had been moved to the rear and forgotten. Now they drew their swords, collected their discarded shields and rushed upon the Roman centre, hamstringing and creating utter confusion and terror.

As at Lake Trasimene, the Romans faced annihilation. Paullus, defended by a small group of the best Roman cavalry, had been badly wounded early on by a sling shot. His guard would not leave him and dismounted in order to protect him from the surrounding masses of the enemy. They refused to surrender and most died where they fought. Paullus was seen by a fellow officer who offered him his horse and begged him to escape, but the consul made a brief reply, "God bless your courage, but... get you gone, and tell the Senate to look to Rome and fortify it with strong defences... Tell Quintus Fabius that while I lived I did not forget his counsel, and that I remember it still in the hour of death. As for me, let me die here amongst my dead soldiers."[4] Even as he spoke, a group of Numidians swept by and Paullus fell under a shower of spears. The officer's horse bolted under him and he survived to tell the tale.

Livy describes the field of battle on the morrow:

"At dawn next morning the Carthaginians applied themselves to collecting the spoils and viewing the carnage, which even to an enemy's eyes was a shocking spectacle. All over the field Roman soldiers lay dead in their thousands, horses and foot mingled, as the shifting phases of the battle, or the attempt to escape, had brought them together. Here and there wounded men, covered with blood, who had been roused to consciousness by the morning cold, were dispatched by a quick blow as they struggled to rise from amongst the corpses; others were found still alive with the sinews in their thighs and behind their knees sliced through, baring their throats and necks and begging who would to spill what little blood they had left. Some had their heads buried in the ground, having apparently dug themselves holes and by smothering their faces with earth had choked themselves to death."[5]

Fifty thousand Romans died at Cannae. A few, who had escaped to the Roman camp, made their way back across country to Rome. The wounded and demoralised in the camp surrendered and were held as prisoners of war. Later, the Senate in Rome refused an entreaty from them to pay the ransoms demanded by Hannibal.

Romans were never sympathetic to their countrymen who had surrendered in battle and, after Cannae, they could not refrain from comparing the prisoners with the fifty thousand dead. Despite the cries of their families and friends, the Senate voted to allow Hannibal to enslave them.

Varro, the man directly responsible for the disaster, had survived, and with a few soldiers marched back to Rome to await judgement for his folly. With generosity worthy of Fabius, the citizens welcomed him and the Senate accorded him a word of praise for his unbroken faith in the power of Rome, for in the full knowledge of the awful disaster and of the fact that the city lay at Hannibal's feet, he had returned to it. Minucius, like Varro a victim of popular foolishness and his own ambition, had died on the field of Cannae, but Fabius remained, his reputation at its height in this moment of uttermost danger, when Rome and all that she had built and stood for hung on the precipice of destruction. The people turned to him, and he took charge of the city in the expectation that within days Hannibal would be at its gates.

The situation appeared hopeless. Rome had no army. Hannibal commanded a force whose morale could not have been higher. Long months of hardship and frustration since the initial successes in the north had turned in a few hours into exultant victory. Everything was within the grasp of such invincibles, led by a demi-god.

The moment passed, as the master of Cannae, of Lake Trasimene, of the Trebia, of the passage of the Alps, haggled over the ransoms of prisoners and the distribution of booty. Hannibal's lack of political wisdom saved Rome, for had he marched instantly to the city, intent upon seizing it as the key to final victory, he could hardly have been withstood for more than a day; but his mind was exclusively that of a soldier, as though destiny had produced nothing more nor less than a perfect instrument for the testing of Rome. No doubt his men were tired; perhaps he failed to appreciate the recuperative power of Rome, or was genuinely unaware how slender were the forces which remained in the city. Whatever the reason, he decided not to press home an attack, but to turn further south in order to destroy Rome's basis of allied support in south Italy. Perhaps the temptation of restoring Carthaginian power in Sicily was too great.

Rome knew nothing of Hannibal's failure of intent. She followed the advice of Fabius, who was seen by all as the only possible saviour in this hour of nemesis. Under his direction no-one was allowed to leave the city, men of seventeen and above were recruited for the army to join Varro's survivors, mourning was limited to thirty days and the festival of Ceres was cancelled to avoid the evident absence of women, since by custom mourning clothes were forbidden at religious festivals. Taxation - the *tributum* - was doubled.

Although the adamant spirit of Fabius was the point to which Romans turned in the days after Cannae, there appeared also the first glimpse of another soldier of genius, whose final victory over Hannibal at Zama in Africa stole the glory of the great defender of the Republic in the Italian phase of the war. Publius Cornelius Scipio was only nineteen when he escaped from the slaughter at Cannae. Shortly afterwards, Scipio heard that some patricians had decided to abandon the struggle and leave Italy by sea. With a few friends he rushed to the house of their leader, burst in upon a meeting at which the plans to defect were under discussion, and raised his sword above their heads.

"I swear with all the passion of my heart that I shall never desert our country, or permit any other citizen of Rome to desert her. If I wilfully break my oath, may Jupiter, Greatest and Best, bring me to a shameful death, with my house, my family and all I possess! Swear the same oath, all of you. If anyone refuse, against him this sword is drawn."[6]

Every man present took the oath and the erstwhile deserters put themselves in Scipio's custody.

The defection of allies to Hannibal, however, could not be stopped by such means. In southern Italy, most of the tribes and cities joined the man who had inflicted a seemingly mortal blow on Rome. The people of the hills, whose villages had been burnt by Hannibal beneath the gaze of Fabius' army earlier in the war, now prepared themselves to fight alongside the men whose torches had set fire to their homes. So, too, most of the Greek cities of the south coast, like Pythagoras's Croton, entrusted their liberty to the philistine Africans.

For some years the tide continued to advance as allies deserted to Carthage, as Sicily fell, as the revenues of Spain were recovered by African armies, but victory came for the revived citizen armies of Rome when wiser leadership and prudent training made them the equals of their weary enemy. Many battles were fought after Cannae in the hills of Campania behind Naples, and further south. The cities of Magna Graecia often changed hands several times, and the war reached new heights of cruelty and bitterness in the slaughter of garrisons and the terror inflicted on citizens. Occasionally, individuals rose above the general degradation. In Capua, the second city of Italy, renowned for its wealth and luxurious life, one man, Decius Magius, stood out against Hannibal's contemptuous treatment of the liberty of the citizens when he occupied the city. Even when dragged away in chains, Decius challenged the Capuans to defend their liberty and only the forcible covering of his face could silence him. By a chance storm when he was being shipped to Carthage as a prisoner, he regained his freedom as a subject of Egypt. Occupying Capua was a hollow success for Hannibal, since his army was weakened by the loose living there, and took the field again with less inclination for the rigours of a campaign.

Fierce fighting took place in Sicily, for which the earlier Punic War had been contested. Syracuse, where two hundred years before the Athenians of Nicias had met total defeat, became once more a site of repeated assaults and counter-attacks. It finally succumbed to the persistent efforts of the Roman general, Marcellus, but only after a long period of incredible defensive operations inspired by the engineering genius of the great mathematician, Archimedes. His machines fired an inexhaustible hail of missiles from the walls at every range and level. When Marcellus ordered a seaborne attack with a giant siege tower carried on a group of barges, the Syracusans brought into play enormous grappling hooks that lifted the bows clear of the water and could drop a small ship stern first into the sea from a height. A huge lens was also used to focus the Mediterranean Sun on to approaching ships and set them on fire. At last the Romans were reduced to such a state of alarm that if they saw so much as a length of rope or a piece of timber appear over the top of the wall, it was enough to make them cry out, "Look, Archimedes is aiming one of his machines at us!"[7]

Eventually, however, treachery gave Syracuse to the Romans, and Archimedes himself died at the hands of a common soldier, impatient with the mathematician's refusal to abandon a problem in order to obey a rough order. Marcellus himself was angry at this crude end to such a genius and honoured him with a tomb, bearing, as Archimedes wished, an inscription referring to the famous discovery of the ratio between the volume of a cylinder and the sphere it contains.

Publius Scipio was the man destined to complete the work of Fabius Maximus. Scipio's father and uncle had both been killed in Spain fighting against strong Carthaginian armies - the commercially minded Carthaginians gave more support to their forces in the wealthy province of Spain than to Hannibal, who was at the lion's throat in Italy. Publius won command of the Roman legions in Spain and fought with an energy and verve stemming from motives of patriotism, revenge and ambition. Fate was on his side. His one mistake in Spain was to let Hannibal's brother, Hasdrubal, slip past him into Gaul. Hasdrubal took his army through the Alps, again with a complement of elephants, descended into Italy and prepared to bring to Rome a war on two fronts within the heart land of Italy. Scipio's mistake, however, led to the heaviest defeat of the Africans in the whole war, for on the River Metaurus in Tuscany Hasdrubal himself died together with 57,000 men, whilst the Romans lost only 8,000. A Roman consul, with his legions in the south facing Hannibal, had slipped away to join the other Roman forces in Tuscany. Hasdrubal had been confident that no Roman general would dare to disengage from containing Hannibal in his southern base. When he heard, not one trumpet call, but two, in the Roman camp near the Metaurus, his long experience of campaigns against the Romans told him that both consuls were present in person with their armies.

No quarter was extended to the defeated Africans. The head of Hasdrubal's corpse was cut off and taken south through Italy. Hannibal's first news of his brother's defeat and death came with the sight of Hasdrubal's head lying in his camp. At the command of the consuls, a Roman soldier had flung it over the palisade, as a portent of the wrath of Rome.

The tide had turned. Hannibal was caged in a small corner of Bruttium; but, for a while, the Romans paused, awaiting the return of Publius Scipio from his successes in Spain. Now it was Hannibal whose true qualities of leadership were tested in adversity:

"Fighting for thirteen years in enemy territory, far from home, with varying fortunes and an army composed not of native troops but of a hotch-potch of the riff-raff of all nationalities, men who shared neither law nor custom nor language, who differed in manner, in dress, in equipment, who had in common neither the forms of religious observance nor even the gods they served, he yet was able, somehow or other, to weld this motley crowd so firmly together that they never quarrelled amongst themselves nor mutinied against their general, though money to pay them was often lacking and provisions to feed them were often short - deficiencies which in the first Carthaginian war had led to many acts of unspeakable atrocity by both officers and men. Surely it was an astonishing thing that there was no mutiny in the Carthaginian camp, at least when all hopes of victory had vanished with the death of Hasdrubal and the destruction of his army, and the abandonment of all Italy except for one little corner of Bruttium."[8]

Inevitably the final act of the play unrolled. Scipio's ambition was whetted by success in Spain. Back in Rome, he now demanded to lead an army in the invasion of Africa and in an assault upon Carthage itself. Would not Hannibal be forced to return home to defend his own city? Fabius Maximus, now an old man, true to type opposed the plan as a product of youthful vainglory and, whilst denying any thought of himself returning to the battlefield, insisted that Hannibal should now be met in a final engagement on Italian soil. Scipio threatened to appeal to an assembly of the people. The Senate gave way, but unduly limited his expeditionary force in men and boats. Scipio responded by directly recruiting more of both on his own account. Then he set sail, leaving Hannibal frustrated in the arid hills of Bruttium.

Scipio's plans did not run smoothly. He was forced to abandon the siege of Utica on the African coast and barely managed to gain the support of the Numidian tribes with their fine cavalry. At last, however, he threatened Carthage, and the city made a truce with him; but the war party there rapidly sent for Hannibal, broke the truce with a treacherous attack on an isolated Roman contingent and brought upon Carthage the full power of Scipio's pent up desires to avenge his father and become the greatest commander of the Republic.

Hannibal returned to the coast of Africa, sailing from Croton with the remnants of his undefeated army. What memories did the dry, brown hills behind Leptis in Africa arouse in his mind: of years campaigning in the Apeninnes, of the field of the dead on the morrow of Cannae, of the exultant slaughter by the waters of Lake Trasimene, of the sudden descent of the icy wall of the Alps, of the hills of Spain, brown too and dry, of his oath as a boy before his father, Hamilcar, and of his brother's head lying in the dust of his camp?

Scipio would not renew the terms of the previous truce; he demanded more recompense for Roman losses in the war than Carthage could accept. Although he and Hannibal met in person, a final battle was Hannibal's due after so mighty a challenge to Rome's emergence as the dominant power in the western world. At Zama, five days travel from Carthage, in 202 BC, the ascendant and descendant generals met on the open field. For the last time, Hannibal grouped his elephants, the terror of cavalry, in front of his army; but their unstoppable charge beat against air. Scipio had left broad avenues between his maniples, through which the elephants were driven by lateral attacks with javelins and other missiles. Hannibal's troops were too much a mixture of races and of loyalties, for with him now were new levies from Carthage and its allies. His own veterans were reserved for the eye of the battle and fought with their experienced valour when the time came. Destiny, and the Numidian cavalry now under Scipio's control, were more than they could withstand. Like their master, many who fell at Zama must have recalled the triumphs of Cannae.

Hannibal, with a few personal guards, escaped from the field of Zama. After trying to mitigate the terms of surrender without success, he fled to Syria where he continued for some years to plot against Rome, during her subsequent campaigns in the eastern Mediterranean; but his role ended at Zama. There the war cry of Scipio's legions had terrified in its unison the disparate forces of Carthage. Under the awful stimulus of a great military genius, who had held a knife at her heart for thirteen years, Rome had been united under two great leaders, one a man of determination, self-discipline, and devotion to duty, prudent and yet magnanimous to lesser men; the other of superb self-confidence, fired by a spirit of dedication to his country's safety and glory, bold and resourceful. Scipio (now named Scipio Africanus), became the hero of the times, to live in high honour, until finally he retired from public life in order to avoid the danger to the Republic of hero worship. Fabius Maximus had died before the battle of Zama.

The peace terms were onerous and marked the end of the Carthaginian empire. Spain was lost with all other territories outside Africa. An enormous indemnity of ten thousand talents was to be paid over the next fifty years. Hostages were given to Rome as security. Carthage retained only ten triremes and no elephants, whilst she guaranteed never to make war beyond her coasts. Even on land she could not fight without Rome's permission, and most humiliating of all - and later the cause of the third and final Punic War - the Numidian kingdom under King Masinissa to the west was made a close ally of Rome, acting as a kind of watchdog over the prostrate city.

Thus Carthage became a tributary of Rome. The principle of foreign states paying large sums into the public treasury in Rome was established, and Rome never freed herself from this tie, which ultimately made her dependent on tribute, whilst her own capacity for work and enterprise was sapped. More harmful still in its consequences was the injustice inflicted on cities which had joined Hannibal, notably those in southern Italy. Their land was seized as Roman *ager publicus*; some was made available for settlement by Roman veteran soldiers, some passed into the hands of landlords and speculators, who wanted land only as a means of exploiting native people or even fellow Romans. The concept of *ager publicus*, which in the early days of Rome was a corner-stone of liberty and strength, ensuring the right of all citizens to the use of land, had become a source of bondage in its abuse. Bruttium, for example, became a region of serfdom, where the population were regarded as unworthy of any independence. Greek cities, like Croton, were made into colonies. Even some Latin cities, previously the special friends of Rome, allied with her in a spirit of self-dependence, were treated now with contempt. Fewer colonies were founded for Latins, as opposed to Romans; higher military contingents were demanded and later, in 187 BC, Latins were even expelled from Rome.

Not all Italian states were so treated, but a division had been created: citizen and subject. There were two ideas of relationship to Rome, where before the Punic Wars there was one. Of course, many men in Rome and in its associated territories had not been citizens - indeed, many were slaves - but the new distinction was the product of empire, of the growth of an imperial conception of Rome. No longer were her wars obviously defensive. Long experience fighting abroad, in Spain, Sicily and Africa, for example, against a power which was aggressive in its pursuit of trade and revenues, had changed the outlook of Romans of all persuasions. Now they looked out beyond the confines of the city, beyond Latium, beyond even Italy. Some saw opportunities for spreading a higher form of government and law, others for glory and adventure, others for commerce and wealth, others for greed and exploitation. Thus in the Punic Wars the seeds of all that was best and all that was worst in the later empire were sown.

### References:

1. Polybius, *The Rise of the Roman Empire*, trans. I. Scott-Kilvert, Penguin, London, 1979, Book I, 57.

2. Plutarch, 'Life of Fabius Maximus', in *Makers of Rome*, trans. I. Scott-Kilvert, Penguin, London, 1972, p. 67.

3. Livy, *The War with Hannibal*, trans. A. de Selincourt, Penguin, London, 1978, Book XXII, 39, pp. 138-9.

4.  Livy, *The War with Hannibal*, Book XXII, 49, pp. 148-9.
5.  Livy, *The War with Hannibal*, Book XXII, 51, pp. 151-2.
6.  Livy, *The War with Hannibal*, Book XXII, 53, p. 153.
7.  Plutarch, 'Life of Marcellus', trans. Scott-Kilvert, p. 101.
8.  Livy, *The War with Hannibal*, Book XXVIII, 12, p. 512.

## Chapter 31

# The Fetters of Greece

## *The Roman Conquest of Greece*

HANNIBAL, ARCH-ENEMY OF ROME, had fled to the East. Though not concerned to pursue him after his thorough defeat at Zama, the Romans were engaged by the year 200 BC in the affairs of the eastern Mediterranean, drawn there by the enmity of an ally of Hannibal, Philip V of Macedon. After the death of Alexander in 323 BC his empire had been divided between his generals, and three dominant states of these "successors" finally emerged in the third century BC: Macedon, Syria and Egypt. When a seven-year old child of the ruling Greek family, the Ptolemies, came to the throne of Egypt in 204 BC, Macedon and Syria conspired to break up the Egyptian empire by taking control of the possessions of Egypt in the Aegean sea and on the Syrian coast respectively. Philip V was clearly an aggressive ruler who saw

*Roman Odeion at Corinth*

himself as a new Alexander. Since the Greek city states still lacked political unity, the stage was set for a descent by him upon the liberty of Greece. There had been four thousand Macedonians on the field at Zama, and Roman resentment at this also influenced the decision to intervene in Greek affairs in 200 BC.

The Roman people themselves were reluctant to embark on another war in a new theatre. Sixteen years of continuous war against Hannibal had taken its toll. Citizen soldiers demanded peace and a return to their homes. Only mercenaries threatened with discharge saw further war as an opportunity. The Roman Senate, however, received urgent appeals for help from the Greek island of Rhodes, from the cultured king Attalus of Pergamum and from Athens, threatened now as in the days of Demosthenes. Such appeals made a deep impression on educated Roman Senators. They decided on war; rumours of Macedonian plans to invade Italy moved the Assembly to support it.

The Macedonian war was brief; yet its implications were of great significance for the future of Rome, for it was the first imperial war, in the sense that Roman forces were fighting outside Italy against a state which had not itself committed any acts of direct aggression against her. Rome was led to fight not really from any strong sense of imperial mission, rather from a decision of the moment that her legions were needed to restore an order which she had a responsibility to maintain. Rome had already been granted Hellenic status as a participant in the Isthmian Games; she had been initiated into the Eleusian mysteries by Athens, when a generation before she had come to her aid. Her finest patricians were schooled in the philosophy of Plato and Zeno, and it was they who decided to fight in Greece in 200 BC.

Though the people acquiesced in this new war, they extracted from the Senate a fateful change in the method of recruitment. Citizens of Rome were freed from any obligation to enrol. The allies were not granted this privilege, so the army consisted of citizen volunteers, mercenaries and Italian allies. Henceforth there was a distinction in this vital matter of war service between Roman citizens and others, which became a cause of conflict between Rome and the Italian allies in the early first century BC. As regards Rome herself, this method of recruitment marked the increasing neglect of the Licinian laws of 367 BC, which limited individual land-holdings of public land to five hundred *jugera* to enable every citizen to remain an independent smallholder, if he so chose. The citizen army defending its own land and people rested upon this principle; thus Rome had fought Etruscans, Gauls and Samnites. Against Hannibal, however, the citizen army had been discredited by appalling defeats under the leadership of ambitious men, like Minucius, and demagogues, like Varro. The new army to fight the Macedonians was not recruited in the spirit of defending the citizen's right to livelihood and liberty. Those citizens who volunteered to go had other motives, of plunder or glory, perhaps of imperial mission. Others had no land left in Italy to defend. A proletarian element began to swell the ranks of Roman armies, just as it made its appearance in the streets of Rome when the armies returned from war.

The army which sailed to Greece in 200 BC was led by Titus Quinctius Flamininus, a young man brought up to recognise in Hellenic culture a form of life superior to the rough virtues of his homeland. In one critical respect, however, he knew that Rome excelled, namely in the art of infantry warfare. For three years the Macedonian phalanx was to confront the Roman maniple and, as in the Pyrrhic war, the maniple was to emerge victorious. The phalanx was a solid block of spearmen, whose spears extended twenty-one feet ahead of each man, so that five lines of men could extend their spears ahead of the frontline, making a hedge where every soldier directly facing the enemy was protected by five spearpoints. When the phalanx charged on level ground, or when it was itself attacked head-on, it was invincible. The Roman maniple, evolved in the Samnite wars, had much greater flexibility. Each of the 120 men in it fought as an individual, yet was bound by Roman discipline to operate as a member of the unit. Face to face with a phalanx, he was weak; free to move round it, to attack it from the rear or sides, to meet it in hilly country or on fields with ditches or other impediments, he was able to break it up with skilled swordplay and agility.

Another example of Roman superiority in military technique was given by the use of palisades. Greek armies found it almost impossible to carry stakes for a palisade when on the march, but the Roman soldier hung his shield on a strap round his shoulder and could carry his javelin in one hand and wooden stakes in the other. The stakes were cut carefully with short branches remaining, so that they could be firmly intertwined, making it very difficult to pull any out of a palisade. In the mobile warfare called for by the second Punic War and now the Macedonian War, when armies manoeuvred through dissected uplands and near indented coastlines, such palisades were ideally suitable for building secure camps.

Philip V's hold on Greece rested on his possession of three strategic fortified cities: Demetrias, commanding the gulf of Pagasaeus on the east coast of Thessaly, Chalcis on the island of Euboea, facing the shortest sea crossing to Boeotia, and Corinth, the gateway to the Peloponnese. These fortresses were known as "the fetters of Greece". Were Philip to evacuate all other areas of Greece, these alone ensured his control, for no Greek army could leave its territory at the mercy of such impregnable garrisons, nor risk the cutting of critical lines of communication. Flamininus, however, knowing the importance of Demetrias to Philip, used this as a means to bring the Macedonians to a decisive engagement in terrain of his own choosing. In 197 BC the Roman consul left a force watching Corinth and, escorted by his fleet off the east coast, marched north and induced Philip to bring his main army south through Thessaly, in case Demetrias was besieged. Both armies manoeuvred westwards in parallel lines into the hills north of Thebes. Skirmishing gradually drew in heavier forces, until finally a battle was upon them at Cynoscephalae. With the help of Aetolian cavalry, the Roman infantry broke up the Macedonian phalanxes. For every dead Roman, over ten of the enemy lay on the field. Philip withdrew from Greece.

The question now for the Greek city states, proud of their traditional independence, wary of every foreign army since the days of Marathon and Chaeronea, was whether Rome would use her power for her own gain or in the cause of Greece. The Roman Senate responded to victory by ordering their armies to leave many of the Greek cities, but the suspicious Aetolians, perhaps resentful of the credit awarded to the Roman maniples after the initial Aetolian cavalry success at Cynoscephalae, spread rumours that Rome intended to retain the "fetters of Greece" and other important cities.

The issue was settled at the Isthmian Games held in Corinth in 196 BC. Rome participated in them as a member of the Panhellenic brotherhood. On the opening day of the Games, as the huge crowd awaited the entrance of the athletes, a single trumpeter stepped into the arena, followed by a Roman herald. A shrill trumpet call brought total silence to the great stadium. The herald took a pace forward and delivered this proclamation:

> "The Senate of Rome and Titus Quinctius Flamininus the pro-consul, having defeated king Philip and the Macedonians in battle, leave the following states and cities free, without garrisons, subject to no tribute and in full enjoyment of their ancestral laws: the peoples of Corinth, Phocis, Locri, Euboea, Phthiotic Achaea, Magnesia, Thessaly and Perrhaebia."[1]

Every Greek present knew this freed "the fetters of Greece" and every other city not so far evacuated by Roman troops. Flamininus, who was in the stadium, was nearly smothered by the accolades of exuberant Greeks. He himself had ensured that the herald's message would be without prevarication. The Games proceeded, but the unfortunate athletes exerted themselves with little chance of attracting the attention of the crowd, lost in a feverish anticipation about the prospect of freedom.

Rome's decision to intervene in the eastern Mediterranean was not to be so easily resolved. Antiochus III of Syria was persuaded by Hannibal to challenge her. He occupied most of Asia Minor, except where kingdoms sympathetic to Rome, such as Pergamum, refused his overtures, and then crossed to Thrace over the Hellespont in the footsteps of the Persians of Xerxes. Rome viewed Syria as the inheritor of Persian hegemony in Asia, and hesitated to pick a quarrel with Antiochus, but his crossing into Greece challenged the very principle proclaimed at Corinth. Another Roman army crossed the Adriatic to fight in Greece.

This time Rome's navy was also committed to the war. Its thorough defeat of Antiochus' navy left his army poorly supported in the peninsula. Having retreated to the pass of Thermopylae, the Syrians were routed when a bold attack led by Porcius Cato surprised them. The Romans followed them into Asia Minor, and at Magnesia in 190 BC, near the Aegean coast, defeated the full panoply of a multi-national Asian host: phalanxes, archers, light cavalry, heavily armoured cavalry (or cataphracti), camel riders bearing six-foot swords, Indian elephants bigger and more ferocious than the African elephants of the Romans, chariots with scythed yokes and hubs - a total force of about seventy thousand men. After Magnesia, Roman influence beyond the Hellespont in Asia Minor was bound to be preponderant, for the group of small kingdoms there, such as Pergamum, Phrygia, Bithynia, Cilicia, Galatia, Cappadocia and Rhodes had never been united against threats from Macedon to the west or Syria to the east. Rome was their natural protector once she had intervened.

Scipio Africanus, the victor of Zama, had taken command against Antiochus, though he was not present at Magnesia because of illness. Earlier in the campaign, on first crossing into Asia Minor, he had taken his army to Ilium, encamped on the level ground below the walls and then climbed to the ancient citadel. There he gave sacrifice to Minerva, the goddess whom the Greeks knew as Athena, their patroness in the Trojan wars, yet a deity who preferred to settle disputes peacably and who was revered as the founder of the Athenian court of the Areopagus, where liberty was preserved. To her divine gifts - protection in war, love of peace, liberty and wisdom - Scipio dedicated himself and Rome in the citadel of Ilium, where Hector had left his wife and boy whilst he fought the invincible Achilles. Scipio's own son had been a captive of the Syrian king, who had tried to bribe Scipio with offers of his release. Roman honour could not be bought; the reply to Antiochus made a nice distinction between private and public responsibilities.

Scipio was the Roman type of such heroes, but he represented a nobility which was passing. Other men were thrusting themselves forward, men dedicated to lower gods, to personal glory, to worldly success, to wealth. Such a man was Gnaeus Manlius Volso, a commander in the war against Antiochus. He had led his army into the heart of Asia Minor after the defeat of Antiochus at Magnesia, and attacked the Gallic people of Galatia. The Senate had not authorised such a war, nor had the *Comitia Centuriata*, no ambassadors had been sent to Galatia to demand restitution - indeed there was no offence on the part of the Gauls - and, worst of all, the Fetiales, sacred heralds to declare war, had not attended upon the war before battle was done. Volso's attack was an act of brigandage, yet he claimed a triumph on his return, and the Senate gave way to his demands and granted him one. Success had eclipsed right and honour.

Timocracy, the rule of honour, had given way to oligarchy, the rule of property. "The flow of gold into private stores," as Plato described the decline from honour to property in what the rulers value, was now swift. The Licinian laws were forgotten. The spirit of sacrifice, briefly common to the whole people of Rome after Cannae, the respect for the dignity of other peoples, embodied in the decree of Flamininus at the Isthmian Games, had given way to the greed for empire and the love of wealth.

Another, with Scipio, who still rendered the Roman magistracy honourable, was Lucius Aemilius Paulus, son of the general who had died at Cannae, bravely declining flight. After his defeat by the Romans, Philip V of Macedon had secretly built up a new army by collecting men, arms and money in the inland cities of Macedon, whilst leaving the ports and border cities, which could be more easily observed, in a state of poverty and lack of protection. The Romans had paid him little attention, for they were pre-occupied in Asia Minor with Antiochus III. When Philip died, his son Perseus succeeded to the renewed military power of Macedon. Perseus was ambitious and unscrupulous. Once more the freedom of Greece was threatened, and again Rome produced a soldier worthy of defending it. Aemilius Paulus was chosen by the people to undertake the task when he was sixty years old, after a career of impeccable honesty and service to the State. At the battle of Pydna in 168 BC the Macedonian phalanxes were again destroyed by the Roman infantry.

Paulus had earned a triumph in Rome. Before it was held he warned his junior officers of the vagaries of fortune, reminding them that now, when they were elated with success and basking in praise, was the best time to remember that on other occasions they would be conscious of defeat and treated with contempt, and that a wise man was indifferent to success and failure. Nevertheless the triumph was held in the most magnificent style. For three days the citizens of Rome beheld the wealth of Macedon paraded before their eyes. Three thousand men carried seven hundred and fifty great jars, each full of gold coins. Displays of captured arms rolled past, some set up in mock battle order with Macedonian spears poised before Roman short swords above heaps of shields, corselets and greaves. Macedonian captives walked past in chains. King Perseus limped along preceded by his small children, too young to understand their plight.

Aemilius Paulus himself rode past in his chariot, wearing a purple-bordered toga, speckled with gold, and the laurel crown of victory. Four hundred gold crowns from Macedonian cities accompanied him as symbols of his rule. Paulus exhibited every mark of joy at the success of Roman arms and worthy honour at the privilege of command; yet his son of fourteen years had died five days before the triumph. Three days after it, his son of twelve years died. Like Scipio Africanus, Paulus knew how to distinguish his public duty from his private feelings. When he spoke to the people after his second son had died, his speech concluded that he found his consolation for personal disaster in the happiness and good fortune of the commonwealth.

After Pydna Rome tried briefly to govern Greece with the help of the Achaean League, the organisation in the Peloponnese, which, together with the Aetolian League in the north of Greece, had preserved some degree of Greek freedom for about a century; but enemies of Rome within the Achaean League provoked yet another war. By now Roman patience was exhausted. In 146 BC Corinth was captured and burnt to the ground. Greece and Macedonia were formed into a single Roman province. The political independence of Greece was at an end.

Roman occupiers of Greece soon began to take Greek art treasures back to Italy to adorn their town houses and rural villas. This tangible sign of Rome's acknowledgement of Greek cultural pre-eminence was a mere token compared to the real benefit that Roman society derived from the Hellenistic world. Stoicism, which sustained the Roman nobility for generations, had descended directly from the philosophy of Socrates and Plato, through its founder Zeno. In the field of cultural achievement the ultimate debt was to the Socratic philosophy of unity and universality, which had inspired the creative outburst of Hellenism. Alexander the Great had spread the culture of fourth century Greece across the face of Asia and North Africa. Now, as the Romans were drawn into the political vacuum which followed the crumbling of Macedonian and Syrian power, they met the full force of Hellenistic ideas, in art and science, in literature and mathematics, in architecture and town planning. For the seeds of Greek classical art, scattered so prodigally on the Acropolis of Athens, had not been stifled by the collapse of the classical world at the end of the fifth century, but had fructified in original forms in the milieu of a new culture, Hellenism.

The Roman consul, Mummius, the destroyer of Corinth, had blithely ordered that any works of art lost on the voyage to Rome should be replaced by equivalent pieces. In sculpture and painting Hellenistic artists were, in fact, producing unique master pieces. The timeless poise and harmony of pure classicism could not be recaptured, but the outward looking, dynamic forces embodied in Alexander the Great and in his vast adventure in the Orient, found their expression in the work of sculptors in Alexandria, Pergamum, Rhodes and Athens. Praxiteles and Lysippos produced nude figures of marble or bronze, which combined physical realism with the idealisation of emotions. The former's "Hermes with the infant Dionysos" portrays the god as a tranquil, almost casual, observer, with the smooth, soft exterior of worldly beauty. His "Aphrodite of Knidos" shows female beauty in the perfection of physical form, yet retaining enough of the ideal to avoid pure sensuality. Lysippos' bronze "Apoxyomenos" (the Scraper) captures the moment of a young athlete using a strigil to scrape the sweat off his arm. In the later Hellenistic work, "The Seated Boxer", naturalism has been taken even further to reveal the full coarseness of the life of a professional athlete, who sits bemused, with a brutal, beaten face, knotted muscles and an anguished turning of the head towards a master, or fellow boxer, though humanity is present in the pathetic aspiration of the boxer's look.

In general, Hellenistic sculpture retains this ideal longing, expressed through powerful emotion: Demosthenes as an aged statesman, pondering over some deep problem in the weary dignity of old age; or Alexander himself (a marble head was found at Pergamum) with a look of intense yearning for the realisation of some great end and the furrowed brow of an intelligent man of action. As in other works of the Pergamene school, the face of Alexander is heavily incised, the eyes deep-set, the play of light and shade enhanced to convey emotion and movement. On the huge Altar of Zeus, which stood in a large court, was carved at eye-level the second largest frieze of antiquity (after the Parthenon frieze), in which the gods and giants fight each other in a welter of writhing, muscular bodies, so infused with energy that they spill out on to the steps of the monument. The battle symbolises the triumph of the Pergamenes over an invading army of Gauls, and shows how Hellenistic artists held to the classical idea of the war of civilisation against barbarism. Equally dramatic is the tragic isolation of the Pergamene figure of a dying Gaul. He lies mortally wounded by a sword thrust in the chest, supporting himself on one arm, his head fallen, but nobly resisting despair, a generous portrayal by the victors of a common humanity.

Such works anticipate the baroque style of the late Florentine Renaissance in their emphasis on powerful emotion and expressive movement, but they never lose the Greek insight into Man's essential yearning for final realisation. Most expressive of all the known works of Hellenism is the "Laocoon and his two sons", probably by three Rhodian sculptors. The priest from the Greek army at Troy is shown struggling hopelessly with a giant serpent, which inexorably engulfs himself and his sons. This work, with its intense muscular strain and agony of spirit, profoundly affected Michelangelo, when it was found in AD 1506. Like him, the sculptors were aware of the compulsive toils of the flesh and similarly portrayed the deep passion of a man struggling to be free of them.

Praxitiles had used the translucent quality of marble to produce the effect of light arising from behind the surface. Hellenistic painters rediscovered light in new techniques, using colours mixed with hot wax (encaustic) or with egg yolk (tempera). Light sources, diffusion, transparency, reflection and shadow could all be exhibited, as the later Roman paintings at Pompeii and Herculaneum prove. No works by the accepted master, Apelles, survive, but a description of his picture of Aphrodite rising from the sea inspired Botticelli's "Birth of Venus." A magnificent mosaic, "Victory of Alexander over Darius III," reproduced a painting of about 300 BC by Philoxenus, and shows clearly the mastery of light, which gleams on armour and horses' flanks and enables the face of a fallen man to be reflected in a shield. Foreshortening is used extensively for the cavalry horses. True to Hellenistic standards, Darius expresses a dignified horror as his army is cut down, and the whole composition is directed towards the majestic figure of Alexander himself. For the Hellenistic culture retained its initial presumption that kings and royalty had replaced independent poleis, an outlook re-inforced by its contact with the Orient.

*Hermes of Praxiteles, Olympia Museum*

The tessera technique of mosaics was an invention of Hellenism; it especially flourished at Pergamum with the "famous *trompe d'oeil*" method of Sosos, but at Alexandria miniature tesserae were used and became very influential in the Roman world, so that the splendid pavements of Roman villas and palaces, such as Fishbourne in England, had their source in Greek ingenuity. The Hellenistic palace was itself a development which united the emphasis on kingship with such new forms of decorative art.

Alexandria is the greatest example of a Hellenistic royal city incorporating a palace complex, though Pergamum was of similar magnificence. Ptolemy I Soter planned the great museum, or *mouseion*, as a shrine of the muses. Despite the fire in 47 BC, Alexandria became a unique centre of Greek culture for the whole of the Hellenistic period. Indeed, its role was contemporaneous with the complete cultural cycle which began in the early fourth century BC and ended about 900 years later. Alexander the

Great's personal architect designed the city; within a century it was the greatest in the western world. The lighthouse, or *pharos*, was 440 feet high and one of the seven wonders of the ancient world. The great library contained almost half a million papyrus rolls, with copies of most of the works held in Athens in the school of Aristotle; hence, like that school, it had a strong scientific leaning, which yielded valuable developments in mathematics, physics, medicine and astronomy. At the same time the library preserved classical literature, contemporary poetry and the first translation into Greek of the Pentateuch. In Pergamum the library rivalled that of Alexandria and saw the first use of parchment, more durable than papyrus. Such libraries were initiated by the Romans; the Roman intelligentsia, men like Cicero, acquired extensive personal libraries.

Town planning, using the grid system initiated by Hippodamus of Miletus in classical times, became a distinctive art of Hellenistic society. The Syrian empire founded by Alexander's general, Seleucus, was especially rich in cities. Antioch, its capital, was built to a completely systematic plan, incorporating a palace, courts, vast staircases, broad streets of large town houses and splendid public buildings and temples. The brilliant, spontaneous irregularity of the Acropolis at Athens gave way to a carefully integrated, functional arrangement. It typified the change from polis to kingdom, from the intuition of Homer to the reason of Plato.

The Corinthian order of architecture became predominant in the fourth century. Polykleitos the Younger first used a complete colonnade of Corinthian columns in the *tholos* at Epidauros in about 360 BC. According to Vitruvius, the Corinthian order began when the tomb of a young girl in Corinth became strangely overgrown with an acanthus plant, which wound itself around a pedestal on the grave. Acanthus

*Wall-painting, Pompeii*

*Temple of Apollo, Pompeii*

*Tivoli gardens, Rome*

became a symbol of immortality and its ubiquity on Corinthian capitals in Hellenistic times, therefore, may have some connection with the Socratic teaching on the immortality of the soul. The greatest temples of Hellenism - the Temple of Apollo at Didyma in Asia Minor and the Temple of the Olympian Zeus at Athens, for example - were distinguished by huge, slender Corinthian columns. Unlike the dark mystery of the interior of classical temples, Hellenistic ones had large open courtyards, full of light, with a sanctuary at one end, as at Didyma, where the scale of the whole interior recalls the immensity of Egyptian Luxor or Karnak.

Perhaps the most characteristic Hellenistic building of all was the stoa. Every great city of the period contained one, often of two storeys. In Athens, of course, the stoa was the home of several philosophical movements, notably the Stoics and the Aristotelian peripatetics. There, in the second century BC, King Attalus II of Pergamum built a magnificent double storeyed stoa dedicated "to the demos of the Athenians," probably the finest example of its type. 115m long and 20m wide, it housed 21 shops on each floor ranged along the double colonnade of Doric and Ionic columns, some with capitals based on the Egyptian palm leaf (Pergamene capitals). At the very centre of Athenian commercial life, the shops attracted high rents, which were received by the state and used to maintain the city centre and for other public services. The elegant, systematic and generous architecture of the Hellenistic stoa, with its cool colonnaded walk, represented all that was best in the urban life of the culture. That the royal houses, not only of Pergamum, but also of Egypt, Syria, Cappadocia and the Pontus, all contributed to Athenian building projects at this time indicates both the predominance of kings and the retention by Athens of cultural prestige well into the period when, politically, Rome had eclipsed it.

Hellenistic architects could not recapture the perfect harmony of the Parthenon, but they showed great originality, even outside the fine urban centres. The superb theatre at Epidauros, a half-cone of 50 rows of marble benches with radiating aisles, possibly built by Polykleitos the Younger, shows an intense interest in pure geometry. The mausoleum at Halikarnassos recalls the Egyptian pyramids, with its burial chamber for King Mausolus of Caria, surmounted by a peristyle and crowned by a pyramid, supporting an immense marble chariot and four horses driven by a giant king. The dramatic, oriental figure, whose drapery is tugged by a demonic wind, contrasts vividly with the serene charioteer of Delphi.

Hellenistic culture, for all its sense of drama and passion, produced, also, major advances in the most intellectual of mental endeavours, mathematics. From about 300 BC onwards, there flourished at Alexandria Euclid, Aristarchus of Samos, Archimedes, Eratosthenes and Apollonius of Perge. Their common root led back to the Academy in Athens, where Plato, inspired by Pythagoras' intuition into numbers, had laid the foundations of Greek geometry. From Plato's proposition that the universe was designed by the Creator on mathematical principles, a whole system of deductive, purely abstract laws was established by such men as Eudoxus of Cnidus, a friend of Plato, who had accompanied him to Egypt. Eudoxus defined the fundamental concept of ratio: a and b have a ratio if there are whole numbers m and n, such that both $ma > b$ and $nb > a$. The value of this definition is that it excludes zero and infinity from ratios and that it can be applied to incommensurable as well as to commensurable magnitudes. This enabled incommensurables, like root 2, the hypoteneuse of a right-angled triangle of unit side, to be used in ratios. Eudoxus' second great discovery was the basis of the method of exhaustion. He stated the proposition that given two different magnitudes, a magnitude smaller than the smaller one could always be found. The method is simply to subtract from the larger magnitude any amount not less than its half and then to repeat the process, until the desired amount is attained.

From such foundations the Hellenistic mathematicians developed a brilliantly systematic geometry, which was most clearly expressed in Euclid's *Elements*. For example, Euclid proved (Book XII, Prop. 1,2) that "circles are to one another as the squares on their diameters," which implies that *pi* is a constant. The measurement of the area of a circle was found by convergence, using Eudoxus' method of exhaustion with inscribed and circumscribed polygons. Hence *pi* was calculated with considerable accuracy.

Greek mathematicians did not develop an algebraic notation. What they managed to prove by pure geometry, rather than by algebra, was astonishing. They solved the general quadratic $ax^2 + bx = S$, for example, by purely deductive constructions. Apollonius created a system of conics from his insight that the three forms - parabola, hyperbola and ellipse - are all sections of a right cone, when the angle with the axis is varied. He came close to anticipating the co-ordinate geometry of Descartes and laid the foundations for the whole subject of conics, including its application to astronomy.

Archimedes was perhaps the most fertile mathematical mind of the ancient world. In addition to his famous principle, he discovered that the volume of pyramids and cones is one-third of their containing parallelepipeds, and invented an amazing range of machines for war and peace, such as the irrigation screw and ballistic weapons, many used at the siege of Syracuse. In his work *The Sand Reckoner*, he anticipated the principle of adding indices to multiply large numbers, a principle upon which modern logarithms are based.

Hellenistic science drew heavily upon mathematics. In astronomy steps were taken upon which the subject depended until the time of Copernicus in the sixteenth century. Aristarchus developed a heliocentric theory - Copernicus himself acknowledged it in a marginal note - but Ptolemy, later at Alexandria, wrote an elaborate account based upon epicycles, which replaced that of his predecessor. The circumference of the earth was calculated by Eratosthenes with remarkable accuracy - 50 miles short of the correct figure - by using observations of the angular height of the sun at Alexandria and at Syene, 5000 stadia to the south at the first cataract of the Nile. Mathematics and astronomy both exhibited the superb systematic thinking of the Hellenistic era. The study of ballistics, inspired by Apollonius and Archimedes, showed the practical application of Hellenistic science. It contributed to the social transformation from poleis, able to withstand sieges, to kings, whose armies could dominate cities and the regions they served.

The beauty and system of Hellenistic art and thought conquered Rome. Though her ferocious maniples might outfight the cumbersome phalanxes of the Greeks, Rome could not withstand the subtle mind of a culture that drew its inspiration from Socrates and its heritage from the brilliance of classical Athens. Roman engineering, architecture, road building and military science would add new scope and resilience to the inheritance of Hellenism, but even they were largely derivative, like Roman literature, sculpture and painting. Even in political organisation and law - Rome's greatest contributions to the civilisation of the Western world - the seeds ultimately were Greek. Only the nature of the Roman people was truly her own, for that was born in the hills of Tuscany and the valley of the Tiber from the Trojan stock of Aeneas and the teaching of the *pater patriae*, Numa Pompilius. When Julius Caesar determined upon a career of public fame and fortune, it was to Rhodes that he went to study under the greatest known contemporary teacher of rhetoric. When the young Horace was recognised as an intellectual of genius by his percipient father, it was to Athens that he was sent to finish his education. The Romans knew that Greece was their mentor, and many, no doubt, were grateful that the noble Flamininus had acknowledged the debt at the Isthmian Games in 196 BC, and granted a brief spell of liberty before the final waning of the free spirit of Apollo.

### Reference:

1.  Plutarch, Life of *Flamininus*, X.

## Chapter 32

# Land and Liberty

## *The Gracchi's Land Reform*

WITHIN SIXTY YEARS from the time when Hannibal had come so close to the destruction of Rome the Republic had acquired an empire, stretching from Spain in the west to the fringes of Asia Minor in the east. Carthage itself had been wiped out after a third and final war, fought in obedience to the terrible refrain of the elder Cato, *"delenda est Carthago"* ("Carthage must be destroyed.") At the heart of the empire, however, there were symptoms of decline. The state was divided; soon there would erupt a long period of civil war. Oligarchy, the rule of the few, lovers of wealth rather than honour, was becoming entrenched at the very time when Roman influence was spreading to every corner of the Mediterranean Sea.

Yet in Rome the principles upon which the nation had been founded still inspired uncorrupted families. Cornelia, a beautiful young lady in the family of the Scipios,

*Circus Maximus at Rome*

had married a member of the Gracchus family who had fought with outstanding courage to restore order in Spain. Amongst their children were two sons, Tiberius and Gaius, noted for their fine physiques, eloquence, intelligence and generosity. Tiberius was nine years older than Gaius, and won a unique reputation for his qualities as a soldier and his prospects as a public figure in Rome.

A glittering public career was open to Tiberius. Like any other well-connected young man of ancient family and high ability, fresh from splendid endeavours on the battlefield, he might easily have been elected to an office of state; as *aedile*, responsible for finance, or *praetor*, for the law courts. From these the road was open to the supreme offices of consul, holder of the *imperium*, or executive power, or of *censor*, the guardian of public morality, or of *pontifex maximus*. Youthful ambition, the encouragement of his family and friends, the adoration of the masses for a popular hero home from war, all these called Tiberius to climb the ladder of an honourable public career.

The Senate was by this time the dominant institution in the Republic. Though in theory an assembly of the people, the *Comitia Centuriata*, held supreme power and had been given the right by the *Lex Hortensia* of 287 BC to make law by its resolutions (*plebiscita,*) in practice the assembly in the Rome of Tiberius' day was largely controlled by the Senate or by the tribunes. For many citizens were uneducated, idle, and open to bribery and the wiles of demagogues. The Senate, on the other hand, was a compact body of ancient families, forbidden by the *Lex Claudia* of 218 BC from engaging in commerce and hence united in their defence of the privilege of landowners. Since the appointment of tribunes to safeguard the interests of the people, the Senate had discovered how to exploit the veto held by each of the ten tribunes over the actions of his fellows. Only one tribune had to be bribed, or otherwise persuaded, to support the Senate against the tribunate for the views of the people to be disregarded.

As a member of an ancient Senatorial family, Tiberius Gracchus thus had every prospect of support from the Senate and of a highly successful career to satisfy his ambition and the hopes of his friends. He underwent, however, an experience which made such expectations of no account. On a journey through Etruria, the region north of Rome in which Lars Porsena had recruited his great army centuries before, Tiberius saw deserted fields and ruined buildings, where many Italian small-holders had once worked their own farms; and, beside them, huge estates, on which toiled gangs of slaves, chained and beaten by merciless supervisors employed by absentee landlords. As men captured in war, or descended from such captives, the slaves had no rights. They were a means of exploiting the land of Italy for the profit of rich men. Many of these latter sat in the Senate in Rome. Most of the original Italian farmers, or their descendants, were now swelling the masses who waited in the city upon the bribes of the Senators. For Tiberius the experience of such injustice drove from his mind any thoughts of personal ambition.

Tiberius' mother, Cornelia, was a cultured and devoted woman. When her husband died she received an offer of marriage from the king of Egypt, but she knew that she had a role of great importance to play in Rome and so refused. She recognised in both Tiberius and Gaius the marks of genius, and once chided them that she was still known in Rome as the daughter of a Scipio, rather than as the mother of a Gracchus. Cornelia herself directed her sons' education. They were well versed in Greek and studied both the philosophy and the history of Greece. In Plato they had read of the decline of states, of the ideals of *The Republic*, and of Plato's remedy for a state fallen into a condition of embittered class division: an end of greed and the rise of justice.

With the memory of the Etrurian landscape in his mind, Tiberius stood for the office of tribune of the people. Despite the decline of the office, he still saw in the tribunacy the principle of protecting the Roman people from oppression by the rich and powerful. Once elected, he proposed the re-enactment of the Licinian laws. No one was to hold more than 500 *jugera* of public land. All public land misappropriated was to be returned to its proper holders. All public land acquired by purchase was to be returned to the state for redistribution, with compensation paid to the purchaser. Most such land had come into the hands of the state originally in the successful wars of Rome. When the Samnites were defeated in the south, for example, their land had been partly made over to Rome for distribution to Roman citizens. The distribution had been by auction or by sharing it out as small-holdings for retired soldiers at a small rent payable to the state. Unfortunately, many soldiers had been the victims of men who acquired their land by cunning or deceit. These had bought the small-holdings from soldiers who did not appreciate their value, even using false names to obviate the Licinian laws.

By the year 133 BC, when Tiberius was elected tribune, open abuse of the law was so widespread that such tricks were hardly necessary. Great estates were spread throughout Italy. The labour to work them came from the slave markets of the Mediterranean, from Sardinia, whose population had flooded the markets after the island's occupation in 175 BC, ironically by an ancestor of the Gracchi brothers, from the Greek island of Delos, once the home of the Treasury of the Delian League formed to defend Greek freedom against Persia and now a slave market selling 10,000 slaves a day, or from Epirus in north-west Greece, whence 150,000 slaves were brought to Italy after the Roman victory of Pydna. Not only war captives became slaves. So, too, did victims of pirates - more numerous after the Rhodian navy had been eliminated by Rome - and also, debtors, criminals and children exposed to die. Aristotle's dictum, that it was natural for inferior people to be enslaved, might have settled some uneasy consciences.

Slaves employed in households were often well-treated, and Greek culture was brought to Roman society partly through the educated Greeks who acted as tutors, doctors or secretaries in Roman homes, but rural slavery was of a different order. Even the relatively humane scholar, Terentius Varro, wrote of three types of farm equipment: "the kind that speaks (i.e. slaves), the kind that cannot speak (i.e. cattle), and the voiceless (i.e. farm implements)." In his work, *On Agriculture*, the elder Cato advised that slaves should be treated in the same way as farm animals and maintained sufficiently to get the maximum work out of them until they died. They were often chained in gangs. In Sicily, in the year 135 BC, this situation gave rise to the first serious slave revolt. Many thousands of slaves from the eastern Mediterranean, under a leader who styled himself King Antiochus, seized part of the island and held out for three years against Roman troops. With atrocious cruelty, the revolt was finally broken in 132 BC, the year after Tiberius Gracchus became tribune.

In 215 BC the Roman state had become bankrupt as a result of the huge need for supplies for the war with Hannibal. Supplies had continued on credit for ten years, then in 205 BC the government had decided to sell public land to pay its creditors.

Most of the land sold had come from confiscations from municipalities in southern Italy, which had sided with Hannibal after the battle of Cannae. Hence many small-holdings in the south had been swallowed up in the large estates of rich creditors or purchasers from them. Moreover, at the end of the war with Hannibal, the government, in order to meet finally its creditors' demands, had paid them in kind with public land within a fifty mile radius of Rome, the economic rent of which was high and certain to go higher.

What added further to the tendency towards the concentration of land in fewer hands was the abolition for all Roman citizens in Italy of the land tax (*tributum*) in 167 BC, after success in the wars to control the eastern Mediterranean. Large stocks of gold and silver from captured royal treasuries, supplemented by regular revenue from tribute from the new provinces, royalties from Spanish mines and rent from the public land acquired after the second Punic War, made the public finances of Rome appear so flushed that the land tax was abolished in Italy, without regard to equity. Owners of land found that, irrespective of its value and its size, they were free of any financial obligation towards the state. After a generation of such immunity, there was an inevitable tendency for the greater landlords, growing rich on economic rent, to buy out, or to undersell in produce markets, the smaller landlords, the yeomen citizens of the Republic. This unseen effect of the legislation of 167 BC reinforced the undertow towards land monopoly created by the removal of so many small farmers to serve in wars abroad, and by the massive sales of public land after the bankruptcy of 215 BC.

These great estates cultivated the vine and the olive to produce wine and oil. Many also were given over to pasture for sheep and cattle. No longer were they cornlands, supplying Rome and the other Italian cities with their essential grain, for the granaries of Rome were now abroad in North Africa, even in Egypt. Transport was easy by sea, though later the growth of piracy endangered the bread supply of Rome. The small holding Roman citizen, or Italian ally, had grown wheat for his own and local use. Now the most profitable yields from the chained gangs were in wine and oil, and the most profitable use of the pastured hills of Etruria and Samnia was the maintenance of vast herds of sheep and cattle by a few herdsmen employed by the distant landlords.

Tiberius Gracchus' proposals for land reform included a land commission to supervise the movement back to the law as stated in the *Lex Licinia*. Very many cases of rightful landholding would need to be considered, for much public land had changed hands several times. The three members of the commission would be Tiberius himself, Gaius, his brother, and Tiberius' father-in-law. Naturally this membership was not popular in the Senate.

It was evident to Tiberius that his agrarian proposals would not be passed by the Senate, and so, relying upon the *Lex Hortensia* of 287 BC, he brought them directly before the people's assembly, the *Comitia*. At this point the Senate played its old game of winning over a tribune to use his power of veto over all legislation. In vain, Tiberius tried to dissuade his colleague from opposing a reform so essential to the welfare of the nation. The Senate had chosen well: the recalcitrant tribune was himself a large landowner. At last, Tiberius proposed the dismissal of the tribune from office for neglecting his duty to serve the best interests of the people. Even when seventeen of the thirty-five tribes of the *Comitia* had voted for dismissal and the rest were about to do so, Tiberius pleaded with the tribune to withdraw his opposition to the reforms rather than be dismissed. Tiberius knew that the dismissal was not clearly in accordance with the constitution of Rome. Magistrates were generally appointed for fixed periods - the consuls and tribunes for one year, the *pontifex maximus* for life, for example - and even their resignation was not generally permitted. The choice before Tiberius was to abandon his present proposals in the face of the veto or carry through, with the full support of the people, a step of doubtful legality. He chose to carry through his reforms.

The tribune was dragged down from office on the eighteenth vote being announced. The agrarian reforms became law as the *Lex Agraria*. The land commission began its work. Much needed to be done, however, and the moment Tiberius' period of office came to an end he could be impeached by the Senate for any misdeeds. The Senate was certain to use this ancient right to attack an ex-magistrate. Tiberius decided that his re-election as tribune was essential, but this, also, was of doubtful legality. By custom no tribune could be re-elected, but in a political crisis could not the people overrule the custom in order to re-elect a tribune whom they regarded as their defender against oppression?

When the time for the annual election of tribunes arrived, Tiberius put himself forward as a candidate, but many of his supporters from the rural districts outside the city were busy with the harvest and could not attend to vote. Tiberius' friends delayed the election for a day by raising some point of law. On the following day, the crowd at the Forum in the city centre, where the election was held, were restless and noisy. It was rumoured that the Senate had hired gangs of thugs, secretly armed. Undeterred, Tiberius walked from his home to the Forum and mounted the rostrum. A message was passed to him that armed men were about to attack him and his followers, so he ordered his friends to stand guard with staves. As he did so, he raised his hand to his head to indicate to the crowd that his life was in danger, whereupon a man in the pay of the Senate ran to the Senate house and shouted out that Tiberius was demanding a crown. This was the constant refrain of those who wished to brand a Roman with the name of tyrant. To seek the throne, to revive the hated monarchy, was the unforgivable crime in Republican Rome. The Senate was awaiting such a cry. Tiberius stood condemned. Except for a few honest patricians, the Senators strode down to the Forum armed with clubs and bench legs. As they went, their hired supporters swelled their number, and the people of Rome fell back before them, out of respect for their office and fear of their anger. Tiberius and his friends were clubbed to the ground. For the first time since the expulsion of Tarquin, blood was shed in civil strife within the city of Rome. Tiberius' body, together with the bodies of three hundred of his followers, was thrown into the River Tiber.

For a time Gaius Gracchus took no part in public life. He was, after all, only about twenty when his elder brother was killed; but when he had distinguished himself by his courage and powers of leadership serving in the Roman army for a few years, he was drawn into politics by popular demand. The people had not forgotten the noble efforts of Tiberius and they recognised his talents in Gaius, whose skill in oratory even exceeded that of his brother. So great indeed was his power of speech that on occasions he was carried away by it himself. It was said that he developed the habit of placing a personal servant behind him on the rostrum, who would quietly sound a tuning fork if Gaius' speech rose above a certain pitch, so that he could return to a more measured delivery.

Gaius was easily elected tribune, when he eventually stood for the office. His energy and popular support at once combined to make him virtual ruler of Rome. He introduced legislation in many fields, all of which was directed at improving the welfare of the nation, regardless of the special interests of the rich group of Senatorial families. Laws were passed to enforce once again the Licinian laws about the distribution of public land, to prevent merchants from deliberately raising the price of corn in Rome, which made bread too expensive for the poorer people, to improve conditions in the army and to allow more citizens to serve on juries (which were previously only open to Senators). These laws ensured Gaius the support of the poor and of many knights, who were wealthier citizens not of Senatorial families, and on the other hand the enmity of the Senate, which found its control of land and public affairs seriously weakened.

Once again unscrupulous members of the Senate set out to defend their interests against the just measures of the Gracchi. This time their weapon was deceit. Again, they used a tribune sympathetic to their cause. He introduced legal reforms even more far reaching than those of Gaius, in order to win over the support of the poor. Promises were made that land would be distributed without any rent at all being payable to the state. While Gaius had proposed founding two new colonies to make land available for landless citizens, a proposal was now made for twelve new colonies. As a result of this kind of political dishonesty, Gaius lost much support amongst the more ignorant people, who could not distinguish between the spirit of justice and mere bribery.

Gaius appealed to the people of Italy beyond the confines of Rome. He told how Roman citizens in Italian cities had been treated with contempt and even gross cruelty by arrogant Senators. There was a case, for example, of a Roman consul who had visited a city and whose wife had wanted to use the public baths, since these were better than the private baths available to them. Everyone else in the city was forbidden to use the public baths during their stay. The consul's wife, however, felt that the baths had not been cleaned sufficiently, so the leading magistrate of the city, a respected and honest man, was ordered to be stripped and flogged, tied to a stake in the market place.

A second case cited by Gaius in his appeal to the Italian people concerned a young man of a Senatorial family, who had served abroad in some minor capacity and was travelling home, carried by slaves on a litter. As he passed through a small village, a local farmer, not seeing who was in the litter, asked in jest whether they were carrying a corpse. The arrogant young man was so offended that he ordered the farmer to be flogged with the leather straps which supported the litter. As a result the farmer died.

Gaius Gracchus knew that such incidents as these reflected the degeneracy of the ruling families of Rome, who wished to hold the position of a ruling elite without honouring its obligations. Gaius knew also that even the ordinary people of Rome often ignored the rights of the Italians who were not Roman citizens. Nevertheless, he tried to form an alliance between the poor in Rome, the Roman knights who wanted to break the Senators' control of the law courts, and the Italian people whose grievances were disregarded. Unfortunately for Rome, the deceitful tactics of the Senators in supporting new laws which bribed the common people, had greatly reduced Gaius' popularity. It was easier now for the Senators, with the aid of consuls and tribunes who sympathised with them, to reverse the reforms of Gaius, which so angered some of the people who sought reform that they made a fatal mistake: they committed a crime which played into the hands of their opponents.

When, on a public occasion in the Forum, an attendant of a consul showed contempt for a group of Gaius' supporters, they killed him by stabbing him to death with styluses, iron tipped writing instruments. Immediately the Senate saw its opportunity. A state of emergency was declared, giving the Senate power to inflict capital punishment without trial or appeal to the people. This contradicted the ancient *Lex Valeria* of 509 BC, the cornerstone of a Roman's freedom from tyranny and a law which Gaius Gracchus himself had been striving to re-instate. Everyone in Rome knew that the crisis had arrived. Everything for which Gaius had fought was now at issue.

Gaius' friends urged him to defend himself. Some armed themselves ready for a fight in the streets of Rome. Gaius carried merely a single dagger beneath his toga, like any public figure of the time. His wife begged him not to go to the Forum. Like Hector's wife, she threw herself at her husband's feet, bewailing her utter dependency upon him, appealing to him to protect his small son, avowing her love. What good could come from deserting his family to offer himself, a helpless victim, to the fury and greed of the Senate and its violent followers? Gaius was unmoved. He bade his wife and son farewell and walked to the Forum.

Already violence had broken out. The Senate had employed a body of archers from Crete, renowned for the skill of its mercenaries. Through the streets of Rome they chased the broken remnants of the reformers. Hearing the tumult, Gaius went with a faithful servant to a quiet grove in the city. The servant killed Gaius with a dagger at the command of his master, and then himself. Later, three thousand of the people who had supported Gaius and his reforms were put to death by order of the Senate. Their bodies, with that of Gaius, were thrown in the Tiber, like Tiberius Gracchus' before them.

Cornelia bore their deaths with noble courage. She did not grieve unduly, for she knew they had died in a worthy cause. Rather than retiring to a life of sorrow and bitterness, she maintained an open house in the town of Misenum on the coast south of Rome, where visitors were always welcome and where she would talk freely of her sons' proud exploits. They had caught a glimpse of justice and seen beyond political struggle and the corruption apparent in Rome. So they had given their lives for the principle of a just community that held land for the benefit of all, as in the days of Numa.

In the city of Rome the victorious Senate consolidated its bloody victory over the reformers by passing laws which ignored the principles of the *Lex Licinia*. Land became essentially under private ownership. All holdings of public land in the occupation of individuals were no longer liable for rent; they were now their property - however they were acquired - which they could buy and sell. An ancient principle that lay at the root of Roman virtue, upon which Rome had been founded and to which men like Spurius Casius, Licinius Stolo and the Gracchi brothers had dedicated their lives - the principle that land is the common heritage of the nation to be held in trust by each generation - was no longer observed in the laws of the Republic.

The principles of justice for which the Gracchi had died were largely forgotten by later generations, even though those claiming to succeed them formed a loosely knit group, called *populares*. Supporters of Senatorial power became known as the *optimates*. During the troubled century that followed, whilst the Republic collapsed, these two factions fought each other for political power. As in most movements of decline, the fundamental questions that the original protagonists debated were forgotten, to become overlain by ambition, revenge and greed. The position of the knights was permanently enhanced, for they continued to serve on juries and to administer the tax farming in the provinces, but these powers were often turned to oppressive uses. Cheap corn for the poor also continued on the political agenda, to be abused by later demagogues; it was, of course, no solution to the underlying question of radical land reform. As for the problem of the Italian allies, which Gaius had identified as political injustice, it was to fester on until the Social War of the early first century AD.

When the Senate built a new Temple of Concord in Rome, soon after the death of Gaius Gracchus, in celebration of the end of ten years conflict between the Senate and the people, a slogan was carved below its name during the night by an unknown hand. It read, "the work of discord."

*Chapter 33*

# Cruel Men of Rome

*Decline of the Republic*

"...how grandly does democracy trample all these fine notions of ours under her feet, never giving a thought to the pursuits which make a statesman, and promoting to honour anyone who professes to be the people's friend."[1]

GRADUALLY THE EFFECTS of ignoring natural justice in the distribution of land were felt throughout Roman society. The gulf between rich and poor became wider, the political life of Rome became subject to the exorbitant claims of the wealthy and the desperation of the mob, and morality declined in the wake of blatant greed and ignorant vengeance. The process of decline was slow but inexorable. It took roughly eighty years, from the murder of Gaius Gracchus to the murder of Julius

*Street in Pompeii*

Caesar. During this time outstanding individuals rose and fell: brilliant generals, like Marius and Pompey, demonic men of action, like Sulla, outright demagogues, like Sulpicius, leaders touched with the spirit of the old nobility, like Sertorius and Cato, men of great elegance and culture like Cicero, and one man whose genius challenged that of Alexander the Great, namely Caesar himself. All of them were caught up in the general turmoil and tragedy of their time. Those who kept free of it did not appear on the stage of history, but prepared for the rejuvenation of Rome, when the blood-letting was ended. For the influence of Platonic philosophy in its Roman form of Stoicism continued and bore fruit under the early Emperors, but philosophers did not intervene in the death-throes of the Republic.

The first man whose career exemplified the deterioration of public life was Marius. He came from humble origins and rose through the army by virtue of his outstanding ability and courage, particularly in the war in Numidia, North Africa, against Jugurtha. His defeat of Jugurtha in 105 BC ensured his appointment by popular acclaim to defend Italy against the huge armies of the German tribes, the Teutones and the Cimbri. These were migrating southwards and swept all opposition before them, until Marius crushed the Teutones in a bloody battle at *Aquae Sextiae* (Aix-en-Provence) in 102 BC and the Cimbri a year later near Ferrara in north Italy. He was acclaimed the third founder of Rome, after Camillus, whose victory over the Gauls in 390 BC had earned him the title of second founder.

Marius' victories owed much to radical reforms of the Roman army introduced under his consulships. The days of the citizen in arms, the self-dependent farmer ready to spring to his community's defence, had gone, as the Macedonian War had indicated a century before. Marius now made the army into a semi-professional force, with the soldiers looking to their *imperator*, or general, for pay and for land on which to retire. When armies were disbanded, they began to demand a *Lex Agraria* under which land was apportioned to them. Generals gained personal ascendancy over their men and allegiance was diverted from the Roman state to the successful general. When generals won wars in the provinces, in Asia, Spain, or Gaul, for example, they became local autocrats, set to threaten Rome itself. The new system of army organisation was thus a potent factor in the later collapse of the Republic.

The tactical reforms of Marius were based upon his own great experience and skill as a campaigning soldier. He re-organised the army into legions of 6000 men in ten cohorts, each of 600 officered by military tribune and six centurions, all under a consul as legion commander. The centurions, especially, were a mainstay of the whole army, for they were always tried veterans, noted for their courage and leadership. Weapons, too, were improved, especially the *pilum*, or throwing spear, which was given a wooden rivet between spearhead and shaft, so that it broke on impact and could not be thrown back by the enemy. Soldiers carried equipment to pitch a fortified camp, making the army much more flexible and rapid in movement. The men became known as "Marius' mules" as a consequence of their extra loads. Training was based on methods used in gladiator schools, in line with the greater professionalism of the troops.

These tactical improvements of Marius made the Roman army into an efficient, fast moving and relentless machine. The granting of silver eagles to each legion further improved its 'regimental' morale. Many Roman soldiers were to give their lives to preserve the eagle and the honour of the legion. It is an irony of history that the creation of such a fighting force coincided with its abuse under the influence of private interests.

The Lex Annalis of 180 BC, which forbad re-election to the consulship within ten years, was ignored by the people in their enthusiasm for Marius. From 105 BC to 100 BC he was elected consul every year. So ambitious had he become that he employed violent popular leaders, notably Sulpicius, to sway the Roman mob in his support. He deliberately antagonised the patricians of the Senate by his arrogant speeches, in order to win the favour of those who were jealous of patrician power and wealth. Yet Marius had no statesmanship and little grasp of political leadership. He became a resentful man, set on recapturing the lost glory of his victories against the Teutones and the Cimbri.

An opponent, equally ruthless and almost as powerful a soldier, rose to confront him, but this man, Sulla, was greatly superior as a politician. Plutarch says of Sulla that he made his quarrel with Marius the first principle of his political life. Certainly he showed on occasion a flagrant disregard of any worthier principles. Like Marius, he acquired a reputation for military success, firstly in Numidia, then in the east and finally in the terrible Social War of 91-87 BC, when the Italian allies fought Rome in a desperate effort to acquire equal political status with the capital. Though citizenship was granted to the Italians, the war cost them and Rome immense suffering and devastation of land.

Sulla, however, had made himself famous by his victories: He marched on Rome, only to find that Marius had seized control of the city with the aid of the demagogue, Sulpicius. Plutarch describes how the rule of law was breaking down under the blows of the lawless rivals for power. The Senate, no longer its own master, did what it was told to do by Marius and Sulpicius. When it was informed that Sulla was marching on Rome, it sent two of the *praetors*, Brutus and Servilius, to forbid him to advance further. These *praetors* spoke somewhat abruptly to Sulla and for this the soldiers were quite prepared to kill them; instead they broke their rods of office, stripped them of their purple-bordered robes, and after subjecting them to many other insults, turned them out of the camp. In Rome there was the greatest despondency among the citizens when they saw their magistrates stripped of their badges of office and heard them report that between Marius and Sulla things had now gone too far for any hope of appeasement.

Sulla's violence won the day. Marius fled from Rome. A foreign war had broken out in the east, against Mithridates, king of Pontus, and Sulla was quick to take Marius' place at the head of the Roman armies. Whilst he was campaigning, Marius once more returned to Rome, this time to ensure his seventh election to the consulship by the use of naked force. As Marius walked through the streets, his bodyguard of freed slaves cut down any man whom he did not greet, so that his own friends were fearful of approaching him in case he was petulant or just slow to acknowledge them. Fortunately for Rome, Marius died before he could bring more degradation upon the Romans.

When Sulla returned to Rome from his successful campaigns in the east, he was confronted with the followers of Marius, aided by some Italian tribes, notably the Samnites. In a long and bloody battle outside the Colline Gate, Sulla defeated them and entered the city, to be met with a populace desperate for a return to peace and order. Three days after the battle, whilst Sulla was speaking before the Senate, cries of terror and pain arose from the nearby Campus Martius. Sulla told the Senators to ignore the disturbance, for it was merely some rebels being punished. He continued with his speech in the knowledge that 6,000 Samnites were being slaughtered in cold blood on his orders. Such calculated violence went beyond even the crude barbarity of Marius and corrupted such men as Crassus and Pompey, who were lieutenants of Sulla.

At Sulla's command, the *Comitia* of the people appointed him Dictator for whatever period he deemed necessary. Such an office in conditions of civil war was far removed from the appointment of a Dictator in the war against Hannibal, which was the last occasion of the use of that ancient office. Now the enemy was within and the Dictator was no longer an exemplar of Republican virtue, like Fabius Maximus. Sulla proceeded to attack all whom he believed to be sympathetic to the cause of Marius. He published lists of names, or proscriptions, several hundred each day; those named were to be hunted down, with rewards for their killers and death for anyone, including relatives, who harboured them. In the town of Praeneste, one man at least showed the Dictator that virtue was not extinguished. Sulla came to Praeneste and at first gave every man there a separate trial before executing him. Finally, however, not having sufficient time at his disposal, he herded them all together into one place and gave orders that the whole lot of them, twelve thousand in all, should be slaughtered. The single exception he made was a man who had been his host; but this man acted nobly indeed. He told Sulla that he would never, for the sake of his own life, be under an obligation to the man who was the murderer of his native place, and joining voluntarily the rest of his countrymen, he was cut down with them.

When Sulla had reduced Rome to abject order by this reign of terror, he passed a series of laws which shifted the balance of power decisively in favour of the Senate, the body which Marius had consistently attacked in the name of the people. These laws showed some understanding of the problems that Rome faced, but they did not deal with the root causes, which included the economic injustice that Tiberius Gracchus had observed so clearly. The Senate was strengthened by the addition of several hundred members, including men of the knightly class, not patricians but owners of land and other property. Sulla was careful, however, to choose as new Senators men who supported him, for he aimed at personal domination, at the same time as seeking to create constitutional safeguards against anyone else becoming singularly powerful. To provide against the rise of another Marius, the *cursus honorum* was strictly defined, with the consulship available only to men of 42 years of age or over. The *Lex Annalis* was re-enacted also.

At the same time Sulla broke the power of the tribunes, who might have frustrated Senatorial supremacy. Their power of veto over legislation was removed; so too was their right to initiate legislation. Most telling of all was a measure which forbad tribunes from holding any other important office after their tribunacy. No ambitious and capable man would stand as a tribune with such a bar attached to it. Sulla also reformed the law courts by returning the right to jury service exclusively to Senators, by prohibiting appeals to the people and by making most of the courts permanent bodies. Some of these judicial changes endured longer than his other reforms; even the Principate of Augustus inherited them.

Finally, Sulla attacked a dangerous abuse, the growth of private interests amongst the provincial governors. By the consistent success of her armies abroad, Rome had by now acquired ten provinces: Sicily, Sardinia and Corsica, the two provinces in Spain, Macedonia, Africa, Asia, Cilicia, Gallia Narbonensis and Cisalpine Gaul. Governors accumulated wealth for themselves, partly by not remitting imperial taxation to Rome, partly by outright plunder. From the east particularly, they shipped immensely valuable art treasures back to Italy, often with little appreciation of their real merits. Worse still, most governors treated the army in their province as personal troops, bound to support them with small regard to allegiance to the Roman state. This was an inevitable consequence of Marius' reform of the army, which made each army commander the pay master of his troops and tied their success in battle to their material rewards. Governors became ambitious, when they saw that they had both wealth and arms at their command.

The fall of the Republic was greatly accelerated by this canker throughout the periphery of the empire, as Plutarch asserts when he compares the ancient Republican generals with those of Sulla's time:

"They thought that to show subservience to their own soldiers was more disgraceful than to show fear in the face of the enemy. But now the generals of this later period were men who had risen to the top by violence rather than by merit; they needed armies to fight against one another rather than against the public enemy; and so they were forced to combine the arts of the politician with the authority of the general. They spent money on making life easy for their soldiers and then, after purchasing their labour in this way, failed to observe that they had made their whole country a thing for sale and had put themselves in a position where they had to be the slaves of the worst sort of people in order to become the masters of the better. This was what caused the exile of Marius and this was what brought him back again against Sulla... And here it was Sulla more than anyone else who set the example. In order to corrupt and win over to himself the soldiers of other generals, he gave his own troops a good time and spent money lavishly on them. He was thus at the same time encouraging the evils both of treachery and of debauchery."[2]

It is hardly surprising that Sulla's attempts to prevent the very evil upon which his own power was founded were of little avail, for he had not undergone a change of heart, only a change of circumstance, which had placed him above the need for those particular corrupt practices. By his legislation provincial governors were prohibited, without the permission of the Senate, from moving their armies outside their province, from starting a war and from leaving the province themselves. Governors were only to be chosen from senior magistrates, like *praetors*, and were to hold office for one year only. All these measures were in themselves admirable, but they could work only with the support of men of goodwill. Self-seeking generals, with wealth and soldiers ready to hand, would soon disregard them. Perhaps it was an indication that the Romans had forgotten the virtues of their forefathers that when Sulla died in the year 78 AD he was given a magnificent funeral and treated like a hero of old.

The pace at which the Republic moved to its doom now accelerated. Shortly before Sulla died, a brave soldier, Sertorius, who retained the ancient respect for justice and temperance, led a revolt in Spain against the dictatorship in Rome, treating his provincial allies and his own soldiers with a humanity that aroused deep loyalty. Since the seizure of Spain from Carthage, a succession of Roman generals had behaved with great cruelty and perfidy in their dealings with the Spanish tribes. For a while Sertorius was the hope of the Romans who still wanted an abiding liberty at home and an empire founded on generosity abroad, but the corruption had gone too far. Sertorius was betrayed and the new star, Pompey - 'the Great', as Sulla had termed him - brought Spain to heel. In Rome itself Cicero spoke out for Republican virtues against the greed and ambition of his generation, but later he, too, would feel the hand of persecution, as his words wounded the rising generation of power-seekers and demagogues.

Whilst Pompey was dominated by ambition, his associate, Crassus, was concerned, above all, with wealth. His immoderate pursuit of it illustrates the unbridled oligarchy of this period. He acquired many silver mines and also large areas of land within the city of Rome itself. Slaves were his victims in the mines, but the people of Rome were as little regarded when they could be exploited by his rapacity. Crassus kept a fleet of fire engines and employed 500 men to watch for fires in the city. When one occurred, he sent his agents to offer a price to the owner of the burning property. Once in his possession, at a derisory price, the building was saved by his fire brigade. By such methods Crassus became the greatest landowner in Rome. The economic rent of land there was far in excess of that anywhere in the empire. So rich did Crassus become that he claimed no man was rich until he could pay for his own army. The wheel had turned full circle from the early days of the sturdy independent farmers, who fought as citizens for the Republic.

In 73 BC the slave population in Italy made a desperate effort to free themselves. Near Capua in the south a revolt began, led by gladiators under a courageous Thracian slave called Spartacus. Since gladiators were trained to fight each other to the death, they had little to lose by revolting. As the slave army grew, it became a formidable force, at first disciplined and well-led. Several Roman contingents were defeated. Spartacus hoped to lead his men northwards through the peninsula to escape to their homes, mainly in Thrace and Illyria. Too many of his men, however, intent on revenge and plunder, broke away into smaller groups. Crassus was appointed to command an army of several legions against the slaves. After a massive engagement, in which 12,000 slaves were killed, of which only two were said to have wounds on their backs, Spartacus knew he had little chance. He died fighting to the last, a noble figure, typical of many warriors captured in Rome's aggressive wars and enslaved for life. Crassus, aided by Pompey, who stole most of the glory, rounded up the remaining rebels and had 6,000 of them crucified along the Appian Way. The road of torment led to the heart of Rome.

To crown their success, Crassus and Pompey were elected consuls together in the year 70 BC. A worse scourge even than the slave army of Spartacus awaited the attention of Pompey. Pirates had seized control of much of the sea and shores of the Mediterranean. Whilst Romans fought each other in civil wars, the power of piracy grew to threaten the existence of the state itself, as Plutarch relates:

"The power of the pirates extended over the whole area of our Mediterranean sea. The result was that all navigation and all commerce were at a standstill;

and it was this aspect of the situation which caused the Romans, who were already short of provisions and expected a real breakdown in supplies, to send out Pompey with a commission to drive the pirates off the seas. Gabinius, one of Pompey's friends, drew up a law by which Pompey was to be given not only the supreme naval command but what amounted in fact to an absolute authority and uncontrolled power over everyone. The law provided that his command should extend over the sea as far as the pillars of Hercules and over all the mainland to the distance of fifty miles from the sea. There were not many places in the Roman world which were not included within these limits; and inside the area also were a number of great nations and powerful kings. Then he was to be given power to choose from the Senate fifteen subordinate commanders to whom he would assign their special tasks, to take from the treasury and from the taxation officials as much money as he wanted, to raise a fleet of 200 ships, and to arrange personally for the levying of troops and sailors in whatever numbers he thought fit."[3]

These were unprecedented powers that were granted to Pompey. Though the "state in danger" is always reason for exceptional concentration of power in the executive government, its abuse in Pompey's case was to be expected. Had he not been a lieutenant of Sulla, quick to observe how ruthless determination, backed by violence, might overthrow law and moderation? In the following year, 66 BC, the Manilian law gave Pompey supreme command in the war against Mithridates in the east. Since he retained control of naval forces, also, "in practice this meant putting the whole of the Roman empire into one man's hands" (Plutarch). Only one member of the Senate, Catulus, had the courage to attack this proposal of Manilius, for Pompey's popularity seemed to place him beyond the reach of Senatorial opposition.

Pompey was immensely successful in the Mithridatic war. By the year 63 BC he had driven Mithridates eastwards to Armenia, conquered Syria and overcome the spirited defence of the Jews, who fought valiantly to preserve their holy city of Jerusalem. Pompey, to emphasise his supremacy, insisted on entering the innermost sanctuary of the Temple in Jerusalem, though he did not desecrate it. His settlement of these eastern conquests, however, was a masterly piece of administration, establishing boundaries of provinces which lasted for centuries. When he returned for his triumph in Rome, he was a popular idol.

Pompey's great gifts, including personal charm and a reluctance to indulge in political scheming, attracted even such men as Cicero, whose support was important, especially after the latter's forthright denunciation of the despicable Catiline. Cicero was consul in the year 63 BC. Catiline was an impoverished noble, who had ruined his life by debauchery and sought to seize power with associates as corrupt as he. By making unscrupulous offers of land and plunder to the dispossessed, they attracted a motley crowd of supporters, whose loyalty proved to be as feeble as Catiline's integrity. Cicero exposed the conspiracy to the Senate, despite his own personal danger, and his prestige in public life later rested mainly on this defence of the Republic. Cicero had been close enough to the assassin's dagger to know that strong government was needed in Rome. Like the extreme Republican, Cato, he probably thought that Pompey was the best man to fill the role of a benevolent dictator.

In the year 60 BC, however, control of Rome and its empire passed to three men, of whom Pompey was one. Crassus and the rising Julius Caesar joined with him to form what has been called the first triumvirate. This union of the greatest soldier of the time, the richest man in Rome and the immensely talented nephew of Marius, who represented the *populares*, or people's faction, was against the spirit of the constitution. It was aimed at supplanting Senatorial authority with naked power. As Plutarch wrote, it was this initial co-operation of Pompey and Caesar, rather than their later hostility, which did more to subvert the legitimate order. Pompey's soldiers virtually controlled Rome. They would surround a building or arrest an opponent at the word of their commander. The rule of law had ended. Its demise marked the approaching close of the chaotic period when generals and demagogues rose and fell, like corks on the turbulent sea of the people's will, a period that Plato would have described as democracy.

For these men - Marius, Catiline, Sulpicius, Crassus, Pompey and the rest - were indeed promoted briefly to honour by professing to be the people's friend, and showed little enough of the statesmanship that Plato had defined. Ambition, not the public welfare, was their incentive. They seized the tiller of the ship of state, not in obedience to its rightful owner, the good of all, but to direct it headlong towards the nearest destination demanded by their own faction. These men were the leaders thrown up by the disparate groups in the late Republic, who did not respect Republican virtues or the ancient constitution, but who wanted in one way or another to attack the oligarchy residing in the Senate. They were *populares* opposing the *optimates*, the conservative faction which fought back under the leadership of Sulla and finally, to some degree, under Pompey. What both sides showed by their methods of violence and corruption was that they had each forgotten the real origin of the dispute, namely the land question, which the Gracchi had valiantly sought to resolve.

The final stage in the fall of the Republic has been summed up by a modern historian:

> "An alliance between the Italian bourgeoisie and the Italian proletariat, headed by ambitious politicians and military leaders, resulted in the collapse of the hegemony of the two privileged orders of Rome, the senatorial and the equestrian, which together had formed a class of large half-feudal landowners and business men who owed their material prosperity to the exploitation of the resources of the state and their political power to their wealth."[4]

The move from oligarchy to democracy was beginning when the Gracchi had brought economic injustice before the conscience of the Republic. Their relative failure to awaken Rome to the inequitable distribution of land and to the neglect of the Licinian laws hastened the growth of the two factions, which saw themselves as the protectors of property rights and the opponents of those rights. Hence the *populares* looked for men who would be the party-leaders in the civil war against property, the definition of tyrants given by Plato. Marius opened up a new prospect for propertyless men. The Roman proletariat, whose fathers, or ancestors, had lost the farms which had once provided the premier citizens of the Republic, flocked to join the professional army of Marius, and the precedent was set for the armies of the provincial generals of the first century BC. Each army was a concealed democracy, its general the people's friend, who would provide its soldiers with pay and booty and see to it that the gratuity of land in Italy was offered on retirement. Thus the generals were less the masters than the servants of their armies, and the most powerful of them translated this relationship into the political arena of the capital, where they danced to the tune of the people's will. Innate Roman pride and the dim memory of timocracy, both enhanced by the rhetoric of Cicero and Cato the Younger, disguised the real character of the age, but in fact the seventy odd years after the Gracchi's downfall were akin to a democracy, and they led, inexorably, to tyranny, which Pompey's soldiers foreshadowed in the streets of Rome.

### References:

1. Plato, *The Republic*, trans. B. Jowett, Random House, New York, 1937, Book VIII, 558.

2. Plutarch, 'Life of Sulla', in *Fall of the Roman Republic*, trans. R. Warner, Penguin, London, 1973, pp. 81-2.

3. Plutarch, 'Life of Pompey', trans. Warner, p. 183.

4. M. Rostovtzeff, *Social and Economic History of the Roman Empire*, O.U.P., Oxford, 1957, preface.

## Chapter 34

# But One Only Man

## *Julius Caesar*

ONCE WHEN CAESAR WAS travelling through the Alps with some troops, they came to a small, miserable village, which his officers derided. Whereupon Caesar said that he would rather be the first man in that village than the second man in Rome. Nature endowed Caesar with supreme qualities of leadership. The men who fought under him in Gaul for many years became utterly loyal to him; some of them, when captured by his enemies, were offered the chance to fight against him to save their lives, but preferred death. He led by example; if a battle became desperate, he would go down and fight in the ranks, so that every common soldier knew that he shared the danger and exertions. He trained his men thoroughly and was severe with cowards or laggards, but openly applauded men of any rank who showed bravery in battle, so that many of his soldiers performed astonishing feats of arms. There were

*Forum, Rome*

cases, for example, of men fighting on when transfixed with javelins, or with an arm lopped off.

Caesar's own courage was worthy of Alexander. When he was cut off from his armies in Gaul during a major revolt of the Gallic tribes, he dressed as a Gaul and made his way through the mountains and the enemy lines, so quickly that the Gauls could not believe that he was really there at the head of his men once more. In Egypt, he was trapped on the end of the mole in the harbour of Alexandria. He jumped into a small boat, which was then overwhelmed by enemy ships. Diving into the sea, he swam several hundred yards to the shore with - it is said - a sheaf of official papers held in one hand above the water; this at the age of fifty-two! When Dictator in Rome, though knowing that there were many people there who might try to kill him, he disbanded his personal bodyguard of Spanish cavalry. If he knew fear, he was its master.

Caesar was not born into a condition which gave him undue advantage in Roman society. He was of the Julii *gens*, which traced its ancestry back to Aeneas and hence to the goddess Venus, and members of the Caesar family held office in Rome before and after his birth in 100 BC; but compared with one of the dominating senatorial families, like the Metelli or the Scipios, the Caesars were not important. Caesar's aunt Julia had been married to Gaius Marius. This influenced Caesar in taking the side of the *populares* against the *optimates* when he began his political career, but the decision was his own; he could have become an *optimate*. Already he perhaps knew that at heart he sought radical change in the government of Rome and recognised the *optimates* as beyond reform.

Unlike Pompey, the man who finally became his deadly rival, Caesar pursued a constitutionally correct path of office for many years. After the usual step of prosecuting alleged enemies of the state in the law courts, he embarked on the *cursus honorum*, rising from a military tribuneship to *quaestor, aedile, pontifex maximus* (in 63 BC) and *praetor*, before standing for the consulship in 59 BC. For him the *cursus honorum* was a means of keeping his political irons in the fire, whilst he gained the experience which he knew was required for whatever great task lay ahead. Pompey, six years his senior, had raised a private army to help the Dictator, Sulla, and then demanded a triumph and a succession of offices, including the consulate, without having first entered the Senate - an unprecedented procedure.

An early insight into Caesar's character was given when, en route to Rhodes to study rhetoric under the famous teacher, Molon, he was captured by pirates. His personality so dominated his captors that they were virtually obeying his orders on the voyage to obtain a ransom. Once released, he raised the money to pay them, but also took some boats and sailed after them, in conformity to a promise he had made to their faces to crucify them all. Sure enough, he caught every one of his captors and had them crucified, though mercifully their throats were cut first.

During these early years Caesar gained vital military experience in Spain. It was there, fighting the warlike tribes in the dry hills of Andalusia, that he realised that he possessed great gifts of generalship and perhaps decided on a soldier's route to power. In the year 63 BC he appeared at the trial of Catiline, having partially implicated himself in Catiline's earlier schemes, but now speaking out to condemn him, not to death, but to life imprisonment. These were troubled years for Caesar in his private life. His first wife, Cornelia, daughter of the Marian consul, Cinna, had died - Sulla had ordered Caesar to divorce her, but he refused - and Caesar then married Pompeia, a relative of Pompey. A serious scandal occurred when Pompeia was alleged to have committed adultery with Publius Clodius, a scoundrel whom Caesar himself employed as a political agent in Rome. Clodius entered Caesar's house disguised as a woman, during the festival of *Bona Dea*, a religious rite reserved for women. Whereupon Caesar divorced Pompeia. Ambition made Caesar careless of his financial security. He spent money lavishly on banquets, public games and bribes. His debts mounted, until Crassus came to his rescue and paid many of the creditors. Plunder from Spain paid others.

Caesar reached the commanding heights of power in the year 60 BC. Pompey was returning from the east, his prestige immense after having destroyed the pirates in a brilliant campaign and having settled, with great administrative skill, the new Roman dependencies in Asia Minor and Syria. Crassus was jealous of Pompey and remembered with bitterness Pompey's stealing of the limelight from him over the suppression of Spartacus. Only Caesar could reconcile the most powerful man and the wealthiest man, which he did with sure diplomacy and self-confidence. The triumvirate was strong enough to overawe the *optimates*. Cato and the other extreme Republicans made Caesar's work easier. They persuaded the Senate to deny Pompey both land for the settlement of his veterans and ratification of the eastern borders of the empire.

In 59 BC Caesar was appointed consul, but the Senate allocated to the new consuls for that year the derisory offices of supervising forests and cattle trails in Italy, and secured by bribery the election of an opponent of Caesar, Bibulus. A marriage was then arranged between Pompey and Caesar's only child, Julia, whilst Caesar himself married Calpurnia, whose father, Piso, became consul in 58 BC. As consul for the year 59 BC, Caesar now began a series of legislative acts.

Firstly, land for Pompey's soldiers was secured, though with difficulty. Bibulus used the tactics of preventing public business by watching the skies for portents whenever the Assembly was convened. Three tribunes also used their veto. Eventually Caesar got some of Pompey's soldiers to make a riot, cowering the opposition into giving way. This resort to violence cost Caesar dearly later, for it rendered him liable to prosecution if he became a private citizen again. Compared with the outrageous violence let loose by Marius and Sulla, it was of small proportion, but for Caesar himself it was a dangerous step towards the abyss of tyranny.

Caesar's own share in the spoils of the triumvirate, besides the consulship of 59 BC, was the governorship of two provinces, Cisalpine Gaul, between the Alps and the Apennines, and Illyricum. Shortly before he took these offices, the governor of Transalpine Gaul died. This was added to Caesar's command. Transalpine Gaul was a strip of territory running from the right bank of the Rhone, along the Mediterranean coast to the upper Garonne and the Pyrenees. Northwards, the huge land of Gaul remained closed to Roman control, if not to Roman influence. It was an area of great potential wealth. The Gauls were amongst the most civilised of European peoples outside the area of Hellenism, competent farmers and highly skilled metallurgists, who also traded with their fellow Celts in Britain. Their priests, the Druids, made secret use of a Greek script, professional bards sang at the banquets of nobles and speech was valued second only to valour. Their misfortune, at this time, was their political disunity. The many tribes - Aedui, Arverni, Suessiones, Bituriges, Veneti, Sequani and many others - did not cooperate. Some indeed, like the Aedui, were allies, or *amicitia*, of Rome.

Naturally Caesar was from the first immensely interested in Gaul beyond the bounds of his command. When a Germanic tribe, the Helvetii, decided to move westwards into central Gaul, under pressure from other Germans, Caesar decided to intervene outside his province. In his own words, he justified this armed intervention:

> "He (Caesar) saw that it would be very dangerous to the Province to have a warlike people, hostile to Rome, established close to its rich cornlands, which were without any natural defences..... Unable to protect themselves or their property, the Aedui sent to ask Caesar for help, pleading that they had always been loyal to Rome, and that it was not right to allow their land to be ravaged almost under the eyes of his army, their children carried off into slavery, and their towns taken by storm."[1]

Swiftly Caesar defeated the Helvetii, driving them back into Germany. In the following year he did the same to the German chieftain, Ariovistus, and his people, the Suebi. At this point Caesar probably made the fateful decision to conquer Gaul. He left his legions to pass the winter within the territory of the Sequani, whilst he went to Italy, but when he returned he sent his army northwards to attack the Belgae, who, he claimed, were conspiring against the Roman forces. Though the Belgae were a warlike people, Caesar's legions soon defeated them, only to find more trouble from the Veneti in south Brittany. They were a maritime people who traded with Britain and hoped that their fleet was invincible. Caesar rapidly built himself a fleet on the River Loire, and the Veneti too were defeated. On the grounds that they had not respected the rights of Roman envoys, Caesar executed all the Veneti leaders and sold the people into slavery. It was intended as an example to all the Gallic tribes. Roman hegemony was to be accepted, or to be enforced.

Certainly Caesar began his campaigns in Gaul with a defensive war to protect the country from invasion by German tribes, but within two years he had decided to make Gaul a Roman dependency. He realised how rich was the land, and he wanted security on the borders of Transalpine Gaul. He believed in the benefits of Roman culture. Yet he knew, also, that here was the perfect opportunity to build an unassailable base for his own political future. With a victorious army at his command, with plunder from the territory, with the prestige of a great northward extension of the empire, he would rival Pompey the Great and challenge the decadent power of the *optimates*. What use did he intend to make of supreme power? Only the outcome sheds some light on this question.

Caesar's treatment of two German tribes, the Usipetes and Tencteri, who had expelled Gallic peoples from their homelands near the north coast, became a permanent stain on his character. After the Germans had broken a truce, he himself felt justified in deceiving their envoys and unexpectedly attacking their settlements. Everyone, including women and children, was massacred by the Romans, who trapped those who fled at the confluence of the Rhine and Moselle. If any justification is possible, it can only be that no further German invasions of Gaul were made for centuries.

In 55 and 54 BC Caesar made expeditions to Britain. The first was a small-scale matter, in which his ships were wrecked by a storm on the beaches of Kent, but the second involved five legions and the largest fleet to cross the English Channel until 1944 AD. The Romans took the stronghold of the British chieftain Cassivellaunus, in Hertfordshire, by storm, but guerilla activity continued. Moreover, the weather again took heavy toll of Caesar's fleet. After about three months of facing British intransigence and climate, the expedition returned, claiming hostages and tribute, which were probably not delivered. Caesar had hoped to cut off British help to their Gallic allies - particularly from the recently arrived Belgae in the south-east - but he may have hoped for great prestige from the submission of an unknown and fabulous island, reputed to be rich in pearls and precious metals.

Meanwhile, in the year 56 BC the triumvirate had been renewed at Luca in Cisalpine Gaul, whither Caesar summoned his partners. Crassus acquired from this meeting the province of Syria for five years; Pompey, a similar term in the province of Spain; both became consuls for 55 BC. Caesar was granted a further five years in his existing provinces. Once more the triumvirate was seen to be an unconstitutional proceeding, manipulating the proper conduct of politics in Rome by means of agents, like Clodius and, later, Mark Antony for Caesar and Milo for Pompey, who swayed the Assembly and threatened the Senators with violence. Reactionary *optimates*, led by Cato, began to look for ways to fight back. The skies darkened over Rome, whilst Caesar basked in the successes of his legions in Gaul and his political manoeuvres at Luca.

Suddenly, in 53 BC, the death of Crassus gave a new twist to the situation. He was murdered by the Parthian leaders after his massive defeat at Carrhae, where he had hoped to break the power of Rome's only rival on its eastern frontiers. Caesar and Pompey were unlikely to co-operate for long. Pompey's wife, Julia, Caesar's daughter, had died the year before. In 52 BC Clodius was killed in a brawl with Milo's ruffians. Everything pointed to a showdown between the two greatest soldiers of the time.

Caesar, however, was busy in Gaul. In 52 BC a great revolt broke out, when for the first time a leader was found capable of uniting the Gallic peoples. Caesar claimed that Vercingetorix gathered support by barbaric methods of torture and devastation, but the unity of numerous tribes between the Loire and the Garonne suggests that patriotism rather than fear was the principal motive. Vercingetorix' tactics were intelligent. He knew that though the Gallic cavalry was superior to the Roman, the infantry could not match the superb discipline and tactical skill of the legions, despite the Gallic reputation for good weapons and fierce bravery. Thus he counselled a war of attrition, cutting Roman supply lines, ambushing isolated units, separating commanders from men, as when Caesar was apparently trapped in winter on the other side of the Alps from his army. Gallic indiscipline frustrated the task of Vercingetorix. At Avaricum (Bourges), for example, the Bituriges insisted on a defensive siege and were stormed by Caesar's veterans. At Gergovia, in the heart of the Arvernian highlands, however, Caesar was severely repulsed when trying to take Vercingetorix' fortress. It was Caesar's only major defeat in Gaul.

He recovered, of course, driving the Gauls into a great fortified camp at Alesia (in modern Burgundy). The legionaries now showed their mastery of military engineering by building a massive double ring of intricate earthworks around Vercingetorix' army.

When a huge levy of Gallic tribesmen came to relieve the siege, they could not penetrate the outer ring and were eventually scattered by Roman attacks. Vercingetorix was starved out. The Gallic leader put on his finest armour, had his horse carefully groomed and rode out to meet his conqueror. Caesar received him sitting down. Later, Vercingetorix was taken to Rome to be led through the streets at Caesar's triumph, and some years afterwards he was strangled in the same cell in the Mamertine prison near the Forum where King Jugurtha had been similarly done away with half a century before.

A few minor rebellions kept the flame of Gallic independence flickering. Caesar's patience was running out. He suppressed a rising at Uxellodunum on the river Lot; this is his account of the outcome:

"Caesar saw that his work in Gaul could never be brought to a successful conclusion if similar revolts were allowed to break out constantly in different parts of the country; and his clemency was so well known that no one would think him a cruel man if for once he took severe measures. So he decided to deter all others by making an example of the defenders of Uxellodunum. All who had borne arms had their hands cut off and were then let go, so that everyone might see what punishment was meted out to evildoers."[2]

The supreme test of Caesar's political career was approaching. Despite his intense activity in Gaul, he had kept in close touch with affairs in Rome, partly by exchanging letters with his supporters, partly by the meetings he held in Cisalpine Gaul. Cato remained his implacable enemy. Now the consul for 50 BC, Marcellus, brought forward a proposal to make Caesar lay down his commands unilaterally. A fierce debate began in Rome, centred on the question of how to bring, or prevent, a prosecution of Caesar for earlier illegalities, notably those committed under his consulship in 59 BC. Once his governorships expired he would be liable for prosecution as a private citizen, unless he could obtain a new office to run consecutively. If he went to Rome himself, he could not legally take his army with him. A law of Sulla forbade a governor from crossing into Italy with his army. Rome was a likely death-trap for Caesar unarmed. Could he then stand for office *in absentia*? Only the Senate could give him permission to do this.

Whilst the argument raged, Pompey hesitated. In his hands were the means to control affairs in Italy by force, since he exercised his governorship of Spain, with Senatorial permission, from Rome, and the legions in Italy would scamper to his side, as he said, whenever he stamped his foot. Marcellus knew this. Without consulting the Senate, he went to Pompey, himself no longer a consul, and offered him a drawn sword, symbol of the military command of Rome and of all Italy. On hearing this news, Caesar instantly sent a proposal to the Senate, read there on January 1, 49 BC, that both he and Pompey should disarm simultaneously. It was Caesar's last effort to avoid a bloody civil war, at which he had not connived. The Senate, following the lead of Cato and Marcellus, rejected the proposal and treated Caesar as a public enemy.

Ten days later Caesar took his troops to the little River Rubicon, which marked the boundary between his province and Italy. Here he hesitated and discussed matters with his closest advisors. As never before, perplexity and doubt came upon him. The fate of the Roman world lay in his hands. How much he balanced ambition against the welfare of the people of the whole empire can never be told. He had long realised that Republican government was disintegrating, that a city which had governed itself and Italy with political acumen was running short of the men and institutions fit to govern an empire. Perhaps he believed that a strong monarchy was the only way. Undoubtedly, he believed that if it had to be a monarchy, he was the man destined to be monarch. From Plato had sprung the concept of the aristocratic ruler, the philosopher king, exemplified, however imperfectly, by Alexander the Great and the petty kings of Asia Minor and the east who had succeeded him. Now the Roman Republic was moving inexorably towards government by a single ruler, be he wise or not. What greater challenge could there be for a man like Caesar, aware of his unique mastery of the military and political arts?

An hour or so of doubt was enough for such a man. "Let the die be cast!" he exclaimed, and gave orders for the river crossing. City after city opened their gates to him as he marched to Rome. In the capital the *optimates* panicked. Pompey himself fled southwards and decided to abandon Italy in favour of gathering a strong army in Greece. With coolness, Caesar dealt with his opponents in Spain before he followed Pompey across the Straits of Otranto. After a severe set-back attacking Pompey's fortified position near the coast - when Caesar admitted that Pompey should have defeated him - the two armies met at Pharsalus in Macedonia. Caesar had drawn Pompey into the hills away from his supplies; nevertheless, Pompey had a fine force, especially in cavalry, more than twice the size of Caesar's.

Pharsalus demonstrated Caesar's military foresight. For when he saw the brilliant display of Pompey's cavalry - proud, young men on splendid horses - and anticipated that Pompey intended to win by sending his whole cavalry against Caesar's strongest unit, the famous Tenth Legion, veterans of Gaul, he ordered six specially chosen cohorts to move from the rear of the army and stand hidden behind the Tenth Legion. He told these men not to throw their *pilae* (spears), but to move forward and use them for thrusting upwards at the faces of the enemy riders. The cavalry attack came as expected; the terrible shock of the cohorts tactics broke the spirit of Pompey's best troops. Caesar's infantry completed the task, for Pompey himself was dispirited by the repulse to his cavalry.

Caesar always showed mercy to defeated Romans. When he walked into Pompey's camp and saw the carnage, he groaned aloud and said, "They made this happen; they drove me to it. If I had dismissed my army, I, Gaius Caesar, after all my victories, would have been condemned in their law courts."[3] Many survivors of Pompey's army were welcomed into Caesar's forces, including Marcus Brutus. Pompey himself did not survive for long. He fled to Egypt and was cut down when he stepped ashore by Egyptians who feared the wrath of Caesar.

It took three more years to complete the rout of the Republican forces. At Thapsus, in North Africa, Caesar crushed one army, whilst the forlorn Cato committed suicide to avoid humiliation. At Munda, in Spain, he crushed another. In Alexandria he was briefly in great danger from a civil war, and found time to dally with the beautiful Ptolemaic Greek queen, Cleopatra, possibly fathering her son, whom she called Caesarion. But these were intervals between starting a programme of reform, which, at last, showed what Caesar's real aims were.

From 49 BC, until his death in 44 BC, Caesar took many of the magisterial offices to himself: he was consul for most years, *censor*, commander-in-chief of the army, and he accepted the sanctity of status of a tribune. Like Sulla before him, he took the office of Dictator, at first briefly, then for ten years and, finally, in 44 BC, for life. Above all, he named himself *Imperator*, not merely in the limited sense of a holder of the *imperium*, or military authority, but one worthy to hold the highest office. Hence from Caesar arose the later meaning of 'emperor'.

As a man of action, however, Caesar was concerned, not with titles, but with how supreme power might be used. The germ of universal monarchy which had fructified momentarily in the mind of Epaminondas, then in the fabulous career of Alexander, came to fruition in Caesar. In him, Plato's conception of the philosopher king broke painfully through the mould of practical rationalism and military efficiency which were the natural qualities of this most gifted of all the Romans. For Caesar had a vision of the Roman *imperium* which transformed history. He saw that the ancient Republic had become incapable of governing the empire it had acquired; that the *optimates* were irrevocably corrupt, like Crassus, or narrow-minded, like Cato; that the *equites*, or knights, were inordinately greedy; that the common people, at least, in Rome, were becoming a dispossessed and workshy rabble; and that the army was quicker to serve its next benefactor than the state in the name of which it fought.

*Insula, Ostia*

For five years, therefore, Caesar laboured to put things right. His guiding idea was that of a universal empire, in which Rome and Italy would take the provinces into partnership and feed them with the arts of civilisation which had been inherited from Greece and the east. Citizenship was extended beyond Italy; as early as 49 BC,

Caesar rewarded Cisalpine Gaul, which had supplied him readily with soldiers, by making its freemen citizens of Rome. Where he did not grant full citizenship, he extended the Latin rights, which gave local independence; for example, to Toulouse, Vienne, and Avignon. The new citizens, from Gaul or Sicily or Africa, might even rise to magisterial office, even to the Senate. Moreover, Caesar founded Roman colonies throughout the empire, particularly in the west. Seville, Tarragona, Arles and Lyons were all his foundations, and at Carthage and Corinth he deliberately built colonies upon the ruins of once great cities.

One purpose of these new foundations was to relieve the insidious problem of the landless population in Italy, and especially in Rome. From the capital about 100,000 of this proletariat established new lives in provincial colonies. At the same time Caesar reduced the recipients of free corn to half their former numbers, and yet improved the supply of corn by the construction of a great artificial harbour at Ostia on the mouth of the Tiber. In Rome, he offered the citizenship to all medical practitioners and other liberal professions. Army veterans he settled on land in Italy. In Italy, also, he reformed the government of the *municipia* by standardising local magisterial careers and improving the census. In all such measures, Caesar introduced the same systematic and efficient working which characterised his own life.

Caesar's law which insisted that one-third, at least, of those employed in pastoral farming should be free men, hinted at a recognition of the evils of slavery; but even he, in the five years available to him, did not deal with the land problem, which was responsible for the most fundamental divisions in Roman society and was eventually to bring Rome to destruction. However, he dealt decisively with its most troublesome symptom, the problem of debts. Crassus, the richest man of his time, had made his fortune from buying land cheaply and holding it until its price rose many times over. The proletariat, the poorest in Rome, were the men with no land. In between these extremes were creditors and debtors, whose position stemmed mainly from the claims they held, or lacked, to land or to its economic rent. Catiline and his desperadoes had been a group of debtors who hoped to cancel all debts and win the support of debtors of every rank. Catiline's opponent, Cicero, had emphasised that the preservation of property rights was a condition for the survival of the Republic.

Many supporters of the *populares* had hoped that Caesar would prove as extreme as Catiline in his approach to the debt problem, but Caesar was not a social revolutionary. In two far-reaching, but responsible, reforms, he made all interest payments, even past ones, count as repayments of capital, thus reducing outstanding debts by one quarter. Furthermore, he ordered that creditors must accept payments in land valued at prices before the civil war - which had caused a large fall in land values. Thus the working proprietor, notably the peasant farmer outside Rome, was helped to avoid bankruptcy. For the first time since the Gracchi's legislation, Italian farmers found their situation improving. The great creditors, of course, did not welcome such radical steps.

Caesar's fertile mind teemed with ambitious projects for the benefit of the people of Italy and the empire. The Pontine marshes near Rome and a large mountain tarn in Central Italy were drained. A ship canal would be cut through the Isthmus of Corinth. New roads would drive through the Apennines. The centre of Rome would be relieved of congestion and a new Forum and public buildings would be created there. Only some of these yielded results. A temple dedicated to the clemency of Caesar was built during his lifetime; the Corinth canal on the other hand was only completed in the 1890s! Reform of the calendar was one of Caesar's finest achievements. The existing Roman one was seriously out of step with the seasons. With the aid of an Egyptian astronomer, he introduced the system of 365 days in a year, with an extra day every fourth year.

What had caused the civil war, from which Caesar arose the victor, was the tendency for provincial governors to build themselves independent positions of power. These were based upon the extortion of taxes and plunder from their provinces and the conversion of their armies into personal followers, intent on payment in land and loot for their services. Caesar cut through this anarchic system. He had already tightened up the law against extortion, when he was consul in 59 BC. Now he reduced taxation in the wealthiest provinces - those in the east - and transferred the rights of collection from tax-farmers, usually *equites*, to municipal governments. In Asia and Sicily he introduced a land tax. A shorter limit was placed on the term of governorships. As for the question of military command, Caesar's assumption of the name *Imperator* heralded direct control of all Roman armies by him personally. The governors of provinces became his agents. On recall they could be tried by impartial judges. Moreover, Caesar had learnt in Gaul how to work through a small expert bureaucracy of staff officers, directly responsible to him. This system he expanded to include *legati* or *praefecti* in provinces who could overrule the *de jure* magistrates. It was the beginning of an imperial administration which would last through the centuries into the Byzantine empire.

Such measures were signs of autocracy. So too was Caesar's disregard for the Senate, which he enlarged to about 900 by the addition of many Italian and provincial citizens, and which he treated as no more than an advisory council. Yet, at the same time, Caesar allowed much more local autonomy throughout the empire than ever before. The government of Rome might be an autocracy, but the empire had the chance of becoming a commonwealth. Here again was the universalism of Alexander the Great, when he forced his Macedonians, jealous of their privileges, to accept equality with the Asian newcomers to his empire. Both men were visionaries, whose political ideas raised them above the more parochial minds of most of their contemporaries. Both created bitter enemies amongst those who would not open their hearts beyond the confines of the national state.

Caesar's enemies accused him of aiming at the fateful title of *Rex*, or king. He denied it, though he probably acknowledged to himself that he wanted the substance without the name of kingship. Disaffected Senators gathered around Cassius, a supporter of Pompey whom Caesar had forgiven and promoted to office, and Marcus Brutus, a favourite of Caesar, but known for his Republican sympathies. Caesar was preparing a massive military expedition against the Parthian kingdom to recover the Roman standards lost at Carrhae, where Crassus had died, and to secure the eastern borders of the empire; perhaps even to conquer the Parthians and rival the Asiatic empire of Alexander. A plan was mooted to return via Dacia (modern Rumania) and Germany, to subdue those troublesome areas also. Were he to succeed, Caesar would become an unexampled hero-emperor. Already his head appeared on Roman coins, as no living ruler had yet been portrayed. Divine honours were offered him.

Had the Egyptian queen, who had followed him to Rome after his affair with her in Alexandria, become his evil genius, inspiring him with a new vision of an eastern God-King?

On the Ides of March the conspirators struck, as Caesar sat in the Senate house, conducting public business from the curule chair:

"... those who had come prepared for the murder all bared their daggers and hemmed Caesar in on every side. Whichever way he turned he met the blows of daggers and saw the cold steel aimed at his face and at his eyes. So he was driven this way and that, and like a wild beast in the toils, had to suffer from the hands of each one of them; for it had been agreed that they must all take part in this sacrifice and all flesh themselves with his blood. Because of this compact Brutus also gave him one wound in the groin. Some say that Caesar fought back against all the rest, darting this way and that to avoid the blows and crying out for help, but when he saw that Brutus had drawn his dagger, he covered his head with his toga and sank down to the ground. Either by chance or because he was pushed there by his murderers, he fell down against the pedestal on which the Statue of Pompey stood, and the pedestal was drenched with his blood, so that one might have thought that Pompey himself was presiding over this act of vengeance against his enemy, who lay there at his feet struggling convulsively under so many wounds. And many of his assailants were wounded by each other, as they tried to plant all those blows in one body."[4]

Caesar died as he had lived, by the sword, for he was a man of blood. In the year of his first consulship, he had turned Pompey's soldiers loose in the city. He had allowed Clodius to support him as a client by violent methods. He had slaughtered the German tribes who had settled in Gaul, and treated the Veneti and the survivors of Uxellodunum with barbarous severity. He had crossed the Rubicon, knowing that he thereby plunged Italy into civil war. These things he did as acts of policy. The sword was drawn for a political end: to secure and pacify Gaul, or to defeat his enemies in the civil war. Until the formation of the first triumvirate, he pursued power more or less constitutionally through the *cursus honorum*. After that he operated in the naked arena of power politics, exchanging blows with the other political gladiators who entered the ring: Crassus, Pompey, Cicero, Cato and the rest. They did not all use his methods; Cicero, for example, used only the sharpness of his tongue. Yet Cicero did not achieve supreme power, or, at least only momentarily to dispel the conspiracy of Catiline.

What kind of man was Caesar? Essentially he was a man of action and, like every individual a focus through which the forces of nature were brought to bear upon time and place; but in him these forces were of a unique quality and power. His speed in decision, his knowledge of the right time to act, whether on the battlefield or in diplomacy or politics, amounted to genius, and the charisma of his personality bought men of all ranks to his side. With such ability, driven by a demonic energy, he could not fail to dominate his age. Moreover, Rome had come to a point of decision. The decline of the Republic could have been arrested at the time of the Gracchi; by the first century BC it was too late. A terrible drama was moving to its conclusion, but within the drama a decision had to be made. Marius, Sulla, Pompey - each in turn dominated the scene by the power of arms. So, too, did Caesar, but he intervened to transform the blind clash between over-powerful generals into the emergence of a new form of government, the *imperium* of one man. In addition, he brought to the play a nobility of character which was lacking in the other power mongers. Time and again he forgave his Roman enemies. When he invaded Italy, those who resisted him were welcomed back into his fold when they had submitted. After Pharsalus he took Cassius, Brutus and other former lieutenants of his, who had joined Pompey, and promoted them to office. When the poet, Catullus, abused him, Caesar invited him to dinner. He turned with loathing from the Egyptian who brought him Pompey's head, and burst into tears at his great rival's signet ring, on which was engraved a lion holding a sword in its paws.

His relationships with women were no better or worse than most men of his time. Roman morality, with its ancient emphasis upon the sanctity of family life, was in headlong decline. Like most soldiers, he could not live a regular married life, and he did not regard sexual restraint as a necessary virtue. The wildest stories, such as that he seduced Pompey's wife in the time of the first triumvirate, are hardly consistent with his character as a man who valued the pursuit of power far higher than his own pleasures.

If women did not trust him, his soldiers did. No leader since Homeric times, including Alexander, commanded greater loyalty. Whence did it come? Not from the desire for success, pay or plunder. Roman soldiers wanted those, but they found in Caesar a man they could admire as no other, a man of unquenchable spirit and resolution in warfare, whose energy, courage and speed of decision and movement was god-like; who would never desert them and would always fight at their side as a brother-in-arms. For what Caesar possessed was the power, if not the true nobility, of a *kshatriya*, of the warrior caste. He was never petty. It was he, not Mark Antony, who bestrode the world like a Colossus. No other could do so, as Shakespeare said:

> "Age, thou art sham'd.
>
> Rome thou hast lost the breed of Noble Bloods.
>
> When went there by an Age, since the great Flood,
>
> But it was fam'd with more than with one man?
>
> When could they say (till now) that talk'd of Rome,
>
> That her wide walls encompassed but one man?
>
> Now is it Rome indeed, and room enough
>
> When there is in it but one only man."[5]

### References:

1. Caesar, *The Conquest of Gaul*, trans. S. A. Handford, Penguin, London, 1956, ch. 2, pp. 43-4.

2. Caesar, *The Conquest of Gaul*, ch. 8, p. 257.

3. Plutarch, 'Life of Caesar', in *Fall of the Roman Republic*, trans. R. Warner, Penguin, London, 1973, p. 288.

4. Plutarch, 'Life of Caesar', p. 306.

5. Shakespeare, *Julius Caesar*, act I, scene 2.

## Chapter 35

# A Better Age of Gold

### *The Rule of Augustus*

"I would then have the reader trace the process of our moral decline, to watch, first, the sinking of the foundations of morality as the old teaching was allowed to lapse, then the rapidly increasing disintegration, then the final collapse of the whole edifice, and the dark dawning of our modern day when we can neither endure our vices nor face the remedies needed to cure them. The study of history is the best medicine for a sick mind... for I do honestly believe that no country has ever been greater or purer than ours or richer in good citizens or noble deeds: none has been free for so many generations from the vices of avarice and luxury; nowhere have thrift and plain living been for so long held in such esteem. Indeed, poverty, with us, went hand in hand with contentment. Of late years wealth has made us greedy, and self-indulgence has brought us, through every form of sensual excess, to be in love with death both individual and collective."[1]

*Maison Caree, Nimes*

THUS WROTE LIVY ABOUT twenty years after the murder of Julius Caesar. The degeneration that he observed around him was evident enough, though most Romans chose not to see it, or to call it progress. Sexual immorality, particularly adultery amongst the upper classes, was commonplace; the extensive slums of Rome put to shame the greed and ostentatious living of the wealthy minority; the populace in Rome expected a regular entertainment of barbarous shows in the arena, where men and wild beasts alike were slaughtered in their thousands; in the provinces, despite the brief effort of Caesar, corruption and taxation oppressed all but the privileged.

Yet even before Caesar died, in the period following the rule of Sulla, a beginning had been made in the massive task of regeneration. A Greek philosopher, Panaetius, founder of a Stoic school in Rhodes, had begun to teach in Rome itself. His follower, Posidonius, later hailed as the wisest man of his generation, continued to build a school in Rome and taught Cicero, Cato the Younger and Marcus Brutus. Amongst the Roman nobility he found many other pupils, who deplored the current decline in morality.

Panaetius' teaching was derived from Plato. His recognition of the natural hierarchy of things and men led him to postulate four kinds of duties; the highest was *sapientia*, the search for truth itself; then came *justitia*, the preservation of society; then, *animi magnitudo*, the achievement of greatness of character; and finally, *modestia* or *temperantia*, self-control. *Sapientia*, as Plato affirmed, was a prerogative of the highest class in society, the sages who preserved the traditional knowledge; *justitia* depended upon harmony between classes, when each fulfilled the role for which it was best suited. *Animi magnitudo*, related to the leaders of society; like the courage of Plato's warrior class, it was to be emulated by men of lesser status. Whilst *temperantia* was a quality to which all might aspire, including the *demos* or common people, whose tendency, when badly governed, was towards gross intemperance. When Augustus revived the great religious festivals of Rome, he took care to demonstrate the hierarchy of emperor, provincial governor, local leading citizens and the ordinary people. Memory of a natural hierarchy had been awakened.

Under Posidonius, the Stoic School in Rome derived morality from the idea that everything in the universe was united in an all-embracing power, called *sympatheia*. This power was benevolent and its form was divine fire, a doctrine which recalled the primeval fire of Rome, guarded by the Vestal Virgins. Educated Romans could find reborn the teaching of Numa Pompilius, whilst some felt a connection with a supreme power which enabled them to contribute to the remarkable creative work of the Augustan period. One of these was the greatest Latin poet, Virgil, who expressed this rediscovered unity in the *Aeneid*:

> "... one common soul
> Inspires and feeds, and animates the whole.
> This active mind, infus'd thro' all the space,
> Unites and mingles with the mighty mass.
> Hence men and beasts the breath of life obtain;
> And birds of air, and monsters of the main.
> Th' ethereal vigor is in all the same,
> And every soul is fill'd with equal flame."[2]

Pythagorean ideas influenced Posidonius. His five books on astrology treated the Sun as the controller of the other heavenly bodies and, since it was visible fire, as the symbol of *sympatheia* itself. Later, Augustus adopted the Sun, or *Sol*, as the mark of his own supreme power, identifying it with Apollo, the god under whose special protection he claimed to rule. Posidonius also followed Pythagoras in recognising the transmigration of souls. Virgil assimilated this, too, and expressed it in the great scene where Aeneas is shown the workings of the underworld. After being purged by wind and water and fire of its sins:

> "... the pure ether of the soul remains.
> But, when a thousand rolling years are past,
> (So long their punishments and penance last),
> Whole droves of minds are, by the driving god,
> Compell'd to drink the deep Lethaean flood,
> In large forgetful draughts to steep the cares
> Of their past labours, and their irksome years,
> That, unremembr'ring of its former pain,
> The soul may suffer mortal flesh again."[3]

As Julius Caesar marched inexorably towards worldly glory and some measure of immortal fame, the ground was thus being prepared for a revival of the Roman nation and for the culture which had raised her to greatness. The political instrument was to be Caesar's great-nephew, his adopted son and heir, Octavian. It was perhaps Caesar's most significant decision, to choose a man who would prove to be a great administrator and a master of politics as the art of the possible. Octavian was born at Velletri, south-east of Rome, the son of a senator who reached the rank of *praetor*, and of a niece of Caesar's, but it was his adoption by Caesar, of course, which brought him rapidly to the forefront. He showed his sense of destiny by claiming his inheritance as Caesar's heir directly after the murder on the Ides of March; he was only nineteen and his elders had advised him to remain at his studies in Apollonia in Greece.

For thirteen years he learnt how to command and fight in the hard school of civil war. At Philippi in Macedonia the Republican forces, under Cassius and Brutus, were crushed. Octavian, Antony and Lepidus, the *pontifex maximus*, had already formed the second triumvirate, a grouping given constitutional authority by the Senate. Even before Philippi they had carried out a terrible proscription, worthy of Sulla, killing 300 senators and 2000 *equites* by calculated decision. Cicero was amongst those executed, for his enemy, Antony, persuaded Octavian, against his better judgement, to do away with perhaps the noblest Roman of his time, the man who had laboured to bring Stoicism to a wide audience in Rome and to preserve legal government from the predator warlords. Later, Octavian did not lose the capacity to be cruel when he felt it was necessary, but, like his great-uncle, he was rarely wantonly so.

The civil war came to an end in 31 BC, when the fleet of Antony and Cleopatra was destroyed at Actium, off the west coast of Greece, by Octavian's brilliant admiral, Agrippa. Antony had allowed himself to be seduced by the beauty and wiles of the Egyptian queen. He was a man of great talent, especially as a war leader, and aspired to create a kind of Graeco-Roman empire ruled from Alexandria, but his determination succumbed to his sensuality. As star-crossed lovers, he and Cleopatra committed suicide, though Cleopatra did not take her life until she had tried and failed to win Octavian, as she had won Caesar and Antony. This was not the least of Octavian's many examples of self-discipline!

It took him four more years to pacify the Roman empire. In 27 BC he laid down the extraordinary powers granted him, and, to all appearances, restored the Republic; but Rome was ready for the benevolent rule of one man:

"The Father has loosed upon earth sufficient
snow and hail, smitten with his livid
right hand the sacred heights and terrorised
Rome our city,...
Which God shall the people call to affairs
of tottering empire? With what prayer shall
holy virgins beset pure Vesta not
heeding their hymns?
To whom shall Jupiter assign the role
of atonement? Come at length, we pray,
prophetic Apollo, swathing in cloud
your bright shoulder."[4]

Apollo and Mars were the gods to whom Octavian appealed for help in his great task of restoring equity and Roman arms. Many Greeks lived in Rome and Roman culture was aware of its debt to the great god of Delphi, the light of whose gaze brought harmony and peace to suppliants from every corner of the known world. At Philippi "Apollo" had been the watchword of the army. At Actium a sanctuary to Apollo overlooked the embattled fleets. On the Palatine hill in Rome, Octavian, now Augustus, built a great temple to the Greek god; in it were housed the Sybilline Books. The Julian *gens* had long worshipped Apollo under the Roman name of Vediovis.

*Courtyard of gladiators' barracks, Pompeii*

Octavian "transferred the State to the free disposal of Senate and people," but he retained the consulship to himself for many years and, above all, kept control of the army. His methods were simple and effective. The provinces were shared out between himself and the Senate; he retained those provinces where the army was essential for maintaining security, namely Spain, Gaul and Syria. He also retained the richest province of all, Egypt, appointing there a Roman knight as his special envoy. Senatorial provinces had few soldiers and were governed by pro-consuls appointed by the Senate - though even these had the tacit approval of Octavian. He took the title of *princeps*, or first citizen, to emphasise the Republican form, but to underline his real power, he accepted the name of Augustus. This was derived from the word *auctoritas*, implying his original authority, and related to the practice of augury, symbolic of the ancient prophetic power of the past rulers of Rome from Romulus and Numa.

Virgil in the *Georgics* called upon the great pantheon of Rome to support the new monarch, who held the sacred *imperium*. Mars was the god who would right the wrongs of the old order. When Augustus, in 2 BC, opened the splendid temple of Mars Ultor (the Avenger) at the end of the Forum Augusti, it contained statues of the great generals of Rome, set between the huge white Corinthian columns of the portico and the brightly coloured marble walls of the interior. Every new soldier of Rome was to worship there, dedicating his life to the service of the god who had avenged the mighty Caesar and protected the sacred person of the *Imperator*. Despite tradition, Mars was presented as the consort of Venus, ancestral mother of the Julii *gens*.

After a spell of campaigning in Gaul and Spain, Augustus was taken seriously ill in 23 BC. When he recovered, he revised his position in the constitution, resigning the consulship and accepting instead an *imperium majus*, which gave him unique power over all the proconsuls who governed in the provinces and an undefined superiority over all magistrates. At the same time he took the tribunician power (*tribunicia potestas*) without the actual title of tribune. By this means he acquired the sanctity of a tribune, the power formally to veto legislation and to convene the Senate, and the aura of a democrat defending the interests of the people, even though, for practical purposes, he looked to the upper classes, especially the *equites*, as the foundation of his support. For three years he travelled in Sicily, Greece and Asia, reorganising, exhorting, advertising his *auctoritas* in far domains. Agrippa, now his son-in-law and deputy *princeps*, was his strong right arm, especially in war. In 20 BC the Parthians returned to Agrippa the standards taken from the stricken Crassus after the battle of Carrhae. Nothing pleased Augustus and Rome more.

On his return, Augustus initiated a new step in the revival of Italy and the Empire. He passed laws encouraging marriage and the lawful procreation of children. Adultery by women and the condoning of it by husbands became crimes, and so too were extra marital intercourse with a woman of high status. For at least two generations the sexual morality of the higher classes in Rome had been in decline. The status of women had changed profoundly from the days of the dutiful and virtuous wife of the ancient Republic. Women moved freely in the city, they encouraged their spouses' or lovers' political ambition and played a social role equal to that of men. They could own and manage property in their own right. As a consequence marriage easily became a matter of political convenience. Sulla had five wives, Pompey five, Caesar four and Octavian three. Family life was disregarded in the quest for personal advantage from marriage, liaisons and divorce. Frequent excursions to the fashionable resorts on the Bay of Naples, like Baiae and Puteoli, contributed to the laxity of morals in the capital. Horace was aware of the need for action to correct disastrous conditions:

> "Teeming with sin, the times have sullied
> first marriage, our children, our homes:
> sprung from that source disaster has whelmed
> our fatherland and our people.

> "The generation that dyed the Punic Sea
> with blood and laid low Pyrrhus,
> Anthiochus and Hannibal was not born
> of parents such as these."[5]

and in his Centennial Hymn at the Secular Games in the year 17 BC, held with great pomp of ancient ritual to purify the Roman people of past sins and inaugurate a new age of religion, Horace explicitly assented to the *princeps'* legislation:

"Goddess, rear our young and prosper the Senates' edicts on wedlock, that the new law on the marriage of women produce abundant children."[6]

Augustus' own daughter, Julia, disgraced herself and her father by infamous sexual licence. With a true Roman's regard for the public weal, he banished her to the tiny island of Pandeteria and maintained a rigid control over her personal life, refusing to ameliorate the sentence even when the Senate pleaded for it.

A terrible sense of guilt possessed those Romans who were not so debased as to be beyond redemption. Memories were filled with images of bloody civil war, of the murderous proscriptions of Sulla and the second triumvirate, of the head of Pompey the Great sent to Rome by fawning Egyptians, of the crucifixion of slaves along the Appian Way, of beatings and riots stirred up by Clodius and Milo in the streets of the capital, of the adultery and broken families of the leading members of the state, of the urban proletariat besotted with the gory spectacles of the arena, and of the ruined farmers of Italy, crouching on the ancient land, the farms, where once "every year the earth, untilled, yields corn; and the vines, unpruned, forever bloom; and the never failing sprigs of olive bud; and dusky figs adorn their trees; and honey drips from the hollow oak."[7]

People cried out for a deliverer from their distress. What value was freedom amidst such suffering of guilt and disorder?

> "Whoever may wish to root out
> seditious killings and internecine madness,
> if he aspire to be styled
> on monuments Father of Cities, oh let him dare
> to bridle unbroken licence
> and his fame will shine down to posterity."[8]

Augustus responded to the call of the better men of his generation, of Horace, Livy and Virgil, of Agrippa, his general, of Maecenas, his cultural *alter ego*. Cicero was not there, but his shade nodded approval to the man who had assented to his murder. And so Augustus instituted a complete revival of Roman religion and morality, calling upon the long tradition derived from Numa, the true *pater patriae* of Rome. After reforming the order of *equites* in 28 BC, Augustus had revived the religious rite of the *lustrum*, the solemn purification unused for 41 years. He had revived the Fetiales, makers of just war, even as early as the war against Cleopatra. The *salii* or priests of war, once more danced their sacred martial rites. The gates of Janus were closed three times in Augustus' *principate*; only under Numa and at the end of the first Punic War had they so signified a time of peace. Other colleges of priests were established; some to give annual offerings at the Ara Pacis, the great sculptured altar dedicated by Augustus to the peace of the world. For the common people, the cult of *compita* - rites held at crossroads - met their religious aspirations and assured them of the attention of their benevolent master.

Much religious ritual was centred upon Augustus himself, but he did not allow divine honours to be granted to his person, except in Asia and Egypt, where rulers had long been deified. In Italy and the western Empire, religious devotion reinforced loyalty to the *princeps*; prayers were offered in gratitude for his protection. The cult of his genius developed as a spirit which accompanied each person through life, watching over birth, marriage and death; the *lares* and *penates* - the household gods - of Augustus were honoured in rites. Yet the title of *princeps* precluded the final step of deification. He was the son of a god, the deified Julius, but as a living man he was not himself divine. To encourage religious feeling amongst his councillors - for this is what the Senate now became - Augustus made each senator pour a libation to the god in whose temple the Senate was meeting, before taking his seat. As Livy said, Numa replaced the discipline of war with the discipline of religion. By invoking the *pax deorum* and encouraging the "Augustan peace" within and on the borders of the Empire, the *princeps* recognised this insight of the historian of Rome's greatness. In 2 BC Augustus himself was granted the title *pater patriae*.

The Augustan peace was not universal. Tiberius and Drusus, his wife Livia's sons by her first marriage, fought across the Alps, successfully annexing Noricum and Raetia and extending the Roman border to the Danube. Agrippa finally pacified Spain, and in Germany the border briefly was held on the Elbe, east of the Rhine. Revolts had to be repressed with difficulty in the Balkans, and in AD 9 the worst military disaster of the *principate* occurred, when Varus, with three legions, disappeared without trace in the forests of Germany. The German leader, Arminius, thus succeeded in forcing back the border of the Empire to the Rhine. This tragedy made a deep impression on Augustus. He wept when he heard of the loss of three of his best legions, and when he died he warned his successor, Tiberius, not to seek more territory. For nearly four centuries the Empire remained in extent much as Augustus left it.

Internally he re-organised the administration with speed and efficiency. A central treasury, or *aerarium*, was set up. Tax farming was eliminated, except for indirect taxes, like customs duties, which were held under 2.5%. Direct taxes consisted of a poll tax (*tributum capitis*) and a land tax (*tributum soli*), the latter yielding the greater part of the public revenue. The defect of the system, which proved fatal in the long-run, was the failure to tax Rome and Italy. Citizens there remained exempt from tax, an exemption granted after the Roman conquest of the prosperous eastern Mediterranean. Such injustice was compounded by the fact that Italy was central and that in Rome itself - as Crassus and many other shrewd speculators demonstrated - land values were the reflection of the city's place at the hub of an Empire that stretched from the Atlantic to the borders of Mesopotamia. By this time a superb road system linked the Italian and provincial cities; layers of graded materials made the roads immensely durable and well drained. The local communities through which they passed paid towards their cost - an equitable charge, since most trade using the roads was local. An imperial courier service sped messages throughout the Empire. The army, of course, had priority, when rapid movement of troops was required.

*Street in Pompeii*

Trade and industry flourished under conditions of relative peace and good communications. Woollen goods, metal-working, glass-blowing and pottery were particularly prosperous in Italy. The pottery at Aretium, for example, exported its red-glazed ware extensively outside Italy. In the provinces, cities like Leptis Magna in north Africa, became huge emporia, boasting porticoed market places, theatres and arenas. Coins of Augustus circulated abundantly, but bronze coinage of individual cities was also permitted. Whole provinces, like Gaul, became increasingly Romanised as the native population appreciated the benefits of belonging to a secure and prosperous Empire. Despite all this, however, the underlying lack of economic justice left the majority of people within the Empire poor and often subject to exploitation by the wealthy town-dwellers, who gained most from the growth in communications, trade and urban land values.

Augustus' later years were partly pre-occupied with the problem of the succession. Agrippa, the man most fitted to succeed by ability and experience, died in 12 BC, the same year that Augustus took the office of *pontifex maximus*. His favoured stepson, Drusus, died in action on the German frontier. Augustus' two grandsons, Gaius Caesar and Lucius Caesar, both died young. Only Drusus' brother, Tiberius, remained. He was a capable soldier and was adopted as heir, eventually with equal constitutional rank to Augustus himself. Nevertheless, the succession question was irresolvable.

Augustus was not a king; the Republican tradition had not wavered in its suspicion of any return to outright kingship. Equally, after decades of an ordered society, following the trauma of civil war, no-one looked for a return to outright Republicanism. Somehow a middle way had to be found, whereby the ruler could choose an heir and endow him with the *auctoritas* that Augustus himself had so skilfully acquired. His authority came largely from holding powers without the corresponding offices: tribunician power, censorial power, *imperium majus*, in particular. Could such a subtle system be transmitted? Though the Empire continued for centuries after Augustus death in AD 14, it was perpetually plagued with the succession problem.

*Circus Maximus, Rome*

Reasons of state made Augustus appear harsh and cold on many occasions, as when he banished his daughter Julia, but he was by nature a kindly man. Once, for example, he went especially to visit a senator who had been suddenly struck blind and encouraged him to go on living, when he had contemplated suicide. His habits were self-disciplined and his household remarkably simple in style. He was fond of practising elocution, which he had studied under Apollodorus of Pergamon; he also learnt philosophy and even wrote a book recommending its study. At Athens he was initiated into the Eleusinian mysteries. Intellectuals were always made welcome - unless he judged them positively harmful to the state, as in the case of Ovid - and he would listen patiently to all kinds of writers reading their works aloud. He was a handsome man, with bright blue eyes and a serene expression, which so charmed a fierce Gallic chieftain, who had planned to push the *imperator* off a mountain pass, that he did not have the heart to do it. Indeed, this serenity may have indicated a truly philosophic temperament, for, when Augustus was dying, he summoned a group of friends and asked "Have I played my part in the farce of life creditably enough?" then added the well-known theatrical flourish: "If I have pleased you, kindly signify appreciation with a warm goodbye."

Suetonius, in his *Lives of the Caesars*, suggested that Augustus was given to vices, including adultery, cruelty, heavy gambling and even perversion. His evidence came mainly from enemies of Augustus, like Mark Antony. Nevertheless, charges like the seduction of senator's wives and breaking the legs of a secretary accused of bribery were serious, especially as they implied gross hypocrisy. Even Suetonius allowed that Augustus "easily refuted the charge of unnatural vice by the purity of his life at the time and afterwards," but claimed that lust and gambling were regular vices of the Emperor. Suetonius' method of writing was to record what was said or written about his subject without verifying the source. Moreover, the evidence of Augustus' public policy on Roman morals and the general recovery that marked the growth of the Empire after the Augustan period made it unlikely that the Emperor set such an example of hypocrisy.

Undoubtedly, Augustus deliberately fostered the cult of the *Imperator*. Not only many religious rites, but also the work of the greatest artists of the period were focussed on his person. Portraiture in sculpture was already developing as a distinctively Roman contribution to Hellenistic art; with Augustus, portraiture reached its zenith. An archetypal statue of the *Imperator* stood in the Villa of Livia at Prima Porta. In the pose of an orator, with the right hand raised in a benevolent but commanding gesture, Augustus' face was idealised as an heroic leader intent on his mission, whilst his cloak fell in rich folds to reveal a superb breastplate, sculptored with scenes like the recovery of the standards lost at Carrhae. High above the stage of the huge theatre at Orange in Gaul stood a similar figure, casting a paternal light over the Romanised natives and the Roman officials and merchants in the audience. Thus did the new *pater patriae* watch over his people across the Empire. In a statue of him as *pontifex maximus*, his face, wreathed in the gentle folds of a toga, was transmuted even into the benign wisdom of a man of god.

It was probably after 27 BC that the master architect, Vitruvius, wrote his compendious *De Architectura,* covering every aspect of the art, from town planning to military engineering and astronomy, later to be enormously influential in the Florentine Renaissance. Augustus meanwhile claimed to find the city of Rome made of brick and to leave it of marble. In his *Res Gestae* (or Acts), recording his most notable achievements and carved on his mausoleum, Augustus listed the buildings with which he had adorned Rome: the temple of Mars Ultor, two temples to Jupiter on the Capitoline hill, the temple of Apollo, the temple of the deified Julius, and several others; a new Senate house, the Basilica Julia, the theatre of Marcellus, and, of course, the Augustan Forum and the Ara Pacis. Other great buildings he restored, like the theatre of Pompey. Outside Rome, the *principate* witnessed the spread of buildings of splendid proportions, Hellenic in conception, but thoroughly Roman in their superb adaption to site and function. Southern Gaul, for example, received such fine works as the vast Pont du Gard constructed by Agrippa, a three-tiered aqueduct taking water over a gorge to the city of Nimes. The unadorned blocks of masonry were almost cyclopean, yet produced a harmony of arches and horizontal passageways for water and vehicles. In Nimes was built the so-called Maison Carree,

*Dancing Faun, Pompeii*

*Municipal buildings, Pompeii*

a small temple in the rich Corinthian style, with a delicate vine scroll frieze, reminiscent of the decoration on the Ara Pacis and symbolising immortality. Nimes was but one amongst many provincial cities benefitting from the Augustan building programme.

Roman painting, like every other art, was Hellenistic in its formal use of space and interest in architectural motifs. However, the painters of the Augustan period were eminently skilled in creating illusionary effects, especially on interior walls, where the viewer was led out to elaborate urban porticoes, or, as at Porta Prima, to an exquisite garden in which birds perched amidst foliage of enchanting beauty. At Pompeii, a large tableau of the Dionysiac mysteries in the Villa of the Mysteries rivalled the prosaic still life on the wall of the House of Julia Felix in the skilful treatment of space, perspective and texture. In technical accomplishment and range of theme, Augustan painting was exemplary; and the evidence of Pompeii proves that gracious living was not restricted to a narrow group of families around the *princeps* in Rome.

The most complete expression of the mind of the Augustan age, with its classicism, its longing for a golden past and its devotion to imperial prestige, was achieved in literature. Horace, Livy and Virgil were the most eminent of many fine writers; these three were certainly much helped by Maecenas - Livy and Virgil both receiving commissions for their greatest works. Not all were so fortunate: Ovid, in particular, was banished for his flagrant disregard of the *principate's* efforts to reduce sexual licence. Official sponsorship, however, did not frustrate genius; indeed, Livy was clearly inspired by the need for a history of the Roman people to present all that was heroic and valuable to posterity, even within the confines of a chronological account, whilst Virgil rose above his earlier preoccupation with pastoral poetry to write a verse epic which drew upon the intellectual wealth of ancient Greece, from the wiles of Odysseus to the teaching of Pythagoras on re-incarnation. There can be little doubt about the sincerity of Virgil's belief in the salutary effect of the *principate* on Rome and the world:

> "But next behold the youth of form divine,
> Caesar himself, exalted in his line;
> Augustus, promis'd oft, and long foretold,
> Sent to the realm that Saturn rul'd of old;
> Born to restore a better age of gold."[9]

From the Sibylline books, repositories of the ancient teaching of Greece supposedly derived from the sibil of Cumae and then rehoused on the Capitoline hill, came the prophecy of a new cycle of ages after the passing of the Iron Age. The idea that successive ages of gold, silver, bronze and iron revolve, until the final cataclysm, struck a chord with Augustan writers. Horace held out the hope of transcending the repetitive cycles:

> "Jupiter set apart these shores for a God-fearing race
> When he stained with bronze the age of gold:
> With bronze, then iron, he hardened the ages, from which
> I prophesy, the godly are offered auspicious escape."[10]

but it was Virgil who had the greater vision, for in his *Fourth Eclogue*, written only four years after Julius Caesar's murder, he prophesied the coming of a child to usher in a Golden Age. His birth would be attended by celestial light (the goddess Juno Lucina). He would be the Apollo of the new age, the bringer of harmony, the purifier, the washer away of sin, before whom the gods rise to their feet and all men bow:

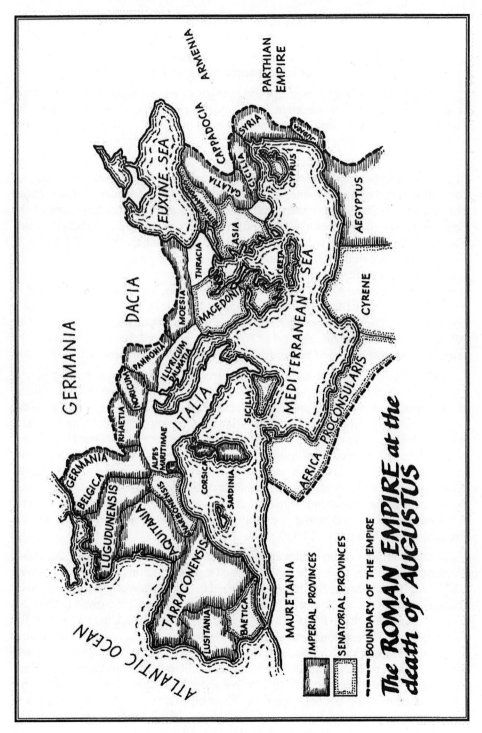

*Roma Empire at the death of Augustus*

"The Firstborn of the New Age is already on his way from high heaven down to earth. With him, the Iron Age shall end and Golden Man inherit all the world.

Smile on the Baby's birth, immaculate Lucina; your own Apollo is enthroned at last ...and the ox will not be frightened of the lion, for all his might."[11]

Is this child the young Octavian, bearing the lyre of Apollo to soothe the discordant voices of civil unrest, or was there a still greater prophesy, of the coming of the Saviour, the Christ who would be born in the reign of Augustus to bring peace, not to a generation and an Empire, but to every generation and to the world?

The Augustan era was not seen by all Romans as a Golden Age, or even as a time of general improvement. Tacitus, writing a century later, represented the feelings of some of his contemporaries when he said that Augustus had seduced the army with bonuses and civilians with cheap food, that he had absorbed the functions of the Senate, the bureaucracy and the law, and eliminated opposition by judicial murder. Slavish obedience had been the route to success. Yet the achievements of the men of the time refute much of the criticism and, as for the charge of suborning the constitution, Augustus had not intervened directly in the judicial process; indeed, he was said to have done so on only one occasion, when he appealed to the plaintiff to drop the charge, as the defendant had saved Augustus by disclosing to him a conspiracy. In Ulpian's *Digest of Roman Law*, written about 220 AD, the sentence "*Princeps legibus solutus est*" appears ("The emperor is freed from the action of the laws,") but Augustus himself had only claimed immunity from some specific statutes.

The real question about his sovereignty over the Roman people and Empire is whether anything better was possible. Failure to reform the law and the constitution in the century preceding the murder of Julius Caesar, especially the land laws, the exemption of Italy from taxation, and the law concerning provincial governors and their control of armies made the demise of the Republic inevitable. Caesar had shown the way forward to a new conception of government. The chaotic democracy of the years after the time of Sulla had to give way to tyranny, as Plato had taught, but the tyranny could be of the foullest kind, as Sulla's rule suggested, or it could be tempered by virtue. It could even turn towards a new aristocracy. Such dawning of a brighter hope was best portrayed by the poets, but it arose from the work of the generation preceding them, notably of Cicero.

In a vain effort to avert civil war, Cicero had called for a union of all the sound elements in the state, a *concordia ordinun*, based especially upon the support of Senate and *equites*. In the year 51 BC, he had published his *De Re Publica*, a book inspired by the reading of Plato, which explicit acknowledged the debt Cicero owed to the Stoic teacher, Panaetius. Like Plato, Cicero upheld reason as "the kingly power in the minds of men", whose dominion allowed no room for passions, anger or rash action. Kingship was the best of the three forms of government - monarchy, aristocracy and democracy - but better still was the harmonious blending of all three to produce equality before the law and stability. Power should be shared between a king, the leading citizens and the whole populace. Kingship and tyranny Cicero regarded as two sides of the same coin, for which he cited the case of the ancient Roman monarchy degenerating from Romulus to Tarquin. *De Re Publica* was widely read as soon as it was published. It brought a measure of the highest political philosophy of Greece into the mind of Rome. When, twenty years later, Octavian took the reins of power, educated men were prepared to recognise a political movement in the direction indicated by Cicero, ironically the man proscribed and executed by the second triumvirate. Some degree of kingship was to be tolerated in the interests of strong government and an end to civil war; yet the forms of senatorial and popular power were to remain. Octavian acknowledged that the state was "at the free disposal of Senate and people," whilst retaining, as *princeps*, control of the army and effective executive power. It was not Cicero's perfect state, but it allowed a degree of blending of the three simple forms.

Cicero followed Plato, also, in placing great emphasis upon the character of the rulers. Reason must be their guide and the reality of the supreme God their true aspiration. As Augustus matured into an experienced ruler of men, he did not fall too far short of Cicero's high ideal, nor did some of his associates, like Maecenas and Virgil. The benevolent reforms of religion and morals, the magnificent art and architecture, the embracing of world peace in the greater *pax deorum*, all these were part of a vision of more than terrestrial things. For the era of Augustus was, in fact, the revival of a culture. The cultural cycle that began with the teaching of Socrates and Plato in Athens was already running down towards the end of the first century BC. The new force required to move it forward was provided by the leaders of Augustan Rome. Amidst the passion of civil turmoil and immorality, it was Cicero who reminded them of the creative source to which they might turn:

> "Strive on, and rest assured that it is only your body that is mortal; your true self is nothing of the kind. For the man you outwardly appear to be is not yourself at all. Your real self is not that corporeal, palpable shape, but the spirit within. Understand that you are god. You have a god's capacity of aliveness and sensation and memory and foresight; a god's power to rule and govern and direct the body that is your servant, in the same way as God himself, who reigns over us, directs the entire universe. And this rule exercised by eternal God is mirrored, in the dominance of your frail body by your immortal soul."[12]

### References:

1. Livy, *The Early History of Rome*, trans. A. de Selincourt, Penguin, London, 1976, Book I, p. 34.
2. Virgil, *Aeneid*, trans J. Dryden, Airmont, New York, 1968, Book VI, p. 166.
3. Virgil, *Aeneid*, trans. Dryden, Book VI, pp. 166-7.
4. Horace, 'Odes, 1, 2', trans. W. G. Shepherd, in *The Complete Odes and Epodes*, Penguin, London, 1983, pp. 70-1.
5. Horace, 'Odes, 3, 6', trans. Shepherd, p. 139.
6. Horace, 'Odes, 3, 6', trans. Shepherd, p. 167.
7. Horace, 'Epode, 16', trans. Shepherd, p. 63.
8. Horace, 'Odes, 3, 24', trans. Shepherd, p. 156.
9. Virgil, *Aeneid*, trans. Dryden, Book VI, p. 168.
10. Horace, 'Epode, 16', trans. Shepherd, p. 64.
11. Virgil, *The Pastoral Poems*, trans. E. V. Rieu, Penguin, London, 1949, p. 41.
12. Cicero, *De Republica*, trans. C. W. Keyes, Loeb, London, 1988, Book VI, 24.

*Part 5*

# The Rise of Christian Civilisation

## Chapter 36
# I Am the True Vine
### *The Life of Jesus Christ*

IN ABOUT THE FIFTEENTH YEAR of the reign of Augustus' successor,
Tiberius, the young Jewish teacher, Jesus of Nazareth, whom some called the Messiah,
walked with his three closest disciples, Peter, James and John, on the Mount of Olives,
over-looking the ancient, walled city of Jerusalem, fortified now by Roman soldiers.
The four men entered the peaceful garden of Gethsemane. Jesus told his disciples to

*Head of Christ, Autun Cathedral*

wait, whilst he went a little way ahead to pray. As he prayed great anguish came upon him, as though his spirit laboured against mighty forces of evil. He returned to his disciples, to find them asleep, and warned them to watch and to pray, lest they succumb to temptation. Again he walked further off and prayed in the same agony of spirit. Returning, he found once more that the disciples were asleep. Yet a third time he moved away, a solitary man, forgotten even by those whom he had especially chosen to follow him. As he prayed the third time, sweat fell from his face, like great drops of blood. "O my Father, if this cup may not pass away from me, except I drink it, thy will be done."[1] When he returned, Peter, James and John had not awoken. Darkness was upon the face of the earth.

Why did Christ, the anointed one, come at that time in history, born in the middle of the rule of Augustus and crucified under Tiberius, with the consent of the Roman procurator of Judaea? Was the glorious Augustan age a time when rampant materialism demanded the coming of a Messiah?

The Augustan revival itself arose to meet the needs of the time, for the Hellenistic culture that had produced the fine art of Pergamum and the learning of Alexandria was in decline. Livy, as the historian of the Roman Republic, knew only too well how his own age was witnessing the degeneration of morals. Augustus and his loyal henchmen in the arts of war and peace laboured to raise once more the standards of Roman integrity. Their efforts bore fruit gradually. In their lifetimes the Roman world was stirring out of the slough into which it had fallen from the days of ancient Republican virtue. Behind the culture of Hellenistic Rome, however, lay the whole civilisation of the ancient world in the west, once vibrant with the wisdom of Apollo and the values of Homer, and now drawing to its close. Even Euripides, in the fifth century BC, had not taken too seriously the religion of his ancestors. As for the Roman nobility of the first century AD, a few might appreciate the philosophy of the Greeks, but they did not revere the Greek pantheon, even when it merged with the gods of Rome. Julius Caesar used the office of *pontifex maximus* as a mere step in the *cursus honorum* which led to the consulate. Augustus took the supreme religious office when Lepidus died and built superb temples on the hills of Rome, but nothing could bring back the true inspiration of the god of Delphi, who had offered harmony and peace to a millennia of Greeks.

The world of Rome contained many symptoms of the decline of civilisation, which even the most intelligent Romans did not often recognise. Slavery at its best was a harmless institution; at its worst it was an abomination. The valiant Spartacus was a Thracian noble, who sought to repatriate the enslaved soldiers of the wars with Rome. Six thousand of his fellows were crucified along the Appian Way. Crassus and Pompey advanced their careers by their success in suppressing the revolt, for, like other such revolts, it shook the complacency of Roman society, which had grown accustomed to the enslaving of war captives since the wars with Hannibal.

Nor had the land question been resolved after the Gracchi had died in the attempt. Marius had recruited an army from the proletariat created by the land accumulations of Roman oligarchs. Such a proletariat, either serving abroad under ambitious generals, or demanding bread and circuses in Rome, was a major source of the political and social instability which brought down the Republic. The *principate* did not deal with the root cause, which was the lack of just laws regarding land holding and taxation. Rent still flowed into private pockets, though Caesar and Augustus removed the worst abuses in the administration of the provinces. By the creation of new colonies and the development of finance and trade, the economic condition of the Empire was improved, so that poverty and unemployment were ameliorated. However, the ancient world had not dealt fundamentally with the question of economic justice. In a lofty speech against the depraved rebel, Catiline, Cicero could refer in the same breath to the Gracchi as a danger to the security of the Republic, when the real danger had lain with those patricians who saw that the land reformers were clubbed to death. When even Cicero was unaware of the problem, or powerless to deal with it, its insidious effect was inescapable. The *latifundia* would grow, until an unbearable weight would topple the fine pillars of Hellenistic society.

The great men of the last centuries of the ancient world took for granted a certain level of violence and coarseness in society. Augustus himself had authorised the proscription of 2,300 leading Romans on his path to supreme power. Mark Antony, a man of immense talent, had succumbed to eastern sensuality. More significantly, the Roman leaders who met the early challenge of Christianity responded to it with a crude ignorance of the real meaning of Christ's teaching, even when some of them were steeped in such an intelligent tradition as Stoicism. The younger Pliny, with the qualified support of Trajan, persecuted the early Christians; so did the most reasonable of all Roman Emperors, Marcus Aurelius. The dying civilisation could not understand the one new-born, and reacted with violence.

As for the place where Jesus himself lived, it probably saw more human suffering than anywhere else in the Roman Empire during the centuries immediately before and after his coming. Since the revolt of the Maccabees in 165 BC against the Hellenic Seleucid dynasty, there had been continuous unrest in Judaea, until Pompey restored order in 65 BC. Herod the Great seized the Judaean throne in 43 BC, but the glories of his rule, including a magnificent new temple in Jerusalem, twice as large as Solomon's, could not erase the memory of murderous conflict within the royal family. Immediately after the death of Herod in 4 BC, probably the year of Jesus' birth, the Roman general, Varus, ordered the crucifixion of 2000 Jews, accused of disturbances in Galilee. Groups of violent nationalists, like the Zealots, went on causing trouble for the Roman procurators. By the time of the Emperor Vespasian, the Romans were provoked beyond measure. As the Jewish historian, Josephus, records, they dealt with the problem of Judaea with unrestrained force, subjecting the Essenes, for example, "to every torture yet invented". After terrible slaughter, Titus destroyed the temple itself in the heart of the sacred city of Jerusalem in the year AD 70. From a local viewpoint - if such is possible - the crucifixion of Christ was just another bloody event in an unbroken series of conflicts. If ever the righteous needed to be protected and the wicked to be destroyed, it was then and there.[2]

The suffering of the world could not be relieved by the unaided efforts of Man. Therefore Christ came as the Word, or *Logos*, to renew the knowledge neglect of which had brought civilisation in the west near to ruin. From his teaching and example a new civilisation would be built, to grow like a mustard seed cast into a garden, until it becomes a great tree in which lodge the fowls of the air, or to ferment like a pinch of leaven hidden in three measures of meal. Around Jesus gathered those few who looked for an escape from the darkness of the time, not for themselves alone but for all who chose to join them. Taught by their Master, they put the kingdom of God before family, possessions and life itself, making themselves fit to transmit his teaching to the world.

Jesus taught the ancient law of the Jewish people. His message that "I am the Way, the Truth and the Life" was a restatement of the first commandment stated by Moses, "I am the Lord thy God." In his emphasis upon the second great commandment to love one's neighbour as oneself, however, he gave a new direction to the Jewish tradition by asserting the fundamental identity of all men:

"this do, and thou shalt live... a certain Samaritan, as he journeyed, came where he was: and when he saw him, he had compassion on him, and went to him, and bound up his wounds, pouring in oil and wine, and set him on his own beast, and brought him to an inn, and took care of him. And on the morrow when he departed he took out two pence, and gave them to the host, and said unto him, Take care of him; and whatsoever thou spendest more, when I come again, I will repay thee. Which now of these three, thinkest thou, was neighbour unto him that fell among thieves? And he said, He that shewed mercy on him. Then said Jesus unto him, Go, and do thou likewise."[3]

Though most of the Jewish people were to deny the Messiah, there were enough to provide the disciples and other followers who would form the early Church in Israel. The Old Testament traces the profound tradition which had prepared such men to recognise the Master when he came. For Christ, like King David but greater, was a high priest after the order of Melchizedek. The unique monotheism of the Jews and the name of God YHWH - "I am that I am" - enabled some to understand the inner meaning of Christ's esoteric words, like "I and my Father are One," referring to the identity of God and the Spirit in Man. The kingdom of God which he preached was not what men expected; he was not a warrior hero to lead his people from political oppression, but the one whom Isaiah had heralded, half a millennium before, as the source of eternal, not temporal, peace and justice. Only the pure in heart, like Peter, James and John, fishermen at Lake Gennesaret, recognised the Messiah as the master teacher.

As the prophet, Micah, foretold, Jesus was born in the city of Bethlehem, a few miles south of Jerusalem, the son of the virgin Mary, who was married to Joseph of the house of David. Of his childhood little is known, except that his family took him into Egypt to escape the wrath of King Herod, who was informed of the birth of a Messiah within his kingdom. Though the ancient teaching associated with Hermes Trismegistus was not evident in Egypt of the first millennium BC, the wisest of the Greeks had continued to return there. In the company of some school or master, the infant Jesus may have first met there the system of knowledge which he needed to express the truth of his incarnation.

When it was safe to return to Palestine, Joseph brought his family back, settling in the remote hills of Galilee, at Nazareth, far from Archelaus, Herod's son. At the age of twelve, Jesus was taken to Jerusalem by his parents. They lost him in the crowd, only to find him discussing religion with the elders of the temple. Until he was about thirty, Jesus was preparing for the three years of his life on earth which would change the whole direction of human history. He may have met the Essenes, a Jewish religious sect with a strict discipline, who were convinced of the immortality of the soul, "teaching the same doctrine as the sons of Greece,"[4] and perhaps conversed with the Pharisees about the transmigration of souls and the rule of their rabbi, Hillel, which resembled the new commandment of Jesus to love one another.

Jesus' ministry began in Galilee, amongst the mixed and mainly poor population. He taught, also, in the coastal areas, and probably then moved south into Judaea, perhaps even to Jerusalem. Many miracles were performed at this time, beginning with the changing of water into wine at a marriage feast in Cana. Blind, dumb, lame and sick were healed by his words and hands. Some, like Lazarus, were raised from the dead. Devils were cast out of those possessed. Soon the priests and scribes of the synagogues became worried by the reputation that Jesus had acquired amongst the people. They considered how to destroy him.

Fully aware of the danger, Jesus entered Jerusalem to the joy of the people, who strewed his path with palm leaves. His first act was to cleanse the temple by expelling the street traders and money lenders, who carried on business there. Then, for a few days, he continued his teaching, both of the people and of his disciples, whom he warned of terrible events to come. It was the time of the Jewish feast of the Passover, celebrating the miraculous escape of the Jews from Egypt. As Jesus sat with his disciples, eating the unleavened bread and drinking the wine, he gave a new meaning to the celebration. The bread and wine would commemorate his own body and blood. Those who partook of them were of one substance and realised their unity in Christ. Then he foretold his own betrayal by a disciple who sat at the table with him.

From this last supper they went to the Mount of Olives, where Jesus prayed in the Garden of Gethsemane. Even as he spoke again to his disciples, Judas Iscariot, the betrayer, came with armed men to take Jesus to the chief priests. He appeared before the Sanhedrin, the high court of the Jewish synagogue, accused of blasphemy. Whilst he was interrogated, Peter, outside in the courtyard, three times denied him. The Sanhedrin sentenced Jesus to death and took him to the Roman procurator, Pontius Pilate, for only he could pronounce sentence legally under the Roman occupation. Pilate was reluctant to confirm the sentence, for he could find no fault in Jesus, but he was a weak man and already worried by Jewish troublemakers, like the Zealots. He offered the crowd, which had been stirred up by the priests, the release of one man, as it was a Jewish feast. They cried out that Barabbas, a convicted criminal, should be released, and Jesus crucified.

And so Jesus was scourged and humiliated by Roman soldiers, made to wear a crown of thorns, and led, carrying his cross, to the hill of Calvary. Seeing that Jesus stumbled, the soldiers made an onlooker, Simon of Cyrene, carry the cross up the hill to Golgotha, the place of a skull. There they crucified him, nailing his hands and feet to the wooden cross. On either side were crucified, also, two common thieves. After nine hours Jesus died, "and the earth did quake and the rocks rent."[5]

Three days later, Mary Magdalene and the other Mary who followed Jesus, came to the tomb where he had been buried and found the stone rolled away from the door and the body absent. When Jesus then appeared before Mary Magdalene, she took him for a gardener, until he called her by name. Similarly, the two disciples on the road to Emmaus did not recognise him when he appeared as a stranger and walked beside them, whilst they spoke of his own life. Only when he broke bread with them did they recognise him. In Jerusalem he appeared before eleven disciples, who supposed him to be a spirit, until he ate a piece of fish and honey and spoke of his fulfilment of the law.

The events of the last days of Jesus' life have the character of a drama. In them the great play of human life is enacted to create the model for a new civilisation. Every man is in himself pure, but in the world he is ensnared by the forces of evil. Betrayed to powers of darkness, he suffers and, through suffering, awakes to recognise that he has sinned. Repentance leads to a new life, which ends in the death of the personal self. In accepting this death, he is resurrected and returns to himself in God the Father. Jesus did not sin, but chose freely to face the consequences of his betrayal by evil, to suffer, die and be resurrected, in order to demonstrate the way of release from the cycle of life and death. Other men may not experience the full cycle of birth, death and resurrection in one life on earth, for the cycle is the life, not of a body, but of a soul which re-enters many bodies.

Jesus and his disciples demonstrated the idea of transmigration of souls in the episode of the healing of the man blind from birth. The disciples asked Jesus, "Master, who did sin, this man, or his parents, that he was born blind?" Jesus answered, "Neither hath this man sinned, nor his parents: but that the works of God should be made manifest in him."[6] The disciples' question contains the assumption, not disputed by Jesus, that the man must have lived before birth in a previous incarnation; for how else could the question make sense? No sin committed during the present lifetime could have incurred the consequence of being blind at birth. Perhaps Jesus had studied with the Essenes, for Josephus describes them as "a group which follows a way of life taught to the Greeks by Pythagoras,"[7] whose teaching on transmigration was most explicit.

The idea of transmigration of souls was common to many philosophies and religions in the ancient world. The Egyptians, the Pythagoreans, Socrates and Plato, and the Stoics, all taught that the soul was immortal and passed from one embodiment to another, until it found its true home in union with the Supreme Power. So, also, did the Jewish Pharisees, as well as the Essenes of Jesus' own time. Only later, probably in the second century AD, did the early Church reject transmigration in favour of an incomplete idea of death and resurrection, which treats a single life on earth as responsible for all the consequences that confront the individual.

The story of Christ's life and ministry, as told in the four Gospels, suggests that there was a clear distinction between the teaching given by Jesus to the disciples and the public teaching given to the people whom he met in the streets and homes and assemblies of Galilee and Judaea. To the people he always spoke in parables, leaving his message to be understood according to the insight of the hearer. To the disciples he often gave the explanation of a parable and, also, an explicit teaching. Shortly before the transfiguration, when Jesus revealed his divine nature to Peter, John and James, he warned the disciples not to speak to the people too directly.

"Whom say the people that I am? They answering said, John the Baptist; but some say, Elias; and others say, that one of the old prophets is risen again. He said unto them, But whom say ye that I am? Peter answering said, The Christ of God. And he straitly charged them and commanded them to tell no man that thing."[8]

Similarly, Matthew relates that Jesus told his disciples that they would know the mysteries of the kingdom of heaven, but that the multitude would not, for "they seeing see not; and hearing they hear not, neither do they understand... for this people's heart is waxed gross, and their ears are dull of hearing."[9]

The public acts and words of Christ, including the miracles, gave great comfort to people who were in need, but the inner teaching created a civilisation. As the early Church grew in numbers and range, it retained enough of this teaching to offer a way "into the measure of the stature of Christ."[10] Beyond the outward trappings - the rites, creeds, doctrines, offices, uniformities - lay the pearl of great price, for which a wise man will sell all that he has:

> "Abide in me, and I in you. As the branch
> cannot bear fruit of itself, except it abide
> in the vine: no more can ye, except ye abide
> in me."[11]

The words of Christ resounded through the civilisation of the west, without intermission, to the present day. By them came the advancement of civilisation. The centres of Christian culture in the Middle Ages - Constantinople and Paris, for example - rediscovered, with the help of Greek philosophy, the inner meaning of Christ's teaching, and found thereby the natural laws upon which the fabric of medieval life was woven: of common law and government, of religious worship, of language in all its manifestations as speech and literature, of art and architecture, even of military science. The hand of the peasant upon his plough relied ultimately upon love of one's neighbour, and provided a few visionaries could remind the world that Christ spoke of unity, not duality, that love remained.

## References:

1. *Matthew*, ch. 26, v. 42, King James Version.

2. See *Bhagavad Gita*, trans. Shri Purohit Swami, Faber, London, 1978, ch. 4, vv. 7-8.

3. *Luke*, ch. 10, vv. 28, 33-7, King James Version.

4. Josephus, *The Jewish War*, trans. G. A. Williamson, Penguin, London, 1985, ch. 7, p. 136.

5. *Matthew*, ch. 27, v. 51, King James Version.

6. *John*, ch. 9, vv. 1-3, King James Version.

7. Josephus, *Antiquities*, XV. 371.

8. *Luke*, ch. 9, vv. 18-21, King James Version.

9. *Matthew*, ch. 13, vv. 11, 13-15, King James Version.

10. *Ephesians*, ch. 4, v. 13, King James Version.

11. *John*, ch. 15, v. 4, King James Version.

# Chapter 37

# When Uricon the City Stood

## *Roman Britain*

STRABO, AN ALEXANDRIAN SCHOLAR of Greek origin and a great traveller, gave a description in his *Geography* of the islands of Britain in the first century AD. He was impressed by the variation of hill and plain and the great areas of forest. Rain prevailed over snow, and on days of clear sky the sun was seen for only three or four hours around midday, owing to fog. It was to this land that Geoffrey of Monmouth in his *History of the Kings of Britain*, written in the twelfth century, claimed a Trojan Brutus had come in times beyond memory:

> "Brutus, beyond the setting of the sun, past the realms of Gaul, there lies an island in the sea, once occupied by giants. Now it is empty and ready for your folk. Down the years this will prove an abode suited to you and to your people; and for

*Mosaic of Romano-British Villa*

your descendents it will be a second Troy. A race of kings will be born there from your stock and the round circle of the whole earth will be subject to them."[1]

Thus did the goddess Diana direct the Trojan hero, Brutus, great-grandson of Aeneas, to sail to the islands of Britain and found a line of kings. This ancient myth, retold by Geoffrey of Monmouth, that the British nation, like the Romans, sprang from people of Trojan stock, conveyed three features of the early Britons. The legend about giants expressed the awe felt for the huge megalithic constructions at Stonehenge and Avebury on the chalk uplands of southern Britain, which related to similar constructions in Brittany, notably at Carnac, in Spain and in Malta. Built at least two millennia BC, they are evidence of a culture in western Europe on a scale comparable with the Mycenaean culture of the eastern Mediterranean. Secondly, the Trojan origin of Brutus also suggested that the culture of early Britain was of the same kind as that which perished with the destruction of Troy, a culture rich with gold and embodying the aristocratic values of priestly and noble castes. Thirdly, the reference to a race of kings implied that the British were governed continuously by kings, rather than by an elite of nobles.

The British were Celts, a race of tall, fair, blue-eyed warriors, whose homeland was central Europe, but who spread westwards and south east, until at the height of their power in the third century BC they occupied a huge crescent of land from Spain to Galatia in Asia Minor. Strabo described the Britons at the time of Augustus:

"I myself, in Rome, saw mere lads towering as much as half a foot above the tallest people in the city, although they were bandy-legged and presented no fair lines anywhere else in their figure. Their habits are ... simple and barbaric ... and they have no experience in gardening or other agricultural pursuits . . . The forests are their cities; for they fence in a spacious circular enclosure with trees which they have felled, and in that enclosure make huts for themselves and also pen up their cattle - not, however, with the purpose of staying a long time."[2]

The word "Celt" may be related to the Gothic *hildja*, meaning to fight; certainly Celts greatly respected the warrior caste, which, with the priests, ruled over farmers and traders in a society bearing many resemblances to that of the *Mahabharata*. The nobility wore fine jewellery, including great gold torques around the neck or wrists. They rode in chariots and fought in them with a speed and verve reminiscent of Arjuna. Their laws were in the tradition of the Sanskrit laws of Manu, oral in origin, written in verse and with features, such as marriage law, which were almost identical with those of ancient India. The relationship between pupil and teacher, in which the pupil became the teacher's successor, was also common to Celts and Hindus. Even the metre system of Celtic verse was very close to that of the *Rigveda*, the earliest Sanskrit poetry.

Unlike the Celts of Gaul, the British Celts preserved the institution of kingship into the period when they confronted in arms the might of Rome. Caesar found in Gaul tribes led by aristocratic warriors, but devoid of kings. When he led his expeditions to Britain in 55 and 54 BC, he met tribes led by fighting kings and queens, who with their successors made their mark on people and events: Cassivellaunus, Cunobelinus, Caratacus, Carausius, Boudicca, Cartimandua and others of more legendary fame, like King Lear and King Lud, who gave his name to London.

Whilst the British kings retained something of the charisma of the *kshatriya*, the British and Gaulish Druids were akin to *brahmins*, the preservers of knowledge and religion, who sanctified the rulers' power. "Druid" comes probably from the Greek *drus*, meaning an oak tree, and from the Sanskrit *wid*, to know. Before the Romans influenced Celtic religion, leading to the development of Romano-Celtic temples, religious ceremonies amongst the Celts were held in woodland clearings, with the oak held especially sacred. Originally the Druids were the wise, who knew the will of the gods, understood astronomy and could prophesy. In short, their knowledge of natural law made them the guardians of legal and moral principles, so that Celtic society turned to them for judgements in all such matters. As with the *brahmins*, the Druids memorised the poetry which preserved their ancient wisdom, thus leaving no written evidence of their oral tradition. By the time of Caesar, this knowledge was corrupt. When the Roman governors of Britain, Suetonius Paulinus and Agricola, destroyed them in their sanctuary on Anglesey, the last flicker of a flame which may have once enlightened a great culture was extinguished.

The Celts in Britain held land as the property of the community. Sections of land were occupied by the king and his associates in return for their public service. Most of the good pasture and agricultural land was retained as the common land of the whole tribe, without individual rights of sale or alienation, whilst some was set aside for the maintenance of poor, old or incapable members. Gavelkind, the ancient system of land tenure found in Wales until the late Middle Ages, under which family land could not be partitioned amongst the sons of a deceased tenant but continued as a working unit of land, was a remnant of the Celtic system. Pliny the Elder, in the first century BC, observed that the Celtic plough, with its mobile coulter, was superior to that of the Romans. In Britain, according to the laws of the legendary king, Molmutius - whom King Alfred acknowledged - the right of the peasant farmer to his plough was inviolable.

Celtic art retained a native awareness of beauty into the period of Romanisation. The style known as La Tene, after the place in Switzerland where it was identified, produced artistic masterpieces of jewellery and armour, flagons and decorated hand mirrors, characterised by flowing curves and brilliant gems and adapting abstract patterns into animal shapes and features, even as human faces disguised in the whirling forms.

Many of these artifacts were found in burial chambers, which bore witness to the great wealth of the Celtic princes. Like the ancient Egyptians and the Mycenaeans, the Celts clearly believed that for their rulers life beyond death required the appurtenances of nobility, for the graves contained chariots, crowns, brooches, robes, weapons and ornaments, all of the finest quality, such as the hilt of a dagger inlaid with amber. This practice was associated closely with the most striking doctrine of the Druids, namely the transmigration of souls. Ancient authors, such as Strabo, Caesar and Lucan, agreed that the Druids taught that the soul was immortal and moved from one body to another. Hippolytus said that the Druids had "profoundly examined the Pythagorean faith" and were instructed in it by the Thracian Zalmoxis, said to have been a pupil of Pythagoras himself. Caesar, who knew the courage of the Celts at first hand, attributed it to their belief in a life beyond death.

When Caesar came to Britain in 55 and 54 BC, he faced only a temporary alliance of some of the tribes of the south-east. As in Gaul, lack of political unity was to cost the Celts their independence and freedom. Probably the unwillingness of the tribal kings to co-operate reflected the general decline in morality and law, which often made them oppressors of their own people. Caesar and other classical authors refer to human sacrifice by the Druids and the practice of hanging freshly cut heads of defeated enemies outside their houses. There were about 25-30 distinctive tribes in Britain by the second century BC; then came immigration by Belgic Gauls, or Belgae, from north-eastern Gaul. These newcomers were energetic and brought customs of cremation and wheel-thrown pottery to Britain. North of the Thames valley, the Belgic Catuvellauni threatened to dominate southern Britain, and south of it the Belgic Atrebates contested this, sometimes with Roman political and economic support from across the Channel.

Caesar believed that the Cantii of Kent were the wealthiest and most civilised of the tribes, but by this he probably meant the most open to Roman influence, for trade between Gaul and Kent was common. To the west, in Dorset, the Durotriges were noted for their great defensive earthworks, probably built to fortify the position of the nobility as much as to defend the tribe from aggressors. Maiden Castle exemplified the huge double circle of ditches, massive ramparts and barbican gateways of such redoubts. In the east Midlands, the Coritani had a capital at Leicester, which traditionally took its name from King Leir (or Lear), whose story of a deliberately divided kingdom and the inevitable tragedy consequent upon it points a finger at the absence of British unity. The mountains of Wales were settled by the warlike Silures in the south and the Ordovices in the north, both tribes who caused the Roman legions much trouble after the invasion. North of the Humber, the Parisi, whose origins were on the River Seine, were a particularly cultured people, proud of their fine war chariots. Across the North of Britain to the Solway Firth, the Brigantes formed an uneasy confederation of many lesser tribes. In Scotland various Celtic tribes occupied the west, whilst to the east were the non-Celtic Picts.

In the century between the invasions by Caesar and by the Emperor Claudius, Roman influence in Britain greatly increased. Britain imported pottery, wine, jewellery, glassware and even exotic goods like red amber, and exported corn, cattle, gold, silver, iron, hides, hunting dogs and slaves. Tin had long been a major export from Cornwall, especially by sea to the Mediterranean, but when Caesar destroyed the Veneti tribe of Brittany he eliminated its carriers. Roman occupation of Gaul, however, greatly enhanced the political significance of Britain, for it became a refuge for Rome's enemies and thus an object of Roman diplomacy. Some of the southern tribes, notably the Atrebates and the Trinovantes of Essex, became, more or less, client kingdoms of Rome, in line with Roman policy along her borders elsewhere. British leaders were perhaps not well informed about the tendency of Rome to swallow up client kingdoms in the drive for expansion and security.

The policy of Augustus had been to consolidate the territory that Rome possessed, especially after the disaster that befell Varus in Germany in 9 BC. His successor, Tiberius, despite his military gifts, held firm to the same conservative attitude on the borders, preferring to reform the administration of the Empire. The brief reign of Caligula saw an attempt to mount an invasion of Britain, which impelled Claudius in 43 BC finally to attempt it. Claudius' motives were probably twofold: to win for himself military glory and to gain for Rome the expected economy of maintaining an army in Britain - which as a province would yield revenues - rather than additional troops in northern Gaul to guard the coast. Military glory had become an integral factor in the life of the Roman nobility. The great families of Rome, including the Emperor's, derived much prestige and status from their ability to fight on Rome's behalf and particularly to extend her conquests. Augustus' policy may have partly frustrated this drive for glory, but there was continuous warfare on the Rhine and Danubian frontiers and the growth of the Empire since the time of the wars with Hannibal made territorial gains the crowning triumph, despite what the ancient god, Terminus, had originally decreed. As for exploiting the wealth of Britain, it was still viewed as a mysterious land of unmeasured prosperity, rich with silver and gold and the delights of the oyster. Roman imagination was not wholly misguided. Roman Britain, with its warm, fertile cereal lands of the east Midlands, was to become the chief granary of the northern Empire; gold would be mined in the mountains of Wales, and a great deal of lead and silver from deposits in the Mendips and elsewhere.

The Catuvellauni, who had led the opposition to Caesar, had encroached upon the Trinovantes and upon the tribes south of the Thames by this time. Princely refugees to the Romans asked for vengeance. Here was the ideal pretext, if one were needed, to cross the Channel in force. Troops were selected from the Upper Rhine (Second Augusta legion), from Pannonia (Ninth Hispana), from the Middle Rhine (Fourteenth Gemina), from the Lower Rhine (Twentieth Valeria Victrix), together with similar numbers of auxiliaries. So much did Romans believe that the civilised world ended at the northern coasts that these troops mutinied at the port of embarkation. The Britons assumed that the invasion would be cancelled and neglected to defend their coastline, but Roman discipline and honour re-asserted themselves after a month. The legions landed at three points on the coast of Kent; then built a great fortress and supply base at Richborough. When the British gathered forces to defend the Medway crossing, they were dispelled after a two day battle, distinguished by the tactical skill of Vespasian, commander of the Second Augusta and a future Emperor. The British chariots could not match the firmness and order of the Roman infantry. At the Thames the Roman Commander-in-Chief, Aulus Plautius, called a halt. Claudius himself was to take command of the final drive to Camulodunum (Colchester). When he arrived, the Thames crossing was efficiently made; the defeated Britains split in two, one group following their king, Caratacus, to join the undefeated tribes in the west. Claudius' triumph was complete. Camulodunum became the capital of a new province and later boasted a huge statue of the deified Claudius. King Cogidumnus in Sussex accepted client status, which he probably exercised from the fine palace at Fishbourne; so too did King Prasutagus of the Iceni in Norfolk.

Vespasian took command of the drive westwards. Cogidumnus ensured his security in the rear, as he attacked the Durotriges. At Maiden Castle a fierce struggle took place; a field cemetery within the ramparts was found by archaeologists to contain bodies slashed by the swords of auxiliaries, thrust through by legionary short swords and pierced through the bone by *pila*. A bolt from a catapult was lodged in the spine of one hapless defender. The Romans themselves must have fought tenaciously to cross the double ditch and surmount the stone and timber walls on the crest of the great earthworks.

Caratacus fought on for eight years, firstly with the brave Silures and then with the Ordovices, with whom he was finally defeated. Escaping to the north, he threw himself on the mercy of Queen Cartimandua of the Brigantes. She had already ingratiated herself with Rome. Caratacus was handed over and brought before Claudius with great ceremony, for the fame of the British warriors roused the people of Rome and enhanced the glory of their conqueror. Caratacus made a speech of great dignity:

> "If to my high birth and distinguished rank I had added the virtues of moderation, Rome had beheld me rather a friend than a captive, and you would not have rejected an alliance with a prince descended from illustrious ancestors and governing many nations. The reverse of my fortune to you is glorious, and to me humiliating. I had arms, and men, and horses; I possessed extraordinary riches; and can it be any wonder that I was unwilling to lose them? Because Rome aspires to universal dominion must men therefore implicity resign themselves to subjection? I opposed for a long time the progress of your arms, and had I acted otherwise would either you have had the glory of conquest or I of a brave resistance? I am now in your power. If you are determine to take revenge, my fate will soon be forgotten, and you will derive no honour from the transaction. Preserve my life, and I shall remain to the latest ages a monument of your clemency."[3]

Unlike Caesar, who did not spare the noble Vercingetorix, Claudius accepted this plea for clemency.

A more bitter conflict arose following the death in the year 59 AD of the client king Prasutagus of the Iceni. Following the practice of rich Romans seeking the favour of the Emperor - especially such a one as Nero, who had succeeded Claudius - Prasutagus left his estates to be shared between the Emperor (one half) and his (Prasutagus') two daughters (one quarter each). This arrangement was misinterpreted by the provincial administrators to mean that the provincial government could take over lands and rights indiscriminately amongst the Iceni. When Boudicca, the widowed Queen, protested, she was flogged and her daughters raped. Outraged, the Iceni people rose in revolt.

The tribe to the south, the Trinovantes, though benefitting from the Roman invasion in their relief from subjugation by the powerful Catuvellauni, also had grave cause for complaint. The provincial capital of Camulodunum was being converted into a model of Roman civic imperialism, with a Forum, theatre, Temple of Claudius and, finally, a *colonia*, or settlement of Roman veterans, as an example for the Britains to emulate in style of life, language and loyalty. The Trinovantes hated the cult of the deified Claudius; they hated even more the arrogant veterans whose land was appropriated from that of the British tribe. The Roman administrators treated Trinovantes' land as disposable in the interests of Rome and the British as little more than slaves to work it. Moreover, some of the wealthier tribesmen were made to become priests of the temple cult at their own expense. When demands came from Rome to call in loans which had earlier been made to the Trinovantes, the tribe were ready to revolt. News of events amongst the Iceni to the north was the spark that was needed.

The terrible violence of the revolt led by Boudicca bore witness to a deeper disaffection than even these injustices would have provoked. It suggests that, for the seventeen years since the invasion, the British tribes profoundly resented the alien rule of Rome. Camulodunum was easily stormed. There was probably a fifth column within the city, perhaps amongst the temple priests. The city was gutted and the garrison massacred. Then the rebels marched on London and Verulamium.

The Roman Governor, Suetonius Paulinus, was occupied in reducing the Druids in Anglesey when he heard news of the revolt. With all speed he marched to London, arriving before the rebels, but saw quickly that there was no chance, with his one legion plus auxiliaries, of defending the city. Abandoning the citizens, he returned to the north to await his opportunity, having meanwhile called in vain for help from the Second Augusta in the west. It was tied by the need to hold down the western tribes. Part of the Ninth Hispania died bravely before being overwhelmed by the British horde as it marched south. And so, not for the last time, the sky above London turned black above the raging flames of the helpless city:

> "Something like 70,000 Roman citizens and other friends of Rome died in the places I have mentioned. The Britons took no prisoners, sold no captives as slaves and went in for none of the usual trading of war. They wasted no time in getting down to the bloody business of hanging, burning and crucifying. It was as if they feared that retribution might catch up with them while their vengeance was only half-complete."[4]

Suetonius Paulinus was an efficient Roman general. He regrouped his ten thousand men in the Midlands and chose a site which suited his mobile infantry. The great mass of the rebels advanced on him from the south, expecting a final victory and careless of where it would be gained. Their women and children followed closely in wagons, and parked behind the army on the edge of the battlefield. The Romans were in a steep defile, protected by thick woods to the rear, with auxiliaries and cavalry on the wings. As the Britons closed in, uphill and with little regard for any order of battle, they were met by a well directed flight of javelins. Then the Roman infantry attacked in systematic wedge formations, cutting through the undisciplined ranks of the enemy. Though there were British chariots on the field, they had none of the well-trained technique which had impressed Caesar. Pushed back against their own wagons by infantry and cavalry, the Britons were brutally massacred, soldiers, women and children alike. Tacitus gives figures of 80,000 British dead, against 400 Romans. Boudicca escaped, to die soon after from poison or illness. Her revolt was a demand for freedom and honour, but it was carried out with methods of barbarism.

This great uprising of spontaneous wrath was an overwhelming condemnation of Roman imperialism as practised in Britain. Rome, however, showed that she still retained the ability to listen and to change. The humane and tolerant strain in the Roman character, imparted by Numa and revived by Stoicism, enabled the Romans to take account of national and tribal demands and to temper the harshest forms of autocratic power. The governor of Britain, Suetonius Paulinus, was recalled, though not until he had hounded down the scattered rebels and avenged the Roman deaths in full measure. A new administration was sent out to the province, men chosen for moderation and free of vindictiveness. In this, perhaps, the hand of the Stoic first minister of Nero, Seneca, a man of the broadest sympathies, who saw beyond the institution of slavery to a common humanity, may be detected.

A process of reconstruction began, of the gutted buildings and of confidence between rulers and ruled. In the year 78 AD, a governor was appointed, Agricola, father-in-law of the historian, Tacitus, who established the province as a civilised extension of the Empire, in which the British people might fulfil their aspirations, short of self-government. Agricola saw his first task as the establishment of security. The original area in the south-east marked out as the province, delimited by the line of the Fosse Way - the Roman road from Exeter to Lincoln - was no longer considered viable. Security meant holding the upland areas to the west and north. Firstly, the formidable tribe of the Ordovices was mercilessly defeated by Agricola's forces; then he advanced northwards and, allied with some British tribes loyal to Rome, he brought the northern British to battle in Aberdeenshire, below the mountain called Mons Graupius. Tacitus records the speech of a British leader before this final attempt by the native tribes to resist the far-reaching tentacles of the Roman *imperium*:

> "When I consider the motives we have for fighting and the critical position we are in, I have a strong feeling that the united front you are showing today will mean the dawn of liberty for the whole of Britain... We, the choicest flower of Britain's manhood, were hidden away in her most secret places. Out of sight of subject shores, we kept even our eyes free from the defilement of tyranny. We, the most distant dwellers upon earth, that last of the free, have been shielded till today by our very remoteness and by the obscurity in which it has shrouded our name... Pillagers of the world (the Romans), they have exhausted the land by their indiscriminate plunder and now they ransack the sea. A rich enemy excites their cupidity; a poor one, their lust for power. East and West alike have failed to satisfy them. They are the only people on earth to whose covetousness both riches and poverty are equally tempting. To robbery, butchery and rapine, they give the lying name of 'government'; they create a desert and they call it peace."[5]

*Roman Theatre at Verulamium*

Agricola's response to such defiance represented the attitude of those Roman rulers, like Seneca and the later Stoic Emperors from Nerva to Marcus Aurelius, who saw Rome's mission in the world as the enlightening rule of the more civilised over the lesser. He won the battle at Mons Graupius and built forts in Scotland to consolidate his position, but he had already begun a process of bringing to the British the solid advantages of submission to the Empire. The British were exhorted to live in towns, where they were given help in constructing public buildings in the Forum, temples - often for gods who were a fusion of Celtic and Roman deities- and private houses. Roman dress was encouraged, even the toga of citizenship being seen frequently. Above all, the children of the leading British families were educated in Latin, by practice in rhetoric especially, which remained the keystone of Roman education despite the demise of the Republic. As Latin speakers, they could act in the law courts and the bureaucracy, and gather together to create a cultural life of the province capable of appreciating the best in Latin literature and art. A Roman British culture grew in which Celtic originality and Roman order mingled to produce fine mosiacs, comfortable villas and such splendid urban developments as the baths at Aquae Sulis (Bath). Gradually a road system was laid down, which radiated out from London, but also linked the major towns, including the *coloniae* at Lincoln, Colchester and Gloucester and the *municipium* at Verulamium, in an efficient system for commercial and military uses. In short, the process which Agricola began enabled Roman Britain to take its place alongside all those other provinces which could boast of their metamorphosis from native barbarism to Roman civilisation.

Tacitus reminds us, however, that civilisation is too strong a word to place upon this change, though his irony was embittered by disgust with the cruelties of the Emperor Domitian:

"And so the population was gradually led into the demoralizing temptations of arcades, baths and sumptuous banquets. The unsuspecting Britons spoke of such novelties as "civilisation", when in fact they were only a feature of their enslavement."[6]

In truth a new civilisation based on the teaching of Christ was already being fostered in the interstices of the Empire. In Britain the remnants of a once great culture, which may have stretched from Malta to Britain, from Spain to Bohemia, was merely succumbing to the late and fading splendor of Hellenism, a development with life enough to sustain four centuries of relative prosperity, until the legions would be withdrawn to defend the crumbling Empire.

## References:

1. Geoffrey of Monmouth, *The History of the Kings of Britain*, trans. L. Thorpe, Penguin, London, 1966, part I, p. 65.
2. *The Geography of Strabo*, trans. H. L. Jones, Loeb, London, 1988, II, Book IV, V.
3. Tacitus, *Annals*, Book XII, 37, quoted in W. S. Churchill, *A History of the English-speaking Peoples*, Cassell, London, 1965, vol. 1, p. 18.
4. Tacitus, *Annals*, trans. M. Grant, Penguin, London, 1962, Book XIV, 33.
5. Tacitus, *Agricola*, trans. H. Mattingly and S. A. Handford, Penguin, London, 1971, ch. 30, pp. 80-81.
6. Tacitus, *Agricola*, trans. Mattingly and Handford, ch. 21, p. 73.

## Chapter 38

# Care of the Churches

### *St Paul and the Early Church*

UPON THE LOVE REVEALED and demonstrated by Christ a new civilisation might be founded; but how could the disciples he left behind continue such a work? On the day of Pentecost, in an upper room where they had met together, the Holy Spirit freed them from the limitations which would have made their task impossible. The gift of speech was miraculously enhanced in them. Even to the many foreigners who dwelt in the crowded city of Jerusalem, they could speak and be understood, for their words came from beyond the multiplicity of tongues.

James, the brother of Jesus, became their leader in Jerusalem. Others were chosen by them to assist in the mission. Some, like Peter, found that even the power of healing was granted to them, so that the sick and lame had faith that the mere passing

*St Paul's Bay, Rhodes*

of Peter's shadow might relieve them of their burdens. It was a time of belief in the power of evil spirits, when the devils that entered an erring mind were legion, and when the power to cast them out was the greatest sign of holiness.

One chosen by the disciples was Stephen, a man of conviction, whose preaching angered the orthodox Jews, who brought him, like Christ, before the Sanhedrin. He was sentenced to death. As he died beneath a hail of stones outside the city walls, one orthodox Jew, a Pharisee from Tarsus named Saul, stood holding some garments for those who cast stones and listening unmoved to the dying prayer of Stephen that echoed his Master's in asking forgiveness for those who killed him.

It was the year 36 AD. Saul was about 26 years old, a proud, intelligent citizen of Rome - for his family had earned that privilege - who had trained as a rabbi at Jerusalem under the eminent teacher, Gamaliel. Learned in Judaic law and history, righteous, zealous and energetic, he saw himself as guardian of the Jewish religious tradition, and therefore as an indignant persecutor of the small sect of Jewish followers of Christ, who threatened to shatter the precious orthodoxy of his people.

After Stephen's martyrdom, Saul set out for Damascus to hunt down a group of the new sect. Then, on the road from Jerusalem, he underwent an experience which totally changed the course of his life. A heavenly light shone about him and he heard the voice of Jesus asking him why he, Saul, should persecute him. "Lord, what wilt thou have me to do?" asked Saul, and Jesus told him to go into Damascus and he would hear. For three days Saul was blind and did not eat or drink. A man called Ananias came to him and pronounced that he would be filled with the Holy Ghost; whereupon he recovered his sight and strength. From this time, for the rest of his life, Saul, or Paul as he now became known (using his Roman surname, instead of his Jewish name), was convinced of the truth of Christ's teaching and of the divinity of Christ Himself. His certainty made of him a new man. Time and again he expressed this absolute faith in Christ:

"For I am persuaded, that neither death, nor life, nor angels, nor principalities, nor powers, nor things present, nor things to come,

Nor height, nor depth, nor any other creature, shall be able to separate us from the love of God, which is in Christ Jesus our Lord."[1]

For a brief time Paul lived in solitude in the desert of Arabia. Then he returned to Damascus to work alongside the men he had previously sought to destroy. His zeal led to conflict with the governor of the region and he had to escape in a basket lowered over the walls of the city. He travelled to Jerusalem, meeting James and Peter, who accepted him as an Apostle ("one sent out") alongside the founders of the church, but soon he moved on again, to Tarsus and then to Antioch, where the name "Christian" was first used of followers of Christ. Antioch became Paul's base for the series of remarkable missionary journeys which he made over the next quarter of a century.

Paul sailed first to the island of Cyprus, preaching in the synagogues there, and then to Pisidia and Pamphylia in Asia Minor, where he met opposition from the Jews and began to teach the Gentiles, who begged him to preach to them also. Paul was faced with a fundamental question which was also troubling the church in Jerusalem. Should the teaching of Jesus, a Jew who had come to fulfil the law of

*Areopagus Hill, Agora at Athens*

*Agora, Athens*

Moses, be offered to the Gentiles? Paul had no doubts on this matter. As he wrote later, in his Epistle to the Galatians:

"There is neither Jew nor Greek, there is neither bond nor free, there is neither male nor female: for ye are all one in Christ Jesus."[2]

In Jerusalem Peter wrestled with this question, but it was resolved for him by a vision of all kinds of creatures being offered as food, and the voice of God telling him to ignore the Jewish restrictions concerning "unclean" food, for "what God hath cleansed, that call not thou common." The strict Jews amongst the members of the new church insisted that Gentiles who wished to join the church should be circumcised and told to adhere to all other aspects of Jewish law. Peter's vision led him to the same conclusion as Paul, that no such limitations could possibly be placed upon the universal message of Christ. When Paul went again to Jerusalem to discuss the matter, their joint advocacy led to James, as head of the church, making the portentous decision "that we trouble not them, which from among the Gentiles are turned to God." Paul was free to continue his life's work.

His second great journey led him once more to Asia Minor, and then, in response to a dream of a man from Macedonia appealing for help, he entered Greece, founding churches at Philippi, Thessalonica and Beroea. Paul and his fellow missionary, Silas, faced hostility in Philippi. At the command of the magistrates they were beaten and imprisoned, but, after an earthquake had all but destroyed the prison, they proudly demanded, as Roman citizens, that the bewildered magistrates pronounce them free. In Athens, Paul faced a sophisticated audience when he spoke from the massive rock of the Areopagus, looking down upon the very place where Socrates had taught and faced his own accusers. With the boldness of certitude, Paul cried out to men versed in the tradition of the Greek schools of philosophy, "I perceive that in all things ye are too superstitious." Seeing an altar inscribed "To the Unknown God," he told these heirs of Plato that God "dwelleth not in temples made with hands" and reminded them that their own poets had written that in God all men live and move and have their being. Yet, when he spoke of the resurrection of the dead, the Athenians mocked him, for Paul insisted on the resurrection of the body, which seemed to conflict with the Greek idea of the immortality of the soul alone. His Greek audience had forgotten the Pythagorean teaching on transmigration, which explained the soul's passage through many bodies to immortality.

Athens was a disappointment to Paul. Corinth, on the contrary, was a fruitful ground for the seeds he planted. Arriving there probably in the year 50 AD, he stayed for some while, making lifelong friends with a Jewish Christian couple, Aquila and Priscilla, tentmakers by trade, like himself. In fact, the new church at Corinth later caused him much anxiety. A great trading and sea-faring city, notorious for its cosmopolitan, libertine population, its Christian converts were too ready to interpret Paul's idea of freedom from the Jewish law in a spirit of self-indulgence. His first letter to the Corinthians, therefore, had to deal with serious cases of immorality - incest, divorce, disorderly conduct at the Lord's Supper. He showed his true stature as a teacher, however, by writing, also, of the final transcendence of love, with words which could not fail to elicit it (1 Corinthians 13). He eventually returned from Corinth by sea to Caesarea, and thence to Jerusalem and Antioch.

Paul's third mission took him again to Asia Minor, to found churches in Colossae, Hierapolis and Laodicea, and to remain for a while in Ephesus on the west coast, where the huge temple of Diana bore witness to the power of the ancient tradition of the Greek pantheon. Once more he suffered violence, including imprisonment and the threat of exposure to wild beasts. Once more trouble in Corinth diverted him for a while, but in writing to the Ephesians, he defined the true nature of a church of Christ:

"From whom the whole body fitly joined together and compacted by that which every joint supplieth, according to the effectual working in the measure of every part, maketh increase of the body unto the edifying of itself in love."[3]

From Ephesus, Paul travelled through Macedonia to Corinth. Whilst he dealt with the recurrent problems of the Corinthian church, he found time to write a long letter to the Christians in Rome, explaining many of the central ideas of the faith. Just as Paul saw that Christ's teaching was for all, not only for the Jews, so he saw too that the Judaic law as taught by the Pharisees, which in Paul's eyes previously had been the essence of moral law, was insufficient for the highest end of Man. For this requires transcending human will, which may adhere completely to the moral law, but can never rid itself of selfishness, of its character as the will of a doer of action, of "my" will. Hence it is always tainted with the past and the sins of the past:

"If then I do that which I would not, I consent unto the law that it is good. Now then it is no more I that do it, but sin that dwelleth in me. For I know that in me (that is, in my flesh) dwelleth no good thing: for to will is present with me; but how to perform that which is good I find not. For the good that I would I do not: but the evil which I would not, that I do."[4]

Man as a willing creature has no escape from this snare of the law: "O wretched man that I am! who shall deliver me from the body of this death?"[5] In Christ alone lies the way to fulfilment, for Christ lives in every man beyond the self which wills.

Paul's power of interpretation in his letters and preaching reached out beyond the legal and moral meaning of righteousness to the nature of goodness. His contact with Stoicism in his home city of Tarsus may have given him some conception of Plato's idea of the Good, but his inspiration lay in his awareness of the presence of Christ in himself, from the revelation on the road to Damascus and continuously thereafter. Such a realisation made Paul one of the pillars upon which a new civilisation, offering nothing less than the fulfilment of Man, could be built. In his passionate appeal to Christ as the deliverer from the death of the material world, Paul opened a door into Christian civilisation.

From Greece Paul returned for the last time along the Ionian coast, calling at Rhodes, where he may have preached on the Acropolis at Lindos, high above the tiny bay later named after him. Once more he came to Jerusalem, amidst the perpetual difficulties of the Jewish Christians. The Jews saw him as a troublemaker. He was arrested, probably for his own safety, and taken to Caesarea, where the Roman governor imprisoned him for two years. Paul, as a Roman citizen, appealed to Caesar. In the autumn of 59 AD his voyage to Rome began, only to be delayed by tremendous storms near Crete and then shipwreck at Malta. There he was treated kindly by the people and healed some who were brought to him. A new ship took him to Syracuse and Puteoli for brief stops, before finally he arrived at Rome to face further imprisonment. Paul's eventual fate is unknown. Christian tradition assumes that he was executed in Rome, where Peter may have similarly died. In his own words, the Herculean labours of the Apostle are summarised:

> "Of the Jews five times received I forty stripes save one. Thrice was I beaten with rods, once was I stoned, thrice I suffered shipwreck, a night and a day I have been in the deep; In journeyings often, in perils of waters, in perils of robbers, in perils by mine own countrymen, in perils by the heathen, in perils in the city, in perils in the wilderness, in perils in the sea, in perils among false brethren; In weariness and painfulness, in watchings often, in hunger and thirst, in fastings often, in cold and nakedness. Beside those things that are without, that which cometh upon me daily, the care of the churches."[6]

The manner of living in the early Church was a simple and whole-hearted brotherhood. No one claimed anything as his own, for all was held in common. When a man or woman joined the Church, they sold any valuable property, like land and houses, and gave the proceeds for the use of all. It was a principle that presented the uncorrupted condition of a Golden Age to covetous men. Eusebuis, "the father of ecclesiastical history", who wrote that "James the Righteous, John and Peter were entrusted by the Lord after his resurrection with the higher knowledge,"[7] recorded that the first Christians renounced all material interests, went outside the town walls and lived on lonely farms to avoid the harmful influence of worldly ideas. Philo of Alexandria, a Jewish contemporary of the Apostles, described their life in the area of Alexandria as follows:

> "In every house there is a holy chamber called a sanctuary or 'monastery', where they celebrate in seclusion the mysteries of the sanctified life, bringing in nothing - drink, food or anything else required for bodily needs - but laws and inspired oracles spoken by prophets, hymns, and everything else by which knowledge and true religion are increased and perfected... The whole period from dawn to dusk is given up to spiritual discipline. They read the sacred scriptures and study their ancestral wisdom philosophically, allegorizing it, since they regard the literal sense as symbolic of a hidden reality revealed in figures."[8]

The spread of Christianity to places as far apart as Rome and Alexandria by the mid first century testified both to the power of the message of Christ and to the extent to which Hellenism and Roman imperialism had made of the Mediterranean basin one world with two common languages - Latin and *koine* Greek. It also indicated the acute need amongst the general population of the time for a teaching that could inspire hope and regenerate love. Men longed for the spiritual life implied in Paul's description of the early Church:

> "That there should be no schism in the body; but that the members should have the same care one for another.

> And whether one member suffer, all the members suffer with it; or one member be honoured, all the members rejoice with it.

> Now ye are the body of Christ, and members in particular."[9]

The strength that such a brotherhood generated was to be tested by prejudice and persecution. Ignorance bred fear amongst those who heard of Christian practices without understanding them. The use by Christians of the terms 'brother' and 'sister' led to a belief that they practised incest. The terms 'body' and 'blood' used in the Eucharist were taken to imply cannibalism. Such grotesque ideas were harboured amongst people who believed in the prevalence of demons and had forgotten the real meaning of pagan religion. However, so widespread was the feeling against Christians that in the year 64 AD, when Rome was half destroyed by a terrible fire, the Emperor Nero made them scapegoats. In fact, his treatment of them was so atrocious - some were made into human torches in the gardens of Rome - that sympathy was aroused. Nevertheless, persecution was to continue spasmodically until the fourth century AD.

Early Christianity was one of many new religious beliefs and practices which grew up in the Roman Empire in the first century: cults of the Egyptian deities, Serapis, Isis and Osiris; of Attis from Phrygia in Asia Minor; of Adonis from Syria; and of Mithras from Persia. Only the last of these, with its emphasis on ethical and military efficiency, failed to offer redemption to its devotees, so much did men yearn for release from the grip of sin and the demoniac world. Mystic deities were called saviours; redemption implied deliverance from the perils of life and also from the annihilation of death. The central cult figure was always a youthful god who died and rose again. Firmicus Maximus recorded the mystic utterance:

"Take courage, ye initiates! As the god was saved,
So too for us comes salvation from suffering."[10]

Yet Christianity became the root of a civilisation, whilst the others remained as no more than cults. For a living man, not a mere cult figure, had acted out the full drama of birth, death and resurrection for men to witness. Christ's choice of the path which led to death by crucifixion had shown that he knew what the age demanded in its devotion to so many forms of a sacrificial god. People had come to believe that they were the slaves of fate, or even of the capricious Tyche, god of chance. For this condition the patron deity of a city or the official gods of Rome - some were deified emperors - were no remedy. To master fate or chance, powers beyond the control of individuals, a greater power was needed, a grace beyond the world and the will of man. The Word made flesh offered redemption.

Another form of mystic religion entered the Roman Empire at this time from the Orient, namely Gnosticism. The name is a term of modern scholarship, derived from the Greek term *gnosis*, meaning secret knowledge. Opposition to Gnosticism in the writings of Church fathers, like Irenaeus and Hippolytus, show that it was prevalent in the second century AD. So pervasive was its influence upon other sects, including Christianity, that it cannot be defined as one cult amongst others. Its roots were probably in Persia and Syria, but it appeared in the Jordan valley in Palestine, and was associated with the Phrygian Attis, the writings of Philo, and the teaching of neo-Platonists. Gnostic ideas were so comprehensive that they even seemed to include beliefs of the early Christians.

Essentially, Gnosticism presented a great myth about Man, to be understood on the lines of Philo's reference to allegory. In the beginning, Man was a heavenly figure of light, but by a tragic fall into the world he was fragmented into a myriad of splinters or sparks, each forming the soul of an individual man. The demons of the world of darkness seized upon these sparks, which alone enabled some order to be given to the primeval darkness and chaos of the world. Hence men felt alienated in their lives on earth, yearning for a return to the heavenly state. Some were more aware of their real condition than others, feeling themselves imprisoned in the body. Others slept in the ignorance engendered by the demons. The Supreme Being, whose kingdom of pure light was the original home of Man, took pity on men and sent his own Son to earth, disguising him in a human body to mislead the demons. The Son taught the way of return, identifying himself by such words as "I am the sacred truth," and giving sacred formulae, by which to pass safely the planets and other outposts of the demonic powers. Then he returned to his Father in the kingdom of light to prepare for those who chose to follow him. Hence redemption for Man was made possible not by any event in the world, which could have been within the control of the demons, but by an intervention from beyond, a message from an emissary from the world of light. The work of the Son was nothing less than to assemble the scattered sparks of light. When it is complete, the figure of light of original Man is once more established in heaven. Judgement has been made, light separated from darkness. The myth applied as much to the Egyptian story of Osiris and to Greek Orphism as to the drama of the Christian cycle of the coming of the Messiah, his work, death and resurrection. It was a universal teaching, redolent of the earliest scriptures of the Veda. With the mission of Christ, and in the interpretation of Paul, the myth was made real.

In the centuries after the birth of Christ, the basin of the eastern Mediterranean was the crucible in which the elements of western Christian civilisation were created. Vital new ideas confronted beliefs emaciated by the decline of the ancient world. The labours of St Paul - the constant journeys through Asia Minor, Greece and Palestine, the intellectual struggle with virulent opponents, the unyielding devotion to the teaching of Christ - typified the response of men who had awoken to reality and found themselves placed in that crucible and called upon to act.

### References:

1. *Romans*, ch. 8, vv. 38-9, King James Version.

2. *Galatians*, ch. 3, v. 28, King James Version.

3. *Ephesians*, ch. 4, v. 16, King James Version.

4. *Romans*, ch. 7, v. 19, King James Version.

5. *Romans*, ch. 7, v. 24, King James Version.

6. *2 Corinthians*, ch. 11, vv. 24-8, King James Version.

7. Eusebius, *The History of the Church*, trans. G. A. Williamson, Penguin, London, 1984, Book II, 1, p. 72.

8. Eusebius, *The History of the Church*, Book II, 17, p. 91.

9. *Corinthians*, ch. 12, vv. 25, 27.

10. Firmicus Maximus, *de errore prof rel.* 22.1.

*Chapter 39*

# One True Nobility

## *The Empire from Trajan to Marcus Aurelius*

"If a man were called to fix the period in the history of the world during which the condition of the human race was most happy and prosperous, he would, without hesitation, name that which elapsed from the death of Domitian to the accession of Commodus."[1]

"But do not expect Plato's ideal commonwealth; be satisfied if even a trifling endeavour comes off well, and count the result no mean success. For who can hope to alter men's convictions; and without change of conviction what can there be but grudging subjection and feigned assent?"[2]

FOR JUST OVER HALF A CENTURY the four Emperors who succeeded the great Augustus - Tiberius, Caligula, Claudius and Nero - ruled with a mixture of ferocity and timidity, busyness and neglect which made the demise of the Julian

*Pantheon, Rome*

dynasty inevitable. The end came in the year 69 AD, when Nero was driven to suicide; even the Praetorian Guard abandoned him. For a year a violent struggle continued between rival generals, each holding the throne with the support of their regional armies, until one, Vespasian, emerged as the strongest.

The Flavian dynasty of Vespasian and his sons, Titus and Domitian, saw improvements in Roman government, particularly in Vespasian's reclamation of large areas of public land from private landowners, who had illegally appropriated it (Nero had executed six landowners who between them owned half of the whole province of Africa!), and his determined efforts to raise the depleted public revenue. Domitian, however, degenerated into an outright tyrant, whose murder by palace officials was universally welcomed. In that year, 96 AD, a change came over the *principate* which ushered in almost a century of good government. Five Emperors, devoted to the security and well-being of their people and territories, were elected in succession by the authority of the Senate and the consent of the soldiers. All were followers, to some degree, of the precepts of Stoicism.

*Arch of Severus, Forum, Rome*

The first of these "good Emperors", Nerva, was 66 years old when the Senate chose him. His long record of devoted service to the state and his equable and just character distinguished him, but he had less than two years to serve as Emperor. He may have initiated the generous system of *alimenta* which Trajan later developed, but his finest achievement was the adoption of that soldier-emperor as his successor. There was no question now of a return to a Republican constitution - men were too immured to the idea of ultimate responsibility having passed to one man - but Trajan treated those who had been his peers with respect, honouring the Senate and dealing with his senior magistrates affably and reasonably. After 19 years of firm rule he, or those close to him, chose Hadrian as his successor, thus ensuring that another capable soldier, whose mind encompassed much more than military advantage, would rule. Hadrian was more conservative than Trajan in his vision of the extent of empire, choosing to withdraw from the latter's eastern conquests, but he was a fine blend of man of action and lover of the Empire's cultural heritage. His own choice of Antoninus Pius, with Marcus Aurelius as Antoninus's heir, was masterly, for these, of all Rome's rulers, became the nearest in character to the ideal of a philosopher king.

Underlying this golden century from 96 AD to 180 AD, when Marcus Aurelius bequeathed the throne to his son Commodus, was the teaching of Stoicism. Between the eloquent defence of its doctrines by Cicero in the late Republic and Nerva's accession, the greatest exemplar of Stoicism's practical philosophy had been the chief minister to the odious Nero, Seneca: playwright, essayist, and a man who faced the ultimate test of his beliefs when he was ordered to commit suicide by his master. His death was lingering and painful, but he had long schooled himself to face "the birthday of eternity:"

*Marcus Aurelius*

"'Rehearse death'. To say this is to tell a person to rehearse his freedom. A person who has learned how to die has unlearned how to be a slave... There is but one chain holding us in fetters, and that is our love of life."[3]

Stoicism influenced the educated minority in Roman society in this period in several ways. It taught that the universe was an orderly, rational system, under the guidance of a Supreme Being, whose will was beneficient and whose laws were the expression of that will in nature; that men could read the natural laws if they awoke from sleep; that for each man law was ordained in his own nature; that Reason was one with the Supreme Being and resided in everyone. The world itself, including the body with its desires and feelings and susceptibility to pleasure and pain, was no more than a place of trial, where the wise would remain unfettered, holding fast to rational principles amidst the storms of passion. Though the Roman character had declined from the early Republican days when each citizen had relied on his own plough and spear, the essential love of sturdy independence and natural justice remained. To these Stoicism was perfectly attuned. Now the sovereign power in the Empire was touched with this noble philosophy that traced its original ideas back to the Porch in Athens and thence to the master, Socrates.

Trajan maintained the *alimenta* throughout Italy and even on the imperial estates in Africa. It was a generous system, under which the state made loans to farmers at low rates of interest and the interest was set aside for the education of free-born boys and girls. The intention was partly to encourage the growth of population and to aid agriculture, but public policy was deliberately supporting the education of talented children not born into the ruling class. To further sustain agriculture, Trajan passed a law ordering all senators to invest at least one third of their property in Italian land.

Military affairs, however, were closest to Trajan's heart. The Dacians, north of the lower Danube, had caused trouble under Domitian. Their king, Decabalus, had invaded Roman territory and been bought off with large indemnities. When he again proved troublesome, Trajan decided to settle the matter by force. In 101-2 AD he led a campaign into Dacia, reached the capital, Sarmizegethusa, and came to terms with Decebalus, which fell short of revenge but enforced obedience. The Dacian king was resentful. A few years later he broke the agreement, precipitating a second war. This time Trajan was ruthless. After a bitter conflict, involving the reduction of Dacian fortresses with siege engines taken across the Danube, the barbarians submitted once more, though their king killed himself. Fifty thousand warriors were led southwards in chains to become gladiators in the amphitheatres of Italy. Of the remaining population some fled northwards across the Carpathians, some worked the mines for Roman overlords, and a few, who had surrendered early, were enrolled in auxiliary units of the Empire. Trajan then settled Dacia with people from other provinces. It became a new polyglot province, a useful addition to the Empire, yielding gold and other minerals and forming a buttress north of the Danube, protected by the ring of the Carpathians. Modern Romania bears witness to its Romanisation, as the only Balkan country with a Latin derived language. In Rome the accession of Dacia was marked by the brilliantly original artistry of Trajan's column, on which a spiral bas relief, 650 feet long, depicts the whole story of both Dacian campaigns.

Success in Dacia encouraged Emperor and people to settle a further border problem in the distant east, where the kingdom of Parthia had long presented problems for Rome. The Parthian king failed to acknowledge Roman rights in selecting a king for Armenia, so that Trajan felt justified in occupying Armenia in 114 AD. Then he led an invasion of Parthia down the valleys of the Tigris and Euphrates, took Ctesiphon, the

*Tivoli Gardens, Rome*

*Tivoli Gardens, Rome*

Winter capital, and reached the Persian Gulf, the only Roman Emperor to look thence upon the Indian Ocean. Trajan's imagination dwelt upon the exploits of Alexander, but he knew that the resources and energy were not available for such dreams. Moreover, even as he was redrawing the eastern borders in the sands of the Orient, revolt broke out behind him. Those obdurate subjects, the Jews, had once more struck back at the destroyers of their temple. In Africa, Egypt, Cyprus and Judaea they were aroused to fury, committing such slaughter in Cyprus, for example, that when the island was recovered by Rome, no Jew was allowed to set foot there again.

Trajan left Parthia in order to deal with the revolts. He was a tired man. Though the Jewish risings were suppressed, he could do no more. In 117 AD, as he was returning to Rome to celebrate his eastern successes with a triumph, he died. Later generations of Romans, and medieval writers like John of Salisbury, regarded him as the most virtuous of the Emperors. His correspondence with the friend whom he appointed especially to govern the troublesome province of Bithynia, Pliny the Younger, bears this judgement out. In his replies to Pliny's requests for advice or directions, Trajan shows a remarkable attention to detail and a measured response to the needs of his subjects. He listens carefully to requests for finance for public buildings, decides matters of honours or promotions, gives judgements about criminal proceedings, notably concerning the Christians in the province. They are not to be hunted out, informers are not to be encouraged, but if Christians refuse to recant their beliefs and to acknowledge pagan gods, they must be punished. Clearly Trajan (and Pliny) had no conception of the teaching that was creating a new civilisation within the fading forms of Hellenism, but he treated the miscreants with the dignity that his office allowed him. For though the ancient world was in decline, it retained a respect for *arete* - the Roman *virtus* - so that even the bitterly satirical poet, Juvenal, could write:

> "You may line your whole hall with waxen busts, but virtue,
> And virtue alone, remains the one true nobility."[4]

As a soldier Hadrian was more cautious than his predecessor. The Empire under Trajan had reached its greatest extent, and Hadrian realised that the new conquests in the east could not be held without excessive strain on military and financial resources. He wisely withdrew from Mesopotamia and Armenia. His frontier policy reverted to that of Augustus: to consolidate the existing borders in the interests of a permanent peace. In pursuit of this ideal - the *Pax Romana* - Hadrian travelled with zealous energy to almost every province of the Empire in the course of his reign of 21 years, inspecting defences and ordering improvements. The great wall between Wallsend and Bowness in the north of England and the earthworks of the *limites* in Germany were two of the lasting fruits of his efforts.

Hadrian acknowledged the debt of Rome to Greece. He favoured the cities of Greece in his building programmes; a superb library, a monumental gateway and the half-built Temple of Olympian Zeus below the Acropolis were completed in Athens under his patronage. There, too, he was initiated into the Eleusinian Mysteries. Such emphasis upon Greek culture moved the Empire further towards the day when it would divide into eastern and western spheres, under Greek and Latin influence, a division anticipated also by the growth of Byzantium on the key trading route into the Black Sea.

The reign of Antonius Pius was singularly uneventful, drawing from Edward Gibbon the famous remark that it "furnished very few materials for history; which is indeed little more than the register of the crimes, follies and misfortunes of mankind," but that of his son-in-law, Marcus Aurelius, tested the temperament of the philosopher-emperor to the full. Though Marcus loved peace and had no ambition beyond seeing his people tranquil, secure and happy, he was compelled to face many years of arduous campaigning on the northern borders of the Empire. The Sarmatian Jazyges and the Germanic Marcomanni and Quadi continually burst over the Danubian frontiers, themselves driven forward by migrant barbarians further north and east. In 167 AD the Germans broke right through the *limites,* crossed the Julian Alps and besieged Aquileia. Even the splendid city of Verona trembled at this second Cimbric invasion. Marcus rallied his armies with the determination, if not the zest, of Marius. The situation was saved, but it was a foretaste of what would eventually destroy the whole western Empire.

In the midst of these troubles, Marcus Aurelius played the true Stoic, indifferent to fortune, faithful to his own nature and endeavouring to turn his mind to God and let Reason alone rule his conduct. His so-called *Meditations,* composed during these years of military engagement on the frontier, were actually entitled *To Himself,* they indicate how deeply Stoicism had influenced the Roman ruling class in this period of the mature Empire:

"In the life of a man, his time is but a moment, his being an incessant flux, his senses a dim rushlight, his body a prey of worms, his soul an unquiet eddy, his fortune dark, and his fame doubtful... Where, then, can man find the power to guide and guard his steps? In one thing and one alone: Philosophy. To be a philosopher is to keep unsullied and unscathed the divine Spirit within him, so that it may transcend all pleasure and all pain, take nothing in hand without purpose and nothing falsely or with dissimulation, depend not on another's actions or inactions, accept each and every dispensation as coming from the same Source as itself - and last and chief, wait with a good grace for death, as no more than a simple dissolving of the elements whereof each living thing is composed. If those elements themselves take no harm from their ceaseless forming and re-forming, why look with mistrust upon the change and dissolution of the whole? It is but Nature's way; and in the ways of Nature there is no evil to be found."[5]

The inspired writing of Plato on the idea of a philosopher king came to fruition in this courageous and sensitive intellectual, born to occupy the throne of an Empire at the height of its powers, but already experiencing the early symptoms of decline. Indeed, doctrines of Stoicism retained enough of their original teaching to enlighten Roman society from top to bottom in the second century AD; for, from the accession of Nerva, a new spirit of benevolence in the rulers permeated downwards to bring a greater sense of community and a greater willingness to serve at every level. Even the urbane Pliny the Younger took care of those who worked on his estates, including the slaves, and conscientiously examined everything drawn to his attention as governor of Bithynia, from faulty aqueducts and the need for fire engines to individual cases of hardship or corruption.

The "good Emperors" made great efforts to improve the quality of government. The abuses of the *publicani* system of tax-farming were removed by the appointment of *conductores,* and later procurators for complete provinces, who were directly accountable to the Emperor. Local government was improved by the intervention of imperial councils in the provinces. Though these changes created a tendency towards centralised control, the Emperors were careful to preserve the spirit of independence in local government, encouraging the growth of *municipia* and *coloniae,* which by this time were becoming indistinguishable. Provided defence, imperial taxation and the more serious judicial questions were reserved for the imperial power, Rome was content to leave localities to govern themselves, thus avoiding bureaucratic interference and concern with detail. Marcus Aurelius, in the spirit of the old Republican tradition, had learnt to respect "a community based on quality and freedom of speech for all, and a monarchy concerned primarily to uphold the liberty of the subject."

Rich men were turned by the relative enlightenment of the times to devote much of their wealth to the public good, in the spirit of the Greek liturgies. The Athenian, Herodes Atticus, for example, inherited a large fortune and spent it on a remarkable series of endowments of fine buildings to his native city and elsewhere. He gave half the cost of a new aqueduct for the city of Troas in Asia Minor, a stadium built entirely of white marble for the Athenian games, an *odeion*, or covered theatre, below the south-west wall of the Athenian Acropolis, a temple of Neptune in the Isthmus of Corinth, a theatre at Corinth, a stadium at Delphi on the hillside above the sacred site, a bath at Thermopylae, an aqueduct at Canusium in Italy and other gifts to Epirus, Thessaly, Euboea, Boeotia, the Peloponnese and Asia Minor.

The growth of towns and cities - urbanisation - was the main indicator of the spread of Roman culture throughout the provinces. Italy was no longer seen as pre eminent in status and privilege. Were not the Emperors themselves provincials - Trajan and Hadrian from Spain, Antoninus from southern Gaul, and Marcus of Spanish stock? By the second century the work of pacification of barbarian tribes was over. They were settled in *civitates*, regions each based upon a chief town, linked with the body of the Empire by excellent roads and amenable to the arts of Rome - unifying language, even-handed laws, and tolerant religion. Verulamium, Lugdunum (Lyons), Cordoba, Aquincum (Budapest), Thessalonica, Nicomedia - throughout the length

*Theatre, Ostia*

and breadth of the Empire towns could be proud of their forums, basilicas and temples, their markets for goods which might contain materials from the Baltic coast, like amber, or the distant east, like spices. For although the roads served mainly local traffic, no restrictions, except provincial customs posts, barred commerce from markets in every part of the Empire. The rust-red pottery of Gaul, the brilliant glassware of Cologne, earthenware lamps from Carthage, Spanish wine and Egyptian papyrus, were traded across the urban network, though industry remained essentially small-scale and locally orientated. Border towns, especially, grew fast, some owing their origin to military camps, like those which became the modern cities of Cologne, Mainz, Strasburg, Vienna and Budapest, which all began as *canabae*, the settlements for inn-keepers, winesellers, dealers in the spoils of war and camp-followers, including soldiers' "illegal" wives.

Close to Italy, both geographically and in the native qualities of the people, Gallia Narbonensis lay at the crucial junction of the great waterway of the Rhone and the Roman road, the Aurelian Way, from Italy to Spain. Many of its numerous towns, particularly Arelate (Arles) and Nemausus (Nimes), owed their growth to the bridging of the southward flowing rivers by lateral roads. The whole area was permeated with Greek influence, linked as it was to the city of Massilia (Marseilles), an ancient Greek foundation captured by Julius Caesar in 49 BC.

*Glanum, Provence*

Augustus and his lieutenant, Agrippa, took in hand the Romanisation of Narbonensis. By the second century AD it was a mellowed blend of Gallic independence, Greek artistry and Roman order. Arausio (Orange), Nemausus and Arelate boasted the splendid buildings of major cities: amphitheatres, theatres, temples, basilicas, public baths, triumphal arches. In towns like Glanum (near St

Remy), Vasio (Vaison) and Carpentorate (Carpentras) stood the solid houses of prosperous merchants or smaller landowners amidst the inscribed monuments, minor public buildings and open spaces common to Roman urban culture. Water was delivered to the major cities by aqueduct. That which crossed the Pont du Gard carried water from Uzes 50 kilometres southwards to Nimes, with a fall of only 17 metres. A distributing basin in the city contained large ducts in the bottom for essential civic uses and smaller ones in the sides for private uses (which were metered). Some towns, like Vasio, were built on springs, which were numerous on the edge of the calcareous foothills of the Alps.

The prosperity of Narbonensis was enhanced by a nodal position, but the basis of its wealth was the rich fertility of its agriculture. Here, between the Alps and the Cevennes, the alluvial soil of the floodplain of the Rhone, improved by irrigation, yielded cereals, fruit and vegetables in abundance, whilst on the slopes of the drier hills the vine and olive flourished in the hot summers. Narbonenses' wine was full bodied and resinous. The Greeks had introduced the olive - the immortal tree - and even a decree of Domitian favouring Italian cultivators could not stop the spread of the silver green foliage on the limestone hills. Those men and women of Arausio who looked up from a performance at the theatre to the statue of Augustus in a niche high above the stage could well believe that his benevolent gesture of magisterial blessing was the genuine sign from a god, still honoured by his imperial successors.

"Latifundia have ruined Italy," said the elder Pliny. As Nero's six African landlords showed, they were ruining the provinces also, with their chained slaves and their destruction of the independent farmer, but after Vespasian's reforms the situation on the land underwent some improvement. Slave labour was seen as often inefficient as well as inhumane; the tenant farmer would work harder and without the expensive apparatus of overseers and managers. Thus many estate owners sought small tenants - *colonii* - who would rent a farm or perhaps hand a third of the crop to the landlord. Hence husbandry and pride in the soil could be revived, the basis of any economy and something which Emperors like the Antonines found consonant with their Stoic dislike of slavery. For, as Marcus wrote, are we not all slaves to circumstance and at one with all men in "the brotherhood of all rational beings?"

In this brief interlude of the *Pax Romana*, when civil war was extinguished and the torrents of invasion from the north had not yet descended on the Rhine and Danube, the Roman Empire achieved a rare balance of order and tranquillity, of industry and culture. Greater wealth, not distributed with gross inequality, enabled men to build cities of elegance, where the eye could rest upon stone and brick still moulded to the Hellenistic forms beloved by the Greek cities of the eastern Mediterranean. Rome built on a grand scale, even if her buildings were largely functional. The magnificent aqueducts that leaped for tens of miles over the golden countryside of Latium and Etruria and swept into the capital city with the efficiency of modern motorways, were emulated in Spain, at Segovia and in Gaul at Nimes. The immense spans of the bridges at Alcantara in Spain and at Drobetae on the Danube; the awesome dome of Hadrian's Pantheon in Rome, built as a perfect hemisphere to resemble the heavens, with a circle open to the sky and the invincible Sun; the enormous Forum of Trajan, three times larger than that of Augustus, with its semi-circular market and splendid column; the wall of Hadrian, winding over the windswept moors of Northumbria between milecastles and impregnable fortresses: all these were in harmony with the elements of fire, air, water and earth, the great constituents of the Nature of Stoic philosophy. So, too, the civilised amenities of Aquae Sulis in Britain, of Italica in Spain, of Arelate in Gaul, of Trier on the Rhine, of Aquincum on the Danube, of Palmyra in the Syrian desert, of Leptis Magna in Africa, rivalled those of the more ancient cities of the Greek world - Athens, Ephesus, Antioch, Alexandria - which were themselves adorned with Roman baths and amphitheatres and basilicas to supplement the declining glory of their classical and Hellenistic treasures.

Vitruvius had given the measure of such harmonious development over a century before:

> "Without symmetry and proportion no temple can have a regular plan; that is, it must have an exact proportion worked out after the fashion of the limbs of a finely shaped human body.... In like manner the various parts of temples ought to have dimensions answering suitably to the general sum of their whole magnitude."[6]

It was as though for a moment the world took breath and paused after the wild scenes of horror under Domitian, so that the citizen of Leptis Magna on the African coast could gaze out from the theatre, over the forest of ochre columns of the courtyard and portico enclosing the temple of the deified Emperors, to the azure line of the sea, and feel at one with the centurion who looked from a milecastle on Hadrian's wall northwards, over the snow-filled hollows of the rugged hills to a land that did not know the ease of civilisation and the security of law. The Empire had achieved a passing unity, transient but precious for all that and reflecting, however imperfectly, the unity of Spirit. It was a unity based on hierarchy, on the due recognition of a natural order that ran from the petty tiller of the soil by the banks of the Nile, through the wine and olive oil warehouses of Baetica, the elegant *peristylia* of the town houses of Pompeii, the lovely villas of Pliny with their box hedges cut in the shapes of animals, to the majesty of Rome itself in the austere height of the Senate house and the beautifully poised statue of Marcus Aurelius on horseback in front of the Lateran Palace. That Emperor, above others, knew that the hierarchy was not complete without the recognition of a cultural heritage derived from the Athenian philosophers and the gift of civilisation offered by the Supreme Being.

It was not indeed Plato's ideal commonwealth. The brave warriors of Dacia slaughtered each other in the Coliseum for the amusement of the Roman crowd. Slaves occasionally murdered their masters and the Senate could still order that every slave of the household, guilty and innocent alike, should be put to death for it, even if now soldiers had to line the streets to ensure that the full sentence was carried out. Pliny ordered, routinely, that two women slaves should be tortured to extract from them details of the practices of Christians. Cheaply built *insulae* collapsed from time to time on Roman artisan families, and plague might sweep into the Empire with the soldiers returning from eastern campaigns. Yet nothing could quite break the golden moment, when the rulers of men became briefly touched by the finger of philosophy, reconciling them and their people to death, as it had reconciled the noble Seneca:

> "O Man, citizenship of this great world-city has been yours. Whether for five years or fivescore, what is that to you? Whatever the law of that city decrees is

fair to one and all alike. Wherein then is your grievance? You are not ejected from the city by any unjust judge or tyrant, but by the selfsame Nature which brought you into it; just as when an actor is dismissed by the manager who engaged him. But I have played no more than three of the five acts. Just so; in your drama of life, three acts are all the play. Its point of completeness is determined by him who formerly sanctioned your creation, and today sanctions your dissolution. Neither of those decisions lay within yourself. Pass on your way, then, with a smiling face, under the smile of him who bids you go."[7]

## References:

1. E. Gibbon, *Decline and Fall of the Roman Empire*, Methuen, London, 1905, ch. 3.

2. Marcus Aurelius, *Meditations*, trans. M. Staniforth, Penguin, London, 1964, Book IX, p. 144.

3. Seneca, 'Letter 26', in *Letters from a Stoic*, trans. R. Campbell, Penguin, London, 1977.

4. Juvenal, *Satire* VIII.

5. Marcus Aurelius, *Meditations*, Book II, p. 51.

6. Vitruvius, *Ten Books of Architecture*, Book III, ch. 1.

7. Marcus Aurelius, *Meditations*, Book XII, p. 188.

## Chapter 40
# Saints and Martyrs
### *The Growth of the Church to the Council of Chalcedon*

AFTER THE DEATH OF MARCUS AURELIUS in 180 BC, the throne of the Emperors in Rome became an object to be seized by whoever commanded the strongest army or the largest purse. In the fifty years between 235 AD and 285 AD, twenty-six Emperors wore the purple, of whom one died a natural death. Only an outright military take-over by the hardened Dalmatian soldier, Diocletian, in 287 AD, established a brittle stability, which enabled the Empire to survive further disturbances, until the last Emperor in the west, Romulus Augustus, was deposed by the German general, Odoacer, in 476 AD. At intervals during these centuries of decline men and women were massacred, tortured, thrown to wild beasts or burnt alive for their Christian faith. Waves of barbarian invasion shook the Empire, especially in the Danubian lands, then in every province, and finally in Italy itself. The social hierarchy was wrenched as under

*Medieval Greek Church in the Agora, Athens*

by the rise of peasant soldiers to military commands and barbarians to the highest offices of state. In the realm of morals and religion only the Christians preserved a consistent rectitude - though, in Christian theology, intellectual unrest led to recurrent crises in the statement of the cardinal principles of the faith. Why such turbulence? Why for so long was all in pieces and all coherence gone?

As one civilisation fell and another arose, the twilight of Apollo was at the same time the dawning of Christ. The nine hundred year cycle of Hellenism, from the death of Socrates to the early sixth century AD, constituted the final culture of the civilisation that extended back into the age of heroes; but Hellenism reached forward into Christian civilisation, also, its language and its art becoming a medium for the transmission of the new religion, especially in the matrix of the eastern Mediterranean, where St Paul had laboured so intensively. Hence the last centuries of Hellenism struck a strangely unique note, an uneasy fusion of the fading harmonies of Apollo's lyre and the rising call of the gospel of Christ.

The Church grew up initially in cities, so that the word "pagan", meaning "unbeliever", arose from the primary meaning of "those who dwelt in the *pagus*", the countryside beyond the cities. By the early fourth century these urban Christian communities were especially strong in Asia Minor - the "seven cities which are in Asia" of St John's Revelation - in Syria and Palestine, Alexandria and the Nile Delta, eastern Greece, Italy from Rome southwards and north Africa around Carthage; but even in Gaul and Spain cities like Massilia, Arausio, Lugdunum, Burdigala (Bordeaux), Cordoba and Hispalis (Seville) soon became Christian centres. Christian converts amongst the Roman legions took their faith to Britain and the *limites* on the Rhine and Danube. People of all classes were converted: the superior *honestiores* - senators, civil servants and town councillors - the inferior *humiliores*, who were the majority of the citizens, and even slaves, who found in the Church a genuine equality before God. Christians became a community within a community, a brotherhood who recognised each other by a common devotion to Christ and a common will to live according to Christian precepts:

> "The difference between Christians and the rest of mankind is not a matter of nationality, or language, or customs. Christians do not live apart in separate cities of their own, speak any special dialect, nor practice any eccentric way of life... They pass their lives in whatever township - Greek or foreign - each man's lot has determined; and conform to ordinary local usage in their clothing, diet and other habits... Their behaviour there is more like transients; they take their full part as citizens, but they also submit to anything and everything as if they were aliens."[1]

Each local community was under the guidance of a bishop, or sometimes a group of presbyters assisted by a deacon, but in the first decades of the early Church these were of lesser importance than the apostles, prophets and teachers referred to by St Paul in his first Letter to the Corinthians (12:28), who were called to office directly by the Holy Ghost. Apostles founded new churches and visited others, where they preached, staying for no more than three days and accepting in provisions only whatever would support their journey to the next port of call. Prophets were men inspired to speak, whose words were not to be doubted whilst they were speaking, for fear of blasphemy against the Holy Ghost, though the congregation might judge by their behaviour whether they were genuine prophets. Teachers had special powers of instruction. It was only when such men were no longer present that the authority of the bishops became predominant, a change probably related to the gradual disappearance of the inner teaching of Jesus, which he had given directly to his disciples.

The early Christians met in small groups in houses - not until the late third century were churches built especially for worship. A bishop sat on a dais in the centre of a semi-circle of his clergy, a seating arrangement like that of a Roman judge and assessors, whilst:

> "A chant celebrates the fear of the Law,
> The grace of the Prophets is made known,
> The faith of the Gospels is implanted,
> The tradition of the Apostles is secured, and
> The grace of the Church waxes jubilant."[2]

This suggests that, after an initial reading of Psalms, Old and New Testament readings followed, and finally a sermon. The younger Pliny in Bithynia discovered that the Christians there met before dawn, chanted verses in honour of Christ and took an oath not to commit theft, robbery, adultery, breach of trust or fraud. Later in the day they would meet again to eat a meal together. Pliny admitted that he found "nothing but a degenerate sort of cult carried to extravagant lengths."

Baptism and the eucharist were the principal rites of the early Church. Both were understood as forms of purification. The eucharist was not to be celebrated until the communicants were purified in mind by the confession of sins, and until every cause of dissension between them had been resolved. For, above all, it was a celebration of the true communion of members; nothing should separate them from one another, nor from God. To break bread and to drink wine in remembrance of Christ was to be remembered, to become One. In the central place that the Last Supper held in Christian worship, there was an echo of the Socratic symposium, as well as of the Passover feast of the Jews.

Clement of Alexandria, in the mid second century, stated explicitly that just a few men preserved "the true tradition of the blessed teaching straight from Peter, James, John and Paul." He himself had heard this teaching from the lips of one man in Greece, one in southern Italy, one in the Lebanon and a fourth in Egypt. For the first century or so of the early Church, authority lay with the dwindling number of men such as Clement, third bishop of Rome and Polycarp of Smyrna, a pupil of St John at Ephesus, who had personally conversed with the apostles. This was probably the real meaning of the apostolic succession, namely that there was an oral tradition by which the inner teaching of Jesus had been handed down directly from the immediate disciples. As the link became more tenuous, the Church looked to a secondary source of authority in the Gospels, so that the idea of a written canon developed, giving rise to much debate about which writings were the canon. Certain fundamental ideas, like that of the transmigration of souls held by Clement of Alexandria, and the pre-natal existence of the soul held by Origen, were omitted from what finally became the canon; for example, from St Jerome's translation of the Bible into Latin (the Vulgate). As the Church grew in membership, and particularly when it was granted official recognition by the Emperor Constantine in 313 AD, the need to present a broadly acceptable doctrine became overwhelming, so that the inner teaching disappeared from sight, except in so far as it guided the formulation of what the world required.

Persecution of Christians was spasmodic and often the result of local pagan zeal, mob emotion, or the spite of a provincial official, rather than of imperial policy. The worst persecutions were those under Nero and the Antonines, then under Decius and Valerian in the mid third century and, severest of all, under Diocletian at the end of the third century. Generally, the Roman policy of religious toleration inhibited any continuous and systematic persecution, but the imperial authorities were tested by the nature of the Christian sects. Christians would not accept Emperor worship, even if it only meant a token sprinkling of incense on a shrine; nor would they repudiate the name of Christ. They would not allow any hint of syncretism - such as the assimilation of God the Father with Jupiter, or of Christ with Apollo - the means by which Rome had absorbed all other religions within its borders, except Judaism. Most difficult of all, the Christians' absolute insistence on purification before the eucharist meant inevitably that their services were held in private and were strictly limited to known members. Inevitably the rumours of secret, heinous practices arose, like incest and cannibalism. Such misguided attitudes explain the fury with which the populace in cities like Smyrna and Lyons demanded the torture and execution of Christians, so that often the imperial officers tried, humanely, to persuade the victims of mob fury to go through the form of recantation. A further irritant was the Christian's eschewal of public life, where this involved recognition of pagan gods. Even visiting the public baths, the social centre of urban life, was avoided.

The saints and martyrs of the early Church demonstrated the virtues, especially the courage, which sprang from certainty of the living God within them. Some exhibited an incredible indifference to bodily and mental suffering. Ignatius of Antioch, martyred at Rome in 117 BC, wrote "I am His wheat, ground fine by the lions' teeth to be made purest bread for Christ." At Smyrna c156 AD, Polycarp died at the age of 86:

> "When he had offered up the Amen and completed his prayer, the men in charge lit the fire, and a great flame shot up. Then we saw a marvellous sight, we who were privileged to see it and were spared to tell the others what happened. The fire took the shape of a vaulted room, like a ship's sail filled with wind, and made a wall round the martyr's body, which was in the middle not like burning flesh but like gold and silver refined in a furnace. Indeed, we were conscious of a wonderful fragrance, like a breath of frankincense or some other costly spice."[3]

Ignatius and Polycarp were bishops of major churches in the eastern Empire. Many humbler Christians died with equal courage, like those from Lyons and Vienne in the Rhone valley, during the reign of Marcus Aurelius. Amongst these was a woman called Blandina. She was subjected to humiliating tortures. Having survived terrible beatings, whipping and the rack, she was hung on a post and exposed as food for wild beasts in the arena. When the beasts did not kill her, she was cut down and returned to prison, only to be burnt later on an iron griddle, yet still not allowed to die. She was then brought out once more, dropped into a basket and thrown to a bull to be tossed many times on his horns. Still alive, and sustained by "her hope and sure hold on all that her faith meant, and her communing with Christ," Blandina's sufferings were finally ended by the executioner.

Such sufferings give an extra dimension of meaning to the very word "martyr". The Greek *martyros* meant "one who bears testimony, a witness"; in the case of the early Christians, this meant both those who originally witnessed the presence of Jesus and, later, those who bore witness to the truth of his teaching. Yet as the witnessing of their own sufferings is perhaps the only way in which the martyrs' ability to bear them can be understood.

The Roman city of Verulamium in Britain saw the martyrdom of Alban, a Roman citizen who may have been a soldier. During a period of persecution a Christian priest fled to the house of Alban for shelter, possibly because Alban, although not baptised, may have been preparing to enter the Church. When the authorities demanded surrender of the priest, Alban put on the priest's cloak and allowed himself to be taken away in his place. To shed his blood for Christ he hoped would take the place of baptism by water. The Roman judge became furious on discovering the deception and demanded that Alban sacrifice to the pagan gods, Jupiter and Apollo. He refused and was beaten with rods to make him submit. His persistent refusal and his repeated affirmation of faith in Christ led the judge to order torture and, when that was ineffective, execution. Whereupon he was led out to the place of execution beyond the city wall, crossing the River Ver at a ford and climbing the gentle slope of a hill, which was covered with the wild flowers of early Summer. At the summit, where a large crowd had gathered, the executioner is said to have flung down his sword and urged Alban to pray for him. A second executioner was found, and Alban's head was struck off. The soldier who had first declined the task was then himself executed.

The name of Alban became venerated throughout Britain, and elsewhere in Europe, especially in the Rhineland. The date of his martyrdom is uncertain. It was possibly in the mid third century under the persecution of the Emperor Decius, or even under Diocletian; but it may have been as early as 209 AD, during the reign of Septimus Severus, when the Emperor and his two sons were in Britain. If so, Alban was the first martyr of Europe.

In the year 313 AD, the Emperor Constantine, with his co-Emperor, Licinius, at last gave Christians in the Empire the right to practise their religion without fear of persecution. The Edict of Milan of that year shows a remarkable liberality of mind:

"When we, Constantine and Licinius, Emperors, met at Milan in conference concerning the welfare and security of the realm, we decided that of the things that are of profit to all mankind, the worship of God ought rightly to be our first and chiefest care, and that it was right that Christians and all others should have freedom to follow the kind of religion they favoured, so that the God who dwells in heaven might be propitious to us and to all under our rule. We, therefore, announce that, notwithstanding any provisions concerning the Christians in our former instructions, all who choose that religion are to be permitted to continue therein, without any let or hindrance, and are not to be any way troubled or molested. Note that at the same time all others are to be allowed the free and unrestricted practice of their religions; for it accords with the good order of the realm and the peacefulness of our times that each should have freedom to worship God after his own choice, and that we do not intend to detract from honour due to any religion or its followers."[4]

The Edict went on to order that all places of worship previously taken from Christians should be restored to them.

As in the life of Christ, so in the early church the role of women was of great significance. Many died, like Blandina under Marcus Aurelius, as martyrs, but others contributed by their direct influence upon the leading men in the Church in the early centuries. An outstanding example of this was Macrina, sister of two great figures in the Greek Church in the fourth century, St Basil the Great and Gregory of Nyssa. Macrina devoted herself to the Christian life after the man to whom she was betrothed died when she was twelve. Gregory described her as following the path of philosophy, a term which in the Greek Church of the time meant "the greatest, as it is the most difficult of professions which can be taken in hand by but a few, and only those who have been called forth by a divine magnanimity." (Gregory of Nazianzus). Macrina became the head of a women's community which her brother, Gregory, described:

> "the arrangement of their life, the high level of their philosophy, the lofty regimen of their activities night and day was such that it transcends description... among them was seen no anger, no envy, no hatred, nor arrogance..."

It was Macrina who first drew her brothers to follow a truly devout way of life. Later, when Basil returned from visiting the Christian fathers in the Egyptian desert, the monastery he founded in Asia Minor was built on the opposite bank of the River Iris from that of Macrina's community, and reflected her ideas. Gregory even regarded Macrina as his teacher, depicting her thus in his dialogue *On the Soul and the Resurrection*. It was contrary to the thinking of the early Church that women should be accorded an active role, following the words of St Paul in his epistle to Timothy (I, 2:12) "I suffer not a woman to teach," but Gregory of Nyssa lifted the veil on the part played by such women as his sister. On her deathbed she drew Gregory's attention away from her suffering, and he was inspired by her discourse on the soul explaining the reason for life in the flesh and how death is a release back into a truer life. Consumed by the Holy Spirit, she explained all this "clearly and logically".

There were other women of similar character, such as Melania the Elder, who founded a monastery at Jerusalem, and Paula and Marcella, who were taught by St Jerome and became powerful influences on aristocratic society in the Empire. Jerome summed up the role of such philosophical Christian women in these words on Marcella's work in Rome:

> "In case of a dispute arising as to the testimony of Scripture on any subject, recourse was had to her to settle it. And so wise was she and so well did she understand what philosophers call *to prepon* (what is necessary or becoming) in what she did, that when she answered questions she gave her opinion not as her own, but as from me or someone else, thus admitting that what she taught, she had learned from others."[5]

Until the Edict of Milan the teaching of the Church had developed without much apparent contention, though in the second century the Gnostics disturbed orthodox Christians, and in the third century the dualistic view of good and evil, taught by the Persian religious leader, Mani, caused difficulties. After the Edict of Milan a spotlight was cast upon the Christian faith, for Constantine himself became a Christian and so were all the subsequent Emperors, except Julian the Apostate (361-363 AD). Moreover, the Church became more centralised; the authority of bishops, especially of metropolitans, was enhanced, and general assemblies of bishops, or synods, acquired great authority in settling Church doctrine. As though in preparation for this broadcasting of the faith, a few profound thinkers had formulated ideas by drawing upon both the Christian faith and Hellenistic philosophy. Clement and Origen, both of Alexandria, introduced to the Church a tradition of Platonism derived from their predecessor there, the Jewish philosopher, Philo.

This tradition found its purest expression in the work of Plotinus, a pupil, together with Origen, of a teacher, Ammonius Saccas, said to be the founder of Neo-Platonism. Ammonius, like Socrates and Jesus, wrote nothing. He was given the title Theodidaktos, meaning "taught by God". At a time when the young Plotinus was deeply frustrated by the lack of inspiration in all his other teachers, he heard Ammonius lecture and immediately exclaimed "This is the man I was looking for!" Plotinus studied under Ammonius for eleven years in Alexandria; then joined the expedition of the Emperor Gordian to Persia, in order to find the wise men of Persia and India. When Gordian was killed, Plotinus returned to settle in Rome, where he gathered around him a group of the senatorial aristocracy. Whilst he taught philosophy, he remained a practical and companionable man, arbitrating disputes - without ever making an enemy - acting as guardian of children, and attending to people's personal problems, as when he found who had stolen a lady friend's necklace and when he advised his pupil, Porphyry, to avoid depression by going away for a change of scene and company. "Present at once to himself and others, gentle and at the disposal of all who had any sort of acquaintance with him," as Porphyry described him, he was aware of the eternal, yet careful of the earthly, needs of his friends. The Emperor Gallienus (253-268 AD) and his wife, Salonina, admired Plotinus; perhaps through the philosopher's influence the persecution of Christians was halted during Gallienus' reign.

Plotinus taught that the ultimate reality is the indescribable, unchanging and eternal One; that this One sees Itself; that the One in the form of the soul is the creative principle of the world. Upon this trinity of the One all else totally depends, having no independent existence of its own. In a beautiful analogy, he refers to all three:

> "The One, which contains no otherness, is always present with us, and we
> with it whenever we escape from otherness. It does not desire us, to be attentive
> to us, but we desire and revolve about the One. We are always around it, but
> do not always look to it; just as a chorus, singing in order around its leader,
> may at times turn away from the sight of him, but when it turns inwards again
> it sings beautifully, fully attentive to him. We similarly always revolve about
> the One - otherwise we should meet utter dissolution and cease to exist; but
> we do not always look to him. But on looking to him, then we find our goal
> and our resting place, and around him we dance the true dance, God inspired,
> no longer discordant."[6]

Plotinus called the One the Father, the seeing of Itself Nous, or Reason, and the creative principle the soul. Thus, though he was not explicitly a Christian, Plotinus formulated a doctrine of the Trinity which the Church was able to assimilate at a time when intellectual formulation was becoming essential.

For when Constantine took away the public disability of the Church by the Edict of Milan, its teaching was already in danger of serious division. The central issue was the status and nature of Christ. This was understood in the early Church with a natural simplicity:

> "Though He has existed since the beginning, He came as one appearing newly; though we know Him to be from Old, He is born ever anew in the hearts of His saints. This is He who is from everlasting, this is He who is accounted this day a Son."[7]

The world, however, required a more intellectual and defined statement. Arius, also from Alexandria, put forward the view that the Son was not equal with the Father, because he was created after the Father; nor was he, therefore, of one substance with the Father. This dividing of substance threatened the idea of the divine unity. At the Council of Nicaea in 325 AD, summoned by Constantine and attended by bishops from all over the Empire, the Arian argument was rejected with the formula: "the Son of God, begotten of the Father, only-begotten, that is of the substance of the Father." This Nicene orthodoxy was championed by Athanasius, bishop of Alexandria, but for much of the fourth century, Constantine's successors were Arian in belief, so that Athanasius was exiled.

So feverish did the debates within the Church over Arianism become that the pagan historian, Ammianus Marcellus, was driven to write that, as public transport hurried throngs of bishops hither and thither to attend synods, these attempts to impose Arian conformity only succeeded in hamstringing the postal service. Constantine himself realised that public debate was not the right way to settle points of theology:

> "It was wrong ever to propose such questions as these, or to reply to them when propounded. For points of discussion which are enjoined by the authority of no law, but rather suggested by a contentious spirit which is in turn the consequence of misused leisure, should be confined to our own thoughts, and neither hastily produced in public assemblies nor ill-advisedly entrusted to the public ear."[8]

Only after the brief pagan interlude of the Emperor Julian did the orthodox view emerge triumphant, notably when it was confirmed at the Council of Constantinople in 381 AD. Behind this affirmation of the threefold unity of God lay the teaching of Plotinus. He had insisted that the ultimate reality of the One is indivisible, yet has three forms; hence the Trinity is the three Persons of Father, Son and Holy Spirit, which yet are of one undivided substance. The Son was Plotinus' soul, the creative principle of the world, which St John had long before called the Word, whilst the One seeing Itself was the Holy Spirit.

This re-affirmation of the Oneness of God was vital to the Church's lasting mission, and was particularly vital to its teaching on redemption. How could Christ redeem men if he himself were not God? His role as the mediator between Man and God rested upon his divinity; the separation apparently created by sin could not be bridged by a creature not himself divine. Yet this need for a Man/God led to a further major dispute within the Church. Such Church leaders as Nestorius, Bishop of Constantinople, were accused of heresy for emphasising the humanity of Christ and thus seeming to divide him into two Persons, one human, one divine. In fact, Nestorius taught the intelligent doctrine of prosopic union, in which *prosopon* means self-manifestation with extension. Hence, just as a painter uses a brush to extend his own manifestation, so Christ used manhood without dividing his Person. Nevertheless, Nestorius was accused of heresy and in 431 AD the Council of Ephesus affirmed that Christ was One Person. Twenty years later, under the leadership of Pope Leo I, the Council of Chalcedon affirmed the dual nature of the One Person. Hence the orthodox statement was completed, to remain until modern times, that God is the Holy Trinity of one substance and three Persons, of which the Son has the dual nature of Man and God.

Though the finest minds of the Church in these centuries were turned mainly to the deep questions of the Trinity and the Logos, one of the greatest Church fathers, St Augustine of Hippo, faced a problem of faith which arose immediately out of the historical situation in which he found himself. In 410 AD the city of Rome was sacked by Germanic tribes under Alaric the Goth. Twenty years later the Vandals, who had crossed the straits of Gibraltar, approached Augustine's see of Hippo Regius.

In the interval between these devastating events, Augustine wrote his major work, *The City of God*. The book was dominated by the question of why God should allow the Roman Empire, with its tradition of ordered government, law and culture, to be destroyed by uncivilised barbarians. The pagans - many remained, only a century after the Edict of Milan - claimed that the fall of Rome was the vengeance of the true gods, angered by the apostasy of Christians, and the consequence of the Christians' refusal to serve in the imperial armies. Augustine did not turn this argument round upon the pagans, nor could he deny the omnipotence of God. His answer lay in his understanding of the idea of justice. In this he was greatly influenced by Plato's *Republic* and Cicero's writing on the same theme. Any group of men, even a crowd of pirates, said Augustine, may form a community, if they hold to a common aim. The pirate who answered Alexander the Great, when the king asked him how he dared to molest the seas, was justified: "Because I do it only with a little ship, I am called a brigand: you do it with a great navy and are called Emperor." Yet a true state - the Republic - is founded upon more than this; it is the embodiment of justice. Without justice the state is a mere convention, a man-made contrivance for a common aim. Rome had lacked justice. Hence its fall was no more than the collapse of an organisation set up for the convenience of men, without the divine quality of justice which would render its fall a true cataclysm:

"His foundation is in the holy mountains.
The Lord loveth the gates of Zion more than
all the dwellings of Jacob.
Glorious things are spoken of thee, O city of God."[9]

Augustine's city of God was a spiritual city, where dwelt the souls of the righteous - even of those who lived before Christ. The Church was the pilgrimage of the righteous during their brief spell on earth. The earthly city was founded on selfish love; the city of God on love of God. Therefore, no fall of an earthly city need arouse fear or indignation, whilst the fall of the city of God was impossible. Augustine's ideas were highly influential throughout the Middle Ages. They were often misinterpreted to mean that the city of God was the Church on earth, the institution centred on Rome which became embroiled in political disputes with kings and emperors. When correctly understood, they contributed to a medieval indifference to things of the flesh and to a love of the spiritual, though these could degenerate into a dream of otherworldliness.

Augustine, as a student of Plotinus, retained something of the latter's insistence on non-duality, but Plotinus taught more clearly than Augustine that men could find the city of God within themselves:

> "If it is the soul that makes us lovable, why
> is it that we seek it only in others and not in
> ourselves? You love others because of it.
> Love, then, yourself."[10]

It was a doctrine sorely needed by men and women living through the turbulence of the third and fourth centuries after Christ, when the interlude of the Stoic Emperors had passed and the visible fabric of Christian Europe had not yet emerged from the invisible sources of its growth.

### References:

1. 'The Epistle to Diognetus', (c124 AD) in *Early Christian Writings*, trans. M. Staniforth, Penguin, London, 1968, p. 176.

2. 'The Epistle to Diognetus', trans. Staniforth, p. 183.

3. Eusebius, *The History of Church: From Christ to Constantine*, trans. G. A. Williamson, Penguin, London, 1984, Book IV, p. 173.

4. *Documents of the Christian Church*, ed. H. Bettenson, O.U.P., Oxford, 1943, p. 22.

5. St Jerome, *Epistles*, 127, 7.

6. Plotinus, *Enneads*, trans. J. Gregory, privately published, Book VI, 9, 8.

7. 'The Epistle to Diognetus', trans. Staniforth, p. 182.

8. 'Letter of Constantine to Alexander and Arius', in Eusebius, *The Life of Constantine*, 11. 64-72.

9. *Psalm* 87, vv. 1-3, King James Version.

10. Plotinus, *Ennead*, trans. Gregory, v. 1.

# Chapter 41

# Long Autumn of Empire

## The Fall of the Western Empire and the Creation of Constantinople

"If all the barbarian conquerors had been annihilated in the same hour, their total destruction would not have restored the empire of the West: and if Rome still survived, she survived the loss of freedom, of virtue, and of honour."[1]

THE WESTERN WORLD OF late antiquity exhibited disruption by religious conflict, extremes of wealth and poverty, and foreign invasion, whilst fears of the future and regret for the past obscured the present. Only amongst the Christians were many to be found who saw, in spite of everything, that the kingdom of God was spread upon the face of the earth. The Castalian spring of creativity that had nurtured the arts of Apollo was running dry. Yet the passing of the pagan gods did not occur without a few

*Arch of Constantine, Rome*

valedictory expressions of the old genius of Greece and Rome, for as the poet Claudian wrote at the end of the fourth century AD, "spring has her flowers, autumn her apples: so the year goes by." The Emperor Julian, for example, set an impeccable standard of self-discipline and devotion to duty. A student of philosophy and literature, sober, continent and devout, and a courageous soldier, he reflected the ideals of Lycurgus and Plato. Artists and craftsmen occasionally produced work that shone with the distant light of Athens and Augustan Rome, like the great silver platters found at Mildenhall in England and Kaiseraugst in Switzerland. Even in the fifth century, as Germanic armies penetrated far inside the western Empire, generals like Stilicho - himself a barbarian - and Aetius, showed Spartan resilience in the Empire's defence.

The third century had witnessed an almost mortal crisis for Rome: huge losses of territory on the borders, rapid inflation, economic decline and the murder of Emperors. The low point was reached when the Emperor Valerian was captured by the Persians in 260 AD and probably put to a cruel death. For six years afterwards, Zenobia, the resourceful queen of Palmyra in Syria, had set up a broad empire of her own in territory which Pompey the Great had once so well controlled. In 271 AD the Emperor Aurelian built a massive wall around the city of Rome, for centuries before contemptuous, like Sparta, of foreign infantry.

The martial spirit of Rome, however, had not yet expired. Zenobia's fiefdom was destroyed. Then Diocletian rose from commander of the imperial bodyguard to the imperial throne and set about reforms which turned the Empire, more or less, into a military dictatorship. The last vestiges of Republicanism, in particular the authority of the Senate, were removed. All power was centred upon the person of the Emperor, whose council took over what few duties the Senate had retained. The Emperor's residence was moved from Rome to Nicomedia in Asia Minor (later Emperors in the west often resided in Milan and Ravenna). A central military reserve, called the *comitatus*, was established under the Emperor's command. The finances were strengthened by the issue of a new gold coin, the solidus. Most significantly for the future, Diocletian appointed a second Emperor, or Augustus, in the west, with subordinate Caesars in east and west, to rule alongside himself - though Diocletian retained overall authority until he retired in 305 AD. The provinces of the Empire were grouped into 12 dioceses, whose vicars were responsible to four praetorian prefects. The army of each frontier of the Empire was controlled by a military leader (*dux*), henceforth independent of civilian authority.

This new order set the tone for the final two centuries of Roman power. When further inflation struck the Empire, Diocletian responded with a far-reaching edict of price control. Despite fearful penalties for evasion, economic forces proved too strong for mere legislation. Dictatorship set up new barriers and inhibited the free effort of the people, whilst the stream of decline ran inexorably. To bolster falling production, occupations were made compulsory by law, so that bakers or miners, shipbuilders or weavers, were not allowed to change trades and their sons had to continue in their father's trade. Under Constantine a law was passed allowing farm owners to chain any *coloni* who showed signs of planning to leave the land. Such measures could only weaken the inner resources of the Empire. Beyond its borders enemies were gathering strength for mortal blows upon its frontiers.

On the steppelands of central Asia, a nomadic, primitive people, the Huns, were moving westwards, frustrated by the Great Wall of China from expansion to the east. To the north and west of the Black Sea, large communities of Germanic Goths had settled, after migrating southwards from Scandinavia. Further east were the Alans and the Vandals, harassed by the Huns and ready, like the Goths, to cross the great barrier of the Danube. On the Rhine frontier other Germans - the Alamanni, Burgundians and Franks - troubled the garrisons of the *limes*, whilst by the fourth century, Angles, Saxons, Jutes and Frisians from north-west Germany were crossing the North Sea to challenge the counts of the Saxon shore, who guarded the east and south coasts of Roman Britain. The great finale of the epic wanderings of the Germanic peoples - the *Volkerwanderung* - was approaching.

In the mid fourth century, Visigoths were allowed to settle inside the Danube frontier. Already the imperial armies were everywhere largely recruited from men of German stock; no longer were such barbarian soldiers transferred to frontiers far from their homeland to avoid any natural collusion with invaders. Such a procedure was beyond the financial and administrative resources of the late Empire. If Goths stood in Roman uniforms along the Danubian lines, why not recruit whole armies of Goths to fight for Rome in return for their settlement on Roman land near the frontier? Thus were whole tribes, rather than individual Germans, invited into the very lands they coveted.

Wise statesmanship might still have salvaged peace from such a bargain. The feudatory (allied) Germans showed an inclination to be integrated into Roman society: they respected Roman authority and arms, and appreciated Roman wealth and amenities. Moreover, their assimilation might have been gradual and easy, for their armies were rarely more than 20,000 strong. Even when the Vandals came totally to dominate the Roman people of North Africa, they amounted to only 2% of the population. The mind of Rome, however, was obscured by darkness; no man of broad sympathy came forward to offer to Romans and Germans alike a policy of integration. Feudatory status - land for armed service - was the best that could be offered.

The Visigoths accepted such terms from the Emperor Valens, but immediately the meanness of local commanders created a deep antipathy. Though care was taken to transport the Gothic host across the Danube - Ammianus Marcellus adds, ironically, that even the sick were brought over, so that "none of those destined to overthrow the Roman Empire should be left behind" - the Roman generals, seeing that the Goths were near starvation, forced them to exchange slaves, including the sons of leading men, for dog-meat. Soon after, when the Goths respectfully asked a Roman chief magistrate for food and money to support their transference to another district, he armed the populace and threatened the outnumbered Goths with mob violence. Not surprisingly the Goths broke out into open revolt against their Roman masters. Their barbarian vigour and martial habits took possession of them and the whole region of Thrace was devastated with rapine, pillage and fire.

Valens brought an army against them. Overconfident in Roman power of arms, he was too impatient to wait for help from his co-Emperor from the west. In the year 378 AD at Adrianople in Thrace one of the greatest military defeats of Rome was enacted. The Visigoths were permanently established inside the Empire and embarked upon a westward movement, which would lead them eventually to Spain.

Briefly the Empire was united again under the powerful soldier and dogmatic Christian Emperor, Theodosius I. As a convinced orthodox Catholic, Theodosius removed Arian clergy and allowed the persuasive Bishop of Milan, Ambrose, to dominate the Church, even incurring Ambrose's excommunication for authorising a punitive massacre in Salonika - an event which later churchmen were to cite in claiming the Pope's spiritual ascendancy over Emperors and kings. Theodosius demonstrated how rigid the thought of the later Empire had become. In 384 AD the President of the Senate in Rome, a pagan, asked the Emperor to return the great statue of Victory to the Senate house after it had been removed. Theodosius refused: Victory was a pagan goddess. The reply of the President, given to Bishop Ambrose, showed that ancient intelligence might still outshine the new dogmas of the Christian Church: "So great a mystery cannot be approached by a single road only."

When Theodosius died in 395 AD, the Empire was divided between his sons, Arcadius in the east and Honorius in the west, never to be re-united (though, in theory, Arcadius and Honorius ruled the whole Empire jointly). They were pale imitations of Emperors. In the west the barbarian, Stilicho, was *de facto* ruler. He won many victories over the German tribes, but even he could not stop the massive onrush of Vandals, Alans, Suebi and Burgundians over the Rhine in 406-7AD, which devastated Gaul. The western Empire never recovered from this disaster. In Roman Britain ambitious generals betrayed their trust in order to seek power for themselves, bringing their troops back across the Channel, whilst the Britons remained to brave the German mariners. When the last legions were withdrawn by Honorius to help Rome, the Emperor could only answer the Britons' appeal with an order to fend for themselves. In 410 AD the most symbolic blow of all was struck. The Visigoth leader, Alaric, disgruntled by his Roman paymasters, attacked Rome itself - though Honorius had moved to Ravenna in 404 AD. The city was partially sacked. Not since the Gaullish invasion of 387 BC had the eternal city succumbed to a foreign army.

Nevertheless, Germanic respect for the majesty of Rome prevented any German war leader from assuming the purple. In Africa the Vandals under Gaiseric set up an independent kingdom in Roman territory, built a fleet and dominated the western Mediterranean. In 455 AD they sailed northwards and sacked Rome. The last Roman commander of any standing in the west, Aetius, had fought valiantly until the year before the Vandal raid. He formed an alliance with the Visigoths to defeat even the Huns of Atila, the greatest of all nomadic warlords, on the Catalaunian Plains of eastern Gaul in 451 AD, perhaps saving western Europe from a truly barbarous future. Significantly, it was Pope Leo I who, in the following year, persuaded Atila to withdraw from Italy. The western Empire was in pieces. In 476 AD it came formally to an end, when the German general, Odoacer, deposed Romulus Augustulus in Ravenna and informed the eastern Emperor, Zeno, that the western throne was vacant.

Beneath decline lay a deterioration of leadership and character, disregard for natural law, especially in the economic sphere, and unwillingness to undertake public responsibility. The later Roman Emperors, despite particular virtues in such men as Diocletian, Constantine, Julian and Valentinian I, were of a lesser order than the great men of the Roman Republic and of the Stoic period of the Empire. A state visit to Rome by Constantius II in the year 357 AD exemplified how abject a figure the Emperor had become, if set beside the ideal of the philosopher king that had inspired Hellenistic rulers for over seven hundred years:

"Constantius, behaving as if the temple of Janus were shut and all his enemies over thrown, conceived a strong desire to visit Rome and celebrate the fall of Magnentius by a triumph to which he had no title, since it had been won by the spilling of Roman blood. He had not overcome in person any race that made war on him; no news had arrived that any had been defeated by the valour of his generals; he had added nothing to the Empire; he had never been seen fighting at the head of his men or even in the front rank in moments of crisis. His object was simply to display his gold-inlaid standards and his brilliant retinue in a procession of inordinate length before the eyes of a populace that was living in peace and neither expected nor wished to see any such show."[2]

The Emperor Valens allowed himself to be persuaded that it was beneath his dignity to act as a judge, with the consequence that those who had so persuaded him, and other rich and powerful men, corrupted the courts with the collusion of judges and advocates. Even the virtuous Julian, renowned for his devotion to pagan gods, dwelt on the outskirts of religious truth, since his admirer, Ammanius Marcellus, described him as "superstitious rather than genuinely observant of the rites of religion." His indulgence in animal sacrifice on a large-scale was very far from the bloodless ceremony of King Numa; whilst his regard for the messenger-god, Mercury, exceeded his love for Apollo, god of light.

Emperors had lost touch with the Platonic ideal of a ruler dedicated to the Good and intent upon the wise government, protection and service of the people. Rome had moved through the unruly, divisive era of the third century, when an egalitarian army of professional soldiers had chosen ephemeral rulers - like the Republican armies of the first century BC - to a final stage of tyranny. The throne became an object of unprincipled ambition, so that even Constantine won and held it by bloody battles and the execution of close relatives, and his descendants continued to struggle for the chimera of absolute power. Finally, Diocletian's system had created a military dictatorship. "There is in fact no way of correcting wrongdoing in those who think that the height of virtue consists in the execution of their will", wrote the percipient Ammanius.

The character of the Emperors was reflected in the character of the people. The upper classes gave up philosophy for idle pursuits, dancing with "bird-like evolutions" or manufacturing "water-organs and lutes the size of carriages"; whilst the lower classes developed a passion for the chariot races of the hippodrome, wearing themselves out in detailed discussion of the relative merits of horses and drivers. In the theatre actors were hissed off the stage unless the mob had been first bribed to show them favour. Language generally became foul and senseless; and many people became addicted to gluttony, acquiring thereby names like Gluturinus ('gobbler'), Lucanicus ('sausage') and Porclaea ('pig's belly'). Some devoted their lives to drinking, gambling and brothels.

Constantine showed scant respect for the tradition of Roman Stoicism, which taught that the divine fire resided in every man, when he allowed the chaining of *coloni*. Theodosius I went even further in endorsing the unreserved power of landlords over tenants.

"Tenants... shall be bound by the rule of origin, and though they appear to be free-born by condition, shall nevertheless be considered like slaves of the land itself to which they are born, and shall have no right of going off or of changing their place."[3]

Such disregard for the civil duty of rulers to protect their subjects from unlawful imprisonment was matched by ignorance of the economic duties of government. The fundamental question of how land should be held had never been properly answered by the Roman Republic. Civil war and proscriptions had virtually eliminated the old patrician class by the end of the first century AD, which together with minor land reforms, like Vespasian's, had slowed the rate at which land accumulated in the hands of a few powerful men. Nevertheless, without natural justice in land tenure the inexorable polarisation between rich landowners, on one hand, and impoverished tenants and proletariat on the other, brought its destructive force to bear upon the late Empire. At no time was there a clear recognition that the economic rent of land was the natural fund of taxation, whether in kind or in money. For Crown land, it was acknowledged that tenants should pay rent to the state, but the principle was not equitably administered. Towards the end of the fourth century, perpetual leases of Crown land became widespread, known as *ius privatum salvo canone*, which gave tenures close to freeholds, since the land was removed from the list of Crown lands. The annual rent charge was fixed, making its revenue susceptible to inflation. In 434 AD any arrears of purchase money for Crown land were remitted. By the end of the western Empire all Crown land was held on perpetual leases and most of it was in the hands of wealthy men. One early fifth century Emperor issued a pathetic call "to prevent our eternal house being stripped of all its property." Moreover, land which lapsed to the state on the death of owners without heirs, or by confiscation of criminals' land, increasingly passed to rich men who claimed it before the state was told. Sometimes informers (*delatores*) were bribed to pass their information about vacant land to private individuals, rather than to the state.

Diocletian regularised the tax levied on private land by creating the *iugatio*, a tax on agricultural land. This left land not used for agriculture, but for houses and gardens, for example, free of tax, thus accentuating the burden on the poor, most of whom were peasant farmers. When Constantine added a poll tax to the *iugatio* assessment, the effect was to make mainly agricultural tenants liable for that also, though it only amounted to about 5% of the land tax. These taxes were levied in kind out of agricultural produce. Rich landlords often gained lower assessments by bribery of officials. Constantine also introduced a tax on trade, like the poll tax yielding about 5% of the land tax in total, which caused hardship, especially for small traders.

The general effect of all this was to break the back of the poor tenant farmer, the *colonus*. By the fifth century, between one third and two thirds of agricultural produce was taken in taxation, a much higher proportion than under the Republic. Such a huge levy went to support a massive bureaucracy, a completely mercenary army under excessive strain on most borders and the maintenance of a city proletariat in Rome. Meanwhile, landowners grew richer as they grasped Crown and vacant land, acquired virtual freeholds, and reaped the economic rent where it was untaxed, especially on urban land. Patterns of landholding became increasingly complicated. Senators held land in many provinces; for example, Melania held land in Italy, Sicily, Africa, Numidia, Mauretania, Spain and Britain, including one holding which contained 62 hamlets. Land-holding by the Church grew apace after the Edict of Milan, so that it soon held land in all the central provinces of the Empire. These rich landowners leased land to tenants - usually on short-term leases - who collected rent from the *coloni*, the actual tillers of the soil. After tax and rent, these *coloni* received a mere subsistence share of the produce, and their consequent attempts to move elsewhere, especially from marginal land, were frustrated, if necessary by chaining. By contrast, wealthy landowners were only lightly troubled by the *aurum oblaticum*, payable by Senators on the Emperor's accession and at certain festivals and the *aurum coronarium*, payable by cities on accessions only.

This debilitating economic situation was more serious in the western than in the eastern Empire, for several reasons. In the east, after 444 AD, land falling vacant could not be claimed by private landowners, so that it reverted to the Crown. In parts of the east, notably Syria, the land tax was assessed equitably by using *iugera* (the unit of assessment for the *iugatio*) of more or less equal value, taking into account land use and quality. Elsewhere - in Italy, for example - *iugera* were equal sized units, irrespective of use and quality. Thus in Italy rough pasture paid the same rate of tax as highly productive vineyards and olive groves, with the inevitable result that poor land went out of use or supported at the margin the very poorest of tenants. Syria, on the other hand, was one of the most productive regions of the whole Empire. Particularly after the calamities of the third century, the western Empire was generally poorer and yet, by the fifth century, Italian farmers were paying taxes of up to two thirds of the crop, whilst Egyptian farmers rarely paid more than one third. In 498 AD Constantine's tax on trade was abolished in the East. Finally, there was a huge and iniquitous difference between tax collection fees between east and west. In the east, these amounted to a modest 1-2% of the land tax; in the west they were 35% by the time that the western Emperor was deposed in 476 BC. The western Emperor, Valentinian III, had described his own tax collection system, with despairing eloquence, as a "smokescreen of minute calculations involved in impenetrable obscurity." In such conditions it is surprising that the western Empire did not succumb earlier to barbarians, whose vigour and simplicity had no truck with artificial barriers to beneficial use of land. That the warm, fertile, well-watered province of Gaul, for example, should contain so many marginal farms, where hungry *coloni* eked out a living, invited the German tribes to restore the natural prosperity of the land.

Hand in hand with the growth of the immense *latifundia* of the senatorial class went a disinclination to accept public leadership by the very people who had the time and resources to participate. By the late fifth century, when it was too late to save the western Empire, Senators were returning to their public responsibilities, mainly because the Emperors were weaker than they were; but, in the century before, they were content to enjoy their gains from land without offering service in return. Even the threat of barbarian invasion induced them merely to fortify their own individual estates. They ejected imperial collectors of taxes, harboured deserters from imperial armies when they were short of labour, and often took the law into their own hands, even to the extent of building private prisons. A visitor to Rome from the east wrote:

> "There is in the city a Senate of wealthy men . . .
> Every one of them is fit to hold high office.
> But they prefer not to. They stand aloof,
> Preferring to enjoy their property at leisure."[4]

The counterpart to this dereliction of duty by the senatorial class was a growth of bureaucracy, particularly in the fourth century, when civil servants became a hereditary caste. As standards of morality declined in society generally, so corruption spread amongst officials, who had permanent security and every opportunity for collusion.

One major case of corruption, in the province of Tripolis in Africa in the late fourth century, illustrates the extent of this. The city of Leptis was besieged by fierce local tribes, upset by the execution of one of their leaders, who had stirred up trouble. The citizens sent desperately for help from the local Roman commander, Count Romanus, recently appointed governor of the province. He refused to help, unless the besieged townspeople gave his army large supplies, including 4,000 camels. This they found impossible, and, left to their fate, sent two envoys with an appeal to the Emperor, Valentinian I. Romanus, however, hearing of the appeal, wrote to a high-ranking associate of his in the capital to arrange that the appeal should be frustrated. Valentinian was diverted from giving the matter his full attention, but he did agree that a government lawyer, Palladius, should go to Tripolis to investigate the whole matter, and also to pay the army its arrears of wages. Meanwhile, Count Romanus was informed of Palladius' visit. He gave confidential instructions to his agents in the army to see that most of the money for the soldiers should be left with Palladius. When Palladius heard of Romanus' failure to assist Leptis he was very indignant, but, on reprimanding Romanus, he was met with the insinuation that he himself would be exposed for corruption if he took the matter further. Palladius gave in. He returned to the imperial court and told Valentinian the outright lie that the complaints from the citizens of Leptis were quite unfounded. Orders were sent out to punish the envoys from the city. One was executed; one managed to escape. The local tribes, by this time, had withdrawn, without succeeding in breaking into the city. Later, the Emperor Theodosius uncovered the details of this nefarious matter.

At the level of government below the excessive bureaucratic ranks of consuls, praetorian prefects, vicars of dioceses and governors of provinces were the city councillors - the *curiales*. These middle class local officials were squeezed between the corrupt, greedy upper classes and the hard-pressed, regimented lower classes of small traders, craftsmen and peasants. On the *curiales* fell the burden of collecting taxes from individuals and generally ensuring that all other orders from on high were enforced. So unpopular did their task become that they would go to almost any length to avoid the position. Unfortunately for them, membership of a *curia*, or city council, was made hereditary. Under the Code of Theodosius II, they were forbidden to travel abroad or sell their property (15 acres of land was a requirement for a *curiale*), and they were denied asylum in churches. In some cases men were flogged for refusing the office; whilst one imperial edict ironically ordered governors to cease from appointing *curiales* as a punishment for offences, so hated was the office. No doubt some councillors escaped by joining the army or the Church or by evading the inefficient system altogether. Such conditions did not induce the sense of social responsibility required for good local government.

Leadership and character, recognition of natural law in economic matters, and a sense of responsibility to the community: these were the essential qualities which slowly disappeared from the late Empire, leaving it weak and impoverished, and in the west, headless. A more general cause, noted by Gibbon, hastened the effect of their disappearance:

"The decline of Rome was the natural and inevitable effect of immoderate greatness. Prosperity ripened the principle of decay; the causes of destruction multiplied with the extent of conquest; and as soon as time or accident had removed the artificial supports, the stupendous fabric yielded to the pressure of its own weight."[5]

Yet the years of turmoil contained a profound growth of human enlightenment, ultimately to flourish as Christian civilisation. Moreover, a new culture was soon to unfold within the dying organism of the old. Before the creation of Hellenism in the early fourth century BC, the finest forms of the previous culture were concentrated in one place, Athens. So, too, when Hellenism was drawing to its close, a point of concentration gathered many of the forces for the making of the succeeding culture. The Emperor Constantine not only realised that Christianity had overtaken paganism in its power to meet the religious needs of the time; he also recognised that the city of Rome was defunct as an imperial capital and that a new capital was required for the old Empire. In 324 AD he founded the city of Constantinople, on the site of the existing ancient city of Byzantium.

*Baths of Caracalla, Rome*

This was a political and military masterstroke. So crucial was the role of Constantinople to become in defending Christendom for eleven hundred years that Constantine's belief that he was divinely inspired in the choice of the site, and even in the exact extent of the city boundaries, was justified by history. He had defeated his last rival for the throne, Licinius, in 324 AD at Chrysopolis in Asia Minor, thereby gaining control of the eastern Empire, when almost immediately he gave orders for the foundation of the city.

Rome was inadequately positioned for the defence of the Danube and Persian frontiers, where the main threat to the Empire would be felt. Her effete senators were of no political significance. Italy itself was no longer a recruiting ground for the armies of the frontiers. Rome had immense prestige and little else. The site of Byzantium, on the other hand, was ideal for the guardianship of the eastern Empire. It lay at the confluence of north-south routes through the Black sea to the Aegean and east-west routes from Europe into Asia. It dominated the narrow straits of the Bosphorous, the sea of Marmara (or Propontis) and the outlet to the Aegean, the long, river-like passage of the Dardanelles. On its northern side the Golden Horn, an inlet from the Bosphorous, formed one of the finest natural harbours in the world, where large ships could moor on the almost tideless water. On the landward, western side of the triangle of the city, a few miles of walls could make it impregnable from land attack. For trade, imperial communications and military strategy its site was as though divinely appointed. Only when it was betrayed to a Christian army in 1204, and stormed finally by a Moslem one in 1453, was Constantinople ever taken. For over a millennium it prevented the enemies of the Empire from gaining simultaneous control of European and Asian imperial territory. It was a citadel, an arsenal, a naval base, a platform from which to send administrators and soldiers forth on either flank; and it became also the preserve of Greek culture, when Greece and its other appendages were lost. Constantinople alone was almost sufficient cause of the survival of the eastern Empire, after the western Empire fell.

By the fourth century the educated classes of the Empire were no longer bilingual, except for a few scholars, but the language of the new capital was unhesitatingly Latin rather than Greek, and remained so until the late sixth century. Constantine established there, also, parallel institutions to those of Rome: a Senate, one consul (Rome retained the other), a forum, public games, a corn-supply from Egypt (rather than Africa), a pro-consul for the government of the city (not a prefect, like Rome), and a collection of art treasures, culled from all parts of the Empire. The new public buildings, parks and roads were adorned with the finest antique sculptures, so that Christian bishops complained of the prevalent nudity!

Forty thousand Gothic feudatories laboured on the building of the new city, which was largely completed in five years, from 325 AD to 330 AD. The existing Hippodrome was reconstructed; a royal palace with courtyards and gardens adjoined it, and a new church of St Sophia (the Holy Wisdom) completed this central nucleus of major buildings near the eastern apex of the triangle by the sea of Marmara. On the central spina of the Hippodrome stood the column of three intertwined bronze serpents brought from Delphi, where it had been dedicated by thirty-one Greek poleis after the great victory of Plataea in 479 BC which preserved Greek freedom from the Persians. Slightly to the west of this complex of buildings stood the Milion, a square made of four triumphant arches supporting a cupola, above which was set what was believed to be the True Cross. Constantine's mother had found the cross in the Holy Land, in a cistern beneath a temple of Aphrodite. All distances throughout the Empire were measured henceforth from the Milion. Near it stood the first church of the new capital, dedicated to the Holy Peace of God, St Eirene. Further west, where the main road, the Mese, crossed the old walls built by the Emperor Severus, was the splendid new forum, oval shaped and paved entirely in marble. At its centre rose a hundred foot column of porphry, the purple feldspar used only for royal sculpture, bought from Heliopolis in Egypt and now crowned with a statue of a body of Apollo made by Phidias, with a head of Constantine himself!

This imperial, god-like figure carried a lance in its right hand and an orb in the left, surmounted with a cross. A crown of radiant sunbeams adorned the head. Probably by choice, Constantine here presented himself with religious ambiguity. He was the mediator of the new religion, Christianity, and yet also resplendent as a figure of the Invincible Sun-God, the Sol Invictus, whom many of his pagan subjects still worshipped, as he himself once had. Constantine's conversion was allowed to remain obscure until his baptism on his death-bed, for he used the term "supreme divinity" rather than the name Christ, and even retained the pagan title of *pontifex maximus*.

Much of the building and new artwork of Constantinople, however, was shoddy, for "the impatience of Constantine soon discovered that, in the decline of the arts, the skill as well as the numbers of his architects bore a very unequal proportion to the greatness of his designs."[6] The Arch of Constantine, for example, owed any beauty its sculptures possessed to their transference from Roman monuments of the time of Trajan, Hadrian and Marcus Aurelius, though the heads were re-carved into portraits of Constantine and his generals! On the same Arch, sculptures by contemporaries showed tiny figures with huge, stiffly posed heads and toy-like buildings in the background. Crude channels in the togas replaced the graceful, classical folds. Earlier masterpieces brought from across the Empire compensated for the lack of spontaneous talent. Works of Phidias and Lysippus were exhibited freely. Rome, Athens and Antioch yielded their art treasures. Nevertheless, as Gibbon concludes:

> "It is not in the city of Constantine, nor in the declining period of an empire when the human mind was depressed by civil and religious slavery, that we should seek for the souls of Homer and of Demosthenes."[7]

Constantinople was unambiguously a Christian city, the capital of an Empire that in the course of the fourth century gradually became undeniably Christian, despite the efforts of Julian, the continued adherence of pagan intellectuals to the memory of an unseen divine world controlled by the ancient pantheon, and the obstinate belief amongst simple peasants in magical powers. The birth of Constantinople was not a renaissance - the time was not ripe - but it was a marker that rose above the flood-waters of the barbarian invasions, indicating that God had not abandoned his people, that the new convenant was unbroken. Into the city Constantine had brought peoples from many regions of the Empire - Italy, Greece, Africa, Egypt, Arabia, the Danubian territories, Asia Minor, Syria, Palestine - and they would multiply and cultivate the land when the floods receded.

When the ancient world drew to an end in the fifth century AD, the beauty to which it gave expression did not cease. The Doric knife-edge still cut its sharp shadow on the smooth marble of the temple floor, the olive groves of Apollo still shimmered under the midday sun below Mount Parnassus, and the great wall of Hadrian still wound through the mists of the Northumberland moorland. The music of Homer and the words of Socrates, as he prepared himself for death, did not lose their resonance, nor the thunderous drama of Sophocles its power to purge the guilty mind. The brilliant reasoning of Apollonius and Archimedes was not invalidated by the mere passage of time. Alexander and Caesar would live in the memory of valorous youths, and the sacrifice of Lucretia still marked the triumph of innocence. Later ages would draw upon the ancient world like ardent treasure seekers at a pot of gold, finding there wisdom reflected from the primeval ages of Man and works that were honed upon the blade of Truth itself. The white limestone hills and mountain oak, the eternal vine and pale olives, the wine-dark sea, and "the brazen sky that stays a fixed habitation for ever" remained with the unending Mediterranean sun; and those who see them, though they are not ancients,

> "... can in greatness of mind
> Or of body be like the Immortals,
> Tho' we know not to what goal
> By day or in the nights
> Fate has written that we shall run."[8]

### References:

1. E. Gibbon, *The Decline and Fall of the Roman Empire*, Methuen, London, 1905, ch. 35.

2. Ammianus Marcellinus, *The Later Roman Empire*, trans. W. Hamilton, Penguin, London, 1986, Book XVI, p. 99.

3. Quoted by M. Grant, *The Fall of the Roman Empire: A Reappraisal*, Weidenfeld & Nicolson, London, 1990, p. 106.

4. Quoted by M. Grant, *The Fall of the Roman Empire*, p. 126.

5. Gibbon, *The Decline and Fall*, ch. 38.

6. Gibbon, *The Decline and Fall*, ch. 17.

7. Gibbon, *The Decline and Fall*, ch. 17.

8. Pindar, 'Nemean VI' in *The Odes*, trans. C. M. Bowra, Penguin, London, 1988, p. 206.

# Bibliography

**(Main Works Consulted)**

**Ancient Scriptures**

*The Ramayana of Valmiki* (3 vols.) trans. H. R. Shastri, Shantisadan, London, 1962.

*The Mahabharata*, adapted and trans. C. V. Narasimhan, Columbia U.P., New York, 1965.

*Srimad Bhagavatam*, trans. Swami Prabhavananda, Sri Ramakrishna Math, Madras, 1972.

*The Geeta*, trans. Sri Purohit Swami, Faber, London, 1978.

*The Way of Hermes*, trans. C. Salaman, D. van Oyen and W. Wharton, Duckworth, London, 1999.

*The Divine Pymander of Hermes Trismegistus*, The Shrine of Wisdom, Godalming, 1978.


**Classical Authors**

Aeschylus, *The Oresteian Trilogy*, trans. P. Vellacott, Penguin, London, 1961.

Ammianus Marcellinus, *The Later Roman Empire*, trans. W. Hamilton, Penguin, London, 1986.

Aristotle, *The Politics*, trans. T. A. Sinclair, Penguin, London, 1964.

Caesar, *The Gallic War*, trans. J. F. Gardner, Penguin, London, 1964.

Cicero, *De Republica*, trans. C. W. Keyes, Loeb, London, 1988.

Demosthenes, *The Crown*, trans. A. N. W. Saunders, Penguin, London, 1974.

*Early Christian Writings*, trans. M. Staniforth, Penguin, London, 1968.

*Early Greek Philosophy*, trans. J. Barnes, Penguin, London, 1987.

*The Epic of Gilgamesh*, trans. N. K. Sandars, Penguin, London, 1977.

Euripides, *The Bacchae and other Plays*, trans. P. Vellacott, Penguin, London, 1973.

Eusebius, *The History of the Church*, trans. G. A. Williamson, Penguin, London, 1984.

*Greek Literature: An Anthology*, ed. M. Grant, Penguin, London, 1982.

Herodotus, *The Histories*, trans. A. de Selincourt, Penguin, London, 1972.

Hesiod, *Theogony and Works and Days*, trans. D. Wender, Penguin, London, 1982.

Homer, *The Iliad*, trans. E. V. Rieu, Penguin, London, 1972.

*The Odyssey*, trans. E. V. Rieu, Penguin, London, 1970.

Horace, *The Complete Odes and Epodes*, trans. W. G. Shepherd, Penguin, London, 1983.

Josephus, *The Jewish War*, trans G. A. Williamson, Penguin, London, 1985.

    *Latin Literature: An Anthology*, ed. M. Grant, Penguin, London, 1987.

Livy, *The Early History of Rome*, trans. A. de Selincourt, Penguin, London, 1976.

    *The War with Hannibal*, trans. A. de Selincourt, Penguin, London, 1978.

Marcus Aurelius, *Meditations*, trans. M. Staniforth, Penguin, London, 1964.

Pausanias, *Guide to Greece* (2 vols.) trans. P. Levi, Penguin, London, 1984.

Pindar, *The Odes*, trans. C. M. Bowra, Penguin, London, 1988.

Plato, *The Dialogues*, trans. B. Jowett, Random House, New York, 1937.

Pliny, *Letters of the Younger Pliny*, trans. R. Radice, Penguin, London, 1981.

Plotinus, *Enneads*, trans. J. Gregory, published privately.

Plutarch, *Plutarch on Sparta*, trans. R. J. A. Talbert, Penguin, London, 1988.

    *Fall of the Roman Republic*, trans. R. Warner, Penguin, London, 1973.

    *Makers of Rome*, trans. I. Scott-Kilvert, Penguin, London, 1972.

    *The Age of Alexander*, trans. I. Scott-Kilvert, Penguin, London, 1979.

    *The Rise and Fall of Athens*, trans. I. Scott-Kilvert, Penguin, London, 1976.

Polybius, *The Rise of the Roman Empire*, trans. I. Scott-Kilvert, Penguin, London, 1979.

Seneca, *Letters from a Stoic*, trans. R. Campbell, Penguin, London, 1977.

Sophocles, *The Theban Plays*, trans. E. F. Watling, Penguin, London, 1984.

Staugustine, *City of God*, trans. H. Bettenson, Penguin, London, 1984.

Strabo, *The Geography of Strabo*, trans. H. L. Jones, Loeb, London, 1988.

Suetonius, *The Twelve Caesars*, trans. R. Graves, Penguin, London, 1978.

Tacitus, *Imperial Rome*, trans. M. Grant, Penguin, London, 1962.

    *The Agricola*, trans. H. Mattingly, Penguin, London, 1971.

Thucydides, *The Peloponnesian War*, trans. R. Warner, Penguin, London, 1976.

Virgil, *The Aeneid*, trans. J. Dryden, Airmont, New York, 1968.

Xenophon, *The History of My Times*, trans. R. Warner, Penguin, London, 1981.

    *The Persian Expedition*, trans. R. Warner, Penguin, London, 1981.

**Modern Authors**

Bettenson, H., *Documents of the Christian Church*, O.U.P., Oxford, 1943.

Bowra, C. M., *The Greek Experience*, Weidenfeld & Nicolson, London, 1985.

Bultmann, R., *Primitive Christianity*, Thames & Hudson, London, 1983.

Bury, J. B. and Meiggs, R., *A History of Greece*, MacMillan, London, 1979.

Camp, J. M., *The Athenian Agora*, Thames & Hudson, London, 1986.

Carter, C., *The Tomb of Tutankhamun*, Book Club Associates, London, 1972.

Cary, M. and Scullard, H. H., *A History of Rome*, MacMillan, London, 1989.

Crawford, M. and Whitehead, D., *Archaic and Classical Greece*, C.U.P., Cambridge, 1988.

Ellis, P. B., *Caesar's Invasion of Britain*, Bookclub Associates, London, 1981.

Finley, M. I., *The World of Odysseus*, Penguin, London, 1962.

Gibbon, E., *The Decline and Fall of the Roman Empire*, Methuen, London, 1905.

Grant, M., *History of Rome*, Faber, London, 1979.

Graves, R., *Greek Myths*, Bookclub Associates, London, 1981.

Green, P., *Ancient Greece*, Thames and Hudson, London, 1987.

Hammond, N. G. L., *A History of Greece to 324 BC*, O.U.P., Oxford, 1977.

Hartt, F., *Art: A History of Painting, Sculpture and Architecture*, Thames & Hudson, London, 1976.

James, T. G. H., *Introduction to Ancient Egypt*, British Museum, 1979.

Johnson, P., *History of Christianity*, Weidenfeld & Nicolson, London, 1976.

Kelly, J. N. D., *Early Christian Doctrines*, A&C Black, London, 1985.

Kerenyi, C., *The Heroes of the Greeks*, Thames & Hudson, London, 1978.

Kitto, H. D. F., *The Greeks*, Penguin, London, 1962.

Maffre, J. J., *L'Art Grec*, Presses Universitaires de France.

Meiggs, R., *The Athenian Empire*, O.U.P., Oxford, 1999.

Murray, O., *Early Greece*, Fontana, London, 1993.

Myres, J. L., *A History of Rome*, Rivingtons, London, 1947.

Richmond, L. A., *Roman Britain*, Penguin, London, 1971.

Rostovtzeff, M., *Rome*, O.U.P., Oxford, 1999.

   *Social and Economic History of the Roman Empire*, O.U.P., Oxford, 1957.

Salway, P., *Roman Britain*, Clarendon, Oxford, 1984.

Scullard, H. H., *Roman Britain*, Thames & Hudson, London, 1991.

Stobart, J. C., *The Glory That Was Greece*, Bookclub Associates, London, 1971.

   *The Grandeur That Was Rome*, Sidgwick & Jackson, London, 1961.

Syme, R., *The Roman Revolution*, O.U.P., Oxford, 1989.

Tarn, W. W., *Alexander the Great*, C.U.P., Cambridge, 1979.

Toynbee, A., *Mankind and Mother Earth*, O.U.R, Oxford, 1976.

Vasiliev, A. A., *History of the Byzantine Empire 324-1453 AD*, University of Wisconsin Press, Madison, 1958.

Warner, R., *Men and Gods*, Heinemann, London, 1967.

# Index